THE
ISO 9000
HANDBOOK

Fourth Edition

Edited by

Robert W. Peach

McGraw-Hill, Inc.

New York   San Francisco   Washington, DC   Auckland   Bogotá
Caracas   Lisbon   London   Madrid   Mexico City   Milan   Montreal
New Delhi   San Juan   Singapore   Sydney   Tokyo   Toronto

Printed in the United States of America. The publisher of this book was Paul Scicchitano. It was set in Palatino and GillSans by Suzanne DuBose.

Acknowledgements

A special thanks to Douglas Parr and Henry Gryn for their assistance with the first section of Chapter 13, "Automotive QS-9000 Quality System Requirements." Parr works for the customized training services division of Riverland Community College in Southern Minnesota, where he also serves as an internal consultant to the college's quality and continuous improvement initiative. Gryn represents DaimlerChrysler on the QS-9000 Task Force and the International Automotive Task Force, which developed ISO/TS 16949.

The publisher also thanks QSU Publishing Company's Big Ten registrars for kindly submitting their ISO 9001:2000 transition guidance, found on the *Handbook*'s accompanying CD-ROM.

Table of Contents

SECTION III
THE REGISTRATION AND AUDIT PROCESS

CHAPTER 5

CHAPTER 6

SECTION IV
Implementing ISO 9000

CHAPTER 10
CONVERSION — MOVING FROM
ISO 9001:1994 TO ISO 9001:2000.........421

SECTION V
Industry Applications of ISO 9000

SECTION VI
Conformity Assessment and Laboratory Accreditation

SECTION VIII
Environmental Management

SECTION IX
Opportunities and Challenges

CHAPTER 26
COMPARING ISO 9000, MALCOLM
BALDRIGE AND TQM

CHAPTER 27
CHALLENGES FACING THE ISO 9000
INDUSTRY

SECTION X
Appendices

THE ISO 9000 HANDBOOK
BONUS CD-ROM

STANDARDS
   ISO 9000:2000
   ISO 9001:2000
   ISO 9004:2000

BIG TEN TRANSITION GUIDANCE
   BSI Inc.
   Quality Management Systems Inc.
   Underwriters Laboratories Inc.
   Perry Johnson Registrars Inc.
   Bureau Veritas Quality International
      Inc.
   DNV Certification Inc.
   Lloyd's Register Quality Assurance Inc.

   SGS International Certification Services
      Canada Inc.
   ITS Intertek Services
   National Quality Assurance Ltd.

OTHER QSU PUBLISHING PRODUCTS
   View QSU Publishing's Electronic
      Catalogue
   Get the Latest Third-Party Registration
      Counts on QSUonline
   Contact QSU Publishing Customer
      Service
   Contact QSU Publishing Technical
      Support

Preface to the Fourth Edition

The 21st century has arrived, and business continues to face expanding international competition. The economic superpowers of the United States and Far East have been joined by the unified market of the European Union.

A major factor in economic success in this global marketplace is higher quality products and services. This emphasis on increased quality is demonstrated by the growing acceptance of international quality standards, and perhaps none more so than the ISO 9000 series. In many industries, meeting and exceeding the requirements of ISO 9000 standards is recognized as essential to succeed in an ever more competitive marketplace.

This fourth edition of *The ISO 9000 Handbook* is a complete update of the third edition. Complete revision has been particularly necessary because of the significant changes made in the year 2000 editions of the international standards, compared to the previous version published in 1994. In a single, comprehensive source, this fourth edition contains, or references, all the information that an organization needs to understand the ISO 9000:2000 series and to initiate the process of implementing the standards. Also included in this edition is information about industry-specific standards, including: QS-9000, the American auto industry's quality system requirements and the designated replacement ISO/TS 16949; Aerospace Standard AS9100; and Telecommunication Standard TL 9000.

This book also describes developments in the European Union in the "bigger picture" of product standards, product certification and conformity assessment.

Whatever the motivation, whether to protect sales to the European Union, to respond to the requirements of large customers or to adopt the standard on the basis of good quality practice, there is a need to understand not only the content and use of the standard, but also the marketplace factors that are influencing adoption of the ISO 9000 standards worldwide.

In addressing my responsibility as editor in carrying out this process, input has been solicited from a variety of knowledgeable contributors. While many of the conditions affecting registration to the standard are constantly changing, each contributor has made every effort to be as current and as accurate as possible in discussing the subject matter of this *Handbook*.

In addition, the staff of *Quality Systems Update*, a journal published by QSU Publishing Company, has provided some material that has appeared in previous *QSU* issues. The reader should find this input invaluable in understanding the requirements of the international standard.

The contributors to this *Handbook* come from a variety of backgrounds and thus reflect somewhat different points of view regarding quality system standards issues. Most of these differences are not substantive and will, I believe, contribute positively to the reader's appreciation of the broad spectrum of factors that influence the application of the ISO 9000 quality standard series. In a few cases, however, the opinions of the contributors conflict, or may seem to conflict. As long as the facts used by the contributors are correct, no attempt has been made to resolve these differences. Rather, such differences reflect the diverse judgments and perspectives of people throughout American industry and should contribute to the comprehensiveness of the *Handbook*.

Underlying the increasing level of ISO 9000 registration activity is the fact that the ISO 9000 standards describe a technically sound quality system for use by manufacturing and service organizations. The standards have proven to be a valuable foundation for expanded quality practice to which principles of Total Quality Management (TQM) are applied. Many companies initially make use of the standards in response to external demands — customer requirements, regulatory compliance or market competition. They soon find that meeting all requirements of the standard results in significant internal benefits and that the rewards are well worth the necessary cost and effort.

I trust that this *Handbook* will provide the information readers need to apply the standard successfully in their own organizations and to achieve the benefits of an improved quality system, and that readers will discover that this is only the beginning of an era of continual improvement in the quality capability of all segments of commerce and industry.

— *Robert Peach*

How To Use This Handbook

The fourth edition of *The ISO 9000 Handbook* is fully updated and expanded from the third edition, published in 1997. The 27 chapters in this edition include expanded chapters on uses of the standard in specific industries including automotive, aerospace and telecommunications, industries that have developed supplemental requirements based on ISO 9001. Chapters on documenting and implementing an ISO 9000 system have been completely revised and expanded, and now include aid to organizations already using the 1994 version of ISO 9001 or ISO 9002, but who are now faced with converting to use of the ISO 9001:2000 publication. These additions make the fourth edition an even more useful industry guide.

As with the third edition, the fourth edition also includes the verbatim text of ISO 9001:2000, ISO 9000:2000 and ISO 9004:2000. These documents are the complete international quality standards, and are the verbatim equivalent of the ISO 9000 series.

The fourth edition's resource section has been modified compared to the third edition. The *Handbook* continues to provide readers with information on obtaining standards and directives. However, lists of profiles of consultants and training services are no longer included. Instead, Appendix C consists of a Webliography, where such information can be referenced.

Understanding and implementing international quality system standards can be complex. This challenge is confronted in Chapter 3 by restating the requirements of the standard in simple, practical language. Another popular feature of the third edition, interpretations of the ISO 9000 standard, is continued here, appearing throughout Chapter 4 as information boxes.

The accompanying CD-ROM not only features the actual standards, but also includes exclusive transition guidance from each of the North American Big Ten Registrars as ranked by QSU Publishing Company. This will allow you to compare the various approaches of the largest registrars to the new standard.

We hope that readers of this book will find *The ISO 9000 Handbook, Fourth Edition*, a useful tool in implementing their ISO 9000-based quality system.

About the Editor

Robert W. Peach is principal of Robert Peach and Associates Inc., Quality Management Consultants, Cary, North Carolina. He was a member of the US Delegation to the ISO TC 176 Committee on Quality Assurance at its formation in 1980, and continued serving as Convener of the Working Group that developed ISO Quality System Standard 9004 *Quality Management and Quality System Elements - Guidelines*. He was the first chairman of the Registrar Accreditation Board (RAB), which he helped form and where he served for ten years. He also was a member of the Executive Committee of the American National Standards Institute (ANSI) Z-1 Accredited Standards Committee on Quality Assurance and the Electronics Components Certification Board (ECCB). At intervals, Mr. Peach has evaluated and planned quality management training in developing nations for the World Bank.

Mr. Peach established the quality assurance activity at Sears Roebuck and Company and managed it for over 25 years. In this capacity, he and his staff worked with quality systems in the plants of hundreds of Sears suppliers.

Mr. Peach is co-author of *Memory Jogger 9000:2000* and *ISO 9000:2000 Paraphrased*, published by GOAL/QPC, as well as editor of *The ISO 9000 Handbook*. In the year 2000 he was the first recipient of the ASQ's Freund-Marquardt medal for holding positions of responsibility for development of standards that focus on the management system of an organization. Previously, he received the Edwards Medal of the ASQ for leadership in the application of modern quality control methods. Past service in the ASQ includes: vice president, publications; technical editor, *Quality Progress*; chairman, Standards Council; deputy chair, General Technical Council; chairman, Textile and Needle

Trades Division; and chairman, Awards Board. Through ASQ he aided in the evaluation of contractor quality programs for NASA's Excellence Award for Quality and Productivity.

For its initial three years, Mr. Peach served as project manager of the Malcolm Baldrige National Quality Award Consortium, which administered the awards program managed by the National Institute of Standards and Technology (NIST). He chaired the writing of the ANSI/ASQC Z1.15 standard *Generic Guidelines for Quality Systems*, one of the standards upon which ISO 9004 is based. He was a delegate to the International Laboratory Accreditation Conference (ILAC) and served on the board of the American Association for Laboratory Accreditation.

Mr. Peach received degrees from Massachusetts Institute of Technology and the University of Chicago. He is a Fellow of the ASQ, a certified quality engineer and registered professional engineer in quality engineering. He also has been an instructor in quality control in the Graduate School of the Illinois Institute of Technology.

INTRODUCTION TO ISO 9000

ISO 9000 — The Second Decade of Marketplace Development

1

by Robert Peach

Celebrating its 15th year anniversary in 2002, ISO 9000 has become a powerful force in the international marketplace. It is a prerequisite for any number of major contracts in such important sectors as aerospace, automotive, medical devices, telecommunications, defense and electronics with users found in more than 120 countries and on every continent of the world. More importantly, for those companies that have truly embraced its intent, ISO 9000 has become a brilliant beacon along the sometimes-twisting quality path.

But the ISO 9000 phenomenon has also drawn its share of criticism, some of it deserved, much of it not. Its doom has been predicted and its importance inflated. Yet, despite the misunderstanding and misinterpretation of the purpose and promise of the standards, registration continues to grow, not only in the United States and Canada, but worldwide. Entire industries have adopted it, including the chemical processing and semiconductor industries and much of the electronic components manufacturing industry.

Pinpointing a single reason for interest in ISO 9000 is difficult. Companies seeking registration in the early 1990s were reacting to either customer demand or an impression that the developing European Community (now European Union) would soon demand ISO 9000 registration as a prerequisite to doing business in Europe. Today, companies still seek registration for marketplace and competitive reasons; however, a growing number of companies now pursue ISO 9000 registration as a valuable business and process management tool.

Yet, neither inflated promises, effective marketing campaigns or a growing sense of business management utility can sustain any movement for long. The real value, and ultimately the reason behind the continued marketplace success of ISO 9000, is its ability to deliver an organization-specific map for building a continually improving quality management system. In short, ISO 9000, effectively applied, has demonstrated itself as a foundation for a quality management program. (See Chapter 26 for a comparison of ISO 9000 to Malcolm Baldrige National Quality Award criteria and to Total Quality Management.)

The importance of the ISO 9000 standards extends well beyond simply providing a universally understood measure of process quality consistency. ISO 9000 is part of a much larger fabric of international trade and the rapidly developing technology that supports the production and delivery of goods and services around the world. The ISO 9000 standards are a natural and necessary result of the global economy. Integration of ISO 9000 with other emerging standards, such as ISO 14000 on environmental management, will further underscore the importance of the ISO 9000 family as baseline international process management standards.

ISO 9000 has become a pervasive catch phrase throughout the US economy. Dozens of government agencies either are studying the standard for use within their agencies or have adopted it outright. The Department of Defense (DoD) and the National Aeronautics and Space Administration (NASA) have both

Figure 1-1

ISO 9000 Registration Growth in the United States, Canada and Mexico from 1999-2002.*

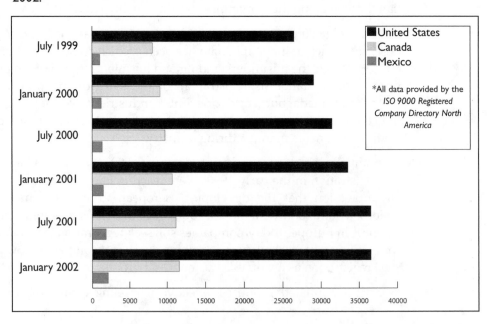

adopted ISO 9000 and dropped long-standing quality standards such as MIL-Q-9858. Federal agencies that do not use voluntary consensus standards such as ISO 9000 and ISO 14000 have been required to provide a written explanation for their position. Experts say that such requirements are likely to push more government agencies toward ISO 9000 and ISO 14000. (See Chapter 24 for more information on government agencies adopting or using ISO 9000.)

In the private sector, the Big Three automakers (Ford Motor Company, DaimlerChrysler Corporation and General Motors) and certain truck manufacturers have created related quality system requirements for their suppliers, known as Quality System 9000 (QS-9000). At the time of this writing, thousands of suppliers to the auto and truck manufacturing industry, are being asked to transition to ISO/TS 16949, which incorporates the verbatim text of ISO 9001:2000 plus industry specific requirements. Both the manufacturers and the suppliers supported the concept of an industry-wide quality requirement to reduce cost and resource burdens. (See Chapter 13 for more on QS-9000 and the history of its development.)

The success of ISO 9000 as an internationally accepted process management standard has also aided in the enthusiasm that the international business and government community has shown for the ISO 14000 series of environmental management standards. ISO 14001, the standard used for registration, is certainly a first cousin to ISO 9000, since they share a common management framework. Although important differences exist between the standards (as explained in Chapter 25), the general consensus among those involved in international standards is clearly that the ISO 14000 series could not have been developed as rapidly without the success of ISO 9000 in the world marketplace.

In fact, the success of ISO 9000, ISO 14000 and related industry initiatives like QS-9000, ISO/TS 16949, AS9100 and TL 9000 have driven debate toward a single process management standard that would encompass both quality management and environmental management. While that goal seems lofty, many regis-

Table 1-1

Top Industries Registered to ISO 9000 in the United States as of January 1, 2002.

Industry SIC*	Description	Total Certificates
3400	Fabricated Metals	4,383
3600	Electronics Industry	3,664
3500	Machinery and Computer Equipment	3,418
3000	Rubber and Plastics Products	2,771
2800	Chemical	2,236

trars are offering integrated audits for ISO 9000 and ISO 14000 and emphasize the use of the term "management systems" rather than specific standards.

The reason for this move to integrate standards is simple — implementing two or three unrelated or marginally related management systems does not add business value, especially for those companies that will have to meet ISO 9000, QS-9000, ISO 14000 and perhaps additional ISO 9000-based standards in other fields. Certainly, an integrated approach to these standards is part of the natural evolution process toward an efficient global marketplace.

ISO 9000 and the Future

Having passed the test of time, it is clear that ISO 9000 is not just another "flavor of the month" quality system standard. ISO 9000 and the related standards it has spawned are fast becoming part of the "glue" that holds the world economy together. It is just as vital as negotiated trade pacts and agreements between countries. Yet, there are challenges to the viability of international voluntary consensus standards.

Some of these challenges include the credibility of third-party registration, interpretation of the standard and industry-specific interpretations of ISO 9000. The long-term viability of these voluntary standards is also challenged by those who serve the "ISO 9000 industry" — trainers, course providers, consultants, accreditation bodies, registrars, auditors, publishers and others who are part of the organizational bodies that contribute to making the system work. Inconsistency among any of these players — whether in the provision of consultant, registration or other services — slows the process that will allow ISO 9000 and related standards to have positive impact on the global marketplace.

Despite these and other challenges to the system, a new global trade language has developed that is changing the way all companies plan their business strategies and allocate resources. Some consolidation is taking place among registrars. A global auditor and training certification program is fully in place, as well as agreements to recognize ISO 9000 registrations in any marketplace. Thousands of suppliers around the world now meet the QS-9000 requirements and additional thousands of companies around the world have ISO 14000 registration certificates. Stopping this train will require more challenges than anyone can dare to imagine.

Taking Care of Business with ISO 9000
by Greg Hutchins

Many organizations are chasing fads such as downsizing, re-engineering, outsourcing and customer-supplier partnering. Each of these initiatives has its place to achieve certain goals. Yet, another marketplace trend is also emerging. Some of these same companies are discovering they must go back to basics — simple but effective organizational, managerial and operational processes, techniques and methods embodied in the ISO 9000 standard.

Contrary to many naysayers, ISO 9000 is not disappearing. Many companies that have been striving for "world-class" quality now realize that they must first ensure that they have the foundation of an effective quality system. Since the publication of ISO 9000, focus has shifted from looking at it as a family of compliance documents to now recognizing it as a set of commonsense business systems and processes.

Benefits can accrue through ISO systems implementation as well as formal ISO 9000 registration. ISO 9000 benefits can be categorized in terms of three broad areas: customer-marketing benefits, internal benefits and customer-supplier partnering benefits.

Customer-Marketing Benefits

- Assists in developing products
- Provides access to markets
- Conveys commitment to quality and partnering and allows for promotional credibility.

Internal Benefits

- Guarantees that new and existing products and services satisfy customers
- Facilitates business and quality planning
- Provides a universal approach to quality and business
- Assists in establishing operational baselines and operationalizes and proceduralizes quality
- Provides insights into organizational interrelationships, encourages internal focus, facilitates internal operational control and helps employees understand and improve operations
- Encourages self-assessment and maintains internal consistency

- Controls processes and systems and establishes operational controls
- Makes internal operations more efficient and effective
- Ensures that product development and design changes are controlled
- Creates awareness of the need for training and encourages operational problem solving.

Customer-Supplier Partnering Benefits

- Forms the basis for a common language of quality
- Ensures a minimum level of quality
- Facilitates development of seamless operations
- Reduces supplier base and assists in selecting suppliers
- Facilitates just-in-time delivery
- Assists in monitoring suppliers.

Background and Development of ISO 9000 Standards

2

by Donald W. Marquardt

Editor's Note: Mr. Marquardt was one of the most highly regarded pioneers of ISO 9000 who continued to influence the standards until his death in 1998. This historical perspective remains one of the best available sources on the original intent of the standards. It has been updated to reflect the year 2000 revision.

This chapter provides an overview of the background and development of the ISO 9000 standards. The chapter includes:

- The development of the ISO 9000 standards
- The development of third-party registration systems
- A brief description of the European Union and the EU Conformity Assessment System
- Reasons for the marketplace success of ISO 9000 and some related concerns about the implementation of the standards
- The basis for the 2000 revisions of the ISO 9000 standards.

Introduction

International Standards and the Development of the Global Economy

During the second half of the 20th century, profound changes occurred in the way companies do business. Although importing, exporting and international trade have gone on for hundreds of years, such trade was peripheral to the everyday business activities of most companies.

As the 21st century begins, products offered for sale typically involve raw materials, parts, design know-how, assembly operations, software, services and other inputs from multiple countries. Most products now incorporate added value from various countries and very few products are produced entirely in a country of origin. "Domestic content" percentages more accurately reflect where and how a product is produced. Automobiles and computers are good examples of products produced for the global marketplace. Yet, these changes in trade and commerce are not confined to large companies. Small companies, with only a handful of employees, often do business in multiple countries; they form joint ventures, produce products, market and implement competitive strategies in the international marketplace.

The Technological Basis of the Global Economy

The global economy could not have developed without two dramatic technological advances:

- Information technology — the ability to move large amounts of *information* rapidly, accurately and inexpensively to any part of the world

- Transportation technology — the ability to move *people and goods* rapidly, safely and inexpensively to any part of the world.

The Impact on Standards and Regulations

People in any economic system need standards for designing the things they make and use and for the ways people work together; otherwise the system becomes chaotic. Figure 2-1 illustrates how this reality has impacted the world of standards and regulations during the second half of the 20th century.

In the 1950s, most business activities focused within a local economy and/or within a specific company. In such a setting, the most useful standards were those devised locally, often specifically for use within the company. Such standards often dealt with both technical aspects of products and management procedures

Figure 2-1

What's Happened in the World of Standards and Regulations

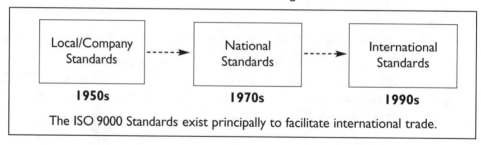

The ISO 9000 Standards exist principally to facilitate international trade.

for the company's activities. Standards were viewed as proprietary information because they formed part of a company's unique competitive position.

By the 1970s, many company-specific standards were being replaced by national standards, as a vast number of companies expanded their operations beyond local borders. Many US companies began to sell US-designed and -produced products in the international market. US standards also gained stature internationally and were exported and sold; this enabled other countries to use effectively the products of US industry.

Today many countries have the technology and economic infrastructure to compete effectively in the global marketplace. Company-specific or country-specific standards have become nontariff barriers to trade. Countries can no longer succeed economically by insisting that their standards are better than the standards of other countries. Such differences make contract negotiations more difficult and create barriers beyond the inevitable language translation problems. These problems can lead to costly, non-value-adding activities in the conduct of trade.

Need for Global Standards

The ISO 9000 Standards and the Global Economy

The ISO 9000 standards are a natural and necessary result of the global economy. The ISO 9000 standards, with their internationally harmonized requirements and guidelines, remove the nontariff trade barriers that arise from differences and inadequacies among national, local or company standards. Here are some basic tenets of the ISO 9000 standards:

A primary purpose of the ISO 9000 standards is to facilitate international trade. All activities within any nation's economy take place in the context of the global economy. Consequently, the use of harmonized standards both within individual countries and among these countries produces a valuable economic benefit. Companies around the world representing a wide variety of industry and economic sectors are using the ISO 9000 standards as a fundamental basis for their own operations as well as their trading-partner relationships.

The roles of the ISO 9000 standards and product technical standards are "separate and complementary." The founding principle of the ISO 9000 standards is the concept that the assurance of consistent product quality is best achieved by the simultaneous application of two kinds of standards:

- Product standards (technical specifications)
- Quality system (management system) standards.

This may be called the "separate and complementary" concept. The two kinds of standards, when implemented together, can provide confidence that products will meet consistently their requirements for quality.

Product standards provide the *technical specifications* for the design of the products and often of the process by which the product is produced. Product standards are specific to the particular product — both its intended functionality and the end-use situations the product may encounter.

The ISO 9000 standards are *management system* standards exclusively and are not related to any product's technical specifications. Organizations use the ISO 9000 standards to define and implement the management systems by which they design, produce, deliver and support their products. While the ultimate purpose of the ISO 9000 standards is to achieve and assure the quality of products, the ISO 9000 standards focus directly on the management system of an organization.

The ISO 9000 Standards Apply to All Industry/Economic Sectors

The ISO 9000 standards are being applied in a wide range of industry and economic sectors and in government regulatory areas. One of the characteristics that make the standards so widely useful is that they apply to all generic product categories, namely hardware, software, processed materials and services.

The ISO 9000 standards provide guidelines or requirements on *what* features are to be present in the management system of an organization, but do not prescribe *how* these features should be implemented. This nonprescriptive characteristic enables the ISO 9000 standards to have wide applicability for various products and situations of use. Each organization is free to determine how individual ISO 9000 requirements/guidelines will be incorporated in its own management system.

Background of the ISO 9000 Standards

The Initial (1987) Series of ISO 9000 Standards

The ISO 9000 standards are prepared and maintained by Technical Committee 176 of the International Organization for Standardization (ISO TC 176). The committee had its first meeting in 1980. The vocabulary standard for the ISO 9000 family was first published in 1986. The initial ISO 9000 series of standards was published in 1987. The original ISO 9000 family consisted of:

- ISO 8402, the vocabulary standard
- ISO 9000, the fundamental concepts and road map guideline standard
- ISO 9001, ISO 9002 and ISO 9003, three alternative quality system requirements standards to be used for quality assurance

- ISO 9004, the guideline standard to be used for quality management purposes.

These six initial standards were quickly adopted as national standards by many countries and immediately began to have enormous impact on international trade.

The revised publication in the year 2000 has consolidated ISO 9001, ISO 9002 and ISO 9003 into one requirements standard, ISO 9001. See Subclause 1.2 of ISO 9001 and Chapter 9 for an explanation of how to provide for exclusions of requirements that are not applicable in specific cases.

National Adoption of International Standards

ISO standards are published in English, French and sometimes in Russian, the three official languages of ISO. Adoption by a country as a national standard involves three steps. First, the standard must be translated into the national language. Second, the formal procedure for adoption of a national standard is followed. Third, the standard is given a national identification number and is published.

Those familiar with earlier editions of the *ISO 9000 Handbook* may recall a map showing the 101 countries of the world that had adopted the standard, with unshaded areas in portions of Africa, the Middle East and South America. Today, some 150 countries have adopted the standard; such a map now would merely demonstrate that essentially all of the major nations of the world (and a host of smaller nations as well) have adopted the standard as a national standard.

Standardization: Standards and Their Implementation

Standardization Defined

"Standardization" encompasses activities in two interrelated areas:

- The conception, planning, production, periodic revision, promotion and selling of standards
- The conception, planning, establishment, control and maintenance of standards implementation.

Both areas of standardization generate challenges and opportunities. In practice, the implementation activities of standardization often give rise to more challenges than the standards themselves.

The Role of Regional Blocks of Countries

International and Regional Approaches

Developing and implementing international standards requires the interplay of many forces, including technology approaches, economic issues and political alignments. The development of the ISO 9000 standards has taken this "international" approach, allowing each member body to participate according to individual technology, economic and political circumstances.

As shown in Figure 2-2, the implementation of the ISO 9000 standards is following a mix of two approaches, global and regional. The *international* approach to implementation is happening simultaneously with a European *regional* approach. In a regional approach, the countries that constitute a regional bloc act in a relatively unified, regional manner.

It is not clear what the future will bring. In recent years other regional blocs of countries have been formed in various parts of the world. The NAFTA treaty is one example. The "mixed" approach to standards implementation is likely to expand to some degree in these other regional blocs.

Figure 2-2

Implementation Approaches

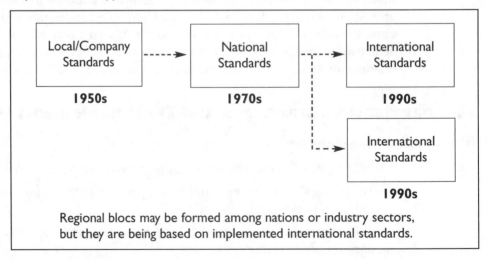

The Early Role of the European Union in Worldwide Implementation of the ISO 9000 Standards

The European Union (EU, formerly the European Community) played a decisive role in the early, rapid implementation of the ISO 9000 standards. Perhaps the single most visible factor driving the early acceptance of the ISO 9000 series

What Is ISO?

ISO is short for the International Organization for Standardization, founded in 1946 to develop a common set of manufacturing, trade and communications standards. According to ISO officials, the organization borrowed the name from the Greek word *isos*, meaning "equal." *Isos* also is the root of the prefix iso, as in "isometric" (of equal measure or dimensions) and "isonomy" (equality of laws or of people before the law). Its selection was based on the conceptual path that leads from "equal" to "uniform" to "standard."

The Geneva, Switzerland-based organization is composed of approximately 100 member countries. In ISO each country is represented by its member body, the national organization that coordinates national standards. Each member body has a single vote, irrespective of the size of the country. The American National Standards Institute (ANSI) is the US member body to ISO.

All standards developed by the International Organization for Standardization are voluntary; no legal requirements force countries to adopt them. However, countries and industries often adopt ISO standards as national standards. In some instances countries attach legal requirements to ISO standards they have adopted, thereby making the standards mandatory in that country. The International Organization for Standardization develops standards in all industries except those related to electrical and electronic engineering. Standards in these areas are made by the Geneva-based International Electrotechnical Commission (IEC), which has more than 40 member countries, including the United States. In practice, ISO and IEC cooperate closely in their activities. They publish a common set of directives governing standards development.

ISO is structured into approximately 200 technical committees that draft standards. Member nations form national committees — in the United States these are called technical advisory groups (TAGs) — that develop national negotiating positions and strategies and select delegates that provide input into the ISO standards development process. Through this mechanism ISO receives wide input and establishes consensus from industry, government and other interested constituencies before promulgating a standard.

has been the effort to unify the 15 major European nations that form the EU into a single internal market. The full members are Austria, Belgium, Denmark, Finland, France, Germany, Greece, Ireland, Italy, Luxembourg, the Netherlands, Portugal, Spain, Sweden and the United Kingdom. New members will be joining the EU over the next several years.

The European Union originated with the 1957 Treaty of Rome, which was established to abolish tariffs and quotas among its six member states and to stimulate economic growth in Europe. (The original members were France, West Germany, Italy, Luxembourg, the Netherlands and Belgium.)

Economic growth slowed during the 1970s and early 1980s, and Europe began to fear that the US, Japanese and Pacific Rim economies would dominate the world economy of the 21st century. The European nations were concerned that they would fall behind, partly due to the differences among their technical standards and requirements.

Differing national product certification requirements made selling products in multiple national markets in the European Union a costly undertaking, requiring duplication of tests and documentation, and separate approvals from national or local regulatory authorities.

In response, the European Union called for a greater push toward a unified market — a single internal market — and for the removal of physical, technical and fiscal barriers to trade. In 1985 the EU Commission presented a program for establishing a single internal market. The goal was to create a single set of procedures for conformity assessment that is simpler and less costly for manufacturers.

The single internal market program was based in part on the 1979 Cassis de Dijon decision of the European Court of Justice, which established the principle of mutual recognition. This principle states that products that meet the requirements of one EU member state could freely circulate in other member states, a concept similar to the interstate commerce clause of the US Constitution, unless the products presented a health, safety or environmental threat.

The 1985 program, presented in a white paper, drew upon the rationale of the Cassis de Dijon decision and created EU-wide directives that would replace national laws governing health, safety and the environment. The move to a single internal market was further expedited by the Single European Act, adopted in February 1986. This act amends the 1957 Treaty of Rome. The combined intent of the white paper and the Single European Act was to abolish barriers to trade among the (then) 12 member states and to complete an internal European market by the end of 1992.

The single market — known as EC 92 — became effective at midnight on December 31, 1992. Its goal is to encourage trade and to increase confidence in the safety and reliability of products marketed in the European Union. To better understand this framework of standards and product certification — and ISO 9000's role in that framework — it is important to understand the European Union's conformity assessment program.

European countries have extensive trade with countries worldwide. The EU single market approach was introduced into international trade before any other regional blocs had anything comparable. As a result, the European conformity assessment model has had a major effect on all international trade, whether or not any of the trading partners are European.

European Union Conformity Assessment

In preparation for EC 92, the European Union began developing a comprehensive framework for conformity assessment activities. Conformity assessment refers to all processes — product testing and certification, quality system registration, standards and laboratory accreditation — that may be used to ensure that a product conforms to requirements. The conformity assessment system, when successfully completed, will give customers confidence that products conform to all requirements.

This system has the following three major components:

- EU-wide directives and harmonized standards
- Consistent conformity assessment procedures
- Competent certification and testing bodies.

EU-Wide Directives and Harmonized Standards

In the European system, products are classified into two categories: regulated and nonregulated.

Most products sold in the European Union are nonregulated. Nonregulated products are those not covered by EU legislation. The European Union's strategy for removing technical barriers to nonregulated products is to rely on the principle of mutual recognition and on product certification by a third party.

In effect, a US exporter of a nonregulated product can certify to a US standard for technical specifications, and if these standards are accepted in at least one EU country, they will be accepted in the European Union through the principle of mutual recognition.

Regulated products are those that have important health, safety or environmental implications. Their requirements are spelled out in directives — official EU legislation — that are binding on all member states of the European Union.

Each directive deals with a class of regulated products and spells out the essential requirements for compliance. However, directives do not list specific technical requirements; they reference appropriate technical standards that are being developed by the major European or international standards organizations.

The EU Regulatory Hierarchy

The 15 nations that make up the European Union (formerly the European Community) are bound by its regulations. The regulatory process begins with the European Commission. A proposal is drafted by the Commission and is sent to the European Parliament. The Parliament, with its 626 members, votes on the proposal. However, this vote is not binding on the European Council.

The European Council comprises many working groups, each of which consists of civil servants from the member states. These groups examine the proposals and, if necessary, make changes. The proposal is then forwarded to the Committee of Permanent Representatives, made up of civil servants from the member states. When the Committee reaches agreement, the proposal is forwarded to the Council of Ministers. The makeup of the Council depends on the subject matter of the proposal. The Council of Ministers decides whether to adopt the legislative proposal. It acts by majority vote. As a result of the process, regulations and directives are created.

Regulations are directly binding on the member states; they do not require any action on the part of each state. Directives do not directly create a new law but instruct member states to amend their national legislation within a prescribed period.

The European Court of Justice has judicial oversight. It interprets and applies European Union law.

(These organizations are developing "harmonized" standards to eliminate the jumble of standards of the individual 15 member states.)

Consistent Conformity Assessment Procedures

Depending upon the requirements of a particular directive, which takes into account the health, safety and environmental risks of the product involved, conformity assessment can require one or more of the following:

- Type-testing of the product
- Third-party audit of the quality system
- Testing of regular production
- A manufacturer's self-declaration of conformity.

This approach, known as the modular approach to conformity assessment, provides manufacturers with options from which to choose in order to demonstrate compliance with a directive. (Refer to Chapter 21 for an in-depth discussion of conformity assessment procedures.)

Accreditation, Certification and Registration

Terms such as "accreditation," "certification" and "registration" are often used interchangeably, creating some confusion. To clarify the meanings, the Conformity Assessment Committee of the International Organization for Standardization, in its *ISO/IEC Guide 2: General terms and their definitions concerning standardization and certification*, defines the terms as follows:

Accreditation: Procedure by which an authoritative body gives formal recognition that a body* or person is competent to carry out specific tasks.

Certification: Procedure by which a third party gives written assurance that a product, process or service conforms to specific requirements.

Registration: Procedure by which a body indicates relevant characteristics of a product, process or service, or particulars of a body or person, and then includes or registers the product, process or service in an appropriate, publicly available list.

Although certification and registration are slightly different steps in the same process, the terms are used interchangeably. In Europe the term "quality systems certification" is used widely; the term "quality systems registration" is the preferred US terminology.

* In particular, a certification body. — Editors

The Quality Assurance Route to Conformity Assessment

Some EU directives require quality system registration. For other directives, quality system registration is not an absolute requirement. However, to ensure confidence in the quality of products circulating throughout Europe, the European Union has strongly emphasized quality assurance.

The European Union has adopted the ISO 9000 series as part of its conformity assessment plan to establish uniform systems for product certification and quality systems registration. Registration involves the audit and approval of a quality system against ISO 9001 by a third-party independent organization known as a *certification body* in the European Union or as a *registrar* in the United States.

For some businesses, achieving ISO 9000 registration satisfies an immediate customer requirement. However, for many companies, ISO 9000 registration is only an important first step for doing business internationally. Additional regional, national or trading bloc requirements may exist with respect to product technical requirements that are outside the scope of the ISO 9000 standards, in accordance with the "separate and complementary" concept.

Competent Certification and Testing Bodies

The European Union has recognized that confidence in the conformity assessment system and in the products sold throughout the European Union depends on confidence in the competence of certification and testing bodies. Thus, the European Union has encouraged the development of standards such as the EN 45000 series. The EN 45000 standards establish requirements for testing, certification and accreditation bodies. (See Chapter 21 for more on EN 45000.)

The European Union has also encouraged the formation of organizations such as the European Organization for Testing and Certification (EOTC) to promote consistent practices in testing and certification and to promote the mutual recognition of test results.

Implication for the United States

The economic implications of the European Union's efforts are far-reaching. The European Economic Area (EEA) Treaty became effective January 1, 1994, extending the European Single Market to include three of the four European Free Trade Association countries: Iceland, Liechetenstein and Norway (Switzerland is the fourth), which have structured their relations with the Economic Union in the form of the Agreement on the European Economic Area, and through which they participate in the EU Single Market.

This expanded European Single Market is now the largest free trade zone in the world, comprising 380 million people and 18 countries. The treaty reinforces the free flow of goods, services, people and capital throughout the EEA.[1]

Interest in European integration has also extended to other countries, with the signing of Association Agreements with Poland, Hungary and the Czech and Slovak Federal Republic. With the inclusion of other Eastern European countries and the former Soviet republics, the European Union could eventually develop into a multitrillion dollar market of 500 to 800 million people.[2]

The United States is the European Union's biggest foreign supplier, exporting well over $100 billion in goods annually to the countries of the European Union. About half of all sales of US subsidiaries overseas are in Europe.[3]

US companies are understandably eager to gain and maintain an economic foothold in this market. Manufacturers can anticipate millions of new customers for goods and services. The challenge is to meet both product and quality system standards and conformity assessment procedures necessary for unrestricted trade within this market.

Table 2-1

ISO Quality Management System Standards and Other Publications

Core Standards	
ISO 9000:2000	Quality management systems — Fundamentals and vocabulary
ISO 9001:2000	Quality management systems — Requirements
ISO 9004:2000	Quality management systems — Guidelines for performance improvements
ISO 19011	Guidelines for auditing management systems
Other International Standards	
ISO 9000-3:1997	Quality management and quality assurance standards — Part 3: Guidelines for the application of ISO 9001 to development, supply and maintenance of computer software
ISO 10012-1	Quality assurance requirements for measuring equipment — Metrological confirmation systems for measuring equipment
ISO 10012-2	Quality assurance for measuring equipment — Guidelines for control of measurement processes
ISO 10015:1999	Quality management — Guidelines for training
Technical Reports	
ISO TR10006:1997	Quality management — Guidelines to quality in project management
ISO TR10007:1995	Guidelines for developing quality manuals
ISO TR10014:1997	Guidelines for managing the economics of quality
ISO TR10017:1999	Guidance on statistical techniques for ISO 9001:1994
Quality Management and Quality Assurance Standards	
These standards may be discontinued in the future (depending on user demand).	
ISO 9004-2:1991	Guidelines for services
ISO 9004-3:1993	Guidelines for processed materials
ISO 9004-4:1993	Guidelines for quality improvement
Guidelines for Auditing Quality Systems	
Standards replaced with ISO 19011 (above)	
ISO 10011-1:1993	Auditing
ISO 10011-2:1993	Qualification criteria for quality systems auditors
ISO 10011-3:1993	Management of audit programs

The ISO 9000 Family of Standards

Table 2-1 lists the standards in the ISO 9000 family as of the beginning of 2002. The three standards, ISO 9000, ISO 9001 and ISO 9004, are referred to as the ISO 9000 "series." The first revision of the ISO 9000 series was published in 1994.

Origins of ISO 9000

In the past several decades, "quality" has emerged as an important concept. Various national and multinational standards were developed in the quality systems arena for military or nuclear power industry needs. Some standards were guidance documents. Other standards were quality system requirements to be used in contracts between purchaser and supplier organizations.

In 1959, the US Department of Defense (DoD) established the MIL-Q9858 quality assurance program. In 1968, the North Atlantic Treaty Organization (NATO) essentially adopted the tenets of the DoD program in the NATO AQAP1, AQAP4 and AQAP9 series of standards. In 1979 the United Kingdom's British Standards Institution (BSI) developed from the predecessors the first quality assurance system standards intended for commercial and industry use. These standards were designated the BS 5750 series, Parts 1, 2 and 3.

Despite the commonality among these predecessors to the ISO 9000 standards, there was no real consistency until Technical Committee 176 (TC 176) of ISO issued the ISO 9000 series standards in 1987.

Since the initial series was published, ISO TC 176 has published a number of additional standards. Some are numbered in the 10000 range. Others are currently numbered as "parts" of ISO 9000 or ISO 9004. Part numbers are shown in abbreviated form by a dash before the part number. For example, ISO 9000-1:1994 described the 1994 revision of the former ISO 9000:1987. Part numbers -2, -3, etc. designated other standards numbered as part numbers to ISO 9000.

The term "ISO 9000 family" refers to all the standards published by ISO TC 176. As shown in Table 2-1, there are a variety of additional standards. However, only ISO 9001 is a requirements standard. All others are guideline standards. The decision has been made to consolidate and, in some cases, to renumber several of the standards, with changes to be made at the time of the next revision of those documents. All ISO standards are reviewed at approximately five-year intervals and are reaffirmed, revised or withdrawn.

Quality Management and Quality Assurance — Similarities and Differences

In the early years of ISO TC 176, one of the most pressing needs was to harmonize internationally the meanings of terms such as "quality control" and "quality assurance." These two terms, in particular, were used with diametrically different meanings among various nations and even within nations.

During the1980s, the term "quality management" was introduced into the ISO 9000 standards as the umbrella term for quality control and quality assurance. The term "quality management" was defined, included in ISO standards and adopted internationally, and it is now used worldwide. This, in turn, enabled agreement on harmonized definitions of the meanings of the terms "quality control" and "quality assurance."

The commonalities and distinctions between quality management and quality assurance are still not universally understood, despite the existence of internationally agreed definitions. This may be due to the expansion of ISO 9000 standards use to many more countries than participated in the early 1980s, to lack of widespread reference to ISO definitions or to deficiencies in the definitions. Undoubtedly, all these reasons have contributed.

Quality management is defined in ISO 9000:2000 Clause 3.2.8 as "Coordinated activities to direct and control an organization with regard to quality," with a note stating, "Direction and control with regards to quality generally includes establishing of the quality policy, quality objectives, quality planning, quality control, quality assurance and quality improvement."

These six quality management activities have important relationships to the classic Plan-Do-Check-Act management cycle. Quality policy, quality objectives and quality planning focus on the "Plan" step; quality control focuses on the "Do" step; quality assurance focuses on the "Check" step; and quality improvement focuses on the "Act" step. Many quality assurance activities are internal to the organization and therefore fall within quality management; internal quality audits are an example. Other quality assurance activities involve parties external to the organization; third-party audits are an example.

For simplicity, it is common today to use the term "quality management" when referring to internal activities (i.e., quality policy, quality objectives, quality planning, quality control, quality improvement and/or quality assurance for internal purposes) and the term "quality assurance" when referring to activities related to second- or third-party audits.

Table 2-2 describes the prime focus of quality management and quality assurance. The quality *control* aspects of the umbrella term "quality management" are focused on the word "achieving," but all bullet points in the left-hand column of Table 2-2 relate at least indirectly to quality control. The right-hand column of Table 2-2 shows that the quality *assurance* aspects of the umbrella term "quality management" focus primarily on the notions of demonstrating and providing confidence, through objective evidence.

These terminology distinctions need to be understood to use the ISO 9000 standards effectively.

Table 2-2

The Prime Focus of Quality Management and Quality Assurance

Quality Management	Quality Assurance
Achieving results that satisfy the requirements for quality.	*Demonstrating* that the requirements for quality have been (and can be) achieved.
• Motivated by stakeholders internal to the organization, especially the organization's management.	• Motivated by stakeholders, especially customers, external to the organization.
• Goal is to satisfy all stakeholders.	• Goal is to satisfy all customers.
• Effective, efficient and continually improving overall quality-related performance is the intended result.	• Confidence in the organization's products is the intended result.
• Scope covers all activities that impact the total quality-related business results of the organization.	• Scope of demonstration covers activities that directly impact quality-related process and product needs.

Three terms currently in use are defined in ISO 9000:2000 with essentially similar meanings:

- "System" is the term defined as "a set of interrelated or interacting elements."
- "Management system" is the term frequently used in the daily language of business, defined as a "system to establish policy and objectives, and to achieve those objectives."
- "Quality management system" is the term coming into increasing use for discussing an organization's management system, when the focus is on the organization's overall performance and products in relation to the organization's objectives for quality. It is defined as the "management system to direct and control an organization with regard to quality."

A benefit of the term "quality management system" is its effectiveness in emphasizing both the commonalties in management system features and the differences in the objectives for the results of an organization's management system for various areas of application. For example, the terms "quality management system" and "environmental management system" describe two such areas of application.

Roles of the ISO 9000 Standards

The ISO 9000 standards have two primary roles:

Quality management — ISO 9004 and related guideline standards provide guidance for producers of all types of products who want to implement not only effective but efficient quality systems in their organizations or to improve the performance of existing quality systems.

Quality assurance — ISO 9001 provides quality system requirements against which a customer, or a third party acting on behalf of customers, can evaluate the effectiveness of an organization's quality system.

These two roles are complementary. In the context of programs for quality system registration, the quality assurance role is more visible, but the business value of both roles is important.

The Growth of Third-Party Registration

Origins

The earliest users of quality assurance requirements standards were large customer organizations such as electric power providers and military organizations. These customers often purchase complex products to specific functional design.

In these situations the quality assurance requirements are specified in a two-party contract, where the providing organization (the supplier) is referred to as the first party and the customer organization is referred to as the second party. Two-party contract quality assurance requirements typically include provisions for the organization to have internal audits ("first-party audits") sponsored by its own management to verify that its quality system meets the contract requirements.

Two-party contracts typically also include provisions to have external audits ("second-party audits") sponsored by the management of the customer organization to verify that the supplier's quality system meets the contract requirements. Within a contractual arrangement between two parties, it is possible to tailor the requirements as appropriate and to maintain an ongoing dialog between customer and supplier.

Unfortunately, two-party quality assurance arrangements become burdensome once the practice is widespread throughout an economy. Soon each organization in the supply chain is subject to periodic management system audits by many customers and is subjecting many of its subsuppliers to such audits. The supply chain is burdened by redundant audits for essentially the same requirements. The conduct of audits becomes a significant cost element for both the auditor organizations and auditee organizations.

Certification-/Registration-Level Activities

The development of quality system registration/certification is a means to reduce the redundant, non-value-adding effort of multiple audits. A third-party organization — a certification body or a registrar — conducts one or more formal audits of an organization to assess conformance to the appropriate quality system standard, ISO 9001, or one of the specific industry quality system requirements documents..

When the organization is judged to be in complete conformance, the third party issues a certificate to the organization and registers its quality system in a publicly available register. The terms "certification" and "registration" carry the same marketplace meaning because they are two successive steps signaling successful conclusion in the same process. To maintain its registered status, the organization must pass periodic surveillance audits by the registrar.

Hundreds of registrars operate worldwide. Most of them are private, for-profit companies. It is critical that the registrars operate competently and objectively and that all registrars meet standard requirements for their business activities. The registrars are, in fact, supplier organizations that provide a needed service product in the economy. As long as these registration services add value in the supply chain, these audits will be valued by both the organization and its customer.

Accreditation-Level Activities

To ensure the competence and objectivity of the registrars, systems of registrar accreditation have been set up worldwide. Accreditation bodies audit the registrars for conformity to standard international guides for the operation of certification bodies.

The quality system of the registrar comes under scrutiny by the accreditation body through audits that cover the registrar's documented quality management system, the qualifications and certification of auditors used by the registrar, the record keeping and other features of the registrar's office operations. In addition, the accreditation body witnesses selected audits done by the registrar's auditors at a client organization's facility.

In the United States the registrar accreditation is carried out by the Registrar Accreditation Board (RAB) under a joint program with the American National Standards Institute (ANSI). This joint program is called the American National Accreditation Program for Registrars of Quality Systems. (See Chapter 7.)

Other ISO 9000 Implementation Considerations

Customer Requirements

The role of ISO 9000 standards in the global market is well established. Customer expectation of ISO 9000 registration by an organization is now commonplace. Customers are asking companies to become registered to ISO 9001 as a precondition to placing a purchase order.

Legal Requirements

For companies whose products are subject to EU directives, registration to ISO 9001 is a legal requirement to enter the regulated EU market. Registration might also help a company meet a domestic regulatory mandate.

Liability Concerns

Liability concerns are also driving registration. Some companies register a quality system, at least in part, for the role ISO 9000 registration may play in product liability defense. Companies that sell regulated products in Western Europe may be subject to increasingly stringent product liability and safety requirements that are moving toward the strict liability concepts prevalent in the United States. (See Chapter 23 for more information on these aspects of registration.)

An EU product liability directive, for example, holds a manufacturer liable, regardless of fault or negligence, if a person is harmed or if an object is damaged by a faulty product. In addition, an EU product safety directive requires manufacturers to monitor product safety. A possible consequence of these directives would be the necessity for companies to document that they have adequate quality systems for their production processes. These procedures would demonstrate more thoroughly that products meet specified requirements, thus minimizing liability claims.

Registration of Suppliers

The ISO 9001 standard requires the organization to ensure that materials purchased from suppliers conform to specified requirements. As a consequence, increasingly many companies are requiring that their suppliers become registered, even though the ISO 9001 standard does not specifically require quality system registration of suppliers.

Internal Improvement

Although external market pressure has stimulated many companies to seek ISO 9000 registration, other companies have implemented the ISO 9000 standards to gain internal benefits. Companies that have implemented the standards have often discovered that internal improvements in facility performance and quality have lasting value at least equal to the market value of ISO 9000 registration. A well-established quality system can increase productivity and reduce costs associated with inefficiencies.

The ISO 9000 standards can also be used as a foundation or building block for implementing broader quality systems such as Total Quality Management (TQM) and for meeting more stringent quality goals, such as the criteria of the Malcolm Baldrige National Quality Award in the United States. (See Chapter 26.)

Marketplace Competition

Marketplace competition is a great impetus for implementing ISO 9000 standards. Companies are implementing ISO 9000 standards to keep up with registered competitors and to distinguish themselves from nonregistered competitors.

Concerns About Registration

Despite the worldwide acceptance of the ISO 9000 standards, the issue of ISO 9000 registration has raised some concerns.

Are Standards and Product Certification Barriers to Trade?

Standards facilitate a common international industrial language, provide consumer confidence and promote product safety. Standards can also facilitate and encourage trade. Used improperly, however, standards can hinder worldwide trade.

One argument is that standards generally lag behind the development of the latest technology and thus become nontariff barriers to trade. Although standards may not reflect the latest technical innovations, periodic review and revision prevents them from becoming nontariff barriers to trade.

A related argument states that, like standards, product certification systems adopted to facilitate trade within an area can consequently act as a trade barrier for trading partners outside that area.

In the early 1970s, for example, Europe developed a regional certification system for electronic components. This system, in effect, became a nontariff barrier to trade for American and Japanese manufacturers. The groups adversely affected petitioned the international electronics standards body, the IEC, to develop an international system to replace the regional one.

A major misunderstanding about the ISO 9000 standards is revealed, however, when examples like this are cited. The ISO 9000 standards deal only with quality systems, not with a product's technical or performance specifications. (See the discussion of the "separate and complementary" concept earlier in this chapter.) The above example deals with product certification to regional technical specifications. These specifications can become nontariff trade barriers for suppliers in other countries that have different technical specification standards for the same class of products.

Time and Costs

Achieving registration to ISO 9001 requires money and time. It takes companies an average of somewhat more than a year to prepare for their first registration, while the average cost for registrar fees alone was about $20,000, according to the *ISO 9000 Survey '99*. Some companies have established quality systems considered to be above the level provided for in ISO 9001. In such instances, the ISO 9000 standards may appear to add cost without adding real value. However, many companies that believed their quality system exceeded the requirements for ISO 9001 registration subsequently discovered that this was not true for all elements of their systems.

A Level Playing Field

A related concern is whether a level playing field will hurt companies that already produce high-quality products. According to this argument, all products manufactured by ISO 9000-registered companies may be viewed favorably. This recognition may benefit the manufacturer that previously produced to lower product technical standards, because now its products are viewed on a par with all others.

Another misunderstanding of the ISO 9000 standards is revealed by this example. While ISO 9000 does represent a universal standard, no expectation exists that two companies' products are the same just because both companies are registered.

Registration means that in both companies the quality system has elements that at least meet the scope of ISO 9001 and each quality system element meets the requirements of the standard and is consistently deployed.

Ample opportunity remains for organizations to succeed in the marketplace if they offer products that conform to better technical specifications and if they are better at meeting customer expectations than their competitors.

Differences Between the US and the EU Systems

The EU regional product certification system has also created a good deal of uncertainty, making it difficult for some US companies to plan. The status of directives and which products they cover is complex, as are the conformity assessment requirements for specific products.

These are genuine problems affecting both European and non-European suppliers. However, these problems concern the procedures for implementing the testing, accreditation and certification systems and are not related to the content or structure of the ISO 9000 standards themselves.

US companies are not as familiar as European companies with a government-driven standards system such as the system being implemented in the European Union. Unfamiliarity with the system, coupled with the uncertainties about the EU system for conformity assessment, may leave some US manufacturers with the perception that Europeans have an advantage. However, ingenuity and flexibility have always been a cultural advantage for the United States. Many US firms have proven their ability to become registered and to compete effectively.

Some perceive the European Union to be exploiting the differences between US and European standard-setting systems and government-business relationships to its advantage. The European system is government-oriented with an emphasis on third-party verification, while the US system is driven by the private sector and has often relied on manufacturers' self-declarations of conformity.

Outlook for the Future

Both the European system and the US system have their unique advantages and drawbacks. The world scene is likely to be a paradoxical, simultaneous mix of approaches to standards for the foreseeable future. Despite the challenges, companies around the world will continue to benefit from the increasing use of international standards, to compete and prosper in the global marketplace.

Endnotes

[1] "European Single Market Expands," *European Community Quarterly Review*, Vol. II, Issue 2 (Spring 1994).

[2] Timothy J. Hauser, "The European Community Single Market and US Trade Relations," *Business America*, 8 March 1993.

[3] Ibid.

THE ISO 9000 SERIES STANDARDS

Overview of the ISO 9000 Series Standards

3

This chapter contains two articles related to the ISO 9001:2000 series of standards. The first one, by Robert Peach, describes the ISO 9000:2000 series, its uses and defines the various guidance standards in the ISO 9000:2000 family. Peach also discusses key terms and definitions that must be understood in order to apply the standard, including:

- Organization
- Supply-Chain Terminology
- Product
- Hardware
- Software
- Processed Material
- Service.

The second article, by Lawrence A. Wilson, discusses ISO 9004:2000 — *Quality Management Systems — Guidelines for Performance Improvements*. Wilson details the differences between the 1996 and 2000 versions of the document and discusses how the application of ISO 9004:2000 can be a vehicle for improving an organization.

The ISO 9001:2000 Series

by Robert W. Peach

Here we provide an overview of the currently available standards in the ISO 9000:2000 series (which also includes standards with designations in the 10000 and 19000 series.) The contents of guidance standards ISO 9000:2000 and ISO 9004:2000 are discussed in detail. Since Chapter 4 contains a comprehensive discussion of requirements standard ISO 9001:2000, only an overview of that standard is presented here. The verbatim English text of these three standards is provided in Appendix F and on the included CD-ROM.

Introduction

The ISO 9000 series consists of a set of generic standards that provide quality management guidance and identify generic quality system elements necessary to achieve effective control. They are independent of any specific industry or economic sector. Each individual organization determines how to implement these standards to meet its specific needs and the needs of its customers.

The ISO 9000 series covers a broad scope of quality system elements that are basic and uncomplicated. An organization that has achieved registration to ISO 9001 can attest that it has a documented quality system that is fully deployed and consistently followed. This does not necessarily imply, however, that the company produces better-quality products than those of its competitors.

ISO 9001 does not establish requirements for product or contain any technical requirements. The quality system requirements in the ISO 9000 series are not substitutes for distinct product technical requirements.

Basically, the ISO 9001 standard requires a company to have documentation appropriate to what it does, to do what it documents, to review the process and to change it when necessary. To illustrate an objective of ISO documentation: if a company were to suddenly find it necessary to replace all of its personnel, their replacements, properly trained, could use the documentation as a guide to continue making the product or providing the service as before.

ISO 9001 identifies basic requirements of a quality management system, in effect providing the essential building blocks for such a system. While the ISO 9000 standards identify what must be done, they do not dictate how to do it. The choice of methods is left to the management of the organization.

Uses of the Standards

Primary uses for the ISO 9000 standards include:

- Guidance for quality management
- Contractual agreements
- Second-party approval or registration
- Third-party certification or registration.

In both *contractual* and *noncontractual* situations, organizations want to install and maintain a quality system to strengthen competitiveness and to achieve the needed product quality in a cost-effective way. Thus, the ISO 9000 standards offer valuable guidance for internal quality management.

Additionally, in a *contractual* situation, the customer wants to know whether its supplying organization can produce products or services that consistently meet necessary requirements. In a contractual situation both organization and customer must agree on what is acceptable.

In a *second-party* approval or registration situation, the customer assesses the quality system of its supplier and grants formal recognition of conformance with the standard.

In a *third-party* situation, a registration body evaluates the quality system for conformance.

A particular organization can be involved in one or more of the above situations. For example, an organization may purchase some materials *without* contractual quality system requirements and purchase others *with* contractual requirements.

Definition of Terms

Before discussing the ISO 9000 series further, it is necessary to define common terms that are used in the standard. One purpose of the ISO 9000 family of standards is to create a consistent international "language of quality." Most of the definitions quoted below are taken from ISO 9000:2000, *Quality management systems — Fundamentals and vocabulary.*

What Is an Organization?

For the purposes of the standard, an organization is "a group of people and facilities with an arrangement of responsibilities, authorities and relationships, for example, a company, corporation, firm, enterprise, institution, charity, sole trader, association, or parts or combination thereof." This is a broad definition, making the point that the quality system elements in the ISO 9000 family apply to essentially any type of organization, whether or not incorporated, public or private.

Supply-Chain Terminology

ISO 9001 Clause 3 describes the supply-chain terminology and is illustrated in the following way. It improves terminology in the previous versions of the ISO 9000 series, which were not consistent between standards.

$$\text{Supplier} \longrightarrow \text{Organization} \longrightarrow \text{Customer}$$

Requirements of ISO 9001 and the guidance in ISO 9004 now similarly address the organization's relationship to its suppliers and customers.

The organization provides products/services to its customer(s). In a contractual situation, the customer is referred to as the purchaser and the organization as the contractor. The organization receives goods and services from its suppliers.

What Is a Product?

A product is defined simply as the "result of a process." A product can be *tangible*, such as assemblies or processed materials, or *intangible*, such as information, or a combination of both, often occurring in service delivery. Products can be classified into four generic product categories: hardware, software, processed materials and services.

Hardware

Hardware refers to a tangible, discrete product with distinctive form, such as an engine mechanical part. Hardware products normally consist of manufactured, constructed or fabricated pieces, parts or assemblies.

Software

Software consists of information, generally intangible. Software can be in the form of approaches, transactions or procedures. Some examples are computer programs, the content of a dictionary, automobile engine control software or a driver's manual.

Processed Material

A processed material is a tangible product generated by transforming raw material into a desired state, such as a lubricant. This state can be liquid, gas, particulate, material, ingot, filament or sheet.

Service

A service is a result of at least one activity performed at the interface between the supplying organization and the customer and is generally intangible. Examples include auto repair, an income statement needed to prepare a tax return, the delivery of knowledge, even ambiance in a hotel or restaurant.

The activities of many companies fall into more than one generic product category. Often, hardware, software and services will all be part of the organization's offering to its customers. ISO 9000:2000 cites as an example an automobile, which includes hardware (tires), software (engine control software) and, at the time a car is purchased, service by the salesperson.

What Is Quality?

The word "quality" has a variety of meanings — many of which are subjective, such as the concept of "excellence." In the quality management field, however, the meaning is more specific. According to ISO 9000:2000, quality is "the degree to which a set of inherent characteristics fulfills requirements." In a contractual situation, requirements are specified by contract and translated into product features and characteristics with specified criteria. In other situations, implied needs are identified and defined by the company, based on knowledge of its marketplace. The requirements of the customer, of course, change with time. Thus, organizations should review quality requirements periodically.

Quality in a product or service often refers to "fitness for use" or "fitness for purpose." Most organizations produce products to meet specific criteria, such as technical specifications. However, the existence of a specification may not in itself guarantee that a customer's requirements will be met consistently.

Each of the following four facets of quality should be addressed:

- Definition of needs for the product
- Product design
- Conformance to product design
- Product support.

An effective quality system will address all four facets of quality.

What Is a Quality System?

A quality system is the organizational structure, procedures, processes and resources needed to implement quality management. It should be only as comprehensive as needed to meet the quality objectives.

Earlier in the industrial era, product quality was associated primarily with inspection after the fact. To improve quality control and prevent problems, manufacturers developed tools such as statistical process control and established quality control departments. Quality systems standards such as the ISO 9000 standards series are based on the idea of building quality into every aspect of the enterprise with an integrated quality management system.

The quality system involves all processes in the life cycle of a product that affect quality, from initial identification of market needs to final satisfaction of requirements.

What Is Quality Management?

Quality management refers to "the coordinated activities to direct and control an organization with regard to quality, generally including the quality policy, quality objectives, quality planning, quality control, quality assurance and quality improvement." Quality management is not separate from general management. When used effectively, quality management should be an integral part of an organization's overall management approach.

What Is Quality Assurance?

Quality assurance is that part of quality management focusing on increasing the ability to fulfill requirements.

The purpose of a quality assurance system is to prevent problems from occurring, detect them when they do, *identify the cause, remedy the cause and prevent recurrence.* A common way to summarize the basis of a quality system is to say what you do, do what you say, record what you did, check the results and act on the difference.

A summary of this process is as follows:

- Plan your objectives for quality and the processes to achieve them.
- Do the appropriate resource allocation, implementation, training and documentation.

Check to see if:

- Implementation is as planned
- The quality system is effective
- Objectives for quality are being met
- The system is being improved as needed

Types of Standards in the ISO 9000 Series

The core standards in the ISO 9000 series consist of ISO 9000:2000, ISO 9001:2000, ISO 9004:2000 and ISO 19011. ISO 9001 is a conformance standard; the other three are guidance standards. Table 2-1 lists the international standards in the ISO 9000 family.

Conformance Standard

ISO 9001 - Quality Management Systems - Requirements

ISO 9001 is used when the organization must ensure product conformance to specified needs throughout the entire product cycle. It is principally used to provide confidence to the customer that the organization's quality system will provide a satisfactory product or service. It applies to manufacturing or processing industries and can also apply to services such as construction, or to professional services such as architecture and engineering. The requirements of ISO 9001 are discussed in detail in Chapter 4.

Guidance Standards

ISO 9000 and ISO 9004 are *guidance standards*. This means they are descriptive documents, not prescriptive requirements. ISO 9000 and ISO 9004 provide guidance to all organizations for quality management purposes. These documents are used for internal quality management, which are activities aimed at providing confidence to the management of an organization that the intended quality is being achieved.

ISO 9000 — *Quality management systems — Fundamentals and Vocabulary* defines key terms and provides guidance on selecting, using, and tailoring ISO 9001 for external quality assurance purposes. It also provides guidance on using ISO 9004 for internal quality management. It is the "road map" for use of the entire series.

Topics Covered in ISO 9000:2000

ISO 9000:2000 is a remarkable consolidation and expansion of ISO 9000:1994 *Guidelines for selection and use* and ISO 8402:1994 *Definitions* into a standard entitled *Quality management systems – Fundamentals and Vocabulary*. This standard should always accompany ISO 9001 and ISO 9004, for the user will find it of significant help in understanding how to make use of the other standards in the series. ISO 9000:2000 is included in the appendix of this handbook; the reader is encouraged to look through that material and become familiar with its content.

Table 3-1

A Comparison of ISO 9001:2000 and ISO 9004:2000 Table of Contents

ISO 9001:2000	ISO 9004:2000
Quality Management Systems Requirements	Quality Management Systems
Foreword	Foreword
Introduction	Introduction
0.1 General	0.1 General
0.2 Process approach	0.2 Process approach
0.3 Relationship with ISO 9004	0.3 Relationship with ISO 9001
0.4 Compatibility with other management systems	0.4 Compatibility with other management systems
1 Scope	1 Scope
1.1 General	
1.2 Application	
2 Normative reference	2 Normative reference
3 Terms and definitions	3 Terms and definitions
4 Quality management system	4 Quality management system
4.1 General requirements	4.1 Managing systems and processes
4.2 Documentation requirements	4.2 Documentation
4.2.1 General	
4.2.2 Quality manual	
4.2.3 Control of documents	
4.2.4 Control of records	
4.3 Use of quality management principles	4.3 Use of quality management principles
5 Management responsibility	5 Management responsibility
5.1 Management commitment	5.1 General guidance
	5.1.1 Introduction
	5.1.2.1 Issues to be considered
5.2 Customer focus	5.2 Needs and expectations of interested parties
	5.2.1 General
	5.2.2 Needs and expectations
	5.2.3 Statutory and regulatory requirements
5.3 Quality policy	5.3 Quality policy
5.4 Planning	5.4 Planning
5.4.1 Quality objectives	5.4.1 Quality objectives
5.4.2 Quality management system planning	5.4.2 Quality planning

Table 3-1 (continued)

A Comparison of ISO 9001:2000 and ISO 9004:2000 Table of Contents

ISO 9001:2000	ISO 9004:2000
5.5 Responsibility, authority and planning	5.5 Responsibility, authority and planning
5.5.1 Responsibility and authority	5.5.1 Responsibility and authority
5.5.2 Management representative	5.5.2 Management representative
5.5.3 Internal communication	5.5.3 Internal communication
5.6 Management review	5.6 Management review
5.6.1 General	5.6.1 General
5.6.2 Review input	5.6.2 Review input
5.6.3 Review output	5.6.3 Review output
6 Resource management	6 Resource management
6.1 Provision of resources	6.1 General guidance
	6.1.1 General guidance
	6.1.2 Issues to be considered
6.2 Human resources	6.2 People
6.2.1 General	6.2.1 Involvement of people
6.2.2 Competence, awareness and training	6.2.2 Competence, awareness and training
	6.2.2.1 Competence
	6.2.2.2 Awareness and training
6.3 Infrastructure	6.3 Infrastructure
6.4 Work environment	6.4 Work environment
	6.5 Information
	6.6 Suppliers and partnerships
	6.7 Natural resources
	6.8 Financial resources
7 Product realization	7 Product realization
7.1 Planning of product realization	7.1 General guidance
	7.1.1 Introduction
	7.1.2 Issues to be considered
	7.1.3 Managing processes
	7.1.3.1 General
	7.1.3.2 Process inputs, outputs and review
	7.1.3.3 Product and process validation and changes
7.2 Customer-related processes	7.2 Processes related to interested parties
7.2.1 Determination of requirements related to the product	

Table 3-1 (continued)

A Comparison of ISO 9001:2000 and ISO 9004:2000 Table of Contents

ISO 9001:2000	ISO 9004:2000
7.2.2 Review of requirements related to the product	
7.2.3 Customer communication	
7.3 Design and development	7.3 Design and development
7.3.1 Design and development planning	7.3.1 General guidance
7.3.2 Design and development inputs	7.3.2 Design and development input and output
7.3.3 Design and development output	
7.3.4 Design and development review	7.3.3 Design and development review
7.3.5 Design and development verification	
7.3.6 Design and development validation	
7.3.7 Design and development changes	
7.4 Purchasing	7.4 Purchasing
7.4.1 Purchasing process	7.4.1 Purchasing process
7.4.2 Purchasing information	7.4.2 Supplier control process
7.4.3 Verification of purchased product	
7.5 Production and service provision	7.5 Production and service operations
7.5.1 Control of production and service provision	7.5.1 Operation and realization
7.5.2 Validation of processes for production and service provision	
7.5.3 Identification and traceability	7.5.2 Identification and traceability
7.5.4 Customer property	7.5.3 Customer property
7.5.5 Preservation of product	7.5.4 Preservation of product
7.6 Control of monitoring and measuring devices	7.6 Control of measuring and monitoring devices
8 Measurement, analysis and improvement	8 Measurement, analysis and improvement
8.1 General	8.1 General guidance
	8.1.1 Introduction
	8.1.2 Issues to be considered
8.2 Monitoring and measurement	8.2 Measurement and monitoring

Table 3-1 (continued)

A Comparison of ISO 9001:2000 and ISO 9004:2000 Table of Contents

ISO 9001:2000	ISO 9004:2000
8.2.1 Customer satisfaction	8.2.1 Measurement and monitoring of system performance
	8.2.1.1 General
	8.2.1.2 Measurement and monitoring of customer satisfaction
8.2.2 Internal audit	8.2.1.3 Internal audit
	8.2.1.4 Financial measures
	8.2.1.5 Self-assessment
8.2.3 Monitoring and measurement of processes	8.2.2 Measurement and monitoring of processes
8.2.4 Monitoring and measurement of product	8.2.3 Measurement and monitoring of product
	8.2.4 Measurement and monitoring of satisfaction of interested parties
8.3 Control of nonconforming product	8.3 Control of nonconformity
	8.3.1 General
	8.3.2 Nonconformity review and disposition
8.4 Analysis of data	8.4 Analysis of data
8.5 Improvement	8.5 Improvement
8.5.1 Continual improvement	8.5.1 General
8.5.2 Corrective action	8.5.2 Corrective action
8.5.3 Preventive action	8.5.3 Loss prevention
	8.5.4 Continual improvement of the organization
Annexes (Informative)	Annexes (Informative)
A Correspondence between ISO 9001:2000 and ISO 14001:1996	A Guidelines for self-assessment
Table A.1 Correspondence between ISO 9001:2000 and ISO 14001:1996	A.1 Introduction
	A.2 Performance maturity levels
	A.3 Self assessment questions
Table A.2 Correspondence between ISO 14001:1996 and 9001:2000	A.4 Documentation of self-assessment results
	A.5 Linking potential benefits of ISO 9004 to self-assessment
B Correspondence between ISO 9001:2000 and ISO 9001:1994	B Process of continual improvement

ISO 9000:2000 (in Clause 0.2) lists eight quality management principles.

1. Customer focus
   - Understanding current customer needs
   - Understanding future customer needs
   - Meeting customer requirements
   - Striving to exceed customer expectations

2. Leadership
   - Establishing unity of purpose and direction for the organization
   - Establishing the organization's internal environment

3. Involvement of people
   - Developing abilities fully
   - Using abilities to maximum benefit

4. Process approach
   - Managing resources as a process
   - Achieving desired results more efficiently

5. Systems approach to management
   - Identifying
   - Understanding
   - Managing the interrelated processes of a system to effectively and efficiently attain objectives

6. Continual improvement
   - Making improvement a permanent objective

7. Factual approach to decision making
   - Analyzing data and information logically

8. Mutually beneficial supplier relationships
   - Creating value through mutually beneficial, interdependent relationships

Clause 1, *Scope,* lists potential users of international standards, including producers, systems assessors, registrars, regulators, training organizations and users of the products.

Clause 2, *Fundamentals of quality management systems,* addresses the following elements of QMS:

2.1 Rationale: customer satisfaction can be enhanced where continual improvement of processes and products is a way of life.

2.2 Understand the distinction between requirements for quality management systems (as in ISO 9001) and product requirements, established by customer requirements or by regulation.

2.3 Eight elements contained in the approach to developing, implementing, maintaining and improving a quality management system, including determining customer need, organization's quality policy and objectives, processes needed to attain the objectives, methods to measure processes effectiveness and efficiency, prevention of nonconformities and providing for continual improvement of the quality management system.

2.4 The "process approach" is introduced that forms the basis for the structure of ISO 9001 and ISO 9004. A diagram illustrates the interrelation and interaction of process elements, which are essentially the primary clauses of the standards. (This contrasts with the "manufacturing sequence" structure of ISO 9001:1994.)

2.5 A discussion of the need for and value of establishing a quality policy and quality objectives.

2.6 Nine items encompassing the role of top management, essentially putting the various quality management elements into practice.

2.7.1 The value-adding features of documentation, including meeting customer requirements, confirming appropriate training, assuring repeatability and traceability, providing objective evidence and providing evaluation of effectiveness and suitability of the quality management system.

2.7.2 Types of documents used in the quality management system, with a listing of factors determining the extent of and selection of type of documents to be used.

2.8.1 Questions to be asked when evaluating the quality management system: are processes defined, are responsibilities assigned, are procedures implemented and maintained and are results being achieved?

2.8.2 Types of audits — first-, second- and third-party audits — with a reference to ISO 19011 that describes auditing practice. (See Chapter 6 on auditing.)

2.8.3 The role of top management in reviewing the quality management system.

2.8.4 Definition and value of self-assessment by organizations.

2.9 Actions to take to accomplish continual improvement, consisting of analyzing the situation, setting objectives, searching for solutions, deciding upon which course of action to achieve a solution, implementing action, evaluating and verifying results, then putting the change into permanent use.

2.10 The role and value of applying statistical techniques to measure, describe, analyze, interpret and model variability.

2.11 Discussion of the focus of quality management systems and its relationship to other management systems, such as ISO 14001.

2.12 The relationship of quality management systems to excellence models, identifying similarities (identify strengths and weaknesses, provide for evaluation against generic models, provide for continual improvement and external recognition) and differences (requirements for quality management systems [ISO 9001:2000] and guidance for performance improvement [ISO 9004:2000], while excellence models provide a basis for comparative performance with other organizations).

Clause 3 *Terms and Definitions* contains:

- Some 80 carefully crafted definitions of quality terms
- A multipage informative annex describing the methodology used in the development of the vocabulary that will aid users in their application of the many definitions
- A bibliography of selected international standards.

Other Standards in the ISO 9000 Family

A number of other guidance standards have been published, either as part of the ISO 9000 series or in a form that complements the primary standards. Some standards previously published are scheduled to be discontinued, on the basis that the revised set of ISO 9000, 9001 and 9004 in their year 2000 edition adequately addresses material in a past standard. Others are being revised and updated to be compatible with the year 2000 series. Several are to be designated as technical reports or brochures, a category that provides greater freedom in their preparation, approval and use. At the time of this writing, some of these standards were in a final draft stage, ready to be published. Following is a description of these standards.

ISO 10012 — Quality Assurance Requirements for Measuring Equipment

Revision of ISO 10012-1:1992 and ISO 10012-2:1997.

In many products or processes, quality depends upon accurate measurements.

ISO 10012-1, Quality assurance requirements for measuring equipment — Part 1: Metrological confirmation system for measuring equipment includes detailed guidance for a supplier's measurement system to ensure accurate and consistent measurement. (See Chapter 6 for more information on ISO 10012.)

ISO 19011 — Guidelines on Quality and/or Environmental Management Systems Auditing (to be published)

Revision and expansion of ISO 10011:1994 series, a document that includes auditing for both quality management and environmental management disciplines.

ISO 19011 is a guidance standard for establishing an audit system for quality and/or environmental management. It considers the overall process of establishing, planning, performing and documenting quality and environmental system audits. It lists definitions of audit terms, includes general principles to be followed in carrying out an audit and identifies auditor qualifications. (See Chapter 6 for more information on the ISO 19011 standard.)

ISO 9000-3:1997 — Quality Management and Quality Assurance Standards — Part 3: Guidelines for the Application of ISO 9001 to the Development, Supply and Maintenance of Software

This standard provides guidance to supplier organizations that produce computer software or products that include a software element. The primary rationale for this standard is that software development, supply and maintenance — unlike other manufacturing processes — does not have a distinct manufacturing phase. The key process is the design phase. ISO 9000-3 offers suggestions regarding appropriate controls and methods that apply to the design phase. (ISO 9000-3 is discussed in detail in Chapter 19.)

ISO 10006:1997 — Quality Management — Guidelines to Quality in Project Management (to be revised and published as ISO Technical Report [TR] 10006)

This publication provides guidance on quality systems elements, concepts, and practices important to the achievement of quality in project management, supplementing guidance given in ISO 9004. It is suitable to a wide range of applications. Ten sets of project management processes are presented.

ISO 10007:1995 — Guidelines for Configuration Management (to be revised and published as ISO TR 10007)

Ideally, design and development processes end with a design that is "frozen." In practice, changes are frequently made in the design after production is under way. The collection of activities needed to accomplish these changes is called *configuration management*. This document describes the configuration management process (identification, control, accounting and audit), structure of config-uration management and specific procedures for identification, control and audit. It is applied over the life cycle of a product to provide visibility and con-trol of functional and physical characteristics. Configuration management pro-vides a rigid discipline for identification of product and part status, applicable for products with large numbers of component parts, where identification of design status is critical. This process is particularly applicable to industries such as aerospace.

ISO 10013:1995 — Guidelines for Quality Manuals (to be revised and pub-lished as ISO TR 10013)

This guideline standard describes the development, preparation and control of quality manuals, tailored to the specific user. Quality manuals developed in accordance with ISO 10013 will reflect documented quality system procedures required by ISO 9001. The standard does not cover detailed work instructions or quality plans. The standard may be used to develop quality manuals relating to quality system standards other than the ISO 9000 series.

ISO 10014:1998 — Economics of Quality (to be revised and published as ISO TR 10014)

ISO 10014 provides guidance on how to achieve economic benefit from the application of quality management. It approaches the subject from the organi-zation's view (identify process activities, monitor and report costs) and from the customer's view (identify factors causing dissatisfaction, satisfaction and delight). It then provides a basis for managing the improvement process.

ISO 10015:1999 — Continuous Education and Training (to be revised and pub-lished as ISO TR 10015)

This document provides guidelines to help organizations and their personnel address training issues based on a commitment to continuous improvement. It covers the development, implementation, maintenance and improvement of strategies and systems for training that affect the quality of products supplied by an organization. It follows sequential stages in the training process (identify and analyze needs, design and plan, deliver, evaluate, improve and monitor).

ISO 10017:1999 — Guidance on Statistical Techniques for ISO 9001:1994 (to be revised and published as ISO TR 10017)

This document provides guidance for application of statistical techniques when following ISO 9001 and lists where statistical techniques can be used, clause by clause, in ISO 9001. It describes 12 specific statistical methodologies, with state-ments of how to use, benefits, limitations, cautions and examples listed for each technique.

The following ISO documents are to be published as ISO brochures:

"Quality Management Principles"

"Selection and Use of Standards"

"Handbook for Small Business."

The following standards are being or have been discontinued, because they are considered no longer necessary with publication of the ISO 9000:2000 series.

ISO 9000-2:1997 — Generic guidelines for the application of ISO 9001, ISO 9002 and ISO 9003

ISO 9004-2:1991 — Quality Management and Quality Assurance Elements — Guidelines for services

ISO 9004-3:1993 — Quality Management and Quality Assurance Elements — Guidelines for processed materials

ISO 9004-4:1993 — Quality Improvement

ISO 10002 — Quality Principles

ISO 10005 — Quality Plans

ISO 9004:2000 – Quality Management Systems – Guidelines for Performance Improvements

by Lawrence A. Wilson

On November 14, 2000, balloting of ISO 9004:2000, *Quality management systems — Guidelines for performance improvements*, concluded, and it was approved as one member of a consistent pair of quality management standards, the other being ISO 9001:2000.

Both are based on a set of quality management principles that have been integrated into the content of each standard.

While most of the attention in the quality community has been focused on ISO 9001:2000 because it is a directive standard against which an organization's quality management system (QMS) can become registered, ISO 9004:2000 has a great deal to offer to any organization, whether it has been using a QMS for years or is just beginning the implementation process.

ISO 9004:2000 provides guidance that permits the management of an organization to go beyond the baseline requirements of ISO 9001 in pursuit of performance improvement of the QMS and ultimately of the organization itself, thus benefiting the organization and its interested parties.

The recommendations and content of ISO 9004:2000 can be used as a tool to move the organization as far toward improved performance as desired by its management and as permitted by its resources. ISO 9004 also has two annexes — one for guidance on self-assessment and another for generic guidance on the continual improvement process.

Gaining a better understanding of how ISO 9004:2000 compares with its predecessor, its relationship with ISO 9001:2000 and what it contains and offers to organizations seeking an effective and efficient QMS will benefit your organization, whether you plan to improve the performance of your existing quality management system or plan to implement a QMS from the beginning.

Can You Compare ISO 9004:2000 with ISO 9004-1:1994?

The answer to this question is "Not really." There is a very limited relationship between the newly released ISO 9004:2000 and ISO 9004-1:1994, *Quality management and quality system elements — Part 1: Guidelines*, its numbered predecessor.

A completely different approach has been taken regarding the nature and application of the technical content of the new version of ISO 9004. A needs analysis of potential users of the consistent pair determined that a clear departure from previous approaches to ISO 9004 was essential. The new approach was deemed necessary for the following reasons:

1. There was little user interest in the 1994 version as a guideline, which was demonstrated by the lack of sales and low user acceptance of the 1994 document.

2. The analysis identified an interest in having suitable guidance on going beyond the basic ISO 9001 requirements available to potential users of the consistent pair to enable the management of an organization to pursue performance improvement of the organization and achieve benefits for the organization's interested parties.

The ISO 9004-1:1994 document was intended to provide basic guidelines for quality management and quality system *elements*. ISO 9004:2000 is cast in a different role, that of providing the guidance to management for the performance improvements identified in its title, first by improving the processes of the QMS and subsequently by improving the organization itself.

The 1994 version concentrated on a set of 20 separate system elements that are judged to be instrumental in any quality system.

The year 2000 standard recognizes that all 20 elements — and many more activities — are involved in the many realization and support processes, the operation and performance of which represent the truly dynamic nature of any organization.

ISO 9004:2000 presents the quality management system as being composed of many interrelated processes that form a comprehensive QMS process network. All operations of an organization are based upon its processes, and such processes are managed by the process approach.

The Consistent Pair of QMS Standards

In response to the needs analysis of potential users, 1S0 9004:2000 and ISO 9001:2000 have each been developed to be members of a planned "consistent pair of quality management system standards." They may be used as stand-alone documents or together, as a pair of complementary standards having different but consistent purposes and scopes.

By design, the latter usage is preferred. Remember, ISO 9004:2000 provides guidance to management for developing a comprehensive QMS whose application can enable management to improve the performance of the QMS and eventually the organization itself.

In a different plan for application, ISO 9001:2000 identifies the basic requirements within the system that are necessary to ensure that the organization meets specified requirements and can demonstrate such compliance.

Each member of this new consistent pair is based on a set of eight Quality Management Principles developed by ISO Technical Committee (TC) 176, the TC responsible for the ISO 9000 series. These principles are typically found in use in successful organizations. They are also often associated with candidate organizations competing for excellence awards programs, such as the Malcolm Baldrige National Quality Awards.

The eight quality management principles represent the concepts that should be applied by the management of any organization in pursuit of continual improvement of its processes, the QMS and the organization. These concepts have been integrated within the clauses and text of both standards.

For user convenience, these principles may be found, with brief descriptions, in Clause 4.3, Use of Quality Management Principles, of ISO 9004:2000 and are discussed in greater detail in an ISO brochure by that name.

The eight principles are:

- Customer focus
- Leadership
- Involvement of people
- Process approach
- System approach to management
- Continual improvement
- Factual approach to decision making
- Mutually beneficial supplier relationships.

As noted previously, ISO 9004:2000 is directed towards performance improvement of an organization and the satisfaction of its interested parties. Interested parties are those individuals and/or groups having a stake in the success of the organization, usually because they benefit in some way from such success.

The interested parties of a typical organization include:

- Customers and product/service end users
- People in the organization
- Owners and investors

- Suppliers and partners
- Society and the community.

In a departure from common practice, *all* the requirements in ISO 9001:2000 are also provided within ISO 9004:2000 for informational purposes. The ISO 9001:2000 requirements are clearly identified, included verbatim and enclosed within separate and distinguishable boxes in ISO 9004:2000.

The boxes containing the ISO 9001 requirements have been placed adjacent to the related text of ISO 9004. On this basis, users can first examine the directive text from ISO 9001 to determine what is expected for meeting specified requirements.

The users can then refer to the related ISO 9004 guidance for the recommended management actions that can result in continual performance improvement of the entire organization.

A Vehicle for Improving the Organization

ISO 9004:2000 has been written for management, with the focus on top management as being responsible for both the success of the organization and the satisfaction of its interested parties. This statement is so basic that no prudent manager can disagree; thus it is clear that the standard is for actual application by management.

The standard provides guidance to management but has no stated requirements. It offers suggestions and recommendations for the management to use as it determines the application of the standard to the organization's QMS.

ISO 9004 is generic in nature, which means that the management of each organization will utilize its own frame of reference to determine the nature of the standards application. The guidance conveys the benefit to the organization of taking steps beyond simply meeting the specified requirements in ISO 9001:2000.

ISO 9004:2000 focuses on effective and efficient performance improvement that is both cost-effective for the organization and will benefit its interested parties.

If properly applied, ISO 9004:2000 can be used to move an organization toward improvement on a continual basis. The strategy for best use of ISO 9004:2000 is to first concentrate on improving the QMS. An improving QMS then becomes the engine for achieving performance improvement for the organization as a whole.

The suggested focus is on continual improvement of the QMS processes being used for moving the total organization towards performance improvement, perhaps even toward excellence. Using ISO 9004:2000 will ensure the movement is in a direct line toward the planned improvement.

Direct-line movement means there is no concern for having to retrench or change direction after starting to use ISO 9004:2000, even if an excellence award becomes the goal of management.

Since ISO 9004:2000 contains no actual requirements, only recommendations and guidance to management, there are no mandatory compliance points. With no mandatory compliance points being identified in the standard, there is no basis identified by which conformity assessment can be legitimately performed.

Acceptance of any or all of the contents of the standard for application is completely up to the management of an organization. Only the organization's management is in the position of deciding the suitability of the recommendations for application or implementation. In fact, Clause 0.3, Relationship with ISO 9001, states that ISO 9004:2000 "is not intended for certification or contractual purposes."

A second disclaimer that is clearly stated in ISO 9004:2000 is that the new edition is not a guide for the implementation of ISO 9001:2000. Although the two standards have similar structures, integrate the concepts of the quality management principles within their texts, present the process approach for managing the organization and offer essentially the same process model, these two ISO 9000 standards serve entirely different purposes and have quite different scopes.

The two standards have a consistent structural outline. The similarity or consistency is most notable in the respective tables of content. However, even though the clause titles are often the same in both documents, ISO 9004:2000 and ISO 9001:2000 do not cover the same aspects of textual content within a given clause title.

ISO 9004:2000 addresses a topic from the position of the effective and efficient improvement of the realization and support processes within the organization to the satisfaction of the interested parties of the organization. By comparison, when ISO 9001:2000 covers the same general topic, it focuses on the effective improvement of the realization processes as they relate to satisfying customer requirements.

It should be clear that there may be material in ISO 9004:2000 that will aid the user of ISO 9001:2000 as implementation is being planned, but only the management of the organization can make a decision to go beyond the minimum requirements of ISO 9001.

Progressive management within an organization may well decide to use some of the ISO 9004 recommendations, particularly when going beyond ISO 9001 requirements is in the organization's best interest and in keeping with its strategic plan.

Implementing the "Guidelines for Performance Improvement"

The majority of the content of both ISO 9004:2000 and ISO 9001:2000 is arranged in four identical key sections:

- Clause 5, Management Responsibility
- Clause 6, Resource Management
- Clause 7, Product Realization
- Clause 8, Measurement, Analysis and Improvement.

Although they share the same major titles, each standard examines and presents each section — and even each clause within the sections — from a different viewpoint. These different viewpoints tend to highlight the major discriminators between the two standards.

The discriminators in ISO 9004:2000 show that the standard:

- Is clearly a guideline standard without any requirements specified
- Provides guidance for performance improvement of the QMS and the organization
- Has been written for the use of top management
- Focuses on improvement of all realization and support processes in the organization
- Addresses both effective and efficient improvements in the organization's processes
- Seeks to achieve the satisfaction of all the organization's interested parties
- Looks beyond ISO 9001 toward the pursuit of organizational excellence
- Displays all ISO 9001:2000 requirements within separate, identified boxes
- Offers guidelines for "self-assessment" of the effectiveness and efficiency of an organization's QMS in its Annex A
- Contains guidance on the process for "continual improvement" of an organization's QMS in its Annex B
- Is not designed or intended to be an "ISO 9001:2000 implementation guide"
- Prohibits its use for certification registration or contractual purposes.

Examples of Performance Improvement Guidance

Within each of the key clauses of ISO 9004:2000, there is guidance that clearly goes beyond the requirements of ISO 9001:2000. This guidance may play one of four roles:

1. Extend the basic ISO 9001 intent to a level beyond the stated requirements

2. Consider such aspects as satisfying all of an organization's interested parties

3. Pursue efficiency in addition to effectiveness in all processes and activities

4. Provide unique points for consideration as the management of an organization pursues performance improvement.

Tables 3-1 to 3-4 contain some typical examples of the performance improvement guidance from each of Clauses 5-8. For each section, there are examples of concepts typical of those found in ISO 9004:2000 that would not be found in ISO 9001:2000. By glancing through the list of these "discriminator" concepts from ISO 9004:2000, one can quickly develop an accurate view of the nature of the new edition's content.

Table 3-1. Concepts Unique to Clause 5, Management Responsibility, of ISO 9004:2000

Responsibility to society and the community

Identification and pursuit of market opportunities

Financial effects of quality activities

Benchmarking and third-party evaluation

Use of quality policy to lead organization

Planning and gaining competitive advantage

Risk assessment and risk mitigation data

Continual improvement of the organization

Exceeding compliance with statutory/regulatory requirements

Encouragement of feedback and communication

External evaluation of the organization

Empowerment of the organization's people

Determination of the organization's competitive weaknesses

Quality objectives as part of strategic plan

Identification of the benefits to interested parties

Use of reviews to create platforms for new ideas

Table 3-2. Concepts Unique to Clause 6, Resource Management, of ISO 9004:2000

Leverage of partnerships to aid mutual improvement

Involvement of people in setting objectives

Leading, problem solving, and teambuilding

Objective setting and decision making

Consideration of environmental issues (e.g., pollution)

Control of heat, humidity, light, airflow and noise

Top management responsibility for ensuring future resources

Project and matrix management needs

Conversion of data into information, which can become knowledge

Maintenance of the availability of natural resources

Evaluation of product failure, warranty rates and lost markets

Management/workforce succession needs

Table 3-3. Concepts Unique to Clause 7, Product Realization, of ISO 9004:2000

Protecting the value of customer property

Compliance of realization process networks

Pursuit of process improvements to benefit interested parties

Purchasing practices that include function, price and delivery

Role of people within processes

Design reviews that evaluate potential hazards

Supplier financial reviews

Inclusion of both materials and energy in resource management

Consideration of the needs and expectations of end users

Market research, with sector/end-user data

Perceiving that support processes add value indirectly

Designing, which includes life cycle, usability and risk

Elimination of process error by foolproofing

Development of operating plans to define opportunities

Identification of resources to maintain product

Ensuring people's health and safety

Verification within processes to identify variation

Traceability for product recall or statutes

Table 3-4. Concepts Unique to Clause 8, Measurement, Analysis and Improvement, of ISO 9004:2000

Recording support process nonconformities

Ongoing continual improvement/breakthroughs

Measurement of the organization's perception by society

Use of valid and purposeful measurements that add value

Self-assessments to determine maturity of QMS

Satisfaction surveys from interested parties

Customer, regulatory or third-party verification

Involvement of people in pursuing improvement

Mitigation of losses with loss-prevention plan

Use of corrective-action teams to define problems

Application of process measures, including throughput and yield

Collection of satisfaction data from focus groups

Management efforts to create an environment for improvement

Excellent audit results for motivation/reward

What Does Annex A Contribute?

Annex A, Guidelines for Self-Assessment, provides a method for evaluating the status of the organization's QMS. This method is designed to determine whether the system is accomplishing what is intended for the organization and how well it is doing it. The evaluation rates the level of the organization's success on a predetermined scale (e.g., 1- 5).

Self-assessment is actually a judgment based on a simple evaluation made by knowledgeable people who go through a process of asking and answering key questions. It is anticipated that the evaluators or assessors would be the top management of the organization. The assessment may be performed remotely, cover all or part of the QMS, done when convenient, performed by one person or several or used as a simple indicator to be combined with other measures.

Annex A is not expected to be used as competition with other self-assessment approaches, since it is a guide to developing a self-assessment rather than a comprehensive self-assessment plan.

Sample or typical questions are provided in the Annex, although the user would be better served to develop questions that would be directly relevant to its organization's operations. As such, an organization using Annex A as its guide can develop questions related to its own concerns and interests.

By using the resultant answers, the organization can determine approximately where it stands in relation to where it wants to be. Using the Annex A method of evaluation over a period of time, management can monitor any apparent change, plus the direction and rate of the change.

Over time, the evolving maturity of the QMS as well as the organization itself can be monitored.

Annex A also contains sections that:

• Deal with the benefits to be derived from a maturing QMS

• List the benefits to be expected if the questions being asked on a given subject reveal successful movement toward improvement.

As the QMS demonstrates increasing maturity, the organization can also check to see if the expected benefits are being encountered. If the expected benefits do not start to appear, the organization will need to reevaluate the cause and effect of the question/benefit relationship.

It may reveal that the questions need to be more focused or that there is no direct cause and effect between questions and expected benefits.

The self-assessment approach is not a substitute for the formal internal audit process defined in the consistent pair of standards. The standards present the internal audit process as being used to determine the technical conformance (or nonconformance) of the organization to its defined QMS.

The internal audit process assigns trained auditors to compare specific requirements as stated within the QMS with the organization's actual conformance to those requirements, with the decision based upon objective evidence gathered by the auditors.

This process is in contrast to the self-assessment method presented in Annex A, which is subjective in that it relies on the opinion of one or more experts within the organization.

What Does Annex B Provide?

Annex B, Process for Continual Improvement, presents a generic process that is suitable for use by any organization. Annex B covers the continual improvement process, whether it involves ongoing and incremental activities or breakthrough projects. The basic process utilizes the same sequential activities for achieving improvement, regardless of whether the improvements are incremental or breakthrough.

Annex B also makes it clear that one of the best ways to reap the most benefit from continual improvement is to involve all the people in the organization. For the continual improvement process to be successful, top management must create the environment for people to be responsive and innovative.

The process steps shown in Annex B, when followed in the sequence presented, can be used by the management of any organization to quickly develop a continual improvement program. The need to allocate and prioritize projects and resources for the continual improvement process is the responsibility of top management.

Key Points

ISO 9004:2000 — A Standard Comes of Age

ISO 9004:2000 provides guidance to management to go beyond ISO 9001's basic requirements in pursuit of performance improvement of the QMS and the firm itself.

The quality management principles are typically found in use in successful organizations.

In summary, ISO 9004:2000:

- Is a quality management system standard for performance improvement of the QMS and the organization, for use by top management, and offers guidance without specifying any requirements
- Is not an "ISO 9001:2000 implementation guide" but focuses beyond ISO

9001 as management pursues organizational excellence and the satisfaction of all interested parties

- Offers guidelines for self-assessment (Annex A) and continual improvement (Annex B) as additional tools to increase the effectiveness and efficiency of all the organization's realization and support processes

- Prohibits its use for certification/registration or contractual purposes, while maintaining a user-friendly consistency with ISO 9001:2000.

The ISO 9001:2000 Standard

4

by Robert W. Peach

This chapter discusses the requirements of ISO 9001:2000 in detail. While certain specific documentation requirements contained in ISO 9001:1994 have not been carried over to ISO 9001:2000, some new requirements have been added. These are identified in this chapter as "Additional ISO 9001:2000 Requirements."

Various guidance documents had been published in recent years to supplement the ISO 9000 family of standards. Portions of the material contained in these standards have been incorporated into ISO 9000:2000, ISO 9001:2000 and ISO 9004:2000. At the time of the publication of ISO 9001:2000, the supporting guidance standards had not been reissued with the new clause structure of ISO 9001:2000, but much of their content remains appropriate as guidance for applying ISO 9001.

ISO 9001:2000 and ISO 9004:2000 are a "consistent pair," which means that they have a similar primary clause structure and are designed to complement each other, but can be used independently. While ISO 9004:2000 provides guidance for efficient quality management practice, it does not contain requirements. ISO 9004:2000, *Quality Management Systems — Guidelines for Performance Improvement* contains much valuable content, of use as requirement elements are adopted, but particularly as an organization seeks to improve its quality management capabilities. Frequent references are made in this chapter to ISO 9004:2000 content, primarily alerting the reader to additional guidance elements. On occasion, reference is made to lists of items in ISO 9004:2000, which are to be found in the standard itself, contained on the *Handbook*'s CD-ROM.

In addition to referencing ISO 9004:2000, this chapter also draws on contents of other standards and documents. This information is for guidance in application and is not to be confused with the requirements specified in ISO 9001:2000. The documents, which are clearly identified as guidance, include:

- ISO 9000-2:1997, *Quality Management and Quality Assurance Standards — Generic Guidelines for the Application of ISO 9001:1994*

- ISO 10013:1995, *Guidelines for Developing Quality Manuals.*

These guidance documents can be invaluable to organizations as they apply the content of ISO 9001:2000, for they provide suggestions for obtaining maximum benefit from the quality management system.

Certain clauses contained in ISO 9001:1994 have not been carried over into the 2000 edition or have been condensed. In cases where this earlier content may be of use to some readers, that material is included and clearly referenced.

In addition, this chapter includes references taken from QS-9000 *Quality System Requirements*, a document originally prepared by the US Big Three automotive producers, Ford, General Motors and Chrysler (now DaimlerChrysler). For many suppliers in the automotive industry, QS-9000 is a requirement. (For background on these requirements see Chapter 13.) Unlike QS-9000, the recently issued ISO Technical Specification (TS) 16949 second edition incorporates the revised ISO 9001:2000 clause structure. This chapter references QS-9000 requirements as an aid to applying ISO 9001. QS-9000 content applies specifically to certain suppliers in the automobile industry and *not* to other users of ISO 9001. However, QS-9000 contains many elements of effective quality practice that are worthy of consideration by all organizations.

This chapter also includes interpretation of ISO 9001 elements by experts in the field. These interpretations take two forms: comments by The Victoria Group, a management consulting company in the quality field, and question-and-answer interpretations that have appeared in the highly regarded ISO 9000 industry's journal, *Quality Systems Update*.

As mentioned in Chapter 3, the structure of the standard is quite different from ISO 9001:1994. The 1994 structure can be characterized as a quality assurance model, which follows the flow of a manufacturing process from design and purchasing through manufacturing and delivery. The year 2000 revision is called a process model for quality management, which groups the organization's functions into five process categories. The standard observes that this process approach emphasizes the importance of:

- Understanding requirements and meeting them

- Expecting to receive added value from application of the various processes

- Achieving effective performance
- Using objective measurements of processes that demonstrate improvement.

Foreword

The foreword section of ISO 9001:2000 notes that the term "quality assurance" is not used in the revised standard. This reflects the intent of the quality management system.

Introduction

Reinforcing the statement of the foreword, the introduction to ISO 9001:2000 states the ways in which the standard may be used to address satisfying customer requirements, meeting regulatory requirements and fulfilling the organization's own requirements. It can be used internally by the organization or by external bodies to determine the organization's ability to meet such requirements.

I Scope

The statement of scope emphasizes the generic nature of the standard. It applies to organizations regardless of type, size or product. The introduction states that "it is not the intent … to imply uniformity in the structure of quality management systems or uniformity of documentation."

With the consolidation of ISO 9002:1994 and ISO 9003:1994 into one standard, ISO 9001:2000, provision is made for permitting exclusions of requirements that do not apply in a given situation. Such exclusions are permitted only in Clause 7, Product Realization.

2 Normative Reference

ISO standards alert the user to make use of the latest revisions of other standards that are referenced.

3 Terms and Definitions

Successive updates of ISO 9001 have contained changes in the use of the words "supplier," "subcontractor" and "organization." In earlier publications, use of these terms has varied even between ISO 9001 and ISO 9004. ISO 9001:2000 resolves those differences and should prevent further possible confusion. The producing organization making use of the standard is consistently referred to as "organization." Purchases are from "suppliers." Sales are to "customers." The term "subcontractor" is no longer used in the standard.

The main body of ISO 9001:2000 requirements appears in five primary clauses, numbered 4 through 8. These contain 23 subclauses. The numbers in parentheses reference ISO 9001:1994.

4 Quality Management System

4.1 General Requirements (4.2.1)

This clause states the requirement that a quality management system (QMS) shall be established, implemented and maintained, with appropriate documentation, and that its effectiveness shall be continually improved.

In implementing the QMS, the organization is to identify and manage processes, determining their sequence and interaction. The organization is to do the following:

- Determine those criteria and methods that will ensure effective process operation and control.

- Provide the needed information to operate, monitor, measure and analyze these processes.

- Take action, if necessary, to attain planned results and to improve these processes.

- Processes are to be specifically managed to conform to ISO 9001:2000 requirements.

Additional ISO 9001:2000 Requirements

- Actions shall be taken to continually improve the QMS.

- The quality management system shall identify outsourced processes affecting quality and ensure control over such processes.

ISO 9004:2000 Guidance

ISO 9004:2000 lists examples of activities that can help establish a customer-oriented organization. It makes reference to Annexes A and B, which contain examples of self-assessment and continual improvement processes.

4.2 Documentation Requirements (4.2)

4.2.1 General (4.2.1)

The QMS shall include the following documentation:

- Quality policy and quality objectives
- Quality manual
- Documented procedures required to implement ISO 9001:2000
- Optional documents to ensure process operation and control
- Quality records, as called for in Subclause 4.2.4.

In a note, the standard states that the term "documented procedure" means that the procedure is to be established, documented, implemented and maintained. This clarification enables positive identification of instances where documentation is required.

A second note observes that the amount of QMS documentation necessary will depend upon the size of the organization, type of activities, process complexity and their interactions and employee competence. This note is apparently in response to concerns of smaller organizations that less comprehensive documentation may be permissible.

A third note states that documentation can exist in any form or type of medium, hard copy or electronic.

Subclause 4.2.1: Electronic Control of Documents

Reprinted courtesy of Quality Systems Update

Question: How can electronic documents be controlled to meet the requirements of ISO 9000 series standards?

Answer: All three experts agree that generating and tracking documents electronically is allowed by the ISO 9000 series standard, according to Note 3 in Clause 4.2.1, which states, "Records may be in any form or type of media," though the phrase "such as hard copy or electronic media" no longer appears in this clause.

Advantages of Electronic Media

Robert D. Bowen, president, r. bowen international, inc., says that ISO 9000 series document control principles apply equally to all media. He also points out four distinct advantages of electronic media:

- Accuracy: Immediate on-line review of proposed changes by all knowledgeable persons and a transaction history file showing the date and nature of changes.

- Authenticity: Secure sign-on functions to ensure controlled access to read and write functions.

- Completeness: Online edit-checks that ensure all required information is complete before a document is released.

- Currency: Instantaneous removal of all obsolete documents. Uniform startup of all concerned persons when initiating procedures or changes.

Other strengths, notes Bowen, include immediate update of an organization's documents through electronic data interchange. In addition, "many organizations find it easier to establish a planned review system of quality-related documents if those documents are online." He notes that setting up a database reminder to review documents at specified, agreed-upon intervals is easy to accomplish.

Charles McRobert, president, Quality Practitioners, Inc., says that he worked with "nearly paperless" companies whose document-control systems were excellent. He agrees with Bowen's contention that electronic control of documents makes review and approval of documents and highlighting of changes easier.

McRobert notes that "some auditors with misguided zeal have requested hard copies of all controlled documents with approval signatures." He suggests that any company whose auditor suggests this approach "immediately seek relief" from this requirement.

Document Control

Ian Durand, [then] president of Service Process Consulting Inc., points out that controlled documents can include mechanical assembly drawings, circuit schematics, process flowcharts, physical reference samples, pictures of reference samples or videotapes illustrating proper work methods. He agrees that using electronic media for document control has many distinct advantages. He says the complexity of such systems should not be a roadblock, pointing to the demanding access and control requirements of electronic fund transfer financial-control systems and security and administration systems.

Durand notes that a number of software programs are currently available to handle documentation and quality records of an ISO 9000-based quality system.

4.2.2 Quality Manual (4.2.1)

A quality manual defining the documentation structure of the quality system shall be established and maintained. It is to include the scope of the QMS, include or make reference to all QMS elements and procedures and describe the interaction between processes included in the quality system. The quality manual shall be part of the overall organization documentation; it is not necessarily a separate document, and it may be electronic.

Additional ISO 9001:2000 Requirements

4.2.2a The quality manual is to cover the scope of the QMS, including details and justification for any exclusions.

ISO 9004:2000 Guidance

ISO 9004:2000 lists ways to satisfy the needs and expectations of interested parties.

It also lists criteria for evaluating the effectiveness and efficiency of the use and control of documentation.

ISO 9000-2:1997 Guidance

The quality manual can be structured as a tiered set of documents, with each tier becoming more detailed. Quality policy, defining approach and responsibility, would be the top tier, while detailed procedures and work instructions and record-keeping forms would be in lower tiers.

ISO 10013:1995 Guidance

ISO 10013:1995, a reference publication, provides guidance in the preparation of quality manuals. Remember: this publication is only advisory. The guidance contained in ISO 10013 is not to be interpreted as part of the requirements of subclause 4.2.2.

4.2.3 Control of Documents (4.5)

Documents required by the QMS shall be controlled and a procedure shall be established. Each must be reviewed and approved for adequacy before being issued. To avoid using invalid and/or obsolete documents, organizations should identify the current revision status of the documents. Subclause 4.2.3 also requires that:

- Documents shall be reviewed, updated as needed and reapproved.
- Documents shall be legible, easily identified as to current version and available at all relevant locations where needed. Documents originating from outside the organization shall be identified and controlled.
- Any obsolete documents retained for legal and/or knowledge-preservation purposes shall be suitably identified to prevent unintended use.

A basic requirement is to identify changes in documents and to review and approve all changes. The review and approval process should normally be performed by the functions or activities that performed the original review. The intention is to ensure that changes made in documents already issued follow the same approval process as conventional industry practice. This would be a system in which a document is issued by a designated originating activity (department) before it passes through one or more approval stages. These stages may organizationally be in the same department or another department. One situation where waiving the approval process might be acceptable is if an organization had field-installation responsibilities and its qualified personnel were empowered to modify a product or practice on the spot, in which case an approval mechanism might not be available or practical.

ISO 9000-2:1997 Guidance

Documentation is usually subject to revision. This requirement applies both to internal documentation and to external documentation, such as national standards. Organizations should consider the effect that changes in one area may have on other parts of the organization and the actions that should be taken to assess this effect. Other things to keep in mind include:

- Planning the circulation of a change proposal to avoid disruption
- Timing implementation of the changes.

The standard specifically mentions that documents of external origin shall be included within the controlled system. This means customer specifications, national and international specifications, regulatory documents, etc.

Document control shall apply to all documents and/or computer records pertinent to design and development, purchasing, realization, quality standards, inspection of materials and other internal written procedures. Internal written procedures for document control describe the following:

- How should documentation for these functions be controlled?
- Who is responsible for document control?
- What is to be controlled?
- Where and when is it to be controlled?

QS-9000 Automotive

Document and Data Approval and Issue (4.5.2)

Examples of appropriate documents include:

- Engineering drawings
- Engineering standards
- Math (CAD) data

- Inspection instructions
- Test procedures
- Work instructions
- Operations sheets
- Quality manual
- Operational procedures
- Quality assurance procedures
- Material specifications.

Engineering Specifications (4.5.2.1)

A procedure is to be established for timely reviews (days, not weeks or months) of all standards and specification changes, with a record of implementation date.

4.2.4 Control of Records (4.16)

The organization shall:

- Establish documented procedures for identification, storage, protection, retrieval and disposition of quality records
- Store records effectively and to prevent loss or damage
- Establish and record retention times of quality records
- Make quality records available for evaluation by the customer or its representative.

As with documents, quality records shall be legible and identifiable to the product involved.

ISO 9000-2:1997 Guidance

Throughout ISO 9001 there are references to quality records. The purpose of quality records is to demonstrate required quality and the effectiveness of the quality system. Effective quality records contain direct and indirect evidence that demonstrates whether the product or service meets requirements. The records should be readily accessible. They may be stored in any suitable form, either as hard copy or on electronic media.

Sometimes customers may be required to store and maintain selected quality records that attest to the quality of products (including services) for a specified part of the operating lifetime. The organization should provide such documents to the customer.

International standards do not specify a minimum time period for retaining quality records. Organizations should consider the following:

- Requirements of regulatory authorities
- Product liability and other legal issues related to record keeping
- Expected lifetime of the product
- Requirements of the contract.

Aside from these considerations, it is common practice to retain records for five to seven years.

Examples of quality records potentially requiring control, contained in ISO 9004-1:1994, Clause 17.2, are:

- Inspection reports
- Test data
- Qualification reports
- Validation reports
- Survey and audit reports
- Material review reports
- Calibration data
- Quality-related cost reports.

QS-9000 Automotive

Records Retention (4.16.1)

- Production part approvals, tooling records and purchase orders shall be retained one calendar year after the part is active for production and service.
- Quality performance records are to be retained one year beyond the year created.
- Internal quality system audits and management reviews are to be retained for three years.

The above record retention requirements do not supersede customer or government regulations. The specified periods are "minimums."

Superseded Parts

The "new part" file is to contain documents from superseded parts if they are required for a new part qualification.

Business Plan (4.1.4)

The plan should cover short term (one to two years) and longer term (three years and beyond) and should:

- Be based on competitive analysis and benchmarking
- Have methods to determine customer expectations
- Use an objective information collection process
- Ensure use of plan through documented procedures
- Use data to drive process improvement
- Provide means for employees to be empowered.

Note: Contents of the business plan are not subject to third-party audit.

Analysis and Use of Company-Level Data (4.1.5)

The organization shall:

- Document quality and performance trends
- Compare your data with competitors' data and/or appropriate benchmarks
- Take action to solve customer-related problems
- Support status review, decision making and long-term planning.

Subclause 4.2.4: Control of Quality Records

The ISO 9001 standard continually refers to the need for records to demonstrate completed actions. Subclause 4.2.4 does not call for the creation of additional records, but points out that records must be identified, legible, stored, protected and maintained in a manner that makes them easily accessible.

The difference between the quality records filing system and any other in a business is that a great deal of the information contained in these records should be decentralized to be instantly available when required. This means that the maintenance of the defined quality records will need to be monitored by the process of internal audit to ensure that everyone is doing what they should. It is easy to become paranoid about fulfilling the requirements of this element, which are quite basic.

Contrary to popular belief, the clause does not require fireproof safes, bank-vault storage, microfiche or other similar methods of storage. The level of protection required for records depends upon the nature of the business, as well as any contractual or statutory requirements. The records connected with the construction of a nuclear power station need to be kept somewhat longer, and under more secure conditions, than the records for making a compact disc.

Some registrars have definite ideas about record-retention times. It is a good idea to establish whether the company's record-retention policy agrees with the registrar's demands during an initial meeting. The record-retention policy should be clarified and agreed upon before the audit team arrives on site.

Procedures for Access

The methodology in use must provide for appropriate access to records as required. Specific references may be required for access arrangements, particularly when records have to be maintained for extended periods of time or in compliance with specific contractual requirements.

— *The Victoria Group*

5 Management Responsibility (4.1)

5.1 Management Commitment (4.2.1)

This clause describes the requirement for commitment of top management to develop and improve the quality management system. Top management shall:

- Establish a quality policy
- Establish objectives
- Conduct management reviews
- Provide necessary resources.

Additional ISO 9001:2000 Requirements

5.1a Making certain that everyone understands the importance of meeting needs of customers and regulators.

ISO 9004:2000 Guidance

Ways in which management responsibility can be furthered are listed as follows:

- Actions by management to establish, sustain and increase customer satisfaction
- Methods of measuring organization's performance
- Activities in which leadership can be demonstrated
- Ways in which management may analyze and optimize interaction of processes.

Clause 5.1: What Constitutes Evidence of "Commitment"?

Reprinted courtesy of Quality Systems Update

Question: Clause 5.1, Management Commitment, requires companies to define their policies for quality, including objectives for quality and commitment to quality. What objective evidence will establish this commitment to quality in the eyes of an auditor?

Answer: *Quality Systems Update*'s panel of experts say objective evidence ranges from success in meeting measurable objectives to involvement of top management in the operation and implementation of the quality system.

Moderator Reginald Shaughnessy, [then] general manager operations of Samuel-Acme Strapping Systems Inc., says the term "commitment" can be demonstrated by showing that measurable objectives have been met.

"The intent of the clause is that there would be measurable objectives," he says. But there isn't a consensus on what constitutes measurable objectives. "The knowledge in managing the business is the top line. To produce the products and services effectively and efficiently is the middle line. The sustainability of the company is the bottom line. To me that's what it's simply all about. It's not about building up reams and reams of concepts."

Shaughnessy says objectives may include an overall reduction in numbers of complaints and claim levels and an improvement of customer service. "There's no point in telling people, 'Well, I got a policy to be better,'" says Shaughnessy. "How much better?"

Shaughnessy says the clause is not solely about management participation in the implementation of the quality system. "The quality system is management," he says. "You haven't even got a quality system if that's an issue. Every company to whatever degree knows it's business first."

The intent of the clause is to drive improvement, he says.

"Commitment and involvement are for a purpose: to drive the quality objectives, to lead and to manage the organization," says Shaughnessy. "Without a vision, the people perish. Without a policy to drive the vision with a sense of mission and a sense of purpose measured by the quality objectives, there would be no point. It becomes an add-on and just a cost of doing business to get a certificate."

Bud Weightman, president of Qualified Specialists Inc., an ISO 9000 and QS-9000 training and consulting organization, interprets "commitment" to mean the commitment of top management in the operation of the quality system.

"Commitment is not just finding an individual and assigning an individual who is going to be the management representative and then dropping the ball," says Weightman. "It really begins with executive management introducing the concept to the company's management team and letting it be known that he totally supports the quality effort, not the ISO effort, in his organization and that he will support the management representative throughout the implementation of the quality system."

Weightman says that executive management can show its commitment through weekly, monthly or periodic steering committee meetings, company publications, and memos and by demonstrating interest in the establishment of goals and objectives in conjunction with the development of a quality policy and manual.

"That's not just a sign-off, but demonstrated interest," Weightman explains. "I like the words 'demonstrated interest' because if executive management is interested and they're visible, then the rest of the management tends to fall in line."

Commitment implies that executive management set aside time for problem resolution between the management representative and other managers, according to Weightman.

"It also means that executive management holds other managers accountable for their part in quality system activities," he adds.

Weightman says objective evidence may include management reviews, signatures, minutes of steering committee meetings, internal memorandums and newsletters.

5.2 Customer Focus

This clause is not contained in ISO 9001:1994.

Additional ISO 9001:2000 Requirements

The organization shall ensure that the needs and expectations of customers are thoroughly defined, understood, translated into requirements and met, resulting in customer satisfaction.

Customer expectations include product-related requirements, such as meeting regulations. Refer to Clause 7.2, Customer-Related Processes.

ISO 9004:2000 Guidance

ISO 9004:2000 lists identifying needs and expectations of interested parties.

- Actions of an organization to understand needs of interested parties
- Actions to understand needs and expectations of customers and end users
- Examples of customer and end user needs and expectations

- Actions key to establishing partnerships with suppliers
- Actions to consider in an organization's relationship with society.

QS-9000 Automotive

Customer Satisfaction (4.1.6)

The organization shall:

- Document the process for determining the frequency, objectivity and validity of customer satisfaction information
- Document trends in customer satisfaction and key indicators of dissatisfaction
- Compare trends to competition and benchmarks
- Review trends (task of senior management)
- Consider both immediate and final customers.

5.3 Quality Policy (4.1.1)

Quality policy is defined in *ISO 9000:2000, Quality Management and Quality Assurance — Vocabulary*, as "the overall intentions and direction of an organization related to quality, as formally expressed by top management ... The quality policy shall be consistent with the overall policy of the organization ..."

Top management shall ensure that the quality policy:

- Is appropriate to organizational goals, and includes a commitment to meeting requirements and to continual improvement
- Provides a framework for establishing and reviewing quality objectives
- Is communicated to and understood by everyone affected
- Is reviewed for suitability.

The standard refers to "top management" being responsible for establishing the quality policy. This emphasizes the importance of management with executive responsibility being involved in the quality system development process. The words "top management" are repeated throughout the standard.

The clause emphasizes a commitment not only to meeting requirements but also to continual improvement.

Additional ISO 9001:2000 Requirements

5.3b Quality policy is to include a commitment to continual improvement.

5.3c Provision for establishing and reviewing quality objectives.

ISO 9004:2000 Guidance

ISO 9004:2000 lists factors to consider in establishing quality policy and factors to consider when using quality policy as a means for making improvements.

ISO 9000-2:1997 Guidance

ISO 9000-2 recommends that management ensure that the quality policy is:

- Easy to understand
- Relevant to the organization
- Ambitious, yet achievable.

Since commitment to a quality policy starts at the top of an organization, management should demonstrate its commitment visibly, actively and continually.

5.4 Planning

5.4.1 Quality Objectives (4.1.1)

The requirement to set objectives is continued from ISO 9001:1994.

Additional ISO 9001:2000 Requirements

Quality objectives are to be established at each appropriate organizational function and level, including meeting requirements. Objectives are to be measurable and consistent with quality policy.

ISO 9004:2000 Guidance

Clause 5.4.1 lists considerations by management when establishing objectives. (See *Handbook* CD-ROM.)

5.4.2 Quality Management System Planning (4.2.3)

Planning necessary to meet quality objectives and requirements stated in Clause 4.1 shall be carried out. Planning is to ensure that the quality management system is maintained during organizational changes.

ISO 9004:2000 Guidance

Clause 5.4.2 lists inputs to be considered for effective and efficient quality planning and outputs of quality planning, defining product realization and support processes to be considered. (See *Handbook* CD-ROM.)

ISO 9000-2:1997 Guidance

Quality plans define how quality system requirements will be met in a specific contract or for a specific class of products. An example might include a detailed sequence of inspections for a particular product, types of inspection equipment and quality record requirements.

QS-9000 Automotive

Quality Planning (4.2.3)

The *Advanced Product Quality Planning and Control Plan* reference manual shall be used for:

- Planning
- Product design and development
- Process design and development
- Product and process verification
- Production
- Feedback assessment and corrective action.

Use of Cross-Functional Teams

Internal cross-functional teams are to use techniques in the *Advanced Product Quality Planning and Control Plan* reference manual.

Special Characteristics

Appropriate process controls shall be established for special characteristics.

Feasibility Reviews

Manufacturing feasibility is to be confirmed prior to contracting.

Product Safety

Factors affecting product to be considered at design control and process control stages.

Process FMEAs

Efforts are to be taken to prevent rather than detect defects, using techniques in the *Potential Failure Modes and Effects* reference manual.

The Control Plan

Control plans consist of the output of the advanced quality planning process and shall be developed for:

- Prototype (may not be required from all suppliers)
- Pre-launch
- Production.

Clause 5.4: Meeting the Requirements of Quality

Reprinted courtesy of Quality Systems Update

Question: Clause 5.4 of ISO 9001, Planning, requires objectives to "include those needed to meet requirements for product." Is it sufficient to list a set of quality objectives? Or must we also define how the objectives are to be achieved? What do registrars look for when auditing this clause?

Answer: *QSU's* panel of experts disagreed as to whether companies must define how quality objectives will be achieved.

Moderator Arthur Gold, [then] an industry sector specialist with the New Jersey Manufacturing Extension Program (MEP), says the standard doesn't specifically state that companies must define how their quality objectives are to be achieved, but companies must do so nevertheless.

"It's somewhat implicit," explains Gold. "They wouldn't have to go into detail but they've got to define some methodology and accountability."

He says ISO 9000 registrars look for objective evidence that companies give ample consideration to their quality objectives. "They're looking for some policy statements and general strategies to do that and they're also looking for some objective evidence that that has happened," says Gold. Such evidence may include the minutes of meetings at which quality objectives were discussed.

Gold says companies should attempt to define how quality objectives will be achieved as early on in the implementation process as possible. "This may act as a template to drive other sections of the standard in implementation," he says. "You want to lay your general framework first, and have consistency through a quality management system."

James R. DiNitto, president and chief executive officer of International Quality Systems (IQS), an ISO 9000 and QS-9000 training and consulting firm, says he too believes it is necessary for companies to show how quality objectives will be achieved.

"I think the company's quality objectives should become an integral part of the management review process and should have plans backing up the objectives," explains DiNitto. The plans should include some type of metrics to measure progress in meeting the objectives.

"Otherwise they become meaningless," he says of the objectives. DiNitto says registrars are looking for evidence of quality improvement as opposed to more general business objectives.

"They want to get a feeling that a company is using its quality system effectively," he says, "and that certification isn't just a one-time accomplishment, but a continuing involvement.

Lanny Gookin, president and senior consultant of QMR Consulting Inc., an ISO 9000, API Spec Q1 and QS-9000 consulting and training firm, agrees that quality planning must include an explanation of how quality objectives will be met.

"Quality planning involves determining objectives and methodology required to achieve those objectives," Gookin says. "And then within the context of 5.4 they need to determine whether that methodology is consistent with the remainder of the methodology used by the company to achieve other stated objectives of management."

Gookin says the methodology and activities that support quality planning should be appropriate to the nature of the business. For example, he says, organizations that perform project work or that have constantly changing products require a more active quality planning function than most organizations.

In such organizations, he explains, "quality planning is much more of an ongoing activity that is either project-by-project or order-by-order based."

For other companies, quality-planning activities might be constant.

Gookin says registrars typically evaluate quality-planning activities based on the business type, scope of registration and quality objectives.

Joseph Murphy, North American operations manager with ISOQAR, an ISO 9000 registrar, says he does not believe companies are obliged to define how quality objectives will be met, since the standard does not specifically address this. "They would not have to state how they are going to achieve them," says Murphy of quality objectives. "But we would just be reviewing them to see how in fact they are being met."

Auditors need to verify that there is some planning taking place relative to the quality system, he says.

"That doesn't necessarily mean that they have specific quality plans," he explains. "To us quality plans are where you have a set of specifications that embody particular processes that the customer requires."

For example, Murphy says, medical device companies may be subject to certain US Food and Drug Administration (FDA) requirements. In such cases auditors would attempt to verify that the company has a way of ensuring that FDA requirements are being met in their quality-planning activities.

"If they don't have those, then we seek to determine if, for example, through their management review meetings, or any other periodic quality meetings they might have, they plan for directions they're moving in and improvements in their quality systems," according to Murphy. "We kind of look to see if it is luck that they're moving ahead or if they actually have a master plan."

For example, he says, companies that undertake an expansion might be expected to demonstrate that they took into consideration things like training needs of the new personnel.

"When you take a look at the records and review them and talk to [employees], does this come through?" Murphy asks.

5.5 Responsibility, Authority and Communication (4.2)

5.5.1 Responsibility and Authority (4.1.2.1)

The organization shall define and communicate the responsibilities, the authorities, and the interrelation of all personnel affecting the quality of product and service to customers. This refers to personnel who must prevent the occurrence of product nonconformity, identify and record any product quality problems, recommend solutions, verify their implementation and control further processing, delivery or installation of nonconforming products until the problem has been corrected.

Additional ISO 9001:2000 Requirement

Roles and their interrelations are to be defined and communicated so that quality management can be effective.

ISO 9000-2:1997 Guidance

Individuals in the organization should:

- Be aware of the scope, responsibility, and authority of their functions.
- Be aware of their impact on product and service quality.
- Have adequate authority to carry out their responsibilities.
- Understand clearly their defined authority.
- Accept responsibility for achieving quality objectives.

QS-9000 Automotive

Organizational Interfaces (4.1.2.4)

Systems are to be in place during advanced planning stages. (See the *Advanced Product Quality Planning and Control Plan* reference manual.)

The organization shall use a multidiscipline approach for decision making.

Information and data are to be communicated in customer-prescribed format.

Subclause 5.5.1: Defining Responsibility and Authority in ISO 9000

Reprinted courtesy of Quality Systems Update

Question: Subclause 5.5.1 of ISO 9001, Responsibility and Authority, states, "Top management shall ensure that the responsibilities, authorities and their interrelations are defined and communicated within the organization." What is meant by "defined" and what kind of communication will auditors be looking for?

Answer: Our panelists agree that this element of the standard requires that personnel be identified and their responsibilities spelled out and documented in a textual or hard-copy format, such as an organizational chart.

"Documentation requirements were contained throughout ISO 9001:1994, and many of these requirements are carried over into ISO 9001:2000," explains Robert W. Peach, our panel moderator. "However, the intent of ISO 9001:2000 is to reduce the required amount of documentation; that is one of the issues being addressed by TC 176."

According to Peach, there have been a number of complaints with respect to too much prescriptive detail in the previous standard. "This may well be, but does not take away from the requirement that methods of operation are to be documented in some way," he adds. "That certainly means in writing, hard copy, or computer or some other method."

Peach says that people who are involved in the quality management effort must know their authority, scope, responsibility and function.

"You can't do that just by word of mouth; management is to have authority to carry out its responsibilities and that authority must be in writing someplace," he says. "But the method by which it's done is up to management; it can be in a manual, in directives, but it's got to be available."

Peach says that any statement defining authority must be understandable to those reading it, to effectively define limits of authority.

"This includes people with the assigned task, as well as those for whom they work and those who work under them. Lines of authority must be clear; otherwise authority can be confused," Peach concludes. "How far suppliers must go in documenting lines of authority is intentionally not detailed in ISO 9001. It is up to management to establish and document practices suitable for their business."

Peach says the absence of the word "documentation" in parts of ISO 9001:2000 does not take away the need for defined responsibility throughout the organization.

"The word 'defined' means it needs to be understood within the organizational structure who has responsibility for doing what," says Greg Hansa, [then] vice president of technical development for SGS International Certification Services Inc. "And that needs to be assigned to specific people and they need to have the appropriate responsibility and authority."

Hansa says that it's hard to redefine "defined." But essentially, that's what it means.

"'Definition' can be in any of a number of formats," he adds. "It can be verbal, in other words, in text format; it can be written out; or it can be charted in a flowchart or organizational chart," he says. "Generally, within documentation for an ISO 9000 system, the definition should be textual to some extent, enough to provide stability and coherence to the system.

"Communicated" has always been a very controversial topic with regard to ISO 9001, says Hansa.

"In this case, 'communicated' means to avoid any confusion that might arise with the change in personnel or a change in management structure or changes that occur," he explains. "Essentially, what 'communication' is trying to do is to provide an amount of stability to the system, as well as an amount of discipline."

Hansa says that a baseline is established in documented format and all changes that are made to the system must be made in a controlled manner. This prevents any loss of control or any confusion within the system.

"With regard to this specific clause, 5.5.1, what we're talking about is overall responsibilities and authorities," he says. "The upper-level responsibilities and authorities are defined within an organizational chart that indicates who is responsible for what issue and to whom they report."

Further down within the organization, he adds, responsibilities and authorities are typically delineated within quality system procedures and/or work instructions. They indicate who is responsible for executing a particular procedure or instruction, as well as where lines of authority meet.

The initiation of action to prevent nonconformities, while not necessarily addressed in a specific clause or quality system element relating to responsibility and authority, will probably be addressed within specific work instructions and/or within specific procedures for handling nonconformities, he adds. This is a much bigger issue in ISO 9001:2000.

A particular weakness that is found in many quality systems is the definition of the 'functions and their interrelations,'" Hansa concludes. "In other words, the particular function is assigned to particular tasks and responsibilities, but their relation to other tasks and responsibilities within other parts of the organization is not well defined."

W. Bruce Walker, a lead assessor for Quality Systems Registrars Inc., says the clause refers to three different areas in the organizational structure and how these interact with each other. Companies that do a good job of defining responsibility and authority usually have thought these activities through and are committed to producing a product or service that meets customer requirements.

"Defined," he says, means to specify the extent of responsibility and authority for:

Managers who affect quality. Usually this is documented in the quality system under the management sections as statements defining general responsibility and authority for each management position in regard to quality of the product/service. Specifics are stated in the procedures that a particular manager is responsible for.

Performance of work that affects quality. This is generally documented in the quality system in the section defining process control and other quality-related activities. Specifics for performance of work are more defined in the procedures or instructions that further describe the process, servicing, handling, storage, packaging, preservation and delivery functions.

Verification activities that affect quality. These are generally documented in the sections of the quality system defining inspection and tests or internal audits or, in some cases, where the process operators are tasked with verification (inspection and testing) activities in process control. Specifics are defined in the procedures, which describe the verification activities (inspection and testing, internal audit, inspection and test status, etc.).

"The more thought put into the interaction of personnel within the organization generally results in less wasted time and energy in addressing design, purchasing, manufacturing and product/service acceptance issues," says Walker.

5.5.2 Management Representative (4.1.2.3)

Top management shall designate a member of the organization with defined responsibility and authority to establish, implement and maintain QMS processes and to report on QMS performance and improvement needs. A note observes that management representatives can interface with outside parties on quality issues.

Additional ISO 9001:2000 Requirements

5.5.2c Management representative is to ensure that customer needs are well known throughout the organization.

Subclause 5.5.2: The Management Representative

Reprinted courtesy of Quality Systems Update

Question: ISO 9001 Subclause 5.5.2 states: "Top management shall appoint a member of management who, irrespective of other responsibilities, shall have responsibility and authority ..." What does the term "irrespective of other responsibilities" mean? What background or qualifications should this person possess and where should the position fall in an organizational structure?

Answer: A panel of experts disagreed on whether the management representative may oversee ISO 9000 series registration as a secondary responsibility. Elizabeth Potts, quality director, Ashland Chemical, maintains that the term "irrespective of other responsibilities" does not preclude the representative from having other duties and from those other duties taking precedence.

"This phrase allows companies the flexibility and opportunity to structure their organizations to meet their needs and not be forced to comply with an imposed requirement to have a person assigned only to the quality system," she says. "This further enhances a wider application of the standard to all types of organizations and organizational structures."

While agreeing that the management representative may have other responsibilities, the three other panelists say the quality system has to be the first priority.

As a Primary Responsibility

Stephen Gousie, operations director, Information Mapping, Inc., says the term "irrespective of other responsibilities" means that the management representative must assign equal or higher priority to ISO 9000 relative to other responsibilities. The management representative's primary responsibilities are to ensure that the requirements of the ISO 9000 series standard are implemented and maintained, Gousie says.

This would include primary responsibility for ensuring that the organization is prepared for the initial registration audit and for the periodic, ongoing audits to maintain registration, he says. That person should be familiar with the requirements of ISO 9000 and the appropriate external quality assurance standard. He or she should also be familiar with the company and be able to show how the organization meets each of the requirements of the standard, Gousie says.

"Most organizations have their management representative attend one of the lead assessor courses," he says. "While this will help the representative to better understand the registration audit process, it is not an absolute requirement. Knowledge of the requirements of the standard can be obtained by attending one of the many ISO 9000 overview seminars or working closely with an ISO 9000 consultant."

The position should be considered a management position and the person in it should be given direct access to the most senior person in the organization, Gousie says. In most cases, he adds, the management representative is also the quality assurance manager. "There is no specific requirement that the management representative be the quality assurance manager," Gousie says. "Where the quality function is closely meshed with production, the production manager might fill this responsibility."

Must Have Defined Authority and Responsibility

Robert Hammil, of Excelsior Consulting, says the management representative must have "defined responsibility and authority" for ensuring that the requirements of the ISO 9000 series are implemented and maintained. "Ultimately, the management representative is the facility's quality system overseer, sponsor, and champion," Hammil says. "He or she is the person whom others, both within the facility and outside of it, consult on any matter pertaining to the quality management system."

Hammil says the management representative shoulders a heavy burden. "Though the management representative may have duties apart from the quality system, the person assuming this role must, in order to be effective, make a serious and long-term commitment to the activity." According to Hammil, candidates should posses a number of qualifications, including the following:

- Be knowledgeable about traditional quality assurance and quality control technologies.

- Have an understanding of the series standards and the strategic role ISO 9000 plays in the company.

- Have a commitment to the importance of ISO 9000.

- Be an authority figure, ideally with seniority and experience that cuts across departmental lines, though not necessarily from senior management.

- Have superior communication skills.

- Carry the backing of the chief executive officer or general manager.

"He or she must have the trust, confidence and backing of the highest authority in the facility," Hammil says. "This could and often does mean that the management representative reports directly to the chief executive officer, at least insofar as quality management system responsibilities are concerned."

Prioritizing Job Responsibilities

John Cachat, president of IQS, Inc., agrees that "the highest priority for the individual's time will always be to ensure that ISO requirements are implemented and maintained. The larger the organization the more full-time the job becomes."

Cachat says the management representative should have a broad understanding of the organization and products or services offered. That person should also have excellent communication, interpersonal, and sales skills. "Knowledge of the ISO specs can be gained over time," he explains.

The position's standing within the company hierarchy may vary, according to Cachat. "If a positive, quality- and customer-oriented environment exists, he says, the position in the structure is less important. "If ISO, organization, structure and discipline are lacking, the position should be a high — if not the highest — ranking member of management."

Selecting the Management Representative

Selecting the management representative is entirely up to the company, according to Potts. The background and qualifications of the person are up to the company. "For organizations with a distinct quality department, it is typically the quality manager, but management representatives have ranged from lab supervisors to presidents of corporations," she says.

The decision regarding where to place the position on the corporate hierarchy is also left to the company, Potts says. "What is most important is that the individual be able to demonstrate that he or she has the authority and responsibility for implementation and maintenance of the ISO 9000 quality system and has access to all appropriate personnel — including top management — to raise issues and ensure resolution relative to that implementation and maintenance."

Subclause 5.5.2: Management Representative

The management representative is an individual who, irrespective of other responsibilities, has the responsibility and authority to ensure that the quality system is established, implemented, and maintained. The management representative must belong to the organization's management team and not be an external person (i.e., a visiting consultant). Apart from ensuring that the system is effectively maintained, he or she must also report on the performance of the system to the management, not only for review purposes, but as a basis for assuring the awareness of customer requirements. The management review requirement is often mishandled. It is now required to be performed by executive management. Management must be concerned with the overall process, not just with audit results. The following questions can serve as guidelines:

- Is the system working effectively?

- What are the quality metrics, both internal and external?

- Will changes be made within the operation of the company that will radically affect the system?

- Is technology changing in a way that necessitates rewriting documentation?

- Is the company achieving its stated quality policy and objectives?

- Is the company recognizing opportunities for improvement and taking action?

— The Victoria Group

5.5.3 Internal Communication

This clause contains requirements not specified in ISO 9001:1994.

Additional ISO 9001:2000 Requirements

Top management shall make certain that effectiveness of the quality management system is communicated within the organization.

ISO 9004:2000 Guidance

Clause 5.5.3 lists ways in which management can communicate internally. (See *Handbook* CD-ROM.)

5.6 Management Review (4.1.3)

5.6.1 General

Top management shall periodically review all elements of the quality management system to make sure that it remains suitable, adequate and effective.

Top management shall assess opportunities for improvement and whether modifications in the quality management system are needed, including policy and quality objectives. Management review records shall be maintained.

5.6.2 Review Input

This subclause is not contained in ISO 9001:1994.

Information included in management review shall include:

- Audit results
- Feedback from customers

- Performance of the process and conformity of the product
- Preventive and corrective actions
- Follow-up from previous reviews
- Changes affecting the quality management system
- Improvement recommendations.

Additional items are listed in ISO 9004:2000. (See *Handbook* CD-ROM.)

5.6.3 Review Output (4.1.3)

Management review of output shall include decisions and actions concerned with effectiveness of the QMS and needed resources.

Additional ISO 9001:2000 Requirements

5.6.3a and b Management reviews shall look for ways to improve the effectiveness of the quality management system and the product, based on customer needs.

ISO 9004:2000 Guidance

Clause 5.6.3 l lists examples of outputs to enhance efficiency. (See *Handbook* CD-ROM.)

ISO 9000-2:1997 Guidance

The scope of management reviews should encompass the following elements:

- Organizational structure
- Implementation of the quality system
- The achieved quality of the product or service
- Information based on customer feedback, internal audits and process and product performance.

The frequency of reviews is not specified but depends on individual circumstances. In terms of follow-up, problems should be documented, analyzed and resolved. Required changes to the quality system should be implemented in a timely manner.

6 Resource Management

6.1 Provision of Resources (4.1.2.2)

The organization shall identify and provide resources necessary to establish and maintain a quality management system.

Additional ISO 9001:2000 Requirements

6.1a Resources shall be provided for improvement of the effectiveness of the quality management system.

6.1b Resources shall be provided to enhance customer satisfaction.

ISO 9004:2000 Guidance

Clause 6.1.2 lists resources to be considered to improve the performance of the organization. (See *Handbook* CD-ROM.)

6.2 Human Resources (4.18)

6.2.1 General (4.1.2.1)

All personnel with activities affecting quality shall be qualified as to education, training, skill and experience.

6.2.2 Competence, Awareness and Training (4.18)

Competency needs shall be identified and the organization shall train to satisfy these needs or shall take alternative action.

Additional ISO 9001:2000 Requirements

6.2.2a Competency needs shall be identified.

6.2.2c Training effectiveness shall be evaluated.

6.2.2d All employees shall be made aware of the importance of their work and the impact they have on meeting quality objectives.

6.2.2e Relevant records shall be maintained for education, experience, training and employee skills.

ISO 9004:2000 Guidance

Clause 6.2.2.2 lists (see *Handbook* CD-ROM) ways in which an organization can do the following:

- Encourage the involvement and development of its people.
- Identify competence of people.
- Enhance competence.
- Increase employee awareness.
- Consider elements of training plans.

ISO 9000-2:1997 Guidance

Training is essential to achieving quality. Training should encompass the use of the quality management approach of the organization and the underlying rationale. The training process should include the following:

- Evaluate the education and experience of personnel.
- Identify individual training needs.
- Provide appropriate training, either in-house or by external bodies.
- Record training progress and update to identify training needs.

ISO 9004:2000 (Clause 6.2.2.2) lists ways of encouraging involvement of people, ways to identify competence of people, factors enhancing competence, ways to increase employee awareness and elements to be considered in training plans.

QS-9000 Automotive

Training (4.18)

Training effectiveness is to be periodically reviewed.

Clause 6.2: Documenting Personnel Competence

Reprinted courtesy of Quality Systems Update

Question: Most quality systems (especially to ISO 9000) are adopted after a company has been in business for quite some time and where employees may have been working at a job for years. How should personnel competence be determined as per Clause 6.2?

Answer: The panel of experts agreed that companies have a certain amount of discretion in documenting personnel qualifications.

Identifying Training Needs

Raymond P. Cooney, of Cooney and Mori Associates, says the organization determines the appropriate mix of education, training and experience needed for personnel to perform certain tasks and to ensure that personnel are properly qualified. He says that, when implementing ISO 9001, companies frequently upgrade or "tighten up" training and qualification procedures. "If employees' experience on the job qualified them without needing to go through the new system, a note to that effect in the employees' personnel files or other appropriate place would be an adequate record."

Training and Testing Criteria

Dean Stamatis, president, Contemporary Consultants Co., says the intent of the clause is to establish requirements for training, certifying, and recertifying employees involved in performing critical and specialized functions at a given organization.

"It covers all employees performing routine, critical and specialized functions related to deliverable items. This includes both the management and nonmanagement personnel. In addition to this general impact, the clause may also include requirements specified by the customer's contract."

"As part of the audit and the Clause 6.2 requirements, it is also essential to look at the responsibility for developing training and testing criteria," Stamatis says. "Here, the auditor looks for consistency in operating the training sessions for normal/generic, special, certification and recertification sessions."

Stamatis says the criteria for such an evaluation probably are contained within the quality manual under the heading for the quality management and administration department. He says auditors may also be interested in addressing customer-imposed requirements while auditing this section.

Stamatis lists the following information as typical with respect to appropriate records:

- Employee's name and identification number
- Employee's department
- Date and duration of training
- A check mark for certification or recertification
- Location of training
- Type of training
- Name of the course
- Certification number
- Function of the certification
- Expiration date
- Name of the instructor.

Auditors may also be interested in viewing records and verification documents of training for employees who are unable to attend or be present at a scheduled session. "Although the concerns of Clause 6.2 may be very frightening to some companies, in reality they are nothing more than a substantiation of the quality system that the company itself has defined in its own quality manual," Stamatis says.

According to Raymond Cooney, "the system for keeping qualification records need not — should not — be rigid or onerous. The simplest, easiest, most flexible system that works is the best. Competence records can take many forms."

Cooney says that competence records must have credibility and utility. "This implies two things," he says. "Responsible people must sign off on the records. Oftentimes this means both the employee and appropriate management. Secondly, records need to be readily accessible to those who need to use them."

Good business practice, he says, dictates that an organization be able to answer the question: How do we know that a person doing or being told to do a job is qualified to do it?

Job Descriptions

Kirk Eggebrecht, executive manager, Geo. S. Olive & Co. LLC, says it is important to consider any single element of ISO 9001 in the context of the document as a whole. "The organization's method of addressing training and work assignments will be a function of the approach used to address other ISO 9001 requirements, such as Design and Development (7.3), Production and Service (7.5), Internal Audit (8.2.2) and many others," he says.

"In addressing these requirements, many organizations conclude that job descriptions are needed for each unique position in the organization." Typically, he says, these job descriptions prescribe the specific skills, training, and experience required for that position. "The makeup of these job descriptions then determines the makeup of the information needed in each employee's personnel and training file," he says.

"Naturally, the key to any quality system is that there is a match between the job requirements as documented and the employee's qualifications as documented," Eggebrecht says. "If there is a mismatch, the organization should have procedures implemented to provide the appropriate training and supervision until the prescribed qualifications are met."

In the case of employees who have been performing a job for years without any formal training, he says, registrars allow organizations to "grandfather in" experienced workers, exempting them from prescribed training or educational requirements. However, to qualify for this treatment, the employee must have demonstrated a proven capability.

New employees should be trained by a designated instructor and a record of training should be kept. There should be a sign-off procedure authorized by a designated person or position, who may or may not be the instructor, Eggebrecht says. When hiring skilled employees, companies must have specific procedures that address the employees' placement in the organization along with a transition period for them to become familiar with the position.

Clause 6.2: Must Training Be Ongoing?

Reprinted courtesy of Quality Systems Update

Question: Clause 6.2 of ISO 9001, Human Resources, requires companies to establish and maintain documented procedures for identifying training needs and to provide for the training of all personnel performing activities affecting quality. Must this training be ongoing?

Answer: *QSU's* panel of experts was divided as to whether training must be ongoing.

Moderator Robert Peach says he believes the training must be ongoing.

"The standard does not explicitly say you must have an ongoing training program, but there is no conceivable way that most organizations can continue to meet the requirements of the standard if they don't have it," Peach explains.

Peach says companies should not only train new workers but they should provide refresher training for employees who have been with the company over time.

"Assuming that your processes continually improves, then there must be a backup training for those new processes," he says. "There's no way organizations can just have one-time training and stop it."

One way to track training needs in a company is to create a matrix showing required training modules by job title, according to Peach.

"Match the job titles down one side of the matrix to the various training program modules and you continually administer training modules for each job," he says. "Any sharp company is routinely doing that."

Lawrence Turk, president of Quality System Solutions Inc., an ISO 9000 training and consulting organization, says he does not believe training must be ongoing to satisfy ISO 9000 requirements.

"What the standard says is that the personnel who are performing activities affecting product quality must be competent to do so," Turk explains.

According to Turk, training is one way in which personnel can be deemed qualified, but not the only way. "You can also use education and/or experience," he says.

Although he does not believe the standard requires ongoing training, Turk says businesses may benefit by implementing ongoing training requirements.

"It is certainly to the benefit of a business to have a training program that provides ongoing confidence in the qualifications of the people performing the work," Turk says. "Ongoing training will reinforce the use of approved procedures and instructions while reducing the variance in individual work."

If the business establishes a policy for ongoing training, ISO 9000 auditors will he looking to see that the policy is enforced, he says. "If the business says that they provide necessary skill training at regular intervals, then the auditor will expect to find records documenting that training," Turk says.

Bryce E. Carson, Sr., [then] quality program manager with Kemper Registrar Services Inc., an ISO 9000 registrar, says ongoing training may or may not be a requirement based on the type of business or service the company provides.

"It depends on the nature of the product or service that's being manufactured or provided," he explains. "Any training that is ongoing would be predicated a lot on the activity that was being performed."

Carson says certain regulated industries such as the healthcare industry are required to have ongoing training.

"The training that would be required under such regulations and regulatory requirements would mandate ongoing training in that particular service sector," he says. "Ongoing training would also depend on whether the manufacturer's or the service provider's procedures indicate that the training would be ongoing or not ongoing."

In other industries, there may be no such mandated requirements for ongoing training.

"It may not apply to … maybe, let's say a manufacturer that performs die punching and die stamping where the activity is repetitive," according to Carson.

He says the need for ongoing training also depends on the criticality of the task being performed. "The evaluation of that training also would be predicated on the severity of the tasks that are being accomplished," he explains.

Some companies may have internal requirements for ongoing training. "The specific training that's required or necessary for performing specific tasks and for general training is required to increase the awareness of the quality objectives of the organization," Carson says.

He adds that employees should be made aware of the rationale behind training requirements in order to build incentives and heighten quality awareness. Companies should continually reevaluate training needs, he says.

H. Pierre Salle, president of KEMA-Registered Quality Inc., an ISO 9000 registrar, says his firm has taken the position that training must be ongoing in most instances.

"In general KEMA will focus on training needs, quality objectives, with an eye toward continuous improvement," Salle explains. "Customers who feel that their training needs are static will be required to provide evidence to that effect. In general, training must be ongoing."

Salle says the issue of whether training must be ongoing is directly related to the training needs cited in subclause 6.2.2 and whether those needs change over time.

"Speaking absolutely, it is possible that training needs for a particular employee or corporate function could be static," Salle says. "However, a static business situation is difficult to imagine and the likelihood is that the training will be ongoing."

Salle says the same holds true for identifying training needs in addition to the evaluation of personnel with respect to performance versus past training.

6.3 Infrastructure (4.1.2.2, 4.9)

To ensure conformity, the organization shall identify, provide and maintain facilities, which are defined to include buildings, work areas and related facilities, and necessary equipment, hardware and software. While ISO 9001:2000 provides less specific detail on facilities requirements than ISO 9001:1994, it places on management the obligation of determining all resources required, making them available and putting them into effective use to meet demands.

Additional ISO 9001:2000 Requirements

6.3c Supporting services shall be provided for activities where needed. This extends the facilities requirement beyond product realization into service areas, such as transportation, communication, warehousing, delivery and repair.

ISO 9004:2000 Guidance

Clause 6.3 lists elements to be included when defining the infrastructure needed to achieve effective and efficient product realization. (See *Handbook* CD-ROM.)

6.4 Work Environment (4.9)

To achieve product conformity to product requirements, the work environment shall be determined and managed. ISO 9001:1994 contains a similar statement.

ISO 9004:2000 Guidance

ISO 9004:2000 identifies resources available to the organization:

Human resources (Subclause 6.4)

Information as a resource (Subclause 6.5)

Suppliers and partnerships (Subclause 6.6)

Natural resources

Financial resources.

7 Product Realization

7.1 Planning of Product Realization (4.2.3, 4.9)

Process planning shall be consistent with the quality management system. The organization is to do the following:

- Set objectives and product requirements.
- Provide the processes, resources and documentation for the product.
- Establish verification, validation, monitoring, inspection and test procedures.
- Establish the criteria for acceptability.
- Provide needed records to demonstrate conformity of the processes and product.

This brief clause condenses requirements that appeared in ISO 9001:1994 Clauses 4.2.3, 4.9, and others. Rather than reducing requirements, it emphasizes the need for the organization to understand its processes and to build a quality management system to effectively manage all activities.

One note states that documentation on how the quality management system is to apply to a specific product, project, or contract may be considered a quality plan.

A second note observes that design and development requirements in Clause 7.3 may be applied to product realization processes.

Additional ISO 9001:2000 Requirements

7.1a Quality objectives and requirements shall be determined for the product.

7.1c Validation procedures shall be conducted as appropriate.

ISO 9004:2000 Guidance

Clause 7.1 contains extensive lists of ways in which documentation can support effective and efficient operation:

- The role of people within the various processes
- Elements of an operating plan
- Examples of support processes
- Process input issues

- Examples of topics for periodic review of process performance
- Issues to consider in product and process validation
- Processes meriting particular attention to validation
- Examples of tools of risk assessment
- Examples of process information related to interested parties.

7.2 Customer-Related Processes

7.2.1 Determination of Requirements Related to the Product (4.3)

The organization shall determine customer requirements, including details of delivery and the extent of product support functions. It shall also identify all regulatory and legal obligations related to the product and identify any other requirements set by the organization.

Additional ISO 9001:2000 Requirements

7.2.1b The organization shall identify any product requirements that, while unspecified by the customer, are necessary for use.

7.2.2 Review of Requirements Related to the Product (4.3.2)

All customer requirements and other requirements shall be reviewed before making a commitment, such as submitting a tender or accepting a contract order. This is to be done to be sure that requirements are defined, verbal agreements are confirmed, changes from the original tender or quotation are resolved and all requirements can be met. Results of reviews and follow-up actions shall be recorded.

Where requirements change, necessary documentation shall be updated and personnel involved shall be notified.

A note observes that where a formal review is not practical (such as with Internet sales) the review can cover specific product information available to customers such as advertising and catalogs.

ISO 9000-2:1997 Guidance

Contract review process steps are:

- Review the contract.
- Achieve agreement.
- Discuss results of contract review.
- Discuss draft quality plan (if existing).

The contract review procedure should have the following features:

- An opportunity for all interested parties to review the contract
- A verification checklist
- A method for questioning the contract requirements and addressing the questions
- A draft quality plan
- Provision for changing the contract.

7.2.3 Customer Communication

This clause is not contained in ISO 9001:1994.

Additional ISO 9001:2000 Requirements

Customer communication channels shall be established related to product information and handling of inquiries, orders, contracts and amendments. Provisions shall be made for feedback from customers, including complaints.

7.3 Design and Development (4.4)

The essential quality aspects of a product — such as safety, performance and dependability — are established during the design and development phase. Thus, deficient design can be a major cause of quality problems. ISO 9001 establishes separate requirements for design review, design verification and design validation. The standard includes the following subclauses:

7.3.1 Design and development planning (4.4.2)

7.3.2 Design and development inputs (4.4.4)

7.3.3 Design and development outputs (4.4.5)

7.3.4 Design and development review (4.4.6)

7.3.5 Design and development verification (4.4.7)

7.3.6 Design and development validation (4.4.8)

7.3.7 Control of design and development changes (4.4.9)

Clause 7.3: A Road Map for Design and Development Control

"Design output meets design input" sums up the entire intent of the design and development requirements. Clause 7.3 can be met following this suggested road map:

1. Plan what is to be done.

2. Document that plan.

3. Assign someone to review the contract, document the designated person, and ensure that this person feeds data to the task of design input.

4. Create an input specification that includes "applicable statutory and regulatory requirements" and is unambiguous and adequate.

5. Follow up as progress is made and make sure that the plan is still being followed.

6. Review how the system is working with the involved employees and document the progress. Perform design reviews at previously defined stages in the evolution of the design.

7. At the end of the task, make sure the output matches the input.

8. Conduct tests and keep records. Do these in accordance with the "acceptance criteria" in step 4. above.

9. Make sure that a good method of tracking changes is in place and that everyone understands the rationale for all changes made.

Design Validation

Subclause 7.3.6 contains a requirement for design and development validation. The standard distinguishes between verification and validation. The software engineering profession, for example, has long made this distinction. There is a recognition that much in process design verification may well have little direct linkage to the defined requirements. Thus it is possible to have a design project that has succeeded in every verification phase but fails to meet the user requirements in any way. This requirement may cause some design organizations to rethink some of their strategies to ensure that their design-proving methodologies take sufficient heed of customer operational environments. It may require some reorganization of test methodologies, even if there is no actual increase in the amount of testing being performed.

Design Changes

Subclause 7.3.7 calls for approving changes and modifications "before implementation." One important consideration for companies is that they ensure that their systems provide the necessary levels of authorization to allow for implementing essential changes or modifications quickly to meet production or customer needs.

— *The Victoria Group*

Clause 7.3: Must All Projects Be Subject to Design Requirements?

Reprinted courtesy of Quality Systems Update

Question: I work in a research and development facility that has attained ISO 9001 registration. Not all of our projects are geared to product development. Is it necessary to subject all products to the same design requirements if they do not affect product quality?

Answer: *QSU*'s panel of experts agreed that projects must not be subjected to the same design requirements if they do not affect product quality.

Moderator James Highlands, president of Management Systems Analysis Inc., an ISO 9000, QS-9000, and ISO 14000 consulting and training organization, says those projects that do not fall within the scope of a company's registration need not undergo the same type of design development as projects which do.

"All organizations are allowed to define the scope of their program," says Highlands. "Some research facilities will exclude certain research activities for just that purpose."

The challenge is knowing which projects to treat differently, he explains, adding that typically companies should plan to follow design requirements on projects that are within the scope of their registration. However, a company may differentiate between creating a concept for new products or services and simple engineering projects based on existing technologies within the scope of their program or registration.

"It's the difference between saying I'm going to invent a new antibiotic as opposed to saying I'm going to design a new stereo," according to Highlands. "One is conceptual, where you are starting from a zero knowledge base, while the other is simply a design project of arranging existing components to produce a new product."

Gary Lewis, director of quality systems with Amoco Polymers Inc. in Augusta, Georgia, says it is critical for companies to understand their scopes of registration in determining whether design requirements are applicable to a given situation.

"You want to integrate the system into the business, but you also want to make sure that you define in your scope what the system needs to be inclusive of," he explains.

Lewis says an ISO 9001 system being implemented in one of his company's research and development facilities will initially apply only to certain product lines because of time and resource limitations. He says the registration may be expanded in the future to cover the entire facility.

"It's a case of understanding and being flexible," he says. "If it's value added, I think you have to do that. If someone could describe a case where they felt it does not make business sense to go across the whole R&D area, then I could understand."

In general, he adds, companies should try to incorporate their ISO 9000 systems across their entire operation even if the scope of third-party registration covers only a limited area.

Frank Caplan, president of Quality Sciences Consultants Inc., a quality sciences consulting and training organization that also offers ISO 9000 implementation assistance, agrees it is not necessary to follow the same design requirements with every project. But, he advises companies to do so anyway.

"A lot of organizations have faced the problem or question of what do you do with lower-value product lines where your major product line has stringent quality requirements," Caplan explains.

"In many, many cases they found that it's economically and sociologically wise to have just one system."

The reason, according to Caplan, is that this approach tends to give companies more flexibility in scheduling and an overall consistency that is beneficial to the organization.

"This provides a ready transfer of personnel from one kind of project to another kind of project, both from the suppliers' standpoint and from the company's standpoint," he says. "It's simpler if you have the same level of requirements for everything."

Companies that choose to employ a less rigorous system on certain projects also run the risk of losing any financial savings through other costs.

"Some of those costs can eat up the dollar difference from maintaining a single system," Caplan maintains. "What I've advised clients to do who raise a question of this nature and have a respectable reason for wanting to do this is to encourage them strongly to think about setting up a separate facility. Even then they may want to transfer people, and that can bring confusion."

Caplan says compliance with ISO 9001 requirements is determined largely by the way in which registration certificates are worded.

"You should look at that to make sure that you have the option of excluding projects," explains Caplan. "You may not. Even though the standard itself may not require you to do this, your registration may."

7.3.1 Design and Development Planning (4.4.2)

The organization shall develop design plans for each stage of the design and development activity. The plans shall define each activity and assign implementation responsibilities and authorities to qualified personnel who have adequate resources. Design plans shall be updated, as necessary.

ISO 9004:2000 Guidance

Clause 7.3.1 lists tools for risk assessment. (See *Handbook* CD-ROM.)

ISO 9000-2:1997 Guidance

Design activities should be sufficiently specific and detailed to permit effective verification. Planning procedures should take into account:

- Sequential and parallel work activities
- Design verification activities
- Evaluating the safety, performance and dependability incorporated in the product design
- Product measurement, test and acceptance criteria
- Assignment of responsibilities.

QS-9000 Automotive

Required Skills (4.4.2)

As appropriate, design personnel are to have specific required skills:

- Geometric Dimensioning and Tolerancing (GD&T)
- Quality Function Deployment (QFD)
- Design for Manufacturing (DFM)/Design for Assembly (DFA)
- Value Engineering (VE)
- Design of Experiments (Taguchi and classical)
- Failure Mode and Effects Analysis (DFMEA/PFMEA, etc.)
- Finite Element Analysis (FEA)
- Solid Modeling
- Simulation techniques
- Computer-Aided Design (CAD)/Computer-Aided Engineering (CAE)
- Reliability Engineering Plans.

Subclause 7.3.1: Documenting Design and Development Planning

Reprinted courtesy of Quality Systems Update

Question: Subclause 7.3.1, Design and Development Planning, requires companies to assign design and development activities to qualified personnel equipped with adequate resources. What documentation is needed to satisfy this requirement and what will ISO 9000 auditors be looking for?

Answer: *QSU's* panel of experts agree that each company must define the appropriate qualifications and level of resources necessary to conduct its design and development planning.

Moderator Ronald A. Muldoon, president of RAM Consulting Services, an ISO 9000 and ISO 14000 training and consulting firm, says auditors typically will ask to see a project quality plan or equivalent documents detailing the scope of work, project schedule, specifications, procedures, drawings, codes, standards, regulations and work instructions applicable to the project.

"You want to find out what's contractually required to be done and then verify that the schedule and the right people have been assigned to the project and they have the right information and equipment to do the job," he explains.

Muldoon says companies also should be prepared to produce a project quality plan or equivalent documents describing the department/disciplines, scope of work and activities to be performed. Also available for review should be a resource schedule or equivalent documents complete with man-hour estimates, costs, equipment, components and materials needed to meet contractual requirements and dates.

Muldoon recommends performing a review of the project resource schedule and project personnel records — i.e., project orientation, training, professional qualifications, degrees and experience of workers — to verify that qualified personnel are assigned to the project.

"Let's say you have nothing but mechanical engineers and you have a civil engineering portion of the project," Muldoon says. "You need to verify that proper personnel are assigned to the project. You need to look at your resources."

Robert W. Belfit, president of Omni Tech International Ltd., an ISO 9000, QS-9000 and ISO 14000 training and consulting organization, says he looks for a flowchart of these activities, from contract review through the requirements of section 7.3.1, when specifically addressing the question referenced above.

"From the contract review, the education/training required to meet the specific technical needs ought to be established," says Belfit. He adds that he expects to see notes on qualifications of the personnel and resources in the margins of the flowchart.

"These should be identified and referenced to the responsibilities and authorities section (4.1.2.2) of the standard and also in the training records as required in section 4.16," he says. "Much of this documentation will be found in the references to procedures in tier two and will be cross-referenced consistent with the flowchart."

Jerry Paradis, director of ISO 9000 and QS-9000 services with Information Mapping Inc., an ISO 9000 and QS-9000 training and consulting firm, says auditors will be looking to see that companies have a system and processes in place to control the design of new products.

"They're really looking for a description of what we call in this country a process, not step-by-step on how to do it," he says. "They're looking for sequential activities: How the design is verified. And then an evaluation of the performance: How dependable is it?"

According to Paradis, auditors also may want to see input requirements for designs in an attempt to verify that inputs match design outputs.

"How do they know that they match the output requirements?" he says an auditor might ask. "Designating who is responsible is another thing they would look for."

Paradis recommends that companies have a section of documentation labeled "responsibilities."

"One person could be designated as the person who does the verification," he says.

"Another person might be responsible for some related activity: validation, change. If the process changes for some reason, who would be responsible?"

Paradis says typically the person closest to the procedure in terms of responsibility participates in approving related documentation.

"Ultimate responsibility gets pushed back to whoever heads up that function in the organization," he says. "Management basically ends up designating the resources that will be used for a particular design through the chain of command."

He says an auditor might want to know how a company determined that a particular person was qualified to do the work assigned.

The key to satisfying an auditor's curiosity, according to Paradis, is to have sufficient documentation on hand to demonstrate that all the "shall" statements in the clause have been addressed.

Michael Demma, a partner in the firm of Demma, Davis and Reding Consulting, an ISO 9000, QS-9000 and ISO 14000 training and consulting organization, says many companies are confused about how they should approach ISO 9000 design requirements in general. "The design planning is really project management," Demma explains. "What I feel the standard is really looking for and what auditors will be looking for when they come in ... is, What is your design planning process?"

How companies manage their design process activities varies by industry, he says. "It's how you are going to manage that design process," according to Demma.

Demma says one way auditors might verify that qualified personnel have been assigned to the design-planning function is by examining the qualifications of personnel assigned to a particular design-planning project.

"In some cases that's probably going to be tied very heavily to management responsibility," he says. "Who are the individuals and what are their qualifications to flow down through those various activities of design control?"

He says personnel involved with the design function in companies tend to have similar academic backgrounds. "It could be chemical engineers. It could be research type people," he says. "I'm going to look for them to describe their process. Then I'm going to look for them to determine, based on the process that they have, what they feel that the skills, qualifications and requirements are of the people to manage that process and facilitate that activity. And then I'm going to verify that they have in fact matched up the people with the jobs."

Says Demma, "It could be years of experience working as a design project manager. It could be some specific training on a phase four design activity or specific training on project management that the company has sent someone to."

Demma says auditors can be expected to follow the paper trail on at least one completed design cycle to determine how resources were assigned, what qualifications were required and how responsibilities and authority were defined and assigned.

"Resources can be looked at two ways, in my opinion," he says. "One is qualified resources. And then the other is an adequate number of resources to get the job done. Are things getting done from the company's point of view in a manner which customer clients are happy with?"

Demma says more emphasis tends to be placed on the qualification of personnel involved with design planning than the availability of adequate resources.

"In a lot of cases, especially when you're talking design qualifications of resources, in large part it's an academic thing," he says. "People have been academically trained to do certain things." On the other hand, the availability of resources is an issue that tends to require more of a subjective judgment on the part of an auditor, according to Demma.

7.3.2 Design and Development Inputs (4.4.4)

Design inputs are usually in the form of product performance requirements or product descriptions with specifications. The inputs shall define and record requirements pertinent to the product, including:

- Function and performance
- Relevant statutory (statute law) and regulatory (government agency) requirements
- Other requirements necessary for design and development

Incomplete, ambiguous, or conflicting requirements shall be resolved.

Additional ISO 9001:2000 Requirements

7.3.2c Information from previous similar designs shall be used.

ISO 9004:2000 Guidance

Clause 7.3.2 lists external and internal inputs relating to product requirements. (See *Handbook* CD-ROM.)

ISO 9000-2:1997 Guidance

A design description document can serve as a definitive reference throughout the design process. It should quantify all requirements as much as possible, with the customer and the organization agreeing on details. The document should identify design aspects, materials and processes that require development, including prototype testing.

QS-9000 Automotive

Design Input — Supplemental (4.4.4.1)

The organization shall have appropriate resources for computer-aided product design, engineering, and analysis (CAD/CAE).

7.3.3 Design and Development Output (4.4.5)

Design and development outputs are the final technical documents used throughout the process, from production through servicing. They can include drawings, specifications, instructions, software and servicing procedures.

The requirement is to record design output in a manner that can be verified against design and development input requirements. The design output shall:

- Meet design and development input requirements.
- Contain or reference acceptance criteria.
- Identify design characteristics crucial to safety and correct application.

Additional ISO 9001:2000 Requirements

7.3.3b Suitable information for purchasing, production and service activities should be provided.

ISO 9004:2000 Guidance

Clause 7.3.3 lists outputs related to product requirements. (See *Handbook* CD-ROM.)

QS-9000 Automotive

Design Output — Supplemental (4.4.5.1)

Evaluation of design and development output shall include:

- Simplification, optimization, innovation, waste reduction and environmental conditions
- Geometric dimensioning and tolerancing
- Cost/performance/risk analysis
- Feedback from testing, production and field
- Design FMEAs.

7.3.4 Design and Development Review (4.4.6)

The standard requires formal documented reviews of design results. Participants at the design reviews shall include representatives from all functions concerned with the design stage. Subclause 7.3.4 requires the organization to maintain records of the design reviews, covering both findings and subsequent actions.

Additional ISO 9001:2000 Requirements

7.3.4a The design and development review should evaluate the ability of the design to completely meet requirements.

7.3.4b A purpose of design and development reviews is to identify potential problems and to propose actions for their resolution.

Subclause 7.3.4: When Must Design Reviews Be Conducted?

Reprinted courtesy of Quality Systems Update

Question: Subclause 7.3.4 of ISO 9001, Design and Development Review, requires companies to conduct systematic reviews of the design results at appropriate stages of design. My company manufactures pulp and paper converting rolls. If a customer provides us with incomplete design specifications, for example, the length and spleen configuration of a drive shaft but not the material, must we conduct our own design review? In general, under what circumstances are we required to conduct a design review?

Answer: *QSU's* panel of experts disagreed as to whether the company is obligated to perform a design review in this case.

Moderator William Harral, director of Arch Associates, an ISO 9000, QS-9000 and TQM consulting and training organization, says he believes the company must perform a design review appropriate to the design effort required if the supplier has ISO 9001 design capability and customer authorization to complete the design. He adds that this situation would not exist without multiple previous quality system failures at the customer and supplier level.

"Customer review of design output failed to identify the omitted material specification and design verification could not have considered any design input," says Harral.

He says questions over design review should be resolved during the normal contract review process. "If you do not have the expertise to conduct one and to identify the implied needs [of the customer], then apparently you've failed to do a correct and thorough contract review because you are not really capable of performing this type of design service," Harral explains.

"Material specification acts as a change to the original design through its act of completion," he says. "Material specification is basic to satisfaction of many design inputs, for example, load or torque, corrosion resistance, etc."

"You have to review changes, period," Harral concludes. "The extent of review would be appropriate for the significance, or criticality, of change."

If the organization does not have an ISO 9001 design capability, then the material specification must be defined by the customer through either contract review actions or the corrective and preventive action process to overcome their error of incompletion.

Terri Halpin, principal of the International ISO Group, an ISO 9000 and QS-9000 consulting and training organization, says the company not only would have to conduct some form of design review, but also would need to get customer approval on the design changes.

"You need to write up what you think it should be, based on your previous experience with them, and then get them to sign off on it," Halpin says.

If the customer provides only verbal approval, she explains, the supplier should follow up with written confirmation of the change. "If you really want their signature, then you have to say that you are not going to go any further until you get that," she said.

"We describe ISO and QS-9000 quality systems as specification-based verification systems. Your quality system needs the material specifications to be able to verify the manufacturing process," she continues.

"This question needs to be resolved either at contract review or during the design review. Contract review should have at least identified who was going to specify the material," said Halpin. "An effective design review must consider materials as an input to the design."

Moderator Harral agrees that it is necessary to get customer concurrence; however, he notes that a customer signature is not required under ISO 9001. While it may be good business practice to get a signature, he says, it is only necessary to maintain records of the agreement or review. However, QS-9000 does require customer signature of concurrence.

Duane Dodge, president of DLS Quality Technology Associates Inc., an ISO 9000 registrar, says the company does not have to perform a design review if it consults with the customer about the change prior to filling the order.

"They should not have to do a design review on that," Dodge says. "What they should do is take it back to the customer to supply the material." Customer approval negates the need for design review, he says. "If the customer agrees that this is the right material that you're going to put in there, then that becomes part of the customer's design," he explains. In general, Dodge adds, companies must perform design reviews whenever they make a substantive contribution to the design of a product or service. "If they had to add part of the design, then of course they would have to have design reviews for that portion to prove that they got from point A to point B — the input and the output — and everything matched."

Dodge says ISO 9000 auditors usually look at some design review documentation during an audit. "Usually you'll take a package for design review and you'll go right through from beginning to end, looking at the documented steps," he says. "If there's a glaring error, you'll pick it up."

Richard Randall, president of Randall's Practical Resources, an ISO 9000 and ISO 14000 training and consulting organization, says companies should review their contractual obligations in determining whether design reviews are required.

"It depends on whether the customer has subcontracted design or just manufacture," he says. "It also depends on whether the company is performing a complete design or simple design configuration management."

He says ISO 9000 auditors typically respect a company's judgment call on whether something constitutes design work or merely configuration management. In the case of the customer who failed to specify the material, he says, the work would probably fall into the category of configuration management and as such would not require a design review.

"I would pretty much have to consider it configuration management, because the customer considered those missing specifications to be so insignificant that they could be left up to the discretion of the manufacturer," says Randall.

Moderator Harral says it is important to note that configuration management requirements are not specified in ISO 9001 except as required by contract.

"When applicable, configuration management responsibilities almost always fall on the primary design party," says Harral. "This isn't the case at hand."

Harral also says most internal specifications are never insignificant and are basic to satisfying design input requirements.

Subclause 7.3.4: Which Functions to Include in Design Review?

Reprinted courtesy of Quality Systems Update

Question: Subclause 7.3.4 of ISO 9001, Design and Development Review, states that at suitable stages systematic reviews of design and development shall be conducted. The standard requires that participants in such reviews include representatives of those functions concerned with the design and development stages being reviewed. Who specifically should be included and how broad should the review be?

Answer: *QSU*'s panel of experts agree that the specific attendees may vary based on the complexity of the design and size of organization.

Moderator Ira Epstein, president of Value Management Associates, who also serves on the US Technical Advisory Group to ISO Technical Committee 176, says that in the case of "extremely large and complex designs" almost all functions in the organization should be represented at some point.

"Reviews of large, complex designs often occur in stages and different functions may be represented at different stages," he says. "The most obvious functions involved ... are the design, project management, manufacturing and quality functions."

Often overlooked but extremely important are representatives of the customer and major suppliers, Epstein adds. Customer representatives can provide insight and clarification of customer needs and expectations and should also be able to represent the ultimate user, according to Epstein.

Major suppliers can also provide valuable input as to their capabilities and limitations and cost drivers, he says. They can gain a better insight into the needs and expectations of the organization performing the design.

Epstein says there may be other functions that might be able to provide valuable input into the design review process. Technical training personnel may be able to contribute to the design by promoting ease of training equipment operators, he says.

Maintenance personnel can assess whether equipment is easy to maintain, while installation personnel can assess the ease of installation. Packaging engineers can make a determination as to whether equipment will be adequately protected during shipping and storage. Materials handling engineers can assess whether equipment will be protected during handling.

"One could go on, but I think the point is made," he adds. "Everyone in the organization looks at the design from a different perspective. That is the perspective for which each representative has expertise and responsibility."

As the size and complexity of the design diminishes, so too does the need for numerous representatives and the need for formality, he says.

Epstein says that the expense of a thorough design review is offset by its added value. He says that the cost of fixing a design flaw found during the design stage might be a small fraction of the cost of fixing that same problem during production or operations.

"Design reviews are a critical element of design control that, in turn, is a critical element of the product life cycle," concludes Epstein. "They should be given appropriate attention."

Design review participants may also vary depending on the number of reviews and when in the design process a particular review occurs, says Gary Minks, certification manager for TUV Management Service, the registrar division of TUV America Inc.

"For example, a review in the early stages of a project could consist solely of a design engineer and the project manager," he says. "It is preferable to include all concerned functions as early as possible."

However, he notes, ISO 9001 does not require any specific number or format of reviews. The clause can be satisfied with one comprehensive review before a design is released, according to Minks.

There should be as many interested parties as possible, and actual participants may vary based on the impact a design could have on a concerned party. Design reviews can include internal departments, customers and regulatory agencies, he says.

"For example, purchasing may need to determine if component cost or availability would affect product pricing or market launch plans," says Minks. "Production will likely review a design for manufacturing ability and tooling requirements."

Assigned personnel will need to verify that design inputs are being satisfied. Other specialists may also be called upon as needed. For example, he explains, an external consultant could be called upon to review a specific technical aspect.

"The scope of each review should be determined in advance of the meeting," concludes Minks. "Actual and potential problems should be identified and actions recorded for later follow-up and closure."

Dwayne Breaux, audit program director for Quality Systems Registrars Inc., says management must focus on adding value to the process. While design reviews are intended to ensure compliance of the design phase with specified requirements, attendance and breadth of the review are normally determined easily, he says.

On the other hand, it should be understood that not all situations are the same; each particular design project defines its own requirements for attendance and depth of review, he says.

"The depth of a design review is commonly dictated by the complexity of the design itself," says Breaux. "Key agenda items in the review should be the organization's progress in meeting design input requirements and the identification of problem areas."

Breaux poses three questions that must be addressed:

Are the customer's needs being met?

Are product specifications in compliance with requirements?

Are process requirements adequately addressed?

Depending on the design phase being reviewed, areas that should be thoroughly analyzed may include manufacturing, product handling, inspection and testing, delivery and servicing.

Once the depth of the review is determined, participants should be easily defined, Breaux says. The group/function responsible for the design of the product/process must be in attendance. Participants should be those individuals who have responsibility for the quality of the product/process at that stage of the design.

Representatives from manufacturing functions should attend review meetings when the review includes processing capability, inspection and testing representatives should attend discussions on testing of product, and so on.

"Of course," Breaux concludes, "the best method of determining just how broad a design review should be and who should attend is to remember the intent of the standard. The audit question that must be answered is: Will the records of the review provide adequate evidence that responsible individuals have reviewed the product and/or process and found it acceptable to defined requirements? If not, were actions taken to correct nonconformances?"

The design review is the documented, comprehensive and systematic examination of a design to evaluate its capability to fulfill requirements for quality, to identify problems and to propose the development of solutions, adds Ron Ness, a quality assessor for Entela Inc., Quality Systems Registration Division. The representatives should be appropriate to the phase of the project.

This is, he maintains, dependent on the size of the firm and the complexity of the design project. Smaller firms with less complex design projects are going to have fewer functions represented. The entire team might consist of only management and engineering personnel. The stage of the process may dictate who will be involved.

At the early stages of the defined design plan, Ness adds, the various functions could include marketing, financial, legal, engineering, safety engineering, human resources, manufacturing, quality, laboratory, purchasing, information technology and senior management. These early reviews are crucial to the up-front planning of the defined design plan. Involvement of the customer and subcontractors is also desirable; the expectations of subcontractors should be the same as for the supplier. Plans for the realization of the product should be expected from subcontractors as well.

Later in the design process, it may not be necessary to involve as many functions. This is due to the previous progress of the project and the stage of the design. Tooling and equipment stages may require only the tool engineer, subcontractor and equipment provider. The quantity of these reviews also depends on the complexity of the design and the size of the firm. There may be as few as one or two or as many as 18 or 20 reviews lasting over one year.

It is important to note that there is not just one review. As called out in Subclause 7.3.1, interfaces between different groups shall be managed to ensure clear assignment of responsibility. The team formation establishes communication with all involved, including customers and suppliers. The timing plan and the formulation of the team are an essential first priority.

"The extent of the review, again, is dependent upon the complexity of the design and the stage being evaluated," says Ness. "At the early stage, the scope of the design is discussed, as well as the responsibilities of the various functions. Defining customer requirements, with the customer present, includes elements from the contract review conducted previously."

Marketing brings together the areas of test results from research and competitive studies. Engineering maintains the design record of requirements, including data and analysis of warranty reports of surrogate parts. Quality maintains customer complaints, internal reports of scrap, rework and subcontractor problems on surrogate problems, he says.

Purchasing assesses the selection of suppliers based upon the results of past performance.

The finance or accounting group assesses costs, then updates and tracks to ensure that the project meets the goals of the money allocated. Human resources will account for personnel needed to be hired and trained or present personnel training requirements.

The legal department, if the firm is large enough or it is subcontracted, would be involved with contract review, safety-related areas and human resources. Manufacturing brings experience from established production proven processes.

Industrial/manufacturing/production engineering would be involved with floor plan layouts, bills of materials, flow of manufacturing, control plans and FMEAs.

"The participation, frequency, breadth and depth of these reviews are dependent upon the design project and the maturity of the organization," adds Ness. "It is important that at each review all open issues are evaluated as to project progress. All functions are to be notified as to the resolution and timing; the role of management is to coordinate, resolve issues and keep the project within the timeline and financial restraints."

7.3.5 Design and Development Verification (4.4.7)

A design verification process shall be established to ensure that the design output meets design input requirements. Various design verification activities may include alternative calculations, comparisons with proven designs, tests and demonstrations and reviewing the design stage documents before release.

Additional ISO 9001:2000 Requirements

Verification follow-up actions are to be recorded.

ISO 9000-2:1997 Guidance

In most cases, two or more measures are used. Design reviews and/or type-testing may be a regulatory requirement. Design verification should involve personnel independent of those who did the work under review.

ISO 9000-2 includes many questions that the design review can address. Some of these include the following:

- Do design reviews satisfy all specified requirements?
- Are product design and processing capabilities compatible?
- Are safety considerations covered?
- Are the materials and/or facilities appropriate?
- Are components or service elements standardized?
- Are purchasing, production, installation, inspection and testing plans technically feasible?
- Has software been validated, authorized and verified?
- Where qualification tests have been performed, were the conditions representative of actual use?

QS-9000 Automotive

Design Verification — Supplemental (4.4.7)

The organization shall:

- Perform alternative calculations
- Compare with similar designs
- Conduct tests and demonstrations
- Review documents before release.

Subclause 7.3.5: Verification Versus Validation

Reprinted courtesy of Quality Systems Update

Question: Subclause 7.3.5 of ISO 9001, Design and Development Verification, requires that verification be performed to ensure that output meets the input requirements and that verification measures shall be recorded. However, the standard further says, in Subclause 7.3.6, that validation shall be performed to ensure that product meets the requirements for the intended use. What is the difference between design *verification* and design *validation*?

Answer: Moderator Ronald A. Muldoon, president of RAM Management Systems Consultants, an ISO 9000 and ISO 14000 consulting and training organization, says a particularly good explanation appears in the American Society for Quality's Design and Construction Division Interpretive Guidelines.

"Design verification is the process of ensuring that the specified requirements have been fulfilled," says Muldoon, quoting from the document. "Design validation is the process of ensuring that requirements for a specific intended use are fulfilled."

In other words, design validation is conformity with the users' needs rather than with only specified requirements. In most cases, he says, and particularly in the case of an architectural, engineering and construction organization, companies cannot determine if clients' "needs" have been fulfilled until the project is complete.

"Design validation seeks to ensure that the final product conforms to the purchaser's needs," Muldoon adds. "In general, [architectural, engineering and construction organizations] receive this by having a formal acceptance of the contract deliverables by the purchaser or client."

Organizations could have a process for seeking feedback from the client, after construction and commissioning, on the functionality of the design of the facility or system, he concludes. The information could then be used to confirm refine and/or improve the organization's design methods.

"Verification is the confirmation that a product meets identified specifications," adds Vic Halpin, principal consultant of the International ISO Group, an ISO 9000 training and consulting firm. "Validation is confirmation that a product appropriately meets its design function or the intended use."

In practice, says Halpin, the distinction is difficult for companies to comprehend.

"One of our clients makes an epoxy material that is used to form the head gasket of an engine," he says. "There are a variety of specifications — including formulation, specific gravity, flow characteristics and temperature resistance — that apply to the epoxy." Testing that ensures conformance to these specifications is verification, he explains. When the epoxy is applied to an engine properly, it must withstand the working pressures of an engine and perform as a head gasket. If the epoxy leaks when the engine is pressurized, it would fail validation.

In other words, Halpin says, it may have met all the material specifications (verification) but it did not work as a head gasket (validation).

"Obviously, almost all properly designed products will pass validation testing if they pass verification testing," Halpin adds. "But some products are difficult or impossible to verify by the manufacturer."

He cites as an example the engine mounts on a car. Their design function is to physically support the engine and decouple engine vibration from the chassis.

"The only way to validate the engine mount is to assemble it in a car and determine if it isolates engine vibration," Halpin notes. "None of the specification testing — verification — can absolutely assure that the mount will provide sufficient vibration decoupling, or validation."

It should be noted that the engine mount manufacturer cannot perform validation testing because it usually does not have access to a test vehicle. The vehicle manufacturer is reluctant to take responsibility for the validation activity and provide objective evidence of the validation process, even though it is the only party that can validate the product.

"In a ISO/QS-9000-registered system, this leads to difficulty," Halpin says. "There is a clear requirement for validation, but it may be impossible for the manufacturer to perform."

In the case of the engine mount, he says, even if the manufacturer could get a test vehicle, their judgment about the adequacy of the vibration decoupling would usually not satisfy the customer; the customer would want to make that judgment, that is, to perform the validation.

Although the distinction may now be clear, a solution may not be evident in cases where the manufacturer does not have the ability to perform validation. One solution would be to consider the final customer as a supplier for the purpose of design validation.

"This would require customer agreement," says Halpin. "A second solution would be to identify verification testing that is logically linked to the specific design characteristics that require validation."

One way to accomplish this would be to establish a test series beyond verification testing that logically would establish confidence that the usage requirements can be met.

"This approach is also difficult, because, strictly speaking, it only approximates validation," says Halpin. "You will need to convince the registrar that this is appropriate and all that is possible.

"I believe most of the confusion between verification and validation does not result from a lack of understanding of the difference as much as the difficulty of implementing appropriate validation in some circumstances," Halpin concludes.

According to Mark Ames, president of Applied Quality Systems, Inc., the design verification requirements accomplish a beneficial business function that serves the needs of suppliers and their customers.

"The performance and control of design verification activities [are] intended to ensure [that] design activities result in outputs that meet input requirements," he says. "This verification often takes place through the use of measurements of expected results against actual results."

Since design activities are often conducted in stages or in pieces that must be brought together to work as a whole, design verification activities that compare design outputs (or output measurements) with design inputs at each stage are critical, Ames says. Failure to bring discipline to this important activity often results in completed designs that do not meet intended requirements.

But not all verification activities involve measurements, he adds. "Measurements are less common in low-cost, low-technology, low-risk product designs or where design output is binary — it is or it isn't there."

Keeping records of these measurements provides suppliers and their customers with confidence in the results for this important activity, Ames adds. Any organization that designs products will see dramatic benefits through reduced "design rework," design cycle time, costs and other considerations, he says.

"Design validation is the activity of ensuring that the completed design meets the needs of the end user," says Ames. "While design verification may be accomplished by performance measurements of partially completed designs, design validation is more often a check on the performance of a completed design under actual operating conditions."

This check may also include the use of measurements. In effect, design validation is a test of the completed stages or pieces of the design process as they are functioning as a complete design.

While both design verification and design validation check for results during the design process, he adds, design verification is normally thought of as the checks prior to design completion. Design validation is the check that is made after design completion and is conducted under expected operating conditions.

7.3.6 Design and Development Validation (4.4.8)

Unlike design *verification*, which matches the design output to input requirements (the producer's point of view), design *validation* ensures that the product conforms to defined user needs and/or requirements as planned in Subclause

7.3.1 (the customer's point of view). Validation shall be completed prior to delivery or implementation, as applicable.

Though not stated in the standard, validation may take place not only on the final product but also at earlier stages, as necessary, and multiple validations may be necessary if there are different intended uses of the product. Thus, in addition to the end product, there may be major product components that can be validated from the customer's point of view.

Additional ISO 9001:2000 Requirements

Validation results and follow-up actions shall be recorded.

7.3.7 Control of Design and Development Changes (4.4.9)

Designs may be changed or modified for many reasons. The requirement is for authorized personnel to identify, record, review and approve all design changes and modifications before their implementation. Results and follow-up actions are to be recorded.

Additional ISO 9001:2000 Requirements

Before release, changes shall be verified and validated as appropriate. An evaluation of the impact of changes on parts and delivered products shall be made.

ISO 9000-2:1997 Guidance

Design changes in one component should be evaluated for their effect on the overall product. Sometimes, improving one characteristic may have an unforeseen adverse influence on another. The new design output should be communicated to all concerned and the changes documented.

QS-9000 Automotive

Design Changes — Supplemental (4.4.9.1)

Customer must approve all design changes and impact on form, fit, function, performance and/or durability must be determined.

Design Change — Impact (4.4.9.2)

The impact of a design change on the system is to be considered.

7.4 Purchasing

7.4.1 Purchasing Process (4.6.1)

The basic purchasing requirement shall be to establish and maintain controlled processes to ensure that purchased products conform to specified requirements. The nature of this control will depend on the effect of the product upon later processes and output. Suppliers shall be evaluated on their ability to meet requirements.

Additional ISO 9001:2000 Requirements

Criteria shall be developed for selection and periodic evaluation of suppliers.

Processes to make sure that purchases meet requirements shall be established.

A record shall be kept of supplier evaluations and follow-up actions.

ISO 9004:2000 Guidance

ISO 9004:2000 Clause 7.4.1, Purchasing Process, discusses the procurement process in detail. The listing of activities to consider includes the following elements:

- Identifying the purchasing needs of the organization
- Determining the total cost of product, not just actual purchase cost but also impact on performance and delivery
- The process of initial inquiry, obtaining quotations, tendering an offer, and ordering
- Verifying quality and quantity of purchased products
- Selection of suppliers, development, and control
- Documentation and administering contracts.

ISO 9000-2:1997 Guidance

Planned and adequately controlled purchasing procedures ensure that purchases from suppliers, including services, conform to specified requirements. Organizations should establish effective working relationships and feedback systems with all suppliers.

The organization may employ several methods for choosing satisfactory suppliers, including the following:

- Reviewing previous performance in supplying similar products (including services)
- Satisfactory assessment of an appropriate quality system standard by a competent body
- Assessment of the supplier by the organization according to an appropriate quality system standard.

The organization's quality records should be sufficiently comprehensive to demonstrate the ability of suppliers to meet requirements. Factors can include the following:

- Product compliance with specified requirements
- Total cost for the organization
- Delivery arrangements
- Suppliers' own quality systems
- Performance of suppliers (should be reviewed at appropriate intervals).

QS-9000 Automotive

Approved Materials for Ongoing Production (4.6.1.1)

When required, your organization shall purchase materials from suppliers that have been approved by the customer.

Government, Safety and Environmental Regulations (4.6.1.2)

The organization is to provide materials that satisfy government requirements for:

- Restricted, toxic and hazardous materials
- Environmental factors
- Electrical and electromagnetic requirements.

The organization is to have a process to ensure compliance with these requirements.

Evaluation of Suppliers (4.6.2)

Supplier Development (4.6.2.1)

The organization will perform supplier quality system development.

Supplier assessment options include audit by:

- The organization, in accordance with ISO 9001 and QS-9000
- The OEM customer
- An OEM customer-approved second party
- An accredited third-party registrar.

Note: Responsibility for ensuring supplier quality always remains with the organization.

Scheduling Suppliers (4.6.2.2)

- 100 percent on-time delivery performance is required of suppliers.
- Organizations shall plan and commit accordingly.
- Supplier delivery performance and premium freight costs are to be monitored.

Subclause 7.4.1: Assessing Suppliers

Reprinted courtesy of Quality Systems Update

Question: Subclause 7.4.1, Purchasing Process, requires organizations to evaluate and select suppliers "based on their ability to supply product in accordance with the organization's requirements." Can we satisfy this requirement simply by requiring that our suppliers be registered? What responsibility do we have for their suppliers?

Answer: Our panelists agree that requiring registration alone is not sufficient to meet the requirements. A majority also agree that responsibility for the suppliers' sub-suppliers is not addressed in the standard.

Moderator, the late Jim Bigelow, vice president of TQM Consulting, says "simply" is the key word to understanding the first question.

"The panelists generally agree that ISO 9001 registration alone is not sufficient, although it may be useful in some situations," he notes. "The key words in the second question are 'their suppliers' and the panelists disagree on the supplier's responsibility in regard to its own suppliers."

Bigelow says it is important to know how significant the purchased product is to the company's operations. "What is the track record of the supplier? Is this a new supplier or one you have been dealing with for some time?" he asks. "What is the size and nature of the organization? How clearly have I, as an organization, transmitted my requirements to the supplier?"

How companies ensure that the supplied product is appropriate will often depend on their response to the above questions, Bigelow says.

If an organization is considering a new supplier, does ISO 9001 registration alone indicate ability to meet the organization's requirements? Probably not, he says.

"If I am filing 50 complaints a year on the supplier, ISO 9001 registered or not, then something is wrong," he adds. "Likewise, if I am rejecting a lot of deliveries ..., something is wrong. My customer is not likely to offer much forgiveness if my supplier causes me to fail to meet my customer's requirements and I say, 'Well, they are ISO 9001 registered.'"

On the other hand, he says, if a purchased product is not that critical to his operation and there are well-established standards — for example, he needs a case of SAE 30 oil — then perhaps his asking that the supplier be registered is complete overkill.

As to the second question, Bigelow says, he does not find anything in ISO 9001 to suggest that companies must take any action in regard to their suppliers' suppliers. "As a businessman, I would tend to change suppliers rather than formally help them work out problems related to sub-suppliers. Of course, my answer might be different if they were a sole source for the purchased product in question."

Requiring suppliers to be formally registered by a third party as being compliant with the requirements of quality management system standards such as ISO 9001 is a very sensible decision that has a number of benefits, according to Stewart Thackray, [then] operations manager for the Southwestern United States for BSI Inc., an ISO 9000 registrar.

The first question is difficult to answer, says Thackray. Whether such registration satisfies the requirements of the standard depends upon the nature of the organization.

"It puts the responsibility for quality squarely where it should be — with the supplier responsible for supplying the product or service," he says. "It provides the supplier with a solid incentive to properly adopt and maintain the management systems approach to quality, something which requires commitment, investment and, in a lot of cases, a fairly radical change to their business culture."

Further, adds Thackray, it saves money for the organization by removing the need for routine quality audits that may be duplicated by the supplier's other customers. It has the added benefit of the third-party approach, which focuses on the supplier's system without being diluted by second-party interests that may not be truly relevant to the task at hand.

Recognizing the commitment of suppliers through their adoption of third-party registration requires some cultural change by organizations that have traditionally been much more directly involved in the systems side of supplier quality, says Thackray. Experience shows this to be a good move that frees the organization to focus resources on those areas that may genuinely require close involvement.

The organization has full responsibility for meeting the requirements of the contract with their customer, which includes the quality of the product or service that they provide, regardless of the use of suppliers, the number of suppliers or the length of the supplier chain, he adds.

This responsibility exists at all levels of the chain, which may make it attractive to rely on the legalities of the contract and maintain a distance, expecting the supplier to take care of everything.

"In reality, this is not good practice," says Thackray. "For reasons generally based on size and specialization, suppliers do not necessarily have the experience, resources or expertise to fully control the performance and integrity of their own suppliers; the organization is required to define the type and extent of control that they exercise over their suppliers, and the ability of those suppliers to assure confidence in lower levels of the supply chain should certainly be considered."

If the supplier evaluation reveals that an otherwise desirable supplier has shortcomings in this area, then it may be necessary to initiate action, either by encouragement or by enforcement through supplier conditions, he adds.

"One obvious, and increasingly popular, option is to extend the requirement for registration with a properly accredited, third-party registrar down through the supply chain," he concludes.

We would not accept an organization limiting its control of suppliers to their being registered, says John R. Sedlak, general manager of Smithers Quality Assessments Inc. This approach means abdicating the organization's responsibility. In short, Sedlak says, suppliers are not required to be registered.

Ralph D. Schmidt, director, Thornhill USA, recommends that organizations make a list of suppliers and divide it in two — those critical to the quality of the organization's services and those having minor or no impact on the organization's quality. For example, he says, vehicles used as rental cars are critical to quality, but the products used to clean them are probably not.

Schmidt says suppliers on the critical list should be given written quality requirements. "The ideal is a survey for them to fill out to determine their ability to conform," he says. "Critical suppliers not complying with your needs should be replaced with ones that are capable. If the supplier is the only one of its kind, visits, discussions and audits are in order to assure conformance. You may have to invest money and training in the supplier to assure your quality."

He says that a supplier-receiving system is "vital" to tracking supplier performance. The system should keep track of receipts, deviations, rejections, complaints, test reports and certificates of compliance, which in turn become part of the supplier performance file. "Suppliers may furnish organizations their quality manual for review and may be certified or registered under a system," Schmidt says, adding that in such cases supplier audits may be waived if registration is pertinent and the manual covers critical subcontract aspects.

Developing a Supplier Validation and Verification System

To satisfy this clause of the standard economically, Kevin Drayton, senior consultant of Kevin Drayton Associates, suggests companies should have a supplier validation and verification system in place. The system must ensure that the organization has chosen a supplier that is capable of producing product to its requirements and that the organization has an auditable, documented quality system as part of its overall business strategy. Drayton says the validation and verification system typically includes surveys, on-site audits, capability studies performed by the supplier and verified by the organization and a review of products and processes via statistical techniques. "It is quite obvious that when a system such as the one described here is implemented, the objective evidence of the supplier's ability to meet requirements is quite easy to gather and maintain," Drayton says.

Methods of Assessment

"Suppliers should not usually be selected simply because they are certified to one of the ISO 9000 standards, although in some cases this may be adequate," comments Roderick Goult, president and CEO of The Victoria Group. Goult says, "It is common for organizations to believe that ISO 9000 registration is all that is needed from their suppliers."

Goult says that "all the relevant issues need to be addressed in determining which suppliers to use, including all the subcontract requirements for technical capability, delivery time frames, cost and possibly post-sales support." Goult says that if the supplier items constitute high-value purchases or they have a significant impact on the organization's own deliverables, it is very common for the potential supplier to have financial stability verified as well. "The extent of control required should take all these issues into account and may be more than a monitor of performance, including regular audits and product verification," he notes.

Dennis Arter, owner, Columbia Audit Resources, says other possible assessment methods could include a listing in a register for a particular product line or written responses to a questionnaire. He says the process of evaluating potential suppliers must be documented in an in-house procedure and the results recorded. He notes that this record usually takes the form of an "Approved Supplier List," but it may be as simple as a notation or signature in the supplier's file folder.

Arter says organizations must have a program for keeping approved suppliers on a list. Arter says supplier performance "needs to be evaluated on a periodic basis." He notes that some suppliers need an annual evaluation, while others might be evaluated every three years.

Required Documentation to Demonstrate Supplier Assessments

The panel gave the following examples of documentation to demonstrate that an adequate assessment has been performed of suppliers:

• Receiving reports, test reports, specifications, and certificates of compliance

• Copies of complaints, investigations, and implemented changes that have been agreed to

• The supplier's quality manual, recognitions, audits, third-party registration and scope

- Periodic scheduled supplier reviews, internal and on-site

- Documentation of completed corrective actions as referenced by the audit reports

- Statistical evidence of capability and control

- Periodic assessment of process output and effective implementation of quality plans as supported by the supplier ratings program.

Guidance for Specific Industries

Joseph Tiratto, president of Joseph Tiratto and Associates, points out that guidance documents helpful in this area have also been prepared for specific industry sectors, such as chemicals and software. For example, in *ANSI/ASQC Q90 ISO 9000 Guidelines for Use by the Chemical and Process Industries,* an assessment of the supplier's ability consistently to meet requirements may be based on the following evidence:

- On-site assessment of supplier's quality and/or performance data (current and historical)

- Trials or demonstration in the organization's laboratories or plant; for example, the organization may have to rely on inspection and testing when a supplier's appraisal is not feasible (i.e., spot purchases of bulk material)

- Documented evidence of successful use in similar processes

- Third-party assessment and registration of the supplier's quality systems to an acceptable standard.

Developing a Teaming Relationship

Drayton says assessment and selection of suppliers is good business practice, in addition to being a requirement of the ISO 9000 series standards. "Materials-driven businesses have long relied on quantity of suppliers to make up for poor quality," he says. "Today's marketplace is rapidly changing that philosophy. Time and time again it is proven to be more cost-effective to slim down the number of suppliers and form what are known as 'teaming relationships' with them."

Drayton defines this relationship as one where both organization and supplier understand and respect their interdependence and interreliance. "Rather than the adversarial relationships which characterized the old-style vendor-contractor relationship, businesses who team have quality as a focus and success as a mutual goal," he argues.

7.4.2 Purchasing Information (4.6.3)

Purchasing documents shall describe what is ordered, including, as appropriate:

- Requirements for approval of product, procedures, processes, and equipment
- Requirements for qualification of personnel
- Quality management system requirements.

The organization shall make sure that purchase documents adequately specify requirements prior to release.

ISO 9004:2000 Guidance

Clause 7.4.2 lists examples of input to the suppler control process. (See *Handbook* CD-ROM.)

ISO 9000-2:1997 Guidance

The purchasing data should define the technical product requirements to the supplier to ensure the quality of the purchased product. This can be done by reference to other applicable information, such as national or international standards or test methods.

Organizations should assign appropriate personnel responsibility for reviewing and approving purchasing data.

7.4.3 Verification of Purchased Product (4.6.4)

Organizations shall verify that purchased product meets purchase requirements.

When the organization or customer verifies product at the supplier's site, purchasing documents shall describe plans for verification and how the product is to be released.

7.5 Production and Service Provision (4.9)

7.5.1 Control of Production and Service Provision (4.9)

Preventing problems by controlling the production process is preferable to discovering them at a final inspection. Process control activities often include statistical process control methods, procedures for accepting materials into the process and the proper maintenance of process equipment and essential materials.

The organization shall plan and control production and service operations. It is to:

- Have available information describing product characteristics

- Provide work instructions as needed, for work that affects quality
- Use and maintain suitable production and service equipment
- Provide and use suitable measuring and monitoring devices
- Implement monitoring functions
- Operate defined processes for release, delivery and activities after delivery.

ISO 9004:2000 Guidance

Clause 7.5.1 lists ways to improve the effectiveness and efficiency of the realization process. (See *Handbook* CD-ROM.)

ISO 9000-2:1997 Guidance

The adequacy of production process control should take into account the adequacy of the measurement processes. When effective process control depends upon consistent operation of process equipment and essential materials, the organization should include within the scope of the quality system the proper maintenance of such process equipment and essential materials. Organizations are well advised to consider conducting process capability studies to determine the potential effectiveness of a process in delivering product to meet requirements.

All products are produced by processes. "Special processes" are those whose results cannot be fully verified by subsequent inspection and testing of the product and where processing deficiencies may become apparent only after the product is in use. Special processes are particularly common in producing processed materials. Critical product quality characteristics in this area include the following examples:

- Metal parts (strength, ductility, fatigue life, corrosion-resistance following welding, soldering, etc.)
- Polymerized plastic (dyeability, shrinkage, tensile properties)
- Bakery products (taste, texture, appearance)
- Correctness of financial or legal documents/software.

Special processes may require:

- Comprehensive measurement assurance and equipment calibration.

QS-9000 Automotive

Designation of Special Characteristics (4.9.d.1)

Documentation is required to show that the organization is meeting specific customer requirements. "Special" characteristics may affect safety, regulation compliance, fit, function, appearance or quality of later manufacturing operations.

Preventive Maintenance (4.9.g.1)

The organization shall develop a planned preventive maintenance system requiring:

- Procedures
- Schedule maintenance
- Predictive maintenance methods
- Packaging and preservation of equipment, tooling and gauging
- Replacement parts
- Documenting, evaluating and improving maintenance objectives.

Process Monitoring and Operator Instructions (4.9.1)

The organization shall develop and maintain explicit instructions according to the *Advanced Product Quality Planning and Control Plan* reference manual. Instructions are to include, as appropriate:

- Operation name and number keyed to process flowchart
- Part name and part number
- Current engineering level/date
- Required tools, gauges and other equipment
- Material identification and disposition instructions
- Customer-/supplier-designated special characteristics
- SPC requirements
- Relevant engineering and manufacturing standards
- Inspection and test instructions
- Reaction plan
- Revision date and approvals
- Visual aids
- Tool change intervals and setup instructions.

Maintaining Process Control (4.9.2)

Process capability or performance as set forth in the *Production Part Approval Process* reference manual is to be met or exceeded. Requirements include implementation of the control plan and process flow diagram, which include measurement technique, sampling plans, acceptance criteria and reaction plans when acceptance criteria are not met. These requirements are contained in the *Advanced Product Quality Planning and Control Plan* reference manual.

- Significant changes should be noted on control charts.
- Customer can permit revision of control plan when high degree of process capability is indicated.
- A reaction/corrective action plan is required when the process is not stable or capable.
- When required, plans are to be reviewed with and approved by customer.

Modified Process Control Requirements (4.9.3)

The control plan is to be annotated if customer requires higher or lower capability requirements.

Verification of Job Setups (4.9.4)

- Job setups are required to show that all produced parts meet requirements.
- Documentation available for setup personnel.
- Last-off part comparison recommended.
- Some customers may require statistical verification.

Process Changes (4.9.5)

- A record of "change effective" dates is to be maintained.
- Changes to promote continuous improvement are encouraged, but may require customer approval.

Appearance Items (4.9.6)

The organization shall provide:

- Adequate/suitable lighting in inspection areas
- Master standards for appearance items, as needed
- Adequate care of physical standards and equipment
- Qualified personnel.

Inspection and Testing (4.10)

ISO 9001:2000 does not specifically address process inspection stages (incoming, in process and final inspection) as covered in ISO 9001:1994. This omission is apparently because such processes apply only to certain manufacturing organizations and are not applicable universally. There is no indication that these requirements have been eliminated, only that ISO 9001:2000 is less prescriptive. For the use of those organizations to which these inspection stages apply, the ISO 9001:1994 requirements are included in the following section.

ISO 9001:1994 (4.10.1)

The "organization shall establish and maintain documented procedures for inspection and testing activities" to ensure that product requirements are met. This includes documenting the inspection and testing procedures in the quality plan or documented procedures.

QS-9000 Automotive

Acceptance Criteria for Attribute Characteristics (4.10.1.1)

Zero defects shall be the acceptance criteria for attribute sampling plans. Other situations require customer approval.

Receiving Inspection and Testing (4.10.2)

ISO 9001:1994

Receiving inspection allows organizations to verify that suppliers are fulfilling their contractual obligations. The organization is required to do the following:

- Ensure that incoming products are not used or processed until they have been inspected or otherwise verified.
- Verify in accordance with the quality plan and the documented procedures.
- Consider degree of control at suppliers' locations and evidence of conformance.

ISO 9000-2:1997 Guidance (4.10.1.1)

This subclause does not imply that incoming items must be inspected and tested if the organization can use other defined procedures that would fulfill this obligation. These defined procedures should include:

- Provisions for verifying that incoming items, materials or services are accompanied by supporting documentation
- Provision for appropriate action in the event of nonconformities.

ISO 9004-1:1994 Guidance

Receiving Inspection Planning and Control (9.7) notes that the "extent to which receiving inspection will be performed should be carefully planned ... The level of inspection should be selected so as to balance the costs of inspection against the consequences of inadequate inspection."

Receiving Quality Records (9.8) stresses that appropriate records should be kept to "ensure the availability of historical data to assess subcontractor performance and quality trends." Companies should also consider maintaining "records of lot identification for purposes of traceability."

ISO 9000-2:1997 Guidance (4.10.1.2)

The release of incoming product subject to recall should generally be discouraged as a matter of good quality management practice. There are two exceptions:

- An objective evaluation of quality status and resolution of any nonconformities can still be implemented.
- Correction of nonconformities cannot compromise the quality of adjacent, attached or incorporated items.

The organization's procedures should accomplish the following:

- Define responsibilities and authority of people who may allow incoming product to be used without prior demonstration of conformance to specified requirements.
- Explain how such product will be positively identified and controlled in the event that subsequent inspection finds nonconformities.

QS-9000 Automotive

Incoming Product Quality (4.10.2.4)

One or more of the following methods shall be used:

- Statistical data
- Receiving inspection and/or testing
- Assessment of subcontractor by second or third party
- Part evaluation by accredited laboratory.

In-Process Inspection and Testing (4.10.3)

ISO 9001:1994

The organization is to do the following:

- Inspect and test product as required by the quality plan or by the documented procedures.
- Hold the product until the required inspection and tests have been completed.

The exception is when the product is released under positive recall procedures. The release under positive recall procedures, however, would not preclude the inspection required above.

ISO 9000-2:1997 Guidance

In-process inspection and testing applies to all forms of products, including services. It allows for early recognition of nonconformities.

Statistical control techniques are commonly used to identify product and process trends and prevent nonconformities. Inspection and test results should be objective — including those carried out by production personnel.

ISO 9004-1:1994 Guidance

In-Process Verification (12.2) lists the following types of verification checks:

- Setup and first-piece inspection
- Inspection or test by a machine operator
- Automatic inspection or test
- Fixed inspection stations at intervals through the process
- Patrol inspection by inspectors monitoring specified operations.

Final Inspection (4.10.4)

Inspect and test product in accordance with quality plan or documented procedures.

Product is not to be released until:

- All required inspections and tests have been carried out
- Results confirm that all specified requirements have been met
- All activities of the quality plan and documented procedures have been carried out
- All data and documentation are available and authorized.

QS-9000 Automotive (4.10.4)

Conduct layout inspection and functional testing requirements as established by the customer.

ISO 9004-1:1994 Guidance (12.3)

Either or both of the following forms of verification of finished product may be used as appropriate:

- Acceptance inspections or tests such as 100 percent inspection, lot sampling and continuous sampling
- Product quality auditing of representative units selected from completed lots, continuously or periodically.

Servicing (4.19)

ISO 9001:1994 (4.19)

The basic servicing requirements call for the organization to do the following:

- Establish and maintain documented procedures for servicing (when required by contract).
- Verify and report that servicing meets specified requirements.

ISO 9000-2:1997 Guidance

In planning procedures for servicing, organizations should:

- Clarify servicing responsibilities
- Plan service activities (organization or externally provided)
- Validate design and function of necessary servicing tools and equipment
- Control measuring and test equipment
- Provide suitable documentation and instructions
- Provide backup technical advice, support and spares or parts supply
- Provide competent, trained service personnel
- Gather useful feedback for product or servicing design.

ISO 9004-1:1994 Guidance

After-Sales Servicing (16.2) notes that instructions for products should be comprehensive and supplied in a timely manner. Instructions should cover assembly and installation, commissioning, operation, spares or parts lists and servicing of products. In the area of logistical backup, responsibility should be clearly assigned and agreed upon among suppliers, distributors and users.

QS-9000 Automotive

Feedback of Information from Service (4.19.1)

Information from service shall be communicated to manufacturing, engineering, and design.

Clause 7.5.1: Control of Production and Service Provision

Suitable Maintenance of Equipment

The standard includes a requirement for "the use of suitable equipment." Many companies have formal, planned maintenance programs and activities, but these are rarely included in the management system. ISO 9001 requires them to be incorporated. For those that have no such program, creating one need not be complex or onerous. They will need to lay out planned maintenance, define the activities to a level appropriate to the skills and training of the maintenance staff and keep records of the work performed.

Where the appropriate maintenance is "run it until it breaks and then fix it," that should be stated. It is, after all, the company's system — not the auditor's. Examples of "run until it breaks" equipment could include process control computers, some forms of automatic test equipment, hand tools and similar items. Where "routine maintenance" is basically operator-driven, such as lubricating and cleaning metal-working equipment, then this activity can now be referenced in work instructions.

The term "suitable" is open to interpretation. The organization has the absolute right to determine suitability, but a process-knowledgeable auditor equally has the right to question the program that has been defined. The key to the success of this requirement lies in auditors recognizing that they have to prove "unsuitability" by providing evidence of adverse effects on deliverables before writing up a noncompliance and in the company making sure that the "continuing process capability" requirement is adequately covered.

Work Instructions

Work instructions, which are referred to in subclause 7.5.1b, can take the form of anything from a representative sample to a detailed, written document. A work instruction can be a videotape. It can be a model of the work on display by the operator — a common technique in high-volume electronic manual assembly that can work very well.

It is important to assess the training and skills of employees when evaluating where to make use of work instructions. In determining their use, the standard cautions companies to make the decision based on consideration of "where the absence of such instructions would adversely affect quality." In assessing whether an employee knows how to perform his or her job correctly, there are three possible ways this can be demonstrated:

• A work instruction exists that details these responsibilities.

• Records exist proving the individual was hired with a particular skill.

• The employee has received on-the-job training and records exist to document the training and prove it has been performed.

The scope of subclause 7.5.1 also covers service activities, so when such work lies within the registered scope of a company, all the requirements of this clause need to be applied to such activities.

— The Victoria Group

7.5.2 Validation of Processes for Production and Service Provision (4.9)

Process validation for production and service processes is required in cases where output cannot be verified by measuring or monitoring after production. Validation is necessary in particular where deficiencies are seen only after the product is in use or the service has been delivered. Process validation is a demonstration of the capability of a process to deliver an acceptable product or service, fully meeting all requirements.

Steps in the validation process are:

- Pre-qualification of processes, ensuring process capability before production actually begins
- Qualification of equipment and personnel
- Use of defined methods and procedures
- Maintaining records of validation actions taken.

Additional ISO 9001:2000 Requirement

Processes are to be revalidated as necessary.

Subclause 7.5.2: Validation of Processes of Chemical Producers

Reprinted courtesy of Quality Systems Update

Question: Does the Subclause 7.5.2 requirement that "the organization shall validate any processes for production and service provision where the resulting output cannot be verified by subsequently monitoring or measurement" encompass all production processes used by chemical producers? Some auditors have affirmed that it does, basing their decision on the interpretation that all processes are "one, large, special process."

Answer: The experts agreed that the requirement in Subclause 7.5.2 could cover all production processes used by a chemical producer. Robert W. Belfit, president, Omni Tech International, Inc., however, says he interprets this subclause differently. Belfit suggests that, when proceeding through the registration process, a chemical producer should interview potential registrars to ascertain the possible interpretation.

Belfit cites the example of a product that is manufactured under as much control and testing as possible, but requires that the manufacturer delay the shipment until the customer has used the product in his process and then release the product for shipment.

Belfit says these special processes are generally not run on a regular basis and "therefore the processing parameters and testing parameters have not or cannot be defined precisely to ensure that the product will perform in the customer's application." He concludes that the requirements for process validation in the chemical industry imply that it is not possible through process control, in-process testing or final testing to establish whether the product will perform in the customer's application.

On the other hand, Belfit points out, "the production of benzene, styrene, ethyl alcohol, polystyrene or polyvinylidene chloride are processes that are run on a continuous basis. These are, in reality, commodity products." He says the performance of these products in the customer's application is predictable based on the process controls, the end-process analysis, and/or the product analysis of the final product. "These products are covered by Clause 7.5.1 in the general statement under 'control of production,'" Belfit says.

Prevention Versus "Find-and-Fix"

Ian Durand, [then] president, Service Process Consulting, Inc., notes that examining the central theme of the ISO 9000 series is important in interpreting the need for process validation. He says the overall emphasis of the ISO 9000 series is on "preventing quality problems before they occur, rather than relying on 'find-and-fix approaches.'" For this reason, Durand says, "it is not unusual for registrars to look for, and prefer to find, attention given to controlling all processes that affect the quality of the 'total market offering,' i.e., both the tangible goods and accompanying services."

Durand notes that "in the real world there are always trade-offs between process control and inspection and testing." In establishing the balance between the two approaches, Durand says such factors as the feasibility of subsequent inspection, the relative effectiveness and costs and the specific processes and products being considered should be evaluated.

To illustrate, he notes that in some chemical industries, skilled operators assess color, granularity, texture and handling characteristics to complement process control. Durand concludes that assessing relevant factors and establishing a balance between process control and inspection requires working knowledge of the industry and the specific processes and products under consideration. For example, Durand says that keeping levels of airborne contaminants below specified thresholds during production of solid-state devices is essential. "Complete reliance on inspection and testing is generally not a viable alternative to cleanliness and sanitation during food preparation either," Durand adds. He says that both of these examples are types of chemical processes.

Process Validation of Chemical Processes

Terry Heaps, [then] audit program manager, Vincotte USA, Inc., also agrees that a case could be made for including process validation as part of all production processes. Heaps notes that any confusion that arises may be in the manner in which auditors approach the need for process validation, since there is little difference between the requirements for process validation and process control in ISO 9001.

Heaps says ECIC guidelines state that chemical processes may be considered special processes for a variety of reasons, including the following:

- A characteristic can be measured only during the process and not in the finished product.

- A characteristic of the product changes (matures) after the product has been delivered.

- The complete characteristics of a product are not known.

- There is no satisfactory method of measuring a product characteristic.

"There may be a greater emphasis on the results of the in-process inspection and testing and calibration of the equipment used to make or test the product than may be required for a conventional process," Heaps says. Heaps cites other ECIC guidelines concerning customer requirements. For example:

- A specification is agreed upon for certain characteristics inspected or tested during the process.

- Before accepting the contract, the product is evaluated after use in this product or process.

- The process and/or the source of raw materials is not changed without the customer's agreement.

- Specified statistical process control methods are used.

Special skills, capabilities and training personnel may be needed to meet any additional quality requirements.

Joseph Tiratto, president, Joseph Tiratto and Associates, Inc., says that "processes of the chemical process industry generally will require validation." He cites ECIC guidelines as a reference. In addition, Tiratto cites *ANSI/ASQC Q90 ISO 9000 Guidelines for Use by the Chemical and Process Industries*. These guidelines include equipment used to make or measure product; operator skill, capability and knowledge; environmental factors affecting quality; records of qualifications.

7.5.3 Identification and Traceability (4.8)

In some cases, contracts require the organization to trace specific materials or assemblies throughout the process of their development, through delivery and/or installation. Product (and service) traceability refers to the ability to trace the history, application or location of an item or activity by means of recorded identification.

Where appropriate, the organization shall identify the product during all stages of production and (where applicable) service, which may include delivery and installation. This includes measuring and monitoring activities. To the extent that traceability is a specified requirement, individual products or batches of products are to be controlled, with a unique identification.

A note observes that identification and traceability are maintained by configuration management in some industries.

ISO 9004:2000 Guidance

The clause for identification and traceability (7.5.2 in ISO 9004:2000) lists circumstances that may create the need for traceability. (See *Handbook* CD-ROM.)

ISO 9000-2:1997 Guidance

There are many identification methods, including marking, tagging or documentation, in the case of a service. The identifier should be unique to the source of the operation. Separate identifiers could be required for changes in various aspects of the production process.

Traceability may require identifying specific personnel involved in phases of the operation. This can be accomplished through signatures on serially numbered documents, for example.

The status of a product should be indicated as follows:

- Not inspected
- Inspected and accepted
- Inspected and on hold awaiting decision
- Inspected and rejected.

The most certain method of ensuring status and accurate disposition is to separate these product categories physically. In an automated environment, however, other methods can be used, such as a computer database.

QS-9000 Automotive

Inspection and Test Status (4.12)

The organization is required to do the following:

- Identify the inspection and test status of the product by suitable means throughout production, installation and servicing, to ensure that only acceptable product has been used, per quality plan (control plan).

- Identify the inspection authority responsible for the release of the conforming product.

- The test status must be indicated by suitable means. The physical location of the product in the production process is not sufficient to indicate inspection status, unless it is clearly obvious, such as with an automatic process.

Supplemental Verification (4.12.1)

The customer may set additional requirements.

Subclause 7.5.3: Product Identification and Traceability

Reprinted courtesy of Quality Systems Update

Question: Subclause 7.5.3, Identification and Traceability, requires organizations, where appropriate, to identify the product by suitable means through the stages of product realization. How do companies determine what level of product identification and traceability is necessary? Is this likely to vary by industry, and can you give some examples of creative ways to meet this requirement?

Answer: *QSU*'s panel of experts agrees that organizations should closely examine their customers' basic requirements and what is appropriate and customary to the specific industry.

Moderator Robert Peach, principal of Robert Peach and Associates, says manufacturers today must go beyond second-guessing their customer's requirements.

"Companies should not just say, 'What does my customer demand on traceability and I will meet that, and that's it,'" says Peach. "They must go beyond that .... They should say, 'What can be done with the lower costs of being able to identify product through whatever technology is available today?'"

Bar-coding is widely used today, he adds. Today you can identify parts automatically by computer and know what you've got and where it is. Being able to routinely trace parts back to suppliers and their sub-suppliers is an important part of control.

"I don't know how many companies are learning that," Peach says. "I recall the example of the well-known bottled water producer that neglected to provide traceability — date of filling — on their product.

"When a problem occurred, they could not limit the extent of a product call-back, and it put them out of business for weeks. Today, they identify every bottle with the time of filling to the minute, using a four-digit time, the actual moment of filling."

That company lost market share because their product wasn't traceable in distribution, Peach says. Now most bottlers and food packagers realize that it is good business to place an open date on their product for all to see. All in industry should learn by this experience and provide product traceability for their own benefit.

"That may include tracing components as well," Peach concludes. "ISO 9001 traceability questions relate to identifying materials and components from the time received from sub-suppliers. The standard merely says to meet what your customer wants and meet regulatory requirements. You start there. You must do that, but then you determine whether additional controls are needed."

Says Terry Heaps, [then] audit program manager for AV Qualité, the essence of traceability depends on a complete understanding of how each component impacts critical functional properties of the product and, in turn, how the product is utilized by the end user, thus allowing each member of the supply chain to determine the appropriate level of traceability.

"Even within the same industry, the extent of traceability depends on the products supplied," she says. "Specialty chemicals designed for a specific use need a greater degree of control on raw material lot numbers, since formulations depend on the tight interactions of raw-material properties.

"General-purpose chemicals may need traceability back to only one of the raw materials, since their interaction does not greatly affect the product function," she says. "I believe this example holds true regardless of industry."

Aside from product functionality, safety considerations may also need to be taken into account in the case of pharmaceutical products, she adds. In this case, traceability back to the raw materials may not be enough. The packaging used, the equipment in which it was processed and any cleaning supplies that came into contact with the product have to be tracked.

"Understanding your product, the critical aspects of the components and the end use is the key to establishing traceability systems that serve a purpose," she concludes.

Reg Blake, [then] director on the board of BSI Inc. and manager of sales and marketing, says the key words to the interpretation of this clause are "where appropriate."

"These are often overlooked, resulting in the use of elaborate methods, which are both unnecessary and costly," he says. "Companies are free to select those methods that serve their needs and often those required by their customers.

"Adequate solutions are often the simplest and the method employed should complement the complexity and type of product process or service. Product identification and traceability should also address issues and requirements such as criticality, regulatory, statutory, contractual and the nature of the product, such as composite materials used in the aerospace and automotive sectors," he adds.

Blake says that different industries require different levels of identification and traceability based on various degrees of risk and the type of product or process. Also, shelf life or curing times may be critical for safe use.

"The whole of the transportation industry is a good candidate for failures that necessitate grounding of aircraft or vehicle recalls," Blake says. "There is no substitute for good identification and traceability at such times. This is also true of the pharmaceutical, drug and food industries."

Methods include labels, color-coding, bar-coding, batch-numbering, stamping, molding, printing, marking, engraving and other technologies, he adds. Often, much of this data is stored in computers, so records, files and software should be clearly labeled and traceable as well.

"Some creative ways could be genetic coding of organic products and the use of taggants, small pieces of color-coded plastic used in explosives," Blake concludes. "Small shreds of plastic from a bomb can be analyzed to determine the source and batch of the explosive material used."

Vern Portell, [then] lead auditor for AV Qualité, an ISO 9000 registrar, says an important first step is to look at codes and regulations already applicable within the industry in question. There are major differences, he says by way of example, applicable to manufacturers of boilers and pressure vessels and, to use another example, manufacturers dependent on the requirements of the Federal Aviation Administration.

"Being knowledgeable of these requirements forms the essential core of traceability requirements," Portell says. There is also, he adds, the need to understand the expectations of customers and the customary specifications and practices of the particular industry.

"Finally," adds Portell, "there is the need to look at potential exposure to liability to protect oneself against unforeseen circumstances." He uses as an example a drug company that manufactures its products in 10,000-dose lots. Regulatory requirements mandate tight controls, including traceability and identification for all components.

"In contrast to this, chemical processors who are manufacturing or blending chemicals are typically not required to have the same level of traceability," Portell says. "If the products are produced in a continuous process, it may be impossible to provide traceability for the precise raw materials used. In this case, if a purchaser requires a certificate of analysis, a unique lot number identification, or 'pedigree,' can be created by isolating, sampling and assaying the contents of the storage container or tank."

The difference between these two approaches, he says, is the result of regulatory requirements and market demands. The manufacturer must understand both his customer and business environment to ensure that requirements are met most efficiently.

"When traceability is required throughout production, simplicity works best," Portell says. "Lot number identification codes can be used on a simple scheme, such as one that uses the Julian calendar date, shift number and a sequence number. A system like this is easy to use, easy to verify and reduces the probability of error."

Bar-coding is an excellent and proven technology for identifying and tracing materials, he adds. Bar-coded tags or labels can be printed for each raw material package when it is received. This gives them a unique identifier that can be scanned on batch records or retained as an electronic record.

"In industries such as pharmaceuticals, aircraft and defense contracting, 100 percent traceability for all materials is the norm," Portell concludes. "In the chemical industry, there are widely varying practices, but many can provide full traceability to the raw materials and lot numbers that were used."

7.5.4 Customer Property (4.7)

While customer property is being used or controlled by the organization, it shall exercise care, by identification, verification, protection and safeguarding of products supplied by the customer. Products that are lost, damaged or unsuitable for use shall be recorded and reported to the customer.

Additional ISO 9001:2000 Requirement

Customer property includes intellectual property.

ISO 9004:2000 Guidance

Examples of customer property are listed in ISO 9004:2000 Clause 7.5.3. (See *Handbook* CD-ROM.)

ISO 9000-2:1997 Guidance

Customer-supplied product is any product owned by the customer and furnished to the organization for use in meeting the requirements of the contract. The organization accepts full responsibility for the product while in its possession.

Customer-supplied product could be a service, such as the use of a customer's transport for delivery. The organization should make sure that the service is suitable and that its effectiveness can be documented.

QS-9000 Automotive

Control of Customer-Supplied Product (4.7)

"Customer-supplied product" includes customer-owned tooling and returnable packaging.

7.5.5 Preservation of Product (4.15)

Internal processing and delivery is not to alter conformance with customer requirements. Attention should be given to product identification, handling, packaging and preservation. As appropriate, the organization should:

- Establish and maintain procedures for identification, handling, packaging, storage and preservation
- Provide methods to prevent damage or deterioration
- Provide secure storage and stipulate appropriate receipt and dispatch methods
- Control packaging, packing and marking processes
- Provide appropriate methods for preserving and segregating products when they are under the organization's control
- Protect product quality after final inspection and test, including delivery to destination.

Additional ISO 9001:2000 Requirement

Preservation requirements shall also apply to product parts.

ISO 9000-2:1997 Guidance

The requirement applies to incoming materials, materials in process and finished product. The procedures should provide proper planning, control and documentation.

Handling methods should include provision for the transportation unit, such as pallets, containers, conveyors, etc., to prevent damage. Another factor to consider is the maintenance of the handling equipment.

Suitable storage procedures should take into account the following:

- Physical security
- Environmental control (temperature and humidity)
- Periodic checking to detect deterioration
- Legible, durable marking and labeling methods
- Expiration dates and stock rotation methods.

Packaging procedures should:

- Provide appropriate protection against damage, deterioration or contamination as long as the material remains the responsibility of the organization
- Provide a clear description of the contents or ingredients, according to regulations or to the contract
- Provide for checking packaging effectiveness.

For some products, delivery time is a critical factor. Procedures should take into account various types of delivery and variations in potential environmental conditions.

QS-9000 Automotive

Inventory (4.15.3.1)

An inventory management system shall be used to optimize inventory turns, minimize level and ensure stock rotation.

Customer Packaging Standards (4.15.4.1)

Packaging requirements are established by customer.

Labeling (4.15.4.2)

Labeling requirements are established by customer.

Supplier Delivery Performance Monitoring (4.15.6)

Systems are to support 100 percent on-time shipments. When 100 percent on-time is not maintained, corrective action to improve delivery performance is necessary, with notification of customer.

Lead times are to be established and met.

Performance to delivery requirements is to be tracked.

The organization is to conform to customer-specified transportation mode, routing and containers.

Production Scheduling (4.15.6.2)

Current orders are to drive production scheduling. Small lots (synchronous one-piece flow) are encouraged.

Shipment Notification System (4.15.6.4)

On-line transmittal of advanced shipment notification is required, with a back-up method available.

7.6 Control of Monitoring and Measuring Devices (4.11)

To ensure product conformity, the organization shall identify and define needed measurements and provide required monitoring and measuring devices. It shall make certain that such devices are used properly, to meet requirements. Where needed to ensure valid results, the organization shall:

- Calibrate and adjust such devices at prescribed intervals, or prior to use, to standards with a valid relationship to international or national standards. If not, the basis used is to be recorded.
- Protect the devices from being adjusted in a way that would cause the settings to be incorrect.
- Provide identification to determine calibration status.
- Protect such devices from damage, by providing suitable methods of handling, maintenance, preservation and storage.
- Review the validity of previous measuring and monitoring results when equipment is found out of calibration and take necessary actions.
- Maintain calibration and verification records.

Reference is made to ISO 10012, *Quality Assurance Requirements for Measuring Equipment*, for guidance.

Additional ISO 9001:2000 Requirement

Monitoring and measuring software shall be validated prior to use.

ISO 10012 Guidance

Part 1, Management of Measuring Equipment, offers guidance for the management of measuring equipment. However, the guidance in ISO 10012 does not add to or otherwise change the requirements in ISO 9001, except where conformance to ISO 10012 is required.

Measurements may include less tangible instruments, such as polling, questionnaires or subjective preferences.

The requirements of this clause also should be considered when applied to measurements subsequent to producing and inspecting a product (e.g., handling, storage, packaging, delivery or servicing).

QS-9000 Automotive

Inspection, Measuring, and Test Equipment Records (4.11.3)

Calibration/verification records shall include:

- Revisions following engineering changes
- Out-of-specification readings as received for calibration
- Statements of conformance after calibration
- Customer notification of suspect material.

Measurement System Analysis (4.11.4)

Statistical analysis of variability in results of measuring and test equipment is required. Customer may approve other analytical methods and acceptance criteria. (See the *Measurement System Analysis* reference manual.)

Clause 7.6: How Far Do You Take Calibration Programs?

Reprinted courtesy of Quality Systems Update

Question: Do the requirements of Clause 7.6 imply that all inspection, measuring and test equipment must be put on a calibration program? Or does it merely require the calibration of certain equipment?

Answer: In general, the panel of experts agreed that the standard does not require all inspection, measuring and test equipment to be put on a calibration program. However, one panelist, Robert W. Belfit, Jr., president, Omni Tech International Ltd., disagreed, maintaining that no such equipment should escape periodic scrutiny. Nevertheless, he says, there are varying levels of calibration and not all equipment need be subjected to the same degree of scrutiny. "Why would one want to produce data and not know the accuracy and precision?" asks Belfit. "The question should be, 'How do we keep the measurement process under process control?'"

Level of Calibration Required

Belfit says the level of calibration required varies with each piece of equipment. He says it is important to consider the following factors:

- What the measurement will be used for
- The required tolerance versus equipment capability

- The ruggedness of the equipment

- Working conditions

- Frequency of use

- Possible malfunctions

- Whether the measurements will be supported by other data

- Whether the measurements will be used to support a specification or claim.

Bud Weightman, president, Qualified Specialists, Inc., says it is not necessary to put all such equipment on a calibration program, provided "objective evidence exists" to substantiate that the organization made a "conscientious" decision. "It is the organization's responsibility to identify those characteristics of the design and processes which could have a direct effect on quality," he says. "Characteristics could include specific product dimensions and process-related elements that require an inspection, test or measurement to verify conformance to the stated requirements of the design output."

Peter M. Malkovich, president, East Concord Associates, observes that if the equipment does not control and/or verify quality, it does not have to be included in the calibration program. "Hence, there is equipment that may not affect quality and equipment that may be used as a work aid or indicator only. Such equipment can be excluded from the calibration program and should be identified as 'Not Calibrated' with the reason why it is not included." For example, he says, it is not necessary to calibrate gauges and equipment used to monitor the condition of the plant or to indicate that something is operating. They still must be checked periodically to establish that they do work.

Malkovich says firms should calibrate all equipment that affects quality and other equipment used for important measurements. Nevertheless, he says, firms must be prepared to demonstrate why excluded equipment does not affect quality.

Weightman suggests that organizations back up their decision not to calibrate certain pieces of equipment through documentation. Examples include affixing "calibration not required" stickers to them; stipulating which types of equipment will be used in design output documents; including an evaluation of the inspection, measuring, and test equipment in-process capability studies; and having procedures that document which types of equipment will be calibrated and which will not.

He also suggests that organizations evaluate "all potential sources" where inspection, measuring, and test equipment are in use to determine their potential effects on quality. Such sources include equipment owned by the firm, equipment owned by employees, equipment on loan, equipment provided by the customer, and equipment used in vendor processes or operations.

Clause 7.6: Must Calibration Procedures Be Kept on Site?

Reprinted courtesy of Quality Systems Update

Question: Clause 7.6 requires companies to define the process employed for the calibration of monitoring and measuring equipment. Our company does not have its own calibration laboratory. However, an outside laboratory has been selected in accordance with the requirements of Clause 7.4.1. Must we maintain calibration procedures for each piece of measurement equipment even though we outsource this work?

Answer: *QSU*'s panel of experts agreed it is not necessary to keep calibration records on-site for every piece of equipment if the work is performed by a contractor.

Moderator Ira Epstein, president of Value Management Associates, an ISO 9000 and QS-9000 training and consulting firm, says companies must maintain calibration procedures only on those measuring and test instruments for which they actually perform the calibrations.

"Where calibration is done by an outside source, then the calibration procedures need not be maintained by the organization," he explains. "These procedures refer to the specific procedures to calibrate individual instruments."

Epstein says all companies must maintain calibration procedures for the overall control of measuring and test instruments.

"These system-level procedures are required to be maintained by the organization even though the actual calibration is done by an outside source," he says. "The system-level procedures contain requirements for identifying the measuring and test instruments, for identifying the interval between calibrations, identifying the recall methodology and how the instruments are calibrated generally."

Epstein says it is important for companies to document who in the organization is responsible for making sure that equipment has been placed on an appropriate calibration schedule.

Peter Merrill, president of Strider International Inc., a quality management consulting firm that offers ISO 9000 and QS-9000 services, says companies must treat their calibration vendors as they would any supplier of a critical component. He says they should refer to subclause 7.4.1, which establishes requirements for the evaluation of suppliers.

"If you are subcontracting your calibration activity, it still does not let you off the hook in terms of adequate calibration," says Merrill. "You must satisfy yourself that the calibration house is performing adequately."

According to Merrill, companies must have a procedure to ensure that calibrations are being performed in an acceptable manner. "You may have certain equipment which is highly specialized," he says. "There's no way that you can have the in-house skills to do that calibration. Providing that you can show someone is doing it adequately, I would say you met the requirements of the quality system."

Merrill agrees that it is not necessary to maintain copies of the actual calibration procedures being performed by the supplier.

"The rub, as Hamlet says, is monitoring your supplier's performance. I think that's the bigger issue," he explains. "It's the same way that you measure the performance of any supplier. I think you have to in fact monitor the actual physical calibration activity when the house comes in to do it."

If the equipment is sent off-site for calibration, Merrill suggests, companies should schedule regular visits to the supplier's facility. "On a regular basis you need to visit your supplier and satisfy yourself that they are doing the job properly," he says.

Even suppliers with ISO 9000 registration should not be given a free ride. "Is the person doing the calibration properly trained?" he asks. "Do they themselves have a well-documented procedure? Do you experience difficulties in equipment going out of calibration?"

But the standard does not require companies to understand how equipment is calibrated. "I don't think you need to have the skill of doing the calibration yourself," he says. "But I think you have to have the skill of evaluating supplier performance. That's fundamental business. This is one of the areas where most companies make their biggest improvement in the ISO journey."

Thomas F. Haney, president of EAQA USA Registrars, an ISO 9000 and TickIT registrar, says, "Where organizations choose to outsource calibration work, which is becoming more and more common, particularly in the government sector, it needs to be perceived as a supplier control issue," he says. "The approach we would take as a registrar would be to trace or follow the origination of the requirements through the purchasing process into the purchase orders."

Haney says registrars might want to visit the supplier's facility. "Depending upon the size of the organization's calibrated equipment pool, the type of the measurements being taken, as well as the criticality of the products involved, we might ask to pursue this into the supplier organization where there is concern that it's being performed as required," he says.

According to Haney, calibration figures prominently during an ISO 9000 audit. "This issue is significant because calibration of monitoring and measuring equipment is often seen as one of those core functions of any organization, not unlike the outsourcing of other critical processes such as design and contract review," he says.

Haney says all critical functions in an organization call for a level of control to be exercised that is proportional to the risk of product or system failure. "This includes an activity the organization chooses to outsource, whether it be the outsourcing of calibration services or the use of temporary employees to perform work affecting quality."

Dave Fleischli, executive director responsible for the ISO 9000 and QS-9000 consulting practice with ALAMO Learning Systems, agrees that organizations are not required to maintain calibration procedures for each piece of equipment that is calibrated by the supplier.

"You do need a procedure for how the process for calibration within your organization occurs," says Fleischli. "In this situation, the procedure would address the identification of items to be included within the scope of work for the calibration house performing the calibration."

Fleischli says the procedure must also address the maintenance and storage of quality records with respect to equipment calibration and the steps that must be taken when a piece of equipment is found to be out of calibration.

Clause 7.6: Control of Monitoring and Measuring Devices

Clause 7.6 discusses control of monitoring and measuring devices. The standard requires that the organization establish a process to ensure that monitoring and measuring can be carried out in a manner consistent with requirements.

It is easy to misread the requirement laid down in this section. It does not require calibration of all equipment, only equipment used to demonstrate the conformance of product to the specified requirements. Equipment that is used for in-process measurement need not necessarily be calibrated, provided that the measurements made are not the last opportunity to record some item that is a deliverable specification. The same measurement, repeated at final release test or inspection, must be made on calibrated equipment.

Remember the words "to provide evidence of conformity." If any measurement taken in-process is part of providing evidence of conformity or, in other words, measuring a specified deliverable, the equipment used must be controlled. In one example, an audit team demanded that each of 35,000 gauges and meters at a certain refinery be calibrated in a manner traceable to national standards. The company correctly calibrated only those gauges that influenced the quality of the product and were used to demonstrate conformance to specified requirements.

Providing evidence of conformity is not confined to a single site in the company. Test and inspection equipment must be under traceable calibration control at those locations or places in the process where conformance can be demonstrated.

Portable Transfer Standard

External calibration to recognized national standards by the National Institute of Standards and Technology or a recognized, accredited laboratory or test house is expensive. Normal practice, therefore, is to have a certain amount of the critical equipment calibrated externally and then to use this equipment to calibrate the rest. This is known as using a "portable transfer standard."

It is an economical way of establishing calibration of all test and inspection equipment without breaking the bank. When adopting this approach, it pays to remember that the equipment providing the "portable transfer standard" should, whenever possible, be an order greater in its measurement capability than the equipment being checked. This ensures the accuracy of the secondary equipment measurement capability. In summary, the requirement is as follows:

• Identify equipment that ensures compliance.

• Uniquely identify each piece of equipment.

• Define the accuracy and precision required of each piece of equipment.

• Define the calibration method.

• Define the reference standard.

• Keep records of calibration performance.

• Be able to identify the calibration status of any measuring equipment.

• Know what to do about previously tested material if an item is found out of calibration.

ISO 10012: Quality Assurance Requirements for Measuring Equipment is referenced as a guidance document for structuring calibration systems, but this will be excessive for most companies unless they operate a full calibration laboratory system.

— *The Victoria Group*

8 Measurement, Analysis, and Improvement

8.1 General (4.10)

All necessary monitoring, measuring, analysis, and improvement functions shall be planned and put into use, to demonstrate that product meets requirements and quality management system requirements are met. Necessary methods shall be identified, including statistical techniques.

Additional ISO 9001:2000 Requirements

One purpose of such processes is to continually improve QMS effectiveness.

ISO 9004:2000 Guidance

ISO 9004:2000 provides examples of measurement of performance and lists issues to be considered.

8.2 Monitoring and Measurement

8.2.1 Customer Satisfaction

This clause is not contained in ISO 9001:1994.

Additional ISO 9001:2000 Requirements

Information on customer perception of satisfaction and dissatisfaction shall be tracked as one indicator of quality management system performance. Methodologies for how such information is to be obtained and used shall be defined. This wording implies that other methods of tracking quality management system performance should not be overlooked, including internal performance measures.

ISO 9004:2000 Guidance

- Examples of customer-related information (see 8.2.1.2)
- Examples of sources of information on customer satisfaction.

8.2.2 Internal Audit (4.17)

The organization shall have a defined internal quality audit activity, to determine if the quality management system conforms to the plan and to the ISO 9001 standard, is in effective operation and is being maintained.

- Audit planning shall consider the status and significance of the audit target and previous audit results.
- The audit criteria, scope, frequency and methodologies shall be defined.
- Internal quality audits shall be carried out in an objective and impartial manner, with auditors not auditing their own work.

A documented procedure for audits shall cover:

- Responsibilities
- Requirements
- Planning
- Records
- Reports of results.

When deficiencies are found, there shall be timely corrective action, verification of implementation and a report of results.

A note states to see ISO 19011 *Guidelines for Auditing Quality Systems* for guidance.

Additional ISO 9001:2000 Requirements

Audit shall determine if practice conforms to ISO 9001 requirements.

Audit criteria, scope, frequency and methodologies shall be defined.

A procedure shall document responsibilities and requirements.

ISO 9004:2000 Guidance

Examples of subjects for consideration by internal audit are listed in Clause 8.2.1.3. (See *Handbook* CD-ROM.)

ISO 9000-2:1997 Guidance

The purpose of an audit is to make sure the system is working according to plan, to meet regulatory requirements or to provide opportunities for improvement. Auditors should be selected and assigned according to the criteria contained in ISO 9001.

Internal audits may also be initiated for other reasons, including the following:

- Initial evaluation of a system for contract reasons
- When nonconformities jeopardize the safety, performance or dependability of the products
- Verification of corrective actions
- Evaluation of a system against a quality system standard.

Subclause 8.2.2: Internal Audit

Internal quality audits are the mainstay of system conformance. The quality system audit is a powerful tool for continuous improvement. The standard requires a planned, well-defined, ongoing process of audits to ensure that the documented system is effectively implemented and that corrective actions are taken in a timely manner. The audit process ensures that the system is working as planned and that corrective action is taken when it is not.

It is normal to expect that every area will be audited at least once a year, with areas that receive bad audit reports receiving more frequent scrutiny. The full audit plan and the audit reports should be properly documented, complete with details of the effective implementation of any corrective and preventive actions. Follow-up activities are required to be performed, with the requirement to record and review corrective action and preventive action taken.

— The Victoria Group

Subclause 8.2.2: Auditing the Auditors of Your Quality System

Reprinted courtesy of Quality Systems Update

Question: Subclause 8.2.2, Internal Audits, requires companies to establish and maintain documented procedures for planning and implementing internal quality audits to verify whether quality activities and related results comply with the planned arrangement and to determine the effectiveness of the quality system. Must the internal audit function itself be audited? If so, who in the company may be responsible for auditing the internal audit function, since all departments are audited by internal auditors?

Answer: *QSU's* panel of experts agree that the internal function itself is subject to audit under the standard and offer several innovative solutions as to who should be responsible for the audit.

According to moderator Ira Epstein, president of Value Management Associates, the answer to the first question is "a definite yes."

"You actually do have to audit the internal audit function," he says. "Who can perform this audit is really up to the organization. There are two provisions which must be met for all internal auditors, whether they are part of the audit function or they are auditing the internal audit function.

"First, all auditors must be qualified. The determination of qualifications is the responsibility of the organization," says Epstein. "Secondly, the individuals who audit the audit function must be independent of the audit function. If they are part of the audit function, it would appear to be a conflict of interest.

"Where could the organization obtain independent auditors?" asks Epstein. "They could possibly go outside for that."

Epstein says some large multidivision companies have the internal audit function from one division audit another and vice versa.

"The organization could, of course, hire an external auditor, such as an independent consultant," he explains. "In addition to providing independence, this may also have the benefit of bringing fresh new ideas to the organization. Consultants normally have a broader perspective of the ISO 9000 quality system requirements."

Epstein says the most common approach is to have individuals from within the organization, appropriately trained and qualified, who are not in the internal audit function, perform the internal audit of this function.

"The concept of independence has long been very controversial and you can carry this to an extreme," he says. "One might argue that since all personnel work for the organization's leader, everyone in the organization is interdependent."

As with other parts of ISO 9000, Epstein notes that the quality system will not work effectively without proper leadership from management.

"Management should understand the intent of this requirement and assure the intent is satisfied," he says. "I've seen companies where they forget to audit the internal audit function. The internal audit function schedules the audits and they schedule everybody except themselves. Some registrars overlook this as well," he adds. Theoretically, the registrar should pick this up. Organizations must show that the audit was scheduled.

In other words, "It has to be planned," according to Epstein. "They would also have to show records that the audit of the audit function was performed. They would have to show an audit report. Of course, you have to show records of qualifications of the auditors. "You have to show corrective action of audit findings and the follow-up to assure that the corrective action was effective. You have to show the same objective evidence the internal audit function would require," Epstein concludes.

Robert G. Hofer, ISO 9000 consultant for Bert Gibson Quality Associates, agrees that not even the internal quality audit functions should escape scrutiny in a quest to determine the overall effectiveness of a quality system.

Key is finding the right people to do the audits. "I have no problem with internal auditors from departments other than the quality department being used in the audit of Clause 8.2.2," he says. "The quality department has direct responsibility for the implementation of internal quality audit activities and should not be involved in that audit."

There are a number of alternatives that can be used. "Since most of the employees have been through a basic ISO 9000 orientation program, some companies arrange internal auditor training (formal or on-the-job, as observers) for a number of employees," he says. "This provides a pool of auditors from which to draw in case of emergencies."

Some personnel who normally are not used as internal auditors but who may be a good substitute in such situations, according to Hofer, are the following:

1. Managers or supervisors of departments that have been the subject of internal quality audits and have been instrumental in determining appropriate corrective action. They should be familiar with the requirements of clauses 8.2.2, 8.5.2 and 8.5.3 (Corrective and Preventive Action) and be capable of leading or participating in an audit of the system effectiveness.

2. Financial management personnel. They are a useful resource since their familiarity with auditing techniques enables them to evaluate the procedural requirements and their effective implementation.

"In organizations with multiple locations, the audit of Clause 8.2.2 can be performed by qualified auditors from another facility or the headquarters," concludes Hofer. "In some instances, the quality procedures may provide the option of allowing for the audit of Clause 8.2.2 by independent outside agencies, such as consultants, third-party auditors or other qualified personnel."

Stefan Heinloth, president of DQS, Inc., the German American Registrar for Management Systems, echoes in agreement.

"The standard requires [organizations] to plan and implement internal audits to verify whether quality activities and related results comply with planned arrangements," he says. Internal audits are certainly an important quality activity. In addition, it will be necessary to determine the effectiveness of this important part of the quality system.

But some companies believe it is difficult to find qualified internal auditors who do not have direct responsibility for the area audited, Heinloth adds.

"To clarify this situation, the company may ask, 'Who has direct responsibility for planning and implementing internal quality audits?' In many cases the answer will be 'The quality director or the management representative for the quality system,'" he explains. "In these situations any other employee may perform the internal audit."

A general rule, according to Heinloth, is that it will be necessary to assign an internal auditor who does not report directly to the quality director or the management representative. An internal auditor from the engineering department or the customer service department may be a good choice to audit the internal audit function.

"Some smaller organizations have implemented a different approach," he says. "They subcontract the internal audit function to an independent external auditor. This approach allows a smaller company to select a highly qualified auditor to perform internal audits, without sending their own employees to external training seminars. An organization should always verify qualification and references before subcontracting auditors. Corrective action responsibilities will always remain with the company."

Larger companies have more options. "They can share internal auditors from different sites," he says. "This cross-site auditing has been found valuable by many of our clients. Many have observed a significant learning effect on both sides."

Heinloth says it is important that executive management question whether internal audits are meaningful.

"If not, change your approach, because internal audits are a management tool," he says.

Stewart Thackray, a quality systems auditor with BSI, Inc., another ISO 9000 registrar, says internal auditing is a critical activity at the heart of any ISO 9001 quality system.

"Properly planned and conducted audits provide significant benefits by objectively testing the effectiveness of the quality management system and identifying both deficiencies and opportunities for improvement," he says. "Auditing is a 'quality activity' as described in Clause 8.2.2 of ISO 9001 and so must be subjected to auditing just the same as the rest of the quality system."

At first glance, "auditing the audits may seem like an overkill, but on further reflection benefits over and above the basic ISO 9001 requirement become apparent," he explains.

The practice supports an important perception by all personnel within the organization that the audit activity is no different than any other part of the system and subject to the same checks and controls.

"This is important, since getting the maximum benefits out of adopting the ISO 9001 model means adopting all parts of it as business as usual," says Thackray.

Internal auditing is one of the requirements of the standard that typically may be a new activity for companies, so attention must be paid to making sure that it is speedily and clearly understood and accepted throughout the organization.

The following, he adds, are examples of the kinds of aspects that should be considered during an audit of the internal auditing function:

1. Is the audit function operating in accordance with documented procedures?

2. Are auditors adequately trained, technically competent and suitably independent?

3. Do audit plans provide satisfactory depth and frequency of coverage?

4. Do records prove that samples audited and trails followed were numerous enough to ensure a realistic audit conclusion?

5. Where deficiencies have been identified, is the recorded evidence clear and unambiguous?

6. Are corrective action proposals and time scales realistic enough to ensure that corrective action is both timely and effective?

7. Have audit follow-ups been thorough enough to ensure that corrective action has been taken and is effective?

8. Are there any opportunities to improve the audit process?

9. Are there any activities going on within the audit function that are worthy of special mention or praise?

"A common perception, particularly in smaller organizations, is that it is difficult to find somebody trained and competent to carry out this activity who is suitably independent," according to Thackray. "After all, aren't the experts normally part of the audit function itself?"

Citing the standard, Thackray says ISO 9001 requires that personnel conducting audits should not only not audit their own work but also not audit anything that directly involves their immediate-line management.

He suggests the following alternate sources of internal auditors:

1. In technically oriented organizations, use personnel from design, project or manufacturing engineering functions. These people generally have an adequate level of technical competency and are receptive to the competence requirements for effective auditing.

2. Other personnel worth considering are to be found in functions such as finance, where experience of auditing (although of a different sort) already exists, or purchasing, where a disciplined approach is a part of everyday activities.

3. External personnel may also be considered, either from other companies or from facilities within the same organization or from independent sources such as consultants.

"Whichever source is selected," adds Thackray, "the key focus should be on ensuring that the personnel concerned have adequate training and time to conduct meaningful and effective audits."

Thackray says some companies don't see the need to invest in auditor training or allow audit personnel adequate time for preparation, auditing, reporting and follow-up.

"This is a false economy, since the benefits of good auditing cannot be overstated," he says. "An additional benefit of investing auditor training in personnel who are not mainstream 'quality people' is the quality management system awareness and 'buy-in' that it generates."

Thackray says forward-thinking companies tend to view auditor training and audit participation as a fundamental part of career progression and succession preparation. "Organizations looking for personnel to 'audit the audits' should experience little difficulty in finding willing volunteers!"

Subclause 8.2.2: Should Some Areas Be Audited More than Others?

Reprinted courtesy of Quality Systems Update

Question: Subclause 8.2.2, Internal Audits, requires organizations to schedule internal audits on the basis of the status and importance of the activity to be audited. Typically, how frequently should internal audits be performed? Should some areas be audited more frequently than others?

Answer: *QSU's* panel of experts agree that most companies should audit each area in the organization at least once a year. Experts also agree that some areas may be audited more frequently than others.

Elizabeth A. Potts, vice president, business development, Ashland Chemical Company, a worldwide manufacturer and distributor of chemicals and related products, says most companies either schedule internal audits throughout the year or conduct them all during a set time period.

"I would not advise doing critical items such as management review, internal auditing and corrective and preventive action less frequently," she says. "However, it is up to the company."

Potts says the audit results should determine the frequency of future audits. "If no, or minor, deficiencies are repeatedly detected in an audit, that section of the standard or that portion of your operations should be audited less frequently, similar to adjusting calibration frequencies," she explains.

Companies benefit the most from internal audits by using the results to correct problem areas, according to Potts.

"Internal audits should be a tool for continuous improvement, not just something done to comply with ISO 9000," she says.

Tom Arnold, president of IRA Certification, an ISO 9000 and QS-9000 registrar, says many companies develop auditing charts to make certain all parts of the organization are audited at least once a year.

"There may be certain items they've identified to be audited every time the audit team goes around, which may be once a month or once every two months," he explains. "But when they do go around, they have a partial list of items which are only checked every six months or only checked once a year."

Arnold says some areas may be looked at more frequently than others. "It's a judgment call on behalf of the organization to determine what items have a greater degree of tolerance or tendency to fall out of control," he says.

Auditing parts of the system more frequently than others mirrors the approach taken by registrars.

"The registrar always checks records of management meetings and records of internal audit activity," he says. "There are other things within the ISO requirements that are only checked once or twice within the three-year term of the contract. But at the end of the three-year term of the contract, all phases have been checked."

Vincent Zottola, managing partner of Tri-State Quality Systems Inc., an ISO 9000, QS-9000 and ISO 14000 consulting and training organization, agrees that companies have discretion in deciding the frequency of internal audits.

But in practice, he says, most registrars require clients to audit their entire system at least once a year.

"Before they'll register a system, they require that all elements be audited," he explains. "It is incumbent upon an organization to set up a schedule where they will cover all elements before they schedule their registration audit."

When scheduling internal audits, companies should be cognizant of the fact that registrars will audit parts of the system more than others. For example, he says, auditors check management responsibility more frequently than other areas to determine if there have been any changes to the quality organizational structure since their last visit. Auditors also check the internal audit system, corrective and preventive action systems and management review process more frequently than other areas.

"One can see that they're placing most of the emphasis on those elements," he says.

As a rule of thumb, problem areas should undergo more frequent internal audits than nonproblem areas.

"It's all driven by performance of the system," he says. "The results of your customer service internal and external nonconformance reporting should alert you to target certain problem areas."

Mike Delpha, director of consulting services with r. bowen international inc., an ISO 9000 and QS-9000 training and consulting firm, says a company must define both the status and the importance of its activities when scheduling internal audits.

"These terms must be clearly understood by the internal quality audit coordinator," he says.

According to Delpha, "status" means the current state or condition of any activity with regard to recent audit or operating results.

"Is the activity new? Or does the activity include new equipment or new operators or a new location, etc., which may have substantially impacted process capability, average outgoing quality or other critical performance measures?" he says. "Changes such as these ought to result in more frequent internal audits of the activity than may have been originally planned."

Delpha says importance is determined by the criticality of the process or activity with respect to the deliverable product or service.

"For example, a company that has a substantial design and engineering activity and a small purchasing function would want to schedule more frequent internal audits in engineering than in purchasing," he explains.

Delpha says the importance of activities should be reflected in the company's annual internal quality audit plan. Status considerations should result in ongoing changes in audit scheduling.

8.2.3 Monitoring and Measurement of Processes (4.9, 4.20)

The quality management system processes shall be monitored and measured at appropriate stages. When planned results are not achieved, corrective action shall be taken, as appropriate.

This clause greatly reduces the detailed listing of requirements for process control compared with ISO 9001:1994, but it is not intended to reduce the requirement of effective process monitoring. Rather, it is the responsibility of the organization to determine the amount of process monitoring appropriate, to include such activities in the quality management system and to demonstrate that they are being followed.

Additional ISO 9001:2000 Requirements

Monitoring and measuring processes shall be conducted to assure that activities meet their intended purpose.

ISO 9004:2000 Guidance

Clause 8.2.2 lists examples of measures of process performance. (See *Handbook* CD-ROM.)

8.2.4 Monitoring and Measurement of Product (4.10.4, 4.10.5)

Product characteristics shall be measured and monitored at appropriate stages to demonstrate that requirements are met. Evidence of conformity with acceptance criteria shall be recorded. The authority responsible for the release of product shall also be recorded. Unless otherwise customer-approved, the organization shall not release and deliver product until all required activities have been satisfactorily accomplished.

ISO 9004:2000 Guidance

Clause 8.2.3 lists considerations when selecting measurement methods and examples of product measurement records. Clause 8.2.4 lists examples of measuring and monitoring of satisfaction of interested parties. (See *Handbook* CD-ROM.)

ISO 9000-2:1997 Guidance

Inspection and test records facilitate assessment according to specifications and are useful for regulatory requirements and possible product liability problems.

Clause 8.2.4: Must Product Shipment Await Testing?

Reprinted courtesy of Quality Systems Update

Question: Based on statistical control of process and historical product test results or on performance, is it acceptable to release a product before all testing has been completed? For example, test results normally take up to one month, and there is insufficient storage space for more than a week's production of bulk product. If so, must the customer be notified and under what ISO 9001 clause should notification take place?

Answer: The panel of experts agreed that there are times when product may be shipped prior to completion of testing, but they disagreed as to the circumstances under which that shipment may take place.

Elizabeth A. Potts, quality director, Ashland Chemical, says there is little room for interpretation. "The standard means exactly what it says," she explains. "Product release ... shall not proceed until all the planned arrangements have been satisfactorily completed, unless otherwise approved by a relevant authority, and where applicable by the customer."

The organization would be deviating from the terms of the agreement by shipping before completion or documentation of all tests, according to Potts. "The organization must get consent of the other party to the agreement, namely the customer, to do so," she says.

Potts says that the organization and its customer would also have to address issues such as limited storage or lengthy reliability testing well in advance of shipment. "These issues should be addressed in the organization's quality system to meet the requirements of Clause 8.2.4," Potts says.

Shipping with Notification

Bud Weightman, president, Qualified Specialists, Inc., acknowledges that Subclause 8.2.4 prohibits a product from being dispatched until the required inspection and testing are completed. However, he says, the organization may elect to ship before that with proper notification. In such cases, the customer should provide documented evidence that it will accept the product without complete test results at the time of shipment.

"The organization's decision to ship product with incomplete test results should be based upon historical product test results, product performance data and documented evidence of statistical process control, which could be submitted to the customer as an added assurance that the product test results will comply with stated requirements," Weightman explains.

Contract Requirements for Extended Testing

Dan Epstein, senior advisor, Quality Management Consulting Services, Inc., says there are circumstances that would allow shipping the product prior to completing the testing, but the example of limited space is not one. "Contractual obligations may require extended testing in the form of endurance, reliability or life testing," he says. "In addition, satisfactory completion of these tests may determine product acceptability."

Moreover, percent defect allowable (PDA) — the customer-defined acceptable quality level — and Six Sigma requirements — a statistical quality level equating to approximately three defects per million — may be contractually imposed, Epstein says. These allow an organization to compute an acceptance limit only after a period of time, possibly after many shipments. The customer, he says, may have specified a delivery schedule that is in conflict with the supplier's ability to determine acceptability. Potts notes that both partners should understand that this is an issue at the time of contract and should address it under contract review procedures.

If the original contract does not provide any of these conditions (i.e., purchase order, performance specification, etc.) and the customer is expecting products and services from an ISO 9000 registered facility, Epstein says, it is the obligation of the organization to notify the customer of the system noncompliance. "Ideally, every attempt should be made to avoid these sorts of problems during the contract review process," Epstein says.

Shipping and Traceability

Stephen S. Keneally, president, Scott Technical Services, Inc., says the clause appears to require that all testing be completed prior to shipping. Nevertheless, many industries, such as aerospace, defense, and integrated circuits, routinely ship and assemble while samples from the production lot continue to be tested, he says.

"Depending on the product and industry, elaborate systems of maintaining traceability are used in the unlikely event if 'life testing' or long-term reliability or environmental tests result in the product being rejected and the lot being recalled," Keneally explains.

In regulated industries such as defense electronics, medical devices and pharmaceuticals, the traceability and testing requirements are part of the product approval cycle, according to Keneally. He says any changes to the manufacturing, inspection, and testing process would require re-approval by the appropriate regulatory agency or the customer.

In commercial industries, he says, the revised quality plan should reflect reduced inspection, skip-lot inspection or periodic versus 100 percent lot-by-lot testing. It should also reflect an analysis of whether statistical process control data and historical product test results justify changes.

"The manufacturer develops the quality plan and test procedure and has the option to change them when warranted," Keneally says. "It is common sense and good business practice to reduce non-value-added activity when processes are under control and statistical or other data support reduction of inspection or testing activities. Obviously, sufficient history should be available before radical changes are made."

Keneally says customers need be notified only if their contract or specification indicates what tests are to be performed or if catalogs and other sales literature reflect specific tests, with the implication being that organizations conduct such tests in every case.

8.3 Control of Nonconforming Product

ISO 9001 Requirements (4.13.1)

The organization shall maintain a documented procedure to prevent the inadvertent use or installation of a nonconforming product. Nonconforming product shall be identified and controlled. Response when nonconforming product is detected is first to act to eliminate the nonconformity and then to take disposition action, such as to regrade for alternate application or to authorize acceptance for use (by the appropriate authority and, where applicable, the customer). Other obvious alternatives include reworking to meet specified requirements, reject or scrap. Nonconforming product that is corrected, such as by reworking, shall be reverified to ensure that requirements are met. If detected after delivery, further necessary action shall be taken. There may be situations in which the proposed solution is reported for concession (confirmation of action) to the customer, user, regulatory body or others. Corrected nonconforming product shall be reverified to requirements.

ISO 9000-2:1997 Guidance

A nonconforming product — either an intermediate or final product or service — is one that fails to meet specifications. This applies to a nonconforming product that occurs in the organization's own production as well as nonconforming products received by them. The procedures for controlling a nonconforming product should include the following:

- Determine which product units are involved in the nonconformity.
- Identify the nonconforming product units.
- Document the nonconformity.
- Evaluate the nonconformity.
- Consider alternatives for disposing of the nonconforming product units.
- Physically control the movement, storage and processing of the nonconforming product units.
- Notify all functions that may be affected by the nonconformity.

Organizations should consider the procedures in ISO 9001 in relationship to the risk of failure to meet customer requirements. Each action carries a degree of risk. In the long term, rejecting or scrapping may carry the lowest risk.

QS-9000 Automotive (4.13)

Suspect Material or Product (4.13.1.1)

This clause applies to suspect product as well as nonconforming product.

Visual Identification (4.13.1.2)

The organization shall provide visual identification of any nonconforming or suspect material or product and any quarantine areas.

Prioritized Reduction Plan (4.13.2.1)

A plan for reducing the amount of nonconforming product is to be in operation and progress tracked.

Control of Reworked Product (4.13.3)

Rework instructions shall be available to and used by appropriate personnel.

Product supplied for service applications is to have no visible evidence of rework without prior approval.

Rework produces an item that is in every way indistinguishable from a "first-time through" acceptable item.

Repair makes the item meet requirements but it is different in some way, e.g., welded, from the original design.

Engineering Approved Product Authorization (4.13.4)

Changes in product or process require customer approval and apply also to supplier purchases. Records are to be kept with specific product identification, including the time interval or quantity for which the change is authorized.

Clause 8.3: Control of Nonconforming Product

Even in the best of all possible worlds, things still go wrong. That being the case, there is a need to design the system so as to prevent the unintended use or installation of *any* nonconforming product or service. There must be a clear, unequivocal method of making sure that nonconforming product is properly identified and isolated until such time as the procedures that have been created to manage the review and disposition of this unacceptable product or service have been put into effect.

The procedure to be followed must be defined. Questions to guide the process include the following:

• Who has the authority to sentence nonconforming product?

- How is the review to be carried out?

- What are the options for disposition?

- Are processes and authorities the same across the entire company? Or are there different authorities and responsibilities in various areas of the operation, from design to after-sales service?

All of the above must be defined and documented.

— The Victoria Group

8.4 Analysis of Data (4.20)

The organization shall gather data to measure the effectiveness of the quality management system, obtained from monitoring activities and elsewhere.

Additional ISO 9001:2000 Requirements

Data shall be gathered to do the following:

- Target improvement opportunities.

- Determine customer satisfaction.

- Determine how well requirements of customers are being met.

- Determine characteristics of processes and products and their trends.

- Look for ways to identify and prevent potential problems.

- Provide information concerning suppliers.

ISO 9004:2000 Guidance

Clause 8.4 lists possible actions to be taken based on data analysis. (See *Handbook* CD-ROM.)

ISO 9000-2:1997 Guidance

Statistical techniques are useful in every aspect of an organization's operation. Useful statistical methods include:

Graphical methods to help diagnose problems

- Statistical control charts to monitor and control production and measurement processes

- Experiments to identify and quantify variables that influence process and product performance

- Regression analysis to provide quantitative models for a process

- Analysis of variance methods.

QS-9000 Automotive (4.20)

Selection of Statistical Tools (4.20.3)

Statistical tools to be used are to be identified during quality planning and shall be included in the control plan.

Knowledge of Basic Statistical Concepts (4.20.4)

As appropriate, concepts such as variability, control (stability), capability and overadjustment should be understood. Consult the *Fundamental Statistical Process Control* reference manual.

8.5 Improvement

This clause is not contained in ISO 9001:1994. References to improvement are made throughout the standard as follows:

- 4.1 General Requirements
- 5.3b Quality Policy
- 5.6.2g Review Input
- 5.6.3a, b Review Output
- 6.1a Provision of Resources
- 8.1 Measurement, Analysis and Improvement
- 8.4 Analysis of Data

8.5.1 Continual Improvement

Additional ISO 9001:2000 Requirements

The quality management system shall be continually improved by using quality policy, quality objectives, audit results, data analysis, corrective/preventive actions and management reviews.

Clause 8.5: Improvement

The clauses pertaining to nonconforming products and analysis of data are followed, logically, by a clause on continual improvement, corrective action and preventive action. Often the weakest part of quality systems, corrective action loops are frequently designed only to address the immediate problem while failing to act to avoid its recurrence. Another common problem is that they often deal only with matters of processes, products or services while overlooking the system. ISO 9001, Clause 8.5 addresses all three. The standard requires a rigorous examination of all the quality data and records to detect and remove all potential as well as actual causes of nonconformance. This is proactive quality, not reactive.

The division of Clause 8.5 into continual improvement, corrective action and preventive action reinforces the primary intent of the standard, which is preventing nonconformity at all stages.

Subclause 8.5.3, Preventive Action, creates extended requirements for preventive actions and all such actions.

Most companies will need to create procedures specifically designed to address the requirements of subclause 8.5.3. Companies should carefully consider the matter of the comprehensive analysis of all available data. It is very easy to end up with a procedure that, while being very comprehensive in its coverage, requires too much time and effort to fulfill. The preamble statement in 8.5.2 and 8.5.3 must be the guide: that actions "shall be appropriate to the effects of the nonconformities encountered and potential problems."

— The Victoria Group

8.5.2 Corrective Action (4.14.2)

ISO 9001 Requirements (4.14.2)

Focus shall be on eliminating causes of nonconformities, to prevent their recurrence and taking corrective action appropriate to the problem.

Procedures shall specify the following:

- Identify nonconformities, including customer complaints.
- Determine causes.
- Evaluate actions to avoid recurrence.
- Implement corrective action.
- Record the results.
- Review action taken.

Corrective action is directed toward eliminating the causes of *actual* nonconformities. Preventive action is directed toward eliminating the causes of *potential* nonconformities.

ISO 9004:2000 Guidance

Clause 8.5.2 lists sources of information for corrective action consideration. (See *Handbook* CD-ROM.)

QS-9000 Automotive

Problem-Solving Methods (4.14.1.1)

The organization is to follow disciplined problem-solving methods for product that has been identified as nonconforming and respond as prescribed by the customer for external nonconformances.

Mistake Proofing (4.14.1.2)

Use process or design features to prevent manufacture of nonconforming product, as appropriate.

H4 ISO 9000-2:1997 Guidance

This clause explains what an organization must do when things go wrong. Analysis of nonconformities can be performed by using inspection and test records, process monitoring, audit observation and all other available feedback methods. Corrective action procedures should include the following:

- Establish responsibility for taking corrective action.
- Define how the action will be carried out.
- Verify the effectiveness of the corrective action.

Procedures should also take into account nonconformities discovered in a product designated as satisfactory, but that has already been shipped.

QS-9000 Automotive

Returned Product Test/Analysis (4.14.2.1)

Parts that are returned from the customer are to be analyzed, with records kept, and appropriate corrective action and process change are to be taken.

Corrective Action Impact (4.14.2.2)

Apply identified corrective actions and controls to other similar processes and products.

Clauses 8.3/8.5.1/8.5.2: Immediate Solutions vs. System Fixes

Reprinted courtesy of Quality Systems Update

Question: Clause 8.3, Control of Nonconforming Product, and Clauses 8.5.1 and 8.5.2, Corrective and Preventive Action, both appear to be addressing systems problems that result in nonconforming product. Can you explain the relationship between these two clauses?

Answer: Our panelists generally agree that the requirements of Clause 8.3 are intended to provide for an immediate solution to the problem at hand, while Clauses 8.5.1 and 8.5.2 are intended to provide a more thorough investigation and treatment of the underlying systems issues that may result in a particular problem.

Moderator Mark Klugiewicz, of Excel Partnerships, Inc., says confusion between these clauses is common. "The confusion probably originates from the fairly common reference to corrective action, even before the existence of the ISO 9000 standards, and the difference in the applied definitions," says Klugiewicz. "Most often people refer to corrective action as something done to 'right the wrong.' In fact, in plain terms, the ISO definition of corrective action is 'right the cause of the wrong,' while 'right the wrong' is considered disposition of nonconforming product."

Under Clause 8.3, correcting the product, accepting by concession or rejecting are all ways to eliminate the nonconformity, Klugiewicz says. Once these actions have been taken, the fire is out, the refund issued, an apology given, and/or assurances offered to do better in the future. The nonconformity has been dispositioned and, as such, is likely to disappear from the corporate radar screen.

"However, even though the nonconformity is now gone, corrective action in accordance with the requirements of the standard has not yet begun, because action to address the cause of the nonconformity — what caused the fire — has yet to start," Klugiewicz adds. "In addition, part of the confusion between the clauses may also lie in the misconception that corrective action must be taken for every nonconformity that arises."

Clause 8.3 requires nonconformities to be identified and controlled, with necessary documentation, he says. This requirement is applicable to all incidences of nonconforming product. Clauses 8.5.1 and 8.5.2, on the other hand, indicate that any action taken shall be dependent upon the magnitude of the problem and the risks encountered.

In other words, all nonconformities must be dealt with appropriately, but the corrective action associated with those nonconformities should be motivated by an analysis of the frequency, severity, cost, criticality, or other self-imposed resource or business impact issues, he says.

Very frequently the term "root cause analysis" is used when referring to corrective action. In fact, this is a redundant term within the requirements of the ISO 9001 standard, according to Klugiewicz. Disposition of nonconformity addresses the need to resolve the issue at hand, while corrective action addresses the need to resolve the cause (root or other subterranean level notwithstanding) of the issue at hand.

"For those issues that are 'trending' in the wrong direction or cause enough physical or mental pain that the motivation to ensure they never happen again is significant, corrective action is warranted as the next step beyond the immediate fix," he concludes.

Dennis Arter, a trainer and consultant with Columbia Audit Resources, adds that Clause 8.3 may lead to corrective action, but it doesn't have to. "Remembering that 'nonconforming product' is something that failed a test, it must be branded, kept away from good stuff and then formally taken care of, or dispositioned," he explains. "When going back to the origins of ISO 9001 found in MIL-Q-9858, one automatically thinks of: repair, rework, reject, recycle or retain."

All of those actions deal with the bad item, Arter says. At this point, we aren't worried about why it happened; we are worried about keeping the line running. The disposition decision can be made by a process engineer or a more formal material review board, but it generally cannot be made by the operator or inspector.

"Sure, it's a hassle to identify this stuff, move it, call for the engineer and check it again," he says. "It's supposed to be a hassle; we don t want nonconforming stuff to be routinely produced and then 'fixed' or adjusted. That's much too expensive, frustrating and inefficient."

Corrective action is used to address the underlying cause of the bad stuff, according to Arter. It takes resources and serious mental energy. Not everything is worth all of this effort. The problem or problems must be important enough to expend the energy. The hassle factor must be high and getting higher, he says.

"On the other hand, corrective action must be started soon enough to avoid a plant meltdown," he adds. "Classic criteria for this initiation of corrective action are cost, opportunity (production) and risk. Sometimes, a nonconforming item just isn't worth it."

Once the issue or item is defined as needing corrective action, the mental juices start flowing, Arter says. In asking, "Why is this happening?" we need to remember those universal process affectors: methods, material, manpower, measurement, machinery and environment. We need to use all of our quality engineering skills. We need to change the processes and usually the system. This takes time; rarely can corrective action be completed in less than a month.

"In summary, nonconforming action takes an hour," concludes Arter. "Corrective action takes a month."

Stephen V. Zakrzewski, managing partner of Standard Compliance Consulting Services L.L.C., likens Clauses 8.3 and 8.5.1/8.5.2 to examples of "operational" versus "administrative" activities.

"Most organizations that have been in business for a period of time are used to performing the operational activities pretty regularly, although they may not have them well documented," he says.

Zakrzewski says operational activities all have to do with the "business of staying in business," such as controlling manufacturing processes and delivery systems (7.5.1) or ensuring that product is inspected before it is taken out of or put into a box (8.1). These operational activities are generally well established and may have numerous quality records associated with them. Clause 8.3, Control of Nonconforming Product, is one of those operational activities that an organization must have a good handle on if they are to stay in business for any length of time, he says.

"Most of the activities associated with Clause 8.3 have been *de rigueur* with aerospace and government suppliers for decades," he adds. "Unfortunately, Control of Nonconforming Product activities can clearly operate in a loop independent from the rest of the quality system, becoming a process to themselves: Make, Inspect, Reject, Appraise, Remake (or Scrap), Re-inspect, Ship."

Sometimes, says Zakrzewski, the cause of nonconforming product is clearly a "one-off " due to human error, machine breakdown or other process variation. Clause 8.3 is meant to address this type of isolated occurrence and prevent the use or delivery of product that is not fit for its intended use.

"Economic practicalities being what they are, the small- to medium-sized organization is certainly well advised to take a look at the nonconforming product and make a judgment as to whether it can be salvaged (reworked) or whether a customer can use it any way (concession, regrade), before they toss it away (scrap)," he adds.

What he describes as the "administrative" activity, corrective and preventive action, kicks in when problems begin to repeat or when different problems begin to cluster meaningfully around certain "assignable causes." According to Zakrzewski, "The analysis of the appraisal on nonconforming product is the bridge between the two clauses. When the organization recognizes that a pattern of nonconformance exists or that a single serious problem has occurred, then root cause investigation must be implemented to ultimately prevent the problem from recurring."

The standard, he says, is clear in this regard. Quoting the standard, he says, "Corrective action taken to eliminate the causes of nonconformities in order to prevent recurrence shall be appropriate to the effects of the nonconformities encountered." Zakrzewski says sometimes bandage solutions are appropriate: "I think that the practice of 'putting a bandage on a cut' is perfectly acceptable, as long as we recognize that the wound is a random paper cut and not the result of a missing guard on a chainsaw."

Subclause 8.5.2: Documenting Corrective Action Investigations

Reprinted courtesy of Quality Systems Update

Question: Subclause 8.5.2, Corrective Action, requires companies to establish and maintain documented procedures for implementing corrective action, including a requirement to investigate the cause of nonconformance. What information should be included to document such investigations?

Answer: *QSU*'s panel of experts agreed that documentation should include all the steps taken to identify and resolve a corrective action.

Moderator Ian Durand, [then] president of Service Process Consulting Inc., an ISO 9000 training and consulting firm, says it is important to distinguish the corrective action requirements of Clause 8.5.2 from the requirements relating to Clause 8.3, Control of Nonconforming Product.

"Every time you encounter nonconforming product, you must bring that into conformance, says Durand. "You find some way to bring it into conformance."

Corrective actions, on the other hand, tend not to be as clear-cut and typically require systemic changes." In some cases "you might find all the product is fine but there is a high level of rework," Durand says of corrective actions. "There's some problem with the way your processes are being controlled."

Corrective actions can be triggered by nonconforming product and also by process-related or system-related failures, Durand explains.

"It's a problem that you find unacceptable to have repeated," he says. "You need to find out, why did this happen? What were the root causes?"

Durand adds that some sort of test data is usually needed to resolve a corrective action.

"The proper corrective action procedure then should be to identify a situation that is not acceptable, initiate a formal corrective action, gather quantitative data that would provide insight into the root cause of the unacceptable problem and postulate a solution," according to Durand. "Implement it and then verify that it really has either eliminated the problem or reduced it to a satisfactory level."

The problem many companies encounter is that they take action to correct a problem but fail to verify the effectiveness of the action. If done properly, he says, corrective actions result in fundamental change.

"A corrective action will always result in a change to the quality system and invariably in the documentation of the quality system," he says. "You're going to change a procedure or policy or work instruction or training levels, which then need to be documented."

Durand says company documentation of a corrective action investigation should include the original data leading to the identification of a problem as well as data collected for a root cause analysis. The documentation, he explains, should answer the following questions:

"What is the presumed root cause? What alternative solutions were considered? Which one was chosen? How was it validated? And what procedures or what documentation was changed to institutionalize this solution?"

Rod Goult, president and chief executive officer of The Victoria Group Inc., an ISO 9000, QS-9000 and ISO 14000 consulting and training organization, says customer complaints often spur corrective actions.

"When you first get a customer complaint or a product nonconformance," he says, "you should basically determine whether it's a valid complaint. Obviously, if it's not a valid complaint, hopefully there is some system whereby you go back to the customer and explain why you don't think you've got a problem."

Regardless of whether the complaint is deemed valid, Goult says, companies should keep records of the complaint and any actions taken as a result.

"If you cannot resolve the complaint in that way or if it is judged to be a valid complaint, then it has to be assigned to somebody for investigation and resolution," Goult says. "There should be some record of to whom it has been assigned or, in some cases, to which company department it has been assigned."

Goult says he believes good management practice will dictate that companies assign deadlines for addressing complaints and nonconformances.

"Depending on the scale of the problem, that response could either be a resolution of the issue or the presentation of an action plan to resolve the issue," according to Goult. "Of course there should be provision for those due dates to be revised when necessary because of other priorities, with a suitable level of management agreement."

Goult says the action might include a comprehensive investigation to determine the cause of a particular problem. "The action taken should be, to a degree, appropriate to the magnitude of the problem and commensurate with the risks," he says. "In large measure the degree of detail that all those things will encompass will depend on the nature and severity and significance of the declared problem."

In the case of minor nonconformances or where there is little risk of affecting product quality, he says, supporting documentation should be minimal. "All of the things could be encapsulated in a few words basically," he says.

For example, if a customer complains of a product malfunction, supporting documentation might consist of the date and summary of the complaint and date and summary of the company's response, possibly including a return authorization number and the date on which a replacement was shipped.

Goult says companies should document the condition of the returned item.

"All too often people forget that those returned items should really be investigated to find out why they failed," he says. "Sometimes it's something obvious, like it's been run over by a bus."

But the amount of documentation varies by the seriousness of the incident.

"In the case of a very simple occurrence, it's going to be a single, one-page form or an entry into a log book that has columns for the various stages," Goult says. "It can be a simple record."

Goult acknowledges that his approach might exceed the minimum requirements of the standards. "Arguably that level of detail exceeds the minimum requirements of the standard," he explains. "But if you look at the data, it can feed continual improvement."

According to Goult, the accumulation of failure data over time can serve as the basis for trend analysis. "In general, people will forgive you an error if you respond to it in a timely manner and effectively," he says. "It enables a monitor to be kept of the level of complaints and product nonconformities."

Jane K. Wolfe, lead auditor with Smithers Quality Assessments Inc., an ISO 9000 and QS-9000 registrar, says companies must maintain those records that support their decisions with respect to a particular corrective action.

"I would say all information that would affect the decision as to the corrective action would be necessary," explains Wolfe. "My personal opinion is that all of the information that you gather in your quest for corrective action needs to be a part of the documentation for that corrective action."

She says the purpose of maintaining such documentation is to prevent companies from making the same mistake twice. "Although it makes sense to you now, six months from now you may not understand why you made the decision you did and you might change it again," she says. "It's kind of a history file on that particular activity."

For example, she says, in the case of a defective part, companies might want to record the time of year the failure occurred, the name of the person who was running the machine, the revision level of the procedures being used, the weather and anything else that might conceivably affect product quality.

"When you've evaluated and determined what the cause of the nonconformance was, then you record that and document what you think will prevent a recurrence," says Wolfe, "because later on you may find out that that was not at all what caused the nonconformance."

Cohn Gray, president of Cavendish Scott, an ISO 9000 consulting organization, says companies should produce procedures for corrective actions, document the results and ensure effectiveness.

"They absolutely have to make certain that the documented procedures they generate as part of their quality system actually describe the mechanism they use for conducting the investigation and recording it," he explains.

Once a decision is made to investigate a possible problem, he says, companies must record all relevant data.

"If we're investigating an issue which has low impact on product quality, low cost, low risk, then the amount of effort and the amount of records we devote to that should reflect a lesser importance," says Gray. "If the nonconformance that we're investigating has a serious impact on product quality, high risk, high consequence on product quality, then the record should reflect a greater importance."

But Gray warns companies to avoid overdocumentation.

"It's important that people just don't document things for the sake of it," he says. "I think this is perfectly normal, that companies would devote more effort to serious problems than they would to minor problems."

"If it was a minor corrective action we were investigating, I would expect handwritten notes on a copy of the corrective action report explaining what was done," he says. "If it was a serious corrective action, I would probably expect to see more details of the investigation, maybe a report, maybe test results, and then to back that up, maybe the minutes of the meeting that analyzed that information and a record of what actions were going to be taken."

Gray says he would expect to see documentation of the company's follow-up effort.

Companies should also ensure that the actions they take are effective, according to Gray.

"Some form of failure caused the corrective action in the first place," he explains. "To have repeated failures for the same thing, although the corrective action is in place, implies that the action was not effective. The standard specifically requires that actions should be controlled to be effective and failure to do so indicates noncompliance with the standard."

8.5.3 Preventive Action (4.14.3)

A documented procedure shall provide for the following:

- Identify causes of potential nonconformities.
- Evaluate the need for action.
- Determine and implement such action.
- Record the results.
- Make certain that the action is effective.

Additional ISO 9001:2000 Requirements

Steps shall be taken to identify the causes of potential nonconformities, to enable appropriate preventive action to be taken.

ISO 9004:2000 Guidance

Clause 8.5.3 lists sources of data for evaluating potential for loss prevention. (See *Handbook* CD-ROM.)

THE REGISTRATION AND AUDIT PROCESS

Steps in the Registration Process

5

by Lane Hallenbeck and Elizabeth Potts

Introduction

This chapter describes what to expect during the registration process. Regardless of the registrar selected, registration to ISO 9000 generally consists of the following six basic steps:

- Application
- Document review
- Preassessment
- Assessment
- Registration
- Surveillance.

This chapter also considers the time and costs of registration.

Integrated Management Systems

When the first edition of the *ISO 9000 Handbook* was published, making a decision to become ISO 9000 registered was in some ways less complicated. Fewer than 200 ISO 9000 certificates had been issued in the United States. As of the end of 2001 there were over 36,000. Companies seeking registration for the most part were doing so for very practical reasons. They could afford to keep their efforts very focused on achieving ISO 9000 compliance.

Today, this focus on a single standard is a luxury for many companies operating in the global marketplace. The automakers have gone beyond QS-9000 to ISO TS 16949. In the aerospace market, AS9000 is a priority, and in the spring of 2000 the first accredited certificates were issued for the telecommunications standard TL 9000. These sector schemes include all of ISO 9001. While a company implementing these is still registering to ISO 9000, additional sector-specific requirements must be met to achieve registration.

In addition to these standards, other complementary management standards have been developed or are being considered for development, including a standard for occupational health and safety and one for medical devices. There is even a management system standard for social accountability in international labor markets, designated SA 8000. These developing standards certainly add another level of complexity to registration decisions.

Many companies also face the prospect of registering to ISO 14001 in addition to multiple sector-specific documents. The ISO 14000 series of standards for environmental management, a close cousin of ISO 9000, has seen steady growth in demand for certification since 1996. Companies must now tackle the complex task of integrating these requirements into a single management system. (For example, consider semiconductor companies with data book components of planes, phones and automobiles.)

ISO 9000 Registration

Most registrars require a completed application, sometimes called a contract, to begin the registration process. The application should:

- Define the rights and obligations of both the registrar and the client
- State the registrar's access rights to facilities and necessary information
- Address liability issues. *Note:* Companies considering integrating ISO 14000 registration into their system should pay close attention to the issues of confidentiality and liability
- Define confidentiality policy and advise the client of the right to appeal a decision and/or file a complaint
- Offer instructions for the use of the registration certificate and associated marks
- Define conditions for terminating the application.

Selecting a Registrar

First, make sure that the registrar's accredited scope of operations covers the business to be registered. Different methodologies are used to identify a registrar's accredited scope. In the United States, Standard Industrial Classification (SIC) Codes are used. In Europe, a similar system of codes, Nomenclature Générale des Activités Economiques Dans les Communautés Européennes (NACE), is used to define a registrar's operational scope. There is also a set of unified codes to be implemented fully in the near future.

Scope definition is critical to the success of an organization's registration effort and essential to successfully meeting the needs of the customer. The registrar should be willing to work with the organization to define the extent of registration and how it will be achieved. Without a clear understanding of the project's scope, all the stakeholders will be adversely affected. Companies that must also seek QS-9000 approval will discover that careful scope definition enables the registrar to more efficiently audit for both ISO 9000 and QS-9000 compliance using auto industry guidelines. *Note*: Registrars must receive separate accreditations to offer audits for different EMS and QMS sector-specific certifications. A company that expects to develop an integrated standards management program and use the same registrar should carefully consider registrar choice.

Registrars, like any other business entity, have different internal policies. For example, some registrar policies make it difficult to use two different registrars at the same facility. Be wary of restrictive policies that may cause delays and add cost for a large company with centralized functions, such as purchasing or design, that elect to use more than one registrar.

Document Review

Once the application is completed, listing basic information including the standard of choice, the company's size, scope of operations and desired time frame for registration, the registrar typically asks the company to submit documentation of its quality system.

Most registrars are interested in first reviewing the quality manual that describes the existing quality management system. Every company procedure is not required to be in the manual, only referenced. The manual is compared with ISO 9000 requirements to determine summary documentation compliance. Some registrars prefer to perform an on-site document review. However, an off-site manual review (preferred by most registrars) saves travel costs and the internal costs of hosting the registrar.

The costs for this manual review should be discussed up front, along with circumstances that would require a follow-up review. For example, if the company adds an additional site under the same quality system, some registrars may require a second review. Quality manuals that have been extensively revised often require new reviews. These iterations may or may not have recurring costs.

Although the quality manual is not expected to fully define the details of an organization's quality system, an effective manual will provide enough information to allow the registrar to determine if a quality system exists. Companies are required to describe the structure of the quality system and refer to supporting procedures. Questions raised during the document review frequently refine the scope of the registration and ensure that the company sets realistic certification goals.

Preassessment

Most registrars either recommend or require a facility preassessment. To some registrars preassessment means a complete assessment that determines the current status of a company's operations. To others it is an aid in audit planning (number of auditors required, audit days required) that is used to determine preparedness for a full assessment. For some registrars preassessment means a client-paid sales visit and facility tour.

Remember: not every company will need a preassessment, but every company should carefully consider the benefits. Years of data indicate that a preassessment is the best way to ensure a successful initial audit. A preassessment can identify major system deficiencies (or inadequate documentation) before a full assessment. Preassessment will increase a company's chances of passing a full assessment on the first attempt. On the other hand, the preassessment may point out that a company has overprepared. For example, the preassessment may allow a company to discover that documentation it has prepared is not required for registration.

Ironically, overall costs are often reduced as a result of preassessment. The registrar may determine that the final audit will require a smaller audit team or fewer auditor days. However, the company should make this preassessment decision based on its own agenda and business goals. A company must consider that if a registrar requires a complete quality system preassessment, another full registration assessment will be required, adding internal and external expense. It is also worth mentioning that a preassessment can allow for a low-risk organizational introduction to the registration audit process where the company culture or morale may be tense.

One preassessment caveat, however, is universal among registrars: providing consulting services to the client company during a preassessment and final audit phase is strictly forbidden. Evaluating the adequacy of the supplier's quality system and documentation to meet the requirements of the standard is allowed. However, the registrar cannot provide substantive advice and guidance to the company on system implementation. Use an internal or external consultant to provide this guidance as needed.

It is interesting to note that the developers of sector-specific schemes have reinforced what is meant by "consulting activities." Under these rules, delivery of consulting activities by a registrar or any related organization precludes that registrar from providing registration services. A company may not be able to use its registrar of choice if this boundary is crossed.

Note to companies considering ISO 14001 registration: The preassessment (documentation review/initial assessment) phase of an ISO 14001 audit is *not* optional and is more in-depth than the document review associated with an ISO 9000-based assessment. Review of the organization's environmental management system, including its stated environmental impacts, is conducted and the results are used to plan the assessment phase in detail.

Full Assessment

A full assessment is conducted after the registrar determines that the company's documented quality system conforms to the requirements of the selected management system standard. Typically, two or three auditors spend from two to five days at a facility (i.e., 4-15 audit days). The duration of the audit is stipulated by the registrar's accreditation requirements and depends on the size and complexity of the company's operations and the standard of certification. The accreditor's guidelines are public information and challenging or questioning an overly short or long audit is perfectly appropriate.

The auto, aerospace and telecommunications sector groups have tried to standardize this process by clearly defining the duration of audits. These audit times are typically longer by a significant factor than a comparable ISO 9000 audit.

Before beginning its audit, registrars conduct an introductory "opening" meeting with company management and, among other issues of protocol, request that auditor escorts be assigned. At the end of the audit cycle, a "closing" meeting is held to communicate to management any system deficiencies discovered. Registrars should be expected to leave a final report containing the audit team's recommendations. Some of these recommendations are binding, but others require further internal review and disposition by the registrar. The client should completely understand the implications of the audit team's recommendations.

During the audit, most registrars review any findings daily with the client. The client may wish to respond to a stated deficiency and should not feel constrained about expressing an opinion regarding the validity of the findings. However, in most cases, all detected deficiencies, even if rectified during the audit, will be reported. Auditors will also interview all levels of company personnel to discover objective evidence that the quality system as documented in the quality manual and supporting procedures has been fully implemented.

In the case of most sector-specific audits, the registrar will conduct the assessment in accordance with a Code of Practice, which is meant to enhance and reinforce the accreditation criteria.

Registration

Each registrar has specified outcomes that result from an assessment. Typically, three outcomes are possible: approval, conditional/provisional approval, disapproval.

Approval

A company can expect to become registered if it has implemented all the elements of the relevant standard and only minor deficiencies are detected during the assessment. It should be noted that all deficiencies must be closed out prior to issuing a QS-9000 certificate.

Conditional or Provisional Approval

A company will probably be either conditionally or provisionally approved if:

- It has addressed all the elements of the standard and has documented systems, but perhaps not fully implemented them.

- A number of deficiencies detected in a particular area show a negative, systemic trend.

Conditional approval requires the company to respond to any deficiencies noted during a specific time frame defined by the registrar. The registrar may elect to perform an on-site re-evaluation or accept the corrective action in writing and review the implementation during subsequent surveillance visits. Again, it should be noted that QS-9000 requirements differ as stated above.

Disapproval

The final possibility is disapproval, which usually occurs either when a company's system is well documented but has not been implemented or when entire elements of the standard, such as design control, internal auditing, corrective action or process control, have not been addressed. A comprehensive document review or an in-depth preassessment should identify either problem before the final audit. A disapproval recommendation requires another comprehensive (and successful) re-evaluation by the registrar before it can issue a registration certificate.

Once a company is registered, it receives a certificate and is listed in a register or directory published by the registrar as well as the *ISO 9000 Registered Company Directory North America* in the case of US, Canadian and Mexican sites. The company should also receive guidance for use of the certificate and associated quality marks. The client should also understand the registrar's policy for publishing registrations, including actions taken when registration is suspended or withdrawn. These terms generally relate to truth in advertising and the preclusion of misrepresenting a management system certification as a product certification.

Surveillance

The duration and/or validity of its registration is important for a company to understand. Some registrars offer registrations that are valid indefinitely, pending continuing, successful surveillance visits. Others offer registrations valid for a specific time, such as two to four years.

Most registrars conduct surveillance semiannually or annually. This can be a significant expense factor for small, remote companies. The client should clearly understand the registrar's surveillance policy. Some registrars conduct a complete reassessment at the end of the registration period, while others conduct a less thorough assessment that is more than a surveillance audit but less than a complete re-audit. A six-month surveillance schedule will seldom entail a full re-evaluation at the conclusion of the registration. An annual surveillance audit policy usually requires complete reassessment when the certificate expires. Companies seeking to meet the QS-9000 requirements should note that the automakers have mandated a six-month surveillance policy.

The surveillance visits are designed to ensure that a demonstrated quality system remains effective. The internal quality audit (required by ISO 9001, Clause 4.17) and its review by management (required by ISO 9001, Subclause 4.1.3) are mechanisms that drive this process.

However, rigorous documentation and deployment of an existing system should actually spur continual improvement. Changes toward continual improvement are encouraged, but any change in the system should be specifically documented and may require that the registrar be informed of these changes. Some registrars require notification of major changes to the quality system, while others require that the client apprise them of all changes. The client should clearly understand the registrar's policy and the possible profound impacts on registration maintenance.

Companies seeking to meet automotive requirements should note the registrar is required to identify opportunities for improvement as noted during the assessment. The automakers strongly encourage a company's efforts at achieving continual improvement. TL 9000 also specifically stipulates continual improvement. ISO 14001 specifically requires a continual improvement system to be in place. Accreditation criteria are evolving for "alternate methods" for certification, which reduce registrar audit oversight by a number of days based on the historically verified rigor of a company's management system, especially an organization's internal audit program.

Time and Costs of Registration

Achieving registration is not guaranteed no matter how diligently a company pursues the goal. Management commitment and dedicated implementation efforts are required.

Time

The time required to implement an ISO 9000 quality system depends on the company's current status, its commitment to the implementation of the system and its resources. A realistic estimate (if a company is starting with no system or a poorly documented system) is 18 to 24 months. The time required for actual registration depends upon the number of deficiencies detected during the pre-assessment, document review and/or initial assessment.

It is important to determine registrar resources before selecting a registrar to ensure that the organization can meet the client's goals and deadlines. Registrar schedule lead time can vary dramatically. Also be advised that, in addition to the registrar's industrial SIC/NACE code accreditation requirements, the assigned auditor must have competence in the industry to be audited. This can impact schedule and expenses if your assigned auditor is very distant geographically.

Costs

Many costs are associated with registration. Actually developing and implementing a management system is the first cost. Registration costs are estimated at less than 10 percent of implementation total.

When selecting a registrar, companies should assess actual costs of the registration process, including cost estimates for the following:

- Application and document review
- Preassessment visit
- Actual assessment
- Costs associated with issuing the registration and writing the report
- Surveillance visits
- Reevaluation visits (if required).

A company should also consider that some registrars require application fees, listing fees and registration fees in addition to those costs normally associated with registration. Reimbursed expenses can also vary from registrar to registrar. Some registrars are reimbursed at cost, some charge a fixed fee and others operate on a per diem basis. The costs must be taken into account in order to calculate the full cost of the registration.

The company should also understand registrar surveillance visit costs and the number of days expected for these visits. Other important baseline information includes how long the registration is valid and costs associated with any required full or partial reassessment.

Finally, the client should feel comfortable to openly discuss any issue, such as scheduling and qualification of audit team members. Although it cannot act as a consultant, the registrar should be willing to guide the client through the registration process. Remember that companies seeking ISO 9000-based registration are clients of the registrar and should be comfortable raising issues of concern with the registrar. However, clients must realize that the registrar operates in accordance with the requirements of its accreditors. Both the registrar and the client share the responsibility of seeking to continuously improve processes and operations.

The Audit Process

6

This chapter contains two articles related to the audit process. The first one, by Ross Gilbert, describes the internal quality audit process. It defines an audit and the auditor's role and discusses the phases of an internal audit, including the following:

- Planning an audit
- Executing it
- Reporting your findings
- Applying the corrective action process.

The second article, by Roger Pratt, discusses communication techniques helpful in both internal and external audits. These techniques will help make the audit proceed more smoothly. His article discusses the following issues:

- Putting the auditee at ease
- Helpful techniques to try
- What to do during unusual situations or conflicts
- Ethics involved with auditing.

Internal Quality Audits

by Ross Gilbert

This section is designed to give a brief overview of the key steps in developing, conducting and reporting an internal quality audit.

What Is An Audit?

An audit is the process of comparing actions or results against defined criteria. Internal audits are an integral part of any management system, whether it is focused on quality, safety, the environment or any other business element. A management system audit compares the implementation and effectiveness of the system against a standard as well as against its own internal criteria, as defined in policies, procedures and other documentation.

A quality audit is defined in ISO 9000:2000, *Quality management systems— Fundamentals and Vocabulary:*

> **Quality Audit**: A systematic, independent and documented process for obtaining evidence and evaluating it objectively to determine the extent to which the audit criteria are fulfilled.

ISO 9001:2000 states the objectives of internal audits in Clause 8.2.2:

> The organization shall conduct periodic internal audits to determine whether the quality management system:
>
> • conforms to the requirements of this international standard;
>
> • has been effectively implemented and maintained.

The organization shall plan the audit program taking into consideration the status and importance of the activities and areas to be audited as well as the results of previous audits. The audit scope, frequency and methodologies shall be defined. Audits shall be conducted by personnel other than those who perform the activity being audited.

A documented procedure shall include the responsibilities and requirements for conducting audits, ensuring their independence, recording results and reporting to management.

Management shall take timely corrective action on deficiencies found during the audit.

Follow-up actions shall include the verification of the implementation of corrective action, and the reporting of verification results.

Finally, as noted in ISO 9004:2000, internal audits are an integral part of an effective continual improvement system (8.5.2). Used as part of the management review process, they provide the objective information on which corrective and preventive action can be taken. In fact, these elements form the backbone of the "continual improvement" theme in the ISO 9000 standards. This includes the use of factual information on process performance in management reviews, which result in corrective and preventive actions, subject again to audit and verification.

Simply stated, an internal audit evaluates a company's quality management capability to determine the following:

- Does a system exist?
- Is it implemented?
- Is it effective?

Internal quality audits should be scheduled regularly, but some flexibility may be used in determining frequency, according to guidance document ISO 19011. A company should consider any changes to its quality system (including changes in management, policy or technology) and any corrective actions taken for previous audits. An internal audit system can also be used to support ISO 9000 registration, to provide a basis for improving an existing quality system or to ensure that regulatory requirements are met.

The Role of the Auditor

The role of the auditor is to examine whether or not a company or department is meeting the requirements of a declared quality assurance standard and, by collecting objective evidence, verify that the system is implemented and effective. Determining the system's effectiveness is difficult, but it is key to complying with ISO 9001. By interviewing personnel and witnessing activities, you can identify whether there is a system and whether it is being followed, but without a frame of reference as to what you expect from an effective system, you cannot evaluate effectiveness.

The auditor's role is not merely to report facts. An auditor obtains information from a variety of different people and interprets the data to make an informed judgment about the effectiveness of the quality system.

Many people think that an audit is primarily a policing function that ensures compliance with a set of defined criteria or rules. This perception is often shared by auditors, particularly if they are part of a newly developing audit program within a company. If an audit program has ill-defined objectives or the auditees misunderstand the purpose of the audit, then the "policing" aspect of the audit dominates over evaluating the effectiveness of the quality system.

An example of this misunderstanding is the "gotcha" reaction by an auditor who finds a noncompliance. This reinforces the auditor's image as "policeman" and adds nothing to the business. An internal audit function can, and should, be a process that provides the organization with useful information about its systems and their effectiveness. This information, whether it shows compliance or noncompliance, can be used to improve the system and business performance.

Involving managers and section heads in the internal audit process means convincing them of its value — convincing them that it won't become a fault-finding exercise. People won't believe that the audit system is designed to improve the process unless they see it; as such, your company's first audits may also be its most critical. Audit preparation should begin with educating everyone in the organization on the following topics:

- What the audit process will involve
- The audit's expected benefits
- How it can be used to measure the effectiveness of the links between internal customers and suppliers within an organization
- Everyone's role in the process.

Phases of the Audit: PERC

All types of audits have four basic phases that are listed below:

Planning

Execution

Reporting

Corrective action.

The auditee's perception of the audit is negatively affected by poor planning, inadequate execution, confused reporting or corrective action records. As an internal auditor, you should emphasize each of these four areas to ensure a professional approach.

Planning (PERC)

Planning is perhaps most crucial, since all other steps flow from and depend upon this step. Spending sufficient time in this particular phase will reap benefits when trying to ensure a smoothly run audit process. Planning an audit involves six steps:

- Select a skilled and capable audit team.
- Confirm the audit's objective and scope together with the specific quality assurance requirements with the auditee.
- Identify information sources on which to base the audit, including the quality system standard itself, the quality manual, procedures, etc.
- Develop an audit plan.
- Confirm the plan with the auditee.
- Develop checklists and audit assignments.

The quality management standard ISO 9004:2000 also points out that planning for internal audits should also consider the results of previous audits. Observations and findings from these can provide valuable information on issues and areas that deserve particular attention.

Selecting the Team

According to ISO 19011, whether an audit is carried out by a team or an individual, a lead auditor should be placed in overall charge. The audit team is best developed from a diagonal cross-section of the organization.

People from all levels in the company who perform a variety of tasks from different departments should be included. This team will then audit a function of the company where they are not directly responsible; e.g., marketing should audit manufacturing, sales should audit design, etc. Auditors should have some training in auditing techniques and ethics and remain free of bias.

Objective and Scope

Defining the objective and scope of the audit involves answering the following four questions:

- At what point in the process am I starting?
- At what point in the process am I finishing?
- Where am I auditing from — what are the sources of my information?
- What am I auditing to — what are the stated requirements?

One of the ways to identify the scope of the audit is to obtain the relevant documentation, review the documentation, identify the beginning and ending points of the audit and then use that initial review to prepare a checklist.

However, another strategy is to develop a more proactive approach to preparation; that is, get the auditees involved. It is often more effective to sit down with a department manager, supervisor or section head to identify the key things in their processes that are important to them and then use that as the foundation of your checklist. A checklist should never be a "secret weapon" used to find fault. Rather, preparing and developing the checklist should be part of an open audit process.

Information Sources

Identify the sources of relevant information that should be used in selecting the audit sample to ensure a balanced view of the company's operation. An audit sample is a sample of the documents or processes you may wish to audit; e.g., in purchasing, how many purchase orders will you look at — 5, 10 or 15? In manufacturing, which process will you audit? It is the objective evidence evaluated during the audit itself.

Sources of information from which to develop the audit plan/checklists include:

- Quality manual/procedures
- Management priorities
- Quality problems
- Previous audits/outstanding corrective action
- Product information
- Experience of the auditors.

Planning an Audit Program

Your audit program should identify the duration of the audit, the areas of the organization that will be subject to assessment and generally the people who should be available to answer the auditor's questions. Some of the key issues in developing the program follow:

Is it well planned? Have you thought through the process? Have you identified a beginning and an end? Can you take a sample from the system that will provide representative information and enable you to follow the process in a logical way?

Have you set achievable objectives? Can you verify that something is actually happening? Can you find evidence of an effective system, or are you wasting time following loose ends and trying to establish a pattern? Can you verify that the system or process you are examining is working? If so, how?

For example, you may be in the receiving area and be told that product is tested to a certain specification. How can you verify that the specification is up to date? You can see a date on the specification, but it might not be current. A methodology is necessary to identify a document and to identify whether or not the document is up to date. It is far better to identify those difficulties at the audit preparation stage than during the audit itself.

How long is the audit? Is the audit to last one day, two days, one week? The length depends on the objective and scope of the audit.

The audit itself has tight time constraints. It is important to keep the audit plan on schedule and yet maintain the flexibility to follow up on any leads that develop. Therefore, you must have a planned approach and a firm idea of how to conduct the audit. During the audit it is too late to make decisions about what and where the sample is to be taken. However, a plan that is changed for valid reasons is far better than no plan at all.

Confirm the Program with the Auditee

Be sure to confirm the audit program, including the dates, time and schedule with the auditee.

Develop a Checklist

Details of the sample and where it will be taken are on the audit checklist. The plan is the audit strategy that identifies what areas will be examined and when, whereas the checklist provides the tactical component by identifying how the company complies with ISO 9001.

Thought must be given to structuring the checklist to achieve the stated objective of process improvement. Checklist questions need to be open-ended — ones that will enable the auditee to explain the process and show how that process is documented. Whether the documentation is in a procedure or a flowchart does not matter — as long as it is reflected in the actual process. (See the next section of this chapter for more information on phrasing questions.)

Execution (PERC)

The actual execution of the audit consists of a number of distinct events:

- The opening meeting
- The audit itself: collecting and verifying information
- Recording the discrepancies.

The Opening Meeting

While an opening meeting for an internal audit is far less formal than an opening meeting held for a supplier audit, it still requires preparation. Follow an agenda to ensure that all necessary points are covered in as short a time as possible. Items you should consider putting on the agenda include the following:

- In large organizations it may be necessary to introduce the auditor(s), but departments in medium-sized and small organizations might already know the team.

- Explain the audit's purpose and scope as well as the range of activities to be reviewed.
- Confirm that the details of the program are acceptable to the auditee and that the necessary employees are available at the scheduled times.
- Confirm the status of the procedures and any relevant documents prior to the actual physical audit; clarify any ambiguities.
- Explain the manner of identifying and recording nonconformances.

It is also good practice to record those present at the opening meeting.

Collecting Information

The purpose of the audit is to collect objective evidence regarding the effectiveness of the company's quality system. It is a dynamic and practical tour through the company's quality management system along a path prescribed by the auditor's program and checklists.

The team leader's responsibilities during the audit include the following:

- Introduce yourself and the team to the section/department manager.
- Develop a rapport with the auditee.
- Explain what you want to see.
- Focus on the process/understand the objectives.
- Investigate as much as necessary.
- Get the auditees involved.
- Satisfy your sample.

If you don't find any problems, don't panic — some processes might be correct.

You can gain much information by interviewing the staff, by observing activities or by documenting evidence found in a company's records. Staff interviews should not be limited to department heads and senior managers. Everyone in the company has a part to play within the quality system.

When an employee tells you about another employee, however, that information is hearsay evidence and is unacceptable. During one warehouse audit, the manager, who was under increasing pressure from the auditor, finally burst out in exasperation, "Well if you think this place is bad, just wait until you get to Sales!" You cannot use it as a basis for a discrepancy. You can, however, use the information gained to check if a discrepancy indeed exists. But without the "hard" evidence of your eyes, documented proof or a statement from the person responsible for a particular activity, you must give the auditee the benefit of the doubt.

In gathering information, an auditor should ask open questions — those that cannot be answered by a simple yes or no. For example:

> *"Does this company have a procedure to define the quality audit activity?"* can be rephrased as, *"Can you explain how your audit procedure works?"*

"Yes" and "No" questions do not allow individuals to elaborate on their work and do not give the auditor confidence that the employees understand their operations. Open questions allow you to ascertain what is not recorded in the procedures and to determine the level of understanding of the people who are responsible for undertaking various functions.

To verify facts, it is permissible and indeed desirable to ask several people the same question to evaluate the consistency of responses. Do not underrate the use of silence. When you think you have received an incomplete answer, you can encourage the auditee to provide more information by using body language or simply remain silent. In general terms, people are anxious to avoid a silent pause and will tend to provide more information to fill that gap.

Remember, however, that it is not necessary to always find something wrong; there are areas that might actually be under control.

Verifying Your Observations

Auditors have to examine samples of documents, equipment, products, etc. to verify their observations. These items are part of the audit sample, and the auditor determines the size. However, it is not prudent to select only one sample of a system, nor is it possible to select tens or even hundreds of samples. It is good practice to select a representative sample, rather than one observation. Among the obvious benefits, it will help determine whether any discrepancies found are isolated occurrences or part of a larger problem. If one sample is incorrect, it would be wise to take another sample to determine whether it is an isolated occurrence or a larger problem.

When following an audit trail or selecting samples for examination, politely insist on selecting the sample rather than asking the auditee to do so at random. The samples taken by auditees are rarely, if ever, random, and likely will be the information that the auditee wishes you to see rather than what you might wish to select.

An empty file folder may mean that the record is currently in use, or it could mean the auditee does not want you to examine it. Remember that it is your audit. If a piece of information is missing, you have the right to ask for it, but try to be polite and to remain objective. Also, avoid unduly delaying the audit process; you can always return to a particular point when you have more time.

Nonconformities

Many different words are used to express the same meaning when referring to deficiencies or nonconformities within a company's system. In practice, you are likely to encounter various terms such as discrepancy, deficiency, finding or nonconformity. All mean the same — in effect, they are the "nonfulfillment of a requirement." (ISO 9000, Clause 3.6.2). The international standard ISO 9000 standardizes the term nonconformity, but it will take some time for this standard terminology to be adopted on a widespread basis.

Recording Nonconformities

When you identify a nonconformity and can trace and reexamine it to reveal the scale of the problem, stop and record those facts. You do not have to list every single occurrence of a problem, but state that what you witnessed is repeated in other records or in other areas. The audit is very much a "show me" exercise that looks for factual evidence. In this respect, a nonconformity report is a concise record of the facts relating to the nonconformance.

Ideally, a nonconformity should be recorded and signed by the auditee as agreed at the point of identification. You should explain to the auditee that such an acknowledgment does not necessarily mean that you will issue a corrective action request but that you must evaluate the finding in the context of the entire audit.

How you record those facts is up to you. Remember that phrasing the nonconformity requires some care on the part of the auditor. Stopping the audit to write details in full, well-structured English can destroy the pace and timing of the effort. The actual written nonconformity need not be presented until later in the day.

Some auditors have used recording devices during an audit. In one instance, an auditor decided the best way to use this device was to cover his head with his coat, hide in the corner and talk into the machine. This activity caused some consternation on the shop floor (not to mention various ribald comments). These kinds of activities also reinforce negative perceptions of audits and auditors. They should not be part of any audit.

When recording a nonconformity, the statement should be in a format that can be understood by both the auditor and the auditee, including those members of the department who were not necessarily present when the nonconformity was identified. Adequate references should be included to allow the department to reexamine the observations after the auditor has left the department.

The recorded nonconformity should include the following information:

- Where the nonconformity was found

- An exact observation of the facts surrounding the discrepancy
- The reason why the facts constitute a nonconformity
- Sufficient references to allow traceability.

When writing the nonconformity:

- Use local terminology, i.e., work in the language of the department.
- Make the information easily retrievable for future reference.
- Make it helpful to the auditees.
- Make it concise, yet complete.

Reporting (PE**R**C)

Just as a company has a customer for its product or service, an auditor has a customer for the results of the audit process. With an internal audit, the customer is likely to be the company's own quality assurance manager and the department head of the area under examination. As such, the format of the final report and tone of the closing meeting must be structured to meet the requirements of the department or function.

Before the closing meeting, the audit team should meet to evaluate the information they found during the audit and to ensure the validity of nonconformities. Findings should be recorded in a nonconformity report. (See Figure 6-1.) At this point, only the "Nonconformance" section should be filled out.

The Closing Meeting

Whether an audit has been an internal or external assessment, the auditor/audit team should meet with the department and/or company management to confirm results and to identify the subsequent actions required. For an internal audit, discuss the corrective action with the appropriate department manager who is more involved in the process.

The closing meeting should not last longer than 30-45 minutes, and the following items should be covered:

- Thank auditees for their hospitality and assistance.
- Make a record of the attendees at this meeting.
- Confirm the scope of the audit.
- Identify the audit standard and revision status of the company's documented quality system.
- Discuss any corrective action requests (CARs) in the nonconformity report.
- Explain that the audit has been a sampling exercise of the company's qual-

ity system, and therefore, the fact that noncompliances have not been identified in a particular area does not mean that none exist.

- Ask whether any points need to be clarified.
- Confirm future actions.

The last item is an important — if not the most important — element of the audit process. Both internal and external audits are a complete waste of time unless action is taken to correct failures that have been identified within the quality system. The auditee may provide objective evidence that nullifies a particular finding. The auditor/audit team should evaluate the claim and record it if valid. In addition, the auditee might refuse to acknowledge one of your CARs, in which case the auditor should record the refusal. As an auditor, you should leave the corrective action request forms with the department manager at the end of the meeting.

The Formal Audit Report

The formal report should do the following:

- Show a customer or independent third party that the company's quality management system is periodically checked for effectiveness.
- Evaluate the adequacy of the company's quality system as compared to its past performance.
- Identify the areas of the company's quality management system that need improvement. It should assign responsibilities and apply timetables to monitor the progress of the corrective action.

No auditee expects you to write a dissertation, but your report should provide enough detail to validate your conclusions. A summary is a useful way to bring all these facts together.

A summary statement should contain the following applicable information:

- The department audited
- The audit's scope/objective
- The duration and extent of the audit and the dates it was conducted
- The standard against which the auditee was audited
- The total number of discrepancies and where they were found
- Areas/functions where there were no nonconformities
- The effectiveness of the system
- Recommendations for corrective action
- Report distribution list.

Auditing, by its very nature, looks for areas of noncompliance, and it is important for the auditor to try to provide a balanced report that identifies the positive as well as the negative aspects of a company's systems. Therefore, identify and record acceptable elements of the system. The report should also identify — either by reference to the plan, checklists or within the narrative of the report itself — the areas that were visited and the samples that were taken. It should be possible for someone to retrace the auditor's steps and examine the same evidence by referring to the audit report.

Corrective Action (PERC)

An audit uncovers where the system is not functioning in accordance with management's objectives or in regard to the quality standard itself. As such, it can identify the illness, but does not provide the cure. Auditing for the sake of producing a report will serve little purpose. It must be followed by effective corrective action. It is the responsibility of the audited group, not the auditor, to determine appropriate corrective action to each nonconformity.

In the nonconformity report mentioned earlier, there is a space to record the proposed corrective action. A corrective action/follow-up procedure should include the following elements:

- Identify and agree to the details of the nonconformity between the auditee and auditor.
- Agree to the corrective action.
- Agree to timetables and dates to accomplish the following:
  - Resolve the problem
  - Implement the solution
  - Evaluate the effectiveness
  - Re-audit to confirm completion (i.e., closeout) of the program.

In the case of serious nonconformities generally associated with observed failures of system or products, it will be necessary to re-audit an activity to verify that the corrective action has been implemented and is effective.

A third-party registrar will expect to see evidence that the above points have been addressed.

The corrective action program requires some paperwork — not to create undue bureaucracy, but to provide traceability demonstrating the outcome of an audit, to identify those responsible for its resolution, to monitor progress and to initiate the "closeout" of the nonconformity.

Another important feature of the corrective action system is a management review (refer to ISO 9001:2000, Clause 5.6) of actions taken. This summary of corrective actions can form the basis on which to judge the entire quality system. It is important to try to quantify the benefits derived from the corrective action program. This can be in the form of increased customer confidence, fewer complaints or operational cost savings

Some departmental managers within an organization may not respond positively to the need to implement corrective action. A system for escalation to more senior management should be built into the audit procedures when managers fail to act upon audit findings.

Corrective action and follow-up includes the following tasks:

- Identify the discrepancy.
- Raise and issue a corrective action request.
- Develop timetables with the auditee.
- Evaluate the corrective actions taken.
- Maintain accurate records to verify the corrective action has been completed.
- "Close out" completed corrective action requests in the records.
- Escalate the issue to senior management if the auditees are not fulfilling their duties.

The corrective action program and its implementation demonstrates the true commitment of a company's management. The corrective action system is a highly visible part of the total quality system, and management must ensure that their actions demonstrate commitment to the company's quality improvement objectives.

These audit phases are similar regardless of the type of management system audit being conducted. In fact, many organizations choose to integrate their internal audit systems for quality, safety and/or environmental management.

Throughout the audit process, keep in mind the ultimate goal of a management system audit: to determine whether the system is implemented effectively and is suitable for achieving your goals. The combined audit and corrective action process can be a powerful tool to evaluate the systems and drive improvement, if the audits are done in an effective and positive way.

Figure 6-1

Typical Nonconformity Report Form

Nonconformity Report		
Departments/Areas Audited:		
Department Represenatative:	Auditor:	Nonconformance Report No.:
Nonconformance:		
Cause Identification/Proposed Corrective Action:		
Agreed Time Implementation:	Responsibility for Action:	Dept. Rep.'s Signature:
Auditor's Signature:		Date:
Entered in CAR Log by Quality Manager:		
Signature:		Date:
Corrective Action Completely Satisfactory:	Yes	No
Comments:		
		Signature:

ISO 19011: Guidelines on Quality and Environmental Management Systems Auditing

ISO 19011 offers guidance for establishing a quality and/or environmental management audit system and, although the requirements are not mandatory, they are an excellent resource for establishing consistent audit practice worldwide. *ISO 19011, Guidelines on Quality and Environmental Management Systems Auditing,* is a document that provides guidance on audit terminology, audit principles and practices and auditor qualifications.

ISO 19011 complements the requirements of ISO 9001 by providing consistent guidance for one critical area of implementing the standards, namely auditing. In the same way, it also supports ISO 14001, *Environmental Management Systems— Specification with Guidance for Use.*

The document is composed of several sections, each providing guidance on an aspect of auditing that should be addressed in a competently managed audit system. The content of each section is clear from the headings and includes:

• Terms and Definitions

• General Principles of Auditing

• Managing an Audit Program

• Auditing Activities

• Qualifications for Quality and Environmental Management System Auditors.

The general principles of auditing are key to understanding the basic nature of audits. There are several described in ISO 19011, but the four listed below provide a glimpse of the importance of these principles for effective auditing.

• Audits are an effective management tool to examine activities and processes. The result of an audit is information on which management can act.

• Audits are authorized and authority may result from the decision of management, company policy, provisions of contract, the audit client or legislation or regulation.

• Audits are conducted using established methods and techniques to ensure that audit evidence and audit findings are relevant, reliable and sufficient, such that audit teams working independently of one another will reach similar audit conclusions.

• The relationship between the audit team, auditee and the audit client is one of confidentiality and discretion. Unless required to do so by law, the audit team does not disclose the contents of documents or the nature of any other information obtained during the audit or the final report to any third party, without the explicit approval of the audit client and, where appropriate, the approval of the auditee.

Qualifications for Quality and Environmental Management System Auditors

To ensure that quality system audits are carried out effectively and uniformly, minimum criteria are required to qualify auditors. This section describes these minimum criteria. The criteria upon which an auditor is judged include education and training, work experience, audit experience and personal attributes. These provide a person with the potential to be an auditor. In addition, effective auditors require general competencies in auditing procedures and practices and specific competencies in quality (or environmental) principles, techniques and technologies.

Management of Audit Programs

Companies that conduct ongoing quality system audits should establish a way to manage the process. This section describes the activities that such an organization should address and offers basic guidelines for managing them. It addresses the objectives and authority for audits, resources and responsibilities, and guidance on audit management practice.

Auditing the Internal Audit System

by Bud Weightman

Must a company's internal audit system itself be audited under ISO 9000 series standards?

ISO 9001:2000 refers to the requirements for a supplier's quality system. It holds that a supplier shall carry out a compliance system of planned and documented internal quality audits to verify whether quality activities comply with planned arrangements and to determine the effectiveness of the quality system.

There are 23 basic elements in the standard, all of which are applicable to the supplier. Any of these elements is supported by all of the others. You can't take away one of them and say this requirement doesn't apply. Therefore, you must also do internal audits of the audit system.

If the quality department, for example, is charged with internal audit scheduling and performance, get a qualified individual from another department, possibly manufacturing, to audit the quality department.

In such a case, manufacturing would verify, by using an audit procedure or checklist, that the quality department has implemented the applicable controls established by the quality manual. This is most likely supported by a lower-level procedure and further requirements.

Additionally, manufacturing would verify the audit system requirements and that those personnel responsible for performing the company's internal audit system were qualified and trained to perform the audits and actually independent from the activities they have audited.

Without such a system in effect, the auditors (in this case the quality department) would get a free ride. Every individual and every department must be counterchecked. That includes the department or individuals charged with performing the audits on everyone else.

Interview or Inquisition: Successful Communication Techniques

by Roger C. Pratt

There are certain interviewing skills that auditors — both internal and external — can use to help smooth communications with the auditee. While written from an auditor's point of view, auditees can learn from these methods as well.

Introduction

Although part of any auditor's time is spent gathering information from documents, a significant portion is spent gathering information from people. This field investigation is the core of the audit. It is where auditors make observations, collect data and interview employees. Therefore, much of this article addresses the auditing intangibles, so to speak. These include interviewing techniques, body language and ethical issues.

With a little poetic license: *Audit others as you would like to be audited.*

Putting the Auditee at Ease

The announcement that an organization is going to be audited or that a particular function is going to be surveyed automatically creates a fear of the unknown in those being audited. Therefore, auditors must recognize that their early activities will be suspect. Even though the auditees are aware of the ground rules and the scope of the audit, they may be concerned that they will be singled out and that areas under their responsibility will be lacking.

Change of any sort can be threatening, causing a defensive or hostile attitude. The auditee will probably spend more time justifying the status quo than listening to suggestions for improvement. The auditor has to be sensitive to the anxiety of all auditees by considering each audited individual's personal philosophies, motivational characteristics and individual objectives. An auditor should be able to counter any defensiveness by accepting different methods of compliance to a specific requirement; auditors must avoid the "my way is the only correct way" mentality.

To alleviate some of this stress, the audit team should arrive at the designated locations on time and be mentally and physically prepared to audit. The audit team should appear cohesive and have a leader who sets the tone and pace of the audit. Team members should be enthusiastic, unbiased and confident in their ability to assist the organization.

Interview/Communication Techniques

How auditors ask questions will affect the amount and quality of the information they receive. Preparation is the first and most important step; if the auditor knows in advance what should be discussed, the auditor is more likely to ask appropriate questions.

It is up to the auditor to establish an initial atmosphere of trust and open communication. The goal is to obtain as much valid information as possible in the shortest time possible. Some potential conditions that affect the initial interactions include the following:

- The auditee's perceptions of the audit process: "This is a waste of time; I am being evaluated only to fulfill requirements."
- The auditee's initial feelings of fear and skepticism: "Will this clear up the problems? Will I come out of this looking OK?" (The auditee might have certain predispositions based on past experiences.)

The auditor must recognize that these factors exist and be aware of them during the audit process. Auditors should emphasize that they are there to audit the system or program, not the person. Auditors should explain to the auditee's manager that the audit is not a "search for the guilty." It will identify potential problems and assist in correcting them.

Consequently, auditors should take notes throughout the interview process; memory is unreliable, at best. Note-taking may create small pockets of silence that can induce stress, but most auditees will be comfortable if they understand that auditors are taking notes to ensure that they are recording accurate information.

The importance of listening cannot be overstressed; it is difficult to gather information while talking. Auditors should not formulate new questions when the individual is responding to the previous ones and they should listen for more than the "bottom line." It is important to let the auditee respond with as much detail as possible to get the needed information. One way to accomplish this is to first ask open-ended questions and then move to close-ended questions to get clarification of details.

Questions that can be answered "yes" or "no" should be kept to a minimum. An example of a yes-or-no or close-ended question is, "Do you perform reviews according to your project management procedure Number 51?" The reply would undoubtedly be "Yes." One way to rephrase the question in an open-ended format is: "I've read your Procedure 51, which indicates that a particular type of review process is performed. Explain to me in detail how you implement that procedure."

It is important for auditors to communicate at the same responsibility level and knowledge of the person they are interviewing. The discussions may range from quality philosophy with top management to specific manufacturing techniques with the worker on the production line.

There are several clarification techniques that auditors can use to make sure that the information they receive from interviewees is clear and complete:

- **Probing**: using follow-up questions to further explore something the auditee has said
- **Paraphrasing**: repeating and rewording important points
- **Summarizing**: recapping and repeating a set of major points to make sure all the important information has been noted.

Using these techniques the auditor can demonstrate that he or she is a good listener and is a professional. In addition, the techniques give the auditee a chance to fill in any missing or misunderstood information.

General Considerations

It is appropriate in a business situation to shake hands with all individuals when they are introduced — both males and females. Auditors should also try to use the person's name occasionally in conversation. This recognizes the auditee as an individual and facilitates the free exchange of information

Auditors should use appropriate body language to show that they are listening and receiving the message that the individual is sending. This means maintaining good eye contact, nodding the head, etc., as needed. Eye contact should be maintained about 25 percent of the time, as a rule. Too much eye contact, however, makes the auditee feel uncomfortable; too little makes the interview impersonal. The auditor should smile when appropriate, for it is possible for the auditor to concentrate to such an extent that he or she appears unfriendly.

The audit team's dress sets the tone for the level of professionalism perceived by the audited organization. A suit projects a power image, while blue jeans convey a casual tone. Dress should be appropriate to the organization being audited. It would be inappropriate, for example, to conduct an audit of construction activities in a three-piece suit or a silk dress.

Dealing with Unusual Situations or Conflicts

The goal during the interview portions of the audit is to gain information in the best atmosphere possible. There may be times, however, when conflicts or difficult situations arise. This includes situations when the auditee repeatedly fails to answer a question or answers inconsistently, when the auditee tries to dominate the situation or when the auditee rambles on in an irrelevant monologue. In these cases, it is best to directly confront the individual's behavior and redirect the conversation. The auditor should be persistent and not allow intentional or unintentional avoidance of a topic; it is important to demonstrate control in these types of situations.

It is possible that personnel who are anticipating the audit may develop data, statistics or other information and offer it to the auditor as evidence of a previous corrective action or as evidence that no problems exist. Some individuals are skilled at using statistical data deceptively. The auditor should use and accept such data only if he or she is convinced that it is valid and appropriate. It is usually necessary to obtain validations from other sources before accepting and using such information in the audit.

Occasionally auditees will resort to tactics such as showing new products under development, giving tours of the plant or taking long lunch hours to divert the auditors from their planned activities. The auditor should resist such obvious diversionary tactics.

If a facility is in trouble, and particularly if there are management problems, there may be sincerely ethical people who will indicate an interest in talking to the auditor. This does not mean that these volunteers are necessarily correct in their analysis of the situation. Auditors must take care not to be distracted by the side issues. On the other hand, they should not ignore this information; with proper validation, it may give valuable feedback on system effectiveness.

Ethics

When dealing with the audited organization, there are some key principles to keep in mind that take the above factors into account.

Maintain the self-esteem of the individual; refrain from making cutting or sarcastic remarks. This is important in building rapport between the auditor and the auditee, maintaining an atmosphere of openness and trust and encouraging the flow of information.

Showing empathy and understanding will also help build rapport. This will ease tension so that the auditor can gain information that he or she would not have gotten otherwise. To show empathy and understanding, the auditor should listen for both facts and emotions in what the auditee says. Using the technique of *reflecting*, the auditor states the emotional content of what the auditee has said to show that the auditor recognizes and understands the auditee.

An example might be, "You seem dissatisfied with the manner in which that procedure was implemented."

Also, the auditor should try not to show shock, dismay or surprise if the auditee reveals potentially damaging information. The auditor should simply indicate that he or she understood the facts and then communicate an appreciation of openness and honesty.

Check findings and observations against the "so what?" reaction. This means measuring the perceived problem against potential consequences or risks if it is not corrected. If the consequences are small or nonexistent but are symptoms of a larger system problem, the auditor should investigate. They can then be used as facts supporting a more general finding.

The auditor should maintain a conscious objectivity toward the subject being evaluated. Previous practices or personal beliefs can prevent a full understanding of existing conditions. The auditor will be confronted many times with conjecture, suggestions and leading or distracting opinions expressed by those being contacted. It is essential that the auditor keep his or her personal opinions private and concentrate on elements of observed fact.

Concentrate on the relevant facts. The situation should be evaluated in sufficient depth so that the root cause can eventually be determined. It is not, however, the responsibility of the auditing organization to determine the specific source of the problem or to place blame.

Surprises should not be a part of an auditor's evaluation. An ethical audit is not the place for cloak-and-dagger tactics, for witch hunting or for identifying situations at a critical and embarrassing time (a "gotcha"). These practices violate auditor ethics.

All reported observations and recommendations — including the discussion and supporting data for such recommendations — should be stated impersonally. Avoid using names; substitute instead a definition of the functions that were evaluated and/or the level of the persons in that function.

The auditor should comply to the greatest extent practical with the customs of the audited facility. This includes complying with working hours, mode of dress, observance of lunch hours and other facility requirements or customary procedures.

The auditor should give the benefit of the doubt to the audited organization. When there is significant doubt in the mind of the auditor as to the verifiable facts or the correctness of the auditor's recommendation, he or she should carefully evaluate the item with other members of the team and the team leader. If, in further evaluation, the item is still in doubt, it should be dropped or noted with a degree of uncertainty.

Conclusion

Auditing is not a simple task, for an auditor must gather factual information while at times using "intangible" techniques to effectively deal with an organization's employees. It is important that the auditor learn how to interview the auditee, how to handle unusual situations and how to conduct an ethical audit. The auditor must also be professional, preserve the auditee's self-esteem and inform the auditee of all information gathered during the audit (i.e., create no surprises). The "amended" golden rule applies: *Audit others as you would like to be audited.*

References

R.C. Pratt, D.E. Ryder, and F.C. Hood, "Auditing Methods for Lead Auditors," Quality Training and Resource Center Course #QLT-180010, Rev. 5, US Department of Energy, Richland Operations Office, Richland, WA.

Pacific Northwest Laboratory is operated by the Battelle Memorial Institute for the US Department of Energy under contract DE-AC06-76RLO 1830. Pacific Northwest Laboratory, Battelle Boulevard, Richland, WA 99352.

The Value of Registrar Accreditation

7

by Joseph Tiratto

Registrars perform on-site audits of the quality management systems and issue a registration certificate if they find objective evidence that the systems conform with ISO 9000 requirements. The accreditation of these registrars and the recognition of their certificates are the very foundations of the third-party system.

While there are differences among registration and accreditation bodies in Europe, the United States and other countries, there are a number of international initiatives aimed at promoting mutual acceptance of equivalent registration and accreditation practices.

This chapter examines the following topics:

- Registrar accreditation in Europe, the United States and Canada
- Criteria for accrediting certified bodies — the EN 45000 series (ISO/IEC Guides)
- Recognition of registration certificates
- Auditor certification
- QS-9000 and ISO 14000 registrar accreditation issues
- Interpretations of ISO 9000.

Registrar Accreditation

Companies seek registration for different reasons. Some companies seek registration to meet mandatory regulatory requirements. Others seek registration to gain strategic advantage in the marketplace or simply as a means of improving internal quality systems.

The specific marketplace needs of a particular company often determine which registrar is chosen. For example, some registrars have more influence than others in certain regions of the world or in specific industries. Others may employ more appropriately qualified auditors for a particular industry. Yet, a key difference between registrars is their accreditation — or lack of accreditation in some cases. A registrar gains accredited status by meeting strict internationally accepted guidelines and undergoing an appropriate audit from one or more qualified accreditation bodies.

All issues that surround accreditation have not been settled. Unaccredited registrars can be fully competent to conduct quality system audits and award ISO 9000 certificates. On the other hand, fully accredited registrars offer no guarantee of quality auditing services. Ultimately, it is the job of the accredited registrar to provide confidence to industry regarding competence.

In addition, registrars can be accredited by more than one accrediting body. A registrar that offers multiple accreditations may allow a company to meet the requirements of its customers in different countries. For example, if a company does most of its business with customers in the United Kingdom, then seeking a registrar with United Kingdom Accreditation Service (UKAS) approval makes sense. (See Chapter 5 for more on the process of selecting a registrar). It is important to note that the number and type of accreditations for your certificate may affect the fees you pay and ultimately the acceptance of that certificate by customers. So choose wisely.

Accreditation Bodies in Europe

In Europe, third-party assessors are regulated by governmental or quasi-governmental agencies. The Dutch Council for Accreditation (RvA) in The Netherlands and UKAS in the United Kingdom are two of the best known bodies that accredit organizations to perform third-party quality system audits.

Other accreditation bodies in Europe include Association Française pour l'Assurance de la Qualité (AFAQ) in France, UNICEI (Ente Nazionale Italiano di Unificazione, Comitato Elettrotecnico Italiano) in Italy, and Asociación Española de Normalización y Certificación (AENOR) in Spain. The RvA, the first registrar accreditation body to be established, was until a few years ago the only such body in Europe that would accredit registration bodies outside its own country. UKAS changed its policy in late 1995 and began to offer accreditation to ISO 9000 registrars outside its borders. Today, it is common practice for accreditation bodies to make their services available anywhere there is customer demand.

Accreditation and Registration

The marketplace may be the most important registrar accreditation factor for companies whose products are not affected by a European Union (EU) directive. (Refer to Chapter 21 for more information on regulated and nonregulated products.) Essentially, regulated products are those that affect health, safety or the environment in a significant way.

If the company's product is regulated by the European Union, then often an accredited registrar with notified body status must be used for any quality system registration requirement of a directive. Registrars wishing to become officially notified bodies must meet certain criteria and apply for such status. An appropriately accredited registrar is important in these strictly controlled venues since the results of its audit — the registration certificate — could be a company's ticket to do business in Europe.

Accreditation in the United States

The United States has developed its own accreditation system for several important reasons:

- To establish international credibility for US-based registrars
- To provide assurance to the marketplace of the competence of registrars and of the effective implementation of management systems by the organizations registered by those registrars
- To establish and maintain a US system of accreditation and registration that is compatible with similar systems worldwide.

In late 1989 the Registrar Accreditation Board (RAB) was established as an affiliate of the then American Society for Quality Control (ASQC) to develop and operate a national accreditation program for ISO 9000 registrars. The program was intended to meet the challenge of ensuring the consistency of services offered by a rapidly expanding number of US-based registrars.

Then in late 1991, the RAB program was enhanced through the participation of the American National Standards Institute (ANSI) in a joint program. This National Accreditation Program (NAP) was later expanded to include accreditation of training course providers and to cover EMS as well as QMS activities.

Registrar Accreditation Board

RAB performs initial audits of registrars, issues certificates of accreditation, performs regular follow-up surveillance and maintains a directory of accredited registrars. RAB performs complete reassessments of accredited registrars every four years.

A group of qualified auditors perform the audits of the registrar and an ANSI-RAB council evaluates the audit results to make a final decision on the accreditation of a registrar.

ANSI-RAB Accreditation Criteria

The criteria used by RAB to accredit registrars are the same internationally accepted criteria that are used throughout the world. This commonality of accreditation criteria will enhance the mutual recognition of accreditation systems worldwide. The final goal of these activities is to allow for the mutual recognition of registrar accreditations and the international acceptance of individual supplier quality system registrations. To this end, the ANSI-RAB program has incorporated the following international criteria into its own criteria:

- ISO 19011: Guidelines on Quality and Environmental Management Systems Auditing (replaced ISO 10011)
- ISO/IEC Guide 61: General Requirements for Assessment and Accreditation of Certification/Registration Bodies
- ISO/IEC Guide 62: General Requirements for Bodies Operating Assessment and Certification/Registration of Quality Systems.

ISO's Committee on Conformity Assessment (CASCO) has revised guides ISO/IEC 61 and ISO/IEC 62 to agree with the ISO 9001:2000 standard. The International Accreditation Forum (IAF) has issued additional guidance on the application of these documents by member accreditation bodies.

ANSI-RAB Recognition

ANSI-RAB has signed an initial multilateral recognition agreement (MLA) with 12 other Quality Management System (QMS) accreditation bodies from around the world through IAF.

NIST and the NVCASE Program

The National Institute of Standards and Technology (NIST), through its Office of Standards Services, offers a voluntary program to evaluate and recognize organizations that support conformity assessment activities.

The National Voluntary Conformity Assessment System Evaluation (NVCASE) program includes activities related to laboratory testing, product certification, and quality system registration. After NVCASE evaluation, NIST provides recognition to qualified US organizations that effectively demonstrate confor-

ISO/IEC Guides Pertinent to Certification, Registration and Accreditation

Guide 2, General terms and definitions concerning standardization and related activities. (Part of guide to be revised and issued as 17000.)

Guide 7, Guidelines for drafting of standards suitable for use for conformity assessment. (To be revised and issued as 17001.)

Guide 22, Information on manufacturer's declaration of conformity with standards or other technical specifications. (To be revised and issued as 17050 and 17051.)

Guide 23, Methods of indicating conformity with standards for third-party certification systems.

Guide 25, General requirements for the competence of calibration and testing laboratories. (Revised and issued as 17025.)

Guide 27, Guidelines for corrective action to be taken by a certification body in the event of misuse of its mark of conformity.

Guide 28, General rules for a model third-party certification system for products.

Guide 39, General requirements for the acceptance of inspection bodies.

Guide 40, General requirements for the acceptance of certification bodies.

Guide 42, Guidelines for a step-by-step approach to an international certification system.

Guide 43, Development and operation of laboratory proficiency testing.

Guide 44, General rules for ISO or IEC international third-party certification schemes for products.

Guide 53, An approach to the utilization of a supplier's quality system in third-party product certification. (To be revised.)

Guide 56, An approach to the review by a certification body of its own internal quality system.

Guide 57, Guidelines for the presentation of inspection results.

Guide 58, Calibration and testing laboratory accreditation systems—general requirements for operation and recognition. (To be revised and issued as 17011.)

Guide 59, Code of good practice for standardization.

Guide 60, Code of good practice for conformity assessment. (To be revised.)

Guide 61, General requirements for assessment and accreditation of certification/registration bodies. (To be revised and issued as 17011.)

Guide 62, General requirements for bodies operating assessment and certification/registration of quality systems. (To be revised and issued as 17021.)

Guide 65, General requirements for bodies operating product certification systems.

Guide 67, Fundamentals of product certification. (To be developed.)

Guide 68, Arrangements for recognition of conformity assessment results. (To be developed.)

Future ISO/IEC 17040, General requirements for peer assessment of conformity assessment bodies.

mance with established criteria. The ultimate goal is to help US manufacturers satisfy applicable product requirements mandated by other countries through conformity assessment procedures conducted in this country prior to export.

NVCASE recognition provides other governments with a basis for having confidence that qualifying US conformity assessment bodies are competent and facilitates the acceptance of US products in foreign regulated markets based on US conformity assessment results.

NVCASE does not unilaterally establish program areas. Operational areas are established only after a formal request from a conformity assessment body (CAB) and concurrence of need from the affected industry sector. If another US government agency has domestic regulatory responsibility for a sector, that agency will be consulted prior to any program action by NIST.

Conformity assessment activities encompass three levels: (1) the conformity level (e.g., product testing, product certification and quality system registration); (2) the accreditation level (e.g., the actions of accreditors of bodies operating at the conformity level); and (3) the recognition of accreditors. NVCASE recognition may be sought by a body that accredits other bodies (i.e., an accreditor of laboratories, certifiers or registrars). If acceptable accreditation is not available elsewhere, a body may be accredited directly by NVCASE to perform a function (i.e., to certify specific products).

In the NVCASE evaluation process, an applicant provides NIST with sufficient information to allow thorough assessment. The applicant's management system is thoroughly reviewed based on established internationally accepted criteria, such as the ISO 9000 series. The criteria for technical operation are based on internationally accepted criteria such as ISO/IEC 17025 for laboratories and

ISO/IEC Guide 58 for their accreditors, ISO/IEC Guide 61 for accreditors of registrars (e.g., RAB) and ISO/IEC Guide 62 for registrars.

Each participant must undergo an initial on-site assessment by peer assessors prior to obtaining recognition. All elements of nonconformance must be resolved before recognition will be granted. Once recognized, follow-up assessments are conducted on a regular two-year cycle, with both announced and unannounced periodic surveillance visits. NVCASE recognition is effective until either voluntary or involuntary termination. The NVCASE program is described in Code of Federal Register, 15 CFR, Part 286 after the "Introduction" section.

Designating US Recognized Bodies

NVCASE maintains listings of all recognized bodies, including the name, address, pertinent contacts, and the scope of recognition. The list of provisionally qualified CABs for various sectoral annexes of the Mutual Recognition Agreements/Arrangements is maintained. These CABs will be formally qualified through the NVCASE program. (For further information on the NVCASE program, contact Jogindar Dhillon, Program Manager, NIST, 301-975-5521; e-mail: dhillion@email.nist.gov.)

Independent Association of Accredited Registrars

The Independent Association of Accredited Registrars (IAAR) is a nonprofit association of accredited management systems registrars operating in North America. The organization actively promotes the establishment and maintenance of effective management systems in North American companies through accredited registration. IAAR was formed in 1993.

IAAR works to encourage and facilitate consistent management systems registration through the use of accredited registrars. The association also promotes communication and professional practices among its members and works to educate companies and other organizations about the accredited registration process. In addition, the IAAR promotes the integrity of the management systems registration process through member participation in a group forum and encourages its members to follow appropriate codes of professional practice.

IAAR works with other industry groups, government agencies and other organizations to provide guidance in the appropriate use of international standards and the accreditation process. For example, the Big Three consulted IAAR as it developed the QS-9000 requirements for auto industry suppliers.

All IAAR members are accredited to provide registration services in compliance with ISO Guides 48 and 62.

Accreditation Bodies in Canada

Standards Council of Canada (SCC) has been operating a registrar accreditation program since December 9, 1991. The program, known as National Accreditation Program for Registration Organizations (NAPRO), is voluntary and open to any registrar operating in Canada. The SCC is a federal Crown corporation with a mandate to foster and promote voluntary standardization. This connection gives the organization implicit government recognition of its programs.

Applicants for NAPRO accreditation are judged on a number of attributes, including organizational base, administrative practices, human resources, physical resources, documented policies and procedures and independence of operation.

NAPRO is governed by guidelines contained in a Standards Council publication entitled *"Criteria and Procedures for Accreditation Organizations Registering Quality Systems"* (CAN-P-10). An Advisory Committee on Quality (AQC), made up of experts in the field, oversees the accreditation program and provides guidance to the Standard's Council on matters pertaining to quality.

Registrars that apply to the Standards Council for accreditation submit a written application describing their organization and resources, along with a fee as outlined in the published fee schedule. A team of assessors then carries out a five-step assessment process. The first four steps are as follows:

- A preassessment meeting
- An on-site assessment
- Field observations of the applicant carrying out assessments of two clients
- A final meeting to inform the applicant of the assessment team's findings, including any corrective action required.

When the applicant meets all necessary requirements for accreditation, a report is made to the Standards Council's Registration Accreditation Sub-committee (RASC) and then to the full ACQ. A final recommendation is made by the ACQ to the executive committee of the SCC, which approves accreditations.

The entire procedure, from the completed application to the issuing of the accreditation certificate, takes approximately 11 months. Audits are done annually and reassessments every four years. SCC is working towards formal agreements with accreditation bodies in other countries that would provide official recognition of SCC-accredited registrars. This activity is being promoted through membership in the International Accreditation Forum (IAF) and the Pacific Accreditation Cooperation (PAC).

Criteria for Registrar Accreditation

The complexity of the European system with its many unfamiliar acronyms makes it difficult for any company to evaluate registrar competence. The system used to evaluate ISO 9000 registrars is part of a larger framework established by the European Union for evaluating notified bodies.

The standard to evaluate registrars is known as the European Norm 45012 (see Annex 1.) The standard is part of the EN 45000, which was adapted by two other EU organizations, the European Committee for Standardization and the European Committee for Electrotechnical Standardization (CEN/CENELEC). The guidelines are aimed at increasing the level of confidence in the certification, inspection and testing bodies of the European Union. EN 45012 is identical to ISO/IEC Guide 62.

EN 45012, *General Criteria for Certification Bodies Operating Quality System Certification*, is important to companies seeking ISO 9000 registration. (See Annex 1 for an outline of EN 45012 requirements.)

The EN 45000 Series (Identical to ISO/IEC Guides)

The EN 45000 series consists of documents aimed at ensuring that declarations of conformity, test results and product and quality system certificates from different national testing labs and certification bodies are equivalent. Many of these standards are modifications of ISO Guides, listed elsewhere in this chapter. These guides were written to provide general guidance to countries worldwide involved with certification of products.

EN 45001, *General Criteria for the Operation of Testing Laboratories,* details the issues that laboratories must address to demonstrate competence in product testing. These include test personnel, equipment, test methods, test reports, quality systems and conflict of interest.

EN 45002, *General Criteria for the Assessment of Testing Laboratories,* is designed for accreditation bodies that assess testing labs. EN 45002 incorporates the criteria of EN 45001. It also discusses other requirements for accreditation bodies, including a written accreditation process, published assessment methods, a minimum reassessment period, an opportunity for applicant laboratories to comment on the inspection report, a possible requirement for laboratories to participate in proficiency testing and rules involving subcontracting of testing.

EN 45003, *General Requirements for Laboratory Accreditation Bodies,* includes guidelines for organizations that want to become accreditation bodies. Requirements include, among others free and open to access by applicants, independence of the accrediting body, the establishment of sectoral committees to advise the accreditation body and an appeals procedure.

EN 45010 (ISO/IEC Guide 61), *General Requirements for Assessment and Accreditation of Certification/Registrar Bodies.*

EN 45011 (ISO/IEC Guide 65), *General Requirements for Certification Bodies Operating Product Certification,* includes the criteria required for national or European recognition of a product certification body.

EN 45012 (ISO/IEC Guide 62), *General Requirements for Bodies Operating Certification/Registration of Quality Systems,* looks specifically at the issue of quality system registration (certification). Its basic criteria parallel those of EN 45011. (To be revised and issued as 17024.)

EN 45013, *General Criteria for Certification Bodies Operating Certification of Personnel,* applies to the certification of personnel, according to the same criteria as in EN 45011.

EN 45014 (ISO/IEC Guide 22), *General Criteria for Declaration of Conformity,* goes into detail about the process of actually preparing the Declaration of Conformity to demonstrate conformance with a directive's requirements.

EN 45019, *Guidance on Specific Aspects of Testing and Certification.*

EN 45020, *Definitions.*

[To obtain the above standards, contact the American National Standards Institute, 212-642-4900 (phone), 212-398-0023 (fax).]

EN 45012 (ISO/IEC Guide 62): Criteria for Registrars

Organizations that perform quality system certification activities must be evaluated against the requirements of EN 45012. These criteria address the requirements for certified bodies at a national or European level. Implementation of this standard is the responsibility of the International Certification Network (IQNet).

Further guidance related to EN 45012 (ISO/IEC Guide 62) implementation is contained in the ISO/IEC Guide 40, *General Requirements for the Acceptance of Certification Bodies,* and ISO/IEC Guide 48, *Guidelines for Third-Party Assessment and Registration of a Supplier's Quality System.*

Manufacturers or suppliers involved in ISO 9000 registration efforts should make sure that their quality system registrar has been accredited according to

EN 45012 (ISO/IEC Guide 62). (See Chapter 5 for more information on the process of selecting a registrar.)

The European Accreditation of Certification (EAC)

The European Accreditation of Certification is an association of accreditation bodies from the European Union and the European Free Trade Association (EFTA). The EAC's goal is the creation of a single European accreditation system covering products, quality systems and personnel. The EAC has published its own interpretations of the EN 45000 standards (ISO/IEC Guides). By harmonizing the definitions and interpretations of these rules, the EAC hopes to bring the business practices of all registrars into closer alignment.

Definition of Certification

Quality systems certification has a different meaning to customers, suppliers and registrars within and outside the European Union. The EAC, realizing that mutual recognition of accreditation and quality systems certification requires that a certificate have similar meaning and value to all parties affected by it, has tried to harmonize these differences by defining the meaning of a quality systems certificate.

The EAC interprets EN 45012 (ISO/IEC Guide 62) Clause 1.3.3, Certification/Registration Document, as follows:

The certification should give the market confidence that the supplier is capable of systematically meeting agreed requirements for any product or service supplied within the field specified on the certificate, the 'scope of the supplier.'

This interpretation affirms that a supplier should give the market confidence that a product or service will meet the agreed-upon requirements. A customer who places an order with a certified supplier should expect consistency.

While this does not imply that the product or service meets specific technical requirements, both supplier and customer must understand that quality system certification and supplier conformance to agreed-upon customer requirements go hand in hand. Demonstrated product conformity to a technical standard is a separate issue.

Assessor's Technical Competence

The most effective way to ensure and promote market confidence in a certified supplier and to increase industry belief in the value of the certificate is for the certifying registrar to employ technically competent assessors.

The EAC interpretation of EN 45012 (ISO/IEC Guide 62) Clause 2.2, Certification/Registration Body Personnel, clarifies what is meant by competency. The EAC guidelines state:

> *The assessment team needs a background which ensures that they understand the requirements relating to the system they are auditing. Each assessment team should have a general understanding and background in each technological and industrial sector in which it operates. It should be able to determine whether or not a particular quality system adequately covers the requirements of the standard in the area that it covered.*

An assessor's technical competence should be demonstrated by an understanding of how the product is used, a general knowledge of the product's critical characteristics and the process by which the product is manufactured and tested and familiarity with the appropriate product standards.

This competence can be demonstrated by a recognized industry certification, prior work experience or technical society participation. The ability of a quality systems registrar to employ assessors with the necessary audit skills, technical depth and product use knowledge ensures marketplace confidence in a certified supplier.

Consultancy

Consultancy and conflict of interest is an area of extreme importance to registrars, suppliers and customers both in Europe and the United States. EAC guidelines state that if a registration body is owned by a person or holding company that also engages in consultancy, then that person or company is regarded as a consultant and the registration body must have an appropriate structure to prevent that entity from influencing certification.

In addition, the EAC guidelines prevent registration and consulting services from being marketed together to prevent even the perception of conflict of interest. These guidelines clarify that the registrar and its representatives must in no way imply that any business advantage is gained by using a registrar and consultant from the same organization.

Peer Review

The EAC's harmonized interpretation for applying the EN 45012 standard (ISO/IEC Guide 62) uses a peer review system to ensure that signatories of the EAC are complying with these guidelines. Peer review ensures that the certificates issued by an accreditation board and accredited registrar are "valid" within the EAC community. "Valid" may be loosely defined as a certificate that provides the necessary marketplace assurance.

Recognition of Registration Certificates

The international acceptance of registration certificates is a crucial issue. The ultimate goal is to develop a system that will allow a single ISO 9000 registration certificate to be recognized within an industry and in the rest of the world.

As mentioned earlier, in the private sector, recognition of the ISO 9000 certificate by a company's customers is the primary determinant of a certificate's acceptability. The accreditation status of the registrar and how this status is viewed by the marketplace are another matter.

At the member state level in the European Union, a registration obtained in one EU member state for a regulated product may not necessarily be accepted in other EU states on a bilateral basis. Other member states in the European Union can voluntarily choose to recognize the registration certificate.

Two organizations working on these issues in Europe are the International Certification Network (IQNET) and the European Committee for Quality System Assessment and Certification (EQS).

The International Certification Network (IQNet)

IQNET was formed in 1990 by eight ISO 9000 registration bodies in Europe to promote cooperation among individual members based on bilateral sets of agreements. The intention is to further expand the IQNet with the aid of multilateral contracts. The eight original members of the organization were AFAQ (France), AIB-Vinçotte (Belgium), BSI (Great Britain), DQS (Germany), DS (Denmark), N.V. KEMA (The Netherlands), SIS (Sweden) and SQS (Switzerland). Membership as of March 2002 has increased to a total of 32 international members.

The main tasks of IQNet include the following:

- Cooperate to recognize the certificates issued by other members on the basis of existing contracts and to promote the recognition of certificates.

- Coordinate the certification of border-crossing groups of companies/organizations and the joint conduct of the said certificates in a competent and efficient way.

- Issue several certificates at the same time on the basis of joint certification audits.

European Committee for Quality System Assessment and Certification (EQS)

EQS was formed to achieve the following primary goals:

- Harmonization of rules for quality system assessment and certification
- Overall recognition of quality system certificates
- Efforts to permit mutual recognition of the certificates of quality system certification bodies.

The group's ultimate aim is to avoid multiple assessment and certification of an organization's quality system and to develop confidence in quality system assessment and certification carried out by competent bodies.

The ongoing work of CASCO, IAF, IQNET and EQS will eventually lead to a larger if not complete network of mutual recognition agreements.

ISO's Committee on Conformity Assessment (CASCO)

The work of recognition of registration certificates on an international level has been progressing largely through the efforts of ISO's Committee on Conformity Assessment (CASCO) and the International Accreditation Forum (IAF).

The goals of CASCO are the following:

- Study the means of assessing the conformity of products, processes, services and quality systems to appropriate standards or other technical specifications.
- Prepare international guides relating to the testing, inspection and certification of products, processes and services and to the assessment of quality systems, testing laboratories, inspection bodies and certification bodies, including their operation and acceptance.
- Promote mutual recognition and acceptance of national and regional conformity assessment systems.
- Promote the appropriate use of international standards for testing, inspection, certification, quality systems and related purposes.

International Accreditation Forum (IAF)

The IAF was formed in January 1993 when 10 representatives of various international standards bodies and accreditation bodies met to begin a series of discussions on how international accreditation bodies could better cooperate with one another in the effort to establish a complete network of mutual recognition agreements. The goal is a system whereby accreditations are recognized throughout the world.

At an April 30-May 1, 1994, meeting, IAF considered a master list of 22 topics that members felt should be addressed and whittled it down to the following nine primary areas of focus:

1. Requirements of complete re-evaluation of a supplier's quality system, separate and distinct from surveillance

2. Sphere of influence for accreditation bodies

3. Structure of registrars, including role and makeup on the independent advisory board

4. Use of satellite offices of an accredited registrar and the conditions for issuing registration certificates bearing the registration mark

5. Mutual recognition of accreditation

6. Minimum level of registration activity required before accreditation is granted

7. Misleading ISO 9000 advertising

8. Public announcement of applications for accreditation

9. Allowing registrars to offer suppliers a choice of accreditation body marks and use of a quality mark on packaging.

IAF developed a plan to form a Multilateral Recognition Agreement group among member accreditation bodies. On January 22, 1998, an IAF multilateral recognition agreement (MLA) was signed by the following QMS accreditation bodies:

JAS-ANZ (Australia and New Zealand)

SCC (Canada)

CNACR (China)

DANAK (Denmark)

DAR (Germany)

SINCERT (Italy)

JAB (Japan)

RvA (Netherlands)

ENAC (Spain)

SWEDAC (Sweden)

FINAS (Finland)

SAS (Switzerland)

UKAS (United Kingdom)

ANSI-RAB (United States).

Membership as of March 2002 has increased to a total of 57 including accreditation body members, associate members, regional group members and liason group members.

The European Organization for Conformity Assessment (EOTC)

The European Organization for Conformity Assessment (EOTC), proposed by the European Union for the purpose of dealing with conformity assessment issues, was created in April 1990. Its role is to promote mutual recognition of test results, certification procedures and quality system assessments and registrations in nonregulated product areas throughout the European Union and EFTA. Its primary goal is to encourage equivalency of certificates and to avoid the duplication caused by multiple certifications.

The EOTC is also responsible for providing technical assistance to the EU Commission in the implementation of some EU legislation, especially in the preparation of Mutual Recognition Agreements with non-EU countries.

EOTC Agreement Groups

EOTC aims to recognize the technical competence of the certification bodies (i.e., registrars and laboratories) in certain industry agreement groups. The purpose of an agreement group is to promote mutual recognition of test certificates by certification bodies throughout the European Union, EFTA, and third-world countries. These agreement groups ensure mutual recognition of test reports and certificates by the certification bodies that participate in the agreement group. The EOTC vision is to contribute towards a single market within the European Union and towards the elimination of technical barriers to trade.

As of March 2002, the EOTC has recognized eight agreement groups. The industry sectors covered by these groups vary from fire and security to electromagnetic and radio frequency.

The EOTC's agreement groups bring value to the marketplace and benefit both the customers and agreement group participants by helping establish shared confidence in the test procedures and product and quality system evaluation procedures.

EOTC's Status

The EOTC previously was under the auspices of the European Commission; however, the EOTC signed an agreement with its 22 founding members in December 1992 to establish its independence as a private association. The EOTC is run by a General Assembly with a Board of Administrators responsible for developing policy and strategic planning.

EOTC Recognized Agreement Groups

European Fire and Security Group (EFSG)

International Instrumentation Evaluation Group (IIEAG)

Short-Circuit Testing Liaison Agreement Group (STLA)

Low Voltage Agreement Group (LOVAG)

European Welding Foundation (EWF)

Recreation Marine Agreement Group (RMAG)

Agreement Group for Testing of Quality Schemes in the Aluminum Finishing Industry (QUALISURFAL)

Agreement Group for Electromagnetic Compatibility and Radio Frequency Testing and Certification (EMCRAFT) (formerly EMCIT/EMCEL)

One of the EOTC's sectoral committees, the European Committee for Information Technology Testing and Certification (ECITC) — which oversees the agreement groups for information technology — is primarily responsible for this activity.

Auditor Certification Programs

Companies considering registration to ISO 9000 should also know how auditors are qualified and what criteria are used. The international guideline, ISO 19011, *Guidelines on Quality and Environmental Management Systems Auditing*, replaced ISO 10011.

While ISO 19011 guidelines cover all aspects of the conduct and management of an audit and the training of auditors, perhaps their most important requirement is that only certified lead assessors can lead the audit team and perform the assessment of your company's quality systems. (ISO 19011 is discussed in more detail in Chapter 6.)

The Institute for Quality Assurance

The Institute for Quality Assurance[1] (IQA) in the United Kingdom was the first organization to govern and control the ISO 9000 auditor training and certification process. The program, known as the International Register of Certificated Auditors (IRCA), seeks to recognize the integrity and competence of quality systems auditors as measured against the criteria found in international standards.

Under the IRCA IQA scheme, auditor certification is reviewed every three years, with renewal dependent upon the ability of the registered auditor to meet criteria for assessment experience required at the time of the renewal.

Recognition Arrangements for the Assessment and Certification of Quality Systems in the Information Technology Sector (ITQS)

ITQS is one of the original agreement groups that EOTC had formally approved and a good example of how an agreement group contributes to the harmonization process. Agreement groups are set up along industry lines and allow companies to rely on just one test or assessment that will be accepted throughout Europe.

The assessments carried out by the certification bodies (registrars) cooperating in ITQS are performed in a harmonized way, using common standards, techniques and guidance material. ITQS membership is open to any organization in the world, provided the organization accepts and applies ITQS regulations, including an auditor guide.

The ITQS auditor guide is "unique because instead of being a guidance document for the certification applicant, it is mainly designed to be used by the certification bodies," according to Philippe Caussin of AIB-Vinçotte International, which operates the ITQS secretariat.

The auditor guide "tells the auditors what to look for when auditing an information technology firm, covers software and hardware development, and production and service activities," said Caussin. The purpose of an auditing guide is to ensure that information technology firms certified by an ITQS member are assessed on an equivalent basis. Quality managers at some US information technology firms have cited the lack of experienced information technology auditors as one of the reasons the United States does not, as yet, have a strong formalized system for information technology quality assurance.

Criteria for information technology auditors under the ITQS system include a professional education or training, or practical experience in information technology, as well as specific training in the understanding of quality control applicable to information technology. "ITQS regulations also require that auditors be evaluated on a regular basis by an evaluation panel, possibly from a professional society," according to Caussin.

Registrar Accreditation Board

In the United States, the Registrar Accreditation Board[2] (RAB) has its own program for certification of quality management systems auditors. In addition, RAB operates a program for the approval of organizations that train ISO 9000 series auditors.

This program is the final piece of a complete ISO 9000 series registration and accreditation scheme that includes the accreditation of registrars, certification of auditors, and the recognition of auditor training courses.

Certification under RAB's Certification Program for Auditors of Quality Management Systems (QMS) requires training in an approved course. Two types of courses are offered to meet RAB training requirements for RAB auditor certification:

1. A 36-hour Lead Auditor Training Course that includes ANSI/ASQ Q9000 (ISO 9000) series training, quality system audit training, and an examination that covers this information.

2. A 16-hour Lead Auditor Training Course for ASQ Certified Quality Auditors that includes ANSI/ASQ Q9000 (ISO 9000) series training and an examination.

The Certified Quality Auditor (CQA) credential does not exempt the candidate from the other experience required by RAB, including audit experience. A CQA credential, together with a 16-hour course given by the RAB-approved training organizations, will exempt the candidate from the standard 36-hour course.

The CQA program will not be affected by RAB's quality system auditor certification program. RAB and ASQ are separate organizations with separate goals for auditor certification.

In addition to the certification program for auditors of QMSs who conduct second- and third-party audits, the ANSI-RAB program introduced a QMS internal auditor training course accreditation program on December 18, 1998. On May 24, 1999, RAB announced a QMS internal auditor certification program for auditors who will audit only their own sites.

Applicants for internal auditor certification are asked to provide verifiable evidence of:

- Education
- QMS auditor training course
- Work experience in quality assurance activities
- Personal character attributes
- Demonstrated QMS internal audit experience.

American Society for Quality

The American Society for Quality (ASQ) has an auditor certification program that offers a CQA credential as described above. This certification credential signifies that an applicant has education and/or work experience in a specified field and demonstrates knowledge through the successful completion of a written examination.

Mutual Recognition of Auditor Certification

In September 1993, 16 nations met in Singapore to develop a plan to create a single, internationally accepted set of requirements for ISO 9000 series auditor certification and related course accreditation.

This process was further advanced in July 1995 when the International Auditor and Training Certification Association (IATCA) was created. IATCA is composed of 33 auditor certification and course accreditation organizations from 17 regions or countries. In addition to RAB representing the United States, organizations from the following regions or countries are involved with the IATCA program:

- Australia/New Zealand
- Brazil
- Canada
- China
- Chinese Taipei
- France
- India
- Italy
- Japan
- Korea
- Malaysia
- Philippines
- Singapore
- South Africa
- Thailand
- United Kingdom.

IATCA has developed a set of criteria governing auditor certifications and auditor training course approvals. These criteria are designed to eliminate the need for multiple certifications of auditors and multiple approvals of auditor training courses.

The key to recognition of an auditor certification organization is the IATCA peer evaluation process. Five participating organizations have successfully completed peer evaluations and have signed an IATCA MLA for QMS auditor certification bodies. Additional signatories will be added to the MLA as organizations qualify through peer evaluations. The first five organizations are:

- Quality Society of Australasia (QSA) representing Australia and New Zealand
- China National Registration Board for Auditors (CRBA) of China
- IQA International Register of Certificated Auditors (IRCA) of the United Kingdom
- Registrar Accreditation Board (RAB) of the United States
- Japanese Registration of Certified Auditors (JRCA) of Japan.

Six participating organizations have signed an IATCA MLA for QMS auditor training course approval bodies. Additional signatories will be added to the MLA as organizations qualify through peer evaluations. These six organizations are:

- Joint Accreditation System of Australia and New Zealand (JAS-ANZ)
- China National Registration Board for Auditors (CRBA)
- Japan Accreditation Board (JAB)
- IQA International Register of Certificated Auditors (IRCA) of the United Kingdom
- ANSI-RAB National Accreditation Program (NAP) of the United States
- Quality Society of Australasia (QSA).

The current RAB auditor certification program will remain in place and, although current RAB certified auditors may choose to transfer to the RAB IATCA program, it will not be required. To facilitate the transfer at the early stages, IATCA set up a limited window of opportunity, until February 28, 2002, in which an auditor who was certified on or before March 1, 1999, could have made the transition to the new IATCA grade by meeting certain transfer criteria. Now all applicants for IATCA certification, including auditors currently certified by RAB, must meet the full IATCA program requirements rather than the simplified transitional requirements.

In addition to international acceptance of an auditor's certification to the RAB

IATCA program, an auditor training course provider's accreditation program will also enjoy international acceptance. A course provider will now need to earn and maintain only a single accreditation for its auditor training course.

Under the IATCA program, course providers may choose to offer either a 36-hour or a 40-hour course. If a 36-hour course is taught, all students must have successfully demonstrated prerequisite knowledge of the ISO 9000 series of standards.

ISO 14001 for Environmental Management Systems

ISO 14001 was published as an international standard in September 1996. (See Chapter 25.) ANSI-RAB has published an ISO 14001 national accreditation program for registrars, auditors and course providers. The program includes directions for registrars on the circumstances under which companies may combine their quality and environmental management systems.

Registrars are offering combined registration audits to ISO 9000 and ISO 14000.

QS-9000 Quality System Requirements

The QS-9000 Quality System Requirements were developed by the Chrysler, Ford and General Motors Supplier Quality Requirements Task Force. QS-9000, first released in August 1994 and most recently in its third edition in October 1999, incorporates the requirements of ISO 9001 plus sector-specific requirements and customer-specific requirements. (Refer to Chapter 13.) The requirements were developed to standardize the quality systems requirements, documentation, and assessment tools for suppliers to the automotive manufacturers and certain truck manufacturers.

Agreements have been reached with a number of accreditation bodies (including the RAB) and their accredited third-party registrars to conduct QS-9000 registrations. QS-9000 auditors, in addition to being qualified ISO 9000 auditors, are required to take classes and exams conducted by Plexus Training Corporation through the Automotive Industry Action Group (AIAG). QS-9000 auditors are required to recertify every three years.

As of March 2002, the following is a summary of activity of the QS-9000 program:

- 22 national accreditation programs have been approved to participate.
- 174 registrars have been qualified to issue certificates.
- Over 3,000 third-party auditors have been qualified to perform audits.
- Over 22,500 automotive suppliers have been certified.

ISO/TS 16949

ISO/TS 16949 is an automotive sector initiative started in 1996 to achieve the vision of a single global automotive registration process. The ISO/TS 16949 technical specification requirements document, coupled with the customer-specific requirements, satisfies the following automotive requirements documents: QS-9000, EAQF (French), VDA 6.1 (German) and AVSQ (Italian).

In addition to the common technical requirements document, there are the following common key elements: registration rules, contract language for certification bodies and a third-party auditor qualification process which includes an examination. In addition, there is a common global oversight process responsible for the administration of the overall ISO/TS 16949 requirements and registration process.

A second edition of ISO/TS 16949 to align the document with ISO 9001:2000 was published in March 2002.

The sponsoring group and recognizing body of ISO/TS 16949 is the International Automotive Task Force (IATF). This body currently has the following members: BMW, DaimlerChrysler, Fiat, Ford, General Motors, PSA Peugeot-Citroen, Renault SA and Volkswagen, and the trade associations AIAG (USA), ANFIA (Italy), FIEV (France), SMMT (UK) and VDA (Germany). (See Chapter 13.)

As of March 2002, the following is a summary of activity of the ISO/TS 16949 program:

- 45 registrars have been qualified to issue certificates
- Over 300 third-party auditors have been qualified to perform audits
- Over 1,750 automotive suppliers have been certified.

Interpretations of ISO 9000 and QS-9000

ISO 9001 Interpretations

ISO Technical Committee 176 (TC 176) agreed to take on the role of interpreting the standards following concerns that the ISO 9000 standards were not being implemented uniformly throughout the world. These interpretations will be coordinated and communicated at an international level.

The interpretation process is still being refined within ISO TC 176. Some questions such as the roles of the individual member delegations and the method of distribution of the interpretations need to be resolved.

In North America, a program for publishing interpretations of the ISO 9001 standard has been developed and implemented by the Canadian Technical Committee on Quality Management. Under this program, the request for interpretations is reviewed and a proposed reply is prepared by the Interpretation Task Force. The proposed reply is then reviewed and voted on by the technical committee. If the proposed reply is approved, then it becomes a formal Canadian position. The interpretation is then published and ISO is notified of the interpretations.

QS-9000 Sanctioned Interpretations

The automotive industry has developed and implemented a program for publishing sanctioned interpretations of the QS-9000 requirements. The interpretations are developed by the International Automotive Sector Group (IASG). The consists of representatives from:

- Recognized ISO 9000 accreditation bodies
- QS-9000 qualified registrars
- DaimlerChrysler, Ford and General Motors Supplier Quality Requirements Task Force
- Tier 1 Automotive Suppliers.

Representatives from DaimlerChrysler, Ford and GM must individually agree with interpretations before "agreed" status is achieved following a consensus of all members of the IASG. The interpretations are then incorporated into the "IASG QS-9000 Sanctioned Interpretations" and are considered binding.

Conclusion

Registrar accreditation and auditor certification issues have been addressed and refined, and considerable progress has been made in recent years concerning international acceptance. As the registrar accreditation and auditor certification programs receive international acceptance, remaining unsettled questions will be addressed by US, European and international groups.

Endnotes

1. For more information on the IQA scheme, write to: The Scheme Manager/The Registration Board for Assessors, PO Box 25120, 12 Grosvenor Crescent, London, SW1X 7ZL, England; tel: 011-44-20-7245-6833; fax: 011-44-20-7245-6755.

2. For more information regarding the RAB registration program, contact the Registrar Accreditation Board, PO Box 3005, Milwaukee, WI 53201-3005; tel: 414-272-3937; fax: 414-765-8661.

Editor's Note: Thanks to Andrew J. Bergman, who provided assistance in the prepara-

tion of this article. Mr. Bergman was vice president of the Houston-based management consulting firm Quality Specialists, Inc. QSI is an authorized distributor of European standards and assists companies with compliance. See QSI listing in Appendix C for contact information.

Figure 7-1
Accreditation Pyramid

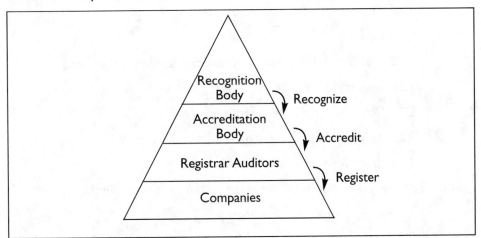

ANNEX I

EN 45012, *General Requirements for Bodies Operating Certification/Registration of Quality Systems (ISO/IEC Guide 62)*

Section 1: General

1.1 Scope

1.2 References

1.3 Definitions

Section 2: Requirements for certification/registration bodies

2.1 Certification/registration body

2.1.1 General provision

2.1.2 Organization

2.1.3 Subcontracting

2.1.4 Quality system

2.1.5 Conditions for granting, maintaining, extending, reducing, suspending and withdrawing certification/registration

2.1.6 Internal audits and management reviews

2.1.7 Documentation

2.1.8 Records

2.1.9 Confidentiality

2.2 Certification/registration body personnel

2.2.1 General

2.2.2 Qualification criteria for auditors and technical experts

2.2.3 Selection procedure

2.2.4 Contracting of assessment personnel

2.2.5 Assessment personnel records

2.2.6 Procedures for audit teams

2.3 Changes in the certification/registration requirements

2.4 Appeals, complaints and disputes

Section 3 Requirements for certification/registration

3.1 Application for certification/registration

3.1.1 Information on the procedure

3.1.2 The application

3.2 Preparation for assessment

3.3 Assessment

3.4 Assessment report

3.5 Decision on certification/registration

3.6 Surveillance and reassessment procedures

3.7 Use of certificates and logos

3.8 Access to records of compliants to suppliers

ISO 9000 Registration Growth and Experiences Around the World

8

This chapter contains two articles related to the growth of certifications to ISO 9000. The first one, by Larry Bauder, describes the worldwide trends in certification to the standard by examining data provided by the International Organization for Standardization, *Quality Systems Update* and the *ISO 9000 Survey '99*. Bauder also discusses what can be learned from the experiences of those implementing the standard, including:

- Average cost of implementation
- Average time from start to finish of implementation
- Cost-to-savings ratios
- Benefits of registration
- Whether or not to use outside services
- Implementation strategies.

The second article, by Bohdan Dyczkowsky, specifically discusses registration trends in Canada, focusing on the registration boom in the early 1990s. Dyczkowsky uses the data from this earlier time period as the basis for his predictions on the acceptance and use of ISO 9001:2000.

Worldwide ISO 9000:2000 Trends

By Larry Bauder

There has been a phenomenal growth in ISO 9000 registrations around the world since the first publication of the ISO 9000 standard in 1987. Fortunately, we have been able to learn much about the experiences of those implementing the standard from user surveys.

Introduction

ISO 9000 standards are developed to meet market needs. ISO committees are not in the business of data collection or reporting. A completely accurate assessment of worldwide ISO 9000 registration activity does not exist. There are several companies that collect data from various sources to generate listings of registered companies and registrars, but all reporting of registration activity is voluntary. Every data source used in this chapter has rather large differences in counts in identical categories. There are a number of reasons for this.

- Companies or their registrars will report their registration to one or more data collectors at different times in different ways. In some instances a single company with multiple facilities or certificates will be counted as a single entity, while in other cases each certificate will be individually counted. On occasion a company may be counted twice in a report due to a name or address change. In other databases the company may not be reported at all.

- A company may have registrations for ISO 9002 and ISO 9003. One service may count this as a single while another might count the company twice.

- A large number of registrars are accredited by multiple agencies. A single customer may receive certificates through a registrar accredited, for example, through Canada (SCC), the United States (ANSI/RAB) and the Netherlands (RvA).

- Some companies may demonstrate conformity to ISO 9000 requirements without a formal certificate from any third-party registrar. These companies would not necessarily show up in any listing.

Information in this chapter is compiled from two major sources.

In late 2001, QSU Publishing Company, which produces the oldest and best-known directory in North America, the *ISO 9000 Registered Company Directory North America*, established what may be the first policy on how certificates will be counted. The policy and current certificate counts are available at www.qsuonline.com.

For worldwide information and comparisons with North America and the United States, *The ISO Survey* of ISO 9000 and ISO 14000 certificates is used. This is a free 20-page report available from the International Organization for Standardization (ISO) in Geneva, Switzerland. It is also available as a PDF file online at http://www.iso.ch.

Discussion of trends and issues in North America is based on QSU Publishing Company's *ISO 9000 Survey '99,* which was prepared by *Quality Systems Update* and Plexus Corporation. This is a 300-page report from a survey of quality managers responsible for about 11 percent of all registered sites in Canada and the United States at the time.

Quotes included in this chapter are from respondents' comments in the survey, provided without attribution.

As an example of the challenges faced in collecting and using these data, consider that both of these sources are reporting on activities that closed December 1999. According to ISO, at that time there were 43,610 registrations in the United States and Canada, while according to *Quality Systems Update* there were about 35,000 registered sites. In 2000, ISO depended on *Quality Systems Update* and another provider for the North American numbers used in the Tenth Cycle report. In July 2001, the web site for *Quality Systems Update* (www.qsuonline.com) placed the North American total at 49,529, based on data collected by the *ISO 9000 Registered Company Directory North America.*

Registration Trends Around the World

The number of ISO 9000 registered companies has blossomed in the last decade according to ISO in Geneva. The number of ISO 9000 certificate holders worldwide has grown from 27,816 in January of 1993 to 408,631 in December of 2000 (Table 8-1 and Figure 8-1). During that same period the number of countries

Table 8-1

Worldwide ISO 9000 Statistics

World Results	Sept. '93	June '94	Dec. '95	Dec. '96	Dec. '97	Dec. '98	Dec. '99	Dec. '00
World Total	46,571	70,364	127,349	162,701	223,299	271,847	343,643	408,631
World Growth	18,755	23,793	32,232	35,352	60,698	48,548	71,796	64,988
Nations	60	75	96	113	126	141	150	158

Figure 8-1

World Total ISO 9000 Registrations

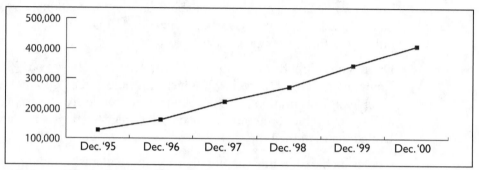

where certificate holders are based rose from 48 to 158. According to the same report, the number of registered companies in North America grew from 1,201 at the beginning of 1993 to 48,296 at the beginning of 2001.

It is interesting to note the regions and countries that saw the greatest growth in numbers of new certificates during 1999 and 2000 (Figure 8-2). On a regional basis Asia/Pacific and Europe had significantly more new registrations issued than did North America in 1999. In 2000, the rate of growth in Europe grew,

Figure 8-2

1999 — New Registrations Worldwide by Region

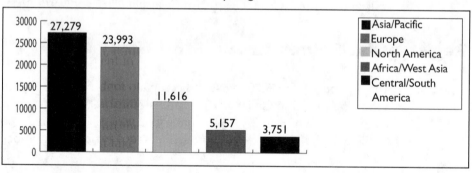

2000 — New Registrations Worldwide by Region

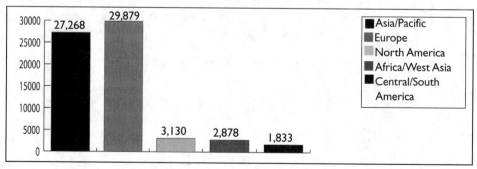

User Quotes
from the *ISO 9000 Survey '99*

As a prerequisite to export our products to the EU and to an increasing number of other countries that require CE certified products...The registration to the ISO 9000 is a requirement by the competent bodies that certify our equipment.

We originally embarked upon ISO 9000 registration as a marketing tool.

I am sure that there are many other companies like us that were required to obtain registration only because of pressure from their major customer.

while Asia/Pacific growth was essentially flat and growth for the rest of the world dropped significantly.

As can be seen in Figure 8-3, in 1999 the United States closely followed Australia and led China when compared on a country basis. In 2000 only China and Japan stayed in the top five. One explanation of this is that many organizations not previously registered delayed registration in anticipation of the release of ISO

Figure 8-3

1999 — Most New Certificates by Country

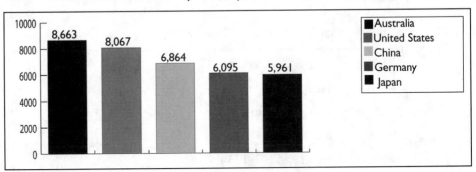

2000 — Most New Certificates by Country

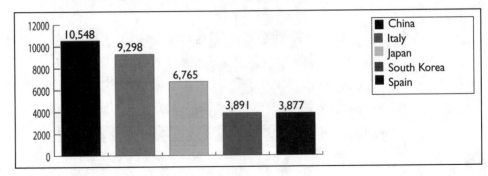

9000:2000. This is supported by the fact that in the first six months of 2001 the new registrations in North America exceeded the total for the previous year.

Apart from the impact of the release of ISO 9000:2000, these reports of recent registration activity are significant to all organizations. It is very clear from several surveys that the two main factors influencing the decision to achieve registration around the world are "Customer Requirements" and "Competitive Advantage."

Figures 8-4 and 8-5 show the relative number of total registrations in the 12 largest countries and by worldwide region. The United Kingdom has always had the highest number of registrations because they started first. (The original ISO 9000 standard was structured on British Standard BS 5750.) In 1993 the United Kingdom had 18,577 registered organizations out of 27,816 in the world.

It is interesting to note that in 1995 nearly 90 percent of the ISO 9000 registrations issued were in Europe. The following year nearly a third of the registrations worldwide were held in Asia/Pacific. It was in 1997 that North America reached 10 percent of the worldwide total. In 1999 the percentage reached 13 percent. With a drop in new registrations in the United States and Canada, the percentage slipped to 12 percent in 2000.

One final set of statistics to review at the worldwide level is the number of certificates withdrawn and reported to the ISO in 2000.

Figure 8-4

2000 — Total Certificates by Country

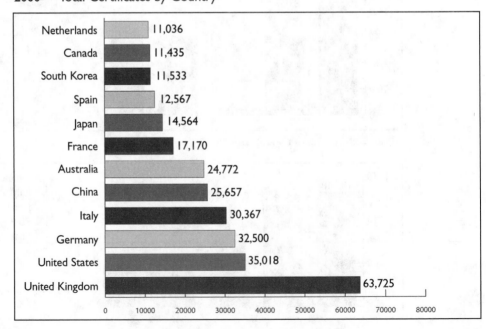

Figure 8-5

2000 — Total Certificates by Region

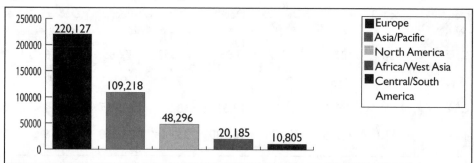

- Nearly 15,000 certificates were withdrawn (a greater than 50 percent increase in withdrawals over 1999), and of that, about 10,500 were withdrawn for unstated or unknown reasons. The United States led with more than 2,200. France and China follow with more than 1,000 apiece, followed by Canada and South Africa with around 800 each.

- Over 2,000 organizations failed their recertification audits and had their certificates withdrawn (more than three times the 1999 count). Spain led in failed recertifications with more than 500, followed closely by Japan and the United Kingdom, with more than 400 each.

- Abandonment of registration by 900 organizations was attributed to poor return on investment or poor business advantage.

- Nearly 1,400 organizations "ceased activities."

User Quotes

from the *ISO 9000 Survey '99*

Hasn't fulfilled its promise. Little or no tangible benefits. Very bureaucratic. Too black and white. Ancient approach — doesn't fit today's business environment.

We are currently reviewing the costs and benefits of maintaining ISO especially with the upcoming increase in expectations set by the year 2000 revision. We desire to continue maintaining our quality system but are reviewing the need to be registered.

Trends in North America

According to the the *ISO 9000 Registered Company Directory*, the number of certificates in North America grew from 1,201 at the beginning of 1993 to 48,296 at the end of 2000.

Table 8-2

ISO 9000 Registrations in North America

Nations	Sept. '93	June '94	Dec. '95	Dec. '96	Dec. '97	Dec. '98	Dec. '99	Dec. '00	Dec. '01
Canada	530	870	1,397	3,955	5,852	7,585	10,556	11,435	11,559
Mexico	24	85	215	412	711	978	1,556	1,843	2,129
USA	2,059	3,960	8,762	12,613	18,581	24,987	33,054	35,018	36,559
Total	2,613	4,915	10,374	16,980	25,144	33,550	45,166	48,296	50,247

While worldwide growth appears to be steadily growing, the rate of growth in the United States experienced a slowdown during the last six months of 2001 as seen in Figure 8-6.

To evaluate trends in North America and the United States, *Quality Systems Update* polled ISO certificate holders in 1993, 1996 and 1999. For the 1999 poll they received replies representing 11percent of the more than 33,000 ISO 9000 certificate holders in North America. The survey was designed to discover costs and savings attributable to ISO 9000 registration, return on investment and why some companies find ISO 9000 registration a rewarding investment and others find it a losing proposition. The 1999 poll data was collected via the internet and contains responses to about 140 questions.

Figure 8-6

United States, Canada and Mexico: Three Years of Growth

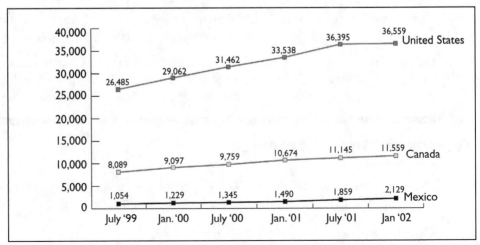

Company Size and Registrations

In 1993, large companies (>$200M) were the highest percentage of certificate holders at 39 percent. In 1996, mid-size companies (<$25-200M>) were the largest percentage of holders at 45 percent. By 1999 more than half (57 percent) of the certificate holders in the United States had less than $25 million in sales.

Only 46 percent of the registered companies are 100 percent registered, meaning that most companies have departments or divisions that are not registered. Eighteen percent of the companies have no intention of becoming fully registered.

Figure 8-7

Company Types Responding to the Survey

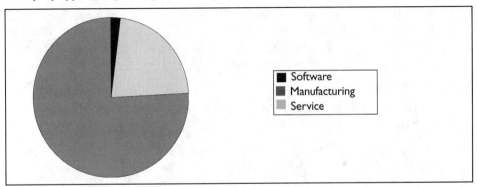

■ Software
■ Manufacturing
■ Service

Registration Experiences

Barriers to Registration

The greatest barriers to maintaining registration are and have been:

- Documentation development and procedure creation
- Lack of management support.

Documentation development is reported to be the largest barrier to registration. Procedure creation, which is an integral part of documentation, is apparently dropping in difficulty according to respondents.

Lack of management commitment is a problem that has grown from less than 10 percent in 1993 to around 18 percent in 1999. At the same time, employee resistance is also increasing from around 8 percent to 14 percent.

User Quotes
from the *ISO 9000 Survey '99*

Over the years ISO has received a 'bad rap' for requiring reams and reams of paper work. It has been my experience that any bureaucracy added to our system was the result of our doing — not the requirement of ISO.

I found that after certification was attained, senior management expected the benefits would be recognized immediately. There were no benefits for the first two years of certification. After realization that the system was not designed effectively for all employees to understand and use, we redesigned the system. Immediately after the new and improved system was implemented, the benefits were amazing.

Good system if used properly. My experience is that in most cases top management is not involved to the point where they understand the system and how it works. The details are left to the lower level managers. This causes a rift when owners or top executives try to change the systems without understanding how it must change and why. They are in some ways undermining the very system they paid to have installed.

Must have total management commitment throughout the organization not just top or bottom.

A company that finds ISO 9000 as a hindrance to operations does not have the management commitment to succeed.

The present system in place is a very effective well-written system that is simply not being used. The culture here is still one that is based on the good old boy network and the suggestions of those people who should be considered experts are never asked for.

Yes, the external benefits such as customer recognition begin to show up relatively early in the process, but the internal cost of employee suspicion, fear and cynicism are heavy for the first 24-30 months. A lot of what finally filters out over the learning curve (minimum time frame) is simply interpersonal trust, respect and a very large capacity for perserverence at the upper management level.

Benefits of Registration

Customer demand and operational benefits are the most compelling reasons given for maintaining registration. Slightly less important is concern about falling behind the competition. Interestingly, when asked about external and internal benefits of registration the answers are slightly different.

The most significant external benefit companies report as a result of registration

User Quotes
from the *ISO 9000 Survey '99*

Even though it was a rough go at the beginning, we strongly believe that the exercise of implementation and registration has benefited our company as a whole. It forced us to evaluate what we do, how we do it and why we do it that way, as well as to ask the question of there being a better way to do it now and in the future. There was no element of our company that did not undergo this examination and we are a stronger and better company for it.

Financial benefits from ISO 9000 are in a lot of cases intangible and cannot be broken out into specific buckets.

Since our company already had a quality system in place the ISO registration did not significantly add value to what we had.

Nothing we did or do now is for the sole benefit of maintaining the ISO quality system. Only the external audit stuff is extra. The quality training, documentation, etc., needs to be done regardless of how your quality system is modeled.

is higher perceived quality of products and services. This is closely followed by an improvement in competitive advantage. A significant number report reduction of customer quality audits as an advantage as well.

The most significant internal benefit of registration reported by companies is improved documentation. This is followed by a beneficial increase in quality awareness by employees. After these two benefits, and related to both, is enhanced intercompany communications. Improvements in operational efficiency/productivity are also reported as a significant benefit.

Figure 8-8

Defect Rate Change Attributed to ISO 9000

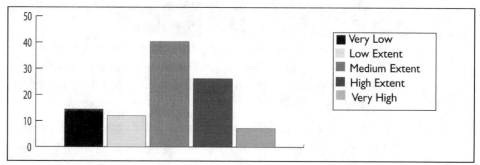

Figure 8-9

Productivity Change Attributed to ISO 9000

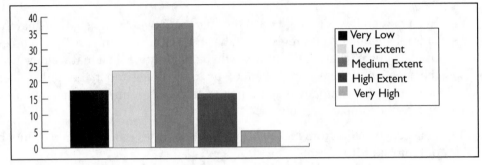

Figure 8-10

On-Time Delivery Change Attributed to ISO 9000

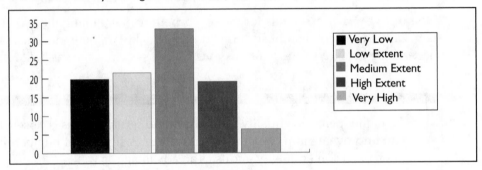

Figure 8-11

Customer Satisfaction Change Attributed to ISO 9000

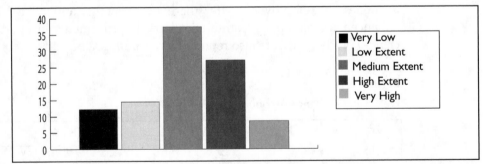

Companies see many other benefits that are attributable to ISO 9000 registration. Beneficial changes occurred since registration, but only a portion of the change is attributed to ISO 9000 registration, as shown in Figures 8-8 through 8-12.

While some certificate holders claim that ISO has helped in all areas, there are some certificate holders that report that the registration has had little positive

Figure 8-12
Market Share Change Attributed to ISO 9000

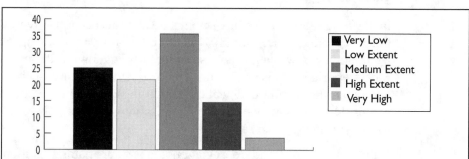

effect with respect to improvements. Improvements that are most attributable to ISO 9000 registration are:

- Defect rate
- Scrap/rework
- Customer satisfaction.

Two additional benefits to note are that 91 percent of the survey respondents report that registration gave them an additional marketing tool that they previously did not have. Fifty-one percent report that registration directly resulted in additional outside contracts.

User Quotes
from the *ISO 9000 Survey '99*

Registration for this particular company did not result in any savings, productivity, etc. This is an established company that has continually refined its processes over the years to ensure maximum productivity.

...our ISO quality management system was more useful to increase productivity and efficiency than it was a marketing tool. We are huge believers in this aspect of ISO! In general, ISO/QS has clearly made our organization a better one. It has been painful at times and not all of the employees are strongly in favor of it, but we are better for it.

Costs and Savings

Savings-to-Cost Ratio

In 1999 the reported average savings-to-cost ratio is a positive 1.2. This means that, on average, for every $100 spent in the program, a savings of $120 is realized. However, while all the respondents are averaged, there is a tremendous range reported in this area. The standard deviation for costs is twice the average while the standard deviation for savings is four times the average. This means that while an average can be informative it cannot be used as an indicator of typical costs and savings.

With such a large standard deviation it is not surprising that there was a broad range of experience reported. Some companies report substantial gains, while others report large losses. By correlating the reported costs and savings to company practices and culture responses the survey demonstrates that the way the requirements of ISO 9000 are implemented significantly affects the results.

User Quotes
from the *ISO 9000 Survey '99*

ISO 9000 is only going to give back what you put into it. You have to commit to it to make it work for you.

There is a tendency to not supply enough manpower to do a good job of utilizing its capabilities and when the paperwork is added to staff already overloaded there is a tendency to do only what you have to do.

I for one believe that for the first time in my career in quality that this department is conceived as something other than overhead...

We do not track 'costs' or 'benefits' as up to this time such tracking would have been done manually only.

You have to worry about too much paperwork and satisfying the registrars, retentiveness on verbiage in your procedures. Resources are used up and there's not enough focus on the real quality problems. I do like the corrective action part of the system.

Generally, the larger companies have a better savings-to-cost ratio and the ratio has improved for all companies between 1993 and 1999. Service companies report a 2.1 savings-to-cost ratio, manufacturing companies report a 1.4 average, while software companies report 0.7. When broken down by market sector the food, tobacco, textile and wood products report the best ratio, averaging 2.3.

This is followed by instruments and electronics at 1.8, manufacturing metals and machinery at 1.7 and petrochemicals and plastics at 1.1.

Expenses

Generally speaking, external costs for registration are less than half the internal costs. Because of their size, larger companies spend more for ISO registration than do smaller companies. External expenses are usually attributable to audit services, consultants and training. Some consultants, and most trainers and registrars, usually charge a daily rate. Company size has the greatest influence on outside expenses. A small company may receive a thorough audit by a single auditor in one day. A large company may require three auditors for a week to do an equally thorough audit. While the total dollars spent by larger companies are larger, they are more likely to have a better savings-to-cost ratio and a better return on investment.

As mentioned above, average reported costs and expenses, especially internal ones, have limited meaning. Averages listed in Table 8-3 have standard deviations $2,000 to $5,000 larger than the number shown for small- and medium-sized companies, and nearly twice the number shown for large companies.

Table 8-3

Average Costs by Company Size

Company Size	Small	Medium	Large
Average Internal Costs	$72,502	$106,890	$299,765
Average External Costs	$29,595	$42,014	$93,104

Reported costs vary for a number of reasons. Internal costs will vary depending on the accounting system and the ability of an organization to accurately track and report the benefit and cost of quality. Different industries have different costs in capital, maintenance, material, production and personnel expenses that dramatically affect quality costs. Software companies rarely have a positive savings-to-cost ratio.

It also appears that ISO 9000 registration costs may be affected by business cycles and by new releases of the ISO 9000 standard. Early adopters often have a harder time achieving a positive savings-to-cost ratio than later adopters. This could be attributed to the later adopters learning from the experiences of others.

How a quality system is implemented and maintained will affect costs and savings.

User Quotes
from the *ISO 9000 Survey '99*

It is extremely difficult to accurately calculate the savings realized from ISO implementation in a service organization.

I answered all the internal cost and money questions with zero dollars. Nothing we did or do now is for the sole benefit of maintaining the ISO quality system.

These efforts are costly due to registrar fees and internal resources for small companies in a very competitive market.

Quality systems that are designed to provide the customer with product that satisfies customer desires, expose and create opportunities to improve quality and/or reduce cost and provide evidence of satisfaction and improvement will cost less than the resulting savings. The next section covers factors contributing to successful implementation.

As might be expected, external costs are higher with companies using external consultants. Companies with lower sales volumes had higher consultant involvement.

One of the most significant general findings is that consultant involvement led to lower savings-to-cost ratios and return on investment when the consultant coordinated and led the ISO 9000 effort. The inverse is the case when trained employees are used. The use of trainers/consultants is discussed further in the section on the Use of Outside Services.

Figure 8-13

Savings-to-Cost Ratio Relative to Consultant Involvement

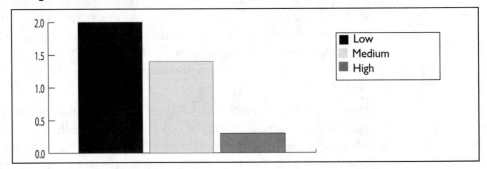

Successful Implementation Strategies

User Quotes
from the *ISO 9000 Survey '99*

> It has been our experience that ISO 9001 has made a tremendous difference in the overall way we do business. Our quality has improved along with our market share. ISO is the way to go.

Survey response identified four implementation and maintenance strategies shown to be significantly correlated with success in using ISO 9000 to improve business. They are:

I. Customizing implementation of ISO 9000 to specific company circumstances.

This is done by

- Working with, and learning from, suppliers, customers, and other registered companies
- Analysis of existing processes and performance and integrating new efforts with existing processes
- Using registration as a springboard to improve existing practices and introduce new ones.

2. Routine use of ISO 9000 documented practices in business.

It has been found that routine use of ISO 9000 practices is the strategy most commonly deployed in successful implementations. Routine use is manifested by:

- Managers valuing internal audits
- ISO documents used in daily work
- Documents regularly modified and updated
- Registration applied to broad areas of the company such as marketing, sales, finance, etc.
- ISO 9000 activities leading to the discovery of improvement opportunities and changing daily practices
- External audit preparations not made at the last minute
- The system not an unnecessary burden
- The system not regularly ignored.

3. Learning, meaning that ISO 9000 practices and findings are used to make improvements in training.

This is indicated by:

- Audit findings are incorporated into training.
- Management uses ISO 9000 data to guide solutions to business problems.
- Management uses ISO 9000 data to discover solutions to technical problems.
- ISO 9000 guidance is helping to prevent problems.

4. Going beyond the minimum requirements for registration.

The practices listed here appear to correspond to the greatest returns on investment. Going beyond minimum requirements is identified as:

- Using ISO 9000 efforts as a starting point for implementing better business practices (e.g., using ISO 9004:2000 to discover improvement opportunities or working toward Baldrige recognition)
- Using ISO 9000 as a catalyst for rethinking business practices
- Perceiving ISO 9000 as an opportunity to innovate.

Results from the survey clearly demonstrate that there is a statistically significant correlation between practices outlined in the above four areas and positive

User Quotes

from the *ISO 9000 Survey '99*

ISO 9000 has improved our quality systems through the three diamonds of the standard which are Management Reviews, Corrective Action and Internal Audits.

Although the ISO 9000 standard focus is to enhance an organization's quality system, unless the organization is committed to quality, being ISO 9000 certified adds little value.

The ISO requirements have provided a very good basis from which we have developed our quality systems. We have expanded way beyond ISO, but the standard was, and still is, the basis of our system.

Prior to our road to ISO our company did not have the discipline needed to improve quality. Since our journey down the ISO road began we have new and improved ways of running and managing our business. Achieving ISO 9001 validated our employees' commitment to quality. It was a lot of hard work but it was a rewarding experience for us. The challenge remains in staying the course on the journey to quality.

return on investment. From the list above, the four single largest indicators of success in ISO registration as measured by return on investment are:

- ISO 9000 activities leading to the discovery of improvement opportunities and changing daily practices
- Using ISO 9000 efforts as a starting point for implementing better business practices
- Using ISO 9000 as a catalyst for rethinking business practices
- Using ISO 9000 registration as an opportunity to innovate.

Of course these four major indicators can be seen as just another way of describing the effects of customization, effective learning and making quality systems practices a routine and integral part of the corporate culture and business practices.

Use of Outside Services

Many companies implementing ISO 9000 make use of outside services in various ways; some don't use them. In some cases, a few key people are sent out for training and all subsequent ISO 9000-related activities are executed by internal employees. Some companies bring in a trainer to deliver different levels of customized training. Or, a company may hire a consultant to provide all the ISO 9000-related project management and develop most of the associated documentation required for registration with limited training provided for employees.

Apart from the actual registration audit services, outside services can be broken into three categories or styles of delivery:

- Training employees for ISO 9000 deployment and development
- External trainers leading ISO 9000 deployment and development
- Consultants leading ISO 9000 deployment and development.

The distinction between an external trainer providing deployment and development services and a consultant might be considered somewhat indistinct. However, the respondents appear to make a real distinction between the two.

Figure 8-14 shows the distribution of respondents sorted by their utilization of these three outside sources in design and development of their ISO 9000 project. There were 1,148 respondents that reported on these three services.

By far the largest group of respondents are the 269 in the lower left corner of Figure 8-14 that reported that they did most of the work themselves. Most (78 percent) of them reported that the effort was coordinated and led by employees who were, for the most part, self-trained and self-developed. Almost the same percent of this block report that the system is used and is not a burden. While 18 percent report that to a medium extent the system is regularly ignored or an unnecessary burden, 12 percent report that the system is ignored to a high or very high extent. Five percent report that the system is a highly unnecessary burden.

The next largest group are the 183 in the lower right corner of Figure 8-14 that purchased outside training but did most of the work themselves. While almost all of them (91 percent) did not provide their own formal internal training, more than half (54 percent) depended on self-trained employees to succeed in the program. Twenty-three percent of the respondents in this category report that the system is regularly ignored to a medium extent. This is slightly higher than the entirely self-developed group. However, those that report that the system is ignored (3.3 percent) or an unnecessary burden (2.8 percent) to a very high extent are a noticeably smaller percentage.

Approximately 500 respondents (nearly half of the total) did not use (or barely used) outside resources for development of their ISO 9000 program. These are the three blocks at the lower back row in Figure 8-14. Thirty-one percent of this row reported that they used self-trained employees to a low or very low extent while 46 percent reported that they used self-trained employees to a high or very high percent. Thirty percent report that the system is ignored to a moderate to very high extent. Twenty-five percent report that the system is an unnecessary burden to a moderate to very high extent.

The 377 respondents that make up the entire top layer of Figure 8-14 reported that they used consultants to a high or very high extent. Roughly two-thirds of them (the front two rows at the top of Figure 8-14) also report that they used an external training provider at least to a moderate extent to design and develop their program. Less than half of the 377 used trained employees beyond a low extent in the development and deployment process.

Of those that did not make use of outside trained employees (the left row at the top of Figure 8-14), most did not use self-trained employees either. While employee participation in development and deployment is much lower than in the "do it yourself" group, the 33 percent reporting a moderate to high extent of the system being ignored or 27 percent an unnecessary burden are not much higher than those that did not use consultants very much, if at all.

The other half of the high consultant involvement group, the one that uses trained employees, reports roughly the same 33 percent ignoring the system to at least a medium extent. About 31 percent report that the system is an unnecessary burden to a medium extent or more which is noticeably higher than the other groups.

As was pointed out earlier, the organizations that used consultants to a high or very high extent reported the poorest savings-to-cost ratio.

There is a correlation between return on investment and the type and style of training received by employees.

Figure 8-14

Extent of Program Design and Development by Consultants, External Trainer or Outside Trained Employees

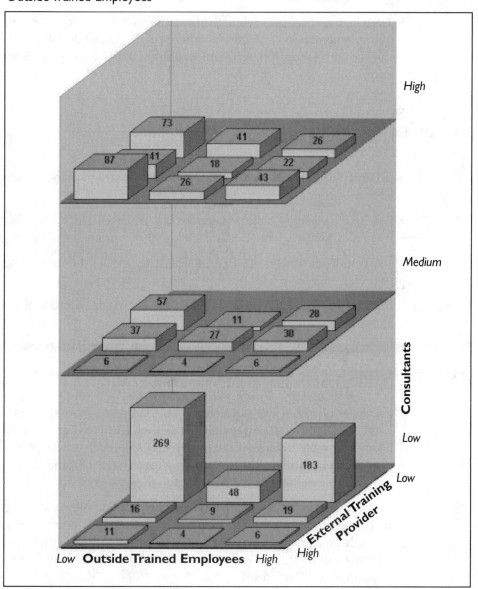

The companies that had the higher return on investment and better savings-to-cost ratio usually had their employees trained and developed through training programs rather than with self-training. These companies also had higher customization of ISO 9000 documentation to reflect corporate business practices than those that provided internal training or self-training.

Employees that were given training, especially from external training providers, were more motivated to make the ISO 9000 registration successful than those who were self-trained.

There is no significant relationship between consultant involvement and types of implementation strategies or other organizational decisions. There is also no significant relationship between consultant use and general company performance.

User Quotes
from the *ISO 9000 Survey '99*

ISO is good for certain companies but it is presently designed to provide a living for auditors and certifiers.

I feel this quality system functions because of the audits. We like to think otherwise. But human nature being what it is, I'll stick with the first reason!

Do we need auditors who are strictly outside observers, or do we want someone who can give us an outside view of how to improve our business?

It is difficult for some small companies to pay the costs associated with obtaining and maintaining registration.

Future Plans

ISO 9000 practices are maturing. A substantial number of organizations have been registered and have maintained their systems for more than six years. Many of the expenses associated with ISO 9000, both internal and external, have dropped as training and service providers have become more plentiful and newer implementers have learned from their predecessors.

In 1993, 57 percent of ISO 9000 certificate holders were planning on pursuing further registration. This percentage dropped to 31 percent in 1999. In most cases those pursuing additional registration are organizations that have registered part of their facilities and expect to expand their efforts to the rest of their departments or facilities.

About 63 percent of the ISO certificate holders are encouraging their suppliers to become registered. This is a value that has fluctuated over time but has never been low. Customer demand is one of the leading reasons that companies seek and maintain their ISO 9000 registration. Nearly half cite this as the primary reason for registration, while almost all report it as one of the top three reasons. Manufacturing customers are far more likely to demand ISO 9000 registration than are service or software customers, and manufacturing companies make up the largest proportion of ISO 9000 registrants.

When the numbers of ISO 9000 registered companies in the United States are compared to US census data, only half of one percent of the enterprises in the United States are currently registered. But about half of the Fortune 100 report at least one registered site according to an analysis by *Quality Systems Update*. If the current rate of growth in registration is maintained, a large majority of companies in the United States will be registered by 2010.

As competitive pressure increases, manufacturing industries will probably continue to lead in growth, followed by service industries. With the changes in ISO 9000:2000 now in place, some of the objections to registration found in the industries outside the manufacturing arena are removed. The publication of ISO 9001:2000 and ISO 9004:2000 as a consistent pair is also expected to increase the utility of ISO 9000 quality systems across industries.

It remains to be seen how fast the new standard will be implemented. Most current certificate holders seem to be in no rush to jump to the new version of the standard. At the time of this writing, transitions of existing registered users are expected to take six to 18 months. New registrations against the old 1994 standard are expected to be issued well into 2002. The complete survey results contained in *ISO 9000 Survey '99* are available from QSU Publishing Company at 1-866-225-3122 ($99.95 plus shipping).

Sources:

The ISO Survey of ISO 9000 and ISO 14000 Certificates — Ninth Cycle. © ISO, 2000-07 / 1 500; ISBN 92-67-10322-9

The ISO Survey of ISO 9000 and ISO 14000 Certificates — Tenth Cycle. © ISO, 2001; ISBN 92-67-10336-9

Naveh, Marcus, Allen and Moon. *ISO 9000 Survey '99.* © 1999. McGraw-Hill, Inc. ISBN 0-07-135972-9

"Bar May Be Too High For Some Companies, Experts Fear" and "North American Registrations Surpass 45,000 Mark."*Quality Systems Update*, Vol. 11 No. 1, January 2001.

"Despite Big Growth, ISO 9000 Touches Few US Businesses." *Quality Systems Update*, Vol. 11, No. 2, February 2001.

"400K ISO 9000 Certificates Worldwide; New Leaders Emerge." *Quality Systems Update*, Vol. 11, No. 7, July 2001.

The Impact of the ISO 9000:2000 Standards on Canada

by Bohdan Dyczkowsky

Introduction

The purpose of this article is to update readers on events and trends in Canada since the 1994 edition of the ISO 9000 standards, highlighting their evolution since the early 1990s. This time frame was chosen because this was the time Canadian organizations began rapidly adopting ISO 9000 in the mid-1990s.

Here we focus on activities in Canada; however, international influences are also factored into the analysis. The approach is to look at the whole registration system as consisting of integrated pieces: trainers, consultants, registrars, government and manufacturers.

Training

To efficiently and properly implement a quality system, training and/or consulting at key milestones is vital. Analysis of training courses provided shows that in the Canadian marketplace there appears to be a very common offering of training course subjects. The standard courses being offered on ISO 9000, QS 9000 or ISO 14000 include Introduction, Documentation/Implementation, Internal Auditor and Lead Auditor. Course providers are from varied sectors, such as community colleges (e.g., Productivity Improvement Centre), registrars and consultants. The question then is, How do course providers distinguish themselves? Some have elected to offer additional courses, such as APQP, FMEA, statistics, etc. specific to the automotive industry, TL 9000 for telecommunications, medical devices, to name a few.

In recent years, the influx of new course providers appears to have subsided. Growth in course offerings is not what it was in the early 1990s. Typically, if an organization selects a registrar early in the process of becoming registered, then the preference is to attend courses offered by that registrar. The rationale is that attendees are getting the official interpretation of the standard that their auditor will use during the registration audit; the perceived benefit is that it increases the probability of passing the registration audit.

A noticeable trend is in auditor training courses. Most course providers are successful in frequently holding internal auditor and lead auditor training sessions.

About three years ago, the majority of attendees in these courses were from non-registered organizations. Now the reverse is true, with the majority being from registered organizations.

With course costs remaining the same and little price slashing, attendance in public courses has been steady. This is particularly important because costs for accreditation of auditor courses are significant.

It should be pointed out that accreditation bodies deem in-house training for a single organization by a registrar to be a form of consulting. Thus this portion of training is being provided by nonregistrars, such as Productivity Improvement Centre and consultants.

With ISO 9001:2000, there will be a short-term increase in course attendance. This increase should diminish in about a year after publication of the standard, the reasoning being that this will coincide with the registrars' time limit within which an organization must convert to the new edition of the standard. After one year, then attendance at courses should go back to the norm. Attendance should not increase greatly, because registered companies have quality system experts now in house. The need to send large numbers of employees for ISO training is not the same as it was in the early 1990s, when the standards were introduced.

Consulting

Networks as a means of achieving registration for groups of organizations became popular in Canada in the mid-1990s. The purpose of networks was to achieve savings on training, consulting and registration, which would not necessarily be available to smaller organizations. Due to the structure of networks, they appealed mostly to small Canadian organizations (less than 50 employees).

To achieve registration, each network utilized training seminars, group meetings and on-site assistance. To apply for provincial government funding, networks were established in such a way as to focus more on training rather than consulting. With the Ontario provincial funding program being terminated in early 1997, networks are not experiencing growth. Some have even wound down after network members became registered and new networks could not be initiated.

With budget cutbacks through various levels of Canadian government, funding for quality initiatives is not readily available. This raises the question: Will small organizations be committed to ISO 9000 standards even if there's no government funding? One reason why small organizations drop out of networks is they may be required by customers to become ISO 9000 registered but not have resources in house or can not afford the higher costs associated with a consultant.

With the publication of ISO 9001:2000, the revival of networks is not anticipated.

Government Funding

Government funding in the early 1990s existed at the federal and provincial levels of Canadian government. However, with budget cutbacks, only a few funding programs still exist. The publication of the next edition of the standard does not appear to have a great impact on government funding of training and registration costs. With the improved Canadian economy, new government funding programs for access into international markets is not foreseeable.

Registrars

The worldwide registration system has now been in place since the first publication of ISO 9000 in 1987. This does not include registrars that were in existence prior to ISO 9000 and offering registration to CSA Z299 or BS 5750 quality standards. With the publication of the standards, there was an initial growth of registrations in the early 1990s. The second growth occurred with the publication of QS-9000 in 1994; this also happened to coincide with the second edition of ISO 9000. Since the publication of QS-9000, the growth of new registrars in Canada has slowed down.

The number of registrars accredited by Standards Council of Canada (SCC) to register quality systems is 18. In recent years there has been only one new SCC-accredited registrar. Thus it appears that the number of new registrars has leveled off. Accreditation formally recognizes the competence of a registrar and provides international acceptance of ISO 9000 and QS-9000 registration. Most of the registrations have been issued by four registrars: Quality Management Institute (QMI), SGS International Certification Services, Intertek Testing Services and Quality Certification Bureau (QCB). However, with what appears to be a polarization between large and small registrars, amalgamation of registrars is foreseeable. This in part will be driven by organizations seeking one-stop registration of ISO 9000, QS-9000, and even ISO 14000.

All Canadian accredited registrars offer ISO 9000 registration. Only one-half provide QS-9000 registration. Only two, International Quality System Registrar and Intertek Testing Services, have conducted AS9000 registrations, whereas only one-third of all these registrars are accredited for ISO 14000 registrations.

With Canadian and international markets moving towards one-stop registration, there is a need for registrars to offer all three types of registrations (ISO 9000, QS-9000, and ISO 14000) at a reasonable cost and from locations closer to the client. Thus registrars have to offer more locations and not just service clients from primarily the Toronto area, where most are concentrated. Travel costs are a significant cost of registration; if this cost is not addressed in the initial proposal to a client, it can be very shocking during the registration process.

With accreditation and maintenance costs being a large start-up cost, new registrars are not starting up frequently in Canada. Thus entry into the registration business would more easily be accomplished through acquisition of existing registrars. To register organizations in new standard industry codes (SIC/NACE), a registrar would have to hire auditors with the industry code experience or use contract auditors. The latter route can be more effective, particularly if a lot of registrations do not develop in a SIC/NACE code. Rather than trying to keep auditors with a few SIC/NACE codes busy, there are lower risks and more benefits in bringing in a contract auditor for the specific code experience. With a growing pool of auditors in Canada, locating an auditor is not difficult unless there is a need for a very specialized code.

A noticeable trend is in the number of organizations that are switching registrars when their three-year registration period ends. Some factors for switching registrars are:

- Not seeing the value of "write me a procedure or instruction" type of audit findings. These types of findings, if not justifiable, may not add value to the quality being produced by an organization.
- "Audits with no findings." Auditors are not finding at least the system findings that are being identified in internal audits.

Basically, an organization that is committed to continuously trying to improve wants auditors to find deficiencies. In the beginning, leading up to the registration audit, and even two surveillance audits after registration, the preference is to use the same lead auditor. This is primarily for the security of knowing the auditor. At the same time, the lead auditor is achieving a deeper understanding of the business practices of the organization being audited. However, complacency can set in during the life of the registration if the same auditor is used. One myth is that organizations prefer to have the same auditor for a lot of audits. If an organization is committed to continuous improvement, the preference is to have new auditors so new findings can be raised. Thus the ideal approach could be to have the same auditor for no more than two audits, so that both organization and auditor stay sharp.

Upgrading to the New ISO 9001 Standard

To see what the future can hold with the new edition of the standard, one should look at what has happened in the past with the publication of the CSA Z299 Quality Management Standards. The Z299s were in existence prior to the first publication of ISO 9000 in 1987. Their use was mostly in the nuclear industry and the application driven primarily by Ontario Hydro and Hydro Quebec on its suppliers.

The Z299s were first published in the early 1970s. By 1985 the third edition was published. With a major increase in requirements between the 1985 edition and the previous edition in 1979, users of the standards re-evaluated the benefits of the new edition. Unfortunately, the major upgrade was not adopted; instead, users stayed with the previous edition of the standard.

The same reaction could also occur with ISO 9001:2000. If the costs of implementing the new standard outweigh its benefits, the standard may lose acceptance. This reaction could be prevalent if major customers no longer specify the standard as a condition of doing business.

With new editions being published on a five-year cycle, users may not see the benefit of incurring additional development and registration costs with each new edition. Thus, prior to publishing future standards, Technical Committee (TC) 176 must survey users as it did for the 2000 edition.

Conclusion

With the publication of the new edition of ISO 9001, it appears that there will be continued acceptance of the ISO standards in Canada. However, this growth does not appear to be comparable to the rapid growth in registered companies that was experienced in the 1990s.

IMPLEMENTING ISO 9000

Basic Guide to Implementing ISO 9001:2000

9

by Roderick Goult*

What Is a Management System?

"'A management system is a collection of resources comprising capital, people, processes and procedures which ensures that a customer's requirements for quality are met by the organization supplying the product or service involved.' To really make sense of that statement, it is necessary to understand what is meant by "quality" in the ISO 9000 context.

"Quality is perceived as conformance to defined specifications in terms of performance, price and delivery. The technique used to achieve that conformance is called quality assurance or quality management, hence the term 'quality management system.' The system allows an organization's management to plan what they are trying to achieve in terms of delivering a quality product to their customers, how they should go about fulfilling that intent, and provide everyone involved with the tools, techniques, training and instruction necessary to fulfill their tasks efficiently and effectively.

"Some companies have the luxury of having their customers tell them precisely what they want before they go about the design process. Other companies must figure this out: in doing so, they must embrace the concept often called 'the voice of the customer' — listen to end-user feedback as well as address the need

*Roderick Goult is chairman of The Victoria Group and much of the material in this chapter has been adapted, with permission, from publications of The Victoria Group.

to comply with today's regulatory requirements. They must anticipate what new regulations may be in force when the product is ready for sale; take note of what the competition is doing now and possibly down the road; and guess where client preference is likely to be by the time the deliverable hits the streets. For some organizations, all this has to be done on a global scale.

"Once the design is determined, the organization then has to create the production process, purchase materials, arrange delivery processes, handle orders and tend to other details which go into the successful development, manufacturing and delivery of a product or service to the customer."[1]

The description given above is as relevant today as it was when it was originally written back in 1996. The year 2000 version of ISO 9001 introduces very few requirements or concepts that haven't been embedded in the standard since its introduction in 1987. There has been clarification of some requirements, while others have been given greater prominence and focus. Most notable is the inclusion of the term "continual improvement," which occurs seven times throughout the document. The essential principles remain unchanged. However, the change in the layout of the document is intended to assist organizations in understanding that an effective implementation needs to be a strategic top-down process-driven activity, not one that merely looks at the standard at an operational level. Equally it is hoped that auditors understand that management system audits need to be process-oriented rather than focused on specific elements.

The new wording is designed to offer greater flexibility to organizations in how their systems are documented. In reality that flexibility has always been available, but use of the term "documented procedure" in the 1987 and 1994 editions has tended to stifle originality and imagination in those who have implemented the standard. Auditors have generally done a poor job of recognizing originality, which has further tended to push system documentation into a particular, easily recognized methodology that has not necessarily always been the best approach for the user.

The Principles Behind Management Systems

Creating an effective and efficient management system isn't about "doing ISO" or becoming certified (registered). It is about creating a functional environment within your organization that will consistently operate a series of basic process steps to achieve customer satisfaction, continually improve the effectiveness of the operation and thereby increase stakeholder value. It is in fact all about money — using it better, not wasting it on rework, making more of it.

ISO 9001:2000 calls itself "Quality management systems — requirements." In many ways it would have been better if the "Q" word had been dropped altogether and the title left as "management systems — requirements." Achieving certification to ISO 9001 in itself will not improve the products or services that an organization provides, nor will it result in greater customer satisfaction or profitability. It will help an organization to be consistent and operate in a controlled environment. That together should result in improved products or services, more satisified customers and improved profitability.

In order to understand why this will happen, it is necessary to understand the ISO definition of quality. Quality, as Crosby and others have been telling us for years, is not goodness, or rightness, or excellence. Quality means meeting a customer's requirements, both stated and implied.

Quality is all too often confused with grade; worse than that, quality is probably the most misused word in the English language. People talk about "high quality" and "low quality" as though there were some abstract absolute standard against which a product or service can be measured with the precision of a calibration process. It is not so. Quality is in the eye of the purchaser, and only the purchaser. Quality, as Crosby stated many years ago, is conformance to specification. ISO 9000:2000 actually says the same thing but uses more words.

Definition 3.1.1 states that quality is the "degree to which a set of inherent characteristics [of a product, system, or process] fulfils [the] requirements."

The only functional difference between these two definitions is that the ISO 9000:2000 definition extends the scope of those interested in a deliverable product or service beyond customers to embrace "other interested parties." These days many organizations do indeed have to consider the impact of their products on "other interested parties," and the interests of those parties may be more significant than those of the actual customer base. Sometimes these other interested parties are the customers wearing different hats. Either way, in the modern world, additional considerations are valid and important.

A core goal of any organization that wants to succeed is to find the best way it can to make money while satisfying its customers, shareholders and other stakeholders. This is where the concept of a formal, structured management system comes into the picture, and that concept leads inevitably to ISO 9001:2000. Starting from some basic principles, the management system concept naturally leads to the standard. The Victoria Group has developed a set of principles called the ten steps to quality management. These ten steps encompass the basic operations of a management system and lead the user into the development of management system visibility.

Before trying to implement an ISO 9001:2000 management system it pays to have a clear picture of the core intentions.

Step 1. Management must plan for quality.

Quality results — those that satisfy customers and other stakeholders — will not happen on their own. Achieving quality results takes time, care, commitment and planning. Any management system will only be as good as the planning behind it, and any system will only achieve what management has committed to in the initial planning of the program.

Step 2. The plan must be recorded and communicated.

Putting a plan together is one thing; making sure that all members of the planning team have the same view is something else. To ensure that the plan has a common understanding and baseline, it needs to be recorded. Once recorded, of course, it must then be shared with those in charge of implementing the plan.

Step 3. The plan must be implemented.

Making plans is relatively easy; making plans come together is the bit that takes the effort.

Step 4. Keep a record of the implementation.

The best-laid plans can go astray. Sometimes plans are unrealistic; sometimes they are the best we can manage without knowing all the facts. Sometimes Murphy's Law gets in the way. Whatever the reason, a good plan will record what was done and what wasn't so that at a later date the activities and results can be compared with the intended activities and results.

Step 5. Measure the results.

Those results are really important. If there is to be any meaningful modification of the plan, then it is vital to have hard data.

Step 6. Keep a record of the results.

Please keep the data. It exists to enable the user to learn from it, so file and forget makes no sense. Anything that provides useful, meaningful data on the output of the plan is valuable, inasmuch as it tells the user what has worked and what hasn't.

Step 7. Management must review records and results.

The plan and the results belong to management. Taking action on those results belongs to management, and that means that the data from the operation of the management system should be regularly reviewed by the management team to see what "lessons learned" can be brought to the table.

Step 8. Make decisions based on recorded results.

Despite protests to the contrary, much management decision making is based on "gut feel." The main reason for this is usually inadequate or unreliable data. A well-operated management system provides the opportunity for management to have accurate and meaningful data available when decisions are made. There is no guarantee, however, that the data will be interpreted correctly, or even used at all. But at least it will be available, and that is a major step in the right direction.

Step 9. Record the decisions and communicate them.

Back to communications again. Once decisions are made they have to be conveyed to the front line where the action is. This is done by changing the system in accordance with the decisions taken by management and ensuring that everyone affected by the system change is notified and, where necessary, retrained.

Step 10. Take account of customer feedback — in Steps 1, 5 and 8.

This whole process is about customers and stakeholders. At every stage in the process where decisions are made as to how things should operate, the customer needs to have a direct or indirect voice. That voice may come from some form of data collection, from surveys, from comments received or from customer advocates present at meetings. It also comes from internal feedback because the organization's staff are primary customers for the management system. These people can provide more added-value input to the structure and operation of a management system than any other single group of individuals. They must not

Table 9-1

Ten Steps to Quality Management

1. Management must plan for quality.
2. The plan must be recorded and communicated.
3. The plan must be implemented.
4. Keep a record of the implementation.
5. Measure the results.
6. Keep a record of the results.
7. Management must review records and results.
8. Make decisions based on recorded results.
9. Record the decisions and communicate them.
10. Take account of customer feedback — in Steps 1, 5 and 8.

be forgotten in the effort to satisfy the external customer and the other stake-holders.

This entire process adds up to one large, organization-wide "Plan – Do – Check – Act" loop, that well-known human activity cycle variously attributed to sever-al twentieth-century quality gurus.

None of this is anything clever, but it does involve creating transparency in the activities and operations of an organization. Every organization has an operat-ing system of some sort because without systems they could not survive. The

Figure 9-1

P-D-C-A — Document, Implement, Audit and Fix

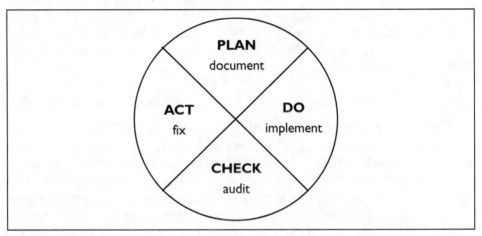

difference between an ISO 9001 management system and others is that in the ISO system the processes have become visible to management, staff and stake-holders alike. Third-party certification gives assurance to the external world that not only is the organization being operated in a consistent manner but it also has a framework in place to drive continual product, process and system improve-ment.

Providing system visibility comprises creating transparency in several ways:

1. The way in which management commitment, responsibility and authority is demonstrated and the system established

2. The way in which resources are managed and allocated

3. The manner of product realization from capturing customer requirements to postdelivery activities of the organization

4. The manner in which the system is measured, monitored and analyzed to create opportunities for improvement in its effectiveness.

Making the Management of Quality Visible

Management Responsibility and Commitment

The very top management personnel in the organization must demonstrate their commitment to the management system. They do this in many ways.

Make the policy known.

First, and most important, they must establish and publicize the quality policy of the organization. This policy should be one that is relevant to the needs and expectations of the organization and its stakeholders as well as its customers, and it should be realistic.

Establish and deploy quality objectives.

Second, top management establishes and deploys the quality objectives of the organization. These need to be measurable and relevant to both customers and stakeholders, including shareholders. The common objective of every organization is to meet customer requirements at minimum cost, so it makes sense for management to be committed to the continual improvement of products, processes and systems. The balancing factor is that improvements must be cost effective. There is no place in any organization for so-called "improvements" that add cost to an operation without adding value.

Establish the importance of customer, statutory and regulatory compliance.

Third, management is responsible for communicating the importance of customer and regulatory requirements to all employees. The only people who can really drive a commitment to customer requirements are the executives in charge of the organization. Satisfied customers have a habit of becoming repeat customers, so a commitment to meeting customer requirements makes very good business sense.

These are also the people who carry a statutory duty to ensure that the organization operates in accordance with the law, so it falls to management to ensure statutory and regulatory compliance across all operations.

Demonstrate management engagement in the system.

Fourth, executive managers have to be engaged in the operation of the system and conduct regular system operational reviews to ensure that it is fulfilling the policies and objectives to which the organization is committed. This review must encompass system output information. To get that, there must be a formal process of management system evaluation. With the commitment that has been made to meeting customer requirements, this is an issue for management to examine.

Ensure availability of resources.

Fifth, management demonstrates its commitment to the system by ensuring that all necessary resources are available as required to fulfill system requirements. This requires that senior management have a comprehensive approach to the planning process and other resource requirements to ensure that the objectives

Table 9-2

Making the Management of Quality Visible

Goals	Activities
Make the policy known.	• Establish and publicize the quality policy. • Ensure it is realistic and relevant to the organization, to customers and to stakeholders.
Establish and deploy objectives.	• Establish measurable and relevant quality objectives for products, customers and stakeholders, including continual cost-effective improvement.
Establish the importance of customer, statutory and regulatory compliance.	• Ensure the entire organization understands management's commitment to meeting customer requirements and all statutory obligations.
Demonstrate management engagement in the system.	• Perform regular systematic reviews of system performance, examining system data, audit data and measures of customer satisfaction.
Ensure availability of resources when required.	• Put planning in place to ensure adequate resources: people, training to fulfill system objectives, equipment, material and finance. • Ensure control of suppliers.
Communicate all of the above to the organization.	• Define responsibilities and authorities. • Document policies and objectives. • Document processes and tasks. • Establish and maintain records. • Define requirements. • Establish system audits.

that have been set can be fulfilled, and that activities designed to improve the effectiveness of the system are undertaken. This planning should include the effective control of suppliers and all outsourced process activities.

Communicate with the organization.

Finally, in order to make all these things happen effectively across the entire organization, management has to define the responsibilities and authorities for the tasks to be performed. This is achieved by creating a documented management system as a means of communicating and ensuring understanding of core policies, objectives and processes to those who perform specific tasks. The system is evaluated through audits, which examine the implementation of the documented process and the records created to evaluate the effectiveness of the operation. The data forms a core part of the input to the management reviews, as does information on changes made in the system to correct or prevent nonconformities. A member of management must be appointed to oversee the system and ensure that every member of the organization understands management's commitment to continually improving the effectiveness of the system.

Once management commitment and involvement is visible, attention must then turn to the provision of resources to which management has committed.

Making the Management of Resources Visible

It is one thing to promise to do good things, and quite another to actually fulfill that promise. A significant part of demonstrating that executive management is going to "walk the talk" is through the commitment of adequate and appropriate resources for the tasks at hand. These resources comprise people, training and facilities; of course, all of these require finance, but the fiscal side of the business is not typically included within the visible management system.

Making resource management visible entails providing fully integrated resource planning as part of the overall management system. Typically, these activities will be integrated into operational planning and process tools.

Management commitment should now be clearly stated, documented and visible to all concerned. Customer and statutory requirements should be included in the statements of commitment, as well as the commitment to provide resources for the activities required to fulfill those policies, objectives and requirements.

The third step in the process is to clearly and unambiguously understand the requirements, plan how to turn the requirements into deliverable products and services and fulfill those deliverables. This step needs top management to establish visible and consistent plans and processes for each of the tasks described.

Table 9-3

Making the Management of Resources Visible

Goals	Activities
Define skills and competencies.	• Establish clear descriptions for individual tasks. • Establish recruitment requirements. • Establish clear training and competency requirements for each position in the system.
Define the training policy.	• Establish a regular needs assessment policy. • Provide for training fulfillment. • Evaluate the effectiveness of training. • Maintain records of training.
Create awareness of policy and objectives.	• Establish understanding of policy. • Establish understanding of objectives. • Establish understanding of customer needs.

Making Customer Requirements Visible and Deliverable

Planning the Process

Everything starts with the customer. The first task for every organization is to identify customer needs. Organizations that produce their own products or services might do this through any manner of processes, from activities like marketing studies, focus groups, examination of current products and services available to simply having a great idea that creates a market need, such as in the case of Rubik's cube. Other organizations exist to fulfill specific customer needs that are precisely defined through contracts between buyers and sellers. Obviously, at some stage the first type of organization also ends up in a direct relationship with a customer based on a contract, but the difference is in who owns the specification. This difference changes the nature of the process that identifies customer requirements and therefore planning of the fulfillment activities.

The core difference between an organization that produces and sells its own product or service and one that creates a deliverable to customer specifications is in the sequencing of events. Ford Motor Company, Hewlett-Packard Printer Division and Hershey's Food Corporation, for example, all plan production capacity based on market research, comparative data and sales estimates of specific products. Such predictions are often based on a mix of reality, guesswork and occasionally even sleight of hand, which is why they are sometimes amazingly accurate and sometimes a disaster. Based on these market predictions, the organizations plan and create a certain level of capacity designed to meet delivery expectations. These have either historically been acceptable to the customer base, or are an attempt to change the expectation on delivery and therefore increase market share. The entire fulfillment process is then driven from these plans and modified if possible to meet the actual market demand that is encountered when the product is launched.

The organization that creates deliverables based on customer-specific requirements operates fulfillment planning in a subtly different manner, but one that is sufficiently different that it requires an alternative approach to sales and marketing. In this latter case the organization anticipates customer demand based on historical data or market research, creates appropriate capacity and then tries to sell to fill that capacity. In this case the requirements review process must look very carefully at capacity and technical issues to make sure that accepted contracts can be fulfilled. Delivery is often customer-critical, and an inability to meet a delivery date might result in the contract going elsewhere. In the previous case the organization is often in a position to negotiate a delivery date for the item the customer wants to buy.

Identifying Customer Requirements

When it comes to accepting an order from a customer, core activities remain the same regardless of how the front-end planning process operates. Customer requirements need to be clearly defined, verified as achievable and interpreted into the products or services offered by the organization. The customer will very often rely on the selling organization to take care of many types of product requirements as well as regulatory and statutory issues, not specifying either. When appropriate, consideration of such matters should form part of the order review process. An example of this would be a distributor placing an order for StarTac mobile telephones with Motorola. If the order comes from the United Kingdom or Europe, the purchaser almost certainly requires GSM phones, whereas if the order comes from Chicago they will more likely have to be TDMA or CDMA. The sales individual receiving the order needs to ask which is required. Equally, those sold to the United Kingdom or Europe must carry a CE mark — but don't expect the purchaser to tell you that.

Obviously availability, price and delivery need to be discussed, clearly identified and documented by the selling organization, and in many cases this information will be documented between the buyer and the seller. Clear lines of communication should be established with customers so that the confusion that can arise from having many different channels of communication is avoided.

Translating Requirements into Deliverables – 1. Design

Those who have no design can skip this part and go directly to section 2.

Organizations that provide design-to-requirements products and services need to operate a complete, controlled design process that extends from the identification of requirements to the provision of design output that has been validated against the user's requirements.

The design activity is a miniature of the big picture — planning the process, identifying requirements, determining who has the skills to perform the design work, monitoring the project as it evolves and then delivering the finished design to the next process stage. The next process stage may be direct to the customer or to a manufacturing operation, whether from the same organization or external to it.

There are six core phases to the design and development process, which frequently run concurrently in today's environment where time to market can mean the difference between a roaring success and almost complete failure. These core phases are program planning, creation of design input requirements, in-process design reviews, development of design outputs, verification and validation activities and configuration management. Control of all six phases is essential if the design process is going to be efficiently and cost-effectively managed to produce a reliable, producible and maintainable product.

Demonstrate design planning.

Design and development planning needs to be systematic and organized, and should provide both the design staff and the management team with a clear picture of the intended staging of the design activities. This plan should identify what review, verification and/or validation activities are appropriate to undertake at each stage in the process, and most importantly, the acceptance threshold for each design stage. This approach will enable the progress of the design to be tracked with some degree of accuracy, and by pre-determining phase acceptance criteria the likelihood of fudging the results to move a design forward because of external pressures is somewhat reduced.

The design planning process should also clearly identify the individual responsibilities and authorities for design activities. In particular the planning process should determine which review, verification and/or validation activities can be undertaken by the design team, and which if any require a degree of independence. Part of this determination is the analysis of participants in each design verification activity to ensure that appropriate disciplines are present at each stage of the review, verification and validation process. All too often design fails to adequately involve other personnel within the organization until it is far too late and the opportunity to influence the outcome to improve, for example, manufacturability or maintainability has been lost.

Demonstrate control of design input.

Good design requires clearly identified requirements that have been agreed to by all contributors to the design input process. These design input requirements should be formally documented and ideally each specific requirement identified and codified in some manner that enables it to be tracked through the review and verification processes. The design authority is also responsible for ensuring that unstated requirements are addressed. These may include statutory or regulatory issues and operational and safety requirements. In a world where environmental issues are increasingly important, the design authority may also need to address the environmental impact of materials and process operations as well as product disposal after use. A well-managed design input process will also take into account the lessons learned from previous design experience.

Once completed, design input documents should be reviewed and agreed by all parties.

Demonstrate control of review and verification activities.

A critical part of a successful design operation is the performance of regular design reviews to ensure that the project is on track and that the requirements are being met. If experience is showing that certain features cannot be provided because of technical, time or budgetary constraints, then these need to be renegotiated with those who have sponsored the design activity.

Reviews should be performed at predetermined intervals appropriate to the scale and complexity of the project. They may precede, follow or form part of a design-stage verification activity depending upon the nature of the project. The scope of the individual review activities should be predetermined and documented in the design plan, as should the required participation in each design review, with any changes resulting in the plan being amended accordingly. Likewise, the design review output should be documented, and any actions arising from the activity clearly identified, assigned and tracked to the next design review stage of the project.

The unique identification of individual design input requirements, which is recommended in the discussion of the input phase of the process, comes into its own during the review, verification and validation processes. The technique will show whether each individual requirement has been verified or otherwise dispositioned at some stage during the design process.

Demonstrate design output and verification.

The outputs of the design process should be documented in a manner that is appropriate for the next stage of the process. This may be paper, electronic or any other form suitable for the organization. The design process must ensure the following requirements are met:

- Ensure that the design output meets the design input requirements.
- Provide appropriate information for production and service operations.
- Contain or make reference to product acceptance criteria.
- Identify any safety characteristics of the product.

It is vitally important that designs are formally released from the process, and that they do not inadvertently "escape." For this reason, design output documents should be subject to a formal approval process prior to release. This will normally be the final design review activity prior to design validation.

The concept of design validation is one of assuring that the end product of the design activity meets the requirements in the intended environment as well as in the design environment. Typically, this activity should be completed prior to the delivery of the design to the customer, but it is not unusual for final validation to be contractually a postdelivery activity. As with any of the verification stages, records of the results of validation and any follow-up activities should be maintained.

Demonstrate control of design change.

One of the most difficult issues in the design environment is determining at what stage in this process formal change control should be implemented. A good rule of thumb is that formal control should be implemented at any stage where a design-stage output is passed from one individual or group of individuals to another. Any hand-off of this nature breaks the continuity of the design and development process, and therefore it is important to have good, formal records of any changes that occur after such a hand-off.

Once a design has been released, formal control is essential and must take into account the full potential impact of the change. This can range from materials on order but not yet delivered to field retrofit of delivered items. Each design change proposal should be formally reviewed and approved before it is implemented to ensure that the full implications of the change have been assessed, and the change itself verified and validated before action is taken. This need not be a lengthy or involved process; the complexity of configuration management will depend upon the complexity of the product and the risks involved.

It is essential that there are full records maintained of all change activity.

Table 9-4

Making Customer Requirements Visible

Goals	Activities
Plan the process.	• Establish clear objectives. • Establish process requirements. • Establish resources and facilities. • Establish verification requirements. • Determine record requirements.
Identify customer requirements.	• Establish customer requirements. • Establish capability to fulfil needs. • Review and clarify requirements. • Review statutory and regulatory issues. • Maintain records of reviews and agreements. • Establish clear communications.
Demonstrate design planning.	• Establish planning processes. • Define responsibilities and authorities. • Define review points for projects. • Define design interfaces.
Demonstrate control of design input.	• Document design input requirements. • Review statutory and regulatory needs. • Review safety requirements. • Evaluate previous design experience. • Evaluate environmental issues. • Review and agree documents.
Demonstrate control of review activities.	• Conduct regular reviews and verification activities. • Conduct defined verifications. • Maintain records. • Track activities.
Demonstrate design output and validation.	• Design output approvals. • Mapping to input requirements. • Validation under user conditions.
Demonstrate control of design change.	• Demonstrate control of design change. • Maintain configuration management. • Validate impact of change throughout the user chain. • Maintain records of change.

Translating Requirements into Deliverables – 2. Realization

Plan product realization.

Plan, plan and plan again! The effective operation of product realization processes requires that there be a well-constructed and time-lined master plan for converting requirements into products or services (realization). For many organizations this starts with materials management. To obtain output that conforms to requirements, inputs have to conform as well, and this means ensuring the purchase of appropriate materials from reliable suppliers.

Assure quality of materials.

It doesn't take a genius to figure out that materials management, of which procurement is a part, is one of the most critical areas of any operation that relies on externally supplied products or services to fulfill customer requirements. Few organizations do a good job of supply-chain management, and yet it is critical to success.

Suppliers should be selected on the basis of their ability to supply to the technical and commercial requirements of the organization, and it is up to the purchasing organization to verify that capability. Every supplier will undertake contracts that exceed their capability if the price is right, so it becomes a case of "buyer beware." The purchaser should examine the requirements for each product or service it purchases and determine the risk to its own deliverables. As a result of that risk assessment, a decision can be made as to the extent of control or oversight that needs to be exercised over the individual supplier.

There is no need to have the same level of control everywhere. If an item is a standard commercial item then price and delivery can be the only factors that need to be considered. Examples of this kind of product would be ordinary nuts, bolts, screws or washers; sheet metal or timber bought to common industry specifications; or pipework made to an ANSI or ASME specification. Any OEM product, from a rivet to test equipment, can be bought where price and delivery make the best business sense if the specification is totally controlled by the outside body or organization.

Typically, input is required from the design authority or production engineering to determine where items can be treated as industry standard or OEM. Certainly any item that is provided against a specification owned by the purchasing organization will require that there is some level of control exercised over the selection and use of the supplier.

As with so many issues in a management system, the decision as to the extent of the effort that needs to be made to control a supplier comes down to risk management decisions. The question that always has to be answered is this: "What is the organization's risk of producing or, worse still, shipping bad deliverables if this purchased item turns out to be no good?"

Once this question is answered, a decision can be made on selection and control and a process put in place. This isn't a one-shot deal. It is important that there be an ongoing process of supplier performance monitoring of some sort to ensure that product continues to be acceptable.

Having selected an appropriate supplier, the next step is to make sure that the right information is transmitted. Thirty years ago, writing in *Quality Is Free*, quality guru Phil Crosby stated that:

"You will find that half of the rejections that occur are the fault of the purchaser — you. Either the item was not described properly in the purchase order, or the wrong requirements were put in, or the test equipment wasn't coordinated properly."

In other words, when there is trouble, it is likely our own fault.

The purchasing process must ensure that complete and correct data is transmitted to the supplier in a timely manner. Put simply, if the supplier isn't told what is required, then no one should be surprised if deliveries are flawed. Typical data to be included with a purchasing document would cover product specification, any special process control information, any special product or process qualifications required (e.g., certificate of conformity to an ANSI or ASME specification, special training requirements or similar) and any requirements for a supplier management system.

As in most areas of activity, some form of check on the accuracy of purchasing documents before they are sent is always a good idea.

Concepts of supplier control naturally lead into consideration of receiving materials and the degree of control that should be exercised there. The two subjects are closely linked, and again the concept of risk management drives the decision-making process.

When the level of control exercised by and with the supplier is greater, then less verification is needed when the materials are delivered. When the item is a standard "off-the-shelf" item, it has to be seriously questioned whether any inspection is worth the effort beyond verifying that the item and quantity received have the same description and quantity as is on the order.

Records of this activity form part of the database that can be used to conduct periodic or ongoing evaluation of the performance of suppliers.

Once materials have been successfully received into the organization, there need to be methods in place to ensure that they are appropriately handled and stored throughout their stay. This requirement for care in the handling of product applies to everything, especially the products being produced by the organization itself.

Part of the handling and storage activity is concerned with product identification and, where required, traceability. Appropriate procedures and records need to be developed and put in place. These issues should all form part of the materials management policies and practices of the organization. When customer product is provided for use in creating the deliverable, that product also requires care and protection.

Assure process controls.

Finally the process reaches the actual product realization operations. These can include everything from provision of services through conventional manufacturing activities to field service operations. Here every organization needs to identify what the processes are and see that they are sufficiently documented to

Table 9-5

Making Customer Requirements Deliverable

Goals	Activities
Plan production.	• Establish materials and resource planning.
Assure quality of materials.	• Establish supplier requirements. • Establish supplier controls. • Establish clear product requirements. • Ensure clarity of purchasing data. • Establish receiving requirements. • Maintain records of suppliers, purchasing and receiving documents. • Establish handling requirements. • Ensure product identification. • Establish traceability requirements. • Control customer property.
Assure process control.	• Establish process requirements. • Ensure adequacy of documentation. • Establish monitoring activities. • Establish servicing requirements. • Establish special process controls.
Assure reliability of measurement.	• Establish requirements for accuracy of monitoring and measurement. • Establish calibration requirements. • Ensure effectiveness of process. • Maintain records of calibration.

ensure consistent and reliable results that achieve customer requirements. There must be clear specifications for the acceptability of products, suitable equipment that is maintained and calibrated as required, defined process and product monitoring activities that can demonstrate conformance and sufficient records to provide confidence that these things have been done.

When processes are used that require any form of specialized control, for example, welding operations for pressure vessels, certain pharmaceutical activities and many bonding processes, then those processes should be verified and validated before they are put into use. Thereafter, all the necessary controls on process and personnel training need to be maintained and demonstrated to provide customer confidence in the delivered products.

Assure reliability of measurement.

Part of providing customers with confidence in the conformance of deliverables to their requirements is the provision of accurate and reliable monitoring and measurement. This is achieved through operating a calibration program that assures the organization and its customers that measuring and monitoring activities produce reliable and repeatable results.

Measurement, Monitoring and Analysis

The effectiveness of any management system depends upon the manner in which it is measured, monitored and analyzed to identify and act on opportunities for cost-effective improvement. A well-operated system will provide management with extensive operational data that will enable product, process and system improvements to be made to the benefit of customers, stakeholders and shareholders alike.

Plan the activity.

Top management needs to be involved in the decision-making process concerning measurement, monitoring and analysis. An organization can turn itself inside-out collecting, collating and analyzing data. It is important to collect only data that is going to be used and has value. Much data collection serves no useful purpose beyond keeping those who collect it in work.

Identify relevant data.

The first step, therefore, is to examine the data collection points available within the system and decide which are likely to provide data that can be usefully applied to preventive and improvement activities. The data should cover the monitoring and measurement of the performance of suppliers, products and processes, and should always include some aspect of customer satisfaction. Where the monitoring and measurement activity is concerned with the demonstration of product conformity, records should be maintained to demonstrate that conformity.

Analyze data.

Once the selected data is established, a regime of analysis is required to provide regular reports that can be reviewed for trend analysis and process, product or system improvement activity.

Perform system audits.

The working of the entire management system needs to be regularly and systematically reviewed through an established and formal program of internal management system audits. These audits should be used to establish that the

Table 9-6

Measurement, Monitoring and Analysis

Goal	Activity
Plan the activity.	• Establish priorities and resources.

Identify relevant data.	• Establish performance data for:
	     - suppliers - products
	     - processes - customer satisfaction

Analyze data.	• Establish data analysis criteria.
Control nonconformity.	• Establish processes for the control of nonconformities. • Establish authority for disposition. • Establish processes for evaluation of reworked items. • Keep and analyze records of activity.
Perform system audits.	• Ensure system conformity. • Ensure adequacy of documentation. • Ensure system adequacy. • Ensure conformity with: - standards - contracts • Provide reports to top management. • Ensure system effectiveness.
Establish corrective and preventive action.	• Establish closed-loop systems. • Track all activities. • Quantify results. • Provide reports to management. • Drive continuous improvement

system is implemented effectively and is being maintained throughout the organization. On an occasional basis the internal audit system can also be used to assure contract, external standards or even statutory compliance as well.

Any nonconformities discovered during audit need to be corrected in a timely manner, and reviews of summary reports of the results of audits form an essential part of the top management engagement with the system.

Control nonconformity.

Unfortunately, even the best systems produce nonconforming results from time to time. The important thing is to ensure that the system has adequate controls to prevent such items from reaching the customer, and has a clearly defined process in place for the disposition of nonconforming items, the recording of the actions taken and the results of re-evaluation once any corrective action has been completed.

The process must also assess what action is required if nonconforming product has been shipped, or may have been shipped, to customers.

Establish corrective and preventive action.

Whenever a problem is encountered, some form of corrective action is required to eliminate the problem. Often it is sufficient if the incident is caught and corrected, but sometimes further analysis is required to identify the cause of the problem and attempt to eliminate the cause from the system permanently.

The same is true of preventive action, only in this case an anticipated problem is hopefully isolated before trouble occurs, thereby removing the need for corrective action.

Both activities need to be applied to products, processes and the system itself. Between them they are key drivers of continuous improvement.

Both corrective and preventive action can take many forms and can involve considerable commitment of the organization's resources. It is important that the level of action taken be appropriate to the risk presented by the incident that has sparked the action. Not every incident requires a full-blown investigation and response. Such an approach would not be cost effective in terms of resources or results.

Records of both corrective and preventive actions need to be maintained. As well as monitoring the results of such actions to ensure that the action taken has been effective, top management should regularly review this activity to ensure that it is appropriate to the goals and objectives of the organization.

In Summary

A good management system will ensure consistency of performance and predictability of results. This provides the organization with a solid framework for improvement of products, processes and systems to enhance stakeholder satisfaction and value.

The fact is this: *It's all about money!*

A good management system will steadily and continually provide opportunities to reduce operational costs while adding to the organization's value to customers, employees, shareholders and society at large. The system either adds value, or it adds cost. If it does the latter, then there is something very wrong. Nothing comes free. There is an initial up-front investment to put the system in place and to achieve certification, and this needs to be recognized and accepted by management. It also has to be recognized that the returns on this investment will not be immediate. Typically it will take between three and five years to recover the costs of installing and certifying the system, according to the *ISO 9000 Survey '99*.

So, with all the philosophical stuff out of the way, how does one start?

Figure 9-2

Doing Things Right vs. Doing the Right Things

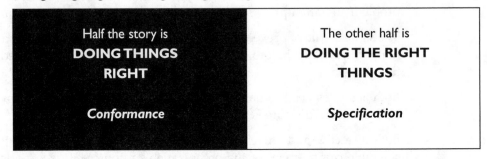

| Half the story is
DOING THINGS RIGHT

Conformance | The other half is
DOING THE RIGHT THINGS

Specification |

Phase One. Creating Executive Management Commitment and Support and Appointing the Project Manager

There are three basic reasons why organizations decide to implement an ISO 9001-based management system:

1. Customer Pressure

The organization is under pressure by major customers. They have a choice, which is to become certified or lose the business. Most choose certification.

2. Competitive Advantage

A second reason organizations choose to seek certification is for competitive reasons. They see certification as a way of getting an advantage in the marketplace and getting ahead of their competitors. A subset of this group: those who see that many of their competitors are ISO 9001 certified and decide that they had better do the same.

3. Opportunity To Improve the Organization

The serious managers are in the third group. They understand that effective management systems make sense and can improve their business. These are the managers who decide to implement ISO 9001 for the opportunities it provides for them to further enhance probably already robust process operations.

One way or another every organization fits into one of these three categories. Hopefully, even if an organization starts out in category one or two, it will develop into category three, for this is the group that gains most from the process. "Trophy hunters" will never reap full benefit from a management system, if indeed they reap any benefit at all other than a short-term benefit of keeping some customers a little longer. Eventually those customers move elsewhere when their own requirements can no longer be met by poorly managed organizations.

Regardless of which group an organization belongs to, the first step is the same: ensure that there is informed top management commitment to system implementation. Even those organizations that seek certification for no other reason than to hang a certificate on the wall have to understand the commitment required.

In order for this commitment to be gained, the executive management of an organization needs to understand:

- The requirements of the standard
- The commitment being made
- The resources required
- The ongoing nature of the undertaking.

While implementation may be a project activity, system maintenance becomes a way of life. Top management must clearly understand this fact regardless of the reason behind their initial interest in ISO 9001.

Once an interest has been expressed, typically a member of middle management is told to take care of things. That individual must first organize a day of executive management training out of which should come a commitment to the process, a commitment to personnel and financial resources and a commitment to ongoing support from all members of the management team. Never miss this step, even in group 3 companies where the management is committed to continuous improvement. They still need to understand their role in an ISO 9001 system and the resources they need to commit to that system.

The executive management overview should encompass the following subjects:

- A discussion of the need to manage the issues, including:
  - Defining what a quality system consists of
  - Necessary steps to effective management of quality
  - Creating visible systems for managers, staff and customers
- ISO 9000 - the structure of the standard, accreditation, & certification.

The executive management team needs to understand the concepts of accredited certification, the roles played by each part of the structure and why accreditation matters in selecting a registrar.

- The registration process — the mechanics and time frame of the certification process should be reviewed and explained.
- A comprehensive overview of the standard.

The training must include a detailed review of ISO 9001 exploring the content and intent of the standard in practical business terms, and demonstrating that this is not a quality thing. All areas of the organization need to be involved in both the creation and the ongoing maintenance of the management system.

The process-driven nature of a competent management system needs to be thoroughly examined and explained, and the interactivity of all the requirements of ISO 9001:2000 has to be understood by the executives.

At the end of this training session, the executive management will have all the knowledge they need to make an informed decision on system implementation. This training session should also be used to gain a statement of commitment to both the process and the resources that will be required.

The goal of the session is that the executive group identify and agree on the following project items:

- A written statement of commitment to management system implementation using the ISO 9001 standard. This may include a commitment to certification. (ISO 9001:2000, 5.0 et al.)
- The appointment of an implementation project leader. (ISO 9001:2000, 5.5.2) This should be a senior manager. The person appointed must have delegated authority to co-opt staff resources as required and have open access to top executive management on system implementation issues.

- A commitment to the provision of financial and personnel resources from all areas of the company to enable the implementation to proceed as a companywide project. (ISO 9001:2000, 5.1 (e)) *Note: at this time these cannot be precisely predicted; what is required at this stage is a statement that the necessary resources will be made available.*

- A commitment to establishing a core team of implementation personnel representing all functions in the organization within a short defined time frame.

Table 9-7

Typical Syllabus for Training Needed by Project Managers

ISO 9000: What is it?

An overview of the ISO 9000:2000 family — the standards, what they are trying to achieve, the systematic process approach and how it fits into an organization.

Overview of the implementation process

Critical success factors and project elements of management structure, communications, implementation action teams, gap analysis and implementation plan.

ISO 9001 - Interpretation

In-depth review and discussion of the standard in order to understand what documentation is needed for conformance. Includes discussion on scope, definitions and quality system requirements.

Scope and boundaries of the system

Explains the scope statement and how to develop one for an organization. Students will leave this chapter with an applicable scope statement for their organization.

Gap analysis

Details what the gap analysis is, how to perform one and how to use the results to show relevancy to the organization; how to plan and develop an implementation strategy. This chapter includes several exercises to enable students to develop a relevancy matrix and an implementation plan.

Quality systems documentation

Details and explains system documentation including quality manual, procedures and work instructions. Discusses procedure administration and control.

- A commitment to meet with the implementation team at a defined interval to discuss and review the project plan, budget resources and agree on system scope.

If all five items cannot be achieved, at minimum the implementation project manager must be identified and named, with his or her authority and access to the executive management team assured on system issues. The chosen individual should either be someone who has taken the executive overview training, or should be sent for ISO 9001 training immediately.

Many companies use a RAB, IRCA or IATCA[2] certified five-day auditor/lead auditor training to build their project manager's understanding of the standard, but this is not an ideal choice. The nature of auditor training is to teach the skills of taking apart and examining an existing operational system, where the project manager must learn how to build a system from the ground up. This is the reverse of auditor training.

The best training for this individual is a "How to Implement ISO 9000" training course offered by a reputable training organization. Choose a course that is offered by an organization that also runs RAB, IRCA or IATCA recognized and certified training programs for auditors. There are competent courses offered by nonapproved organizations, but it is difficult for the beginner to know which training is competent and which isn't; if the training provider offers certified programs, then the chances of their implementation training being effective is much greater. A typical syllabus for the training needed by the project manager is shown in Table 9-9.

Once the project manager has been trained, the organization is ready to move on to Phase Two of the process.

Phase Two. Creating the Implementation Team

Determining System Scope

The first task that needs to be undertaken by the project manager and top management is to determine the scope of the system that is to be created. This will determine from which areas of the organization the implementation team is to be drawn. The decision is an important one for organizations that have multiple products and/or services, and requires a good understanding of the options if an intelligent and sustainable decision is to be made.

An organization can choose to put a management system in place for all its activities, or for only a part of those activities. This is a decision that the executive management should consider with the project manager.

The decision will be driven by a number of factors, basically the same as those that have driven the organization to implement an ISO 9001 system in the first place — customer demand, competitive positioning and overall organizational benefit. Executive management needs to examine the activities that they direct and determine which products and services are to be included. They must then decide which of those activities drive the delivered quality of the deliverables and therefore attract their customers to them. All products and services exist on a "Concept to Disposal Continuum" (see Figure 9-3), and management has to determine which section, or sections, of the continuum need to be addressed by the system.

Figure 9-3

The Concept to Disposal Continuum

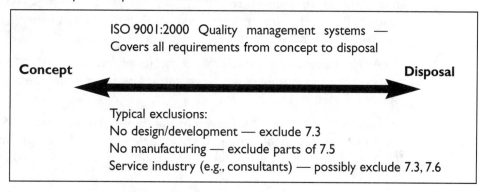

Constraints on "Permissible Exclusions"

ISO 9001 imposes certain constraints and limitations to the extent an organization can exclude activities that directly impact the quality of their deliverables; these limitations are explained in ISO 9001, Clause 1.2, "Application." This states:

"Where exclusions are made, claims of conformity to this International Standard are not acceptable unless these exclusions are limited to requirements within Clause 7, and such exclusions do not affect the organization's ability, or responsibility, to provide product that meets customer and applicable regulatory requirements."

Clause 7 in the standard deals with product realization from the identification of customer requirements through to delivery and contractual postdelivery activities. Clause 4.2.2 describes the mandatory content of the quality manual and requires that, in addition to describing the scope of the quality management system, the manual must also contain "details of and justification for any exclusions."

The intent of the standard was expressed very effectively by the United Kingdom Accreditation Service (UKAS) some years ago, and this guidance remains valid to this day. In a letter to UK-accredited certification bodies dated October 21, 1992, the secretary to the NACCB (The National Accreditation Council for Certification Bodies, now called NACB [National Accreditation of Certification Bodies] and part of UKAS) made it clear as to what was expected with respect to organizational scope. The letter contained the following text:

"Where an individual contract requires design input the assurance which the customer has a right to expect from a certificated quality system rests, in part at least, on the capability of the supplier [organization in ISO 9001:2000] to undertake the design work in such a way that the product or service will meet agreed requirements. To issue a certificate in such circumstances to ISO 9002 risks misleading the market into thinking that the supplier's quality system has been assessed when, in fact, only part of it is assessed.

"NACCB, therefore, requires that certificates of compliance to ISO 9002 should not be issued to suppliers whose customers' orders require them to undertake specific design work."

Although the ISO 9000:2000 series of standards have eliminated ISO 9002, the intent of the statement stands. If customers come to the organization in part because of design capability, then that activity cannot be excluded from the system scope.

Equally, where process capability is part of the deliverable, then process control cannot be excluded; likewise, monitoring and measurement, purchasing, calibration and so on.

Operating within the constraints outlined above, which of the products and services offered by the organization are to be included within the system?

Examples of Legitimate Exclusions

A software developer might have a "legacy" product for which it provides limited technical support for a single customer. This could be excluded from the system because the product is no longer offered.

An injection molding company might produce a range of high-grade telecommunications products, its core business, and have a small line producing pet feeding bowls. The latter could be excluded from the system scope.

A multicolor high-volume printer might also run an operation producing photocopies from customer-supplied print masters and decide to exclude the copy-shop activities.

Once the decision is made as to which products and services are to be excluded, the project manager and the executive team should define the actual scope.

Identifying Management System Scope

The scope statement is the definitive description of a company's registered quality-assured capability. In many countries these statements also appear in nationally compiled registers. For example, in the United Kingdom they are published by the Department of Trade and Industry in a "Register of Firms of Assessed Capability." In the United States there is no government-sponsored register but there is the *ISO 9000 Registered Company Directory North America* produced by QSU Publishing Company, which may be contacted at 866-225-3122.

Each individual registrar also publishes their own list of companies that they have registered. These registers include scope statements which become a public statement of capability, and in the United Kingdom the register is found on the shelves of the majority of professional buyers. Individual registrars also publish their own lists of companies they have registered and these are available from the registrars themselves.

When buyers use these directories of registered firms to source suppliers, or when they ask for details of the certification status of the company, the scope statement is what is used to identify capability. Often it provides the first impression of competency. It may be the only indicator a future customer will have regarding an organization's quality-assured capability. The scope statement communicates to the reader which portion of the business falls within the framework of the quality management system.

Within the organization, the scope statement acts as a definition of those deliverables considered vital for the assurance of customer satisfaction and, therefore, which processes within their control are most significant for the future success of the company. For the management of the company, it identifies the focal points within the quality system for performance monitoring, review and improvement. It is therefore very important that the precise nature and extent of the service being assured to a customer is very clear and unambiguous.

Before documenting the system and during the implementation process, the scope statement acts as a point of focus for determining centers of action. It also can be used as the statement against which achievement and completion may be assessed.

In addition, the scope statement sets the boundaries and key parameters for the external auditors around which they will plan and conduct the formal registration assessment.

Creating the Scope Statement

Quality management systems focus primarily upon the process capabilities of an organization and secondly upon product streams. As such, the determination and creation of an accurate scope statement for a business will depend primarily upon the key process deliverables. These are usually written in generic industry terms describing the actual services, technologies or processes being offered.

The content will typically cover the principal system steps applicable to ISO 9001:

- Design — where design capability is key to assuring deliverables
- Purchase — where purchased items become key deliverables
- Manufacture — when manufacturing is a key capability
- Storage, handling, package and delivery — where stocking is important
- Inspection — if this is an actual deliverable service
- Installation — for those companies that provide this service
- Servicing — for those organizations offering ongoing servicing.

The following are examples of scope statements, including design, for organizations registered to ISO 9001 from the records of the *ISO 9000 Registered Company Directory North America*.

"Design and manufacturer of aluminum and specialty high-voltage aluminum electrolytic capacitors for power supplies, motor drives, UPS, audio, telecom, photoflash, strobe and military applications."

This scope statement identifies the types of capacitors designed and manufactured, and the range of applications for which products are supplied. This range of applications tells the reader more about the nature of the products the company is capable of producing. The reference to military applications also tells the reader that the design capability covers extended operational parameters and rigorous type-testing and approvals.

This next scope statement indicates that the organization has a very wide range of activities included within the scope of the management system, ranging from design to professional services:

"For design, development, production, integration, installation, system support, maintenance of information, networking, communications and switching systems including hardware, software, life cycle support, processes and professional services."

Finally, the third example in this section provides a different kind of information to the reader, but information that is obviously very important to the potential buyer. This scope statement defines the nature of the processes for which the products produced are designed and intended:

"The company specializes in the design and manufacture of packaging and assembly equipment for the household, cosmetic, personal care, pharmaceutical, food, beverage, confectionery, and electronic markets. Equipment solutions include continuous and intermittent assembly, centrifugal and specialty feeders/unscramblers, robotics, line integration, labeling and conveyors."

One of the most significant changes between the 1994 series of standards to the year 2000 documents is that the reduced-scope standards have been discontinued. The ISO 9000:2000 family no longer contains a 9002 or a 9003 variant.

This makes the structure and content of a scope statement even more important. Historically, a potential purchaser who required design would start by looking at organizations in the relevant sector who were ISO 9001. In the future, every organization will be ISO 9001, so now every scope statement will have to be carefully read.

Some Examples of Current ISO 9002:1994 Scope Statements

"Manufacture of uninterruptible power supplies."

This statement specifically excludes any reference to design, installation or to servicing. A study of the quality manual will probably reveal that there are no references to these activities. Once amended to meet the requirements of ISO 9001:2000, the manual will specifically state that none of these activities are undertaken if it does not already do so. Note that this probably isn't an organization where one would go to buy a single item. It is a manufacturer, not a distributor, and the absence of design capability may well indicate that this organization is not in the custom business.

A good example of a scope statement for a distributor is shown next.

"Distribute, service, rent and repair of heavy equipment. Distribute and service recreational and utility equipment (snowmobiles, water-craft, 4-wheelers, lawn mowers, tillers, etc.)."

This clearly indicates that this is purely a distribution organization; it indicates the type of equipment it handles and also that it has repair capabilities. The manual for this organization will indicate that it undertakes no design and no manufacturing.

Here is an example for a wholesale operation. This is a very uncomplicated scope statement and indicates that the manual can be expected to contain many exclusions.

"Wholesale of electrical parts and materials."

The final example in this set is for an organization that could just have easily opted to go for ISO 9001:1994 as ISO 9002:1994. In some operations certain activities are sometimes regarded by management as design, and sometimes not. In this case, a full-service laboratory would typically be an organization that a customer might approach with a request for the development of a particular type of test. This activity is sometimes treated as "design" in the ISO 9001 sense. The new standard specifically speaks of "design and/or development," which clarifies the issue somewhat.

"Full-service laboratory in organic and inorganic chemistry disciplines, with the major focus in environmental, pharmaceutical and material testing."

It is worth noting that from a laboratory accreditation perspective design controls on test validation are essential. Excluding 7.3 is no longer an option in this instance.

An Example of a Current ISO 9003:1994 Scope Statement

Finally there are a few organizations which currently use ISO 9003:1994. This scope statement is another example of an organization that could equally well have used the broader scope of ISO 9002, treating servicing as a process under paragraph 4.9 of the 1994 standard.

"Distribution, sale and service of business equipment."

Each of these scope statements satisfies the requirements of defining:

- The nature of the product and/or service being offered
- The separate product/service streams included
- The boundary (or limits) that apply
- The extent of the scope, within the process flow, from design to service as applicable

Steps in Creating the Scope Statement

The process of creating a scope statement should utilize the following steps:

1. Define key deliverables.

The first step to defining the scope is to flowchart the business process. From that the earlier determination as to whether the entire business will be registered or just a portion of it can be verified. The key process deliverables for which registration is sought should be identified and listed. These should be defined (as in the examples above) in terms of actual processes, technologies or services. Specific product descriptions unique to the organization should be omitted, and recognized generic industry terms are preferable. The list should be checked for completeness and accuracy, and verified for appropriateness.

The organization should now test, from the customer's perspective, if this accurately defines the product or service offerings in terms of the performance requirements of customers. This will help identify if any exclusions can be claimed from the overall requirements of ISO 9001:2000.

2. Process chart the scope.

To ensure that all relevant activities have been captured, create a high-level process chart, as shown in Figure 9-4, constructed of this "customer supply chain" to aid later steps in the process. To ensure that the chart is an accurate representation of the business system, functional or geographic divisions within the organization should be omitted.

Figure 9-4

Creating a Scope Statement

	Design	Purchase	Manufacture (Process Control)	Inspection	Storage Delivery	Installation	Servicing
Part I	Design Development		Product Integration			Installation	System Support
Part II	Information networking, communications and switching systems including hardware, software, life cycle support, processes and professional services						

Part I describes the activities in terms of core process controls.
Part II describes the deliverables from the controlled processes.

Ownership and control over the quality assurance of the complete model should be verified to confirm the boundaries of the system and the registration activity.

The range of activities that can be declared "out of scope" will vary from organization to organization. A few examples of genuine "permissible exclusions" would be as follows (the numbers in parentheses indicate the relevant clause of ISO 9001:2000):

An organization that provides subcontract mechanical assembly services and buys nothing that impacts on the delivered products could exclude purchasing requirements. (7.4)

A consulting and training organization can exclude equipment calibration activities. (7.6)

A manufacturer providing subcontract services using customer-provided designs can exclude design activities. (7.3)

An organization that never uses customer-supplied property could exclude these requirements from their system. (7.5.4)

Organizations that never perform product verification at supplier premises or accept contracts that permit customer access to supplier premises can exclude these requirements. (part of 7.4.3)

The principle to be applied is clear: If an activity is not undertaken, it can be excluded. Otherwise, include everything.

At the conclusion of this activity, the project manager and the executive management have effectively defined the boundaries of the management system which they intend to create.

A Poison Chalice?

Being appointed to the position of project manager for an ISO 9000 implementation project can be a mixed blessing. At the end of the day it is usually reported as having been one of the most interesting and challenging tasks anyone has undertaken, but initially this sometimes isn't the case. A great deal of emphasis has been placed on the need to win and maintain executive management support. This can sometimes be a very real challenge in itself, in that without solid, system-generated data it can be difficult to get top management to believe that failure costs are capable of reduction. However, there are usually other pressures that operate on senior executives to help the decision through.

Gaining the approval and support of the rest of the organization can be a whole different ballgame. This support is as essential as that of top management if the project is to be successful. In this context success is measured by registration at the first certification audit. Gaining this support requires substantial preparation and planning, an understanding of what will enable the organization to succeed and knowing how to bring that about.

Implementing an ISO 9000-based management system is not an overnight activity. For the average company, the journey from project start to successful registration will typically be between nine and 15 months — from the executive decision to proceed to the conclusion of the initial certification audit. This has to be seen as a comprehensive, management-driven, companywide project. The project manager has to create a systematic, cost-effective process for driving the project through.

Unless the organization is under some customer-driven deadline, there is no rush to get the task completed. There are now well over 500,000 registered companies in the world, so it is pretty certain that at least one company in every SIC code is represented. There are no longer any prizes to be won for being first, so it is better to manage implementation on a steady, realistic basis and get it right the first time. A system that is implemented at a comfortable pace will not only prove to be more effective from the start, but will also cause those involved to view it with acceptance — even enthusiasm — rather than with frustration.

There are many problems that project managers commonly experience during system implementation. Some of the most common include.

Unwillingness to recognize that the organization's services or products can be improved

There are many organizations that are proud of what they do, and often with good reason. This is good but it can get in the way of system implementation. There are times when that pride runs so deep and is so intense that staff refuse to recognize or accept that there is any way in which anything can possibly be improved. The truth, of course, lies in the comment made by Henry Ford, that anything a man (or woman) is doing today can be done better tomorrow.

Usually in organizations with this level of pride in their history, traditions and market recognition the solution to the problem is to have the top leadership speak to the benefits which they believe the system will bring. In these intensely proud organizations, the influence and commitment by the leaders usually convinces most staff members.

Finding time and resources to develop and introduce the quality system

In today's "lean and mean" companies there is rarely much spare manpower available, and the task of documenting processes and procedures is often seen as a burden on already overloaded personnel. Part of the solution to this problem is getting lots of people involved — the more of the company's staff who contribute to the project, the less each individual has to do. Most staff will find time to write one document; few will happily write 10 or more.

Difficulties in changing people's behavior, i.e., getting staff to use the documentation

Closely linked to the attitude identified above, it can sometimes be quite a task to get people to actually use the new systems and procedures once they have been created. Despite the fact that the documentation usually represents a formal description of the processes that they have always been following, old habits die hard, and ensuring that the defined process is consistently followed can be a task in itself. Achieving this level of implementation requires the whole-hearted support of supervisory personnel at all levels.

Difficulties in measuring the process improvements and cost savings that result from the implementation of the quality system

Typically this is an issue that only gets raised at management level. The less enthusiastic any particular manager is the more likely that he or she will challenge the benefits, even after the program has started. The problem is that when no systems exist, there is no way of collecting data to report failure costs. Once the system is started, these costs start to emerge. As the system matures and improves its ability to collect and collate data, these costs appear to be rising. They are not, of course; it is just that the system is becoming much more adept at identifying and collecting existing numbers.

There are ways of dealing with these problems, and the recommendations below are based upon the experiences of many organizations covering a variety of industry sectors, size of operation, ownership, technical complexity and management styles. The project elements within the basic recommendations apply to all of the different types of companies. This is a generic approach, which identifies key issues that need to be addressed, and should then be adapted to suit the specific needs, style and profile of the company seeking to implement ISO 9001 and become registered.

Critical Success Factors

Reviews taken at the conclusion of many implementation programs have revealed some key lessons. The following are the findings of many line managers, supervisors and staff involved in creating effective quality management systems, and represent a study made by a major US manufacturing company. They are presented in order of ranking:

- Involve a consultant early.
- Learn and understand ISO 9001.
- Establish and clearly define the scope.
- Flowchart the business process.
- Communicate with the work force.
- Create implementation action teams.
- Perform a gap analysis.
- Develop an overall plan with milestones.
- Release key people from their day-to-day activities.
- Provide procedure-writing training.
- Tackle the interfaces — internally and externally.

• Start internal audits early.

As the above listing shows, an implementation program requires not only that a considerable number of events, activities and tasks be brought together, but also that they span a variety of internal and external groups, management levels and information sources. Each event has to happen at the right time. This is one of the jobs a competent consultant can facilitate — not to take ownership of the implementation process but to guide the organization smoothly through it. A number of effective solutions and processes exist to plan, control and monitor project achievement. Each organization should draw on their own internal expertise wherever it exists within their own staff.

Appoint the ISO Implementation Team

The project manager should now put together an ISO implementation team consisting of representatives from every area of the company that forms part of the scope. These will be the ISO champions during the day-to-day implementation over the following months, and will therefore be required to undertake some ISO training. These people will have to be able to commit anywhere from half-a-day a week to an almost full-time effort, depending on the size of the company. These individuals may not necessarily be managers, but will be people who command the respect of their peers, are knowledgeable about the processes used in their departments and are enthusiastic change agents.

Every functional department should be represented, including those which have little or no direct involvement in ISO 9001:2000, such as finance and human resources. These departments have activities that can impact significantly on customer quality perceptions even though their activities are not usually included within an ISO system. Wise management will include them and integrate

Figure 9-5

Everyone Contributes to Customer Satisfaction

their activities within the management system while excluding them from third-party audit.

One of the most important ideas that ISO 9001 implementation helps an organization get across to its staff is that everyone contributes to the quality of the relationship between the organization and its customers.

Figure 9-5 graphically represents this concept. The entire organization is dedicated to the achievement of customer satisfaction, and each area makes its own contribution to this process. This diagram truly shows what organizational structures ought to look like, with a series of interactive processes all focussing on the same goal.

In reality, such an organizational process would be very difficult to manage despite the obvious advantages in terms of achieving customer satisfaction. One consequence of this difficulty is that just about every organization is structured along the lines of the conventional management structure and responsibility chart shown in Figure 9-6. The different operational groups within the organization all report through vertical command structures, and this structure actually works quite well. Within each vertical structure, operational matters are typically in reasonably good shape if for no other reason than the fact that everyone is trying to keep their own boss happy. Provided that the managers at the first-line reporting level are all reasonably well focused on customer satisfaction, things will go along well enough.

Figure 9-6

The Conventional Organizational Chart

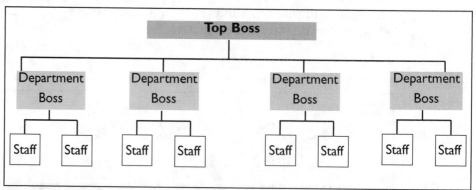

The typical management system documentation structure follows a similar structure, with one significant difference. If the documentation is put together properly, it will formalize the inputs and outputs that create the horizontal process across the vertical hierarchy and thereby achieve customer satisfaction. This process-driven formalization of the internal customer-supplier relationships throughout the organization typically produces significant operational savings. Omission and duplication are eliminated and a level of consistency is introduced, which is to the benefit of everyone.

Figure 9-7

Management System Documentation

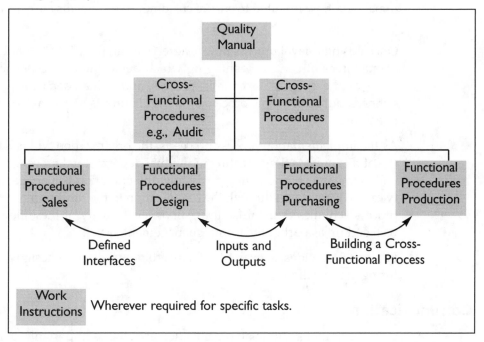

Phase Three. The Macro Process Flowchart, Gap Analysis and the Implementation Plan

Once the implementation team is established, that group should create a high-level macro flowchart of the business process contained within the scope of the system. The flowchart should start with the receipt of a customer inquiry and conclude with a hand-off of the deliverable to the customer. This macro flow-chart serves three purposes. First, it assists in identifying the internal interfaces within the organization that will need to be documented within the system. Second, it can act as a progress indicator as the program moves along. Third, it can provide a visual indication of the "sequence and interaction of the process-es included in the quality management system" when the quality manual is written (ISO 9001:2000, 4.2.2 (c)).

The main purpose in developing this process flowchart is to ensure that the sequence of events that occurs from the time a potential customer contacts the organization through to the completion of all contractual responsibilities is completely identified and captured. Using a flowchart, or process map as they are often called these days, ensures that the processes are organized in a sequential manner, identifies any concurrent activities and starts to define the organizational data-flow required to ensure customer requirements are captured and fulfilled.

Once this high-level process flow is agreed, it can then be subdivided into operational areas of control, identifying which department is responsible for each stage of the activity. From this process, individual departmental roles are defined and the principle process inputs and outputs between departments start to emerge.

As the implementation process proceeds, the organization will make ever more use of this process flow, creating individual departmental process diagrams that will define in ever increasing detail how the operation is managed. This activity can go right down through the organization to the flowcharting of individual process activities at manufacturing floor level. Many of these flowcharts may well end up as part of the formal management system.

Figure 9-8 provides an example of a macro flowchart for a design and manufacturing organization.

Communications

Communications within an organization are always important, so much so that ISO 9001:2000 actually contains a section about communications (5.5.3). During the implementation process it is absolutely vital that everyone in the organization understands the importance of the project, what is being planned, how it will be achieved and what success means for the entire operation. For this to happen there has to be an effective means of communicating with all staff. This may already exist in the form of regular meetings, newsletters, notice boards, internal television services or any one of a myriad of methods. If no such systems exist, something will need to be created. All personnel have to understand, to some level, what is going on and how they will be asked individually to contribute to the activity.

The information that needs to be shared is common to all organizations:

1. Corporate statement of intent, the reasons behind the decision and the perceived benefits from the project. Ideally this is a personal message issued by the chief executive of the company, and in multisite environments should be endorsed by the senior on-site executive.

Figure 9-8

Example of a Macro Flowchart

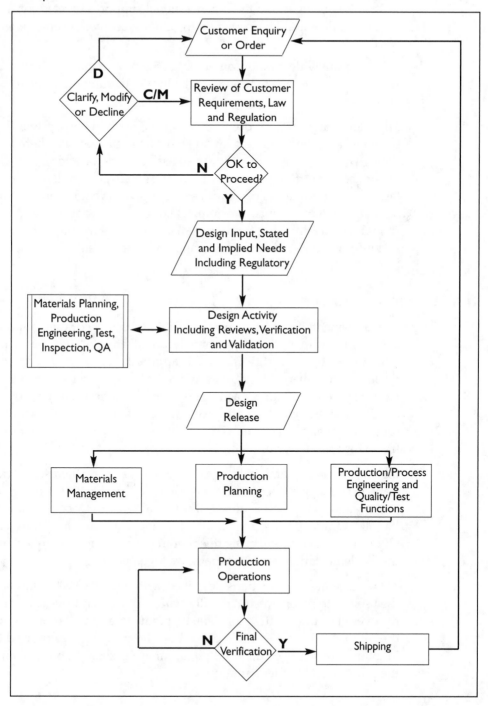

2. A formal announcement of the appointment of the ISO 9001 project manager outlining his/her authority and responsibilities. This should include comments regarding the organizational support expected for the project, and again should be issued by the chief executive or senior on-site executive.

3. Companywide announcement from the project manager outlining the company implementation plan, including naming the implementation team.

There are many ways of doing this and the method chosen will depend upon the scale, and the management style, of the organization. There is no right or wrong way of doing things, and the decision has to be a local one. Once the initial project kickoff announcement has been made, one of the project manager's tasks is going to be to keep staff interest up with regular progress reports and ongoing announcements informing them of the progress of the project. These should include details of training plans, progress of the implementation process and information about the nature and commencement of internal audit activities.

Implementation Action Teams

The implementation process will be facilitated best by drawing upon the expertise and involvement of key personnel from all areas of the organization that are within the scope of certification. This approach has the advantage of spreading the load across many individuals and therefore not overburdening anyone. The lack of spare workload capacity in most organizations has already been noted, and it is important to be realistic about the amount of additional work that any one individual can assume. This must be recognized in developing the time frame for completion of the task.

Job one for the implementation team members is to get themselves trained in the standard and good documentation practices. This, like the initial training for the project manager, is best achieved through a "How to Document and Implement ISO 9001" training program, and the training needs are the same (see Table 9-9). Often organizations will bring this training in-house for the project manager and the implementation team to experience together.

There are some key functions described within the ISO 9001 standard that lend themselves to be operated centrally within any given physical location even if the overall certification is of several disparate locations. According to the size of the company, these may be resourced by allocating an area of need to a specific individual or team, or the total picture may be shared and distributed among the primary ISO implementation team.

System Understanding

Consistency of approach and understanding is fundamental to the success of the project. Because of the way in which the ISO 9001 standard is written, differences in interpretation can arise among staff and it is essential that there is a singular approach. All the different interpretations may well be correct individually, but a single system needs a single approach. Some organizations resolve this issue by appointing a member of the implementation team to be the resident expert for each functional element of the standard, thereby ensuring consistency.

An example of this would be to have one individual act as the reference point or coordinator for the application of calibration across the company. This expert can then coordinate the required activities with the functional/unit representatives.

"The extent of the quality management system documentation can differ from one organization to another due to (a) the size of organization and type of activities, (b) the complexity of processes and their interactions and (c) the competence of personnel." ISO 9001:2000, 4.2.1 Note 2.

A central arbitrator is probably also a good idea for the subject of documentation. The standard largely leaves it open to the organization to determine where documentation is needed. Given the wide variation that will always be found between individuals as to where documentation is required and what level of detail is needed, having a single point of oversight will again help to ensure consistency of approach.

Figure 9-8 provides basic guidance on how to determine the need for, and the level of detail required, in documentation throughout the organization. This issue will be addressed in greater detail at a later stage.

Functional/Unit Representatives

Implementation has to occur within the normal organizational structure and operational divisions that currently exist. Local line managers should be identified to ensure that major operational units have someone to drive the program on behalf of the project team and assist in the transfer of project/program needs via the regular operational chain of command. These representatives should take direction from the implementation team or the individual experts in managing the process within their departments or divisions.

Figure 9-9

Determining the Need for, and Detail in, Documentation

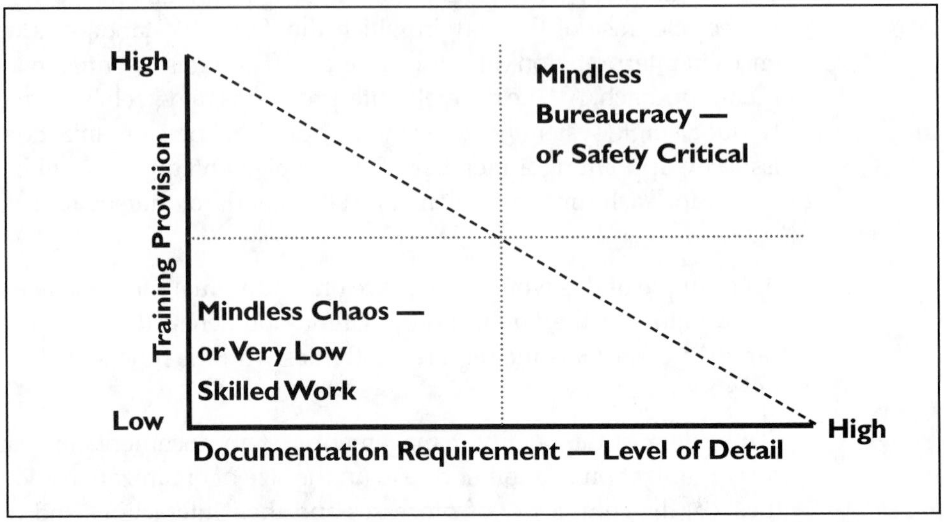

Statutory and Regulatory Interfaces

ISO 9001:2000 appears to place a much greater emphasis on statutory and regulatory issues than the 1994 standard. In fact, the requirements are the same, but they are now much more visible and are likely to attract more audit attention, both internally and externally. It has always made sense to have a nominated individual responsible for issues of compliance; now it is even more important to ensure that someone coordinates the integration of the requirements applicable to current operations, including environmental and safety issues. The responsibility of this individual, or these individuals, is to ensure that the quality management system will cross-reference and incorporate statutory and regulatory requirements accurately and as completely as possible.

The extended references to these issues found in ISO 9001:2000 are in the following paragraphs:

Introduction

0.1 General

The standard "can be used by internal and external parties, including certification bodies, to assess the organization's ability to meet customer, regulatory and the organization's own requirements."

1. Scope

1.1 General

"This International Standard specifies requirements for a quality management system where an organization

> a) needs to demonstrate its ability to consistently provide product that meets customer and applicable regulatory requirements, and

> b) aims to enhance customer satisfaction through the effective application of the system, including processes for continual improvement of the system and the assurance of conformity to customer and applicable regulatory requirements."

1.2 Application

"Where exclusions are made, claims of conformity to this International Standard are not acceptable unless these exclusions are limited to requirements within Clause 7, and such exclusions do not affect the organization's ability, or responsibility, to provide product that fulfils customer and applicable regulatory requirements."

5. Management responsibility

5.1 Management commitment

"Top management shall provide evidence of its commitment … by:

> a) communicating to the organization the importance of meeting … statutory and regulatory requirements…."

7. Product realization

7.2.1 Determination of requirements related to the product

"The organization shall determine

> c) statutory and regulatory requirements related to the product…."

7.3.2 Design and development inputs

"Inputs relating to product requirements shall be determined...

> b) applicable statutory and regulatory requirements…."

Existing Registration/Quality Activities

Many organizations are already operating within a recognized system — DoD, Ford Q1, FDA Quality System Regulation or similar. In these situations one member of the implementation team should be recognized as the catalyst for (a) ensuring the ongoing maintenance of these activities, and (b) reviewing, analyzing and reporting back to the team on any potential philosophical and/or practical divergences that may arise, for example, the more stringent requirements for training and records that apply to a company operating under FDA Quality System Regulation.

The objective must be to ensure that as much of the work committed to the achievement of the alternative quality approval is incorporated into the new system, thereby demonstrating constancy of purpose on quality management issues.

The purposes served by identifying and committing personnel to these requirements are threefold:

1. It provides the organization with a pool of people who can act as points of reference or contact, able to provide guidance and deal with questions, problems and matters of clarification.

2. By creating involvement, it enlarges the population or critical mass of personnel knowledgeable in understanding the ISO 9001 requirements as they apply to local activities.

3. It releases the project manager to focus on the strategic goals and motivational needs for sustaining project momentum.

Identifying and nominating these individuals or groups creates a visible network of helpers within the organization and the project gets a significant increase in visibility. ISO 9001 expertise also becomes more widely accessible to other staff. The demands upon their time should be on an as-needed basis and can usually be absorbed within existing work loads.

Gap Analysis

Once the implementation teams have been established and trained, a gap analysis needs to be performed. This is an examination of the current state of the company's processes and related documentation relative to the relevant requirements of the ISO 9001 standard. The gap analysis provides the baseline for all future implementation activity and is an essential part of the process as the results of the gap analysis drive the development of the implementation plan.

It is very important that those performing the gap analysis have an in-depth knowledge of the standard, and this is one of the activities for which many companies utilize a consultant. Ideally, those performing the gap analysis will be highly experienced ISO 9001 auditors with a knowledge of the processes and methodologies in use by the organization.

One of the worst things that any organization can possibly do is to set about re-inventing their processes and procedures when they already have perfectly adequate methodologies in place. This sort of non-value-added work is what has gained the ISO process a bad reputation, that and the insistence of some consultants that the "correct" approach is to have a single procedure for each element of the standard. That was wrong for the 1994 standard, and would be even worse for the year 2000 approach. The management system should reflect the manner in which the organization does business, and should incorporate every method and process currently in use. The only reason to change a method or process is if it is found to be inadequate or it does not fulfill the requirements of the standard.

The gap analysis examines these issues and makes recommendations for enhancements as well as identifying any absolute gaps. Typically an organization will have, formally or informally, about 75 to 80 percent of the processes required. This is simply because ISO 9001 is really management 101 with some refinements, and without 75 to 80 percent of the processes in place and operating no organization could possibly survive.

The elements that are typically missing to a greater or lesser extent are:

1. Formal review and analysis of customer requirements;

2. Control of documentation that defines requirements and acceptance criteria

3. Formal control of the supplier base

4. Formal collection of process performance data and its analysis and use

5. Formal initiation, follow-up and closeout of corrective actions

6. Any form of formal preventive action process

7. Internal audits of the management system

8. Management review of overall system performance.

These eight items are the activities embedded within ISO 9001:2000 that enable management systems based on this standard and its predecessors to be so effective in driving continual improvement of the product, processes and the system itself. The first ensures that the customer requirements are fully and completely understood, items two to seven drive control and improvement of the internal processes and item eight ensures that the whole process operates in a value-added, cost-effective manner.

Executive Task: Quality Policy and Core Objectives
Team Task: Relevancy Matrix and Implementation Plan

Once the gap analysis has been completed, the next step for the project manager is to work with the executive management team to develop the quality policy statement and the core management system objectives that are to be deployed throughout the organization.

Parallel with this activity, the project manager and the implementation team should develop a relevancy matrix and an implementation plan. The results of the gap, coupled with the high-level process flowchart, will aid in the development of both.

Executive Management Activities

1. Policy Statement

The standard requires that the executive management of the organization (top management in ISO-speak) demonstrate its commitment to the process and the management system through a number of activities, two of which are " establishing the quality policy," and "ensuring that quality objectives are established" (ISO 9001:2000, 5.1, (b) and (c)). The standard goes on to prescribe certain characteristics of the quality policy statement to which the executive must commit. Executive management must ensure that the policy:

- Is appropriate to the purpose of the organization
- Includes a commitment to comply with requirements and continually improve the effectiveness of the quality management system
- Provides a framework for establishing and reviewing quality objectives
- Is communicated and understood within the organization
- Is reviewed for continuing suitability. (ISO 9001:2000, 5.3)

In addition to all this, the policy is also to be a controlled document within the formal management system.

A quality policy statement is an important part of the visible management commitment to the process and the system, and its authorship is not something that should be undertaken lightly. Aspects to consider when drafting a quality policy include the following:

1. Is the policy a clear statement of intent?
2. Is the policy measurable?
3. Is the policy appropriate to the goals and objectives of the organization?
4. Is the policy appropriate to the requirements of the organization's customers?
5. Does the policy commit the organization to continual, value-added improvement?
6. Is the policy easily understood at all levels of the organization?
7. Does the policy represent reality?
8. Will the policy be acceptable to all the stakeholders?

There are few things worse than having a quality policy statement that produces an overwhelming sense of fatigue in those who read it. Policy statements containing phrases like "world-class," or "exceeding customer expectations" or "global leadership" are best avoided. These phrases may be appropriate for the mission statement because they are almost, if not completely, impossible to measure, assess or verify. One of the requirements of the standard is that the policy is regularly reviewed by top management for continuing suitability. This surely means that there has to be some way of measuring achievement of the policy — how else can it be declared suitable?

Examples of some policy statements that address these issues and concerns are shown below:

> *"The ultimate success of our business rests with the consumer. We can earn satisfactory profits only when we can market a product at competitive costs with substantially greater consumer value. It is our intention to increase market share with products of consistent quality delivered on time and at the planned price. We are committed to continuously adding value to our company."*
>
> *Signed: Chief Executive Officer*

(This policy statement brings to mind the comment made by Sir John Egan, the former CEO of Jaguar Cars, when he stated: "Our business is to make money satisfying customers.")

> *"The Happy Valley Company is committed to a policy of total quality in all its business activities. Our performance standard is zero defects. We will deliver products that comply with their specifications, on time and at the agreed price. We will seek opportunities to continuously improve products, processes and systems."*
>
> *Signed: Chief Executive Officer*

> *"We will deliver defect-free competitive products and services on time to our customers. We will continuously strive to enhance the value of our products, processes and systems for all our stakeholders."*
>
> *Signed: Chief Executive Officer*

> *"In order to improve quality we shall provide clearly stated requirements, expecting each person to do the job right the first time in accordance with those requirements, or to cause the requirements to be officially changed. We will seek ways of improving our processes, products and systems to enhance our customers' and stakeholders' experience."*
>
> *Signed: Chief Executive Officer*

2. Core Management System Objectives

"Top management shall ensure that quality objectives, including those needed to meet requirements for product [see 7.1 a)], are established at relevant functions and levels within the organization. The quality objectives shall be measurable and consistent with the quality policy." (ISO 9001:2000, 5.4.1)

What is a "quality objective"?

ISO 9000:2000, the document that now defines the quality vocabulary, provides the following explanation of a quality objective: "something sought, or aimed for, related to quality." In case this is insufficient, two "Notes" provide additional explanations:

> "Note 1. Quality objectives are generally based on the organization's quality policy.
>
> Note 2. Quality objectives are generally specified for relevant functions and levels in the organization."

Organizations may have several types of objectives, ranging from high-level executive objectives to individual goals for production operations. At executive management level, staff are likely to be concerned primarily with core performance objectives and profitability, although these high-level objectives are most effective if they can be deployed down throughout the organization.

Typical high-level objectives could include such considerations as 100 percent on-time delivery, reductions in warranty claims, defined levels of customer satisfaction, profitability goals, sales targets and staff turnover levels. The standard

Figure 9-10

Creating Quality Objectives

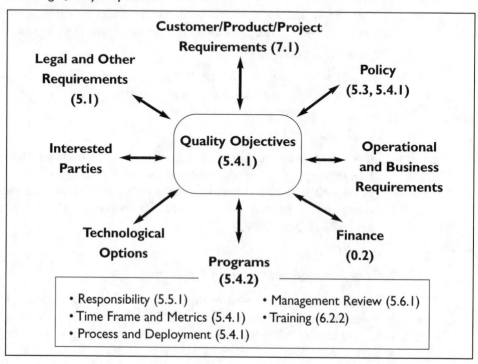

makes reference to objectives in several areas, requiring that in setting its objectives the organization take account of customer and product requirements, statutory and regulatory issues and ensure that the objectives are compatible with the policy statement.

In addition to the requirements created within ISO 9001, there are other issues that drive executive decision making on objectives. They include the views of external stakeholders or other interested parties, financial pressures, operational and business requirements and available technologies.

Out of all these considerations should come objectives that can be translated into action, either through specific programs or through the interactivity of the entire management system. Either way, the objectives need to be capable of being tracked, measured and reviewed.

The overall influences that should drive management objectives are shown in Figure 9-10. It is worth noting that there is a close correlation between the construct of quality objectives as described in ISO 9001:2000 and the Kaplan "balanced scorecard" philosophy.

Implementation Team Activities

The relevancy matrix lists all the elements of the standard on the vertical axis and the pertinent departments of the company on the horizontal axis and identifies which elements are applicable to what departments. An example is shown in Figure 9-11.

The chart is used to plot which elements and requirements are owned by each functional department within the organization, which requirements have an impact on a functional department and which are unique to a particular functional activity.

Thus the quality policy and objectives are owned by every department, as is responsibility for document control and records, for example, but the identification of customer requirements is owned by the sales and marketing department, with an impact on several other departments. Design is owned by design engineering, similarly with an impact on many other departments, whereas calibration activity impacts relatively few parts of the organization, as does shipping.

The matrix helps to sort out and clarify which functional area of an organization should "own" the process and, therefore, in implementation terms be responsible for collecting and collating the data and writing the required procedures and work instructions.

A small part of a completed relevancy matrix is shown in Figure 9-12.

In the diagram, an "O" means process ownership in whole or in part, an "A"

Figure 9-11

Part of a Relevancy Matrix Chart

Functional Department ——▶	Sales & Marketing	Design	Materials Management	Manufacturing Engineering	Manufacturing	Tests & Inspection	Quality	Receiving	Shipping	Top Management
1.1 General										
1.2 Permissible exclusions										
2. Normative reference										
3. Terms and definitions										
4.1 General requirements										
4.2 General documentation requirements										
5.1 Management commitment										
5.2 Customer focus										
5.3 Quality policy										
5.4.1 Quality objectives										
5.4.2 Quality planning										
5.5.1 General										
5.5.2 Responsibility and authority										
5.5.3 Management representative										
5.5.4 Internal communication										
5.5.5 Quality manual										
5.5.6 Control of documents										
5.5.7 Control of quality records										
5.6.1 General										
5.6.2 Review input										
5.6.3 Review output										
6.1 Provision of resources										
6.2.1 Assignment of personnel										
6.2.2 Training, awareness and competence										
6.3 Facilities										
6.4 Work environment										
7.1 Planning of realization processes										
7.2.1 Identification of customer requirements										
7.2.2 Review of product requirements										
7.2.3 Customer communication										
7.3.1 Design and/or development planning ... etc.										

Figure 9-12

A Section from a Completed Relevancy Matrix

Functional → Department	Sales & Marketing	Design	Materials Management	Manufacturing Engineering	Manufacturing	Tests & Inspection	Quality	Receiving	Shipping	Top Management
4.1 General requirements	O	O	O	O	O	O	O	O	O	O
4.2.2 Quality manual	A	A	A	A	A	A	A	A	A	A
4.2.3 Control of documents	O	O	O	O	O	O	O	O	O	O
4.2.4 Control of records	O	O	O	O	O	O	O	O	O	O
5.1 Management commitment	A	A	A	A	A	A	A	A	A	O
5.2 Customer focus	A	A	A	A	A	A	A	A	A	O
5.3 Quality policy	A	A	A	A	A	A	A	A	A	O
5.4.1 Quality objectives	A	A	A	A	A	A	A	A	A	O
5.4.2 Quality planning	A	A	A	A	A	A	A	A	A	O
5.5.1 General	A	A	A	A	A	A	A	A	A	O
5.5.2 Responsibility and authority	O	O	O	O	O	O	O	O	O	O
5.5.3 Management representative	—	—	—	—	—	—	O	—	—	O
5.5.4 Internal communication	A	A	A	A	A	A	A	A	A	O
Etc...										

means affected by the process and a "—" means that there is typically no direct involvement in the day-to-day activity. Although top management is responsible for ensuring the customer focus of the organization, they are not usually involved on a day-to-day basis in the detailed identification of customer requirements. Every organization will have process ownership in different areas, and no general principles should be assumed to be embodied in the example shown.

The implementation plan is a detailed time line for the implementation process, with clearly identified milestones and project reviews. It should be developed once the gap analysis and relevancy matrix are completed and should set the pace for an efficient and methodical implementation process. Some organizations create sophisticated project plans using powerful software tools like Microsoft Project but, while definitely very nice and very useful, this isn't by any means essential. A simple time line identifying key project milestones will serve the purpose perfectly well. One of the most important aspects of the implementation plan is to ensure that it requires regular management progress reviews — top management need to remain engaged. A typical implementation time line is shown in Figure 9-13.

Figure 9-13

Sample Implementation Time Line

Month No.	0	1	2	3	4	5	6	7	8	9	10	11	12
Start-up Activities													
Executive commitment	■												
Appoint project manager	■												
Perform gap analysis	■												
Project Activities													
Define implementation plan		■											
Agree on policy and objectives			■										
Staff awareness		■							■				
Verify control activities		■											
Develop procedure list		■											
Review existing documentation			■	■									
Develop procedures				■	■	■	■	■					
Implement procedures					■	■	■	■	■				
Audit system								■	■	■	■	■	■
Review and amend procedures								■	■	■	■	■	■
Issue quality manual										■			
Management review					▨	▨	▨	▨	■	▨	▨	■	▨
Apply for registration								■					
Registration audit													■

Phase Four. Identifying the Need for Documentation

Requirements for Documentation

Unlike the 1994 standard, in which there are 17 specific requirements for the organization to "establish and maintain documented procedures," the approach in the 9001:2000 standard is somewhat different. The actual stated requirement is that:

"The organization shall establish, document, implement and maintain a quality management system and continually improve its effectiveness in accordance with the requirements of this International Standard." ISO 9001:2000, 4.1

Under the heading "Documentation requirements," the standard informs the reader that:

"The quality management system documentation shall include:

  a) documented statements of a quality policy and quality objectives,

  b) a quality manual,

  c) documented procedures required by this International Standard,

  d) documents needed by the organization to ensure the effective planning, operation and control of its processes, and

  e) records required by this International Standard (see 4.2.4)." ISO 9001:2000, 4.2.1

Note that records are a special kind of document which have their own form of control, identified in 4.2.4; they are not subject to the controls of this paragraph.

Item c) is addressed through the documentation of the six processes that are listed below, coupled with the required quality manual and documented quality policy and objectives.

The term "documented procedure" appears just six times within the requirements. These six references are as follows:

4.2.3	Control of documents
4.2.4	Control of records
8.2.2	Internal audit
8.3	Control of nonconforming products
8.5.2	Corrective action
8.5.3	Preventive action.

The requirements for the remainder of the system are summed up in 4.2.1 d), which mandates "documents needed by the organization to ensure the effective planning, operation and control of its processes." This is where the discretionary powers kick in; it is left up to the organization to determine what documents are required to achieve the defined goals.

The intent is to introduce greater flexibility in the implementation of the management system, but overall the text of the standard is ambivalent on the issue of process documentation. Requirements for information to be documented appear many times; some of these are inputs to processes and some are outputs, e.g., records. But the only mandated procedures are the six processes listed above.

It would appear theoretically possible that an organization could have a management system that complies with the requirements of ISO 9001:2000 and only has a manual, a policy statement, defined quality objectives and six documented processes.[3] Every other activity that the organization undertakes could be defaulted to training and experience. In order to challenge that claim an auditor would have to demonstrate process failures that could be directly and incontrovertibly attributed to the absence of a documented process. This relaxation of mandatory requirements for documentation has the potential to be a source of disputes between auditors and organizations using the standard.

Without clear guidance, how is the user to determine the need for documentation? The new approach and wording is supposed to introduce more flexibility in how a management system is implemented. Specifically, the intention was to help smaller organizations by relaxing the mandatory requirements and leaving more to the judgment, knowledge and experience of the management. Time will tell whether this approach works, or whether it merely provides registration auditors with greater latitude to make unreasonable and unnecessary demands of clients.

The implementation team and the implementation action teams are the people who will have to analyze the processes and determine where documents are required. The decision should be based on the significance of the activity in terms of customer requirements, regulatory compliance, organizational need and overall system risk. These factors can then be balanced against the training provided to the individual performing the task in question, and as indicated in Figure 9-8 the level of detail required in any document can then be established.

Each stage of the macro process flowchart should be examined and a determination made of the inputs and outputs for each operation. The team will then have to decide how those inputs and outputs are going to be correctly transferred across the organization and how much has to be documented to ensure that a consistent process can be established.

Once this operation is completed, the implementation tasks can be assigned to the team members and the process of developing the management system can start. The first two decisions that have to be made concern the typical format, style and layout of documents. Consistency of format, style and layout is not essential, but makes for a much more user-friendly system and is therefore strongly recommended.

Chapter 11 is dedicated to the process of capturing data and creating and controlling documentation. The requirements are therefore not duplicated here, but it is important that the control method is agreed before documentation starts to be created.

The next section is concerned with identifying the system needs and determining requirements.

Implementing the System from Customer Requirement to Fulfillment

Deciding Who Is the Customer and Capturing Customer Requirements

ISO 9001:2000, 7.2

The logical place to start is with the customer. Customers are the reason for the organization to exist, so the first step is to identify who those customers are, and how their needs are captured and correctly transferred into the operations of the organization.

Many organizations have no problem in knowing who their customer is and how they get to understand requirements — it is a straight one-to-one interface through a contract "document" of some sort. This may be a purchase order, a fax or, increasingly these days, an EDI process that is used to notify a supplier of a customer requirement.

Other organizations using ISO 9001:2000 management systems must work at figuring out who is their customer. Who is the customer for a public school, a hospital or a transport agency such as the Washington Metro? Government, in one form or another, pays for schools; it is the people's money through taxation, but the direct paymaster remains the representative government. The same is true to a certain extent for something like the Washington Metro. Hospitals are paid by insurance companies, and by another part of the government. So who is their customer? The paymaster or the patient? The Ford Motor Company doesn't deal with the general public, it deals through agents — dealerships; nonetheless, they see the end user as the true customer.

Why does this matter? It matters because the standard requires that the organization shall determine "requirements not stated by the customer but necessary for specified use or intended use, where known." In each of the cases mentioned, the organization will be receiving direction from the paymaster, and significant input from the consumer of the services or end user of the products. This modifies the whole approach to customer data input and the evaluation of customer satisfaction. Many of the problems in public education stem from the fact that schools are pulled in many different directions by political interference, local concern, parental concerns and educational fashions. Few stop to ask who the true "customer" is.

These issues need to be carefully considered, and then decisions taken on the extent to which the process of capturing customer requirements and transferring them into the organization need to be documented. It is almost a certainty that some form of defined process will be required — there are usually too many different parts of the organization involved for it to be a process that lives off training and records. The recommendation for any organization that is serious about its management system is that the process is documented and authorities clearly defined. The nature of this documentation is in the hands of the implementing organization. It may be a conventional procedure, it may be a detailed checklist of items and interfaces, it may be a flowchart — or process flow diagram as they tend to be called today. As with the 1994 standard, the manner in which a process is documented is up to the organization.

Customer requirements must be clear, understood and achievable. The translation of those requirements into performance and acceptance criteria for the operations of the organization has to be considered. A method must be created for ensuring that this transfer of information takes place every time it is required. This includes customer changes. If the customer requires quantities of product and defined delivery dates, then that is all the information the rest of the organization needs. If the requirements are specialized and technical, then a great deal more evaluation and control is required.

Here are three examples:

1. A wholesale distributor placing an order for several hundred cases of a brand-name product.

The only relevant issues for the manufacturing facility are the quantity and the delivery requirements. The internal processes take care of everything else because the company owns the process, the product design, labeling, packaging and everything else.

2. A major airline placing an order for jumbo jets.

There is obviously a basic design that the manufacturer owns, but the level of customization in the order will be such that the process of transferring the necessary information to the appropriate operational areas will be complex. Everything from galley equipment to avionics to engines is specified by the customer. All that information, together with acceptance criteria, has to be in the right place at the right time to make it possible for the plane to be built to order and delivered according to airline expectations.

3. The mail-order business, including electronic commerce and telephone orders.

Many millions of orders must be placed in one of these three ways every day, particularly if the EDI technologies used by major corporations are included. In these situations, items are ordered from a catalog of available products. This may be a paper catalog, an Internet catalog or, when EDI is in use, the catalog is effectively a listing held on the customer's computer of those items available from each supplying organization. These "documents" become the requirements, and the role of the recipient of the order is to confirm accuracy of data, availability, price and delivery capabilities. The domestic mail-order business often tells the buyer up front what the delivery is — "delivery by parcel post," or "delivery by UPS ground," and there is an extra charge for special delivery arrangements. The only record of the review process will be the fact that the order was accepted by someone and joined the queue for shipment.

Full EDI creates a different set of issues for the process of review of customer requirements. Some EDI systems feed directly into MRP systems with little or no human interface. In these cases, the software packages become the vehicle whereby customer requirements are reviewed for adequacy. Anything that doesn't match causes the data to be rejected and flagged for human intervention to resolve the issues. In a case like this, the only process description required is that which explains what to do when data is rejected.

The bottom line is that the process must ensure that:

- Valid and current product information is provided to customers
- Customer inquiries and contracts are appropriately handled to ensure accurate information is provided
- Clearly defined customer requirements are identified
- The review process involves all necessary parties to ensure that the requirements (quantity, delivery, price, technical) can be met
- The requirements are understood
- Any requirements not stated by the customer but necessary for the intended use have been included
- The organization has considered any statutory or regulatory issues
- There are good records of the requirements and reviews
- Any changes or amendments to requirements are appropriately reviewed and communicated throughout the organization.

Audit Note:

Review of customer requirements contains a number of very clearly defined requirements and is more specific than in the past. Make sure that the records of review address all relevant items, and don't leave any issues mute. For example, if there are no regulatory or statutory issues, then state this somewhere in the process. Likewise ensure that the process takes account of unstated requirements that are necessary for the known intended use.

Implementing Requirements Through Design and Development

ISO 9001:2000, 7.3

Organizations that provide design services now have a further opportunity to refine and clarify customer requirements. Hopefully the design staff will have been involved in the initial discussion of contract requirements. Now they must take those requirements and turn them into an economic, producible product. The 1994 standard used the word "design" in addressing these processes. The new standard uses the term "design and development." For brevity this text uses "design," but the entire commentary should apply equally well to development activities undertaken within the scope of the management system.

Document the Design Plan

ISO 9001:2000, 7.3.1

The majority of organizations try to have a stable design process into which each individual project is fed. There are some which tackle such huge projects that every design plan is unique and separate, but many organizations a single design planning document can be used to outline the process utilized. This procedure or process description is where the various design documents are typically defined, the design review stages of the overall program identified, the responsibilities and authorities laid down and the design planning documentation explained and modeled.

An individual design plan can be as simple as a Gantt chart (see Figure 9-14) identifying the start and finish times of the project phases; where the reviews, verifications and validations take place; the stages at which various other organizational interfaces are triggered and who does what.

Regardless of the nature of the design plan, it should be regularly updated as the work proceeds.

Note the project identifier top left, and date and version number in the top right-hand corner of the plan. These must be controlled documents.

What about very small design jobs, a project that will only take a day or so? Well, the standard doesn't discriminate between task size when declaring that there must be a design plan. But neither does it mandate the nature of the plan, nor that an organization must only have one methodology in use for design plans.

When the design activity is short, typically the design requirements are limited as well, and therefore the design input document that defines the requirements

Figure 9-14

A Design Plan Using a Gantt Chart

Project AGC — Time / Activity	1	2	3	4	5	6	7	8	9	10	11	12	13	14
Project Initiation														
1 Board of Directors Approval	•													
2 Appoint Project Manager	•													
3 Initiate Project Book	•													
Project Plan														
4 Define Project Scope	•													
5 Appoint Project Design Team		•												
6 Initial Project Meeting		•												
Develop Design Input														
7 Identify Customer-Specific Requirements		•••	••											
8 Identify Previous Similar Designs			••											
9 Identify Regulatory/Legal Issues			•••											
10 Identify Environmental Issues			••											
11 Identify Any Safety Issues			•••											
10 Identify Verification Methodology		•••	•••											
Design Activity														
11 Conceptual Design			••••	••••										
12 Detail Design				•••••	••••	••••	••••	•••	•	•	•			
13 Mechanical Design				••••	••••	••••	••••	••••	••					
14 Electrical Design				••••	••••	••••	••••	••••	••					
Design Confirmation														
15 Design Reviews				•	•		•			•		•		
16 Design Verifications					•	•	•	•	•	•				
17 Design Validations										•	•			
18 Pre-Production										••••	••••			
19 Design Release												•		
20 Production Proof											••••	••••		
21 Post-design Review														•

Rev. 1.2/3/XX

might well also act as the design plan. It can identify the design review stages (once completed, for example), responsibilities and maybe even the acceptance criteria. This could be a one-page document with space at the top to write the design engineer's name, and the requirements are fulfilled for both the design plan and the design input requirements.

Planning procedures should always make allowance for every size of activity that the organization typically undertakes. But do not try and create a procedure that is all things to all projects — that will fail. If the organization designs things that literally take from one day to 10 years, then the best approach is to have multiple design planning procedures based on the scale of the project.

Information That Design Planning Should Provide to Users

- How the organization plans and controls design of the product.
- How design planning determines and documents:
    - The stages of design processes
    - The review, verification and validation activities appropriate to each design stage
    - The responsibilities and authorities for design activities
- How the interfaces between different groups involved in design are defined and managed to ensure all the relevant data is available
- How responsibilities for design activities are defined
- How each design plan is updated as the work progresses.

Audit Note:

Design plans can be as simple as the organization wants. There is no need for complicated, complex plans. Ensure that they are adequate for the activity, but keep them simple.

Simple is efficient.

Make sure that they are updated as required. This is a common problem — good initial plans that are not maintained. Remember these need to be controlled documents with a unique identifier, some form of version control and either the document or the process document must state who has authority to issue and change the documents.

Document Design Input

ISO 9001:2000, 7.3.2

Successful design starts with well-defined requirements, clearly documented and ideally traceable through the design process. Where part of the task is to develop the requirements, the process should ensure that there is clarity in the objectives set for that stage of the activity.

Input requirements must take account of

- Customer requirements
- Statutory and regulatory requirements
- Requirements not stated by the customer but known by the organization as necessary for the "known or intended use" of the product

- Life expectancy
- Lessons learned from past experience of similar work
- The "ilities" of design:
    - Produceability
    - Testability
    - Serviceability
    - Maintainability
    - Upgradeability
    - And increasingly often, disposability after use.

The manner in which this input data is documented is up to the organization to decide, and will, in part, be a function of the nature of the work being performed. For some organizations all this data can be captured in a single page whereas for others the input documentation will be a very substantial document. The inputs should also reference any external documents that impact the design. These may be statutory or regulatory, voluntary industry standards such as ISO, ASME or CECC documents, or customer documents.

However the input is recorded, the individual identification and enumeration of each individual requirement is worth the effort, as these can then be tracked one by one through the design process.

Design input documents need to be controlled; they are usually subject to change and therefore typically fall under configuration management. Changes to these documents need to be analyzed and reviewed in the same manner as changes to a finished product, with consideration on time, scaling, cost and producer impacts being performed before each change is accepted. In theory the process used to create design input documents need not, itself, be documented provided that the actual design inputs are.

Information That Design Input Needs to Provide to Users

- How design input requirements are to be documented
- How design input is to address the following requirements:
    - Functional and performance requirements
    - Applicable regulatory and statutory requirements
    - Applicable information derived from previous similar designs
    - Any other requirements essential for the design being undertaken
- How, when and by whom these inputs are to be reviewed for adequacy

- How, when and by whom any incomplete, ambiguous or conflicting requirements are to be resolved.

Nice to have: individual traceability on each requirement.

Audit Note:

Design input need not be complicated or complex, and should use original data sources wherever possible. There is no gain in copying data from one document to another; this simply encourages error. So if the relevant information is in a purchase order from a customer, then use that as the design input document.

Another reminder: Design input documents need to be controlled documents, either as QMS documents or as documents of external origin.

Design Activity

ISO 9001:2000, 7.1

Somewhere between creating design plans, documenting design inputs and documenting design outputs are those mysterious processes called design activity. The ISO 9001 standards have never asked for these processes to be documented, and the latest version is no exception. How the organization moves from design input to design output can remain an "SMH" (Something Magic Happens) box!

In reality, most organizations want a clear process in this area and will choose to define and document at least key areas of the design process to ensure consistency. In some disciplines this is a matter of maintainability; if a software design house doesn't specify code annotation, for example, the resulting product can become almost impossible to maintain. For other organizations it can raise issues of safety or regulatory compliance; examples here would be using defined criteria for printed circuit board design when the product is a modem connecting to a PSTN (Public Switched Telephone Network), or a filter connecting to high-voltage supply lines. In both cases there are strict rules that need to be followed to meet appropriate criteria. These are examples of process controls that are tied to regulatory compliance.

Staying with the same product — a printed circuit board — most professional design organizations have a set of design requirements for things like track widths and spacing. These requirements are based on empirical and theoretical work and exist to minimize risk — risk of "flashover" between tracks carrying power, risk of track burnout from overheating, risk of cross-talk between signal paths and so on. These are all forms of design process control.

Many design organizations try to minimize the level of process controls imposed on designers in order to allow free rein to their imaginative technical capabilities, but this must be done within a framework of acceptable risk. In order to be able to follow the concepts and thinking behind the development of a design, very often individuals are required to keep design logbooks in which they record ideas, sketches, "quick and dirty" calculations to check out ideas and preliminary "breadboard" test data. Once the design has moved past the preliminary stage and comes under formal configuration management a more formal set of process controls is implemented.

Audit Note:

The design process is one of the areas where many companies default to training and generic requirements for design elements rather than documented processes, other than the high-level process stages. But make sure that there are adequate controls to ensure consistency of activity and reliability of output. Designs want to look like they come from the organization, not the individual designer.

When Does Design Go Under Configuration Management?

ISO 9001:2000, 7.3.7

Determining this transition point is one of the most difficult management issues in the design environment. Impose formal control too soon, and the designer becomes mired in unnecessary paperwork, the configuration management department gets buried and everyone gets so fed up with the entire process that it becomes a problem rather than a solution. When this happens it begins to be ignored by everyone, and the next thing is that configuration management has careened out of control and nobody knows what the build-state of anything is anymore.

The other extreme can be just as bad. Impose control too late and configuration status accounting kicks in after the product has moved out of the design environment. By this point no one knows what is going on because there are no records as to what the configured state of the item is supposed to be for any given build-state.

A balance has to be struck.. Experience has shown that so long as a design remains with a single designer, or a single group of designers, the individual or group will maintain reasonable control because they need to know what they are doing. At this stage, control of changes can be as simple as a notebook (or part of the designer's notebook) for the project into which the individual or the team enters information about changes made as the design evolves. At some point the design is handed over to other people. For a small project this may be once it is completed, verified and validated. In other cases it may be for a first formal design verification process.

The design has now become common property, and from this point onwards a much more formal change control process needs to be implemented. Records should be maintained of what is changed, why it was changed, how the change was tested and validated and who authorized the change to be made. Depending on the design stage, consideration of the impact of change may need to extend outside the organization to suppliers who are gearing up to supply parts for volume manufacturing or other organizations whose products interface with the design and who therefore need to evaluate the impact of the changes on their part of the overall project. A large design operation might still be using a development configuration management process that requires a lesser level of change authorization than a postdesign change, but it will still be using formal methods.

Once a design is completed and formally released into the next phase, whether that is delivery to the customer or delivery to the production operation, the level of control over design activities needs to be much greater than during the design process itself. The potential effects of changes are far greater once the product is released to the outside world, and a whole additional level of impact assessment is required.

In all cases, when a designer wants to change the materials being used and decides to try a material that is new to the organization, a good management system will have processes in place that enable the designer to quickly and easily refer the proposed change to other areas of activity for comment. These include procurement, to get input on cost and availability of the materials; production engineering, for an evaluation of the impact of the change on processes; test and inspection, for input on the ability of current techniques to deal with the material, etcetera. The list will be different from industry to industry.

The important thing that needs to be recognized and actioned is that design change never happens in a vacuum, and that it must be an integrated part of the overall process. An example of the process flow for postrelease design change is shown in Figure 9-15, which indicates the activities involved, and the accompanying notes indicate the nature of a design change impact study.

Operation of the Postrelease Design Change Process in Figure 9-15

ECNs can arise from any source: customer, production operations, field experience, obsolescence, etcetera. Items 1 and 3 on the list are typically provided by requestor, item 2 is typically completed by design or configuration management.

All ECNs should be submitted through configuration management for logging and serializing.

Items 4-7 are completed by design engineering, although the requestor may have a suggestion for the nature of the change to be made.

All ECNs are submitted to a Configuration Control Board (CCB) for evaluation once all sections are complete. Members of the CCB must have an appropriate amount of time to complete impact studies prior to adjudication. This will vary

Figure 9-15

An Example of a Postrelease Design Change Process

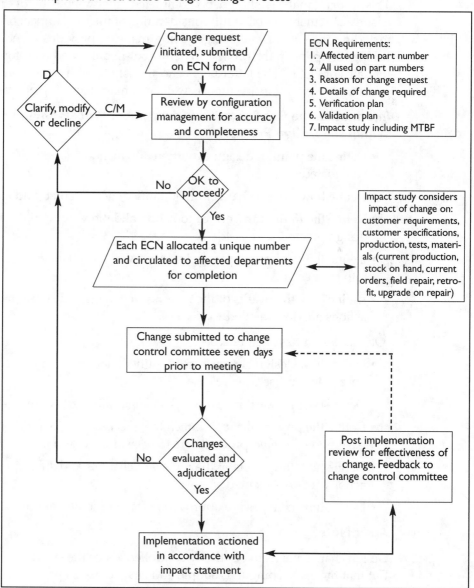

from industry to industry. All this activity can often be "virtual" in the modern company.

The CCB will assess the impact of the change, study the impact statements and determine the most effective implementation, taking account of technical, performance, customer, cost and availability issues. Implementation of change should always consider costs, and seek the lowest-cost option that will satisfy the technical, organizational and customer requirements.

This impact analysis should be completed line-by-line for every ECN. This ensures that there has been full consideration of the total impact of every change including the cost of the changes being made. It provides a vehicle for establishing discipline in the process to define cut-in dates and therefore the effectivity dates of ECNs. The latter helps enormously to eliminate confusion for suppliers and receiving inspectors, as well as in manufacturing operations.

Information the Configuration Management Process Should Provide Users Within the Design Process

- Define the point in design evolution at which formal change control is to be initiated.
- Define how design changes are identified, documented and controlled.
- Define the minimum verification and validation required during the design process.
- Define the minimum approval necessary before changes are implemented into the design.
- Define how the results of the review of changes and subsequent follow-up actions are documented.

Once a design has been released...

- Define how design changes are identified, documented and controlled once a design has been released.
- Define the process through which changes are verified and validated.
- Define the process through which the effects of the changes on constituent parts and delivered products are to be evaluated and by which functions.
- Define how the results of the review of changes and subsequent follow-up actions are documented.
- Define how changes are approved before implementation.

Audit Note:

Design change needs to be strictly controlled. Once the system is created, use it. But that means keeping it as simple and easy to use as possible. This is an area always examined by audit because it is easy to check — everything is documented.

The most common finding: undocumented changes and/or implemented changes that are not fully approved.

This is usually the result of slow, cumbersome processes.

Document Design Output

ISO 9001:2000, 7.3.3

Design output takes two forms. The first is in-process output, the second is final design output.

In-process design output is the stage of the design that is sometimes known as a design stage output, or a process gate, or a phase — there are many terms in current use.

Unless the design activity is small, most design projects take the complete requirement and decompose it into a number of smaller activities, most of which will interrelate in some way and which may all be assigned to different designers or design teams. Each element of the project will reflect different parts of the overall design requirement. Some will directly relate to deliverable requirements and some will be necessary stages in the process. Each part of the activity requires design input documents that reflect requirements as discussed above, and the individual identification of specific deliverable requirements can be a great help when a design is broken down in this way.

As each part of the design is completed, or as each phase concludes, it is essential that the results of the activity can be related back to input requirements and verified against those requirements. Only in this way can the design review and verification activities provide confidence that customer or other design input requirements have been met.

At each stage of the design, design output should verify that the customer requirements have been met. Consideration should be given to the impact of the design phase output on the safe and proper functioning of the product, any regulatory issues and production and maintenance issues. Each stage output should also identify appropriate acceptance criteria for the design stage and, where necessary, for the production process as well.

Once a design has been produced and it undergoes review activities, including verification and validation, it is released to the next stage. For some organizations this is the end of their immediate involvement — the design is the product provided. Future concern with this same product will now be a contractual matter, dependent on whether postdesign support services form part of the contract.

In many organizations, the next "customer" is internal, being the production or manufacturing unit that has to convert the design into deliverable product.

One of the most important single considerations in developing this stage of a management system is to have sufficient control in place to ensure that designs are formally released rather than "escaping." Escaped designs are like escaped convicts: they resist recapture and cause havoc in the outside world. This is particularly true of software.

The system should start by determining the nature of the way in which design output is "documented." In the modern world this is increasingly virtual, with the true design output existing in the form of data files, and paper copy merely being used for convenience in manufacturing facilities or on construction sites, for example.

Design output can equally well take the form of a model or sample item that will be copied by the production process. One example of this would be software, where a copy of the final design is provided for replication. This is also frequently true in the design and print environment and in many aspects of electronic and mechanical engineering, where data files rather than paper copy is increasingly the media of information exchange between customers and potential suppliers.

The increasing use of electronic data makes the entire configuration management process ever more important. Whereas in the days of a paper print it was possible to actually compare two drawings and detect differences if the change control had been lost, it could be done (albeit this was a very slow and laborious process prone to error). Performing the same activity on two enormous data files, which may contain many layers of information about a product, is almost impossible without automated tools.

The design stage output requirements now repeat themselves on a larger scale, with the entire integrated design activity output having to be presented in such a manner that the overall design requirements can be verified against the design output. The full scope of the design brief has to be verifiable while production, product acceptance, servicing and safety issues (where appropriate) must be documented.

Information That Design Output Needs To Provide to Users

- Define how design output is "documented" (i.e., the format of the information).
- Define how design output documentation addresses verification of output against the design inputs.
- Define how design output ensures that:

- Design and input requirements are met

- Appropriate information is provided for production and service operations

- Product acceptance criteria are either included or referenced

- Safety characteristics of the product that are essential for its use are identified.

- The process for ensuring that design output documents are approved prior to release.

- Defines the responsibility and authority for approval of documents.

Audit Note:

Design output must be in a format that allows for verification against design input. Clear links between input requirements and output verifications make the design verification process easy, and also help the audit process, both internally and externally.

Design output documents, whatever their format, must be controlled documents.

Design Review, Verification and Validation

ISO 9001:2000, 7.3.4/7.3.5/7.3.6

In most organizations these three activities are closely interwoven. Typically, design reviews take place at defined stages throughout the process to track and monitor timelines and technical achievement. One of the most important issues that needs to be understood and well defined is when to hold design reviews and who should be at each design review. The attendance at reviews will typically vary as the design evolves; the closer it moves to production, the greater the involvement of manufacturing personnel ought to be.

The stages at which design review, verification and validation are to take place should be contained in the design plan, which is drawn up before starting the design activity. It is important that these processes have clearly defined stages if they are to have credibility later.

The recommended approach is for the design plan to identify the review stages, provide a minimum agenda for each review stage and specify a minimum attendance at each review meeting. This approach ensures that the review, verification and validation activities enjoy a degree of independence from the design personnel. The phase gates are predetermined as are those who will decide if the design activity has met the phase requirements.

ISO 9000:2000 contains no definition of a design review per se, but it does contain a definition of a review, which is as follows: "Activity undertaken to determine the suitability, adequacy and effectiveness of the subject matter to achieve established objectives." This is not a bad set of criteria for a design review baseline, given that the idea of a design review is to have an independent but technically competent pair of eyes examine the process output and help to determine if it is on target. A design review that considers the "suitability, adequacy and effectiveness" of a design-stage output is like a comprehensive analysis of the design activity. It is important that design reviews focus primarily on whether the design achieves the requirements within acceptable limits of effectiveness and efficiency rather than becoming fights over whether a different approach might produce a marginally more efficient output.

Design verification, the process of checking the design-stage input against design-stage output, frequently precedes the final design-stage review activity and is itself subject to verification during final design-stage review.

Design validation is a different concept from design verification. Each stage of a design process might well meet the input criteria, but the completed design, when each module is integrated together, may not meet the overall user requirements. Hence ISO 9001 calls for the user "to ensure that the resulting product is capable of meeting the requirements for the specified application or intended use, where known." (7.3.6) Verification may cover a specific part of the design, and many applications. Validation is asking if the design will perform this particular task.

Once again, the validation process should be predetermined as much as possible. Methods, requirements and authority to accept the design should all be determined before the design activity commences. If a product is intended for several different applications, then validation should be carried out for each intended use unless there is sufficient similarity that designers can offer a cogent argument that data from one validation can be extrapolated to another use.

Records of all three activities must be maintained to demonstrate that the design requirements have been met, and if there are any outstanding issues. Records of those activities and their results should also be maintained. The core issues that the various stages of review, verification and validation should address are shown below. These may be supplemented by ISO 9004, 7.3.3, which provides further commentary and expansion on the areas worthy of consideration.

Design Review Procedures Should Provide:

- Responsibility for defining design review activities for each project
- A minimum frequency of reviews
- A defined design review agenda

- A review process capable of evaluating and ensuring:
    - The ability of the design to fulfill requirements
    - That problems are identified and follow-up actions proposed
- Defined authority for declaring the required participants in design reviews
- Defined authority for declaring and ensuring that appropriate functions for a particular design stage are represented
- A defined process for recording the results of reviews
- A defined process for tracking and following up on actions resulting from design reviews.

Design Verification Procedures Should Provide:

- Defined responsibility and authority for identifying individual requirements for design verification
- Defined processes for design verification
- Clear methodologies to ensure design output meets design input requirements
- Declared processes for recording and maintaining results of verification activities
- Records of any follow-up actions
- Records of the follow-up and closeout of actions resulting from verification activities.

Design Validation Procedures Should Provide:

- Clearly identified requirements for design validation
- Clearly defined methods for the performance of design validation
- Clearly defined processes for ensuring that the product is capable of the intended use
- Defined responsibility and authority to determine if validation is to be completed prior to the delivery of the product (This should be coupled with contract requirements)
- Defined responsibility for releasing product when full validation is a post-delivery activity
- Records of the results of validation
- A defined process and records of any follow-up actions resulting from validation activities
- A defined process to track and close out follow-up activities.

Once the design activity along with final reviews, verifications and validations are satisfactorily completed, the design is ready for delivery to the next stage in the process. Typically it is handed over to manufacturing, which takes over the next stage in the product realization process. An effective management system will have been aligning these activities throughout design. By the time the design is ready for the formal hand-off, manufacturing personnel have actually been working on the project for almost as long as the designers, thus ensuring that the transition from design to manufacture is painless and straightforward.

Audit Note:

Design review, verification and validation are nearly always intertwined activities. To enhance transparency consider process mapping (flowcharting) the process and providing a description of how design proving is accomplished.

Not only will this help prevent auditor confusion, it also ensures clarity in the minds of designers.

Have a very formal hand-off from design to production, even if that is after an extended pre-production phase. Make it clean.

Manufacturing Controls on Product Realization

Procurement

ISO 9001:2000, 7.4

There is an old saying, "You can't make a silk purse out of a sow's ear." It means if you buy junk, you will make junk. This is a fundamental industrial truth, and yet one that is rediscovered by organizations every working day. The inability of many organizations to identify the difference between the cost of procurement and the cost of ownership appears to be as strong today as it has ever been.

The relationship between a purchasing organization and its suppliers should be one of partnership and collaboration. Supplier processes need to be an extension of customer processes, because ultimately these processes are brought together through the products being supplied. If the supplier processes are incompatible with those operated by the customer, then trouble will ensue. The standard recognizes this essential truth by including a strong statement about the control of outsourced processes in the first general statement of requirements. The final paragraph in 4.1 mandates that: "Where an organization chooses to outsource any process that affects product conformity with requirements, the organization shall ensure control over such processes. Control of such outsourced processes shall be identified within the quality management system."

Before going further into the procurement side of activities, it is worth remind-

Figure 9-16

The Customer, Organization, Supplier Relationship

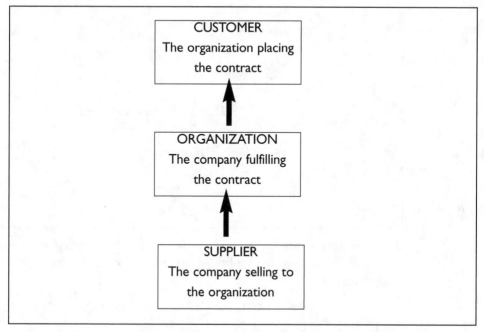

ing those who are familiar with historic ISO terminology of customer/supplier/subcontractor that the language has now changed. The term "customer" remains the same. This is the organization that is buying from the entity implementing ISO 9001:2000. That entity, which was previously called the "supplier," is now the "organization." This body in turn buys from "suppliers," previously known as "subcontractors." The language is consistent throughout the standard.

The entire supply chain is a completely interlinked process, with every stage having the ability to impact the next to a greater or lesser extent.

The ability to procure competent materials and supplies requires three issues to be properly managed.

First, requirement specifications must be accurate, appropriate and adequate. There must be sufficient information included in specifications to enable suppliers to understand the organization's needs. Specifications must indicate any important issues of measurement, process or training.

Second, suppliers must be selected on the basis of their technical ability, capacity and financial soundness to supply materials that meet the specification. Suppliers must be reviewed and evaluated regularly on the basis of their demonstrated performance.

Figure 9-17

The Supply Chain Interaction

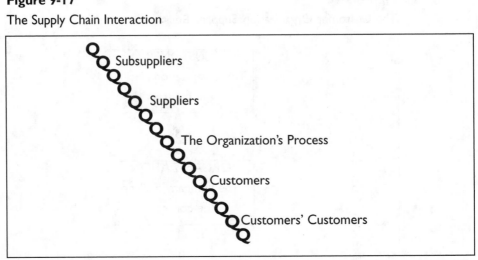

Third, requirements must be identified and orders placed with suppliers in a timely manner, thereby enabling suppliers to operate their processes effectively and completely.

If those three issues are not properly managed the organization will have ongoing problems over supplier performance.

The sequence in which activities are undertaken is also important. There is little point in researching, evaluating and selecting a supplier organization until the technical capabilities required are clearly identified; equally, there is little point in designing or selecting a technical specification that exceeds the known state of the art and then going hunting for suppliers.

Supplier selection can often form an integral part of the design process; for those organizations that do not perform design activity, supplier selection can make or break their efforts at creating customer satisfaction and shareholder value.

Creating Competent Specifications

ISO 9001:2000, 7.4.2 (a)

The quotation that appeared on page 285 from Phil Crosby, that half of rejections are the result of the customer, first appeared in print over 30 years ago. Experience shows that the situation hasn't changed much for many organizations. Even registered firms still tend to cling to the old idea of "buy cheap, buy fast," and fail to see any link between manufacturing problems and poor vendor management activities. The relationship between specification and cost is often not recognized. Remember, the tougher the specification, the more it costs to achieve it.

Overspecifying is an issue for many organizations. It is easy for an engineer to decide to make the tolerances tighter, the performance specification for a component wider, the grade of material to be used higher. It all adds confidence in the performance of the finished product and helps ensure that the specification will be met because it will probably be exceeded. But there is a price tag attached to these tighter specifications, and the price tag is high. In mechanical engineering terms, every figure behind the decimal point typically increases the production cost by an order of magnitude. Hence a tolerance of 0.1" on an item that costs $1 to make will increase to $10 if the tolerance becomes 0.01" and to $100 when the tolerance is tightened to 0.001." In addition to the increased cost of procurement, the cost of the organization's own processes will increase as well — tighter tolerances are harder to work with, to inspect to and to test. The entire cost structure of a product changes when the specification is enhanced.

There is rarely money to be made by exceeding customer expectations, and there are times when an overspecified product can actually disrupt the customer's process in a very detrimental manner.

Typically product specifications, whether for completed items, piece-parts or individual components, come from design engineering. They obviously need to ensure that they specify within the manufacturing capabilities of the organization, and generally within the capabilities of the current supplier base. Anything that is unusual should be flagged early in the design process, hence the need for other departmental involvement in design reviews and design changes in order that steps can be taken, both internally and in terms of sourcing appropriate suppliers.

Selecting Competent Suppliers

ISO 9001:2000, 7.4.1

Once specifications have been defined, the next job is to match them to appropriate suppliers. ISO 9001:2000 doesn't provide much guidance on this process, any more than the previous two versions did. The actual requirement is as follows: "The organization shall evaluate and select suppliers based on their ability to supply product in accordance with the organization's requirements. Criteria for selection, evaluation and re-evaluation shall be established. Records of the results of evaluations and any necessary actions arising from the evaluation shall be maintained (see 4.2.4)."

The first statement is a simple declaration of common sense: "Select suppliers based on their ability to supply … in accordance with … requirements." It is as important for a supplier assurance process to consider the business side of the relationship as it is to consider the product conformity aspect. Timeliness of delivery, cost, willingness to work with appropriate disciplines to resolve any problems that arise and financial soundness are all as important in the supplier base as is conforming product.

The business of supplier management is just like so many other aspects of management; it is all about managing risk in a cost-effective way. This risk management aspect of the control of the supply chain means that for the process to be cost effective it must be variable. This is not a "one size fits all" situation, and the level of control required for individual suppliers can vary from virtually none to having on-site staff performing prerelease tests and inspections on every item of product being provided. ISO 9001:2000 recognizes this fact with the statement, "The type and extent of control shall be dependent upon the effect of the purchased product on subsequent realization or the final product." (7.4.1).

It is worth mentioning that this statement does not only apply to suppliers, it applies to the entire procurement activity. The implications of that statement will be considered further in this discussion of procurement.

The conventional way of managing the supplier chain is to consider the purchased items and to group them into broad areas of risk. Very often a multitier model is used, ranging from virtually no control beyond price and delivery up to full audit and constant monitoring. The degree of variability is something that will vary from organization to organization depending upon the significance of their purchases.

As a consulting, auditing and training organization, for example, The Victoria Group buys very little, other than training materials, that directly impacts its customers and over which it can exercise influence. In consequence the company operates very little supplier control, and that is primarily monitoring by default. Purchased products (training manuals, et. al.) are examined on receipt, and if a problem is discovered the printer is informed and corrective action is taken. There have been few problems over many years, and this very relaxed approach to managing the supply chain is cost effective and operationally simple.

The other end of the scale for the company is hiring a subcontractor — a freelance consultant to represent the company in front of a client. In this case the potential for damage is considerable, and the selection process for subcontract consulting and training personnel reflects that concern.

Such a range of selection criteria is common sense. Note the statement, "The Victoria Group buys very little, other than training materials, that directly impacts its customers and over which it can exercise influence." The last part of the statement is important. If an organization cannot exert influence over a supplier of goods and services, then there is no point in pretending.

Listing the power company because electricity is important is a pointless exercise. Likewise, for The Victoria Group to list the airlines or shipping services would be pointless. The best the company can do with these organizations is to monitor experience and try and use the companies that cause the least grief or have the best prices.

When items are purchased as OEM product, whether it is a computer printer, a brand-name product or even an integrated circuit, the specification of the delivered item is substantially controlled by the OEM source. In this situation, price and delivery are all that matter. Obviously in selecting a distributor for integrated circuits it pays to ensure that their handling and general storage methods are OK, but if major distributors are being used that is a pretty safe bet. These suppliers can be monitored by exception — unless there is a failure report, leave them alone.

The focus of attention needs to be on those suppliers who are producing specified and unique products that have a potential for significant impact on the deliverables from the organization. The selection and monitoring process should separate out the important suppliers and determine the monitoring and control methodology to use. Then use the data collected in a meaningful way.

ISO 9001:2000, 8.4 (d)

Receiving inspection is a dreadful waste of money. Suppliers are paid to provide conforming product. When materials are subject to an additional inspection on receipt, the work is being done twice. It is far better to take considerable care over supplier selection and then monitor performance in process.

Audit Note:

Supplier selection is an area that can be grossly overplayed by auditors, most of whom come from large-company backgrounds. For a small company the ability to influence suppliers is often very limited, and the process should reflect reality. There is no point in the 30-man company trying to change the way that a Fortune 500 company operates. It isn't going to happen. The best that can be done is to monitor performance and adjust processes to deal with reality.

Don't let auditors demand unreasonable activity, but do document what you do.

Providing Reliable Purchasing Information

ISO 9001:2000, 7.4.2

Referring back to the Crosby quotation, once there is a supplier base that can be relied upon, the next concern for the organization is to ensure that its purchasing systems provide those suppliers with accurate and reliable data. If the wrong information is given to a supplier, no one should be surprised if the wrong goods or services are supplied.

Be careful what you ask for — you just might get it.

The use of paper purchasing documents is diminishing quickly. More and more purchasing data is transmitted electronically, often drawn directly from design databases, which are accessed through complex MIS structures. Control of purchasing technical information is now often in hands which are remote from the purchasing process. Good interfaces between relevant groups are essential to ensure that the data required by the supplier are present and are complete.

Key information to be provided on an "as appropriate" basis is as follows:

- A unique and complete description of the product. This could take the form of a catalog part number, a drawing or engineering information provided by the organization, a sample piece to be copied or other form of data. It is absolutely vital that any critical information with respect to measurements, tests or inspections that are important to the purchasing organization are identified in this product description.

- Any requirements for certification or other approval or qualification of the product to be supplied (Mil-Spec, ASME, CECC, UL, etc).

- Any requirements for the use of specific, certified or approved procedures, processes and/or equipment (e.g., ASME welding procedures).

- Personnel qualifications relevant or essential to support the other approvals.

There are times when, either for internal reasons or because of customer requirements, a supplier is selected because that supplier is a registered company with a qualified management system. If this issue is important to the supply of product, then the requirement for product to be provided under the aegis of the certified system must also be included in the purchasing data provided to the supplier.

Make sure that all purchasing data are verified as accurate and appropriate prior to issuing those data to a supplier. The alternative is to receive nonconforming material and to have to live with it because what has been received is what was ordered, even though it is wrong.

Audit Note:

Make sure that purchasing documents contain clear and precise information. A catalog part number is fine, but include the identification of the catalog, e.g., Spring 2001.

When items are ordered to in-house drawings, send a copy of the drawing for the required revision of the item every time.

Verifying Purchased Product

ISO 9001:2000, 7.4.3

The standard addresses issues of verification of purchased product under purchasing, Clause 7.4.3. The process of verifying purchased product is a measuring and monitoring activity and, following a process model, the issues that should be considered in determining the level of verification required for purchased product will be addressed as part of the overall measuring and monitoring activities of the system as a whole. Purchased materials cannot be considered in isolation. The verification processes that should be applied to them depend on three issues:

1. The level of control exercised at the supplier

2. The impact that faulty product would have on the organization's own processes or products

3. The ability of the organization to perform a valid verification.

If the organization intends to perform on-site inspection or tests prior to allowing the supplier to ship product, or if the organization's customer wishes to visit the supplier and perform such tests and inspections, this information must also be contained in the purchasing document. Suddenly turning up at a supplier and demanding access to inspect or test product is not an action designed to win friends and influence people. Allowing a customer to do the same thing is an almost certain way of losing a supplier from the database.

Audit Note:

If the organization doesn't do on-site verification, then say so in the quality manual and be done with the subject. Do not allow an auditor to demand that the issue be addressed on a "maybe" basis. This is a decision exclusively for the organization.

Required Process Controls for Purchasing

Required process controls for purchasing include the following:

- An overall process for purchasing products and services that directly impact the deliverables, with variable levels of control based on the significance of the item being purchased

- An overall process for identifying, selecting and monitoring suppliers.

- Defined selection criteria, directly linked to the effect of the purchased item on the organization's own processes

- Defined processes for periodic evaluation of suppliers based on the importance of the items being purchased

- Records of supplier performance reviews, including any consequential actions

- A demonstrated link between the supplier performance reviews and purchasing activity

- A process for ensuring that if on-site verification activities are required this information is included on the purchase order.

Materials Management and Handling

ISO 9001:2000, 7.5.3/7.5.4/7.5.5

Materials management is a logical progression from procurement activities even though these activities bridge many areas of an organization. The most important single issue to remember is that the safe and proper handling, identification, traceability (when required), preservation, storage and transportation of materials is an issue of concern and significance at all times when product and piece parts are under the control of the organization.

In a well-ordered organization any item that forms any part of the deliverable product will at all times be properly identified as to what it is, whether or not it is able to be used and where it is in the overall process. The item will also be packaged appropriately to enable safe handling, and if necessary it will be traceable to its origins even from outside the organization.

These controls will apply regardless of whether the product belongs to the organization or to a customer.

Audit Note:

This is an area where the process knowledge of the auditor will be in play. Normal industrial practices, taking account of any regulatory issues, are expected unless there are specific contractual reasons for something different. As an example, basic ESD precautions will be expected in electronic assembly operations. The auditor cannot demand anything special!

Product Identification, Status and Traceability

ISO 9001:2000, 7.5.3

Product Identification

From the moment that an item is delivered to the organization it should be appropriately identified. This identification must be adequate for the processes in use, and can be anything from a physical location to a description or part number permanently affixed to the item. Identification must also show if the material is customer property. In this latter case it will often be necessary for the identification to include "used on" information, by way of contracts or equipment. It is very important that customer property is sufficiently well identified to ensure that it will not be used other than for the purpose for which it has been supplied.

Product Status

The second requirement for material is to identify whether or not it can be used — what ISO 9001:2000 calls "status with respect to monitoring and measurement requirements." At any stage in the process from receipt to dispatch it must be possible to identify by whatever means is appropriate for the organization whether an item of material can be used or not. How this is established is up to the organization to determine. It may be achieved by location, by physical identification such as a stamp or other marking, indicated on paperwork that travels with the material or by uniquely identified computer records tracking barcodes etc. The method is for the organization to determine.

Any material that is not suitable for use must also be identifiable, and if it is customer property the customer must be told about it.

Product Traceability

The third issue that has to be addressed is that of traceability. It is very important to keep identification and status separate from traceability. The first two are generally essential in every organization to some level. Traceability, on the other hand, is an activity that many organizations do not require at all. Those who do require traceability need to define the level to which it needs to operate with some care. Traceability is an activity that can cost a great deal of money, often with minimal returns.

The various levels of traceability that can be required of products can range from full source — in the case of an aluminum casting that could literally mean knowing which mine the bauxite ore came from — to tracking the serial numbers of completed products, thereby knowing which customer has received a specific item and finished build-state of a product.

There are an infinite number of possibilities between these extremes, and they are typically determined by contract, regulation or industry practice. The value of traceability is the ability to track where products are if there is a problem that requires postdelivery corrective action. Often this action is declined by the customer even when information on potential failure is known. How many people fail to take their cars in for work even after a manufacturer has issued a recall notice? The Big Three spend enormous amounts of money trying to track owners when there is a serious safety recall, but even when the work is free people often cannot be bothered to have it done.

An organization should not implement traceability unless there is a defined need, as described earlier, or a clear benefit to be gained by the organization. This might be the ability to protect against risk by tracking and tracing products, or the opportunity to sell further products, upgrades or enhancements to customers based on a knowledge of the capability they currently own. An example of this level of traceability and the application of this "up-selling" opportunity is in the registration process for commercial software. The "come-on" that encourages the purchaser to register is usually free technical support for a defined period of time. The benefit to the company is that once the customer information is in their database they have a relatively captive audience to whom to offer enhancements, upgrades and improvements.

Handling

ISO 9001:2000, 7.5.5

The standard calls this issue "preservation of product." In essence the requirement is one of common sense. At all times while product is under the organization's control, appropriate steps must be taken to ensure that it is not damaged. This applies to piece-parts as well as finished products and to all the steps in between. In the 1994 document the activities were called "Handling, Storage, Preservation, Packaging and Delivery," and any organization that has addressed all those issues within its management system should have no problem meeting the new requirements.

Handling issues can involve everything from ESD protection for electronic devices to the use of appropriate equipment for installing a jet engine on an Airbus 370. The management system needs to take care of the appropriate issues through process controls, training and the provision of a suitable working environment to include equipment and facilities.

The same is true for issues of preservation, packaging and storage, all three of which can be closely linked. Very often the assurance of effective preservation of a product is gained through controlling the packaging and storage environment. Examples of this would be the preservation of certain pharmaceutical products through the use of airtight packaging; or the assurance that a side of beef has been maintained at the proper temperature. The quality of many electronic components is assured through the use of conductive materials, while mechanical components are sometimes oiled or greased before being packaged in grease-proof wrappings.

In addressing these issues, the organization must consider product issues, safety issues and regulatory concerns, all of which have a bearing on process activity.

The other activity that is an integral part of materials management but actually receives scant mention in ISO 9001 is that of the storage of materials. In the 1994 standard there was a brief mention of the need to provide authorized methods for the receipt and dispatch of materials from assigned storage areas. Even this brief reference has been dropped from the current text of the standard, leaving the entire activity to be addressed only through reference to protection and storage. An essential part of any competent materials management program is knowing how much of a particular product is available for use at any given moment in time. Whether this is through a stock-management system that relates to a physical count or a measure of volume — buy more when the last box is opened — some method of relating availability to demand is core to successful process management.

Controlling the Processes

ISO 9001:2000 keeps the issues which have been discussed here as three distinct clauses. They are identified as 7.5.3, Identification and traceability, 7.5.4, Customer property and 7.5.5, Preservation of product. The activities are closely linked and where documented processes are developed they will frequently address all of these issues because of the linkage. Product identification, for example, will usually progress from the receiving bay through a storage activity into the production area, and in order to move from receiving to storage the status of the product must be known in terms of inspection. The method of moving invokes handling requirements, and the method of storage will be concerned with both packaging, storage and preservation. The same is true once materials are removed from storage areas into main production areas.

Process Requirements for Materials Management

Identification

- Assuming it is required, the process must provide for product identification throughout all production and service operations.

Status

- The status of the product with respect to monitoring and measurement requirements must be maintained throughout all stages of production, installation and servicing.

Traceability

- If traceability is a requirement then the process must control and record the unique identification of the product at all stages while it is under its control.

Preservation

- Processes must exist that preserve conformity of product with customer requirements during internal processing and while the product is under the organization's control.

- Processes may need to include:

    - Training

    - Delivery

    - Handling

    - Warning notices (ESD, HAZCHEM etc.)

    - Packaging instructions

    - Storage instructions.

- Processes must ensure the protection of product.

- Processes must apply to the constituent parts of products.

Stock Control

- Operating controlled processes includes managing stock to maintain process activities.

Customer Property

- All the controls identified above must be applied to any customer-owned property supplied to the organization.

- Processes must ensure that customer property is:

    - Identified

    - Verified

    - Protected

    - Maintained.

- Processes must ensure that any customer property that is lost, damaged or otherwise found to be unsuitable for use is recorded and reported to the customer.

There is one area of "materials" that has not been addressed, and that is in the arena of customer property. Increasingly often the "property" that a customer passes to a supplier is in the form of intellectual property rather than physical materials. This intellectual property has to be protected just as carefully as hardware, and protected from damage or access by unauthorized personnel.

Audit Note:

Don't confuse identification — essential in every organization to some degree — with traceability, which should only be implemented if there is a regulatory, statutory, contractual or defined organizational benefit; even then, to the minimum acceptable level. It is hugely expensive, so ensure a cost benefit from its use.

The status or "usability" of any product should always be known. Good systems will automatically treat product whose status is unclear as potentially nonconforming, and revalidate before use.

Planning of Realization Processes, Operations Control and Process Validation

ISO 9001:2000, 7.1 / 7.5.1 / 7.5.2 / 6.3 / 6.4

Planning

The new standard has replaced the 1994 clause on process control with an entire section called "product realization," which starts with requirements for the planning of product realization before moving into the capturing of customer requirements, design and so on. Design has its own section on planning, so the application of Clause 7.1, Planning of realization processes, can be largely focused on operational matters.

The issues addressed are mainly those that have historically been called "quality planning" and are concerned with the overall structure and interrelationships of the activities involved in transforming customer requirements into deliverable products.

The overall process that takes requirements from source to delivery has to be an integrated set of activities. Each is interdependent upon many others, just as was demonstrated in the discussion of the engineering input to product specifications and the linking of materials management processes.

The organization needs to examine its operations and determine the process-flow of activities. This is another subset of the macro process flowchart that was developed during the early planning stages. In the operational area it will now become a set of processes that gradually develop the deliverable, testing and inspection at certain defined and predetermined points, until finally the finished deliverable sits awaiting dispatch — pristine, on time and conforming to every customer requirement.

Once the process-flow has been documented and managed through training. the nature and form of that documentation or training must be determined and provided. At predetermined stages in the process, some form of monitoring and measurement will typically occur and these activities must also be decided and documented. Responsibilities and authorities for the ongoing release of product have to be declared and a records regime established sufficient to provide confidence that the products meet defined requirements.

Closely integrated with all this process activity planning has to be a review of facilities and capacity issues to ensure that all the support services, hardware, software and associated equipment are available at the right time to enable the plans to be realized and the customer's delivery requirements to be met. These issues represent the quality objectives for the product, project or contract, and the goal of the organization should always be to fulfill completely all objectives.

Aligned with the facilities and capacity issues are those of statutory and regulatory compliance, including issues of health and safety and environmental compliance.

There are two main ways in which these activities are pulled together. One kind of organization is constantly doing things in different sequences, or even different tasks dependent entirely on customer requirements. The other kind of company basically does the same thing every day, the only variance being quantity and other in-process changes. Depending on the nature of the business, the approach to creating a management system will be different.

The organization that operates differently for each customer usually finds it easier to work in a system based on quality plans. This has a small number of core activities defined within the central management system and the remainder individually documented for each contract in product, process, project or contract specific plans, usually called quality plans.

The more common system is one where the operations of the system are substantially the same from day to day. In this system, the core processes are the main body of the operation, and individual project or contract quality plans are typically little more than the customization by quantity, color and similar minor changes in the specifics for a particular order.

Whichever approach is chosen, documentation should be based on the training versus documentation graph shown in Figure 9-8, and the objective should always be to minimize the amount of process documentation required. The standard leaves the decision to the organization as to how much documentation is needed.

The output from this core planning activity will be the system itself, the determination as to whether to operate on a quality plan basis or a singular system, and the core business operational requirements. There is unlikely to be "procedure" that addresses the issues identified in 7.1. It is far more likely that they will be addressed across the entire suite of documentation with respect to operational processes.

Issues To Be Addressed in the Planning Realization Process, Including Facilities and Work Environment

- The organization needs a defined process for planning product realization.
- The planning process must be consistent and integrated with the rest of the management system.
- Planning must cover all processes and subprocesses.
- The planning process will usually be documented throughout the system.
- The process must determine, as appropriate:
    - Quality objectives for the product, project or contract
    - The need for processes and documentation
    - The need for resources and facilities specific to the product
    - Verification activities
    - Validation activities
    - The criteria for acceptability
    - The records necessary to provide confidence of conformity of the processes and resulting product
    - The need for quality plans.
- Planning must identify the facilities needed to achieve conformity of product.
- Planning must include maintenance to achieve conformity of product, including:
    - Workspace
    - Equipment, hardware and software
    - Supporting services
    - Specific factors in the work environment needed to achieve conformity of product including human and physical factors.
- Planning must consider statutory and regulatory requirements.

Additional issues worthy of examination can be found under 7.1.2 in ISO 9004:2000.

Audit Note:

For most organizations these activities will be an intrinsic part of the operation of the overall management system.

Anticipate that auditors will take time to adjust to the fact that organizations will often not respond to requirements in a unitary manner, but in "bits and pieces" throughout the system.

One way in which an organization can help itself, its staff and auditors understand how and where the response to requirements is to be found is by developing a matrix of conformity during the implementation process.

Operations Control

ISO 9001:2000, 7.5.1 / 6.3 / 6.4 / 8.1

Operations control covers manufacturing, process control, process measurement (including product), installation activities and servicing activities. Everywhere the organization touches the product the requirements of operations control need to be considered and addressed.

The 1994 standard required that the organization provide documentation where its absence could adversely affect quality. The decision was in the hands of the organization. That has not changed. The decision on where process documentation, procedures and/or work instructions are needed remains one which the organization makes based on the training, background and experience of the personnel concerned.

How is this apparently daunting task to be undertaken? The best approach is the same as that for eating an elephant — one bite at a time.

Step 1.

Separate out initial manufacturing from installation and servicing. There will be few similarities and these other activities are best kept apart.

Step 2.

Take the process flowchart for the manufacturing operation and determine where any checkpoints are, or need to be, for processes and products from material receipt to final delivery. These are the measuring and monitoring operations.

Identify any need for statistical techniques and the statistical method to be used.

Identify the necessity for, and frequency of, any process verification or revalidation activities.

Identify any "special processes." These are processes whose output cannot be fully verified and where deficiencies may only be discovered when a product is in use. Typically these are processes that require destructive testing. See below for further information and discussion on process validation for "special processes."

Step 3.

Verify that all the appropriate operations are identified on the flowchart.

Step 4.

Determine which of the process operations, monitoring and measurement activities that have been identified in steps 2 and 3 require support by some form of document or work instruction.

Determine where a record is required to demonstrate conformity, either in the case of a product-related issue or a statutory or regulatory issue.

Determine where training is required to support such activities, including statutory and regulatory issues.

Determine responsibility for release of product between process stages and on completion of relevant activities. The documentation, record keeping and training requirements for the process have now been identified.

Step 5.

Go back over the process and determine what measuring and monitoring equipment is required for process activities or checkpoints. Document those requirements and ensure compliance with any statutory or regulatory issues.

Step 6.

Review the overall process and determine the maintenance requirements for any equipment used that may be needed to ensure continuing process capability. Document those requirements.

Step 7.

Collate all relevant information to the maximum extent possible. Integrated process documentation can be created that addresses process methods, expected outputs, monitoring activities and any statutory or regulatory issues.

Considerations for Operations Control

Operations control must consider, as appropriate:

- How to provide information that specifies product characteristics
- Where work instructions are needed
- What training is required

- What equipment is needed
- How to maintain process equipment to ensure product conformity
- Where in the process measuring and monitoring activities should occur
- What measuring and monitoring devices are needed
- Which measuring and monitoring equipment requires calibration
- The implementation of defined processes for product release.

Audit Note:

As with the planning of product realization processes, different aspects of operations control are likely to be managed in a multitude of different areas of the organization. It may be helpful to show this in the quality manual, in a process map or by using the schedule of conformity mentioned earlier.

An example of this diversity would be measuring equipment, which is likely to be managed through the calibration program rather than through "operations."

Process Validation (Special Processes)

ISO 9001:2000, 7.5.2

There are many processes that cannot be fully and effectively monitored, nor the output reliably tested. These have previously been called "special processes," and they require different handling from activities that are can be fully verified.

Organizations must determine if any processes exist where the results cannot be fully verified. Typically, if the test for the process output is destructive, then the process falls into this category. Examples would be welding, various bonding processes from sticking shoes together to the vulcanization of tires, making matches and — as an extreme example — the manufacture of fireworks or munitions.

In each of these cases, to verify that the process has worked fully the product ends up being destroyed. The only way to confirm that a weld is perfect is to cut it in half. Bonding of shoes or tires is verified by tearing the bond apart, and the other two examples have to be blown up to prove that they are working.

In these cases, a different approach has to be adopted and control has to be established through monitoring and measurement of the process and the equipment used, coupled with training for the personnel involved. Special processes usually require carefully defined processes, the use of qualified equipment and training for the process operators. Typically revalidation of the process is required at regular intervals.

Controlling Special Processes

- Provide for the validation of process capability, equipment capability and personnel training.
- Demonstrate the ability of the process to achieve planned results.
- Maintain records to demonstrate continuing process capability.
- Ensure that validation includes the following, as applicable:

    - Qualification of processes

    - Qualification of equipment, including calibration requirements

    - Qualification and training of personnel

    - Use of defined methodologies and procedures.

- Revalidation requirements for process, equipment and personnel.

Audit Note:

Only declare a "special process" if it is generally seen that way in industry. Welding is typically regarded as such if the welded product requires certification of some sort. This would not be true of the manufacture of a farm gate. Similarly, soldering is not generally regarded as a special process; although everyone provides training in the art few bother to calibrate soldering irons, relying on the skill of an operator to highlight problems. Aerospace, avionics and similar high-reliability products are an exception to this general rule.

The decision is for the organization, not the auditor, unless there is evidence of problems.

Delivery, Postdelivery and Servicing

ISO 9001:2000, 7.5.1 / 7.2.3

The majority of organizations complete their contractual obligations (with the exception of warranty claims) either when the product is shipped or once it has been delivered to the customer. The activities that need to be considered here include control of delivery processes and postdelivery activities, including installation and ongoing servicing (maintenance) of the product, and warranty.

Delivery

The method of delivery can be a contractual issue, and where the customer has the opportunity to select or specify the means of delivery, the customer order review process must ensure that this information is correctly transferred to the operational area of the organization. The level of process control that is required will vary depending on the nature of the operation, but it is important that careful consideration be given to a number of factors.

1. Customer requirements

These must be correctly transferred to the operations area.

They may include such items as a specified carrier, special packaging requirements, special delivery requirements for time and date of delivery, etc.

2. Product requirements

These may include special packaging to protect the product, e.g., ESD, refrigeration or drop and tip indicators. These may also be intended to protect society at large, e.g., lead-lined containers for radioactive products, sealed containers for biological products. Such issues may also be subject to statutory or regulatory requirements.

3. Labeling requirements

Special labeling may be a regulatory or statutory issue — HAZMAT, Bio-hazard — or a matter of product protection — "Fragile," "This way up," "Do not stack more than x high."

4. Packaging requirements

This is another area that is increasingly subject to customer specifications and regulatory requirements. Many customers will not accept anything that is packed in styrene or has disposable packaging. Packaging that uses ozone-depleting chemicals is banned in several countries, as is nonreturnable wooden packaging in others.

Installation and Ongoing Servicing

There are two types of organizations that perform installation and servicing. The first has these activities as part of the overall service they offer, the second provides only installation and/or servicing activities. In the first case the process control of installation is merely a part of the management system and in the second it is the system. Organizations that exist to provide installation and servicing facilities for their customers have to operate a complete system as described in this chapter. Those for whom these activities are a subset of the overall process can support them with a discrete set of processes linked to, but independent from, the core process documentation.

Installation and servicing are typically areas of activity where detail in documentation defaults to high levels of training for personnel performing such tasks. The documentation is often identical to that which accompanies the product, supplemented by customer instructions on location of installation and any special requirements connected with the site. These may include routing of services to the equipment, type of fixtures to be used, ventilation to be installed and any one of many other considerations. Many companies have comprehensive installation requirements that are applied across the industry to any installer working for them even when installing OEM equipment — an example would be the telecommunications industry.

Part of the installation process may include the final validation testing of the product that was left undone at the conclusion of the design phase, and the organization's internal processes must ensure that such information, together with the validations to be performed, are communicated in a timely manner. (ISO 9001:2000, 7.3.6)

Installation activity nearly always requires that some form of testing be performed, and the requirements for the "measuring and monitoring" activities need to be defined, as well as the records to be maintained and the actions to be taken in the event of an equipment failure. Where tests and inspections are performed there is often measuring equipment in use, and this may require calibration in accordance with defined procedures.

The process controls that an organization places on installation activities will obviously vary greatly depending upon the complexity of the activity, in just the same way as the range and depth of process documentation used within manufacturing varies. In considering the scope of the system for installation activities, there are a number of different ISO 9001:2000 requirements that may become relevant, and some of the core areas of consideration are indicated below.

Servicing may be an on-site or an off-site activity. When it is performed at the customer's location, many of the issues are the same as for installation. When equipment is brought back to the organization's location the process controls used can be substantially the same as those for warranty work. The activity and control will be the same; the only difference may be the performance specification that is used for older items as compared to a brand-new item returned under warranty. It may not be possible to restore an old item to original specifications.

Managing Installation and Servicing Processes

The system must define processes for:

- Receiving and managing customer requirements; ISO 9001:2000, 7.2.1

- Identifying and controlling equipment at the customer's site; ISO 9001:2000, 7.5.3 / 7.5.4 / 7.5.5

- Ensuring the use and control of suitable installation and servicing equipment; ISO 9001:2000, 7.5.1

- Physical installation/servicing activities, as appropriate; ISO 9001:2000, 7.5.1

- Inspecting and/or testing items to establish conformance or nonconformance to specified requirements; ISO 9001:2000, 8.2.4

- Maintaining appropriate control of inspection and measuring equipment; ISO 9001:2000, 7.6

- Maintaining records of activities undertaken and performing analyses to identify opportunities for improvement of products, processes or systems. ISO 9001:2000, 4.2.4/8.4

Warranty

Activities connected with warranty claims and repairs are usually managed as part of the core process because such activity is effectively part of the original contractual agreement between the customer and the organization. The warranty is typically part of the initial agreement to supply. Warranty activity is often concerned with rectifying and returning a product to the customer, and that will invoke the processes concerned with the identification, control and safekeeping of customer property which have already been discussed. The customer will expect to receive back the same item that has been sent in for repair, or a brand-new item. Certainly it would not be good practice to return a different warranty-repaired item unless this is clearly stated somewhere in the exchange between the customer and the organization.

The management of warranty issues forms part of the effective handling of customer complaints, and clearly defined processes must be in place to receive and respond to complaints. Records must be kept for customer complaints so that appropriate data analysis can be undertaken and necessary improvement activities initiated. Warranty and field failure information can provide valuable data for the enhancement of current and future products provided that it is collected and analyzed. All too often these data are never subject to any form of critical examination, and repetitive problems dog successive generations of a product because designers have never been told about them. This information is addressed in ISO 9001:2000, 7.3.2 (c), "information derived from previous similar designs."

Warranty activity is a subject that draws on numerous ISO 9001:2000 requirements, and several of these are identified below. This list is not necessarily comprehensive; the intention is to demonstrate the wide scope of this activity in terms of management system requirements.

Managing Warranty Processes

The system must define processes for:

- Receiving and managing customer complaints; ISO 9001:2000, 7.2.3

- Identifying and controlling returned items as customer property; ISO 9001:2000, 7.5.4

- Inspecting, testing, or otherwise reviewing returned items to establish conformance or nonconformance to specified requirements; ISO 9001:2000, 8.3

- Repairing, reworking, replacing or returning the item to the customer (with an appropriate explanation — not specified in ISO 9001); ISO 9001:2000, 8.3

- Maintaining records of activities undertaken, performing analyses to identify opportunities for improvement of products, processes or systems. ISO 9001:2000, 8.4

Audit Note:

Keep all these activities distinct and separate from each other.

When product is brought in-house, whether for warranty or for maintenance, use existing processes wherever possible to eliminate extra procedures, instructions, etc., but be aware of the limitations of doing so.

Ongoing maintenance and repair activity can require that very old documentation is used. Make sure that there is good control of this otherwise obsolete documentation to make sure that it doesn't end up in current production areas.

Measuring and Monitoring of Processes and Products

ISO 9001:2000, 8.1 / 8.2.3 / 8.2.4

The activities discussed in these elements of the standard have previously been called process control and inspection and test. As with other sections of the standard, this one starts with a requirement that the overall approach to measuring and monitoring be planned and implemented in a manner that will assure product conformance and provide suitable data to assist efforts at continuous improvement. Part of this planning process is to identify opportunities for the use of statistics.

The year 2000 version requires that the organization shall "apply suitable methods for monitoring and, where applicable, measurement of the quality management system processes. These methods shall demonstrate the ability of the processes to achieve planned results. When planned results are not achieved, correction and corrective action shall be taken, as appropriate, to ensure conformity of the product." ISO 9001:2000, 8.2.3. A macro view of this statement could be taken to imply a need to have monitoring and measurement activities for every activity within the management system, which is a series of interactive processes designed to assure customer satisfaction. Such a view may well provide ongoing opportunities for system oversight, but the primary goal of these requirements clearly remains product realization activities, i.e., production.

The standard no longer requires the identification of specific inspection and test activities at receiving, in-process and final. The new requirement is that "The organization shall monitor and measure the characteristics of the product to verify that product requirements have been met. This shall be carried out at appropriate stages of the product realization process in accordance with the planned arrangements." ISO 9001:2000, 8.2.4.

During the seven-step activity that was used to map out the operations control activities, the measuring and monitoring of processes and products was identified in Steps 2 and 4. These are two important functions, and there is, rightly, a distinction drawn between "measuring" and "monitoring."

ISO 9000:2000, the repository of quality vocabulary, does not define either word but it does provide a definition of "measurement process." That definition is: "set of operations to determine the value of a quantity." In other words, measurement means establishing an absolute or relative number.

A process or product can only be measured by a device that is capable of providing absolute information relative to an established norm. This will typically require some form of calibration against a recognized national or international standard so that the accuracy of measurement is known. Examples of equipment requiring calibration are calipers, micrometers, feeler-gauges, voltmeters, oscilloscopes and frequency generators.

Monitoring can be performed by devices that will indicate when some characteristic has moved relative to other characteristics within a defined range. This has important considerations for the type of devices used and the manner in which they are maintained, controlled and validated. Typical examples of monitoring devices could include pressure gauges used to assure that there is pressure in a line, wall clocks used to time a process with wide tolerances or mechanical sensors that will indicate if product fails to appear in a location. Monitoring can also be no more complex than an individual watching a process to ensure that product flows through the operation; these days such visual monitoring is frequently performed by machines that "watch" a process and sound an alarm if something goes wrong. A good example of this would be the computer inspection of surface-mount printed circuit board assemblies to ensure that all the components have been placed correctly.

From the information gathered in response to Step 2, the stages of the process where product measurement is to be performed should be identified. These may well start with the receipt of materials from a supplier, and will either end with the final release for shipping or continue into the delivery and installation phase of the contract.

Each measurement stage needs some means of informing those carrying out the task what is to be measured, how to do it and what equipment to use. When test and inspection is performed on receipt of materials from suppliers, the vehicle for these data could be the purchase order, a reference file, the specification against which the order has been placed or a conventional work instruction. The latter can also take several forms, from a chart hanging on a wall to an individual document for each item to be inspected, or a sample item against which the new delivery is compared.

The organization decides for itself, and then puts appropriately controlled activities in place. The same guidelines apply to each and every stage in the organization where measurement is undertaken, whether that measurement is of product conformance or of process capability. Very often a product measurement can also be used to demonstrate process capability. An example of this would be the data typically logged on an X R chart, where often physical measurements of product samples are used to track the operation of the process within predetermined limits. The monitoring of the process is the activity of examining the data on the chart and determining if action is required to ensure the continuing adequacy of output.

Not all monitoring and measurement activities require that records be maintained. Many process monitors can and do operate on an exception basis, only recording out-of-limit conditions. The same can also be true of product measurements. There is no intrinsic value in keeping records of every in-process inspection performed by the organization. There are usually data sources available to provide gross throughput information, and armed with those data and the failure data, process performance can be established quite easily.

The data that must be recorded is that which establishes the conformity of the process or product with "specified requirements." These are the process gates that verify that what is being delivered to the customer conforms to the organization's own specifications or to their requirements. Records of these data, along with information as to the authority for product release, is important, and a requirement of ISO 9001:2000, 8.2.4.

Managing the Monitoring and Measurement of Processes and Products

- Determine and apply suitable methods for monitoring and measurement of processes and products to meet customer requirements.

- Provide suitable process instructions for each monitoring and measurement activity.

- Provide suitable training to ensure that personnel performing monitoring and measurement activities understand the task and the importance of ensuring conformity with requirements.

- Ensure that the methods in use confirm the continuing ability of each process to satisfy its intended purpose.

- Ensure that appropriate monitoring and measurement equipment is available to perform the assigned tasks.

- Ensure the ongoing maintenance of monitoring and measurement equipment; see the section on calibration (below) and maintenance (above).

- Ensure that measurement activities provide evidence of conformity with product or process acceptance criteria.

- When an activity results in the release of product ensure that records indicate the authority responsible.

- Ensure that product release and service delivery do not proceed until all the specified activities have been satisfactorily completed.

- Where there is a methodology to allow for release prior to the completion of all acceptance procedures, ensure that there are appropriate activities identified to manage the situation when subsequent activity reveals that nonconforming product has been released. When such activities require customer approval, ensure that procedures exist for obtaining approval in advance of product release.

Audit Note:

This generalist monitoring and measurement requirement is going to cause confusion to some auditors and to some organizations. It is best addressed through the normal process activities. Follow the seven-step process outlined, and create process maps that highlight the monitoring and measurement activities. Decide which are which, and ensure that the differences are clear. Documenting them is the best way to go, even though there is no stated requirement for a documented process.

Calibration

ISO 9001:2000, 7.6

The discussion on monitoring and measurement draws a clear and necessary distinction between activities that require that a measurement is taken bearing an absolute relationship to an accepted standard and those that merely require that a general sense of well-being is established. The former requires that the measuring equipment is formally calibrated against a known standard. The latter may require no more than that a device is periodically tested and shown to be functional.

Step 5 under operations control involved the identification of the equipment to be used for monitoring and measurement activities. Selection of appropriate equipment is essential. The accuracy and precision required of the measurement activity has to be a consideration in determining what is to be used. In part, the requirements for accuracy and precision also help determine whether the activity being undertaken is a measurement or a monitoring activity.

The selection of appropriate gauging and measuring equipment forms part of the systemic planning activities that ensure the effectiveness of the system. Design activity should be carried out within the framework of the available process capability, which includes measurement capability, or those responsible for managing production need to be involved at an early stage when new capabilities are required to ensure that they are obtained in a timely manner. There is no point in designers requiring production tolerances that exceed a manufacturing facility's ability to measure and control them.

Once the appropriate equipment has been selected and obtained, the decision then has to be taken as to whether or not the devices require to be calibrated, or merely validated as operational.

Calibration is an expensive business, and only those devices that are used to assure product conformity with specified physical or performance requirements need to be calibrated. As far as possible, measuring equipment that requires calibration should be used well within its capabilities for measurement accuracy. This concept is illustrated in Figure 9-18. Calibration requires that the item is compared with known measurements over a range of capabilities, and the relative accuracy of the device compared with a recognized standard — usually a national or internationally recognized standard — is then identified and docu-

Figure 9-18

The Tolerance Funnel

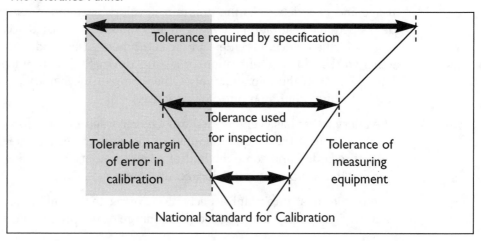

Tolerance required by specification

Tolerance used for inspection

Tolerable margin of error in calibration

Tolerance of measuring equipment

National Standard for Calibration

mented. The measurement uncertainty of the device becomes known. This is an expensive process, and it makes no sense for any organization to calibrate equipment that is not used for purposes of assuring product conformance. Such items typically become "monitoring" items.

The control of monitoring devices is probably best managed as part of an equipment maintenance regime, whereby the item is examined at regular intervals, cleaned and adjusted as necessary to ensure that it continues to operate as required. These items, even though they are not being calibrated, must still be identified and controlled. Some form of register might be an option, with maintenance information recorded for each item. Another valid approach would be a tie-on tag on each device with the date entered each time the item is examined. The method will depend on the extent of the problem; there is no single answer as to how this should be done.

Equipment that requires formal calibration will have to be tracked and controlled more closely. Calibration is a formal process that mandates certain control functions. These include:

1. A unique identification of each item of equipment.

This may be achieved through use of serial numbers (manufacturer's or the organization's), location — probably only a good idea for static devices that are not capable of being moved without considerable effort – or item descriptions. The latter will only be adequate where there are no duplicate items.

2. Determining the calibration interval for each item.

Not every item of equipment needs to be calibrated at the same interval; many items need not be maintained in calibration at all, being classified as "calibrate prior to use." Other equipment might require calibration every three months or three years. The interval should be based on manufacturers' recommendations, usage and experience. As the program develops and an equipment history is developed, the calibration interval can and should be adjusted according to the history of the device. Much electronic equipment in use today is "fail safe." It either works and is in calibration, or it shuts down. Such equipment might well have very long calibration intervals. Other complex mechanical jigs and fixtures might require calibration prior to every use.

The interval that has been decided must be recorded in some form of record or database against the unique identifier of the equipment, the due date for calibration recorded and some method of recall or otherwise alerting users to the fact that the equipment is due for recalibration.

One of the most important aspects of ensuring that a calibration program is effective is to ensure that whoever is in charge of the process has the authority to insist on equipment being handed over for recalibration. If need be, this individual must be empowered to physically remove items from use. Without this authority the program will rapidly fall apart, as there is always a good production reason why an item of equipment cannot be sent away at any given moment.

Obviously the requirements of the calibration and maintenance program must be reasonable. Recalls for calibration and maintenance must be planned, notified well in advance, and can always be marginally adjusted to suit unexpected demands providing that there is historical evidence to support a short variance.

Equipment should, whenever possible, be protected in some way from any form of adjustment or handling that could or would invalidate the calibration. This can be achieved with seals or labels, or requiring that the item is stored in a purpose-made container and handled with care. This is particularly true of equipment taken off-site for the performance of installation, servicing or maintenance work.

Remember that equipment used during design and development also needs to be calibrated; otherwise the results of design activity may well prove to be invalid.

3. Ensure that necessary calibrations are performed.

Having a well-documented and operational monitoring and recall process doesn't help if the equipment is not properly calibrated when it is collected. All items requiring calibration should be examined against a standard having a known, valid relationship with a national or international standard, and the results of this process recorded.

Each item of equipment should be returned to the organization with a certificate of calibration that identifies the reference standard and the results of the calibration process.

Occasionally organizations find that they cannot calibrate against a known reference standard because no such standard exists. In this situation the organization must develop and prove its own method of assuring the measurement accuracy of the device in question, and this technique must then be recorded and followed for all subsequent calibrations.

4. Maintain records of the calibrations performed.

Ideally the actual measurements made during calibration should be maintained as records along with the certificate showing the traceability of the process to a recognized source. Without this information it is difficult for an organization to know how to react to any situation where an item of equipment is found to be out of calibration.

Very often there is nothing that can be done because no records exist as to what products have been tested using any particular item of equipment. This means that the only action open to the organization is to assess the possible results of the out-of-calibration condition, and then monitor customer complaints and customer returns to see if the predicted condition appears. Using the calibration tolerance funnel helps alleviate this situation in that, when it is possible for the measurement accuracy of the equipment to substantially exceed the specification of the product, a significant-of-calibration condition might not have any impact on the conformance of the product.

5. Remember that software needs validation at regular intervals.

Unlike hardware, software doesn't "wear out." Making a lot of use of a program doesn't shorten the life expectancy of the code, or cause it to gradually become less competent as the bits and bytes get worn away or fail through stress fracturing. Basically, once code is working it will keep working unless it becomes corrupted or damaged in some way, or unless there is a basic flaw in the code that causes a malfunction with time. This has been known to happen more than once, with tragic consequences.

Once proved and introduced into use, software that is used for monitoring and measuring products should be periodically retested and revalidated to ensure that it is working correctly and producing the right results. This can be done in several ways. Many automatic test machines run a self-check on the software every time they are started up. The code can be verified by running a test on a special standard item on a regular basis, or it can be compared with a test program. The method is up to the organization but, where software is used to assure the conformance of product, methods of verification need to be identified.

Guidance on the development and management of calibration programs can be found in ISO 10012, and ISO 17025 provides a full management system model for calibration laboratories.

Managing the Control of Monitoring and Measurement Devices

- Identify the measurements to be made.
- Identify appropriate monitoring and measurement equipment capable of the accuracy and precision required.
- Determine which items require calibration.
- Determine a management system for the maintenance of items requiring maintenance but no calibration.
- Establish control of equipment requiring calibration.

- Include the following data in the control records:
  - The equipment type (the identification of the device)
  - The unique identification of the item
  - The location of the item within the system, including any equipment that is off-site
  - The results of calibration activities
  - Whether the device was within specification when received for calibration and, if not, what the measurement error was
  - The traceability record to the national or international standard used for calibration purposes. (This may include details of the calibration method used, and must do so if there is no recognized standard against which to calibrate the device.)
- Ensure that all devices are calibrated and adjusted in accordance with the defined time frames.
- As far as possible safeguard the equipment from adjustments that would invalidate the calibration.
- Institute methods of handling, maintenance and storage that will prevent damage, particularly for items used off-site.
- Have a method to assess the validity of test results if devices are subsequently found to be out of calibration.
- Consider the need for:
  - Traceability from device to product
  - Appropriate corrective action
  - Appropriate preventive action.
- Identify any software used for measuring and monitoring.
- Ensure that software is validated prior to use.

Audit Note:

The only effective way to operate a reliable calibration regime is to operate a documented process. Using externally certified laboratories is usually the more cost-effective option for maintaining calibrated equipment unless there is a great deal of it. Maintaining a facility that can provide true traceability to national and international standards is very expensive.

Do not allow the auditor to demand more of the organization than common sense requires. If an item of measuring equipment cannot be adjusted, e.g., a steel ruler, it does not need to be calibrated, merely verified as undamaged and "fit for purpose." Remember the measurement accuracy is to be "appropriate." A steel rule is not a precision measuring device.

Remember the validation of automatic testers.

Once the calibration process is drafted and placed into use, the core product realization activities have been completed. The significant customer satisfaction controls are in place, from initial customer inquiry to fulfillment of contractual obligations.

Developing the System Infrastructure and Key Improvement Processes

The system is not yet complete. The document control system was developed before starting on the implementation program, so this is already in place. The remainder of the administrative framework needs to be constructed to support the activities in the fulfillment chain, and the core system monitoring and improvement activities need to be created and implemented.

The administrative framework consists of the quality manual, document control, records management and the training needs assessment regime.

The system monitoring and improvement activities encompass control of nonconformity, corrective and preventive action programs, customer satisfaction, internal audit, data analysis and management review.

The quality manual is a significant part of the documentation, being both the introduction to the management system and providing the basic road map through the processes. Many organizations start by writing a manual, but in the absence of the supporting system such manuals end up being little more than a modified copy of the standard and often require substantial rewrites by the time the project is initially completed. The Victoria Group recommends that the quality manual is left until the core systems are in place. This way the manual can describe what the system really looks like rather than what an abstract system can look like.

System Infrastructure

The Quality Manual, Document Control, Records and Training

ISO 9001:2000, 4.2.2 / 4.2.3 / 4.2.4 / 6.2

Chapter 11 deals with documentation, including the quality manual, in some depth, and the information will therefore not be replicated here beyond a brief summary of typical content.

The Quality Manual

ISO 9001:2000, 4.2.2

A manual can serve a number of different functions, some of which are internal and some external. The internal function is one of introducing company staff and recruits to the concepts, principles and objectives of the organization's operational methods. The manual provides an overview of how things operate, who is responsible for what and where supporting information is to be found.

The manual must cover the scope of the system. The manual must also identify any elements of ISO 9001:2000 that have been excluded from the system in accordance with the guidance provided in Clause 1.2. Any such exclusions must be explained and justified.

Typically the quality policy is also contained in the manual, and core long-term management objectives are also likely to be found. The manual then explains the processes contained within the management system and how they interact, and provides information as to where additional information is to be found, i.e., procedures and other documentation that support the system.

The manual therefore acts as an introduction and overview of the fundamentals, beliefs, objectives and operations of the organization and how it is organized.

Externally the manual will provide all the same information to the potential customer. Because it may be used in this context, many manuals also include a brief history of the organization, descriptions of key products and services, the identity of major customers and, sometimes, biographical information of key senior executive staff..

The quality manual can be made to pay its way!

Audit Note:

A quality manual is not required to address every requirement of the standard. It should provide a flavor of the organization and guidance on where other information can be obtained.

It must have:

- Statement of management system scope
- Justification for any exclusions from the system
- Description of the processes used to take customer requirements and turn them into deliverables
- Information on where further details are to be found if not included.

It is nice to have:

- Quality policy
- Responsibilities and authorities
- Key objectives.

The manual must be a controlled document within the management system.

Document Control

ISO 9001:2000, 4.2.3

As has already been stated, a separate chapter of this book addresses the subject of document control in detail. Earlier in this chapter, reference was made to the need to create a control process and document format at the start of the implementation activity. As with the commentary on the quality manual, this section will defer to the later chapter and be limited to brief commentary on the intent of the control mechanism.

The concept is simple: Document control exists to ensure that the right information is available to the right individual at the right time to ensure that the task is performed in the right way. Simple is good, complex will be difficult to maintain and operate.

Responsibility and authority for control and change of documentation is best delegated to a position as close as possible to the task in hand as is compatible with technical competence.

- Avoid centralization whenever possible; it merely produces logjams.
- Strictly limit the amount of material that is considered "controlled."
- Avoid controlling forms as far as possible (see the chapter on document control for guidance on how to achieve this).
- Remember the importance of documentation that provides significant input to the organization but is controlled externally, e.g., national and international standards, industry standards, customer documentation and data.
- Use electronic control and distribution wherever possible and eliminate paper copies.
- Have an easy, accessible system for checking the currency of documents.
- Get rid of old stuff.

Remember that records are not subject to document control because they never change. The standard dictates that they be treated as a "special kind of document" and managed in accordance with Clause 4.2.4.

Audit Note:

Historically an estimated 65 percent of all nonconformities raised by auditors are against document control. Make sure that the system is simple, effective, user-friendly and limited to what needs to be controlled.

Get all those forms out of the system unless they contain "how to" information.

Get everything online and away from paper as far as possible.

Records Management

ISO 9001:2000, 4.2.4

Records are an important part of the management system. They provide the documented evidence of product, process and system conformity, thereby providing the basis for audit and review of the system. Such activities are always reactive; they study historical data on what has happened and what resulted and offer decision-making opportunities that will hopefully prevent repetition of past errors.

When properly used, records can play a far more important role than providing information about past errors. Careful review and analysis of data contained in the records that come out of the management system can provide opportunities for preventive action, detecting trends and acting before a situation develops that causes a problem. This creates a continual process of improvement that can benefit products, processes and systems, adding value to the organization and all its stakeholders.

There are many ways of identifying, collecting and collating records. Over many years of management system implementation, experience has shown that the most user-friendly approach is for individual process documentation to identify the records that result from the operation of that process.

Whether the supporting documentation consists of procedures, work instructions, process flowcharts or any other kind of instructional documentation, it can include relevant information on records to be created and retained as a result of the operation of the process. When the process "documentation" consists of pictorial, aural or sample information — such as photographs or videos, tapes or CDs or a sample work item — this will need to be supplemented in some way with any required information on records generated and maintained.

Not every process within a management system creates a record. The standard requires that "records shall be established and maintained to provide evidence of conformity to requirements and of the effective operation of the quality management system." Within the body of the text the standard identifies 26 specific types of records; these are the ones which, if relevant, must be maintained. Most organizations will require many more than this. An example would be a record of a purchasing document. The standard does not identify these as quality records, but they clearly need to be kept as part of the process of verifying deliveries. In addition, they will often form part of the financial records of an organization, which are a matter of legal compliance.

Processes that may be documented in some way but may not result in records could include individual assembly operations, some inspections or tests where only failures are recorded or machinery set-up operations.

Within the framework of the management system each organization will have to decide for itself what records will provide data which are useful and capable of analysis. There is a tendency for organizations to overdo record retention, keeping records of everything for years. Records are like measurements — only collect information that has some value and can be used, and keep it for as short a time as possible. Keeping records is an expensive business, and the fewer the better.

Deciding What To Keep

The decision-making process on what records should be kept starts with identifying those records that are mandated as a result of law or regulation.

Next come those that are required as a result of contractual requirements, which can often specify both types of records and retention times.

Third, review what the standard requires. The relevant records within the system scope, and subject to any exclusions, must be retained by any organization either seeking certification or wishing to make a self-declaration of conformance.

Finally, when all the above are satisfied, the organization should look at whatever is left and decide for itself whether there is any added value in the retention of these records, and if so, what that value-add is and how long it lasts.

Each and every record should be subjected to this four-point test, and dispositioned accordingly. Dispositioning requires that the responsibility for collection, collation and storage of the record is defined, along with the retention time and any special requirements for disposal at the end of the specified time. All of this information can be included in the process documentation that results in the record being created, as demonstrated in the sample procedures accompanying Chapter 11.

In addition to the information contained in each procedure, a generic records management procedure should be created that defines the options for record retention — paper, electronic, photographic, etc. — and the general disposal methodologies used. This procedure can be used for all generic requirements such as preservation and retrieval policies, and can also be used to create a default retention time, which is used if there is no specific time identified in an individual process document. There are many options and choices open to the organization.

Do not try to create a procedure that identifies every single record contained within the system. Apart from the sheer size of such a listing, it is almost impossible to maintain, and therefore a constant source of audit findings. Distributed data is the way to go.

Records Mandated by ISO 9001:2000 or Requirements for Information To Be Recorded

1. 5.6.1 Management review

   Records of management reviews.

2. 6.2.2 Competence, awareness and training

   Maintain appropriate records of education, training, skills and experience.

3. 7.1 Planning of product realization

   Records needed to provide evidence that the realization processes and resulting product fulfil requirements.

4. 7.2.2 Review of requirements related to the product

   The results of the review and actions arising from the review shall be maintained.

5. 7.3.1 Design planning output — information that shall be recorded

   Planning output is required to be updated as the design evolves. By definition this requires that it is documented in some form.

6. 7.3.2 Design and development inputs

   Inputs relating to product requirements shall be determined and records maintained. Four types of data are listed.

7. 7.3.3 Design and development output — information that shall be recorded

   Outputs from the design process are required to be documented in a manner that permits verification against design inputs. This requires some form of document.

8. 7.3.4 Design and development review

   The results of the reviews and any necessary actions shall be recorded.

9. 7.3.5 Design and development verification

The results of the verification and any necessary actions shall be recorded.

10. 7.3.6 Design and development validation

The results of the validation and any necessary actions shall be recorded.

11. 7.3.7 Design and development changes

The results of the review of changes and any necessary actions shall be documented.

12. 7.4.1 Purchasing process

The results of supplier evaluations and follow-up actions shall be recorded.

13. 7.5.1 Control of production and service provision

Information which describes the characteristics of the product.

14. 7.5.1 Control of production and service provision

Work instructions when these are required.

15. 7.5.2 Validation of processes for production and service provision

Requirements for records [Organization to determine need].

16. 7.5.3 Identification and traceability

The organization shall control and record the unique identification of the product, where traceability is a requirement.

17. 7.5.4 Customer property

Occurrence of any customer property that is lost, damaged or otherwise found to be unsuitable for use shall be recorded and reported to the customer.

18. 7.6 Control of monitoring and measurement devices

Be calibrated or verified periodically, or prior to use, against measurement standards traceable to international or national standards; where no such standards exist, the basis used for calibration or verification shall be recorded.

19. 7.6 Control of monitoring and measurement devices

The organization must assess and record the validity of previous measuring results when equipment is found to be out of calibration.

20. 7.6 Control of monitoring and measurement devices

Records of the results of calibrations are to be maintained.

21. 8.2.2 Internal audit

Records of the audit activity are to be maintained.

22. 8.2.4 Monitoring and measurement of product

    Records shall indicate the authority responsible for release of product.

23. 8.3 Control of nonconforming product

    Records of nonconformities, actions taken, concessions obtained.

24. 8.4 Analysis of data

    The data is collected from the records identified in this list; the analysis itself will also become a record.

25. 8.5.2 Corrective action

    Recording results of action taken.

26. 8.5.3 Preventive action

    Recording results of action taken.

Audit Note:

For most organizations records are an intrinsic part of the overall management system. Auditors rely on records for historic evidence that activities have occurred. With the reduction in required documentation in the new standard, there are now several activities where the production of records of inputs and outputs may be the only way to demonstrate effective control of the process. Records are even more important than before.

Competence, Awareness and Training

ISO 9001:2000, 6.2.2

Training is important to every organization, whether it operates a management system or not. All too often it is one of the first areas to be cut when any pressures arise, including both financial and operational. The standard tries to create an environment in which training becomes more visible at executive management level.

Who Does What?

Clause 6.2.1 states that, "Personnel performing work affecting product quality shall be competent on the basis of appropriate education, training, skills and experience." There are no qualifications to this requirement. It applies to all personnel having any form of assigned responsibility within the management system. This means that everyone from the top executive on-site to the employee emptying trashcans must have appropriate "education, training, skills and experience" for the tasks they perform that are also part of the management system. In all too many organizations training stops dead at shop supervisor level. Once the title "engineer" or "manager" is achieved it appears that many companies believe that no further training is required. Apparently there is no new knowledge required!

ISO 9001:2000 requires that organizations give some consideration to the assignment of tasks to personnel. The fact that this requirement applies at all levels in the organization means that at some level top management must consider the training needs of senior staff. Thereafter, task delegation becomes a responsibility at functional levels.

The overall requirement created in Clause 6.2.1 is expanded and given substance by the associated requirements defined in 6.2.2, "Competence, Awareness and Training."

The first requirement is that organizations must "determine the necessary competence for personnel performing work affecting product quality." Everyone within the scope of the management system is captured in this net, so there needs to be some means of identifying the skills required for each position in the organization. There are several ways of doing this, and as with all aspects of a management system, the simpler the more effective. It is important that the skills identification process be something that is open and accessible to staff.

There are many positions within an organization where the job title effectively identifies the required technical skills. Typically job descriptions provide a range of core competencies, as determined by management. In some industries law and regulation also define some of the required qualifications — the medical and pharmaceutical industries, for example, and some areas of public transport. An organization must capture all of these and incorporate them into processes for determining the required skills for each specific task.

A competencies matrix is one very effective way in which not only to identify required skills, but to also track the training, including an evaluation of effectiveness. A matrix can be created for an individual position or for groups of positions, and in the case of large-scale manufacturing, one competencies matrix might be appropriate for significant numbers of personnel. An example of a competencies matrix is shown in Figure 9-19.

The individual skills are identified across the top of the form, and the names of the individuals inserted down the side. As each skill is acquired and the supervisor is satisfied that the training has been effective, i.e., that the individual is now "competent," the box is filled in and dated. The competencies matrix also serves as a training plan and as a record of training. One major advantage of this system is that the information remains where it is most useful, in the hands of the supervisor in charge of the area concerned.

ISO 9001:2000 goes further than simply requiring training and competency. It

Figure 9-19

An Example of a Competencies Matrix

Skill ➡️	Component Ident.		Hand population		Soldering		Repair	
Individual ⬇️	Date Trained	Date Verified	Date Trained	Date Verified	Date Trained	Date Verified	Date Trained	Date Verified
Anita	03/03/00	04/03/00						
Cindy	05/06/01	06/07/01						
Fred	03/03/00	04/03/00						
Steve	03/03/02	04/03/02						
Chris	05/06/01	06/07/01						
Connie	03/03/02	04/03/02						
John	05/06/01	06/07/01						
Christina	08/09/00	09/07/00						
Howard	05/06/02	06/07/02						

demands that the organization also "ensure that its personnel are aware of the relevance and importance of their activities and how they contribute to the achievement of the quality objectives." This requirement is in addition to the need for the quality policy to be "communicated and understood within the organization" (ISO 9001:2000, 5.3c).

Part of the training regime must therefore ensure that applicable objectives are explained, and individual contributions in satisfying those objectives understood. This process can become a complete operation in itself. Organizations that use Hoshin planning or some similar system will be familiar with an entire management process that deploys corporate objectives down to individual performance objectives. Such activities meet, indeed exceed, the requirements of the standard.

Smaller organizations need not become paranoid. Only high-level objectives set by management are needed to meet the standard provided that all staff understand those objectives are and how they as individuals contribute to the achievement of the objectives.

Finally, appropriate records must be maintained of all training activities, the education, qualifications and experience of all staff.

Requirements for Training, Awareness and Competency

- Procedures must be in place to ensure the competency of personnel who are assigned responsibilities.
- The processes must ensure that:
  - Competency needs are identified

- Training is provided to satisfy those needs

- The effectiveness of training is evaluated

- Personnel are aware of the relevance and importance of their activities in achieving quality objectives

- Records are maintained with respect to education, training, skills and experience

- The quality policy is understood.

Audit Note:

The concept of trained personnel has been replaced with the concept of competent personnel. There is no doubt that many auditors are going to seek definitions from organizations as to what "competent" means.

Word games are an audit nightmare. Can Jane Doe do the job? Is Jane Doe trained to do the job? Has the organization verified that the job Jane Doe is doing is the right job? Is there any evidence that Jane Doe is doing the job wrong? If not, then Jane Doe can be declared "competent."

System Monitoring and Improvement Activities

ISO 9001:2000, 8.3 / 8.5.2 / 8.5.3 / 8.2.1 / 8.2.2 / 8.4 / 5.6

The system monitoring and support activities encompass control of nonconformity, corrective and preventive action programs, customer satisfaction, internal audit, data analysis and management review.

Control of Nonconformity

ISO 9001:2000, 8.3

> *The best-laid schemes o' mice an' men*
> *Gang aft agley,*
> *An'lea'e us nought but grief an' pain,*
> *For promis'd joy!*

> — Robert Burns, 1785

The famous lines from Robert Burns, written over 200 years ago, say it all! However hard we try, things still manage to go wrong and result in nonconformities within the organization. Nonconformities can occur in product, process and system; the 1994 standard isolated product nonconformity for special attention, and focused corrective and preventive actions on all three. ISO 9001:2000 doesn't specifically address process and system in any of these interrelated activities but it refers generally to nonconformities and potential nonconformitites. These can occur in product, process or system.

Nonconforming product is likely to appear from even the best of systems and processes. The trick is to ensure as far as humanly possible that the management system trap that nonconforming product and take it off-line for disposition before it can be delivered to the customer. Hopefully the safety net provided by various forms of "monitoring and measurement" will ensure that anything nonconforming is identified and segregated before there is any risk of use or installation.

The method is undefined; the requirement quite clear. A documented procedure must be produced that defines the process whereby the organization ensures that nonconforming product or service is properly identified and controlled. The control shall prevent "unintended use or delivery" until the procedures that have been created to manage the review and disposition of this unacceptable product have been put into effect.

The documented procedure must provide for notification to all relevant functions inside and outside the organization. It is for the organization itself to identify these functions. Notification may extend to the customer through a contractual requirement. As the standard reminds us, nonconformities may also require notification of a relevant authority. This may be a regulatory body.

Note the quoted text. The word "unintended" is very deliberately used. There are times when organizations will deliberately use nonconforming product, with or without a customer's agreement or knowledge. This should always be done in a controlled manner with the appropriate authority of organizational management. This is one reason for having "production permits" or "waivers."

The new standard retains text requiring the identification of responsibility and authority for the review and disposition of nonconforming product. It states that "the controls and related responsibilities and authorities for dealing with nonconforming product shall be defined in a documented procedure." This is one of the six mandatory procedures.

It is important to remember that this clause applies at all stages of the product realization process, from customer order to final handover. It can apply to service, installation or design just as much as to raw materials, piece-parts or finished goods.

Four options for the disposition of nonconforming product are available. Product can be reworked back to the required specification. Some nonconforming product may be used "as is," with a concession authorized by an appropriate authority identified in the procedure — and which may, when contractually specified, need to be the customer. It can be regraded and specified for an alternate use, or as the standard describes it, "the organization shall …[take action] …to preclude its original intended use or application." Some nonconforming product will be so far off-target that it must be scrapped, an option that the new standard appears to lump in with precluding "original intended use."

Whatever the decision with respect to the disposition of the product, in all cases the organization must take action to eliminate the nonconformity once it has been detected. The procedure must define whether the process and authority are the same across the entire organization, or if there are different authorities and responsibilities in various areas of the operation from design through after-sales service. These things need to be considered, defined and documented.

All nonconforming product is subject to reverification when it has been corrected.

In cases where a nonconformance is identified after "delivery or use has started," the organization is required to take "action appropriate to the effects or potential effects of the nonconformity."

Records are an essential part of the management of nonconformance in many ways, not only to prove that appropriate action has been taken but also to provide process failure data that can then be used to identify opportunities for improvement. The information collected should include:

- A description of the nonconformance
- The authority for disposition
- Details of any rework performed
- Any items accepted "as is" describing their condition and/or any repairs which were authorized.

Any concessions written for the product, whether by the organization itself or an external body, should also be recorded.

The records must in all cases identify the authority for the disposition of the nonconforming product. This is a requirement that comes from Clause 8.2.4, which states that records must "indicate the person(s) authorizing release of product," as well as the 8.3 requirement that "controls and related responsibilities and authorities" be identified in the relevant procedure(s).

Most companies recognize two levels of nonconforming product. The first is routine production rework, for example, the replacement of a faulty component during the testing of a printed circuit board assembly, or the return of an oversized turned part to a lathe operator. This should still be documented to enable process analysis, but the authority to proceed will typically be at shop-floor level. The second involves a more serious nonconformance, one that is beyond the scope of local repair, typically resuting in material review board or similar process. It is customary for most purchased products to follow this route if they are found to be nonconforming when put into use. This is to enable appropriate corrective action to be initiated with the supplier of the faulty product.

Managing Nonconformity

1. Document, implement and maintain a procedure for the control of non-conforming product.

2. Define the responsibility and authority with regard to the disposition of nonconforming product.

3. Ensure that nonconforming product be identified and controlled.

4. Ensure that this control prevents unintended use or delivery.

5. Ensure that nonconforming product is corrected and subject to reverification after correction.

6. Ensure that appropriate action is taken when nonconforming product is detected after delivery or use has started.

7. Ensure that, when necessary, the proposed rectification of nonconforming product is reported for concession to customers, end users, regulatory bodies or others as appropriate.

8. Ensure that records of all activities for the control of nonconforming product are maintained.

Audit Note:

Control of nonconformity is a very important activity in terms of assuring customer satisfaction. Processes need to be well defined and well understood and applied in all areas of the organization.

Note that the standard does not require segregation of material; good identification of nonconforming material is required to prevent inadvertent use. The decision to use nonconforming material is a valid decision provided that it is made at the right technical or managerial level.

Corrective and Preventive Action Programs

ISO 9001:2000, 8.5.2 / 8.5.3

Corrective and preventive action is at the heart of an effective management system. These processes bridge across every other activity and can be initiated from, and provide benefit to, any and every other part of the system. They are the supreme processes, more important even than internal audit and management review because they are the heart of continuous improvement. If the management system is to be effective, these programs have to be completely supported by senior management.

ISO 9001:2000 has individual clauses for these two items; one thing they have in common is that they both require that there are documented procedures describing the activities.

There is obviously a close link between control of nonconformity and this set of requirements for corrective action. The first process identifies nonconforming product, and this provides the method for fixing it. However, it is important to recognize that corrective and preventive action is not limited to product nonconformity. The 1994 standard contained the words "investigation of the cause of nonconformities relating to product, process, and quality system." The absence of this language should not restrict the application of corrective and preventive action processes, which should be freely used in all areas of the business. The positioning of these two activities in the measuring and monitoring section of the standard indicates that they apply to all aspects of the management system, not only to product.

For the sake of simplicity the two areas of activity will be examined separately.

Corrective Action

ISO 9001:2000, 8.5.2

One of the questions that always arises in any consideration of corrective action is, "When should it happen?" The answer is simple: every time anything goes wrong.

Does this mean that the full corrective action process must be initiated for every failure? Absolutely not.

The standard states that the corrective actions taken shall be "appropriate to the effects of the nonconformities encountered."

What this means is that in most organizations there are at least two levels of corrective action. The first level is what might be called "routine production rework." Every process has an anticipated failure rate and a certain amount of anticipated rework for which provision is made in the operational methods of the organization. The sort of activities that can be covered in this way include component replacement after functional testing on items returned because of a missing or untapped hole or minor paint touch-up. They may also involve incorrectly completed forms or letters with typographical errors. All these are examples of minor errors.

Depending on the circumstances, it can be a worthwhile exercise to record these errors. Look at their gross numbers to see if there are any trends worth investigating. Most of these routine rework activities also have process limits set on them; for example, in the electronics industry most organizations place a limit on the number of components that can be changed and on the number of times a single item may be repaired.

Once these limits are exceeded, or the error falls outside the routine rework definition used by the organization, the second tier of corrective action kicks in, and this is the area that ISO 9001:2000 is really interested in. At this level the incident is referred to a more senior authority for disposition. This may initially mean that the decision on rework is taken by an engineer rather than a shop supervisor. It may automatically trigger some form of materials review board. The choice is up to the organization, but it is from this second type of error that the corrective action program is initiated where products are concerned.

In every case, the first priority must be to fix the problem — "correction" — and get the process rolling again — keep the customer happy. Unless it is absolutely essential for the purposes of investigation, products should not be held up by corrective action programs any longer than absolutely necessary.

Once the full process is initiated, it is important that the decision-making process be escalated to senior personnel because it is from this process that root-cause analysis may spring, potentially an expensive activity. The decision must not be taken lightly and must, as the standard says, be "appropriate to the effects" of the problems encountered. It is perfectly acceptable for the result of a review to be that "no further action" is to be taken. There is no added-value in carrying out root-cause analysis on a one-off incident — a statistical "outlier." But the decision must be based on careful consideration of all the facts, including history. That "outlier" needs to be reclassified if it happens every week, or month or each time the product is built.

Once the decision is made to initiate investigation, records must be maintained of all activity undertaken and of the outcome. In particular, the record must show what actions resulted from the investigation and how the action taken was monitored to ensure that it was effective.

Root-cause analysis of failure can be a massively expensive business. If the best judgment of the organization's experts is that an incident is a "one in a million" and the consequences of that failure would not be severe, it is acceptable to determine that the costs of prevention outweigh the costs of corrective action when the incident occurs. On this judgment the records would show no follow-up to corrective action to take any ongoing preventive action.

This is the business of risk management. One very useful tool to employ is Failure Mode Effect Analysis during the design phase. All business is about managing risk; the management of quality is primarily about managing risk, driving the correct prevention techniques to prevent costly failures and reacting quickly if a problem does arise to minimize the impact of the failure on the supplier and the customer.

ISO 9004:2000 provides a list of possible data that can be used as sources of information for corrective action. The list includes customer complaints, non-conformance reports, process data output, customer satisfaction data outputs and management review minutes. The guidance document also includes internal audits, but it is important to remember that there is a completely separate process that deals with the internal audit activity. It is up to the individual organization to determine whether it wishes to use a single corrective action process or have separate processes for product and process. Under no circumstances should anything be done twice.

The corrective action procedure required by ISO 9001:2000 must address, as a minimum, the six specific steps as defined in 8.5.2 sections a) to f):

a) Reviewing nonconformities (including customer complaints).

The process starts by having an identified problem, which may be internal or external. Note that many organizations have completely different processes and personnel to deal with customer complaints, This is fine. The standard makes no attempt to dictate method, merely content.

b) Determining the causes of nonconformities.

Having identified that a nonconformity exists, now the organization must take steps to determine the cause of the problem. This is where judgment is needed with respect to the significance of the event. The next mandated action will take this judgment to the next level.

c) Evaluating the need for action to ensure that nonconformities do not recur.

Having identified the nonconformity and determined the cause to a degree appropriate to the event, the next judgment call comes in determining the need for preventive action; this is where the risk management kicks in as previously discussed.

d) Determining and implementing the corrective action.

Regardless of whether or not any preventive action is to be taken, nonconformities will always require some form of corrective action. Even if the decision is to scrap the nonconforming item and make a new one, this is still correcting the error and therefore corrective action.

e) Records of the results of action taken (see 4.2.4).

Corrective actions are one of those data sources used to drive continual improvement, but that is only possible if there are records of the events and actions available for analysis and review. Records should be as comprehensive as reasonable and possible. Minimum data would include:

- Date of the event
- Item, product or process involved
- Nature of the problem
- Cause (if not self-explanatory)
- Action taken to resolve the issue
- Any preventive action deemed appropriate
- Results of any follow-up action taken to review the effectiveness of the corrective and/or preventive actions taken.

f) Reviewing corrective action taken.

Follow-up to ensure the effectiveness of the corrective actions taken is essential to demonstrate conformance, but this must be planned as carefully as the action itself. It has to be sufficiently rigorous to ensure that there is no repetition of the problem, without being burdensome. Typically this follow-up will take the form of a regular review of reported problems against historical data to ensure that past deficiencies are not reappearing. To do this effectively the reporting system must be able to classify events in a manner that will flag repetitive occurrences.

Key Requirements for a Corrective Action Program

The corrective action program must ensure:

- That there is a documented procedure for corrective action
- That responsibility and authority for dispositioning actions is defined
- That nonconformities are reported and documented
- That each incident is assessed for appropriateness of root cause analysis
- That requirements are defined for:
  - Identifying nonconformities including customer complaints
  - Reporting incidents
  - Determining the causes of nonconformity
  - Assigning tasks to appropriate individuals
  - Tracking activities
  - Evaluating the need for actions to ensure that nonconformities do not recur
  - Determining and implementing the needed corrective action
  - Recording the results of actions
  - Reviewing the results of corrective actions

- That reports of corrective actions taken and their results are reported to management for review.

Audit Note:

A tendency has been noted for some third-party auditors to insist on root cause analysis for every corrective action that an organization initiates. This is not required. The standard specifically makes provision for informed decision making in this regard.

Preventive Action

ISO 9001:2000, 8.5.3

Preventive action is the last step in corrective action, when required... isn't it?

Not quite. Yes, action will frequently be taken as a result of a corrective action and this is part of preventive action, but the preventive action being referred to in this clause of the standard is meant to prevent failure in the first place.

ISO 9000:2000 provides these two definitions to clarify the intent:

[Corrective action is] "action taken to eliminate the cause of a detected non-conformity or other undesirable situation" whereas

[Preventive action is] "action taken to eliminate the cause of a potential non-conformity or other undesirable situation."

The objective is to error-proof systems, processes and products to prevent non-conformities from arising. In its purest form the preventive action approach described in this clause of the standard is "crystal-ball gazing," and really forms part of planning for quality.

Some actions that might be described as "preventive" are also the type of activities that are integral to professionally managed and operated organizations. A well-managed materials management program has a preventive aspect to it; if everything is operating correctly there will be no material shortages to impact workflow. Shipments to customers can be planned earlier than the drop-dead date to ensure on-time delivery; process capability studies can be carried out to ensure that the required product specifications are achievable by the planned method of operation.

These are all examples of preventive actions.

A further source of inspiration for preventive actions includes the analysis of data collected from the operation of the management system. Apart from assisting in the "determination of the suitability and effectiveness of the ... management system" this data also provides an opportunity to detect the development of adverse trends in process or product performance and act to reverse the trend before problems actually occur. Field repair, warranty and field failure data can also assist in trend detection as well as in the initiation of preventive action.

Another valuable source of data comes from the lessons learned from new design introduction; any problems resulting from the introduction of a new product design should be fed back to those responsible for design and/or development work so that similar problems can be avoided in the future.

There are five specific processes that must be addressed by the documented procedure created under this clause.

a) Determining potential nonconformities and their causes.

First, identify the appropriate sources of information that can drive preventive action as discussed above.

b) Evaluating the need for action to prevent occurrence of nonconformities.

As with corrective actions, it is for management to evaluate and determine whether any particular situation requires preventive action to be taken. This is risk management in its purest form, where data is analyzed to seek out possible risks to product, process or management system. This promotes an informed determination as to what is worth doing and what isn't. The wrong decision can easily blow up in management's face; whether the decision is to act or not to act, a wrong call can be very expensive. Risk to the customer should be the first consideration, followed by risk to the organization, and that will often involve a cost analysis. Sometimes the best decision is to do nothing and fix any problems that do crop up because they will be few and far between while the cost of eliminating the risk is much greater. Provided that there are no contractual, statutory or regulatory issues involved and no risk to life or limb, then this can be a valid decision, whatever quality purists may believe.

c) Determining and implementing needed action.

Determine what steps should be taken to deal with any problems that may arise and require that action is taken to prevent them from happening again. Such actions can range from changing a subcontractor to retraining personnel to a process or design change, system restructure and, in an extreme case, withdrawal or discontinuance of a complete product or product line.

An example of a preventive response in the drug industry "commensurate with the risks encountered" would be the total recall of a well-known over-the-counter medication from stores in California during 1992 when it was discovered that someone had spiked a small number of capsules with poison.

On a much smaller scale, there is a constant stream of advisories sent out by car manufacturers to authorized dealers with respect to routine services on vehicles to change things because data indicates a failure risk. Some of these make news when a recall is involved for safety reasons — these are the corrective actions. The vast majority go by and the work is performed unbeknownst to the owners. These are the preventive actions.

d) Keeping records of results of actions taken.

Preventive action, like corrective action, needs data on which to feed, and part of the data is recursive — past preventive actions can feed new and future preventive actions — so good records of perceived problems, what was done to prevent them and the results of such actions are essential.

e) Reviewing preventive action taken.

As with corrective action, there is the need to follow up on preventive actions and confirm that they have achieved the desired results. The same link to management review must exist as in the case of corrective actions. The status of preventive actions must be a mandatory line item on the management review agenda.

Key Requirements for a Preventive Action Program

The preventive action program must ensure:

- That there is a documented procedure for preventive action
- That the responsibilities and authorities for operating the process are defined
- That the organization uses data from the operation of the management system to identify opportunities for preventive action
- That the organization carries out risk assessment to determine if planned preventive actions are appropriate to the impact of potential problems
- That the documented procedure for preventive action defines processes for:
    - Identifying potential nonconformities and their causes
    - Determining the need for preventive actions
    - Assigning tasks to appropriate individuals
    - Tracking the progress of individual tasks
    - Recording results of action taken
    - Reviewing the results of preventive action taken
    - Reporting actions taken to management review.

Audit Note:

Preventive action is frequently a very weak area of activity, only happening when corrective actions are closed.

Expect to see much greater auditor awareness and focus on true predictive preventive action in the future.

Customer Satisfaction

ISO 9001:2000, 7.2.3 / 8.2.1

The year 2000 standard carries a substantial focus on customer satisfaction. The new standard contains a clause specifically called "customer satisfaction," in the hope and intention that this will cause top management to take a more proactive role in reviewing customer perceptions of how well the organization has met their requirements, rather than merely managing dissatisfaction; in other words only worrying about customer complaints.

The requirement that has been created is not onerous, even for the smallest of companies. It is stated in such high-level terms that it can be met by the most simplistic of activities, although this is not the real intent. It requires the management of the organization to "monitor information relating to customer perception as to whether the organization has fulfilled [their] requirements." Note the use of the term "customer perception." This really calls for a proactive approach, as perceptions and realities can be quite different. Sometimes a perception of failure can be corrected by providing hard data. Many of the processes routinely used by a great number of organizations contribute towards the data needed in support of this activity. Examples of this would be data collection with regard to on-time delivery, tracking and analysis of customer complaints, analysis of repeat orders, collection of customer data on future requirements, routine customer visits or calls by sales staff, the use of newsletters and other sources of data to keep customers informed.

Remember that a customer return is a customer complaint even if no "complaint" is made.

If an organization has: (a) some defined methodology for monitoring customer satisfaction, and (b) some methodology for monitoring customer complaints (dissatisfaction), the requirement to monitor information is met.

The methodologies used to monitor customer satisfaction and dissatisfaction will vary enormously depending on the nature, size and complexity of the organization. Such methods can include sampling processes, mail-return card questionnaires, customer surveys or blind customer response studies. Restaurant questionnaires would meet the requirements, as would the training program feedback response form used by many training organizations. Data from formal customer complaint processes can help identify customer perceptions.

In some industries there are independent surveys conducted at regular intervals — the J. D. Powers surveys are examples of this type of activity — and these data also meet the requirements of the standard. There is nothing that states that the organization cannot use externally collected, collated and interpreted data as its information source for customer satisfaction and dissatisfaction. It may even be more reliable as it is independent.

Looking at ISO 9004:2000, Guidelines on performance improvement, another approach is found to the subject of customer satisfaction. ISO 9004:2000 addresses the broader issue of "customer-related information," and under this heading includes not only the customer feedback concepts already discussed, but also such matters as:

- Customer and user surveys
- Feedback on aspects of product
- Customer requirements and contract information
- Market needs
- Service delivery data
- Information relating to competition.

There is a crossover created by the third of these items with activities specifically addressed in another area of the standard; customer requirements and contract information are handled through the processes that support Clause 7.2, customer-related processes. These have been discussed in the context of the heading of identifying customer requirements. Achievement of contract requirements should be monitored directly through the application of these processes, and relevant data on such issues as on-time delivery forms part of that monitoring activity. This is obviously a customer satisfaction issue, but it is important not to duplicate effort.

Studies of market needs and information related to competition are somewhat more fuzzy as measures of customer satisfaction: an organization may well choose to remain in a very small niche market which it feels it can manage effectively rather than move into other areas. Other products may well be in demand by customers, but the organization decides not to try and offer them because it lacks expertise, or doesn't want to grow. Customers may be disappointed that a supplier they like isn't offering a particular product, but that isn't necessarily a matter of dissatisfaction. Equally, knowledge of the competition is a matter for business development rather than customer satisfaction.

The important issue is not the data collection method — the requirement is so open that almost anything meets the intent. The real issue for the system is that the data are being used as an input to management review meetings and are therefore being used as one of the measures of the effectiveness of the management system.

Key Requirements for Managing Customer Satisfaction

The process for monitoring customer satisfaction and dissatisfaction must:

- Identify and implement arrangements for obtaining customer feedback
- Collect internal data on activities that impact customer satisfaction, e.g., on-time delivery
- Collect, collate and monitor and respond to information on customer satisfaction
- Collect, collate and monitor and respond to information on customer dissatisfaction
- Ensure that the methodologies for obtaining and using this information are used consistently
- Apply these measurements to reviews of the performance of the quality management system.

Audit Note:

This is new ground for the majority of auditors. Expect to experience unrealistic auditor expectations. In reality the requirements are stated in such high-level terms that it will be difficult to justify a nonconformity if an organization is doing anything at all in this area, however little it may be.

Internal Audit

ISO 9001:2000, 8.2.2

The conduct of internal audits is one of the most powerful tools for continuous improvement that any organization can ever implement. Used properly, audit activities not only ensure continuing conformity with the processes as documented and intended by the organization, they enable the identification of system weaknesses and the sharing of system strengths.

Most beneficial of all is that they provide a constant measure of the effectiveness of management in assuring the implementation of the management system. By a regular review of all operating documentation, an organization can constantly find new and better ways of doing things, which can then be formally incorporated into the system. Audits of conformity with documented procedures will then ensure that things continue to be done in the way that is defined by those

Figure 9-20

Audit Ensures Continual Improvement Is Maintained

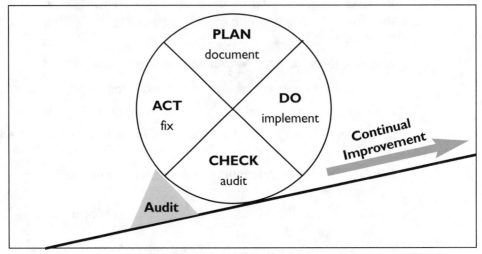

procedures. Gains made by the improvement process are retained. A ball cannot roll back down a slope if there is a wedge jammed behind it; audit is the wedge for systemic improvements in the operations of a company.

Many volumes have been written on the subject of management system audit, and therefore this brief overview will merely focus on the process requirements and records mandated by the standard, rather than on the full implementation of an internal audit program.

There are some key management "do's and don'ts" connected with the audit program, and they will be addressed later.

ISO 9001:2000 requires that the internal audit process ensure that the system "conforms to the planned arrangements, to the requirements of this International Standard and to the quality management system requirements established by the organization." It further requires that the system "is effectively implemented and maintained." The conformity of the system to the standard is a primary responsibility of the management representative, but the internal audit process is required to confirm conformity.

Once a system is certified, it is difficult to see how it will become noncompliant with the baseline standard unless major changes are made to processes, but this check is now a requirement. There is no statement that requires this to be part of every internal audit, so from a practical implementation point of view this can be made an annual or even biannual event. By making the verification of conformity with the standard an infrequent part of internal audit, the core audit activity can remain focused on the system documentation, processes and products. This is where the greatest benefit will be found, not in the sterile comparison of system to standard.

This is one of the six clauses in ISO 9001:2000 that require a documented procedure defining the activity. The requirement defined within the standard is to establish a documented procedure, in which "the responsibilities and requirements for planning and conducting audits, and for reporting results and maintaining records shall be defined ..." The process must also ensure the impartiality of the auditors, and ensure that auditors do not audit their own work.

The operational requirements for the audit program are defined in the third subclause. This states the need for an ongoing planned and organized series of system audits on a regular basis. Typically the plan should provide for every part of the system to be audited at least once a year, but the baseline for the audit schedule is defined within 8.2.2 as being "the status and importance of the processes and areas to be audited, as well as the results of previous audits." Very significant activities may therefore be audited more frequently than less significant activities, and of course those producing bad audit reports must receive more frequent scrutiny.

Audits must be impartial, as already stated. External auditors must remember that this wording intentionally does not create a need for an independent audit group within the organization. The independence of the audit function can be achieved simply by assuring that the individual carrying out the audit performs no part of the activity being audited even if he or she reports to the same functional manager. Obviously the greater the degree of separation within the reporting structure the more visible the independence; however, the basic requirement of the standard can be achieved with reporting structures very close to home. With the trend toward flat management structures over the past couple of decades, a small company will often have only one manager to whom the entire work force reports.

In many cases small organizations have cross-functional staff, and anyone can be performing any task at a given moment in time. In this situation, the independence of the work being performed will be defined in terms of time and space. The task under audit may have been the auditor's job yesterday, and may be again tomorrow, but it isn't while the audit is under way. In such situations the training of the audit personnel will be most important. They need to understand that in reviewing records it is important to select randomly, thereby ensuring that they won't arbitrarily select their own work.

Scope of the Internal Audit Process

Most internal audit programs are limited to the scope of the management system, but this need not be the case. There is no reason why an internal audit process could not be used to examine the consistency and accuracy of all processes including marketing, financial and HR, three areas routinely excluded. There are certain data held by HR which are legally protected and which auditors must not be allowed to see, but there are also large areas of HR activity which could be audited should the organization so decide.

The scope of the internal audit process can be different from the scope of the management system from a registration or third-party audit perspective.

1. Creating an audit plan for the entire system

The full audit plan must be properly documented. The global plan should ensure that every area of the organization is audited once a year, although in very large facilities the program may only cover the entire system on a biannual or triennial basis. This will largely depend upon the allocation of resources. Clearly, the more frequent reviews of the entire system the greater the advantage. But like everything else, this is a risk-management decision. Auditing is an expensive pastime and, despite the benefits, management may not be in a position to commit sufficient resources to a complete system audit every year.

Given that the average certification audit cycle is three years, this should be the absolute maximum for an internal audit cycle.

The audit plan should be structured around core processes, functions and activities. If there are activities that are particularly important to the organization, then these should, initially at least, receive more frequent audits. Once there is a history of audit performance, the program can be adjusted to reflect past audit findings. Those activities or processes that result in more significant audit findings should be audited more frequently than areas that produce few or none.

One approach to macro audit planning is demonstrated in Figure 9-21.

The audit plan should be drawn up as an annual plan and sent to all relevant managers so that they know when audits are going to take place. It can then be updated as audits are carried out, and adjusted according to results. Like other management system documents this plan can be posted on a network or intranet.

The visual impact of this approach is clear: any aberrant activity is immediately obvious, even more so if the key is maintained in color.

Figure 9-21

One Approach to Macro Audit Planning

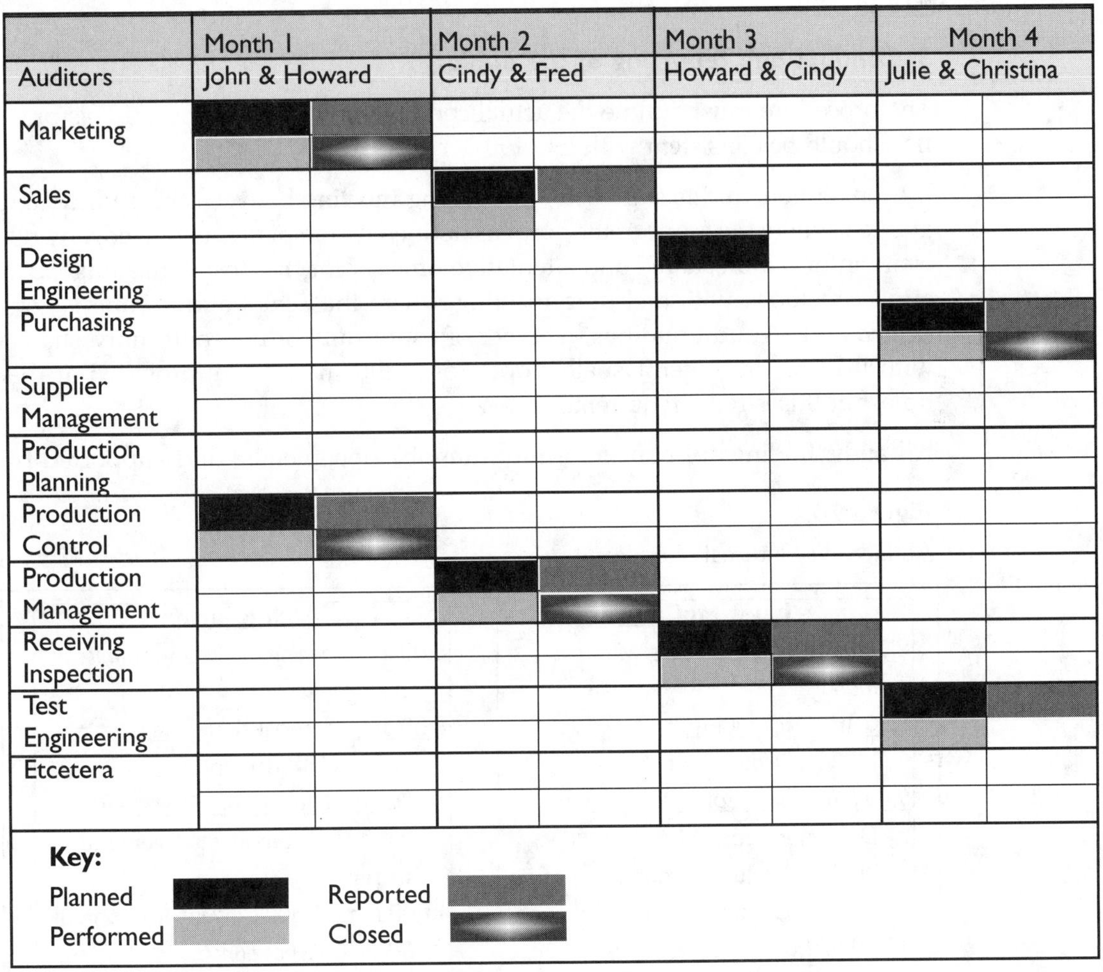

Auditors	Month 1 John & Howard		Month 2 Cindy & Fred		Month 3 Howard & Cindy		Month 4 Julie & Christina	
Marketing	■	▨						
Sales			■	▨				
Design Engineering					■			
Purchasing							■	▨
Supplier Management								
Production Planning								
Production Control	■	▨						
Production Management			■	▨				
Receiving Inspection					■	▨		
Test Engineering							■	
Etcetera								

Key:

Planned	■	Reported	▨
Performed	▨	Closed	▨

2. Individual audit plans

The macro plan provides an overview of the areas which the internal audit will address as the program unfolds. Each of these areas of activity will typically contain many different processes and procedures, and it will not always be possible for an individual audit to cover all of them every time. Closer to the actual time of an individual audit the audit manager or designee should prepare an actual plan for the specific audit activity. This must define the intended scope of the activity, and it will usually also let the auditee know who will be performing the audit.

The plan should be sent to the manager of the area concerned as soon as it is ready. A typical audit plan and audit notification letter are shown in Figures 9-22 and 9-23.

3. Conduct and reporting of the audit

The procedure must outline the actual conduct of the audit process. This practice should be consistent with ISO 19011.

By convention, audits start with an opening meeting between the auditor and auditee, where the scope of the audit as defined by the plan is reviewed, any relevant information shared and a tentative time set for the closing meeting. Each audit concludes with a closing meeting where the actual audit scope is confirmed and all audit findings, whether of conformity or nonconformity, shared with the area manager. Usually copies of audit findings are provided at this time, but this is not a requirement.

All audit findings of nonconformity must be documented and supported by

Figure 9-22

An Individual Internal Audit Plan

Janet McCann	Jack Johnson
8:00 am *Opening meeting with unit manager*	8:00 am *Opening meeting with unit manager*
8:20 am Order input	8:20 am Material scheduling
MP001 Order input	PP001 MRP data input
9:00 am Production management	10:00 am Materials management
Document control	MM001 Materials management
PM001 Production documentation	storage
CM001 Configuration	11:00 am MM002 Inventory control
12:00 to 1:00 pm Lunch	*12:00 to 1:00 pm Lunch*
1:00 pm Production planning	1:00 pm Dispatch
MS001 Production Scheduling	MM003 Materials movement
2:00 pm Material requisition	2:00 pm Purchasing
PC001 MRP shop floor	PR001 EDI control
3:00 pm Production control	3:00 pm Subcontractor control
MR001 MRP requisition	SC001 Vendor management
4:00 pm to 4:30 pm *Final team meeting*	4:00 pm to 4:30 pm *Final team meeting*
4:30 pm to 5:00 pm *Closing meeting with unit manager*	4:30 pm to 5:00 pm *Closing meeting with unit manager*

Figure 9-23

A Typical Audit Notification Letter

Don,

Further to our recent telephone conversation, this letter is to confirm the coming audit of Materials Management, Production Control and Purchasing departments.

The audit will take place on Monday, February 10th, and will be conducted by Jack Johnson and Janet McCann. The usual audit process will be followed, starting with the opening meeting at 8 am with you and, if possible, your two supervisors.

The scope of the audit is all procedures covering the planning, acquisition and allocation of raw materials, shop scheduling and tracking and delivery reporting. This encompasses the procedures and associated work instructions on the enclosed list.

I anticipate that Jack and Janet will be finished by late afternoon, and will probably want to meet with you around 4.30 pm to discuss their findings. If the supervisors can sit in on that meeting as well, it would be much appreciated.

Jackie Blundell,
Audit Manager

---

audit evidence. The documentation of an audit finding must include, as a minimum, the following data:

- A unique identifier for the audit

  This might be as simple as the name of the auditor and the date, or could be a number assigned by the audit manager. The "how" is up to the organization. The important thing is that each audit finding can be related to a specific audit activity identified on the master schedule.

- Date and area being audited
- Name of auditor
- Name of auditee
- Process or procedure being audited
- Precise information on each nonconformity, including a statement of the objective evidence witnessed

This must include direction to the requirement which has not been met, either by reference to a process or procedure and/or a reference to the relevant requirement in ISO 9001:2000

• Signature of the auditee

This may be the area manager at the end of the audit, depending on the way in which the audit process is established. This signature recognizes the accuracy of the data on the form. The individual audit results are then handed in to the audit manager.

4. Follow-up and closeout of the audit

Usually it is the audit manager who distributes the formal audit report to the area after an audit, and typically it is also the audit manager who will agree on the time frame for any corrective and/or preventive action that may be required.

The audit manager or other assigned individual must track audit findings to ensure timely completion. Once the action is completed, the audit manager needs to decide how much time is needed for the process to stabilize before a re-audit is performed. This follows a determination with respect to the effectiveness of the corrective action. Very often this will occur at the start of the next audit of the area, unless the finding is serious.

Once the corrective action has been verified, the audit is closed.

5. Executive reporting

Summary reports of audit activities and the results of those activities, including all corrective and preventive actions taken, form an integral part of management review activity, and it is usually the responsibility of the audit manager (who is often the management representative) to prepare and submit this summary to management.

ISO 19011 is the international standard that provides guidance on the planning, management and conduct of audits. It is intended for both quality and environmental management system audits.

Key Requirements for an Internal Audit Process

An effective documented internal audit process must:

• Have a published audit program covering the scope of the system
• Ensure that the quality management system:

    - Conforms to the requirements of this international standard
    - Is effectively implemented and maintained

- Ensure that the audit program takes into consideration the status and importance of the activities and areas to be audited and the results of previous audits

- Ensure that the scope of individual audits is clearly defined

- Define the audit methodology

- Ensure that audits are conducted by personnel other than those who perform the activity being audited

- Define the responsibilities and requirements for:

  - Conducting audits

  - Ensuring their independence

  - Recording results

  - Reporting to management

- Ensure that management take timely corrective action on deficiencies found during the audits (timely must be defined)

- Ensure that follow-up actions include the verification of the implementation of corrective action

- Ensure that the results of verification activities are reported

- Ensure that summary reports of audit activity are submitted to management review.

Audit Note:

Ensure that the entire system has been audited by internal auditors prior to a certification audit. Third-party auditors will expect evidence of this to be available.

Remember that the internal audit process itself must be audited. Ensure that protected personnel data is kept away from the audit process.

Ensure that the audit record retention time is consistent with the expectations of the registrar, or be prepared to change.

Data Analysis

ISO 9001:2000, 8.4

All too often organizations spend a great deal of time collecting data, only to do nothing with it. The "file and forget" syndrome is one that is frequently encountered. The inclusion of this clause is clearly an attempt to make organizations take more notice of the data generated through the implementation of a management system.

The use of the word "appropriate" means that the organization has wide latitude in determining what data to collect and use. The only specific data that is referenced is that generated as a result of measuring and monitoring activities. Other potential data sources are described as "relevant." Each organization must decide for itself which data sources from the operation of the management system are most likely to provide valuable and usable data that can drive improvement activities.

ISO 9001:2000 identifies five specific data items that must form part of the data analysis activity.

1. Customer satisfaction and customer dissatisfaction

Required data can be collected through the processes that have been put in place to meet Clause 8.2.1, Customer satisfaction.

2. Conformance to product requirements

The data on the organization's level of achievement of conformance to product requirements will come from several sources: the monitoring and measurement of product, as required by 8.2.4, will be one source; monitoring and measurement of process, 8.2.3, will be another (on-time delivery, for example.)

3. Characteristics of processes

The core source of data in this area will obviously be the activities conducted in support of Clause 8.2.3, Monitoring and measurement of processes. The processes referenced in Clause 8.4 are not restricted to "production" processes. The entire system is a series of interrelated processes and the effectiveness of the interrelationships is one of the drivers in ensuring the effectiveness of the overall system. Another source of useful data on the performance of processes is that which comes from the control of nonconforming product (8.3).

4. Trend analysis of products and processes

The two core sources of data on product are 8.2.4 and 8.3. There is substantial crossover between data analysis for conformance to customer requirements and that for products. A significant part of meeting customer requirements involves the production of conforming product. The difference comes in the analysis of data on nonconforming product — which hopefully the customer never sees — and trend analysis on both nonconforming product data and data from the product realization activities. This data can enable the organization to evaluate the effectiveness of the product realization processes and to detect drift in process performance that might otherwise go unseen.

This enables preventive actions to be initiated with all the resultant cost savings associated with eliminating errors before they occur.

These issues were also discussed earlier in the section on corrective and pre-ventive action programs.

5. Suppliers

The significance of suppliers and their potential for having a major impact on the ability of an organization to provide customer satisfaction has already been extensively discussed. The supplier is an extension of the organization's own process, and must be treated as such in the analysis of available data on system performance.

This analysis of supplier performance can be as sophisticated or as simple as the organization chooses. Bear in mind that the extent of supplier control must always be dependent upon the impact of the supplier's products on the organi-zation's own deliverables. This will often mean that the monitoring of supplier performance is carried out on an exception basis.

This is the preferred approach; there are few things more aggravating to a sup-plier than the constant interference of a customer when there are no problems occurring. Unfortunately there is a deep-rooted belief in many large companies that they know better than their suppliers how businesses should be run.

The range of activities that comprise performance data analysis will vary enor-mously depending upon the nature of the organization and its processes. Some organizations have the ability and the sources to carry out extensive, even exhaustive, analysis of many different data sources. Other organizations, partic-ularly small ones with limited resources, will choose to analyze only a few key data points. Either approach is acceptable.

It isn't the volume of data analysis performed within an entity that provides value, it is the quality of the data and the use made of the analysis that makes a difference. It is better to analyze one data source properly and respond to the data than to analyze 100 and file the results unread.

Key Requirements for Data Analysis

To be effective the data analysis process must:

- Define the data to be collected
- Define the analysis to be performed
- Perform the analyses on a consistent basis
- Review and act on the output of the analyses
- Ensure that customer satisfaction measures form part of the analyses
- Ensure that internal audit results form part of the analysis
- Ensure that corrective and preventive action data form part of the analyses

- Examine process characteristics and trends when possible and relevant
- Examine product characteristics and trends when possible and relevant
- Review supplier performance when relevant
- Provide hard data to management for review.

Audit Note:

The formal requirements for data analysis are new and will be new to certification auditors. As with other somewhat loosely written requirements, it is important that the organization doesn't allow an auditor to demand unnecessary activities. This is another instance where there is a risk that auditors will see the commentary in ISO 9004:2000 as identifying what organizations should be doing. Remember 9004 is not a required guidance document for implementation although it can be very helpful. More importantly, auditors need to remember the meaning of the term "Guidance" contained in the title of ISO 9004:2000.

Management Review

ISO 9001:2000, 5.6

Alpha to Omega

Management is key to the start of the system, and management is key to endlessly driving the improvement cycle inexorably forward. Management is the alpha and omega of the process.

Management review is to be undertaken by top management at regular, defined intervals. The purpose is to consider the continuing suitability, adequacy and effectiveness of the management system in achieving the defined objectives that management established, in achieving customer satisfaction and in fulfilling the quality policy — also established by management. As part of this process, management review must consider any potential requirements for changes to the system, the policy or the objectives. None of these should be set in stone, although typically the policy and the core objectives created at top management level are not likely to be particularly volatile. The very fact that every management review should consider the possible need for change acts as a reminder that the world is not a static place. Organizations need to constantly re-evaluate their strategic goals and their management systems to ensure that they are optimized for the market or other operating conditions.

Historically the content of the management review has been largely up to the management representative and the team. The 2000 edition creates mandatory management review agenda items and meeting output requirements. The inputs are contained in Clauses 5.6.1 and 5.6.2. These provide the minimum core agenda items for the meeting, and 5.6.3 the minimum requirements for the meeting output. Records must be maintained of the meeting and of actions that result from each review.

The agenda items are those issues that any competent management review should have been examining anyway — they are core data outputs from the operation of the management system that provide information on system effectiveness, and that drive continual improvement. The review process must examine these items both from the viewpoint of current performance and opportunities for improvement in performance.

Typical methodology for management review involves summary reports of data collected from the system that provides general data on performance, trend analysis that can be gleaned from the data and consideration of any recommendations that may be made by the manager responsible for the task or data under review. This top management review would not typically be expected to look at each individual item of data — that is the task of the process owner. Obviously any particularly significant item, whether positive or negative, would usually make the agenda, but routine items would not.

An item of particular importance in the "Plan-Do-Check-Act" routine is the follow-up process. Management review must follow up actions from earlier reviews if the process is to be effective. There is no point in top management performing reviews, making decisions and initiating actions unless those actions and decisions are then followed up. It is good audit practice to track some of these items to ensure that there is closure on issues raised at review meetings.

All management reviews must actively review "changes which could affect the management system." This involves changes in the operating environment of the organization — technology, standards, regulation — anything that might require that the organization react to accommodate different requirements and necessitate a revision of the management system. All too often there is no evidence available as to whether due consideration has or has not been given to the matter. The inclusion of the very specific requirement means that management review minutes should have at least a line item response to this issue every time.

Other items that are the province of management review are improvements to the processes that comprise the management system, improvements to products and overall resource needs to fulfill the commitments it has or intends to make. Typically top management will not look at the detail of such issues but at the macro picture; the detail is usually delegated!

The minutes of the meeting need to show that all these issues have been discussed and decisions taken — preferably based on data. In considering the resource issue, that review doesn't necessarily mean changing what is available internally when it appears to be inadequate. Equally valid responses to a resource shortfall can be to change schedules to meet resource availability, with appropriate consultation with customers if required, or even to change the operational processes to reduce the resources required. An example of the latter could be something like subcontracting a particular activity or work item, or using past product or process history to reduce the amount of inspection or test being performed on a product. Reviewing and examining resources does not necessarily mean increasing them. Management is the art of managing risk.

Key Requirements for Management Review

An effective management review process must ensure that a defined group of top management reviews the quality management system at planned intervals and that:

- Reviews consider the system's continuing suitability to fulfill policy and objectives
- Reviews consider the system's continuing adequacy to fulfill policy and objectives
- Reviews consider the system's continuing effectiveness in fulfilling policy and objectives
- Reviews evaluate the need for changes to the quality management system, including quality policy and quality objectives
- Review input includes current performance and improvement opportunities related to:
    - The results of audits
    - Customer feedback
    - Process performance and product conformance
    - Status of preventive and corrective actions
    - Follow-up actions from earlier management reviews
    - Changes that could affect the quality management system
- Outputs from management reviews include information relating to:
    - All items listed above
    - Improvement of the quality management system and its processes
    - Improvement of product related to customer requirements
    - Resource needs
- The results of all management reviews are documented and circulated to attendees.

Audit Note:

Ensure that the entire system has received at least one formal, documented management review prior to a certification audit. Registration auditors will expect evidence of this to be available.

Ensure that the management review record retention time is consistent with the expectations of the registrar, or be prepared to change those expectations.

In Conclusion

Structured management systems have proved to be a highly effective and efficient manner of operating businesses ranging in size from The Ford Motor Company, probably the largest certified organization in the world, to a one-man design and build operation in Northern England. The formal disciplines imposed and the logic of defined processes cannot be beaten for effectiveness and reliability.

The management system framework provided by a customer-focused system adapts easily and smoothly to accommodate other considerations, such as environmental or health and safety. The ISO 9001-based system will have accommodated and implemented many of these issues anyway, either as a result of customer requirements — increasingly seen in environmental concerns — or regulatory and statutory issues, which can encompass environmental, health and safety matters.

A management system provides a holistic way of looking at the operations of the organization, giving appropriate and necessary weight to all the stakeholders in the business and seeking to add value to them all, whether customers, shareholders, organizational staff, suppliers or society at large.

Value entails much more than pumping up the stock price.

Footnotes

[1] Excerted from "An Introduction to ISO 9000" by Roderick Goult, 1996.

[2] RAB is the Registrar Accreditation Board, the organization that operates the ANSI/RAB joint National Accreditation Program for Registrars, Training Organizations and Auditor Training Courses. IRCA is the UK-based International Register of Certificated Auditors, currently the largest auditor registration body in the world, which also registers auditor training courses. IATCA is the International Auditor and Training Certification Association, which sets internationally agreed standards for training courses, and to which both RAB and IRCA subscribe.

[3] ISO TC 176 SC 2 Guidance Note 525R makes clear that the documented procedure requirements may be met equally well by a single procedure or by having multiple procedures.

Conversion — Moving from ISO 9001:1994 to ISO 9001:2000

10

by Roderick Goult

Management representatives and others responsible for transitioning their management systems take note: this process is not difficult. Compared to the effort required for the original implementation of an ISO 9000 management system, this task is a walk in the park. Don't be intimidated by those who seek to profit from your fear!

Understand the Timeline

There are currently over 500,000 registered sites in the world. All have to decide whether to convert their systems to the revised standard or surrender their certificates. When the standard was first revised in 1994, there was a one-year transition period. A different model was applied to ISO 9000:2000. A joint IAF — ISO TC 176 — ISO/CASCO Joint Working Group meeting was held in Vienna on September 26, 1999, to discuss the transitional process. The outcome of that meeting was to establish a three-year time frame for certified organizations to convert their systems. The core decisions were as follows:

- Accredited certifications to the Draft (ISO DIS) or Final Draft (ISO FDIS) were prohibited.
- Organizations could choose to have the requirements of either of these documents [ISO DIS or ISO FDIS] considered during an audit that pre-

cedes the official publication of the International Standard, however the certification body could not issue an accredited certificate to the new standard until it was officially published.

- •The user community was given three years to make the transition to the new standard.

- • Audits can continue to be performed against the 1994 document up to and including the day before the third anniversary of the publication of the ISO 9000:2000 family.

(The full text of this communique is contained in Appendix A.)

The basic message was simple: don't panic, there was no need to rush!

The rationale behind the extended time frame for conversion is not altogether clear, but must be largely put down to a (probably justified) belief in the accreditation community that the changes in style and approach contained in the new standard, and the concomitant need for a change in the approach to management system audit, were likely to take a considerable time to accomplish.

Experience of the operations of many certification bodies (registrars) operating in the United Kingdom and the United States would certainly bear out the view that there is a major retraining and realignment required in the cookie-cutter approach previously taken to certification audits. Adding to this, the profusion of "off-the-shelf" management system software packages and books that provide the purchaser with a "fill-in-the-blanks" quality manual and 20 procedures would certainly suggest that a substantial section of the quality community, including many consultants, also needs to undergo a major brain realignment. Every organization that has used such an approach also has a problem on their hands, whether the 20-procedure system has come from a purchased package or poor advice from a book or a consultant.

These are the organizations that will need three years, because they have much to do.

Organizations which have implemented their management systems based on the manner in which they do business, and which therefore have systems based on their operational processes and activities, generally have much less to do and will be able to make the transition quickly and easily.

The Core Changes

Process-Based System

The fact is that there are relatively few changes to the requirements of the standard — the big shift is in style rather than content, in application rather than operation. Instead of the standard mandating documented procedures, it requires that an organization "establish, document, implement, maintain and continually improve a quality management system in accordance with the requirements of this International Standard." In determining the extent of this documentation, in addition to the statement of policy, objectives, manual and documentation of the six specified processes, the organization needs to identify and determine the "documents required by the organization to ensure the effective operation and control of its processes." The decision on what needs to be documented is left for the organization to make, based upon the varied needs of processes, staff and stakeholders.

The objective of the revamped approach to the structure of the standard is to emphasize that a management system is a strategic tool that should reflect the operational processes of the user and is an integral part of the way in which the business is operated. Hence the new standard changes the way in which the quality manual is described; it must now be "a description of the sequence and interaction of the processes included in the management system" rather than a document which covers " the requirements of this … standard" as was stated in the 1994 document.

Management-Driven Quality Objectives

A further change to the requirements mandates that quality objectives be established by "top management," and then deployed throughout the organization at "relevant functions and levels." Management is further required to ensure that all "relevant personnel" are aware of the impact of their activities on the achievement of the objectives. The standard provides guidance and information on the factors to be considered in establishing these management objectives, and that process is discussed in some detail in Chapter 9. There is a blend of required inputs and advisory inputs. These objectives must support the policy, support the concept of continual improvement and be appropriate for the product.

Continual Improvement

The inclusion of the words "continual improvement" is a further change. The ISO 9000 standards have always been based on the concept of the Plan-Do-Check-Act continuous improvement cycle, but it appears that relatively few users have ever recognized that fact. The new wording brings the concept front and center-stage. Any ISO 9000 management system that has been operated even half-heartedly has resulted in management having substantial amounts of data available to them; comparatively few have ever used that data in any sort of meaningful way to enhance the operating systems of the organization to maximum effect.

The activities and data that can be used to drive improvement are all embedded within the standard, and always have been since 1987. They are corrective action, preventive action, customer complaints, product and process performance data collected from processes, inspections and tests, field performance data and internal audit data on the operation of the management system. Using these data sources effectively will provide more than enough opportunities for improvement than most organizations can handle, and once these are mastered there are more available!

Customer Satisfaction

The 1994 standard declared that the "requirements specified are aimed primarily at achieving customer satisfaction by preventing nonconformity at all stages from design through to servicing." The new standard uses slightly different wording, but the intent is identical. The organization is now using the management system to "address customer satisfaction through the effective application of the system, including processes for continual improvement and the prevention of nonconformity."

Customer satisfaction is mentioned frequently throughout the new text; the objective is clearly to emphasize that the focus of the management system should be on assuring customer satisfaction. There is also a new requirement that some effort be made to formally assess and review customer perceptions in addition to customer dissatisfaction so that there are data available for management to review.

Legal and Regulatory Issues

One of the big debates that often raged around ISO 9001:1994 concerned the extent to which the requirements of the standard invoked legal and regulatory issues. At The Victoria Group the view was always that the standard invoked such requirements to the extent necessary for the legal operation of the organization and the production and sale of its products. The comment on regulatory issues under 4.4 (design), and to codes and reference standards under 4.9, coupled with the general comment in the introduction, were always taken as a clear indication that a company had to take account of basic legal and regulatory issues in establishing and managing its systems. An example would be OSHA requirements, which need to be managed and observed even though the safety officer in a company may not appear on the ISO organizational chart. Similarly the handling of hazardous materials requires HAZMAT regulations to be followed, and most operations areas need at least some Material Safety Data Sheets (M.S.D.S.) in place.

ISO 9001:2000 significantly increases the visibility of regulatory and legal issues, including reference to such requirements no less than eight times. The practical impact of this change on most organizations will be minimal, in that any organization bothering to implement ISO 9001 is likely to be taking care of regulatory and legal issues. It may well require the modification of some documentation, including the quality manual, to give the matter appropriate visibility. The references are listed in detail in the implementation chapter and summarized here.

Introduction

0.1 General

1. Scope

1.1 General

1.2 Application

5. Management responsibility

5.1 Management commitment

5.2 Customer focus

7. Product realization

7.2.1 Determination of requirements related to the product

7.3.2 Design and development inputs

8. Measurement, analysis and improvement

8.3 Control of nonconforming product.

Data Analysis

Under the previous versions of the standard it has been very easy for organizations to collect data, file it and forget it. Despite the fact that there have always been clear requirements for data to be used effectively, specifically in the development of preventive actions, this has been an area of weakness in many systems. The requirements are now a little tougher. Subclause 8.4 states that the organization "shall collect and analyze appropriate data to determine the suitability and effectiveness of the quality management system and to identify improvements that can be made."

Data analysis is a clearly defined requirement. It goes on to identify what kinds of data are included, highlighting the output from process control, inspection and test activities — now called "monitoring and measuring" — and specifically requiring that these data are used to develop information on (a) customer satisfaction and/or dissatisfaction; (b) conformance to customer requirements; (c) characteristics of processes, product and their trends; and (d) suppliers.

There is no direct requirement that the results of this analysis are fed back to the management review process, but there are specified inputs and outputs of that activity which can most readily be met by linking data analysis to management review.

In Summary

The changes introduced by ISO 9001:2000 are not dramatic. Any organization with a process-based system that is being effectively operated by a committed management will not have much to do. As for those who have acquired "the badge" and do little to use the system for the overall benefit of the organization, their customers and stakeholders are in for a rude shock. Effectiveness is the name of the game, and systems which are not effective will no longer achieve certification if the accreditation and certification bodies do their job correctly.

There will be a need for vigilance. Auditors are being asked to make more subjective judgements than have been required of them in the past, and this can easily lead to problems. The year 2000 standard will be easy to overinterpret and to misinterpret; too little attention has been paid to the auditability of the requirements. There are plenty of auditors in place who have a hard time separating their opinions from requirements already — when requirements are vague, this situation can only worsen.

Getting Started

Transitioning from current state to full conformity with ISO 9001:2000 needs to be tackled as a project, planned, timelined and progressed. It should not be rushed. This chapter outlines a 12-step process and provides some tools and techniques that can be used by any organization to assist in the transfer. The 12 stages of transition are shown in Figure 10-1.

This 12-step process places substantial emphasis on training. Many organizations are currently being bombarded by their registrars with information and exhortations to attend training sessions and learn all about the enormous task they face in converting their management systems. No doubt many are also being bombarded by other training organizations claiming to have all the answers to this huge problem. The problem is neither enormous nor huge, it is relatively minor and when compared with the full implementation which the organization has already achieved, nothing to worry about.

Registrars, like consultants, are commercial organizations and they are out to make money on their activities. For this reason many of them are moving into the training market, and even into the field of consulting. Several of the major accreditation bodies have drawn up codes of conduct that prohibit accredited registrars from providing in-house training to organizations that they also certi-fy. The conflict of interest is all too obvious — if in-house training is to have real value the trainer must be able to advise the organization on specifics, and there is no way that a registrar could do this and still remain objective when it came time to audit. Organizations are therefore advised to stay away from registrars for training of all kinds, whether in-house or public.

Figure 10-1

Transition 12-Step Process

1) Have the management representative learn and understand the new standard.

2) Review the scope statement, checking for and documenting any exclusions under 1.2.

3) Review and identify the additional / changed requirements that impact the organization, identify them by clause and subclause.

4) Review the quality manual and identify the changes required.

5) Retrain executive management.

6) Retrain internal auditors.

7) Perform a gap analysis on the current system against the additional / changed requirements, take particular note of enhanced record-keeping requirements and data analysis.

8) Develop an overall plan with milestones to enhance the current system.

9) Create a matrix of conformity mapping existing system documentation from the 1994 standard to the new standard.

10) Document plans for revising ISO 9001 references in current documentation as changes / enhancements occur.

11) Review plans with registrar.

12) Retrain all staff.

Transition 12-Step Process

1. Have the management representative learn and understand the new standard.

The ISO 9000 standards have spawned more books than can be imagined. Some of them are very good and very accurate. Some of them are very bad and would cause any organization using them more trouble than enough. For a standard which is not yet formally published, it is remarkable how much literature is already on the streets advising on transitional activity.

The quality community has generally taken an awe-inspired view of ISO 9001:2000, which tells us more about the quality community than it does about the standard. If some commentators are to be believed, this document will create the new age of enlightenment on a scale that will make the original historical period seem positively dull by comparison.

Serious managers must not let themselves be taken in. Much of what has been penned about the great leap forward that this document represents is pure hype, based firstly on a lack of understanding of the true content of the 1987 and 1994 documents, and secondly on a substantive overinterpretation of the 2000 version. On close examination ISO 9001:2000 proves to be almost a case of the emperor's new clothes, and it will be a great shame if the hype and fuss surrounding this really quite ordinary document cause it to be a big letdown for users.

Acquiring objective, authoritative information about the content and interpretation of ISO 9001:2000 requires careful research, even more so than with the previous versions. Make sure that the organization selected to provide the training takes a minimalist view, not a "quality award" view. This is not a quality award yet some of the high-end interpretations of the standard that are appearing make it seem that way. Nor is ISO 9001:2000 any more difficult or demanding than making a decent job of a system based on the 1994 document.

The core areas of change have been identified and discussed above. There are many minor but significant changes that have been introduced and that have to be applied to every system. An example is that the quality manual must now define the scope of the system, and explain and justify any exclusions from the requirements. The elimination of ISO 9002 and ISO 9003 means that organizations previously registered to those standards need to identify carefully the requirements of ISO 9001:2000 that do not apply to their operations and document the exclusions with a brief rationale. The previously commonly found "not applicable" needs a little development and explanation.

The requirement that the manual describe the sequence and interaction of the processes is likely to be a cause for more penmanship than the exclusions clause.

Figure 10-2 shows a clause-by-clause comparison between ISO 9001:2000 and ISO 9001:1994. This chart is going to be an essential tool in mapping and planning the transition of the management system from 1994 to 2000.

2. Review the scope statement, checking for and documenting any exclusions under 1.2.

Any organization currently operating an ISO 9002 or ISO 9003 management system will need to study the new standard carefully to identify which clauses are

Figure 10-2

Cross-reference between ISO 9001:2000 and ISO 9001:1994

ISO 9001:2000	ISO 9001:1994	Change in Requirements
Foreword	Foreword	
0 Introduction		Introduction not part of the standard
0.1 General	No equivalent	
0.3 Process approach	No equivalent	
0.3 Relationship with ISO 9004	No equivalent	N.B. ISO 9004 not guidance on implementation, not intended for certification or contractual purposes
0.4 Compatibility with other management systems		No equivalent
1 Scope		**Section heading only**
1.1 General	1	Customer satisfaction and continual improvement of the system
1.2 Application	1	Limited to Clause 7. No change in intent.
2 Normative references	**2**	**ISO 8402 goes, 9000:2000 takes over**
3 Terms and definitions	**3**	**supplier ➔ organization ➔ customer**
4 Quality management system		**Section heading only**
4.1 General requirements	4.2.1	Mandates the general content of the management system; identifying process interrelationships; outsourcing identified as a specific concern for control in the system
4.2 Documentation requirements		Section heading only
4.2.1 General	4.2.2	Documentation must include objectives
4.2.2 Quality manual	4.2.1	Must include scope and exclusions (1.2)
4.2.3 Control of documents	4.5	None
4.2.4 Control of records	4.16	None
5 Management responsibility		Section heading only
5.1 Management commitment	4.2.1 + 4.1.1 + 4.1.3 + 4.1.2.2	Communicating importance of meeting customer nad regulatory requirements added, also setting objectives
5.2 Customer focus	4.1.1 + 1	No functional change
5.3 Quality policy	4.1	Must include continual improvement of effectiveness of system and provide a framework for review of objectives

Figure 10-2 (continued)

Cross-reference between ISO 9001:2000 and ISO 9001:1994

ISO 9001:2000	ISO 9001:1994	Change in Requirements
5.4 Planning		Section heading only
5.4.1 Quality objectives	4.1.1 + 4.21	Required at all 'relevant' functions and levels
5.4.2 Quanlity management system planning	4.2.3	Continual improvement added, also maintenance of system integrity when changed
5.5 Responsibility, authority and communication		Section heading only
5.5.1 Responsibility and authority	4.1.2.1	Communication added
5.5.2 Management representative	4.1.2.3	Responsible for promoting communication of customer requirements
5.5.3 Internal communication		Approprioate processes to communicate effectiveness of system required
5.6 Management review		Section heading only
5.6.1 General	4.1.3	Assess opportunities for improvement. Review of possible changes to include policy and objectives.
5.6.2 Review input	4.1.2.3 + Note20 + 4.14.3	Defined input requirements.
5.6.3 Review output	4.1.3	Defined output requirements.
6 Resource management		**Section heading only**
6.1 Provision of resources	4.1.2.2	Customer satisfaction added as an actvitity to be resourced, also continaul improvement of system effectiveness.
6.2 Human resources		Section heading only
6.2.1 General	4.18	None
6.2.2 Competence, awareness and training	4.18	Assess training effectiveness and make staff aware of how work contributes to fulfillment of quality objectives.
6.3 Infrastructure	4.9	Maintenance planning required.
6.4 Work environment	4.9	No systematic requirement created.
7 Product realization		**Section heading only**
7.1 Planning of product realization	4.2.3	None
7.2 Customer-related processes		Section heading only

Figure 10.2 (continued)

Cross-reference between ISO 9001:2000 and ISO 9001:1994

ISO 9001:2000	ISO 9001:1994	Change in Requirements
7.2.1 Determination of requirements related to the product	4.3.1, 4.4.4} }	More specific detail of what to consider in contract review and in considerations for
7.2.2 Review of requirements related to the product	} 4.3.2	own products, reference to statutory and regualtory issues. N.B. 'known inteded use.'
7.2.3 Customer communication	Note 9 + 4.3.3 + 4.14.2	Formal fulfillment of existing requirements
7.3 Design and development		Section heading only
7.3.1 Design and development planning	4.4.2+4.4.3	Must now include review, verificaiton and validation stages + responisbility and authority.
7.3.2 Design and development inputs	4.4.4	None
7.3.3 Design and development outputs	4.4.5	Specific reference to production/ purchasing.
7.3.4 Design and development review	4.4.6	Records must include results and actions.
7.3.5 Design and development verification	4.4.7	Records must include results and actions.
7.3.6 Design and development validation	4.4.8	Records must include results and actions.
7.3.7 Control of design and development changes	4.4.9	Specific reference to 'constituent parts and delivered product.'
7.4 Purchasing		Section heading only
7.4.1 Purchasing process	4.6.1+4.6.2	Formal definition of crieteria for evalution and re-evaluation required.
7.4.2 Purchasing information	4.6.3	None
7.4.3 Verification of purchased products	4.6.4	None — less specific.
7.5 Production and service provision		Section heading only
7.5.1 Control of production and service provision	4.9 + 4.10 + 4.12 + 4.19	None
7.5.2 Validation of production and service provision processes	4.9	'Special processes.'
7.5.3 Identification and traceability	4.8+4.12	4.8, 4.12 combined into one.
7.5.4 Customer property	4.7	Broader scope stated.

Figure 10.2 (continued)

Cross-reference between ISO 9001:2000 and ISO 9001:1994

ISO 9001:2000	ISO 9001:1994	Change in Requirements
7.5.5 Preservation of product	4.15	None — less specific
7.6 Control of monitoring and measuring devices	4.11	Less detailed, same intent.
8 Measurement, analysis and improvement		**Section heading only**
8.1 General	4.10 + 4.20 + 4.1	Systemic requirement for planning system, measuring and monitoring for conformity and improved effectiveness
8.2 Monitoring and measurement		Section heading only
8.2.1 Customer satisfaction	4.14.2	Monitoring of customer 'perceptions.'
8.2.2 Internal audit	4.17	Must now consider the standard as well as system. More process detail added.
8.2.3 Monitoring and measurement of processes	4.9	Scope extends acress the entire QMS, not just product reqliation processes.
8.2.4 Monitoring and measurement of product	4.10.1 + 4.10.5 + 4.10.4	Records must identify 'person(s)' performing release activities not 'authority.'
8.3 Control of nonconforming product	4.13	Consider appropriate action when problem discovered after delivery/use starts.
8.4 Analysis of data	4.14 + 4.6.2	Some increased requirements.
8.5 Improvement		Section heading only
8.5.1 Continual improvement	4.1.1 + 4.17 + 4.14.3 + 4.1.3	No systemic requirements created — use the tool the system creates.
8.5.2 Corrective action	4.14.1 + 4.14.2	Reporting to management required.
8.5.3 Preventive Action	4.14.1 + 4.14.3	None.

not relevant to their business. The exclusions are restricted to Clause 7, Product realization, and subject also to the constraints contained in Subclause 1.2. This limits exclusions to "quality management system requirements that neither affect the organization's ability, nor absolve it from its responsibility, to provide product that meets customer and applicable regulatory requirements."

There is a substantial section in Chapter 9 that discusses the issue of scope and system exclusions. Essentially an organization should look at how it fulfills customer requirements, examine Clause 7 of the standard, and identify those activities that do not apply. An organization with no design function would obviously exclude the whole of 7.3. The Victoria Group excludes 7.6, not having any measuring and monitoring equipment to control. 7.5.3, Customer property, is another requirement that many organizations may be able to exclude — but remember warranty and service repairs are customer property — and there are some certified organizations that don't do any purchasing. They could exclude 7.4.

Generally speaking, that probably about sums up the available exclusions. The remaining elements of Clause 7 cover a very wide range of activities and in consequence are likely to apply to the vast majority of organizations.

Having determined the exclusions that apply, these should be carefully checked against the certified scope statement to ensure that there are no conflicts, and then documented. A brief explanation should be written for each exclusion.

3. Review and identify the additional/changed requirements that impact the organization, identifying them by clause and subclause.

Once the exclusions are identified and noted, it must follow that the remainder of the standard applies. This will mean that there is some work to do, because although there is no need to change documents just to map the new layout, there is a need to modify the system to meet changes in requirements. This step in the process is designed to identify the extent of those changes and the additions needed.

Each requirement that applies to the system under review should be examined to identify how it differs from or adds to the system baseline. The charts included in this chapter can be used to identify the changes at a high level; thereafter it is a case of coming to grips with the actual text and seeing what is different.

The best way to identify and track the changes is simply to identify the clause and subclause containing the changed requirement, make a note of the actual change, and cross-reference the original 1994 requirement. Use a separate sheet for each change, and make any relevant notes on the apparent impact of the change on the existing system.

Take particular note of requirements that address the need for requirements to be documented rather than for a "documented procedure." This statement highlights areas in the new standard where a record may be required that is not currently maintained.

These notes will provide a framework for both the next step, the review of the quality manual, and for the system gap analysis that will be performed in step 7 of the transition process.

4. Review the quality manual and identify the changes required.

The quality manual is one document that is likely to need to be completely rewritten. The majority of quality manuals have tended to be written around the 20 elements of the standard. This is for the very good reason that it is the easiest way to write a manual, and if it is done properly it still allows for the document to be a descriptive outline of the organization's operations. However unique to the organization the manual is, it is unlikely to provide the "sequence and interaction of the processes" required by the new standard, nor will it address some of the new requirements.

The reconstruction of the quality manual should be a two-stage operation. The first step is to go through the document working with the notes made from the review of 9001:2000 carried out in step 4. This will help by highlighting the changed requirements and where they occur in the manual.

Take particular note of the fact that the quality policy will almost certainly need to be revised. This is a task that should be passed to top management, as will be the requirement for the development of quality objectives.

Once the additional requirements have been identified, the text may be able to be modified to accommodate them and the changes in the manual then implemented into the system. Alternatively, it may be a case of flagging the areas of the manual that have to change and then waiting until the system is modified before linking the manual to the changed processes.

Once the manual has been suitably modified to reflect the changed requirements the next step is to reorganize the content to reflect the process flow of activities from the initial customer inquiry to the completion of contractual commitments. A detailed review of a suggested approach to the layout of a manual for the new standard is offered in Chapter 11 (Documentation). This approach suggests a four-section manual divided as follows:

Section 1 — Company Outline, Scope, Quality Policy and Objectives

- General statement — the description and sales pitch
- Scope statement
- Quality policy statement
- Statement on the development and deployment of quality objectives
- Details of company organization or structure, both corporate, if a multi-company operation and actual management structures at the highest level
- Statements of responsibility and authority of department heads.

Section 2 — Systems Outline

- A brief description of the operational processes of the organization, how those processes interrelate and what is done to control the significant activities of the company

- Reference to supporting documentation relating to the operation of the organization's processes

- Identification and explanation of any exclusions of requirements in Clause 7 of the standard

- Where responsibility lies for the control of the significant activities.

Section 3 — Procedure Reference

- A description of the organization's processes for supporting the requirements of the six mandatory processes and other supporting documentation.

- Where it is to be found in general terms.

Section 4 — Supporting Activities

- Description of the management-driven activities that support the operation of the management system. These include

  - management review

  - training, competency and awareness

  - analysis of data

  - continual improvement.

At this stage of the transition process the reformatting of the manual need be no more than a rough "cut and paste" of the existing document, complete with the editorial comments about the changes required to meet the standard. This will be perfectly adequate for the purposes of management review of the process in step 5.

5. Retrain executive management.

The initial implementation of an ISO-based management system should always start with an executive training session. Top management must fully understand what it is getting into, and commit to providing the resources necessary for a successful implementation process.

The same is true for the transition process. Although the changes in requirements are not dramatic, some of them will require a significant increase in top management involvement. The policy must include a commitment to continual improvement, and both the policy and the primary quality objectives need to be established by top management.

The "rough cut" revision of the quality manual can be used as a basis for the executive overview training, which probably needs to be at least four hours in length. A full one-day program is preferred, but once an organization is certified getting the executive team to commit that amount of time to a revisit of the requirements of the standard may not be easy.

The focus of attention for the executive (top) management briefing session should be on the primary changes identified, linking each of these enhanced requirements to the quality manual, policy and objectives as well as to the changes in emphasis that will be required elsewhere in the system. Obviously new activities need to be identified and flagged as being resource issues.

The overall increase in the attention being paid to system effectiveness also needs to be addressed, particularly with respect to the role of the internal audit process in contributing to the ongoing development and improvement of the management system. Management needs to understand that internal auditors will be asked to pay more attention to system outputs and system effectiveness than has typically been the case in the past. It is highly likely that the audit reports that come to management for review will in the future contain more commentary on the outputs of the system than simply identifying areas of nonconformity.

There are a number of outputs that are desirable from this training event. They are:

- Obtain a commitment from the management team to provide the necessary resources to complete the transition process.
- Agree a draft time line for the activity including the first management review of the proposed amendments.
- Set a date by which a revised quality policy will be published.
- Set a date for the publication of high level quality objectives and plans for their accomplishment.

6. Retrain internal auditors.

Train, train, train! This is the single most important activity that needs to be undertaken by the organization as it transitions into the new management system. The fundamentals of the audit process remain unchanged. Audit continues to be an independent, systematic, planned process for the examination of objective evidence to determine the conformity or nonconformity of activities to planned arrangements.

There is now an additional requirement placed on the internal audit process, which is to review the ongoing conformity of the system to the standard. This had been one of the defined tasks of the management representative; now it has been placed on the internal auditors. Systems do not of themselves become non-compliant. Some change has to be made for a process or procedure that was compliant to become noncompliant, so it is important that internal auditors do not spend too much time on this aspect of the requirement. The core duty remains that of assuring that the system as planned is being implemented effectively, and reporting on the operation of the system to management.

The internal audit team will require a thorough grounding in the new standard, the changed requirements and the new activities. There is an art to auditing objectives and their deployment throughout the organization. The recommended training for the internal auditors is the two-day transition auditor training program offered by some of the IRCA- and RAB-approved training organizations. The internal auditors need to be at least as well trained as certification auditors, and they will be taking this two-day program. The syllabus that the internal auditors need to understand includes:

- The intent of the revisions
- Third-party implementation of ISO 9000:2000 — the IAF communique
- The eight quality management principles
- The process approach
- How ISO 9004:2000 should help the user — the concept of a "consistent pair"
- The new role of ISO 9000:2000
- Understanding ISO 9000:2000 — an intensive review of the standard and comparison with ISO 9000:1994
- Process-based auditing:
  - The process flow of audit activity
  - Matrix analysis, audit schedules and audit notification
  - Operational analysis, flowcharts and checklists
  - Audit reporting, follow-up and closeout, surveillance.

Organizations which currently base internal audits on the 20 elements will have to completely re-jig their audit planning process and program. ISO 9001:2000 requires a process/department/activity model.

The internal audit process is supposed to be a review and measure of the effectiveness of the management system; this has always been the intent, but it is now more visible and clearly stated than previously. In consequence of this change, internal auditors need to make a more direct contribution to the ongoing improvement of the system by examining and commenting upon the effectiveness of the activities audited. The review of system outputs against inputs and plans will play a bigger role in the life of the internal auditor than has typically been the case in the past.

7. Perform a gap analysis on the current system against the additional/ changed requirements, taking particular note of enhanced record-keeping requirements and data analysis.

By this stage of the process the management representative(s), the top management and the internal auditors have all been retrained. They all share a common understanding of the requirements of the new standard, and the changes required in their own management system as a result of the transition process. Armed with this knowledge, it is time for a comprehensive review of the existing system from top to bottom. This review takes the form of a full-scale gap analysis audit of the system against the new standard.

An ISO 9000 project initiation gap analysis consists of a review of existing documentation and then a review of activities — the presumption is that there will be many more activities than are documented in an organization without a formal management system.

The same holds true for this gap analysis. In many organizations where management take the operation of their system seriously it is highly likely that spread across the organization's operations will be a number of activities that contribute towards conformity with new requirements but are currently informal. It will be important to identify and capture such activities during the audit and later to determine whether they require documentation or whether they can be incorporated into the operational processes in some other way to achieve conformity with ISO 9001:2000.

It is not recommended that the gap analysis be used to identify documentation that can be eliminated. The new standard, without question, reduces the documentation requirements mandated for conformity. It does require a documented system sufficient to ensure consistent achievement of customer satisfaction. The removal of documentation from the system at this stage is unwise. This is an issue that, generally speaking, should be addressed at a later date.

There is one exception. In the early flush of enthusiasm, when organizations started implementing ISO 9001, there was a common misconception that was fostered by much of the bad information going around — and still there to this day — that an ISO system meant that every single thing must be written down. It wasn't true, and it still isn't. Use this gap analysis to identify possibly unnecessary documentation. The test to use is a simple one: Does the operation of this procedure or work instruction produce:

- An output that goes to someone else?
- A record that proves the activity has occurred?
- Any impact if it is left undone?

If the answer to any of these questions is no, then the activity and the document need to be carefully reviewed as a candidate for elimination. This is especially true of the second question, because without a record there is no way of proving the activity has occurred. In considering these options it must be remembered that the record may follow some time later; for example, a test or inspection that produces a record might occur a long time after a production activity — nonetheless the inspection or test record relates to the production work instruction.

The output from the gap analysis should consist of three data elements.

1. Activities that conform to the requirements of the standard. This will com-

Figure 10-3

Transition Implementation Time Line

	Month											
Activity	1	2	3	4	5	6	7	8	9	10	11	12
Steps 1-5	•••	•										
Review Scope	•											
Identify Changed Requirements	•											
Review Quality Manual	•											
Retrain Executive Management		•										
Retrain Internal Auditors		•										
Gap Analysis		•										
Develop Plan		•	•									
Create Matrix of Conformity			••									
Document Plans for Revising Documentation					•							
Review Plans with Registrar					•							
Retrain All Staff						•••	•••	•••				
Implement plans												
a. Policy and Objectives					•	••						
b. Sales and Marketing						••						
c. Materials Management						••	•					
d. Design							•••	•••	•••			
e. Operations								•••	•••	•••		
f. Data Analysis										•••		
g. Customer Satisfaction						••						
h. Continual Improvement								•••	•••			
Management Review											•	
Transition Audit												••

prise 90 percent of the findings if the management system is well constructed and well managed.

2. Activities that require enhancement, or activities that are not occurring as required by the standard. This should be the remaining 10 percent of the output from the audit. Be aware that although enhancement requirements may only be 10 percent of the findings, some of them may require a reasonable amount of work to implement.

3. Activities that appear to fit under the questions above, and are therefore candidates for elimination after careful consideration. With some optimism no percentage is given for these activities!

Armed with this information, the implementation plan can now be created.

8. Develop an overall plan with milestones to enhance the current system.

With all the relevant information on hand, the management representative can now do an intelligent job of creating the overall system enhancement project plan.

A comfortable time frame for the transitional activity will be something in the region of 12 months. Plan the activity around operational structures and processes rather than the standard, and develop any enhanced interface activities as the program proceeds. This time frame allows the usual internal audit activity to assist in implementing the changes and ensuring that they are successfully operational.

At all stages the newly modified processes should be subject to audit activity within a few weeks of implementation to ensure that the planned activity is happening consistently and is appropriate. This is the same process as is used during initial implementation — create the process, place it into operation, review for appropriateness and adequacy, amend as required.

Make sure that there is a comprehensive and thorough management review of the system before the transition certification audit to ensure that everything is operating in the manner management intended, and that the review activity contributes to the ongoing process of improvement.

9. Create a matrix of conformity mapping existing system documentation from the 1994 standard to the new standard.

One of the most cumbersome tasks that confronts the management representative in converting from the 1994 standard to the 2000 version is going to be mapping the existing system into the new layout.

Some requirements are straightforward because they remain clearly identified in individual clauses and subclauses of the standard. Examples of these would include Document control (4.2.3), Records (4.2.4), Management review (5.6), Training (6.2.2), Design control (7.3), Purchasing (7.4) and Calibration (7.6). Note: The numbers in parentheses refer to the year 2000 standard. This is not to say that changes are not required in some of these areas, as will have been revealed by the gap analysis, but at least the procedures that supported the subjectmatter in the 1994 standard are a direct basis for the modified procedure.

The best way to approach this task is to create a matrix of conformity, mapping the existing documents into the standard. The charts provided in the text can be used to help identify where each document fits into the 2000 standard. At this stage there are likely to be blanks in the matrix. Review these against the scope statement, then determine if a document is required by the process.

The process of implementing the changes and enhancements in the system is probably best tackled as discussed above by process, activity or operational area of the organization, using staff training and internal audit as the tools for ensuring accuracy and effectiveness.

During the implementation of the additional or changed requirements careful consideration will have to be given to the method to be used. As the standard provides considerable flexibility in the approach to process implementation and control, each stage of the activity will need to review the options and determine whether documentation is required, and if so what form it should take. There are clear indications in the standard that documented inputs and outputs to and from a process can provide evidence of both the operation and control of a process, and this may be an option that needs to be considered.

10. Document plans for revising ISO 9001 references in current documentation as changes/enhancements occur.

The Victoria Group has always recommended to clients that, with the possible exception of the quality manual, documentation should not contain any numerical references to the standard. A matrix of conformity is the best way to track the relationship between ISO requirements and the organization's system.

The validity of this guidance can now clearly be seen. If a system has cross-references between ISO elements on every document, suddenly they are all wrong. The numbering scheme in the 2000 standard is completely different from the 1994 document, as has been seen from the charts above.

One thing that should definitively not be undertaken at this or any other stage of the transitional process is to start revising existing documentation to remove or change any references to elements of the 1994 standard and replace them with references to the 2000 standard. There is absolutely no added value to any organization in doing this, and it will be a hugely time-consuming task.

References to numbered elements of the standard have no place in documentation and to replace one lot of unnecessary data with another lot is a complete waste of time.

Any organization having direct references to ISO 9000:1994 numbering scattered across their system documentation needs a plan to correct the situation.

The best approach is to establish the matrix of conformity as already described. Utilize the cross-reference charts provided in this text to provide a clear and simple way of identifying the mapping, and make both of these documents attachments to a revised document change control procedure. The revision that is going to be made to the document control change process is to identify that, as procedures, work instructions and other management system documentation is revised, all references to ISO 9000:1994 will be removed from the documents. Until such time as this activity is completed, the attached appendices provide the system user with a cross-reference when required. It is suggested that a three-year limit be put on the completion of this process; any document that has not required any changes in three years is probably either due to be retired, or will just have to be amended to make the world a tidier place!

Note: ISO 9001:2000 4.2.3 b) requires that the procedure for control of documents provide for "review, update as necessary and reapprove documents." This does not mean that a new process has to be invented for a formal review and re-approval of every document on a regular cycle. Use the internal audit activity as the vehicle for the regular review of documents as well as the natural processes of change that operate in the organization.

The one exception to a complete rewrite is the quality manual. Assuming that the manual is the conventional lightweight, high-level document, it is worth the effort to completely revamp this document as a process-driven system outline as discussed earlier. The changes that will be required in most manuals are such that anything short of a rewrite is likely to produce a rather messy, unsatisfactory top-level document.

11. Review plans with registrar.

Light can be seen at the end of the tunnel — and this time it isn't another train. Once the required activities have all been identified, the executive management and internal auditors trained, the gap analysis completed and the transition plans drawn up it is time to discuss the program with your registrar. This can probably be initiated by telephone and followed up by mail. Provide the registrar with copies of the gap analysis and the implementation plan along with the document transition plan, if required. Because of the recommended time line, the majority of organizations will also have a surveillance audit during the implementation of the transitional arrangements, and this can also be used to review activities and progress with the certification body auditor. But in doing this remember that he or she is not a consultant and is not permitted to provide consulting advice. The auditor might draw attention to an aspect that appears to have been missed, or identify something where he or she can draw on experience to suggest that the intended activity may not be very successful, but the one thing the auditor cannot do is to advise on an appropriate course of action.

Verify plans for maintaining records to ensure that the planned retention time is acceptable to the registrar; of course after a number of years working with the registrar the management representative is probably already well familiar with any such aspects of the registrar's approach.

Once the plans are agreed with the registrar, make sure that the agreement is documented, just in case an individual auditor decides to take a different view of the world.

12. Retrain all staff.

Finally the companywide training process is initiated. This activity is not as dramatic as it sounds. Remember that the organization has already been certified for anything up to 15 years by the upper limit of the transitional period (1987 to 2003), so the day-to-day operation of a formal structured management system is nothing new to anyone.

Two aspects that do change for many organizations are the formal deployment of quality objectives and the increased emphasis on metrics and data analysis to provide opportunities for improvement in product, process and system. The revised requirements for training (6.2.2) require that all personnel should understand the importance of their activities in contributing to achieving quality objectives. In many organizations this will mean that employees who have hitherto been asked to do their jobs conscientiously and reliably, but not necessarily with any understanding of how they fit into the greater scheme of things, will need to be shown the links between what they do and what the organization is trying to achieve. Even if this additional training goes no further than to provide a basic level of understanding of how performing according to requirements assures that a product specification is met, it will produce worthwhile results.

Those organizations which go the distance and fit product conformance into corporate objectives and really use the deployment process will definitely benefit substantially. That said, management who want to achieve in this manner will already be doing much more than the Standard requires anyway. These comments also hold true for the use of metrics, legal and regulatory issues and continual improvement. As has always been the case with ISO 9000 based management systems the committed organization will reap substantial benefit from the changes in the Standard as they redouble their efforts on all fronts. The also-ran organization will do just enough to get by and no more. Benefit will accrue, even to them, but at such a low level that no-one will really notice, least of all employees and shareholders.

Recertification

The end point of all this effort is the recertification audit, when the registrar audits the system against ISO 9001:2000 for the first time. This will be a tense moment for the management representative — audits always are. If this 12-step process has been followed, appropriate training acquired and provided to all staff and a careful job done of the documentation transition, the audit should be quite straightforward. The internal auditors can make a massive contribution to ensuring that this is the case by being used continually throughout the transition process. Constant auditing by well-trained staff will ensure that all areas of the system are operating in the intended manner and producing the required results. Coupled with an effective and meaningful management review process, audit is one of the main ways of assuring system operability, conformity and effectiveness. If all three of these are confirmed, the registrar will be happy.

Documentation and Records Management

This chapter contains two articles on the documentation of ISO 9001:2000 and the legal implications of ISO 9001:2000 records. The first one, by Roderick Goult, describes the different ways in which an ISO 9000 system can be documented and the specific documentation requirements of ISO 9001:2000. Goult discusses each clause of the standard requiring documentation and demonstrates the effectiveness of different documentation heirarchies and the ways in which effective information flowdown occurs at an organization using ISO 9000.

The second article, by Jerry L. Whitson and Eugenia K. Brumm, specifically discusses how an organization's ISO 9000 documentation can keep it out of legal trouble. According to Whitson and Brumm, ISO 9000 records can be a legal safeguard against many lawsuits. This article also introduces several considerations on ISO 9000 records that should be considered when preparing a legally protective system, including:

- The importance of records relating to design of products
- Creating a retention schedule for records
- When to suspend records destruction
- Records control vs. document control.

Documentation for ISO 9001:2000

By Roderick Goult

Introduction

The year 2000 version of the ISO 9001 standard was in development for more than six years. The general principles were first outlined in a document called "Vision 2000," which was published in the early nineties. There were a number of different factors considered during the development of the documents, and some of the key issues were commented upon in Clause 1.2 of the printed DIS. Those issues appear to be:

- The adoption of process oriented management

- Problems with the 20-element quality systems model of ISO 9001:1994

- Greater emphasis on meeting the needs of customers and other interested parties

- Difficulties small businesses experience in the application of the standards

- The bias of the current standards towards large manufacturing type organizations

- Supporting organizations in moving beyond merely using the ISO 9000 standards for certification purposes to using the standards to assist in improving their business performance

- The advent of, and the need for, enhanced compatibility with other management systems standards (e.g., ISO 14001).

ISO Technical Committee (TC) 176 has clearly given great weight to implementation issues in that it created a set of implementation guidelines and information documents — an activity that is a departure from its traditonal role of drafting standards. Whether implementation advice is something which an ISO TC should be offering is an issue worthy of discussion in a different forum. It will be too easy for such "guidance" to be seen as "requirements" by some in the certification business. That said, the guidance so far issued by TC 176 is sound and sensible.

No organization should ever create documents for the sole benefit of a certification body. Every document must add value to the organization. If it doesn't add value, it adds cost, and that is completely unacceptable.

The guidance information coming from TC 176 emphasises certain key objectives, the first being a concern to achieve a simplified format that will address small organizations as well as large ones, and secondly for "the amount and detail of documentation required to be more relevant to the desired results of the organization's process activities."

The result of the second of these goals is that the new standard is substantially less prescriptive than the 1994 version, and allows an organization considerable leeway in determining where documentation is needed to ensure control of its quality management system. TC 176 speaks of allowing "more flexibility"; in reality the flexibility has always been there — but few users have recognized or taken advantage of the fact.

The most effective management systems have always been minimalist, and the guidance from TC 176 reflects this fact. The intention of the new standard is to enable "each individual organization to develop the minimum amount of documentation needed in order to demonstrate the effective planning, operation and control of its processes." The more effective the system, the greater the level of continual improvement that will result.

Contrary to frequent ill-informed criticism, the standard has always required a management system to be in place, not just a bunch of documents. That this has all too often not been the case should not be a criticism of the standard, but rather of the manner in which it has been implemented and audited. The quality profession and the certification process bear the burden if the first two versions of ISO 9001 failed to achieve their potential, not the standard itself.

Defined Requirements in ISO 9001:2000

Clause 4.1 of ISO 9001:2000, General requirements, requires that an organization "establish, document, implement and maintain a quality management system and continually improve its effectiveness in accordance with the requirements of this International Standard." It is important to note that the word "document" comes directly before the word "implement." Clearly it is intended that the management system shall be formal, although the combination of different statements does provide a degree of ambiguity.

Clause 4.2, Documentation requirements, identifies certain specific documents which the management system is to include. They are:

- Documented statements of a quality policy and quality objectives
- Documented statements of quality objectives
- A quality manual
- Documented procedures required by the standard

- Documents required by the organization to ensure the effective planning, operation and control of its processes
- Quality records required by the standard.

Elsewhere in the document are six explicit requirements that a "documented procedure shall be established." They appear in the following clauses:

4.2.3	Control of documents
4.2.4	Control of records
8.2.2	Internal audit
8.3	Control of nonconformity
8.5.2	Corrective action
8.5.3	Preventive action.

Clause 4.2 is followed by several "notes." As with the 1994 standard, "notes" are guidance not requirements. Those which follow 4.2 echo the same approach that was taken in the 1994 standard, stating that the nature and complexity of the documentation should depend upon the type of work and the skills and training of personnel. The only change is that the new wording is slightly different. The entire scope, structure and content of documentation will vary from organization to organization based upon the: "size of organization and type of activities; complexity of processes and their interactions; competence of personnel."

This is a reminder that with certain defined exceptions the decision on whether or not a document is required becomes a subjective judgment based on the added value to the organization of defining any specific process. See the balance of training vs. detail in documentation demonstrated by Figure 11-1.

There is little point in having a management system documented unless there can be confidence that all the users of any particular document are in possession of the same information; the reason for documenting a process is to ensure consistency. The documentation in the system must therefore be controlled, and the standard provides a set of basic requirements for the control of documents in Clause 4.2.3. The activity of document control will be discussed in detail later in this chapter.

It is important to understand the difference between "documents" and "records." A required record typically is a document, and it must be controlled, but it is not a controlled document within the meaning of 4.2.3. The reason for this is that a record never changes. A new record may be required, but the old record remains valid. It illustrates certain data which were true at the point in time at which it was created. The data may not have been what was required, e.g., failure to meet a specific requirement. This failure may result in a process being repeated or a repair being undertaken to enable data to be observed that do meet the requirements, but that doesn't change the intrinsic truth of the first record. The requirements for control of records are contained in Clause 4.2.4, and will be reviewed in detail later in this chapter.

Figure 11-1

Training vs. Documentation Detail

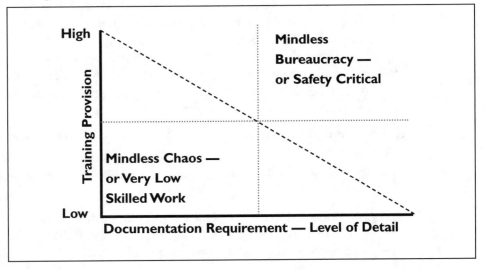

Fulfilling the Basics

This discussion of documenting a management system for conformity with ISO 9001:2000 will therefore start by examining the requirements for these specific, named items.

3.1 A Statement of Quality Policy

Examples of quality policy statements are provided in Chapter 9 of this book and will not be repeated here.

The essential requirements that a policy statement must fulfill are defined in Clause 5.3 of the standard. The first requirement is that the policy statement "shall" be endorsed by "top management," a term defined in ISO 9000:2000 as meaning "person or group of people who direct and control an organization." The executive management of the organization will typically be those held responsible for endorsing policy and objectives, even though those policies and objectives may be driven by the board of directors. In multisite organizations implementing the system on a site-by-site basis, this endorsement may well come from the senior on-site executive manager rather than from "top management" of the organization as a whole.

a) Management are required to ensure that the policy statement "is appropriate to the purpose of the organization."

This implies that the policy statement should relate to the day-to-day activities of the organization and be focussed on some specific issues. Quality policy statements have all too often been confused with mission statements or values statements, both of which are frequently very high-level statements of principle rather than of day-to-day operational matters. The policy statement should be down to earth, directly related to operational activities and contain commitment to measurable targets. Being a "world class" organization is not measurable unless someone writes a definition for the term "world class." Likewise commitments to "exceeding customer expectations" are fraught with danger. Not only is it going to be difficult to measure, but exceeding a customer's requirements can actually cause that customer problems.

Short, simple, measurable, effective. These are the golden rules for a quality policy statement.

b) The policy statement must include "a commitment to meeting requirements."

Closely related to the concept of the policy being "appropriate," which has been discussed above, is a requirement that the policy specifically include a commitment to meeting requirements. These requirements have four primary sources:

"customer requirements — specification, delivery and price";

Example: on-time delivery of conforming product at the agreed price.

"internal requirements — issues known to the organization as important in fulfilling the customer's needs";

Example: metal treatment prior to painting to ensure corrosion resistance.

"regulatory and legal requirements — those requirements imposed by law and regulation which are essential for the legitimate provision and use of the product, including health, safety and environmental issues";

Example – manufacturers installing catalytic converters, seat belts and air bags on cars.

"societal requirements — those which arise from societal demand which may exceed legal and regulatory issues."

Example: many manufacturers offering biodegradable washing powders and detergents in response to a heightened public awareness of environmental issues.

c) The policy statement must include "a commitment to ... continual improvement."

Improvement can occur in products, processes and systems. The concept is that the policy states categorically that the executive management of the organization is committed to continually improving the way it operates. This does not imply that all areas of the organization are going to have improvement programs at all times. Nor does it imply that all processes and products even need improvement.

Improvement at any cost is not the objective — for improvement to be genuine there must be a benefit that accrues to customers, shareholders, the organization itself or to the stakeholders. If one or more of these groups does not obtain benefit, then no improvement has occurred; likewise, if a change is detrimental to one or more of these groups, then there has been no improvement. The name of this game is adding value.

> d) The quality policy must provide "a framework for establishing and reviewing quality objectives."

Clause 5.4.1 defines the requirements for quality objectives. The role of the policy statement is one of committing the management of the organization to declaring, deploying and reviewing quality objectives on a regular basis.

> e) The quality policy is to be "communicated and understood within the organization."

All personnel should be aware of the intent of the quality policy and how they contribute to the fulfillment of that intent by operating in accordance with the management system.

> f) Finally, there is a requirement that the quality policy "is reviewed for continuing suitability."

A quality policy should not be a one-shot deal, cast in stone immutable and unchangeable, never to be revisited. This statement mandates the regular review of the quality policy, and a quick look at the requirements of Clause 5.6.1, Management review, shows that this is one of the essential agenda items for that activity.

3.1.1 Control of the Policy Statement

Clause 4.2.3 states that "documents required by the quality management system shall be controlled." The quality policy is one of the required documents (see Clause 4.2.1); therefore it must be a controlled document.

A quality policy will only be useful if it is shared as widely as possible with members of the organization, its customers and stakeholders. The requirement to ensure control of the policy must not be allowed to interfere with this wide distribution of the policy statement, otherwise the essential value will be lost.

One simple way of addressing this issue is for the "master copy" of the policy statement to contain a disclaimer about distributed copies not being controlled. This approach has long been used with electronic systems and there is no reason why it shouldn't work for the policy as well.

The requirements of 4.2.3 include the statement that documents must be approved prior to use. It must be possible to demonstrate that quality policy has been formally approved by "top management." This does not require that the actual policy statement be signed by an executive manager, although this is an excellent way of demonstrating commitment to the policy. The policy statement can equally well be shown to have been approved by being part of the quality manual, a document that itself requires to be approved prior to issue.

3.2 Declared Quality Objectives

The requirements for quality objectives are defined in Clause 5.4.1 of the standard. This states that quality objectives are to be "established at relevant functions and levels within the organization." This time the use of the term "relevant functions and levels" is beneficial in maintaining flexibility in the requirements. Organizations are now free to determine whether to maintain core quality objectives as high-level, organizationwide issues, or whether to create a layered structure of objectives that is deployed down through the organization to every operational area.

There is a secondary set of quality objectives, directly related to deliverables required by Clause 7.1. The standard goes on to state that "quality objectives shall be measurable and consistent with the quality policy including the commitment to continual improvement." The system must be integrated. Achievement of the policy should be measurable; it follows that the achievement of objectives should also be measurable.

Core organizational objectives may even be embedded in the policy statement; an example of this would be on-time delivery. This can be both a policy and a core objective. A link is drawn between the requirement for a commitment to continual improvement and the objectives. Clearly the objectives are intended to be issues that will stretch the organization and make it strive to do better. This means that once an objective has been achieved, it may need to be revisited, either to enhance the objective or to create a new one that will continue to stretch the organization's capabilities.

The requirement that quality objectives include "those needed to meet requirements for product" is what takes quality objectives down through the system to the level of the deployment of product specifications into the organization's operational planning and processes. A production schedule becomes a deployed quality objective in that it is the means by which the commitment to on-time delivery is implemented. Product specifications become the means of achieving conformance of deliverables.

3.2.1 Control of Quality Objectives

The standard calls for quality objectives to be documented and controlled. Clause 5.4.1 uses the word "established"; in most cases establishing objectives which are then implemented at all relevant levels of the organization is going to require that they are documented. Clause 4.2.3, Control of documents, requires that the organization shall control "documents required for the quality management system." Clearly quality objectives are "required" in the system and, if documented, then those documents must be controlled in some manner.

This does not necessarily mean that the conventional structure of "document control" must be applied. Simpler approaches need to be found and they are available. Objectives that are established as a result of a management review meeting can be documented in the minutes of that meeting. The minutes are controlled under 4.2.4, Control of records.

Objectives that relate to product requirements, such as production schedules, are typically "controlled" by carrying a date of issue. These change every week under the control of the appropriate manager, who is responsible for seeing that everyone has the latest copy.

These are two examples of simple "control" being applied to documented quality objectives.

3.3 A Quality Manual

A management system based on ISO 9001:2000 must have a quality manual. The intent of the manual is that it should describe the manner in which the organization operates, and Clause 4.2.2 identifies specific issues that must be addressed. The first requirement is that the manual must cover "the scope of the quality management system, including details of, and justification for, any exclusions (see 1.2.)."

This statement effectively creates three requirements. The first is that the manual must contain the system scope statement, the purpose and construction of which is discussed in Chapter 9. The second is that the manual must address all aspects of the management system covered by the scope statement, and the third is that any of the ISO 9001:2000 requirements from Clause 7, Product realization, which are not addressed must be explained and justified. Note that the standard only permits exclusions from this one section. Everything else must be included.

A case can be made for saying that the manual must cover all activities contained within the system — the scope of the system — and not neccesarily contain a formal scope statement.

The next requirement is that the manual must contain or reference the documented procedures required of the system, and the final requirement is that the manual provide "a description of the sequence and interaction of the processes included in the quality management system."

The format and structure of the quality manual is not defined, and is left to the discretion of the author and the needs of the organization. A small organization may well operate with a single document that includes the entire management system within a single manual, including all the documented procedures required by the standard.

Large, multinational organizations may need several manuals at the geographical or organizational levels, coupled with a fairly complex hierarchy of documentation.

The traditional approach of the four-tier system of manual, procedures, work instructions and records remains valid and has proved to be an efficient and effective manner of documenting systems for many years.

These concepts are illustrated in Figure 11-2.

Most organizations, particularly middle-sized to large ones, find that the traditional approach is more appropriate than having everything in one manual. The single manual approach tends to result in it becoming large, cumbersome in use

Figure 11-2

Potential Documentation Hierarchies

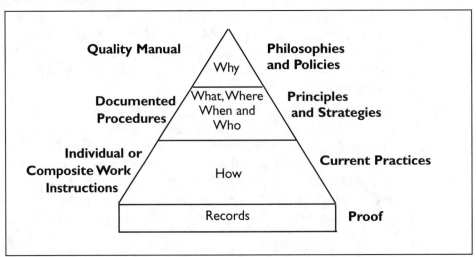

and a nightmare to update and control. The result of this widely recognized problem is that the four-tier documentation structure illustrated in Figure 11-2 has become commonplace.

Is there value in an off-the-shelf quality manual? Afraid not; the quality manual must describe the quality policy, the objectives and system processes actually in use, not just echo the words of ISO 9001 saying that systems have been created. It is important that the manual reflect actual practice, not the system the organization would like to be operating. Every company makes different products in different ways, offers different services and is organized in its own unique way.

The main reason for a quality manual is to provide a high-level overview for internal and external customers on how the management system operates, the scope of the system and the policy and objectives of the organization.

3.3.1 Quality Manual Structure

A quality manual is, fundamentally, a listing of what is done to receive an order and fulfil that order. Ideally, it should be a maximum of 20 to 25 pages long, and typically contains four types of information:

Section 1 - Company Outline, Scope, Quality Policy and Objectives

- General statement - the description and sales pitch

- Scope statement

- Quality policy statement

- Statement on the development and deployment of quality objectives

- Details of company organization or structure, both corporate, if a multi-company operation, and actual management structures at the highest level

- Statements of responsibility and authority of department heads.

Section 2 - Systems Outline

- A brief description of the operational processes of the organization, how those processes interrelate and what is done to control the significant activities of the company

- Reference to supporting documentation relating to the operation of the organization's processes

- Identification and explanation of any exclusions of requirements in Clause 7 of the standard

- Where responsibility lies for the control of the significant activities.

Section 3 - Procedure Reference

- A description of the organization's processes for supporting the requirements of the six mandatory processes, together with reference to relevant documents.

Section Four – Supporting Activities

- Description of the management-driven activities that support the operation of the management system. These include management review; training, competency and awareness; analysis of data; and continual improvement.

Section 1

The requirements for quality policy and objectives have already been discussed.

The quality manual is the traditional place for the policy statement to be formally documented and signed.

Objectives contained in the manual are likely to be high-level, with guidance as to the process for setting and reviewing objectives throughout the system.

Remember that this manual is intended to be read by actual and potential customers as well as the organization's staff. Because of this, many organizations also include a description of the history and background of the company, the products and services it provides and a little marketing piece on what makes them different from the competition.

Company Organization or Structure

Usually this is an organization chart or family tree showing the reporting structure of senior management and the interrelationships of departments and personnel. Organization charts should use job titles, never names; otherwise they could well be continually in need of update. If organization charts are used, the management representative responsible for the quality system should be identified.

Statements of Authority and Responsibility

The standard requires that:

"Top management shall ensure that reponsibilities and authorities are defined and communicated within the organization." ISO 9001:2000, 5.5.1.

The quality manual will often contain a brief description of the key management responsibilities of senior staff; but following the fundamental principle that everyone is responsible for quality, the rest of the system will have to define the way that responsibilities and authorities are deployed throughout the organization. Various ways in which this can be done will be examined later in the chapter.

Section 2

Traditionally there have been two basic approaches to the writing of a quality manual. One follows the processes of the company and addresses the way that the company operates in process-oriented terms. The second approach to writing a manual follows the layout of the standard and addresses the processes of the company in the sequence in which they appear in the ISO 9001 document.

The requirement for the manual to describe the "sequence and interaction of the processes included in the quality management system" now tends to militate against the use of the second approach.

Remember that processes, products and services change; therefore the format of Section 2 should be such that it facilitates the incorporation of change or modification. The control of significant activities should be outlined; let this manual tell the reader something about the way the organization operates, not merely that it has processes in place that do good things.

The following example for reviewing customer requirements is taken from the operations manual of The Victoria Group, Inc.

Review of Requirements
by The Victoria Group, Inc.

Review of requirements operates at three levels within the company. These three levels apply to responses to inquiries as well as to received contracts.

The first level is that of registering students for public training programs. The only criteria for course registration for public training programs is course space availability. The responsibility for contract review at this level lies with the administrative assistant for operations or designee. The registration database provides evidence of review.

The second level of contract review occurs when a standard in-house training, consulting or auditing service is requested by a client. It is the responsibility of the executive vice-president or designee to ensure that suitable staffing is available for the requested dates and that the requirements are clearly documented. The signed contract provides evidence of review.

The third level of review involves discussions between executive committee member(s) and individual consultants (as needed) to determine if the company has the capability and the resources to fulfill the need. Third-level review occurs when the request for services is beyond the provision of standard (second-level review) training, auditing or consulting services. Examples of such requirements include extended demands on resources either in volume or time frame, special training material generation or unusual class configuration or size.

Initial inquiries may be written or verbal. Responses to requests for quotation are maintained by company and contact name to include meeting notes/telephone conversations, proposals and correspondence. Due to the nature of the business, such input(s) and agreement often take place when one or more of the reviewing executives is traveling. Formal sign-off of documents is therefore often neither possible nor appropriate, and the issue of a quotation or a contract signed by a member of the executive management committee provides the necessary evidence of review. Notes maintained in contact databases will record discussions with the authorizing executive and provide evidence in the form of an audit trail.

Any amendments to contract are recorded in the contract database by the executive responsible for the contract administration and communicated to the relevant persons.

Exclusions

Any exclusions must be identified and explained. As previously stated, such exclusions are restricted to Clause 7 of the standard, and can only be activities which the organization does not perform. This constraint is declared in Clause 1.2, which states: "Exclusions do not affect the organization's ability, or responsibility, to provide product that meets customer and appropriate regulatory requirements."

The Victoria Group, as a consulting, training and auditing organization, excludes Clause 7.6, Control of measuring and monitoring devices. None of the measuring and monitoring performed within the system requires "devices."

An organization which performs no design can exclude Clause 7.3, one which never handles customer property can exclude Clause 7.5.3, and so on.

Records

The manual is a useful place to make reference to general requirements for record maintenance.

Section 3 - Procedure References

The quality manual describes the quality system; technical data has no place in it, neither has commercially sensitive information. What it must do is to provide some type of cross-reference such as an index of the operating procedures that support the manual. These procedures may be identified at the end of each section of the manual or a list attached as an appendix to the manual. Whichever approach is taken, the reference should take the reader to a location where procedure names and, where applicable, numbers are available.

Very often a company will also reference the applicable element of the ISO 9001 standard, thereby also creating a schedule of conformity that demonstrates that procedures exist for each of the key requirements of the standard.

There are six areas of activity for which ISO 9001:2000 mandates that there shall be "documented procedures." As identified in section 2, they cover control of documents (4.2.3), quality records (4.2.4), internal audit (8.2.2), nonconforming product (8.3), corrective action (8.5.2) and preventive action (8.5.3).

Each of these areas should be addressed in the quality manual with a brief description of the processes involved and a direct reference to the fact that there are supporting procedures. The commentary may or may not include a specific procedural reference depending on the overall approach that has been adopted. The linkage between the outputs from corrective and preventive actions and continual improvement should be indicated.

The nature of the commentary will depend on the overall approach taken in the manual. A recommended method is to describe the overall process, ensuring that the main requirements specified in the standard are addressed. Identify the responsibilities and authorities for various activities by job title and declare the existence of the supporting procedure or procedures.

Using the approach demonstrated by the earlier excerpt from The Victoria Group, Inc. manual, the section on nonconforming product could be worded as follows:

As with Section 2, Section 3 should contain appropriate references to the records required for these activities.

Control of Nonconforming Product
by The Victoria Group, Inc.

Nonconforming product may be identified at any stage in the process from receiving through shipping. The authority to disposition nonconforming product depends upon the nature of the nonconformity and where it is found in the process. Procedures are maintained that describe the responsibility and authority for the review and disposition of all nonconforming material. These procedures cover receiving, in-process and final, and are on the company Intranet.

Nonconforming product identified at receiving is segregated and documented. Full details of the product and its source are recorded and referred to materials management. Records are maintained of all nonconforming deliveries.

Normal production rework arising from inspection or test rejection is dispositioned by production supervision. Any nonconformance exceeding defined rework limits is referred to materials management.

Materials management is responsible for dispositioning all nonconforming product identified in process. Materials may be returned to the supplier, reworked or repaired, scrapped or recovered for alternative use. Where rework or repair is carried out, quality engineering specify the reinspection required and initiate any concession or waiver activity that may be required.

Finished product that is rejected at final acceptance is referred to quality engineering for review and evaluation.

Records are maintained of all nonconforming material and the actions taken.

Section 4 – Supporting Activities

This section of the manual describes the manner in which management supports the management system by ensuring the competency of personnel, performing analysis and review of the system, and driving the processes that create continual improvement. Section 1 included an overview of the core responsibilities and authorities within the organization; here the manual identifies the commitment of top management.

Competence, Awareness and Training

Clause 6.2.2 of the standard requires that the organization must identify the competencies required for the operation of all aspects of the system and ensure that "personnel performing activities affecting quality" possess those competencies. Everyone in an organization performs activities affecting quality, so these requirements apply to all staff operating within the scope of the management system.

Training is a management issue. It requires to be resourced and supported by top management. The manual must reflect this support and commit the organization to ensuring that all personnel are trained, competent and understand their role in the greater scheme of things. This section should link back to the commentary on the development and deployment of objectives contained in Section 1 and conclude with a commitment to maintain appropriate records.

Analysis of Data

The effective operation of the management system will produce a rich flow of performance data. The manual is the first place where the value of these data is identified and commented upon as the source of information to drive continual improvement of products, processes and systems. The manual can be used to identify the nature of the data analysis performed and how it feeds into the operation of the remainder of the system.

Individual data analysis activities are likely to be identified at numerous points throughout the system, and the manual is a good place to take a bird's eye view of the situation and show how the strings get drawn together.

Management Review

Few managers need processes or procedures to run meetings. Many management systems have no procedure for management review, using instead the quality manual to identify the frequency of reviews, the attendees and the core agenda items.

The definition of the minimum required inputs and outputs for management review that is found in ISO 9001:2000 may inhibit this process, but it remains a valid approach. Records are to be maintained of all management review meetings, and this must be identified in the manual, as should the way that management review uses all the collected and collated data from the system to drive continual improvement.

Continual Improvement

This has been left until last in the manual because effecting continual improvement requires that all the other aspects of the system are in place, operating effectively and feeding data into the analysis process. These data are what enables all levels of the organization, including top management, to review and analyze the effectiveness of the operational systems it has in place and thereby identify and evaluate opportunities for improvement. The manual can be used to highlight the approaches taken and the way in which all the various threads are brought together to provide improvement data.

By the conclusion of this section, all the requirements of the standard have been addressed, and typically most of the 22 types of records identified in Chapter 4 listed in their appropriate activities.

3.3.2 Control of the Quality Manual

The quality manual is a core document in the management system and must be controlled in accordance with the requirements of 4.2.3.

The value of a quality manual comes from its widespread use, and like the quality policy, the fact that is has to be a controlled document must not be allowed to get in the way of making it available to the greatest number of readers, both within the organization and outside.

The method of control must allow for uncontrolled copies to be freely handed out to customers, and for open access within the organization itself.

Note: Remember that most registrars require that they be a designated recipient of the quality manual. Some registrars have been in the habit of physically signing and dating a hard copy of the manual, and requiring that the organization hold that physical document for their ongoing use. With the increasing use of all-electronic systems, this practice will need to be replaced with something more conducive to a virtual world.

4. Procedures and Other Documentation

The new version of the ISO 9001 standard emphasizes the concept of the management system as a series of interconnected processes whereby customer requirements and associated external requirements such as legal, product, health and safety or environmental specifications or needs are integrated to provide a stable methodology for the creation of customer satisfaction. It is called "the process approach" and reinforces the fact that ISO 9001 has always required a documented management system, not a system of documents.

The early ISO 9001:2000 drafts produced an outpouring of articles on how the standard was revolutionizing management systems, taking companies from procedures to processes. This was then, and is now, nonsense. A procedure is one method whereby a process is documented, and the development of effective, economic and concise procedures will remain an effective way of documenting a management system until written language gives way to extrasensory communication!

Figure 11-3 is an adaptation of the grisly graphic to be found in the pages of the standard itself. The concept is essentially a variant on the well-known "Plan-Do-Check-Act" cycle variously known as the Shewart, Deming or human activity cycle. The modifications and additions shown in Figure 11-4 attempt to link the requirements of the standard to the conceptual model.

Starting at the top right-hand side of the page, Clauses 1 through 4 of the standard address issues that effectively shape and direct all the activity within the management system.

On the top left of Figure 11-4 are listed the six clauses within Clause 5 that identify the responsibilities of management within the overall system.

Figure 11-3

The Process Approach as Seen in ISO 9001:2000

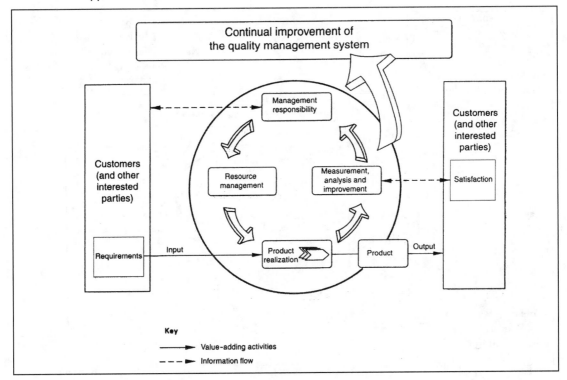

Moving counterclockwise the next set of activities to be encountered are those of resource management. Clause 6 identifies four areas of resource management.

The box entitled "product realization" is where the identification of customer needs and the translation of those needs into deliverables is addressed through the six sets of requirements found in Clause 7.

The final block in the diagram addresses Clause 8, Measuring, analysis and improvement. The five elements here drive value-added improvement of products, processes and the system. Contributing to, and part of the data collection, are (undefined) measures of customer satisfaction.

The core mandatory documents required by ISO 9001:2000 have been identified, and Chapter 9 on implementation provides guidance on how to determine what additional documents are required. The goal is to make the system effective and to be able to demonstrate control of the processes whereby customer requirements are converted into deliverable products.

Figure 11-4

How the Clauses Fit

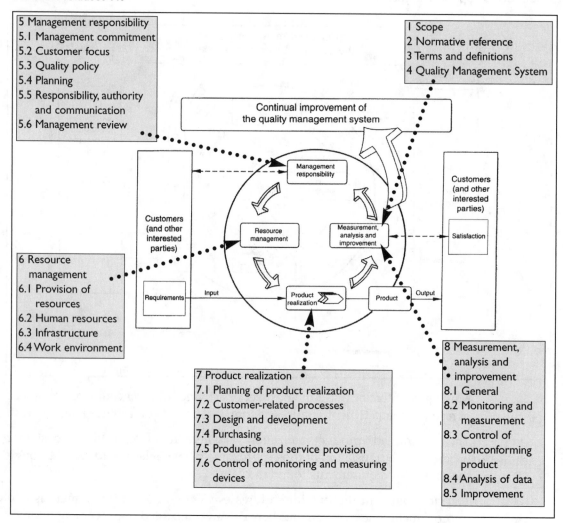

4.1 Why Document the Extra Stuff?

The requirement to "establish and maintain documented procedures..." used to be found in all the elements of ISO 9001. Many organizations struggled with this requirement — "Everyone around here knows what they are doing, why do we need to write it all down?" ISO 9001:2000 removes the mandate, but the reason for continuing to document remains the same as it ever has.

In most organizations, whether or not they have a formal management system, the vertical lines of functionality work pretty well. Each functional manager

Figure 11-5

Organizational Structures vs. Customer Satisfaction Processes

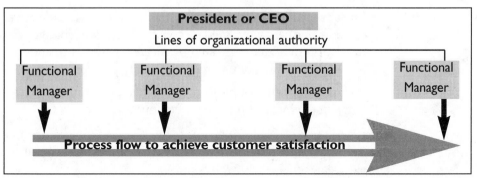

makes sure that the areas under his or her control are operating effectively. Unfortunately, as is shown in Figure 11-5, the process flow required to assure customer satisfaction is horizontal, and requires that each of the vertical operations integrates effectively with the one before it and the one after it. All too often it is this "white space" between functional departments that causes things to go awry, with miscommunication, lack of clearly defined roles and responsibilities and duplication or absence of effort. When an absence of effort arises concerning an essential part of the deliverable requirements of the customer, problems occur. The creation of a documented management system helps to manage this white space.

The creation of effective, user-friendly documentation and data is the key to a successful management system. It is also the part of the system that causes the majority of problems for organizations, in its creation, its maintenance, its use. The reason that documentation is often so problematic is the sheer volume that is to be found in most organizations. Much of the documentation that the system requires to work effectively will already exist in most organizations, and one of the issues to be addressed is the integration of existing materials within the system.

In order for it to be effective, the quality system must be well documented and well controlled. It must describe and communicate to everyone:

- The objectives of the system
- The policies of the organization
- Their responsibilities within the organization
- The operational processes.

Documentation formalizes the quality system and is necessary because it:

- Ensures consistency of action and uniformity of understanding

- Provides a clear, concise definition of company operation
- Is auditable, thereby providing a measure of effectiveness
- Ensures changes in management methodologies are effectively communicated as it is easily updated — consequently, any changes can be incorporated, approval demonstrated by means of signature and the change issued to all points of use simultaneously
- Ensures continuity of performance when personnel changes occur and helps in the induction of new personnel.

Documentation should not be excessive. Quality system documentation is not synonymous with unnecessary paper generation provided it is well planned, simple, clear, concise and well controlled.

4.1.1 Documentation Development

Development of the quality system documentation requires the identification of:

- The scope of the quality system — what deliverables are to be included and the range of activities from the continuum discussed in Chapter 9
- Those processes that impact the deliverables and that therefore need to be controlled.

This in turn requires a clear definition of:

- The functions and areas of activity to be considered in the continuum from customer enquiry to postdelivery maintenance
- What the significant processes and activities are.

These processes and activities then need to be developed into management system documents, some of which will be cross-functional and some of which will be departmental.

Within each operational department there will be a number of specific job activities. The detailed requirements of any particular task may need to be defined in order to ensure consistent working methods and achievement of required quality standards. These individual work instructions need to be developed as the next level of documentation. The work instructions will typically be called up from procedures, and they must be in line with the requirements of the departmental procedures.

Finally, the day-to-day documentation produced as a result of using the management system needs to be considered. This comprises the forms, control charts and records that are completed as work is performed, and provide the evidence of process and product control. These forms and charts must be called up from the procedures, individual work instructions and inspection and test methods documentation; they must be designed to record all of the information required. The information itself will either be defined within the procedure or work instruction, or the form may be used to specify the required data. The implications of these two approaches will be discussed later.

4.1.2 Functions and Areas To Be Controlled

The management objectives for the creation of the quality system will initially determine its scope of application as discussed in Chapter 9 on implementation. Once that decision has been made, it is then necessary to determine which areas of activity require documentation and the extent to which procedural development is necessary. The relevancy matrix, as described in Chapter 9, is a useful tool to drive this process.

Significant Activities

Significant activities should be defined as:

"Those activities of such significance to the achievement of customer satisfaction that they require a systematic approach together with documented and interfacing procedures."

Activities considered significant will impact upon the conformity of a product or service from initial customer enquiry to postdelivery maintenance, and the efficiency with which the product or service is produced or performed.

4.1.3 Documentation Structure

In order to define the quality system, a range of documentation that describes how the system works must exist. Figure 11-2 illustrated the classic management system model.

Level 1

The quality manual has already been discussed in some detail. It must lead the user to the supporting elements of the system.

Level 2

The operating documents are the written definitions of the process flow that defines how the commitment and policy is translated into day-to-day actions. They define the information flows and departmental interfaces, and usually identify the records.

Level 3

The third tier provides the detail of specific operations. These may be work instructions for individual tasks or machines, test or inspection activities, and often also the actual documents — hard copy or virtual — that are filled in to provide the supporting evidence of system and product conformity.

Level 4

The fourth tier is the foundation of the system. It contains the records produced by the use of the documents that form tiers two and three, along with any records that demonstrate the operation of the management system in any areas where processes are undocumented. This tier exists to provide the proof that the system is being effectively implemented.

It must always be remembered, as previously discussed, that records are not "documents" within the scope of the document control requirements of ISO 9001. Records have their own requirements, which are defined in Clause 4.2.4 of the standard.

4.1.4 Outside Assistance

During the process of developing ISO 9000 quality systems, many organizations turn to outside agencies such as consultants for assistance. Beware of any organization offering a "universal quality manual" or ready-made quality systems and procedures. An "off-the-shelf" quality system will rarely fit a particular company's requirements and is unlikely to be of any lasting benefit.

Management systems are an example of where the "one-size-fits-all" approach actually means "one size fits none." Company personnel must be closely involved in the development of all parts of the management system, otherwise they are unlikely to truly reflect the activities concerned. Even if a consultant or technical writer is used to document the information, it must be done in very close cooperation with, and under the control of, company staff and management.

The most beneficial role for a consultant is as an independent assessor during the initial review stages and thereafter as a mentor and advisor. The organization's own policy group should organize and drive the program and involve as many people as possible in producing and implementing the required procedures as discussed in Chapter 9. When staff produce the system they own it. It is their quality system and because of that ownership it will be easier to get commitment to its implementation. A consultant can help to guide this process and help keep the company focused and on track, but at no time should the consultant take ownership of the process. When this happens the system will be doomed for failure as soon as he or she leaves.

The policy group will benefit from having a consultant to turn to for support and guidance and, often, reassurance. Good consultants can also provide practical help with training at all levels in the company and can often help in moving roadblocks out of the way. It is not unusual for some leverage to have to be applied to one or more members of management who are less convinced than the rest of the value of the process, and an outside consultant can often bring pressure to bear more effectively than the implementation team.

Having an independent assessor for the final review phase of the system also ensures a level of objectivity that can be difficult for those who have spent a great deal of their time creating it. Organizations must be encouraged to do as much of the work themselves as is practical; this will result in their reaping the greatest long-term benefits.

5 Documents – Procedures, Work Instructions and the Rest

The documentation required for an effective management system has commonly been referred to as procedures and work instructions. The format in which these are presented has always been a matter of choice for the organization, although typically the default has been to use written documents.

ISO 9001:2000 has moved away from the term "procedure," and to emphasize that the process documentation can take any format, the term "document" will be used hereafter. It is intended to be read to mean any method of providing instruction to a member of the organization in how to perform a task, defining responsibilities and authorities for the task and identifying the records performance of the task creates.

ISO 9001 is very clear as to where the responsibility lies for ensuring that the organization establishes, implements and maintains a system that addresses all relevant aspects of the chosen standard. Clause 5.5.2 lays the burden firmly at the door of the management representative. This individual or group is appointed by the top management of the organization. Clause 5.6 requires that management conduct regular reviews of the system to ensure that it is effectively implemented and is maintaining their policy. It follows that this same management group must take responsibility for overseeing the development of the overall quality system, and for identifying those activities that require formal process documentation.

Documentation is a significant element of the quality management system and plays one of the most important roles in pulling the system together. It creates the bridge across that "white space" referred to earlier in the chapter; it is particularly important that such documents accurately reflect the operations they describe and precisely who is responsible for what. The documentation exists to define how the organization functions in each area and how each area interfaces with other areas. It fulfills a key role in making the management system visible — visible to management, visible to employees and visible to customers.

The documentation must be an accurate reflection of the activities described, meaning that either it be developed by the individuals who perform those activities or, if alternate authors are used, then process validation should be carried out by the user. Only then can there be any certainty that the process is accurately described. Part of the role of management in making the system happen is to nominate authors to develop and write the documents and to ensure that the nominated authors are given time to do the job.

Documents must be user-friendly and effective. They must be vital and useful tools. They must be living documents that are well-known to all who may need them, and referred to whenever necessary. In consequence, the documents will rarely stand still for great lengths of time.

Documents need to be audited regularly and updated as necessary to reflect current practices or process improvements that have been developed. They must become a benchmark for the activities described that can be constantly improved. The standard also provides the primary tool for ensuring that this review and update process happens. It is called the internal quality system audit. During the audit process documents may be used to generate checklists against which the audit can be performed, and this can lead to an enhancement of the function being audited or initiate a change because activity has moved beyond the documentation. This is one of the ways in which the audit process provides significant opportunities for improvement to the management system.

5.1 Advantages of Good Documentation

Documents:

- Provide a process reference point for all members of an organization
- Reduce the amount of verbal and on-the-job training required
- Clearly define responsibilities and authorities for activities
- Provide a method for tracing the cause of errors in process, product or system
- Prevent subsequent errors by communicating changes in activities to all concerned
- Provide an historic record of documents at a given time
- Trigger the creation of records of key activities.

5.2 Planning and Development

Careful planning is an essential prerequisite in developing and writing logical, well-structured and coherent documents. Time spent on the preparation of documents is never wasted if the documents are intended to play a significant role in the effective and efficient working of an organization — and if they are not intended to play such a role, then abandon ISO implementation! The planning of document writing must ensure that the necessary events occur in a sequential and systematic manner. These events include:

- Determining the structure of the document
- Identifying the need — not everything needs a document
- Determining by whom it is to be written
- Determining how it is to be written
- Deciding how it is to be developed
- Deciding how it is to be identified
- Deciding how it is to be introduced and who will receive it
- Deciding how it is to be controlled.

5.3 Document Format and Structure

Documents can take any form a company chooses, and there is no requirement for all system documentation to look the same. Experience has shown that the introduction of a management system is much easier, and the documentation will be more effective, if it is uniform in structure and consistent in presentation. For this reason, an essential first step when starting to implement a management system is to define the structure and format to be used. This structure and format is often defined in a company standard entitled a "Procedure for Documents."

The company standard for procedural documentation will typically define such things as standard headings, typefaces, title indents, line justification, contents sheets, page layouts, etc. and the method of communicating information about the activity being described, e.g., text, flowchart or a combination of flowchart and bullet statements. If the document is to have any value, it should as a minimum define the following:

- Sections that each document needs to have
- What is to be included in each section
- The requirement for the document to follow the company naming and/or numbering convention (which may also be included or may be described in a separate document)
- The page numbering convention
- The choice of method: text, flowchart, graphic or a combination of the these.

A seven-section format has proven to be most effective and is equally applicable to any documentation format. The sections are:

1. Purpose/objective
2. Scope
3. Responsibilities
4. Related documentation
5. Definitions
6. Process description
7. Records and retention times.

The following text describes each of the sections using a procedure for document control as an example.

1. Purpose / Objective

The purpose is a statement that outlines the objective or intent of the document. It tells the reader what will be accomplished by following the instructions. The purpose statement for document control could be written as follows:

This document describes the approval, issue and maintenance of controlled documents.

2. Scope

The scope statement will outline the area, department, group or personnel to which the document applies. For this document control process the scope could be phrased as:

This document applies to all management system and product/service-related documents and work instructions.

3. Responsibilities

This section will briefly define, by function, all personnel who are involved in implementing or using the document. Personnel who have authority over the document and/or process may also be addressed in this section or in the process description section that describes the activity. This section may look like the following:

All Victoria Group employees are responsible for conformance with this document where it applies to their work.

The director of operations is responsible for the implementation and maintenance of this document as well as assigning document numbers.

4. Related Documentation

Any documentation that has an effect on the document or is referenced within the document is listed under this section. This documentation could include any upstream or downstream documents, related work instructions, forms, prints, data or customer specifications that may need to be available for the document to be used effectively. It should also include any statutory or regulatory documents from external sources that need to be referenced when performing the activity unless the necessary information is incorporated into the document itself.

A copy of referenced documentation or an example of any forms may be attached as an appendix to the document itself if the organization so chooses. This may aid in facilitating control of these documents. This section may look like the following:

Document and Work Instruction Log (P&WI)

History of Changes to Documents and Work Instructions (History)

5. Definitions

Words, abbreviations or actions that may be ambiguous, unique to the process or that may not be readily understood by the reader should be clearly defined, e.g.:

QMS Intranet: The location on the company Intranet where all QMS documents are maintained for global access.

6. Process Description

A document details the actions of those personnel involved in an activity. It should also state who does what, where, when and possibly why the activity is carried out. This can be either in the form of a flowchart and/or bulleted statements. The level of detail is determined by the author using the principles discussed earlier. In other words, document the process until it works and then stop.

7. Records and Retention

This section tells the user what records are to be generated as a result of the document and for how long they need to be retained. The organization may also choose to state the physical location where the records will be stored and who is responsible for the maintenance of the files. This information should be general.

5.4 Identify the Need

Once the structure and format for documents is decided and documented the next step for the organization is to determine what needs to be formalized. There are many reasons why processes should be documented and the organization should ask the following questions as a means of determining which processes they need to document:

• Does the standard require a documented process?

- Does law or regulation require a documented process?
- Do any contracts require specific documented processes?
- Does the quality management system itself identify activities where documents are required?
- Do managers wish to formalize activities for which they are responsible?
- Does the person responsible for implementing an activity believe that a clearer definition is required?

Once the need has been identified, a process owner needs to be found.

5.4.1 The Process Owner

When determining who should be the process owner, it is important to try and choose someone who is involved in the activity being described or is very familiar with the process and who also has appropriate technical knowledge. The selection should ideally be by job position rather than by individual as people tend to change jobs.

This position then becomes the process owner for the document.

As process owner the individual is responsible for the implementation and maintenance of the document as well as becoming the authority for any changes that may be required in the future. It is always important to ensure that process owners have a good overall perspective not only of the specific process in question, but also of the other activities with which that process must interface.

Once the process owner is identified, the time line for the creation and implementation of the document needs to be established. This time line will be based on three factors;

- The master implementation program discussed in Chapter 9
- The purpose of the document
- The scope of the document.

5.4.2 Time Line, Purpose and Scope

Establishing a time line for preparation and implementation of the document is an important step in order to fulfill the requirements of the established implementation plan and should always be determined with due consideration being given to the level of activity involved and the complexity of the task to be documented.

Time line considerations should include:

- Defining the purpose
- Defining the scope

- Collecting information relating to the activity
- Preparing a draft document
- Circulating the draft for comment
- Agreement from those concerned
- Authorization for issuing the document
- Incorporation into the control system.

Purpose

The implementation team must define the specific objectives of the activity covered by the document. The purpose should tell the reader why the document has been written and what the document is attempting to control.

Scope

The author must then establish and document the precise scope of activities covered by the document. The scope statement should tell the user exactly which activities are included within the process that the document controls. To do this, he or she must consider:

- Interfaces with other documents or intended documents through the matrix diagram and the implementation plan
- Whether the significant activity being addressed can all be contained in one document
- What procedural information already exists for the activity.

These are the factors that can have the most influence on the time line for completing a process document. If the input to the process is dependent upon the output from several other processes, it may be more efficient to wait to generate this document until the others are completed. Conversely, if this is documenting an early part of product realization it makes no sense to leave it until the rest are done.

The complexity of the task will largely determine whether a single process descriptor is adequate. If the document becomes large and unwieldy it is far better to break the process down into multiple sections. Large documents don't get used. Anything much longer than a couple of pages will have a tendency not to be read unless it is a complex sequential operation where a substantial amount of information is contained in the process documentation.

An example of the latter would be a complex test setup for a piece of equipment where many settings and parametric measurements need to be taken in a strictly sequential manner.

Note: Purpose and scope can be successfully combined into a single statement.

5.4.3 Document Development

Developing the document involves several steps, ranging from identifying what currently happens to providing training on the new document once it is released:

- Establishing current practice
- Documenting current practice
- Reviewing current practice
- Preparing the document
- Approving and issuing the document
- Training people on the content of the document.

Establishing Current Practice

The first step is to review existing practices, whether or not they are documented, and determine how an activity is currently being controlled. If a gap analysis was performed much of this information should already be available.

It is essential to establish what process information already exists for the process, both within the organization and if applicable outside the organization to determine if current activities comply.

Part of verifying the current activity is to establish and record the routine methods of performing the activity. This should include identifying responsibilities, determining existing standards, if any, and how effectively they are being achieved, and ensuring that those aspects of the process that significantly impact on the quality of the output are known. An understanding of how efficiently the desired output is achieved is also important.

Document Current Practice

The existing methods of performing an activity should then be documented in the form of a flowchart. This will allow for ease of revision before the document is prepared.

In order to flowchart activities and develop an effective document, it is important to understand:

- How each step is initiated
- How each activity is carried out
- How one step leads into another.

Information and instructions given in the document about how each activity is conducted must be easy to find and follow.

Review Current Practice

The flowcharts depicting current practice should now be reviewed. This review should involve personnel who are responsible for or involved with the process. The process should be evaluated to determine a number of factors.

- Are the specified objectives being achieved?

Every process should have a defined output requirement. If the existing activities are achieving the desired outputs then leave change for later.

- Are the quality levels adequate?

The specified objectives for the process may be met, but are they themselves adequate to meet the larger requirement of satisfying the process customer? If not, then something will need to be done about it.

- Are there any gaps, duplications or areas of weakness?

Make sure that the current process is complete and that all activities are being performed as planned. Look for any activities that are duplicated from elsewhere in the system, determine where those activities belong and delete the duplicated work.

- Are departmental interfaces adequately addressed?

Make sure that all the inputs and outputs are adequately and completely included, that the inputs from other processes are adequate for the activity under review and that the outputs meet the needs of the internal customer.

- Is there potential for improvement?

All the requirements may be met, but opportunities for improvement might not have been identified. Such opportunities can be noted and put into the system for future action once the system is complete.

- Does it meet the "shall" requirements of ISO 9001?

Despite the fact that there are many fewer mandatory documentation requirements in ISO 9001:2000, each documented process should be examined to ensure that any and all the relevant requirements of the standard are being met, including those for the maintenance of records.

Prepare Document

The first consideration for the author is what the documentation of this process is trying to achieve. Consistency can be assumed. If consistency doesn't matter, then why bother? The consideration is of the level of control required: Is this a process that must be detailed in every minute detail, or is it sufficient to highlight the major activities? Only those instructions that are essential to level of control required should be included.

The "Purpose" and "Scope" statements need to be constantly reviewed to ensure that the process description being created stays within the boundaries of those statements. The instructions contained within the document must support these statements, and must be carefully matched to the flowchart that was prepared for the activity.

Process documents can take any form. The initial flowchart or process map may be adequate as it stands. There may be sufficient information to provide perfectly adequate control if the responsibilities and authorities are also indicated.

Another form of process "document" can be in the form of a videotape or an audio tape, a CD or a soft file of illustrations or a physical model. The same considerations need to be applied to the use of every one of these methods of "documenting" process information. Does it provide sufficient information to ensure adequate control, and does it provide information on the responsibilities and authorities for the process? Typically, photographic or physical process models will require some written supportive information.

When and where appropriate, references to documents that address related activities should be included. If the information contained in one document is too lengthy, more than one document could be written. It is perfectly acceptable, in fact often preferable, for "if-then-else" process routines to refer out to stand alone processes rather than to try and include all the "what if" options in a single document.

The degree of detail required to describe various activities or instructions in the document must always be kept to the minimum that will ensure adequate control of the activity. The decision is based on the complexity of the task, the skill level and training of the personnel performing the task and the criticality of the outcome, as previously mentioned and demonstrated in Chapter 9.

Those affected by the implementation of the document should be involved as much as possible during the drafting stage. This will create ownership and will assist in the introduction of the document; however, it not advisable to have any document written by a committee.

The process owner together with related personnel and departments should then review the draft document to see if it is workable. One way in which this can be done is to issue the process as a "draft" document and let the users loose on it, with a request that any and all problems, however minor, be reported back to the author. Consideration must be given to all comments received regarding the use of the document and implementation of the process; this is especially important if the process has been modified from current practice. Any suggestions regarding modifications or additions should be incorporated, recorded, documented in the standard format and then checked for errors. Once this is completed the final test of the document is its ability to be audited.

One of the core requirements of the ISO 9001 standards has always been that the system should be audited on a regular basis. For any document to be auditable, it should be possible to take any statement of requirement from the document and convert it into a question. An example of this would be as follows:

"The operations director is responsible for maintaining the master record of system documents on the company network."

While auditing the operations director, the associated question would be, "What are your responsibilities for the master record within this process?"

When the document is implemented, the answer to the question would be, "I am responsible for ensuring that the master record index is maintained on the company network." This ability to provide a related answer demonstrates that the requirement can be audited. It is supported by demonstrating the content.

The ultimate test of any document is its ability to provide the consistency and control necessary to achieve the desired result.

Approval and Issue

Once the process document has been through the proving phase and has been agreed upon, the next step is to formally approve and issue the document. Approval and issue should be by the responsible person as indicated in the document control procedure.

Formal issue and distribution to relevant locations can then proceed in accordance with your predetermined method. Staff who will be responsible for operating the process should be given awareness training on the content of the document if they have not already been involved in the review activity.

Training

All personnel who have responsibility within the document must be made aware of the expectations and trained in its use. Each and every individual must understand:

- Their responsibilities within the process
- How these are documented within the process
- To whom they refer when a problem arises
- What records are generated as a result of the document
- What is done with these records once they are completed
- How the operation of this process supports the relevant quality objectives within the management system.

5.4.3.1 The Work Instruction

A work instruction is just another form of document, typically with more specific detail. There is no clear line between work instructions and procedures other than that a work instruction typically has a more narrow scope of application. A work instruction contains the detail of how an operation is performed and it can take the same format as those just described in the document section.

Work instructions are not a requirement of the standard and their use is strictly a company decision. The same factors used in determining the degree of detail contained within a document may be used in determining the content of the work instruction. Pictorial or physical process documentation is often more effective at this level than the written word. It is easier for an individual to glance at a picture, a chart or an engineering drawing from time to time than it is to read text.

When creating work instructions don't forget to include the related document under references. Also, when numbering the work instruction the company may choose to add a different prefix in order to identify it as a work instruction.

5.5 Records

Records are proof that an activity or process is carried out as described by the document, work instruction or quality plan. There are 26 types of records specifically referenced in the standard. These include forms, orders, meeting minutes, design plans etc. Clause 4.2.4 of the standard details the requirements for record maintenance.

The procedure for the control of records can be documented in several ways. One approach is to create a single document control procedure addressing all the requirements of the standard and direct the reader to an attachment identifying every record maintained by the organization. The attachment will then define the type of record, the retention method, the responsibility for collecting the record, the retention time, storage method and disposal. The procedure can be used to describe retrieval, collation and general filing techniques.

The disadvantage of this approach is that all too often things get missed, or retention times are inappropriate, and the record retention activities of organizations do change as processes and requirements change. Major corporations often adopt a modified version of this approach, having a corporate record retention policy and handbook that details specific records that the corporation requires to be maintained and their retention times. Typically, such instructions are issued and controlled by the office of general counsel and the instructions are based on the corporation's requirements for legal defense. Other operational records are left to the discretion of local management.

An alternative approach is to have a general records procedure that outlines the overall collation, storage, retrieval and disposal processes, but directs the reader to individual process documentation to identify specific records, who is responsible for them and how long they are retained. Alternatively, this information could be in the quality manual.

There are a number of variants on these themes; for example, a general default retention time and a standard commercial disposal process can be declared in the procedure, and varied as required by individual process documents. Record retention concepts and the constraints and considerations that go into the determination of record-keeping activities are discussed in some detail in Chapter 9. As a general rule, the disseminated approach is preferable.

5.6 Quality Plans

Quality plans should not be confused with quality planning or, more accurately, planning for quality. ISO 9000:2000 defines quality planning as being "part of quality management focussed on setting quality objectives and specifying necessary operational processes and related resources to fulfil the quality objectives." More simply, quality planning encompasses all the activities that are undertaken by an organization in determining how requirements will be converted into deliverables. This is essentially the operation of the management system. ISO 9001:2000 requires that an organization perform a considerable amount of planning for quality – it is variously described as "Quality management system planning" (5.4.2), "Planning of product realization" (7.1) and "Design and development planning" (7.3.1). Out of all the activities that take place within an operating management system, a quality plan will frequently emerge for the fulfillment of a particular contract, process or product.

ISO 9000:2000 describes a quality plan as:

"[a] document specifying which procedures and associated resources shall be applied by whom and when to a specific project, product, process or contract."

A quality plan is frequently assumed to be a substantial document, but in fact most quality plans are very small documents — a routing card used to take a batch of product through a production process is a quality plan. A printer's "job bag" is a quality plan; a warehouse operator's "pick list" is a quality plan. In each case the document defines in the appropriate level of detail the activities required to fulfil the specific requirements for an individual customer requirement. In all three cases quoted, the document calls on the user to operate certain established quality management system processes. The plan defines the sequence of events, the product required, the quantity required and often the date upon which it is required.

Quality plans can also be very complex. If an organization operates largely on a project basis, fulfilling contracts on a substantially individual basis, then the main management system may contain little detail or information beyond specifying the requirements for each quality plan. Organizations that operate on this basis will obviously produce substantial and complex plans, as each contract is effectively requiring the development of a nearly unique management system.

Project documents may well include:

- Existing documents appropriate to the contract
- Existing documents amended for the contract
- New documents to meet specific requirements for the contract.

Some contracts may call for a combination of all three.

6 Document Administration and Control

The standard imposes a set of requirements for document control, which are contained in Clause 4.2.3, Control of documents. The control must include the following seven core requirements:

a) The approval of documents for adequacy prior to issue

b) The review, updating as necessary and reapproval of changed documents

c) The identification of the current revision status of documents

d) Assurance that relevant versions of applicable documents are available at points of use

e) Methods of ensuring that documents remain legible, readily identifiable and retrievable

f) Methods of ensuring that documents of external origin are identified and their distribution controlled

g) Methods of preventing the unintended use of obsolete documents, and of applying suitable identification to any which are retained.

All of these requirements need to be implemented and maintained through the use of a formal documented procedure that keeps the whole process as simple as possible. Entire books have been written on document control methodologies, and there are many automated processes available to run on network systems, intranets and even the Internet itself for those who have money to spend.

The key is to devolve control to appropriate technical levels throughout the organization, to decentralize as far as possible, to leverage off other processes to ensure control is maintained and to maintain constant vigilance through training and the internal audit process.

The first split to make is between internally generated management system documents and those of "external origin" that need to be controlled because of their impact on product, process or system.

6.1 Documents of External Origin

External documents should be maintained on a library basis, either centrally or by functional departments who need each type of external document. The library system should provide for the formal identification of each copy of a listed document and the revision status of that document as provided by the source. A simple method of tracking who has which document is required — a sign-out sheet is fine — and for each document or group of documents there needs to be a process in place for making "best endeavors" to ensure that the latest copy is available.

The type of document that falls into this category includes national and international specifications, customer drawings, regulatory or statutory documents, codes and regulations, industry standards and product specifications.

Maintaining currency with these documents can be a problem, and individual organizations will have to figure out ways of doing this. There are specialist services that will provide an update service for regulatory issues and published national and international specifications, but these can be expensive. The Internet provides a good tracking tool for documents, and a regular check could be instituted in that manner. For most organizations this is less of an issue than it appears in that these documents usually change fairly slowly and infrequently. However, where environmental regulations are concerned this may not be the case, and customer specifications can be very volatile. In the latter case, the most important factor is to stay in close touch with the customer.

6.2 Management System Documents

The core issue is control of internally generated documents.

There are several key issues that need careful consideration before issuing and implementing a document. These are:

- Who is responsible for the document?
- What is the document identification system?
- How is distribution to be controlled, if at all?
- How is the amendment and revision of documents to be handled?

6.2.1 Responsibilities

There are three primary areas of responsibility that apply to all documents.

1. Responsibility for the review and authorization of each document.

2. The preparation and writing of each document.

3. The administration and control of each document.

Review and Authorization

Once written, documents need to be reviewed to ensure that:

- Any conflicts within or between existing documents are identified and resolved
- The document reflects current practice and provides adequate direction
- Interfaces at both departmental and interdepartmental levels are defined and agreed by means of detailed reviews at both these levels.

Once reviewed, the document must be approved by a nominated or authorized signatory.

Cross-functional documents are usually controlled at the level of the management representative and have senior executive review and approval.

Documents that only apply to an individual functional department can be approved at that level or even delegated down from there.

Approval of work instructions may even be deployed to production supervisory levels.

The decision on the level of authority to review and approve a document will depend upon the nature of the business and the complexity of the activity. Approval must be at a level where the signatory authority not only has the necessary technical skills but also has visibility and understanding of the interfaces between the process under review and the rest of the management system.

Preparation and Writing

As previously stated, this should be undertaken, using the standard typographical layout and format, by personnel familiar with the activities and functions to be controlled or by other nominated staff.

Administration and Control

Management should determine the method for document administration and control and those who will be responsible for the maintenance of the process. This should include:

- Specifying the format in which documents shall be written
- Specifying the identification system for documents
- Specifying how documents are to be reviewed and approved and the steps to be followed in case of review and approval of document changes
- Specifying document storage, distribution and retrieval.

Document Numbering System

An identification system for documents should be developed that allows adequate room for the inclusion of new documents. A numbering system is not mandatory; in a small organization the name of the document may be all that is required. The selected system may be included in the document control procedure or the procedure for writing a document. Typical document identification systems make use of some form of alpha or alpha-numeric numbering system as these provide most easily for expansion and change.

A simple system is best, and if one can be devised that provides an indication of the nature of the document from the identifier alone, so much the better. A typical approach could be along the following lines:

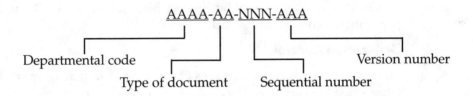

AAAA-AA-NNN-AAA

Departmental code

Type of document

Sequential number

Version number

Departmental codes

    SALE = sales

    MATL = materials management

    DESN = design and development

    PROD = operations control

    QUAL = quality department

    Etc.

Type of document

    WI = work instruction

    DP = departmental procedure

    CP = cross-functional procedure

    QP = quality plan

    Etc.

Sequential and version numbers

    Numbers typically run from 001 upwards.

    Thus a document numbered MATL-WI-003-001 would be a work instruction number 3, version 1 belonging to materials management.

Note: It is best not to link document numbers to ISO 9001:2000 clause numbers — if the standard changes, the number system becomes meaningless. Make it abstract from the beginning.

Cross-functional Documents

There is considerable merit in providing linkages that bring the register of documentation together for large organizations to ensure that naming and coding conventions do not duplicate across the organization. It must also be possible for system users, i.e., the organization's staff, to be able to verify the current issue status of a document if there is a need to verify the status of something prior to use. Even with deployed control there are advantages to having a central master record index system, particularly where project work is involved.

In smaller companies a simple log under the control of a responsible person and in a readily accessible position, from which numbers are allocated and their application recorded, will suffice.

Distribution Control

The one way in which the concepts of a documented management system militate against the generally accepted — albeit maybe never validated — credo of the TQM movement is that in a formal structured management system document distribution is on a need-to-know basis only. This is not to say that every document in a management system should not be open to access by any member of the organization, but the formal notification process limits document "distribution" to those who need specific information.

Whenever possible organizations should use electronic documents and stay well clear of distributed paper copies. The problem with paper is controlling it. It is easy to copy, lose, mark-up and change. It requires that the holders of copies maintain files and be rigorous about updating them with reissued documents and destroying the old ones. It takes time out of schedules that in most organizations are already overloaded. So if the organization has a networked computer system, put the management system documents on it. Make sure everyone knows where the documents are and how to access and read them. The ability to access the documents to make changes is usually restricted to limit the possibility of people making changes by mistake.

When it isn't possible to do this and paper copies must be used, the method and pattern of distribution needs to be carefully thought out to minimize the level of effort required to operate the distribution system.

The intent is to ensure that the correct issue is in the right place when needed. This means that each document, or preferably groups of documents, need distribution lists by job title. Using this approach minimizes the number of copies of documents that are sent out.

Consider having central document controllers in each functional department, and having them as the "official" distribution point, with the authority to determine who needs what. This approach fits in well with the concept of distributed authority for the entire document control process. These document controllers can also conduct regular audits of their own areas to ensure that old documents have been removed from use, that documents haven't been inappropriately marked-up and that they are legible.

The general status of documents and other forms of process descriptors is something that the internal audit process should also examine at every audit. Putting a management system in place is a good thing to do; allowing the documentation to be out of control will make the endpoint worse than the start.

Preventing the unauthorized copying of documents is very difficult and becomes as much a matter of culture and discipline as one of control. When the system is on line, each document can carry a note that states "printed copies are uncontrolled," but when the system is paper based there is no way of completely eliminating unauthorized copying other than through training and vigilance. The vast majority of people go to work to do a good job and to follow the rules. Educating the organization on the importance of accurate data and the correct way to obtain a "legal" copy of a document is the best way to ensure that copies do not get made.

The perfect document control system has yet to be created. There is no system able to completely prevent unauthorized copying. Treat this issue as something to monitor, but don't be paranoid.

Document Amendment and Revision

Good systems change constantly. Process "documents" frequently require amendment or revision. It is vitally important to the effectiveness of the management system that the process whereby change is proposed and introduced be simple and readily accessible to all personnel. The best way to avoid people marking up a document to make it reflect process change — or to correct error — is to make the change process quick and easy.

The change process should ensure that a number of steps are followed.

1. There is a formal change initiation process such as a change note.

Any process document change should be initiated through a process that identifies the precise nature of the change being requested, or the precise reason for a change. This allows the author/reviewer to understand why the change is being requested, and if approved, what has been changed.

Change requests should indicate:

- The required change
- The reason for the change
- What will be affected
- Who is making the request.

Authorization for the change is necessary and the note must be signed by either the author of the document or the manager responsible.

2. That document revision numbers are changed when changes are approved.

There are several ways to indicate revisions to documents. Revisions may be alpha, numeric or a combination of the two. One method is to indicate major revisions that change the process by changing the revision. Minor revisions for grammar or spelling may be identified by changing the letter. (Process is often referred to as "form, fit or function.")

An example of this would be a document that is at issue 1, that has had a major change to the process and could be reissued at issue 2. After reissue the author may decide that it could be more clearly written and makes changes to the document without changing the process. This document could then be reissued as issue 2a.

Another method could be to change the issue number only when major changes occur. Any minor changes that do not affect the operation of the process could be made and the document reissued at the current issue number.

Whichever system is chosen for identifying the revision status of documents, it should be used consistently throughout the organization.

3. That the master record is maintained and updated with every change.

The purpose of the master record is to enable system users to verify and validate the version numbers of documents. It is vital that the master record always be accurate. No document should ever be distributed before the master record is updated.

4. That the personnel responsible for reviewing and approving changes have access to appropriate information, preferably the same information available to the original reviewer.

5. That the document contains some indicator as to what has been changed, either in the document itself or in a suitable and accessible attachment.

Including an indicator to areas of a document that have been revised within the text of the document can be helpful to users. Such a process immediately draws attention to the changes rather than leaving the user to guess or remember what is different. Some commonly used methods include:

- Underlining
- Use of different font
- Vertical line in margin
- Change notification form as a separate document
- Using color in an online system to highlight changes.

Common practice includes a summary record of the revisions made at the start or the end of each document. A record of document revisions may be displayed by means of a revision box on the cover page of the document, by means of an amendment or revision record sheet, or any other process that works for the organization.

6. That the amended document is distributed promptly.

Summary

In summary, to prepare and implement a document, it is necessary to:

- Identify the need for a document
- Confirm the need with those involved
- Nominate and train the author
- Define the significant aspects of the activity
- Prepare the flow diagram
- Write the document in clear and concise terms using the structure and format as defined
- Circulate the document to all involved for comment and review and incorporate comments where necessary
- Obtain approval for the document
- Issue the document
- Review periodically
- Update as necessary.

The single most important point to remember about management system documentation is that every item must add value — to the organization, to the customer, to the stakeholders. Management systems either add value or cost. The latter is unacceptable.

Beyond Compliance — Managing Records for Increased Protection

by Jerry L. Whitson and Eugenia K. Brumm

Properly managing records is not just a smart way to conduct business. Appropriately structured, implemented and maintained records may keep a company out of costly legal proceedings.

To illustrate this point, take the case of: Telectron, Inc. v. Overhead Door Corp.[1] Telectron brought suit against Overhead Door Corp. (OHD) for violation of antitrust laws. On the same day that Telectron's complaint and request for production of records were served on OHD, its chief legal counsel (who was also the secretary of the company), Mr. Arnold, ordered the destruction of massive amounts of relevant records.

The court determined that "... Mr. Arnold ordered this destruction as a willful and intentional attempt to place documentation which he anticipated to be damaging to OHD's interests in this litigation forever beyond the reach of Telectron's counsel."[2] The destruction, also, was conducted in the absence of an established company records retention policy. The court entered a default judgment of liability on behalf of the plaintiff, and the absence of a records retention policy was the reason cited by the court as evidence of bad faith on the part of OHD.

Throughout the case, OHD claimed that it had destroyed records under a company records retention and destruction program. During the testimony, however, a senior vice president of manufacturing stated that he was not aware of any records retention policy in the company. The court concluded that OHD's top management failed to provide any leadership or effective oversight regarding document retention.

OHD's president, who argued ignorance about the company's document retention policy, stated that he believed such a policy had been established in 1966 or 1967. Yet, he knew none of the policy's provisions and he did not know if anybody was formally charged with implementing the policy. In other words, OHD claimed that it operated a records retention program, but could not provide any written policies or procedures to that effect.

The *Wall Street Journal* estimated that the damage phase of the Telectron case could lead to a judgment against OHD as high as $69 million.[3] Telectron did prevail in this case. Although the final judgment is sealed, a valuable lesson is illustrated in this case.

ISO 9000 Records Requirements and Legal Issues

ISO 9000:2000 includes both of the following record requirements:

1. Specific types of quality records must be created and maintained to support the quality operations in an organization.

2. Certain records management activities must be applied to those quality record types.

The requirement for specific quality records is interwoven throughout the standard and appears in statements such as, "Records of contract reviews shall be maintained;" "The organization shall review the requirements … Records of results of the review … shall be maintained."[4] Other sections contain requirements for specific record types. Frequently, however, the requirements for specific types of quality records are implied in statements indicating that the organization must provide proof, without any mention being made of a record.

The second type of record requirement — for conducting records management activities — is clear and evident. Clause 4.2.4, Control of quality records, includes requirements that fall under the following records management activities:

- Retention schedule development and management
- Disposition of records
- Records protection program
- Filing management
- Development of access schemes
- Design of indexing schemes
- Forms management
- Records creation management
- Selection and management of equipment, media (micrographics, optical disk, software, hardware) and supplies.

Not only are records management components required in ISO 9000, they are the same components that have resulted in default judgments and court-imposed sanctions against organizations because they do not exist, are inconsistently practiced or are poorly conducted.

In Telectron and other cases involving documentation, the defendant organizations claimed that they had operated according to a company records retention and disposition policy. In these cases, however, the organizations could not provide any written policies or procedures to that effect and could not demonstrate that:

1. Such a policy was consistently implemented

2. Employees in the organization were aware of such a policy

3. Any records were kept identifying which company records were destroyed

4. Records were officially authorized to be destroyed according to an established and implemented company retention policy.

Judges do not appear sympathetic to defendants who claim an inability to locate specific records.

Importance of Design Process

The importance of the design control process itself is evident in the ISO 9001 standard. Design records serve two basic purposes: (1) They provide evidence about the activities that have occurred, and (2) they collect data for the organization to use in pre- and postproduction analysis. In the fullest sense, design records provide an accumulation of experiences pertaining to the product at hand, and they can serve as a resource for current and future designs.

Quality records related to design, testing, quality control, manufacturing, distribution, customer complaints and other aspects of the development and manufacturing process are those that an organization should be able to produce if cited as a defendant in a product liability case (see Chapter 23 for more information). It is important to identify records that could be used to show how a product's design was developed and approved. Records that could pertain to product liability cases should depict a history of the product so that its design can be explained and the manufacturer can demonstrate that safety and quality were considered at each phase of the design, manufacturing and marketing process.

When a product is released for sale, a product history file should be created and retained for as long as necessary. In such a file, it is important to link information logically, if not physically, since many current products evolve from prior designs and the current design often cannot be explained without references to records about the earlier design. Such records include, but are not limited to the following:

- Design specifications
- Engineering evaluations
- Design reviews
- Prototype testing

- Design assurance testing
- Final design selection
- Quality control procedures
- Inspection procedures
- Product service history
- Performance history.

Development of a Records Retention Schedule

Records retention times should not be assigned carelessly, but should be based on some legal, fiscal, operating and/or historical need. Such basis for determining retention times substantiates the retention schedule and makes it legally acceptable as an operating policy. If records retention times are not grounded in research and/or business need, they can be subject to dismissal in a court of law.[5]

For example, the intended design life of a product is typically a factor affecting record retention time. Consider the different needs of retaining records for automobiles or major appliances versus canned foods or fresh vegetables.

To dispose of records according to the availability of storage space is not a valid approach. Ignorance of retention regulations is no excuse. Part of good business and operating practice is to know what laws apply to certain record categories, and to develop retention schedules based on those laws, as well as internal operating needs.

For these reasons, it is important to develop retention schedules methodically and systematically, by conducting research into the requirements and by interviewing those who use and need the records. Developing a records retention schedule is a difficult, resource-consuming process, especially for those organizations that have been operating for several decades and have never addressed records. Depending on the size, age and complexity of the organization, the preparation of a retention schedule can take from six months to several years.

The following steps, listed in order, should be performed in order to develop a sound records retention schedule:

- Conduct a records inventory.
- Interview key personnel.
- Research records retention periods.
- Appraise the records.

- Prepare a draft schedule.
- Discuss the schedule with affected departmental managers and with legal counsel.
- Obtain the necessary sign-off signatures.
- Duplicate and distribute the records retention schedule.

Organizations should not be establishing retention schedules that have shorter time frames than are expected should courts request those records in litigation. In other words, records retention schedules should not be developed for the explicit purpose of eliminating records that may prove incriminating in a lawsuit.

Favorable Court Decisions

Courts routinely rule in favor of organizations that have records retention schedules in effect and follow them as the procedure dictates, since this does not amount to willful destruction of evidence with the intention of subverting litigation. Routine destruction of records is considered to be unintentional, since the records are being destroyed according to a procedure that was in place before any litigation materialized. Recorded court cases attest to this legal outcome.[6]

It is important for individuals who are responsible for implementing the retention program to be trained in the importance of implementation. Sporadic implementation gives the appearance of impropriety that can have adverse consequences. Scheduling records for destruction requires developing a timetable and preparing records that document the individuals involved and reveal that appropriate review processes have taken place. Under no circumstances should records be destroyed that have been requested for litigation or government investigation, regardless of the time indicated on the retention schedule.

Records About Developing a Retention Schedule

The procedures and methods used in assigning retention times to records become important in litigation. Often, it is necessary to demonstrate the procedures that were followed in developing a retention schedule, by providing evidence on the research that was conducted. The proper development and operation of a retention schedule become evidence that a systematic, methodical approach was followed.

If it becomes necessary to establish the existence of a valid records management program in court, your organization may be asked to produce evidence that proves the existence of such a program. Records managers and/or those responsible for developing the retention schedule and implementing it may be required to testify as witnesses.

When records are destroyed routinely, based on a properly developed and administered retention schedule, their destruction is not considered to be in "bad faith" with an intent of purposely destroying records that may prove harmful to the organization.

Suspension of Destruction When Litigation Is Imminent

Regardless of the soundness of a records retention program, document destruction must be suspended at the first sign of litigation. All units, departments and individuals should be notified in writing that document destruction must cease when litigation is imminent.

The cessation or prevention of destruction has also been extended to include possibly "foreseeable" litigation. Risks inherent in routine evidence destruction when a lawsuit is imminent or reasonably foreseeable are well illustrated in cases involving destruction before a complaint has been filed. The reasoning in those cases suggests that the appropriateness of sanctions rests on whether litigation is foreseeable, rather than whether the destruction was routine. The issue of whether or not litigation is foreseeable becomes most acute when a complaint has not yet been filed.[7]

Personal Records vs. Organization Records

It is important that employees realize that they should not be creating their own individual files from records that are housed or maintained elsewhere, unless these records/files are clearly identified and are brought into the records retention program.

Often, employees feel that they have a need for records pertaining to their jobs, and they create copies for convenience sake or because there is poor access to the records. Because the official records copy and authorized duplicates are part of the records retention program, they can be identified readily when destruction is scheduled. Personal employee convenience copies, unknown to the records manager, are not brought into the retention/destruction schedule. Such records, by their very existence, destroy the credibility and soundness of a retention schedule and call it into question. They can also surface during discovery or when litigation is imminent and cause untold problems for the organization.[8]

Furthermore, employees should be made aware that all records created in the organization, within the scope of its business, are considered to be company records that are open to subpoena should litigation occur. This includes, but is not limited to such items as calendars, appointment books, post-it notes, and so forth.

Terminology

A distinct difference exists between the terms "record" and "document" in the ISO 9000 standards, and in the activities that control them. For purposes of the quality environment, the following definitions for the term "record" are equally valid:

1. The Association of Records Managers and Administrators (ARMA) International, in its glossary, defines a record as "recorded information, regardless of medium or characteristics, made or received by an organization that is useful in the operations of the organization."[9]

2. The *Records Management Handbook* defines a record as "any information captured in reproducible form that is required for conducting business."[10]

The term "quality record" is well defined in ASME NQA-1-1994 as "a completed document that furnishes evidence of the quality of items and/or activities affecting quality."[11] Quality records often carry the distinction of having to be authenticated — bearing an authoritative signature.

Documents, on the other hand, as the term is used in quality activities delineated in the ISO 9000 standards, denotes procedures, policies, instructions or other written or graphically depicted methods or ways of conducting oneself or the operations in a given organization. Documents explain what an organization plans to do and what it intends to do, and they instruct employees how to perform their tasks. They provide information about how the organization and its employees should operate.

Unlike records, documents exist before the fact and provide guidelines, explanations and instructions about how to operate. Records contain information about the activity and, thus, do not exist until after the activity has been performed. They come into being after the fact.

Document control is a system of managing, distributing and keeping records on the documents that have been created by an organization as part of its overall quality system. Those who are unfamiliar with the profession often confuse records management and document control because of the complex series of records that must be maintained about the document control system. Such records, like those in other quality functions, are the only way to prove that a tight document control system has been established and is operating.

Records control includes the following activities:

- Controlling the proliferation of records by instituting procedures to limit the number of copies that are made, reducing the length of records and so forth

- Purging to reduce the number of items that are retained as records (Often nonrecords are retained, e.g., outdated notices about the Christmas party, thank-you notes from colleagues — in addition, multiple copies of a record need not be retained and filed.)

- Determining the retention times of records — analyzing the records for retention based on legal, fiscal, administrative and historical needs

- Deciding between inactive and active records and moving the inactive records to less expensive storage

- Developing logical and efficient access schemes so that records can be retrieved quickly

- Disposing of records that have satisfied their retention requirements

- Ensuring that blank records (forms) are available to those who need them

- Protecting records from deterioration and destruction.

Document control is a different function, and it includes the following set of activities:

- Reviewing and approving all quality plans, procedures and instructions before they are issued

- Formally distributing documents on a need-to-know basis

- Creating and maintaining records that reveal which individuals and/or functions have been issued which documents

- Retrieving obsolete and superseded documents from individuals and functions

- Ensuring that revised documents have gone through the same review and approval process as the original documents.

Records about the document control process can include but are not restricted to:

- Distribution lists for documents

- Master lists of documents

- Requests for documents

- Periodic reviews of documents
- Document change notices.

Records receive minimal attention in most organizations. Some consider records to be a necessary evil, while some consider them to be only evil and unnecessary. At the very best, organizations tolerate records, albeit grudgingly, and devote token resources and personnel to their creation, maintenance, retrieval and disposition. Realization of their innate importance to business operations surfaces only when they cannot be retrieved, when they need to be destroyed or conveniently lost to subvert evidence or the legal process, or when they are subpoenaed, to be used in pending litigation.

The ISO 9000 standards require that organizations create and maintain records about those activities that affect quality — from the development of a quality policy and quality manual, to the design of a product, the processing of materials that comprise the product, through the manufacture/assembly of completed items.

It should be common business practice to record information about the quality activities as required in the standard for internal productivity, for decision making and for sanity. The criticism that the standard requires too many records is ill founded. Reduction in the number of required records in the 9001:2000 standard does not reduce the need for records for most organizations of any size. The fact that organizations balk at common-sense business requirements reveals the gap between common sense and common practice.

Organizations can and do suffer adverse consequences from not properly developing sound records retention programs and from not implementing those that they have developed.

While developing records management programs for ISO 9000 compliance, organizations can also protect themselves legally. Care and thought must be given to records management programs, especially the development of retention times. Used properly, a retention schedule can be a powerful tool in our highly litigious society. Perfunctory assignment of retention times is not tolerated by courts of law.

Endnotes

1. *Telectron, Inc. v. Overhead Door Corp.*, 116 F.R.D. 107 (S.D. Fla. 1987).
2. Ibid.
3. Allen, "U.S. Companies Pay Increasing Attention to Destroying Files," *Wall Street Journal*, September 2, 1987, p. 1. col. 1.

4. Skupsky, Donald S. *Recordkeeping Requirements*. Denver, CO: Information Requirements Clearinghouse, 1988, p. 93.

5 *Lewy v. Remington Arms Co.*, 836 F.2d 1104 (8th Cir. 1988).

6. *Vick v. Texas Employment Commission*, 514 F.2d 734 (5th Cir. 1975).

7. *Lewy v. Remington Arms Co.*, 836 F.2d 1104 (8th Cir. 1988).

8. Allen, op. cit, p. 1, col. 1.

9. Association of Records Managers and Administrators (ARMA International). *Glossary of Records Management Terms*. Prairie Village, KS: ARMA International, 1989, p. 16.

10. Penn, Ira A., Anne Morddel, Gail Pennix and Kelvin Smith. *Records Management Handbook*. Brookfield, VT: Gower Publishing Co., 1994, p. 3.

11. ASME NQA-1-1994. *Quality Assurance Requirements for Nuclear Facility Applications*. New York: The American Society of Mechanical Engineers, p. 7.

A Quality System Checklist

By Robert W. Peach

The generic list that follows offers concise instruction and guidance for translating ISO 9000 requirements into a full-fledged quality system. Together with the previous detailed chapters on implementation and documentation, this "starter list" traces a logical path from the standards to system documentation.

Introduction

Early in the registration process, it is important to understand contents of the ISO 9001 standard that will guide you towards registration and developing quality system documentation.

Teams responsible for developing ISO 9001 documentation face the challenge of making the analysis and developing the documentation—a task they likely have never done before. Not only must they determine how to start the process, but also how to develop a schedule of activities and how to keep on that schedule while remembering how thorough the documentation process should be.

The lists that follow offer specific guidance for team members faced with translating the requirements of the ISO 9001:2000 standard into a comprehensive quality system. Together with documentation (quality manual, quality procedures, and operator instructions), they provide an orderly journey from the standard to system documentation.

Team members should recognize that these lists are generic. The team should first review the content of the implementation lists and then modify them to meet their particular needs. This is a "starter list" to aid teams in their initial task of defining and guiding their assignment.

4 Quality Management System

1. Determine the requirements of the standard, including both documentation and implementation.

2. Plan the structure of the documentation:

- Quality manual (Refer to ANSI/ISO/ASQ Q10013:1995, "Guidelines for Developing Quality Manuals.")
- An outline that includes:
  - Quality policy
  - Organizational chart
  - Quality assurance organization
  - Statement of authority and responsibility
  - Distribution list of controlled copies
  - Quality system: clauses 4–8
  - Procedures index
  - Forms index
- Operating procedures
- Job instructions
- Records, forms and specifications.

3. Establish existing company practices by using:

- Flowcharts
- Procedures (written and unwritten)
- Work/job instructions.

4. Evaluate resources, present and needed, to include:

- Personnel
- Equipment and instrumentation
- Specifications and acceptance standards
- Quality records.

5. Establish a quality planning function to meet requirements for:
    - Products
    - Projects
    - Contracts.

6. Implement the quality system. Consider:
    - Quality plans
    - Needed resources/time frames
    - Updating procedures and instrumentation
    - Identifying extreme measurement requirements
    - Clarifying acceptance standards
    - Compatible elements
    - Quality records.

7. Demonstrate that your quality management system is well administered.
    - Prepare a quality manual that includes:
        - Elements of the quality management system
        - Exclusions, and why they have been made
        - Procedures, or references to them
        - The sequences and interaction of quality management system processes.
    - Provide for control of quality documents.
        - List all documents where a procedure is required.
        - Develop a plan for control of all documents, including review, updating and reapproval.
        - Before being issued, verify that documents are adequate, readable and easily identified.
        - Identify the current revision status of all documents.
    - Ensure accessibility to documents at the work/job site.
        - Establish control over documents that become obsolete, including removal and controlled retention.
        - Identify and control documents originating from outside the organization.
    - Provide for control of quality records.
        - Control to demonstrate that requirements are being met and are effective.

- Establish procedures for identification, storage retrieval, protection, retention time and disposal of records.

- Records are to be readable and easily identified.

- All documents and data required for the quality management system are to be controlled and readily available to users when needed.

- External documents such as standards and customer drawings are to be identified and controlled.

- Before being issued, all documents and data are to be reviewed and approved by authorized personnel.

- A master list (or equivalent control) is to show current revision status of all documents and be readily available to avoid the use of the wrong documents.

- Current documents are to be in use where needed.

- Obsolete documents are to be taken out of circulation.

- Obsolete documents retained for legal or other purposes are to be so identified.

5 Management Responsibility

1. Ensure management commitment (Subclause 5.1).

   - Communicate importance of meeting customer and legal requirements.

   - Establish a quality policy and quality objectives.

   - Conduct management reviews.

   - Provide all necessary resources.

2. Focus on the customer (Subclause 5.2).

   - Demonstrate that customer and regulatory needs are defined, translated into requirements and being met.

3. Establish a quality policy (Subclause 5.3).

   - Assign responsibility to an individual or team to develop the quality policy. It should include:

     - The organization's quality objectives

     - Management's commitment to meet requirements and to continually improve

     - Relevance to organizational goals

- Expectations and needs of customers.
- Ask for input from across the organization to ensure "ownership" of the quality policy.
- Develop comprehensive objectives.
- Verify that the policy is communicated to and understood by everyone affected by it. You can help ensure that the policy is understood, implemented, and maintained at all levels by:
  - Conducting an orientation for new employees
  - Displaying copies of the policy
  - Holding departmental meetings/discussions
  - Reinforcing and following up on the ideas of the policy
  - Verifying that awareness and understanding are uniform
- Periodically evaluate the quality policy for suitability.

4. Create quality objectives and system plans (Subclause 5.4).

- Establish quality objectives throughout the organization.
- Ensure that all objectives can be measured.
- Commit to continual improvement of both product and quality management system.
- Plan to meet product quality requirements.
- Plan actions to meet and document objectives.
- Identify needed systems.
- Document permitted exclusions.
- Provide for resources.
- Ensure that changes take place in a controlled manner.

5. Demonstrate that your quality management system is well-administered (Subclause 5.5).

- Define areas of responsibility and authority.
  - Use organizational charts, as necessary
  - Provide job descriptions for those whose work affects quality
  - Communicate these relationships to everyone affected.
- Appoint a management representative who:
  - Ensures that the quality system is established and implemented
  - Reports on the performance of the quality system

- Ensures that customer needs are well-known

- Interfaces with outside parties on quality issues.

• Provide for internal communication.

- Demonstrate that the provisions of the quality management system and its effectiveness are communicated to all levels and functions.

6. Provide for management review of the quality system (Subclause 5.6).

• Ensure suitability and effectiveness in meeting policy and objectives.

• Determine if quality systems modifications, such as policy and objectives, are needed.

• Review current performance and look for improvement opportunities by:

- Assessing audit results

- Reviewing customer feedback

- Observing performance of the process and conformance of the product

- Assessing preventive and corrective actions

- Reviewing follow-up actions following previous reviews

- Considering ways to improve the quality management system.

• Identify actions to:

- Improve the quality management system

- Improve the product

- Provide resources.

• Maintain records of reviews.

6 Resource Management

6.1 Provision of Resources

1. Identify resource requirements.

• Provide resources and assign trained personnel for:

- Establishing and improving the quality management system

- Work performance

- Verification activities

- Satisfying customer needs.

6.2 Human Resources

2. Identify training needs.
- List all job functions.
- Establish training requirements for each function.
- Include the requirements in job descriptions.

3. Provide training based on:
- Quality plan elements
- Process knowledge requirements: methods, equipment
- Product knowledge requirements: specifications, workmanship standards
- Cross-training
- Extent of trainee's knowledge and skills
- Other requirements: internal customer, delivery.

4. Establish and record personnel qualifications in individual personnel file to include:
- All required training completed
- Education (initial, additional)
- Previous experience
- Physical characteristics and limitations
- Special training (safety, statistical process control)
- Medical records
- Awards, rewards, promotions
- Cross-training.

5. Develop and document a training plan to include:.
- Required training
- Optional additional training
- Qualifications of trainers
- Periodic evaluation of effectiveness and competence.

6.3 Infrastructure and 6.4 Work Environment

6. Define necessary physical resources.
- Equipment
- Infrastructure

- Facilities
- Work environment
- Services (transportation, communication).

7 Product Realization

7.1 Planning of Product Realization

1. Base process control on the quality plan.

2. Identify critical control points.

3. Define factors affecting control of key processes (production, installation and service):

- Equipment
- Work environment
- Hazardous material control.

4. Identify the following product requirements:

- Specifications
- Workmanship standards
- Regulatory standards and codes
- Acceptance criteria.

5. Review existing monitoring techniques.

6. Develop control and approval procedures.

7. Develop work/job instructions.

8. Develop control equipment maintenance procedures.

9. Identify special processes.

10. Develop verification procedures.

11. Develop validation procedures.

12. Establish appropriate record system to provide confidence in conformity.

7.2 Customer-Related Processes

1. Document customer requirements.

2. Identify precontract practice.

3. Establish contract or order review procedures.

4. Verify the capability to meet requirements.

5. Internalize customer requirements and resolve any differences.

6. Maintain control of customer purchase orders that are written under one contract.

7. Develop a plan for deployment.

8. Establish customer purchase order review procedures.

9. Obtain customer agreements.

10. Revise/improve procedures.

11. Evaluate revisions.

7.3 Design and Development

1. Document all customer requirements and any other pertinent requirements (input) (7.3.2).

2. Establish a plan for design control and assign responsibilities (7.3.1).

3. Assign qualified staff; provide adequate resources.

4. Obtain input from all cross-functional activities to establish interfaces (7.3.2).

5. Document the control procedures, with milestones required by the standard (7.3.1).

6. Design output (7.3.3) to:

- Meet input requirements
- Contain reference data
- Meet regulations and statutory law
- Consider safety
- Review documentation before release.

7. Provide output verification (7.3.5) through:

- Alternative calculations
- Comparison with proven design
- Qualification tests
- Review of documents before release (7.3.4).

8. Validate the design (7.3.6).

- Ensure that design verification is successful
- Confirm that the final product meets user needs
- Assess the need for multiple validations.

9. Develop change control procedures (7.3.7).

- Identification
- Documentation
- Review
- Approval.

7.4 Purchasing

1. Evaluate existing purchasing specifications and requirements.

- Review the process for developing and approving specifications.
- Update the procedures, if necessary.

2. Begin upgrading specifications as required.

- Prioritize criticality in meeting requirements.

3. Prepare, review and approve purchasing documents.

- Refer to the updated specifications.

4. Establish criteria for determining supplier acceptability.

- Evaluate and select suppliers based on their ability to meet requirements, including:
  - Product requirements (What is the supplier's product quality history?)
  - Delivery dependability
  - Quality system capability (via audit/ISO 9001).

5. Develop a supplier classification system.

- Start with a list of acceptable suppliers.
- Define the extent of control to be exercised over suppliers based on:
  - Type of product
  - Impact on final product quality
  - Results of previous quality audits
  - Previously demonstrated quality capability.
- A qualified supplier list should include providers of:
  - Raw materials

- Tooling

- Equipment

- Business service, such as consultants and registrars (auditors).

6. Establish a record system.

- Keep records on:

  - Supplier's quality capability

  - Established procedures for communicating requirements and perform-ance with suppliers

  - Results of periodic supplier review

  - Purchase contracts and supporting data

  - Review and approval of purchasing data.

7. Deploy the plan.

- Develop a schedule.

- Coordinate with receiving inspection.

- Assign responsibility for administration.

8. Revise/improve procedures.

9. Evaluate revisions.

7.5 Production and Service Provision
7.5.1 Control of Production and Service Provision

1. Identify customer service requirements.

2. Document the service requirements.

- Establish procedures.

- Perform the service.

- Report and verify that the requirements are met.

3. Revise and improve procedures.

4. Evaluate revisions.

7.5.2 Validation of Processes for Production and Service Provision

1. Identify all process factors (potential variables) that may affect the capability of the product or service to meet customer requirements.

2. Ensure that all equipment requirements are identified and that equipment and facilities meet these requirements.

3. Verify that requirements for operation and administration of each production element have been verified.

4. Confirm that adequate training is available for all personnel.

5. Verify that documented procedures are adequate for all production requirements.

6. Ensure adequate record keeping to demonstrate that procedures are being followed.

7. Provide for process revalidation when there is a significant change in product or production method.

7.5.3 Identification and Traceability

1. Establish customer and/or regulatory requirements.

2. Document existing traceability practices, including:
   - From your supplier
   - In your plant
   - To your customer
   - Installation and after.

3. Revise/improve traceability procedures.

4. Consider types of traceability/identification:
   - Unit identification (serial number)
   - Lot identification
   - Production date code.

5. Consider methods of identification:
   - Paper versus electronic
   - Labeling
   - Bar codes.

6. Determine the following about the records to be kept:
   - Availability
   - Retention times
   - Responsibility.

7.5.4 Customer Property

1. Determine the existence of customer-supplied property (including test equipment).

2. Establish practice for:
   - Verification
   - Storage
   - Maintenance.

3. Revise/improve your procedures.

4. Evaluate revisions.

7.5.5 Preservation of Product

1. Identify the critical points in the process.

2. Review available information, e.g., damage rates, shelf life.

3. Generate documentation for:
   - Packaging designs
   - Unique customer packaging requirements
   - In-process handling procedures
   - Packaging, packing and marking processes
   - Warehouse procedures
   - Inventory/stock management procedures
   - Transportation techniques/carrier selection
   - Storage, preservation, protection and segregation methods
   - Environmental impact.

4. Revise and improve procedures.

5. Evaluate revisions.

7.6 Control of Monitoring and Measuring Devices

1. Identify all inspection and test requirements.
   - Measurements to be made
   - Accuracy requirements.

2. List equipment and software available to conduct inspections/tests (fixed and portable).

- Laboratory equipment
- Inspection and test equipment
- Production machinery
- Jigs, fixtures, templates
- Test software.

3. Identify recognized calibration requirements and verification procedures for each piece of equipment.

- Fixed and portable equipment
- Required measurement capability
- Known measurement uncertainty
- Calibration schedules.

4. Review and flowchart existing procedures and documentation for:

- Measurements to be made
- Calibration procedures
- Measurement uncertainty
- Identification of calibration status on equipment
- Out-of-calibration action
- Work environment control
- Handling and storage
- Safeguarding against unauthorized adjustment
- Rechecking intervals.

5. Revise/improve procedures.

6. Consider hard copy versus electronic records.

7. Establish an effective record system.

8. Evaluate revisions.

8 Measurement, Analysis and Improvement

8.1 General

1. Define, plan and implement the elements listed in the remaining portions of Clause 8. These include:

- Monitoring and measurement of:
  - Customer satisfaction
  - Quality management system (internal audit)
  - Processes
  - Product
- Control of nonconformity
- Analysis of data
- Continual improvement
- Corrective action
- Preventive action.

8.2 Monitoring and Measurement
8.2.1 Customer Satisfaction

1. Reference the procedures called for in Subclause 7.2, Customer-Related Processes, and Subclause 7.2.3, Customer Communication, in particular.

2. Establish a procedure for compiling, analyzing and acting upon information contained in customer feedback data, reflecting the level of customer satisfaction (Subclause 8.4).

3. Incorporate customer satisfaction measures into continual improvement efforts (Subclause 8.5).

4. Constantly look for additional sources of information reflecting the perception of customer satisfaction appropriate to your type of business. This may include service calls, product returns, repair parts usage, changes in market share and downtime affecting customers.

5. Consider practicality of conducting customer satisfaction surveys, using interviews with customers and consumers.

6. Where your product is used by your customers as a component of their product, consider working with your immediate customers to develop feedback from later production or distribution stages.

8.2.2 Internal Audit

Refer to ISO 19011 (ISO 10011), "Guidelines for Environmental and Quality Auditing."

1. Identify the activities to be audited.

2. Establish the qualifications of audit personnel, including:
   - Experience
   - Training
   - Skills
   - Availability
   - Independence.

3. Develop (or update) audit procedures to include:
   - Planning
   - Responsibilities
   - Requirements
   - Records
   - Report of results.

4. Conduct an initial (trial) quality audit.
   - Evaluate the adequacy of procedures.
   - Determine the effectiveness of the procedures.
   - Verify compliance.
   - Determine the suitability of the working environment.

5. Establish a permanent quality audit program.

8.2.3 Monitoring and Measurement of Processes

1. Evaluate the monitoring and measurement needs of each stage in the realization process.

2. Consider alternative monitoring and measurement methods appropriate for each stage.

3. Put into use appropriate monitoring and measurement procedures. Provide for adequate administration, training and documentation.

4. Continually improve practices.

5. Evaluate revisions.

8.2.4 Monitoring and Measurement of Product

1. Establish a separate plan or procedure for each of the following that apply:
   - Receiving inspection and testing (consider the existing level of supplier control)

- In-process inspection and testing
- Final inspection and testing.

2. Determine the policy, e.g., "Do not use until verified."

3. Identify categories of the product that are affected.

4. List all quality characteristics that are subject to inspection and test.

5. Ensure that the procedures for identifying specified requirements are available.

6. Provide for complete and current procedures at the point of inspection/test.

7. Provide for positive product identification/recall for urgent release.

8. Release product only when successful tests/records are complete.

9. Revise/improve procedures.

10. Evaluate revision.

8.3 Control of Nonconforming Product

1. Review and document your procedures for:
   - Identification
   - Documentation
   - Control
   - Segregation
   - Prevention of inadvertent use/installation.

2. Document the procedures for disposition, notification, and classification.

3. Assign authority for disposition approval.

4. Document the procedures for reinspection of repairs or rework.

5. Document the concession reporting and handling procedures.

6. Revise and approve your procedures.

7. Evaluate revisions.

8.4 Analysis of Data

1. Identify existing applications and procedures.

2. Review status, correctness, and effectiveness of data collection and analysis applications such as in:

- Establishing process capability
- Identifying potential problems
- Verifying product characteristics.

3. Examine the quality plan for additional applications.

4. Provide for additional applications.

5. Evaluate the effectiveness and value of new applications.

8.5 Improvement

1. Separately identify procedures for corrective action (actual nonconformities) versus preventive action (potential nonconformities).

- Corrective action: go to step 2.
- Preventive action: go to step 3.

2. Carry out corrective action.

- Assign responsibility to an individual or team.
- Review the number and significance of complaints and returns. Evaluate their importance.
- Prepare a flowchart of the present system.
- Evaluate the effectiveness of present practice.
- Provide resources:
  - Expertise
  - Records, instruction procedures
  - Defective product (for analysis).
- Revise/improve procedures to:
  - Investigate the cause of nonconformities
  - Analyze all processes
  - Determine a final "fix" (i.e., an action plan)
  - Initiate action to prevent recurrence
  - Apply new controls.
- Make permanent changes.
- Evaluate revised procedures.

3. Carry out preventive action.

- Assign responsibility to an individual or team.

- Review existing preventive action activities.
- Prepare a flowchart of the present system.
- Evaluate the effectiveness of present practice.
- Identify appropriate sources of information:
  - Reports of purchased material quality
  - Processes
  - Waiver concessions
  - Audit results
  - Quality records
  - Service reports
  - Customer complaints.
- Identify activities in which preventive action activities can be established or enhanced. Examples:
  - Product design
  - Process development
  - Process control.
- Make use of preventive action tools such as Failure Mode and Effects Analysis (FMEA).
- Modify and continually improve procedures to:
  - Identify potential nonconformities
  - Initiate action to prevent occurrence
  - Apply new controls.
- Report preventive actions that are taken.
- Evaluate revised procedures.
- Follow up on the effectiveness of the actions taken.
- Submit actions for management review.

Industry Applications of ISO 9000

Automotive Requirements

13

While the ISO 9000 family of standards has gained worldwide acceptance across a broad spectrum of industries and organizations, no single industry can claim more influence on the ISO 9000 phenomenon than the automotive sector.

In North America, the Big Three Automakers — DaimlerChrysler, Ford Motor Company and General Motors Corporation — led the way with the development of QS-9000 and its accompanying registration program.

At this writing, the industry reports some 23,000 third-party registration certificates to QS-9000 and automakers have announced their intention to transition all QS-9000 suppliers to the higher-level requirements of ISO/TS 16949:2002 no later than December 15, 2006, unless an earlier date is specified by a subscribing OEM. In that regard, DaimlerChrysler subsequently released a letter requiring its suppliers to complete their transitions no later than July 1, 2004. The ISO/TS 16949:1999 document contains the verbatim text of ISO 9001:1994 supplemented with additional industry requirements such as design and development, production and service provision, employee competence, control of monitoring and measuring devices, and continual improvement.

The International Automotive Task Force (IATF) produced the ISO/TS 16949:1999 document, intended as a replacement not only for QS-9000, but also European automotive quality requirements AVSQ, VDA6.1 and EAQF. The OEMs participating in the development of ISO/TS 16949:2002 included DaimlerChrysler, Ford Motor, General Motors, BMW, Fiat, PSA (PeugeotCitroen), Renault and Volkswagen. Participating supplier trade organizations included the Automotive Industry Action Group, Associazione Nazionale Fra Industrie Automobilistiche (ANFIA/Italy), Fédération des

Industries des Équipements pour Véhicules (FIEV/France), Society of Motor Manufacturers and Traders (SMMT/UK) and Verband der Automobilindustrie - Qualitätsmanagement Center (VDA-QMC/Germany). The IATF also partnered with the Japan Automobile Manufacturers Association (JAMA) under the auspices of ISO Technical Committee 176, which is responsible for the ISO 9000 family of quality management standards.

Important changes to the ISO/TS 16949:2002 document include mapping based on ISO 9001:2000. In addition the automotive requirements place additional emphasis on product realization integration, organization performance and supplier development.

Among the most visible changes for QS-9000 certificate holders will be a new process-based approach of auditors. This will include a more rigorous approval process for registrars and additional emphasis on meeting customer requirements as measured by delivered part quality performance, customer disruptions and delivery schedule performance, including incidents of premium freight and special status customer notifications related to quality or delivery issues.

While it is clear that the emphasis is shifting away from QS-9000 to ISO/TS 16949:2002, we felt it important to include articles on both requirements in this *Handbook* since the transition is just getting under way. In addition, some suppliers subject to QS-9000 supplements, such as the Tooling and Equipment supplement, have been instructed to continue with their present certifications.

Automotive QS-9000 Quality System Requirements

by Joe Bransky

Introduction

QS-9000 is the quality system standards requirement developed by the US automakers General Motors Corporation, Ford Motor Company and Chrysler Corp. (now DaimlerChrysler DCA). The objectives are automotive supplier compliance and certification to these standards utilizing third-party assessment of supplier quality system capability and implementation. QS-9000 is built upon ISO 9000, i.e., QS-9000 is organized around the ISO 9000 (1994) 20 elements and its content. However, QS-9000 includes significant additional automotive content based on the Original Equipment Manufacturer (OEM) requirements for production parts and related services received from a large and multitier base of suppliers.

Key to the effectiveness of the QS-9000 standards and registration process is that automotive suppliers achieve improved quality system capability, delivered part quality, reductions in supplier disruptions and field performance of purchased components. In addition, the process provides valuable information for OEM sourcing decisions. This chapter will endeavor to provide an overview and insights to QS-9000, as contrasted with ISO 9000, and a discussion of related future developments.

Background and Development of the Requirement

Chrysler, Ford and General Motors released the QS-9000 Quality System Requirements in 1994 as a response to reduce multiple customer (second-party) audits by the individual OEMs to evaluate supplier capability. QS-9000 is a harmonized standard based on Chrysler's Pentastar, Ford's Q-1 and GM's Targets for Excellence programs. In addition, across the entire supply chain there existed significant market impetus for improving product quality and reducing costs associated with customer quality problems.

The QS-9000 Quality System Requirements (QSR) was developed by the Supplier Quality Requirements Task Force (SQRTF). This task force, made up of one representative respectively from Chrysler, Ford and General Motors, worked with subject matter experts as well as supplier representatives in developing the standards and registration process.

The QSR document employs the organization and content of the International Standard ISO 9001(1994) as a base. Each element is then enhanced and augmented with automotive requirements. In general, the added automotive requirements of QS-9000 provide greater specifics and detail to focus on quality issues related to automotive manufacturing processes and parts production.

In addition, QS-9000 includes customer-specific requirements from Chrysler (now DaimlerChrysler), Ford and General Motors. Along with meeting the general standards requirements of QS-9000 (Section I), suppliers to each of these OEMs must be in compliance with the customer-specific requirements, detailed in Section II of the manual. Also contained in the manual are appendices addressing important topics such as implementation, codes of practice for certification bodies who contract with supplier clients to conduct the certification audit, control plans, QS-9000 standards changes and accreditation body requirements. A comprehensive glossary is also contained in the manual.

There have been a number of associated supplemental and reference manuals developed to support the QS-9000 manual and its compliance and implementation. Six reference manuals — the Quality System Assessment (QSA), Advanced Quality Planning and Control Plan (APQP), Potential Failure Mode and Effects Analysis (FMEA), Measurement System Analysis (MSA), Production Part Approval Process (PPAP) and Statistical Process Control (SPC) — are considered essential for comprehending and applying the specific compliance requirements of the QSR. These reference manuals are generally guidance documents except for PPAP, which includes mandatory part submission requirements for each of the OEMs. QS-9000 (Third Edition) is the manual currently in effect as of the issuance of this Handbook. Reference manuals have also undergone revisions, and the reader is advised to confirm the most recent editions.

When QS-9000 was released, Chrysler(DaimlerChrysler), Ford and GM defined specific deadlines and compliance requirements for suppliers. As of this Handbook Edition, all current and new Tier 1 production part suppliers are required to be registered by GM and DaimlerChrysler. Ford requires compliance to QS-9000 of its current suppliers, but new suppliers must now be registered. Because QS-9000 requires supplier development of Tier 2 suppliers, many sub-tier suppliers are now implementing QS-9000 within their organizations.

The formal accreditation of QS-9000 registrars (certification bodies) is the reponsibility of accreditation bodies recognized globally. However, policy development, changes and general oversight of QS-9000 are the responsibility of the SQRTF. This group operates on behalf of DaimlerChrysler, Ford and General Motors and also works with the automotive supplier association, Automotive Industry Action Group (AIAG). The AIAG provides administrative support for QS-9000 training and manual distribution. In addition the AIAG provides coordination support for automotive suppliers to tackle industry issues such as, e-commerce, manufacturing, quality and other special projects. The SQRTF has designated Plexus Corporation of St. Paul, Minnesota, as the QS-9000-sanctioned training provider for auditor qualification training and examination.

The SQRTF also works through a special body called the International Automotive Sector Group (IASG). The purpose of this body is to provide official sanctioning statements for clarification of requirements or to address new and special issues related to registrations and implementation of QS-9000. The IASG coordinates receipt of questions or issues and oversees the process for release of QS-9000-sanctioned interpretations. IASG representation includes the SQRTF, representatives from QS-9000- recognized accreditation bodies and selected registrars(certification bodies). The IASG reviews submitted issues or questions and, as necessary, communicates its findings through periodic release of IASG Sanctioned Interpretations. The Sanctioned Interpretations are available on the AIAG website, http://www.QS-9000.org/quality.

The QS-9000 "7 Pack"

The QS-9000 Manual (QSR) combined with the previously mentioned six key reference manuals are identified as the QS-9000 "7-Pack." The overarching purpose of these documents is to describe the necessary tools for the supplier in order to establish a capable quality system. Following is a summary of the content and description of each manual and its relationship to the establishment of system capability and implementation.

Quality System Requirements (QS-9000 Third Edition)

Published in March 1998, the QSR Third Edition manual includes Section I containing the standards and Section II incorporating the sector-specific requirements along with 10 appendices. The Third Edition contains appendices, an expanded glossary and also includes some added requirements based on the addition of certain European automotive quality requirements.

The QSR contains the auditable requirements of QS-9000. All of the other reference manuals except PPAP, which is a requirements document, are guidance documents to support the QSR compliance requirements. Each manual is specifically identified within QSR and is referenced as applicable as a "should" or recommended method to achieve the required results. Except for PPAP, the effect is that the process or methodology within each manual is provided to the supplier as a recommended technique, but other techniques that accomplish the intent are acceptable. It is also clearly the intent of QS-9000 that the methods described in the reference manuals be applied for continuous improvement.

Quality System Assessment (QSA)

The QSA is used to determine the level of conformance to the QS-9000 Third Edition. Proper use of the manual will promote consistency between activities and internal personnel determining QS-9000 conformance gaps. This manual contains defining questions related to all "shalls" (mandatory) and "shoulds" (recommended) consistent with the QS-9000 Third Edition. Questions are designed with an optional 10-point scale that may be used to assist in evaluating the supplier's curent status against the requirements.

Advanced Product Quality Planning and Control Plan (APQP)

This manual communicates to internal and external suppliers and subcontractors the common Advanced Product Quality Planning and Control Plan guidelines. These guidelines were developed jointly by DaimlerChrysler, Ford and General Motors. The guidelines are designed to assist the supplier in developing a product quality plan for new or changed products that will support the development of a product or service to meet customer requirements.

The APQP reference manual is central to accomplishing the intent of QS-9000. The APQP process is modeled on the Plan-Do-Check-Act cycle. It is a closed-loop process, carried out by multidisciplinary teams, that encompasses the entire cycle of product quality planning, realization and communication. Depicting product quality planning as a cycle illustrates the continual improvement that can only be achieved by taking the experience in one program and applying that acquired knowledge to the next program.

Properly implemented, APQP provides suppliers with common guidelines for Product Quality Planning and Control Plans covering a comprehensive and structured approach to product realization. There is a requirement for control plans to be created, which demonstrates the importance OEMs place on the APQP approach and tools. In addition, in order to achieve maximum benefit of these guidelines, DaimlerChrysler, Ford and General Motors place great emphasis on the effective application of APQP, including efforts to improve the knowledge and understanding of suppliers, third-party auditors and OEM internal personnel in engineering, manufacturing and in the supply quality.

Potential Failure Mode and Effects Analysis (FMEA)

This manual introduces Potential Failure Mode and Effects Analysis (FMEA) and gives general guidance in the application of the technique. An FMEA is a systemized group of activities intended to: (a) recognize and evaluate the potential failure of a product/process and its effects, (b) identify actions that could eliminate or reduce the chance of the potential failure and (c) document the process. The manual covers both design and process FMEAs.

Formalized and documented Failure Mode and Effects Analyses have been shown to be a powerful tool for reducing costs by identifying design and process changes early in the product life cycle. A critical factor in the successful use of FMEAs is to conduct them at the appropriate time. FMEA implementation links directly into the early APQP phases involving design, development and validation of the product and related processes. The objective, specifically stated in QS-9000, is to achieve defect prevention rather than defect detection.

Properly applied, FMEAs become "living" documents that are meant to be periodically reviewed through the life of the product. Review of FMEAs is beneficial at many points in a robust quality system, including corrective actions, audits, improvement initiatives and even development of other products and processes. The use of FMEAs in the development of new products or the application of processes to new parts allows the organization to avoid the pitfalls of incorrect process parameters or missing process steps. These pitfalls have been clearly shown to be the highest cost factors to suppliers in the launch of new product or parts. This is a powerful incentive to apply this useful tool regardless of whether or not it is required by the customer. FMEA, Third Edition, was released in July 2001. The technical aspects of this edition are the equivalent of the SAE J 1739 document.

Measurement Systems Analysis (MSA)

This manual presents guidelines for selecting procedures to assess the quality of a measurement system. The manual is not intended to be a compendium of analyses for all measurement systems. Its primary focus is measurement systems where readings can be repeated. Topics include gauge R&R, ANOVA calculation and control chart constants, among others. The MSA addresses both essential as well as some advanced tools related to measurement uncertainty.

A measurement system should reflect the voice of the process. If the measurement system isn't effective, it will provide useless or, perhaps worse, misleading information concerning quality. The MSA reference manual provides tools for analysis of measurement methods, human factors, the environment, instruments and gauges, and the production part. All of these can have critical effects the conclusions and decisions resulting in a measurement system. (Note: This on manual is currently under revision as of this publication and scheduled for release in the Fourth Quarter, 2001.)

Production Part Approval Process (PPAP Third Edition)

This manual is a requirement for production parts suppliers to DaimlerChrysler, Ford and General Motors. The Third Edition incorporates a number of important revisions which include:

- Use of "auditable" language and a format consistent with QS-9000 Third Edition to support third-party audit
- A reordering of the PPAP requirements aligned with the typical process flow
- Revision of "Preliminary Process Capability Requirements," now called "Initial Process Studies," to provide for the use of either Cpk or Ppk, depending on the amount and type of data available, consistent with the Statistical Process Control, SPC, reference manual
- Clarification of when customer notification and/or submission is required
- Incorporation of IASG Sanctioned Interpretations specific to PPAP
- Requirements for bulk material (see Bulk Material-Specific Appendix)
- A Heavy Truck Manufacturer-Specific Appendix
- An enhanced glossary.

Although a required activity, suppliers have found that the PPAP process, when followed and utilized properly, can expedite the approval process for new parts or change orders. This is important as approvals are required before tooling money, normally the highest single-cost item to a suppler, can be released. PPAP, if appropriately applied, has been shown as a good predictor of "run at rate" or other first-run acceptance criteria.

Statistical Process Control (SPC)

This manual describes several basic statistical methods associated with statistical process control and process capability analysis. SPC is used to measure the predictability of processes used in manufacturing. Appropriate use of SPC can help the supplier ensure that quality parts are being produced and help eliminate waste in the manufacturing environment. The SPC manual is aimed at practitioners and managers beginning the application of statistical methods. It provides guidance on selection and application of appropriate statistical methods. SPC methodology and tools in this manual can also be effectively applied to processes outside of manufacturing.

The Registration Process

QS-9000 follows a third-party certification process similar to ISO 9000. Currently, there are over 160 certification bodies who conduct third-party certification of suppliers to QS-9000 on a worldwide basis.

Registration to QS-9000 is focused on the "site" where the value-added production processes occur. Remote locations, such as engineering, purchasing or warehousing, cannot obtain independent certification to QS-9000. They are, however, subject to audit as they support a site.

In order to achieve initial certification, a supplier must be in compliance with the third-party audited standards and all identified nonconformities must be satisfactorily closed. To maintain certification, surveillance audits of certified suppliers are required to be scheduled at regular intervals according to the requirements and the entire quality system must be assessed within three years.

There are conditions in which suppliers can have their certification placed on "probation" or even revoked. For example, if the registrar issues a major nonconformity, or there is issuance of a number of minor nonconformities that are judged to represent a total breakdown of the system, certification probation can result. In addition, each of the OEMs has established its own designation for placing problem suppliers in a special status: Ford — "Q-1 Revocation," DaimlerChrysler — "Quality Rating only — not Total Rating," General Motors — "New Business Hold — Quality." Notification of this status to the supplier from one of the respective OEMs results in QS-9000 certification probation of the supplier.

A supplier that is placed on QS-9000 probation is required to take corrective action to be removed from such status. Failure to meet the timing requirements (generally four months) or failure to satisfy the exit criteria for special status suppliers can result in the revocation of the supplier's QS-9000 certification by their registrar. A process of appeal for disputes related to the identification of supplier nonconformities, probations or revocations exists in the certification rules.

The accreditation process of third-party registrars/certification bodies includes evaluation of the registrar's capability to audit to ISO 9001 and the additional automotive requirements of QS-9000. Accreditation of registrars is performed by accreditation bodies recognized by QS-9000 as well as ISO 9000. Currently there are 22 accreditation bodies worldwide who provide the service of evaluating and certifying registrar capability to satisfactorily audit automotive suppliers.

Auditors of registrars are required to fulfill additional requirements in order to become qualified and certified as QS-9000 auditors. Auditor candidates must pass written and performance examinations administered by AIAG. Auditor certification must be renewed every three years.

Keys to Achieving Certification

The process of achieving certification generally includes the following steps:

- Management Commitment — This includes recognizing the customer requirement of certification or compliance and appropriate deadlines. In addition, management commitment includes support for the value-added quality system assessment and improvement in the organization, providing resources and monitoring progress.

- Organization Alignment to Support the Process — This includes assigning responsibility to specific individuals accountable to coordinate essential activities, implement a cohesive plan and report on progress.

- Training — This includes achieving expert training and general training within the organization. Such training is essential to to provide the leadership, subject matter and process knowledge within the organization to efficiently and effectively achieve the organization goals.

- Gap Analysis — This includes coordinating and implementing appropriate comparative analysis to determine the breadth and depth of the organization's task to achieve certification.

- Gap Closure — This includes identifying, implementing and monitoring reaction plans to close the gaps identified on the Gap Analysis including resources, timing and responsibility.

- Preassessment — This includes the formal warm-up assessment to determine the immediate readiness of an organization to successfully achieve QS-9000 certification. This is generally performed by an outside agency.

- Third-Party Assessment — This is the initial formal audit conducted by an accredited third-party registrar/certification body.

- Certification — This refers to the formal notice and recognition of certification based upon having completed the initial audit of demonstrating compliance to the QS-9000 QSR as determined by the registrar. Celebrate and recognize the organization!

- Surveillance and Continuous Improvement — The quality journey requires ongoing quality system capability and performance evaluation and improvement.

Keys to Maintaining Certification

QS-9000 initially places a high emphasis on assessing the quality system capability of the supplier. A very important aspect of maintaining certification is to demonstrate that the quality system continues to be effective as determined by surveillance audits and by the supplier's performance over time. In other words, the initial certification is the conclusion of the third-party audit that the quality system is capable. The product quality output of the system also provides direct evidence that will confirm (or refute) the capability or execution of the quality system. Furthermore, because QS-9000 requires continuous improvement, the supplier will also be expected to document improved results over time, especially with respect to delivered product quality. An internal audit program that focuses on the compliance of the system to QS-9000 requirements and system performance is a crucial element in assessing the robustness of the system and maintaining certification.

Another area where certified suppliers will be scrutinized in surveillance audits is the application of the core tools (reference manuals). As noted above, in addition to the development of the QS-9000 QSR, there are six important reference manuals. Achieving initial certification requires the supplier to demonstrate that the core tools are in place. Maintaining certification requires the supplier to demonstrate that the quality system is operating effectively in conjunction with the application of the core tools.

Impact of QS-9000

The Big Three automakers have continued in their commitment to QS-9000. A number of key objectives have been achieved including a harmonized quality system standard, an agreed third-party certification process, additions or clarifications that enhance the process and, most importantly, improved quality system capability and supplier performance. Suppliers to the Big Three can expect the commitment to the third-party assessment of a harmonized quality standard to extend for the foreseeable future. For example, as of the first quarter of 2002 there were over 22,500 suppliers registered to QS-9000 worldwide. This represents a large portion of automotive suppliers to the Big Three. However, QS-9000 requirements will continue for the ongoing surveillance of suppliers already registered as well as initial certification for new suppliers. In addition, the level of interest and participation continues, as evidenced by the distribution of over two million QS-9000 related manuals since the launch of QS-9000 (1994).

The benefits of QS-9000 include achievement of improved quality system capability and significant reductions in ppm levels at the automotive OEM manufacturing and assembly centers. Supplier surveys confirm similar findings. For example, in 1997 AIAG and the American Society for Quality (ASQ) conducted a survey of 613 registered suppliers to determine the impact of QS-9000. Suppliers reported process and quality improvement (76 percent of those surveyed) and better understanding of jobs and tasks (75 percent). They also reported reductions in ppm defects (54 percent of suppliers reported an average of 46 percent reduction from preregistration levels). Other highlights of the survey results were fewer parts returned (54 percent), reduced cost of nonconformance (53 percent) and improved on-time delivery (53 percent).

In 1998 AIAG and ASQ surveyed 205 North American suppliers resulting in highly positive findings comparing the financial benefit versus investment in QS-9000. Results of this survey showed suppliers on average invested about $120,000 to achieve QS-9000 registration. Cost factors included internal preparation such as in-house training and gap closure, as well as outside costs including third-party registrars, software, external training and consulting fees. The average annual investment for a supplier to maintain registration was about $40,000. The average benefit reported from QS-9000 was 6 percent of sales, or almost 10 million dollars for the average company surveyed.

ISO/TS 16949

In fact, the success of QS-9000 has led to the development of ISO/TS 16949, currently an ISO-based, global technical specification intended to evolve as a standard specific to the worldwide automotive industry supply chain. This technical specification moves the global automotive OEM sector closer to its vision of a single, global automotive certification process of quality system capability.

The ISO/TS 16949 process includes OEMs from Europe as well as North America. A supplier who chooses the option must meet the ISO/TS 16949 catalog requirements combined with the OEM customer-specific requirements. Choosing this option gives automotive suppliers an alternative through registration that is equivalent to QS-9000, AVSQ, EAQF or VDA 6.1.

Future Direction of Automotive Sector ISO-Based Standards

The development of ISO/TS 16949 leads to several areas of consideration important for automotive suppliers. As noted above, this new standard allows an option for suppliers facing the challenge of supplying to multiple automotive customers globally. Because ISO/TS 16949 is a harmonization effort encompassing a large number of separate standards and requirements schemes, it defines a basic catalog of common requirements for a very broad group of subscribing OEM customers. However, it will be necessary for the supplier to understand and discuss the customer-specific requirements of each OEM beyond the TS standards catalog. With ISO/TS 16949, the customer-specific requirements are separate OEM requirement documents or part of the supplier purchase agreement with the customer, but nonetheless equally important. The responsibility is significant for the supplier to communicate closely with each customer to understand these additional expectations.

Another important difference represented in the ISO/TS 16949 process is that the oversight offices of the International Automotive Task Force (IATF) contract directly with third-party certification bodies (registrars). Only suppliers who are registered through IATF contracted certification bodies will be recognized by the IATF. Contracted certification bodies (registrars) accredited to QS-9000 may not necessarily be under contract and therefore recognized by the IATF for purposes of ISO/TS 16949 registration. Contracted certification bodies (registrars) are required to comply with the terms of the IATF contract and "Rules of the Road." The purpose of the "Rules of the Road" is to:

- Spell out the qualifications, restrictions and expectations for certification bodies.

- Define the audit process in terms of applicability, scope, methods and timelines.

- Define audit team responsibilities and qualifications.

- Set requirements for witness audits, man-days, notifications and surveillance audits.

- Define IATF recognition and oversight of certification bodies.

- Define certificate contents requirements.

- Establish required reporting from certification bodies to IATF.

- Define the phases and steps to be followed in conducting the audit.

- Define qualifications for third-party auditors.

The "TS" designation means that a technical specification has been sanctioned by ISO but it is not a sanctioned general standard. The IATF plan is to monitor the launch activities and the supplier response to ISO/TS 16949. The IATF, working in conjunction with the Technical Committee of ISO (TC 176), will evaluate the process to determine how well the overall objectives are met, including an evaluation of supplier achievements as the result of certification to ISO/TS 16949. In early 2002, an ISO work group made up of interested OEMs and trade associations, including representation from Asia-Pacific, aligned ISO/TS 16949 with ISO 9001:2000. At this writing, DaimlerChrysler, Ford and GM have all recognized ISO/TS 16949 registration as a valid alternative to QS-9000.

Implementing ISO/TS 16949:2002

by Alan J. Peterson

The automotive industry's approach to quality system management can be summed up by what might best be described as three "sights."

- Oversight
- Line of Sight
- Foresight

This approach is evident in the formation of the International Automotive Task Force (IATF) and its subsequent release of ISO/TS 16949:2002 and companion documents: Rules for Achieving IATF Recognition, QMS Assessment Checklist and IATF Guidance to ISO/TS 16949:2002.

Oversight

It's no secret that the worldwide effectiveness and consistency of the third-party registration system, as a key element of supply chain management, has fallen short of expectations, not the least of which being the unmet expectations of the automotive OEMs.

By 1994, many European and North American OEMs had already curtailed their second-party audits or were in the process of doing so. Consequently, OEMs were becoming increasingly reliant on the third-party system for supplier selection and retention.

With the experience gleaned from developing several national and/or OEM-specific supplier quality standards/requirements, the automotive industry embarked on an ambitious worldwide harmonization of supplier quality management requirements and third-party auditing resources at that time.

They did this by

- Agreeing to write a unified specification, and
- Planning to take a more active role in the oversight of the certification bodies/registrars who would audit automotive organizations to the yet-to-be-written technical specification, ISO/TS 16949:2002 (a process that actually began with an earlier first edition).

The first step was to form an alliance of automakers around the world. Once established, such a group would provide the leadership and commitment to develop a plan to improve third-party auditing and supplier certification for the

Figure 13-1

Relationships

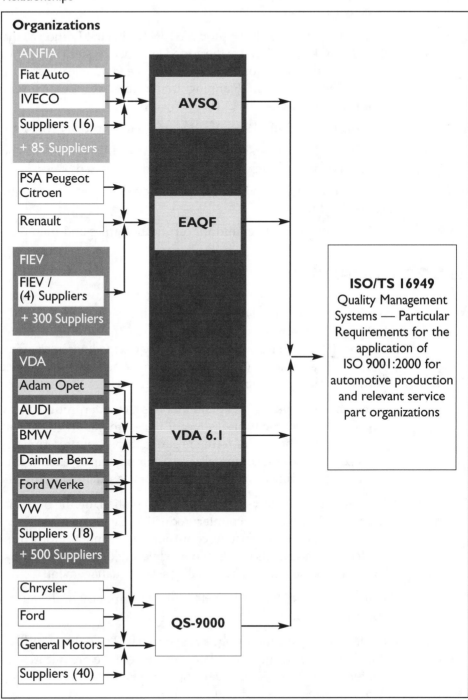

industry on a global scale. The relationship among the OEMs, national standards groups and quality management system standards/requirements in this initiative is depicted in Figure 13-1.

As mentioned earlier, IATF produced TS 16949 First Edition as the forerunner of ISO/TS 16949:2002. But it is the added level of oversight and the decision to seek international recognition that truly sets the 2002 release apart from the early days of the first edition. Planning around the 2002 release essentially involved four primary activities of IATF:

1. Write the technical specification and seek approval from ISO.

2. Establish five oversight bodies in the five IATF member nations — United Kingdom, Germany, France, Italy and the United States.

3. Contract directly with certification bodies/registrars through the oversight body offices.

4. Develop and deliver auditor certification rules and training.

ISO/TS 16949:2002

At its core, ISO/TS 16949:2002 incorporates the complete text of ISO 9001:2000. But like other sector-specific documents, ISO/TS 16949:2002 adds to the foundational ISO standard where the industry deemed necessary for more specificity and/or clarification. (See Figure 13-2.) The action of supplementing the standard with more prescriptive elements is not without controversy.

Some standards purists maintain that it is a counterproductive to add prescriptiveness to a document that is meant to assure quality management at a foundational level. They point to the negative impact of prescription on instructing organizations toward continual self-sustaining improvement. They contend that prescription diminishes, rather than enhances, quality improvement.

Proponents of industry-specific supplementation, on the other hand, agree that too much prescription is counterproductive. But they also believe that too much flexibility leads to confusion: confusion they cannot afford in a supply chain made up of thousands of suppliers delivering thousands of parts. They see this confusion as the antithesis of quality system management.

Found in each section of ISO 9001:2000, a summary of the automotive supplementation includes:

Exclusions — The added language states that "The only permitted exclusions for this Technical Specification relate to 7.3 where the organization is not responsible for product design and development. Permitted exclusions do not include manufacturing process design."

Figure 13-2

IATF Implementation Path: 1997-2002

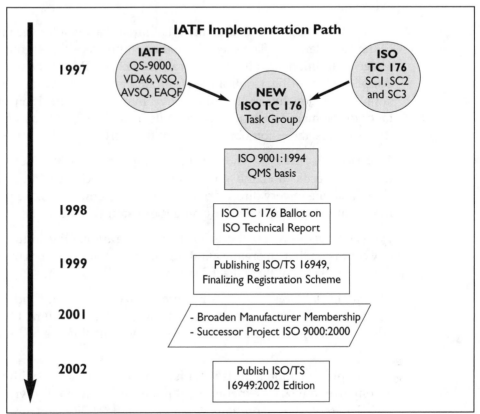

The automotive industry makes it clear that it does not want supplier organizations to be confused about design. While the design of the product may not be within their areas of responsibility, the design of the process certainly is.

Management's Responsibility for Process Efficiency — It has been understood that management was responsible for conformance of the system and effectiveness of the system. But efficiency, while implied, and certainly an integral part of a business management system, was not addressed by ISO 9001:2000. The technical specification stated the responsibility; now, hopefully, there is no confusion.

Customer Representative — This is actually a carryover from each of the national automotive requirements/standards. Though this appears to be a minor element when it is first mentioned in the technical specification, one should not miss the point. Customer orientation is a theme that runs deep in the technical specification. It may very well be the most important focus of the technical specification.

Employee and Site Capability — Several additional clauses are added to the basic standard in the areas of employee training and site-specific requirements and expectations.

Product Realization — This is an area that far and away adds the most language to the base standard. The specific areas of emphasis, either through added language or additional requirements, are: Product and Process Design, Purchasing, Supplier Monitoring, Control Plans, Tooling and Laboratories. These pieces of supplementation reflect the automotive industry's recognition of the importance of the manufacturing process to its overall success in assuring quality to its customers, the automobile drivers of the world.

Customer Satisfaction — Though this is emphasized in the ISO portion of the technical specification, the automotive industry decided to remove any confusion by stating in very direct terms the minimums they would expect and therefore what to measure when assessing the customer's satisfaction.

Types of Audits — Again, this is an effort by the automotive industry to clear up any confusion that an organization might have about the types of quality audits that are expected of them. Each is identified and described.

Monitoring and Measurement — ISO emphasizes monitoring and measurement; TS emphasizes what to monitor and measure (at a minimum). Once again, this addition has the purpose of clearing up any confusion the organization might have.

The supplementation reflects what has and has not worked with respect to the automotive industry's experience with the standard and its own requirements. ISO/TS 16949:2002 represents a balance of flexibility and prescription and, hopefully, captures the inherent strengths of both.

Oversight Bodies

Like the technical specification itself, oversight bodies supplement the already established third-party registration infrastructure. Their role should be viewed in the context of the overall system: ISO writes and publishes the standard. Accreditation bodies in member countries and/or regions oversee the activities of certification bodies/registrars and witness the auditing of their auditors. Certification bodies/registrars manage the auditors they hire and contract with organizations to provide certification services.

In the context of the technical specification, oversight bodies act as a type of accreditation agency. The oversight bodies witness the auditing of the certification bodies'/registrars' auditors in their member country (there are exceptions to that rule, but the main point for this explanation is the concept of national oversight). The automotive industry feels compelled to follow through on its issuance of a technical specification certificate by monitoring the third-party auditing of the automotive supplementations to the ISO standard (including the reference manuals). The oversight bodies, through the use of witness audits, provide the eyes, ears and voice of the automotive industry's interests to a system of certification bodies/registrars and automotive supplier organizations.

Contracts

To insure that the oversight of certification bodies/registrars is clear and indisputable, the oversight bodies, representing the interests of the IATF, contract directly with certification bodies/registrars that wish to do business with automotive supplier organizations. A contract lays out the requirements for acceptance as an ISO/TS 16949:2002 qualified certification body/registrar and details the expectations for performance. Failure to meet the criteria excludes a certification body (CB) from signing the contract or, if already under contract, provides a means for the oversight body to end the CB's participation.

Under the basic third-party system, the relationship between the CB and an ISO-registered organization is subject only to the guidelines of an applicable accreditation body or bodies. There is no contract per se between the accreditation body and the CB. CBs cannot be excluded from the system if they can meet the certification guidelines. Removal of a CB's accreditation is a slow and painful process. In the United States, the National Accreditation Program operated jointly by the American National Standards Institute and the Registrar Accreditation Body, for example, had not permanently revoked a single accreditation as of this writing.

In short, the automotive industry will gain more control by requiring contracts with certification bodies/registrars. Unacceptable performance can be dealt with much more quickly, and the needs of a particular region or segment of the manufacturing community can be accommodated in a more flexible manner. The automotive industry need not depend on a third party to deal with a third-party problem; they can deal with it directly.

In 2002, more than 125 accredited certification bodies/registrars are operating worldwide. But fewer than 50 of these firms have been qualified for ISO/TS 16949:2002. Of those that have qualified, several have already been suspended for their failure to meet all requirements of their contracts by their respective oversight bodies.

Auditor Certification and Rules

In addition to the oversight bodies, the IATF also established two other groups that assist in the oversight of auditors and their certification. The Training Commission and the Exam Commission are responsible for designing and developing certification training programs and examinations for the certification/qualification of the certification body/registrar auditors. Both groups were developed concurrently with the development and promulgation of rules by the oversight bodies.

The key objective of the Training Commission is to create and maintain an auditor-training program that reflects the intentions and requirements of the IATF, as detailed in the technical specification and other IATF rules and guidance documentation. The Training Commission is comprised of directors from designated oversight bodies, representatives of the IATF and representatives from the training organizations nominated and accepted by the IATF to deliver the training. Current auditor certification training is comprised of three days of training and one day of two examinations and an assessment. Upgrade training for current ISO/TS 16949 First Edition auditors is two days of training followed by a day of testing.

It is the Exam Commission that develops and maintains the three types of exams and assessment that are administered on the final day of the certification session. The Exam Commission has developed a written exam to test knowledge, a performance assessment to test behavior and an oral examination to test understanding. A satisfactory grade on each one of the exams and assessment must be achieved before the auditor candidate is certified.

Line of Sight

Line of sight refers to the notion that makers of products can achieve the best quality by keeping the customer in their line of sight. Regardless of the function, regardless of the relative level of authority and responsibility within the organization, each individual employee must have a clear line of sight to the customer.

Joe Bransky, General Motors representative to the Supplier Quality Requirements Task Force and US member of the International Automotive Task Force (IATF), succinctly stated the international automotive industry's position in a speech to the ASQ World Congress in 2002. He said in part:

"The focus on product realization and the process approach is the way we [automotive industry] do business. We think there was legitimacy to the complaint that the current quality system requirements were too oriented to procedures based on an element-by-element approach (and subsequent element-by-element assessment). What we have here (the automotive "single/unified" process approach) is an approach that sets up the system (and audit trail) based on the line of sight from the agreed-upon customer requirements to the operator instructions, and back to what was delivered to the customer. It's a better correlation with the way a business, any business, operates."

Process Approach

While product realization, and the tools, forms and procedures that support it, has been a focus of the automotive industry's quality leaders for several years, the process approach is relatively new. Processes have long been recognized as the lifeblood of the manufacturing system, but an understanding of all the workings of an organization as processes is relatively new. This new recognition is called the process approach. ISO 9001:2000 defines the process approach in the following manner.

> For an organization to function effectively, it has to identify and manage numerous linked activities. An activity using resources, and managed in order to enable the transformation of inputs into outputs, can be considered as a process. Often the output from one process directly forms the input to the next.
>
> The application of a system of processes within an organization, together with the identification and interactions of these processes, and their management, can be referred to as the "process approach."

This new understanding is also graphically depicted in ISO 9001:2000 in a graphic entitled the "Process Model." (See Figure 13-3.)

The process approach definition and the conceptual, graphic depiction of the approach, as a process model, are fully embraced by the automotive industry. But both have been supplemented by the automotive industry.

Unlike most of the sector supplementation found in ISO/TS 16949:2002, the additional language concerning the process approach is not a requirement. The information provided by the automotive industry in this area should be seen more as advice or instruction.

The quality leaders of the automotive industry recognized that though they embraced and encouraged the process approach there was a problem. A preponderance of anecdotal evidence indicated to them that the automotive industry's supplier quality management leadership did not understand the process approach; the quality leadership within the OEMs themselves did not under-

Figure 13-3

The Process Approach as Seen in ISO 9001:2000

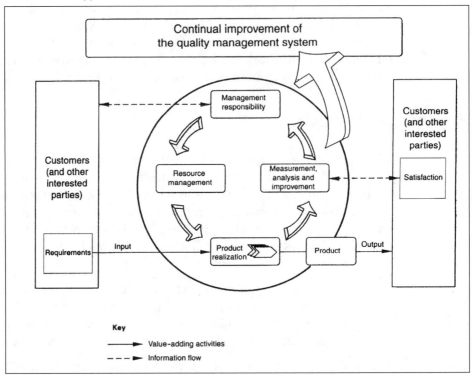

stand it and, perhaps even more surprising, the third-party certifiers did not understand it. This recognition provided the impetus for the development of an automotive position regarding the process approach and a plan to communicate that position to stakeholders.

IATF's Position

There was an early recognition by the IATF that the process approach, if properly understood, implemented and audited, could provide substantial value to the OEMs and to the organizations that supplied them. As Joe Bransky acknowledged in his speech: "It's...the way a business operates."

The IATF had little trouble integrating the requirements, clarifications and guidelines it perceived as necessary to spell out the quality management needs of OEMs and the supply chain associated with them. As stated earlier, while the effort culminated in the creation of ISO/TS 16949:2002, the oversight bodies created a series of companion documents to support the technical specification,

Rules for Achieving IATF Recognition, QMS Assessment Checklist, IATF Guidance to ISO/TS 16949:2002.

IATF recognized that the process approach, the lynchpin to the other pieces developed to improve quality system performance, was not well defined, that perhaps, it was not defined at all.

It recognized that the process approach could not be legislated. Measuring, monitoring, providing certain system elements, submitting pieces of evidence, etc., were parts of a quality system that could benefit from common rules. But processes were an entirely different matter. While individual processes may have common characteristics and elements, when interlinked and networked to create a complete system, their complexity, variability and uniqueness preclude

Figure 13-4

Internal/External Interface Between an Organization and a Customer

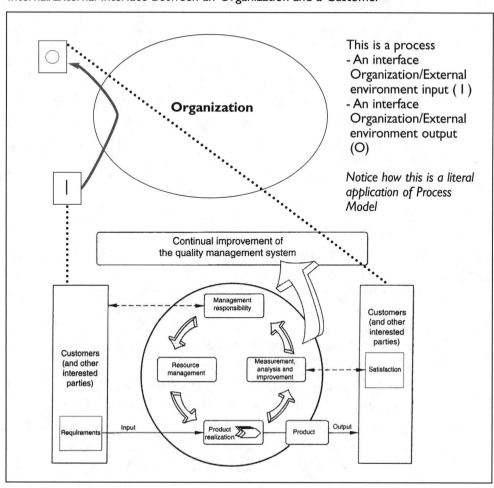

the use of prescriptive rules. IATF reasoned that too much regulation in this area would prove counterproductive.

The IATF turned to the Training Commission to provide a solution, since its mission is to develop and maintain a certification training program for certification body/registrar auditors.

With such an important role to play in the process — auditing the quality management systems of each and every organization that sells parts and products to the automotive OEMs at least once a year — it is critical that auditors understand the process approach. Their actions, questions and modeling while conducting an on-site audit convey a clear indication of OEM expectations with regard to the process approach. And suppliers to OEMs, in an effort to align themselves with OEM expectations and to adopt the most useful business practices, look to the third-party audit function to provide a clear picture of what the OEMs want and what the OEMs deem important.

There is a clear recognition within the IATF that auditors who talk the talk and walk the walk of the process approach will be a key influence as to how the supply base will gain value from the process approach. Additionally, auditor training that has been given a worldwide stamp of approval provides a basis for the development of supplier training to ISO/TS 16949:2002 around the globe.

The IATF's Training Commission attempted to develop a certification training program that will not only assist auditor candidates in understanding the requirements and intentions of the technical specification and its companion documents (including customer-specific requirements) but also promotes development of a fundamental and nonrestrictive structuring of the process approach in an organization.

Automotive Process Approach

The first stumbling block in attempting to conceptualize a process approach that would meet the definition (and expectation) stated in the Technical Specification "…a system of processes within an organization, together with the identification and interactions of these processes, and their management…." was to make sense of the process approach definition.

It is relatively simple to identify a process. It has an input, a transformation and an output. It can be illustrated in a simple diagram. (See Figure 13-5.)

But this simplicity and applicability, though making the concept accessible, also constitutes a problem. Since processes are inherent in all human activities, one might conclude that nearly everything that happens in an organization, partic-

Figure 13-5

A Process

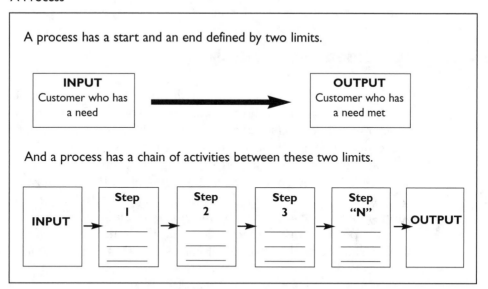

ularly a manufacturing organization, is a process. If true, which it certainly is, then one might ask, How can identifying processes be helpful to a quality management system? Isn't a quality management system at its heart about control, consistency and improvement? If everything is a process, how does an organization get its collective arms around a system in a way that it will gain control, provide consistency and support improvement? How indeed!

The IATF definition of the process approach, as detailed by the Training Commission, is more of a reflective illustration of the process approach than a prescription of how it must be structured. The process approach, according to the IATF, must be fundamental in its method and generic in application. In that way it provides a type of benchmark that can be applied directly and/or can be used to compare the organization's unique application of the process approach.

IATF recognized that it could not afford to stand back and do nothing. The fear, based upon a collective memory of past events, was that any void would be filled by interpretations delivered by all-too-willing individuals and groups with little or no understanding of automotive processes. Further, the process approach, if applied inappropriately, can create confusion and damage the dream of a worldwide quality management system for all automakers and their suppliers.

The subsequent automotive consensus of the process approach can be described as a single or unified approach to processes.

The method to define the process approach began as a question. That question: How does an organization account for all its processes in a single, unified, understandable process approach?

Customer-Oriented Process

The "process model," as defined and illustrated by the writers of ISO 9001:2000, ISO/TC 176, provided the first part of the answer. On the input side are customer requirements (specifications, expectations, etc.); on the output side is the level of customer satisfaction (needs met, expectations fulfilled, etc.). In the middle are the processes of the organization. The problem was that the illustration depicted the interaction between the customer and the organization as having a single occurrence. That simply was not a realistic portrayal of the number of customer interactions with the organization over the span of a typical product realization process. It is more realistic, at least in terms of the automotive industry, to consider several sets of requirements and several times when the customer satisfaction level can be affected. There are several of what have come to be known as Customer-Oriented Processes (COP).

A simple definition of a COP is those processes that begin with a customer requirement/specification (input) and end in the requirement being met (output).

Notice that there is no specific mention about the importance or criticality to the organization or key role in all that happens within the organization. Why? Because this is simply an identification process. They are what they are. COPs are a straightforward and simple means of identifying those processes that exist due to a specific interface with the customer. They are a direct application of the process model with the exception that the recognition of Customer-Oriented Processes adds a critical dimension — number. There are several interfaces between customer and organization. The following illustrations attempt to describe the adaptation of the process model to the COP application.

If we apply the COP definition to something generic like an automobile dealer and service center we might wind up with something like Figure 13-6.

The car dealer and service center example illustrates the central tenets behind the need for the recognition of multiple interactions between the customer and the organization. The tenets are:

- Each interaction has the potential to be successful or not.
- Each interaction has the potential to lead to customer satisfaction or not.
- Each interaction has the need for a network of processes to support it.

Figure 13-6

The Process Approach for a Car Dealership Service Center

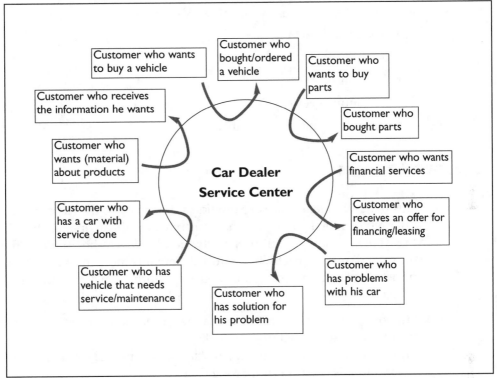

- Each interaction must be supported by the organization, but the customer may not use them all and may enter into any one of the interactions as a first interaction.

COPs exist in every organization whether or not the organization chooses to formally recognize them in its quality or business management system. This realization sets the stage for the need to establish a process approach that is able to bring about the "identification and interaction of [the] processes, and their management," which can lead to an improved quality management system and improved performance by the organization.

To assist organizations in identifying these processes, IATF developed a list of generic COPs. It is not meant to be exclusive and exhaustive but is provided to give organizations some direction. The list, stated as descriptive labels not inputs and outputs, is as follows:

- Market Analysis/Customer Requirements
- Bid/Tender

- Order/Request
- Product and Process Design
- Product and Process Verification/Validation
- Product Production
- Delivery
- Payment
- Warranty/Service
- Post Sales/Customer Feedback

Support Processes

Customer-Oriented Processes provide a direct link to the customer, but they do not present a total picture of what transpires within an organization. They comprise only a small portion of the activities; however, they serve as the impetus (or should) for other activities within the organization. In reality, the lion's share of activities within an organization is performed by processes that support COPs.

Supporting processes are those planned processes whose input, output and transformational activities are established and maintained by an organization in order to comply with requirements/specifications and/or in order to meet the organization's needs in supporting COPs.

While the role of COPs are more for identification than invention, this is not the case with support processes. They are sometimes mandated by requirements, regulations and/or standards, but the organization still has significant discretion in creating, organizing and maintaining them.

As a general rule, organizations need to recognize and apply two truths about support processes: 1) they are in place to support COPs or other support processes, and 2) they are in place to mitigate risk. Because most organizations that implement ISO/TS 16949:2002 are not implementing a quality system for the first time, these truths are used most appropriately to analyze the processes already in existence.

No one set of analytic questions concerning the processes in an organization are able to fit every situation, but the following sets of questions provide a helpful foundation for establishing the need for, and adequacy of, processes.

Need

- Does the process support a COP and/or another support process?

- Does the process mitigate any current or potential risk?

Adequacy

- What is the customer requirement? (Input of both internal and external customers)

- What must be delivered to the customer? (Output of both internal and external customers)

- Who will be involved in the process? (What is their training need? Knowledge? Skills?)

- What technology is needed to support the process? (What equipment, infrastructure and so forth are needed?)

- How will the specifics of the activities be communicated? (What instructions, procedures and methods/tools are needed?)

- What will be measured and how will it be measured? (What are the performance indicators?)

These questions can be asked at any level of the system processes, even at the COP level. In the case of COPs, simply substitute the following for the first question under the heading: "Need." Does it support a customer interface (input and output)?

At other levels (support, and support of support [what some refer to as sub-support]) the first and second questions regarding adequacy often refer to an internal customer. The final, external customer is kept in mind at all times, but the most immediate need is to fulfill the need/requirement of the receiver of the process's output.

The closer to the COP (and, of course, the COP itself) the greater the chance that a process will need to mitigate risk. Each process may require additional processes in order to mitigate potential risks; but regardless, each process must always be able to competently fulfill the questions listed earlier regarding need and adequacy.

In summary, risk is handled two ways by a system dependent upon the process approach structure:

- Establishing processes that are needed to support other processes

- Competently and thoroughly answering the questions regarding need and adequacy.

The bottom-line goals for a system aligned with the process approach are that all risk be mitigated in a way that the organization and customer find acceptable, and that all processes be in place to mitigate risk. Both goals will ultimate-

Figure 13-7

Customer-Oriented Process and Support Process

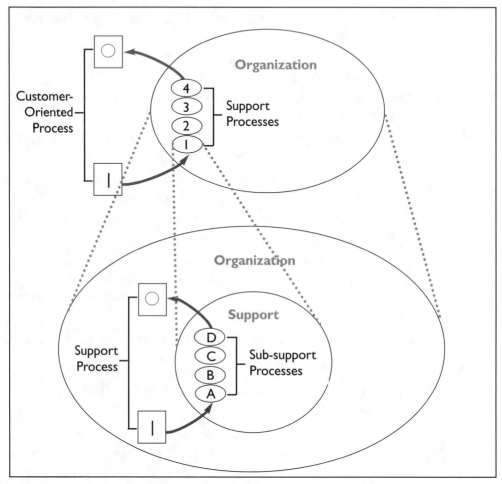

ly lead to effectiveness and efficiency, both of which are requirements to organizations wishing to align themselves with ISO/TS 16949:2002.

Stated simply: the goals must be that "it works, and time, money and effort was not wasted in getting it to work."

A simple, conceptual picture of a Support Process is shown below. Both the Customer-Oriented Process (COP) and the Support Process are shown in Figure 13-7 to give a relative picture of their relationship.

Perhaps the most important element to consider when attempting to understand the process approach — in this case as represented by abstract models of COPs, Support Processes and Sub-Support Processes — is to understand what is being sought and what is being found. If control is being sought, it will not be found. However, it is safe to say that to the extent that increased predictability is inherent, control will increase. But what will be found (and should be sought) is order. Once the order, pattern, outline, model, blueprint, mold, prototype, by whatever label it is given, is understood, then individuals, groups and organizations (as well as the technologies that serve them) can participate more effectively and efficiently with one another.

The pattern of the process repeats itself again and again in the organization (and any system); the pattern of the process itself — input, transformation, output — and the pattern of linkages and interconnections — COP (or equivalent interfaces with the external environment) to processes which support the interfaces to processes, which in turn support the support processes to processes, which in turn support the support processes of the support processes, and on and on, until the processes are indistinguishable, or to distinguish them is of no value.

There is relatively little difference in the questions that need to be asked about the processes of an organization:

- What is the pattern of processes that make up my business/ my work?
- What processes are connected?
- Why are they connected?
- Why aren't they connected?
- How are the processes connected?
- What is predictable and unpredictable in those connections?

Notice that little has been stated or asked about performance as yet. That is for a reason; the pattern, the order, needs to be understood before performance can be anticipated, measured, monitored, altered, improved, etc.

The all-too-often truth is that organizations, like individuals and groups, begin to measure, monitor and change before they have a clear picture of order. Or they move in another direction that is equally hurtful over the long term, which is to not attempt to improve what is not broken ("if it ain't broken, don't fix it"). The inaction by the organization, group or individual is because the "ain't broken" process is not fully understood as to why the it works in the first place; so, an attempt at improvement could very well end up hurting what it was intended to help, or so it is concluded.

An automotive organization exists because it has processes in place that can support its interactions with its customers. It will improve and prosper when it is able to fully understand the pattern of those processes and the patterns of their interconnections with one added ingredient.

Figure 13-8

Management Processes

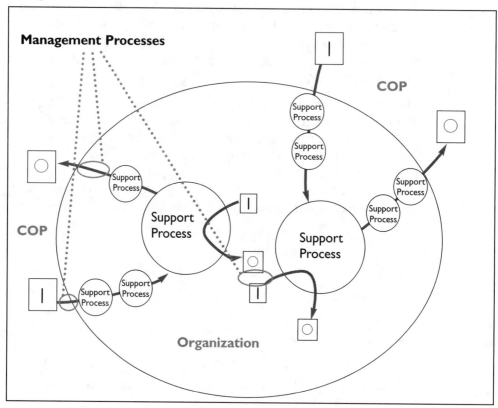

A third type of process is needed because this process category is instrumental in assuring that improvement and change are able to take place. The third type of process in the single/unified process approach is Management Process.

Management Processes

Management Processes are defined like this: all processes determined to be management processes in order to comply with the requirements of the Standard/Technical Specification and/or determined by the needs of an organization. These processes focus upon the determination of the quality policy, objectives, related responsibilities and the means by which they are implemented, and are those processes that are developed for the purpose of making decisions based on the data generated by all other processes (COPs and Support) in an organization's system (a network of processes) in order to direct and lead the organization.

A simple, conceptual drawing of the Management Processes, along with their relative relationship with COPs and Support Processes, might look something like Figure 13-8.

What the drawing attempts to point out is that Management Processes function in those situations that are required by the customer and/or needed by the organization, that determine standards of quality and that have a need for decisions based on quality data. Some of the situations are a planned and repeated activities within a quality management system like management review and internal auditing. Others are unplanned (but anticipated), like problem solving, mentoring, etc.

The three categories of processes, Customer-Oriented, Support and Management, form a "Single/Unified Process Approach." Single and unified are the terms used to describe the automotive view of the process approach because it draws attention to the need to classify processes according to one, consistent, unified theme. The theme chosen by the IATF to illustrate its point is the concept of customer orientation as the central premise. All processes within the organization can be tracked to these oft-repeated processes. In the converse, if the processes in an organization (each in its own fashion) do not contribute in some manner to understanding what the customer requires, as to how that requirement can be met and making sure the requirement is met, then perhaps the process (or processes) is not needed.

With this understanding of the process approach, the organization can determine that each process within the organization can be placed in one of the three categories. In this way, the IATF's application of the process approach allows for all members of the organization to see "where they fit" and to establish and maintain a "line of sight" to the customer. Also, the relationships of inputs and outputs, the dynamics of processes feeding other processes, and the measurements necessary to manage and improve each, become more and more obvious.

ISO/TS 16949:2002 Requirements

As a general rule, the best way to think about the Technical Specification's application to a quality management system, which is structured according to a process approach, is to recognize that each of the five sections of the Technical Specification apply to each of the processes in the organization. Like the fundamental questions regarding need and adequacy, each of the sections must be considered when assessing the compliancy of each process. Are the expectations for a quality management system met by the process? Do they need to be? (4 Quality Management System) Are the expectations for managing the process met by the process, or the processes, which support it? Do they need to be? (5 Management Responsibility)   Are the expectations for resources to support the process contained within the process or somehow met by other processes in the system? Do they need to be? (6 Resource Management) Are the expectations for the product's realization achieved by the process? Do they need to be? (7 Product Realization)   Are the expectations for measurement, analysis and improvement achieved by the process? Do they need to be? (8 Measurement, Analysis and Improvement)

It is important to remember that the requirements and expectations of ISO/TS 16949:2002 must at all times be considered in the context of the process approach. Without the context of the process approach, considerations regarding the quality management system will be without basis. Decisions arrived at based on those considerations will not be based on fact because facts are in most cases dependent upon context. As a result, what is a problematic issue in one system may not be in another system. A process that seems to be compliant, when checked in isolation, may not be, when checked in the context of the processes to which it is linked and interconnected.

In total, the process approach to be implemented well, maintained well and audited well requires a significant amount of effort. That is bad news for organizations having to work harder with fewer resources. The good news is that it appears it is an effort well worth expending. Early indications suggest that the dividends are real, that the effort is worth the investment. Though not perhaps quite as dramatic as the improvements realized during some of the first implementations of quality management systems, the impact is significant. Careful, comprehensive and well-adapted implementations of the process approach are yielding benefits that are significant on any measurement scale. Reduction in non-value-added processes and redundant processes are the first level of savings. A better understanding of outputs leads to less rework. A measurement system that actually understands what to measure and how to measure it can be calculated in saved time and resources. It is harder for management, when confronted by information that is timely and factual, to deny the obvious and easier to make the right decision at the right time.

But there is a dark side. What if the organization does not respond appropriately to the Technical Specification? What if the Certification Body auditors do not audit in a manner that ensures that critical nonconformances are detected and value is brought to the organization that goes beyond the certification of the organization? What if the customer arrives at the conclusion that their words have fallen on deaf ears; that the supply chain and the groups that audit the chain do not understand and do not appreciate the customer's objectives and the processes in place to achieve them?

Foresight

ISO/TS 16949:2002 adds the following words to the ISO 9001:2000 text to clarify what is meant by customer satisfaction in the automotive industry.

"Customer satisfaction with the organization shall be monitored through continual evaluation of performance of the realization processes. Performance indicators shall be based on objective data and include, but not be limited to:

- delivered part quality performance,

- customer disruptions including field returns,

- delivery schedule performance (including incidents of premium freight), and

- customer notifications related to quality or delivery issues.

The organization shall monitor the performance of manufacturing processes to demonstrate compliance with customer requirements for product quality and efficiency of the process." (8.2.1.1, Customer satisfaction – Supplemental, ISO/TS 16949:2002)

Although only four phrases in total length, the minimum expectations listed by this portion of the Technical Specification are sweeping. Directly and succinctly, they direct the organization to consider, as a minimum, those matters that are truly important to the customer. What are they? 1) Good parts — parts that work and fit the way they are supposed to; 2) good parts delivered on time and durable — parts that meet the expectations of #1 and do not shut down assembly plans due to other avoidable screw ups; 3) good parts that don't cost more — elimination of screwups that cause delays in shipping and as a consequence must be shipped by the most expensive means; 4) a customer that is kept informed about any issue related to #1-3.

A critical examination of the four statements reveals that, though the statements are stated as minimum expectations, they are really more than that. Yes, the customer is saying that, from a customer's perspective, this is the entirety of what the customer really needs. Yes, these statements aren't fabrications; the customer is telling the organization the truth. But, what often is misunderstood by the organization reading these four phrases is the significance of what the customer is asking the organization.

Perhaps it is easiest to ascertain their significance by posing a question: Can these four, which are end results not processes, be achieved without a full network of processes that fully support a quality management system? The answer is — not likely. Consequently, what looked like a small matter, a reduced, bare bones scope of the elements that are essential to the customer, is in reality a succinct, results-oriented statement of customer expectations.

The Future

What does the future hold? What changes are on the horizon? No one can predict what decisions will be made by the automotive industry regarding quality management systems in the future.   At present, speculations about the future range from an internationally recognized, transportation-specific quality management system (aerospace, cars, trucks, trains, etc.), which includes a universal set of support tools, to no quality management system requirement.

Perhaps the best action, and what organizations should do in most instances, is to review the past in order to better understand the future. What does the automotive industry's quality management system's past tell us about its future? Are there trends that can be detected over the history of the automotive quality management standards and their applications?

Trends

There are three trends. First, and foremost, the automotive industry has sought tighter and tighter control over the third-party audit system since their acceptance of the notion of a third-party audit system in the early 1990s. This will continue.

Second, and related to the first, the automotive industry has raised the bar for the expectations of performance and understanding for automotive auditors as opportunities to do so have presented themselves. This will continue.

Third, and related to the first and second, the automotive industry has raised the standard of performance for its suppliers and has increasingly put suppliers on notice when their performance did not measure up to expectations. This will continue.

What do these trends indicate? The automotive industry is serious about quality management. They have invested a significant amount of time and effort into the formulation of their version of the standard — the ISO/TS 16949:2002 — and its predecessors. They have invested a huge amount of time, effort and money ensuring that their supply base has integrated, or is in the process of integrating, quality management within each organization. They have invested a significant amount of time, effort and money in creating a program to train and certify auditors, and to provide oversight to the certification bodies that employ the auditors.

The automotive industry believes that a critical component toward improving the overall performance of the supply base is to improve the quality management auditing of their suppliers. These quality audits can be improved by their getting more directly involved in overseeing the actions of the certification bodies and the qualification of the auditors who represent the certification bodies. This effort has carried along with it a substantial price tag.

The automotive industry's patience is running thin. Unknown to most constituencies is the ongoing research being conducted by the automotive industry regarding their return on investment into quality management system implementation, auditing, maintenance and upgrading. Thus far, the results have been mixed. The terseness of 8.2.1.1, Customer satisfaction, indicates a no-nonsense approach. "[T]he organization shall be monitored through continual evaluation of performance of the realization processes." "Performance indicators shall be based on ..." "The organization shall monitor the performance..."

When viewed in composite with the other indicators of the customers' needs, wants and desires, the amount of investment by the automotive industry, the provisions for training and certification of auditors, as well as organizations, and the directness of language and expectations spelled out in the Technical Specification, the conclusion that the automotive industry is giving the system one more try before moving to some other means of quality improvement is not a huge leap.

Conclusion

Oversight, Line of Sight and Foresight are three key concepts in understanding the content, directions and future of ISO/TS 16949:2002 in the worldwide automotive industry. Each concept will play a watershed role in what is envisioned to be critical years in the application of international quality requirements/standards, including third-party auditing, in the automotive industry.

Key Terms

Customer-Oriented Process (COPs) — those processes that begin with a customer requirement/specification (input) and end in the requirement being met (output).

Support Process — all planned processes whose input, output and transformational activity(ies) are established and maintained by an organization in order to comply with requirements/specifications and/or in order to meet the organization's needs in supporting Customer-Oriented Processes.

Management Process — all processes determined to be management processes in order to comply with the requirements of the standard/technical specification and/or determined by the needs of an organization. These processes focus upon the determination of the quality policy, objectives, related responsibilities and the means by which they are implemented; and are those processes which are developed for the purpose of making decisions based on the data generated by all other processes (COPs and support processes) in an organization's system (a network of processes) in order to direct and control the organization.

Quality Health Care — A Path Forward

14

by Dan Reid

Early in 2001, a new tool, "Quality Management Systems — Guidelines for Process Improvements in Healthcare Organizations," based upon ISO 9004:2000, was released for use by health care organizations in implementing or improving their quality systems. This international guidance document is the result of efforts over the past few years by the American Society for Quality (ASQ) Health Care Division, with over 2,000 health care practitioners, and the Automotive Industry Action Group (AIAG), which includes Daimler-Chrysler, Ford, General Motors and the United Auto Workers, with help from the US health care accreditation bodies.

Why the Automobile Industry Cares...

There are a couple of reasons why the automobile industry is driving a health care initiative. In 1997, a senior GM executive asked if ISO 9000 could be applied to health care as it had been to the automotive production supply chain with QS-9000 for significant gains in quality and cost. In supplier surveys, it has been documented that QS-9000 has provided up to a 3:1 return for all (internal and external) compliance-related costs, and nearly 17:1 return for out-of-pocket certification costs.[1] In the most recent survey, the suppliers, who averaged $130 million in annual sales, reported average savings of 6 percent of sales, or about $8 million as a result of QS-9000. In addition to cost and quality, suppliers also reported as benefits of QS-9000: improved processes and delivery, better understanding of jobs and tasks and improved morale. Note that health care represents the largest single cost to each vehicle we make. Health care costs run billions per year. Even a 1 percent reduction in this cost would save millions annually.

Further, several groups met with President Clinton in December 1999 to discuss plans to improve patient safety in the United States through medical error reduction. The discussions stemmed from an Institute of Medicine (IOM) report on medical errors that estimated as many as 98,000 people die annually from preventable medical errors in hospitals. This is reported to be more than the number who die from car accidents, AIDS, workplace injuries or breast cancer.[2] Of the people GM covers, on average, this equates to more than one life each day. Research shows that almost every tenth patient suffers from preventable harm and adverse effect related to their care and that variation among health care providers is big. This cannot be explained by patient characteristics.

Isn't Health Care Accreditation Enough?

In the United States, health care organizations are accustomed to accreditation. Considering the number of errors and variation in health care, the basic principles of process management are still a challenge.[3] In the June 2000 issue of *Quality Progress*, Dr. Paul Schyve of the Joint Commission for Accreditation of Healthcare Organizations (JCAHO) wrote: "Quality approaches initially developed for other industries hold promise for improving the performance of health care organizations."[4] ISO 9000 was specifically mentioned. Separate crosswalks between ISO 9001 and the existing health care accreditation criteria published by JCAHO, the National Committee for Quality Assurance (NCQA) and the American Accreditation Health Care Commission (URAC) respectively, have revealed significant gaps in the health care criteria to the ISO 9001 elements. These include requirements for document control, purchased product control, control of inspection, measuring and test equipment, inspection and test status and internal auditing. Also, it has been reported that the accuracy of medical technology, e.g., calibration of equipment and/or devices, is poorly managed in a health care organization.

Adding ISO 9001 to the Equation...

ISO 9001 defines the generic minimum requirements for a fundamental quality system. The ISO 9000 series is written to apply to all types of companies, but the new revision, ISO 9001:2000, improves the standard's applicability to service sectors, e.g., health care.

The model now being offered by the joint ASQ Health Care Division and AIAG group is that ISO 9004:2000 should be used to define the fundamentals of the quality system and should support the use of the existing relevant health care sector documents, e.g., accreditation criteria, regulatory requirements. There is concern that some health care organizations opting for ISO 9000 certification will use it as a substitute for accreditation criteria. Both are required to address specific quality management needs of health care organizations. In fact, the Malcolm Baldrige National Quality Award criteria for health care can also be added to the fundamentals in defining a world-class health care quality system.[5]

Use of ISO 9000 in health care is on the rise globally. There are now over 600 ISO 9000 certifications worldwide that we know of. In the United States, the Centers for Medicare and Medical Services (CMS) reportedly require ISO 9000 certification for purchases over a specified value. A recent study revealed that there are at least seven different documents created by national bodies as guidelines for the interpretation of ISO 9001/9002 for health care. The countries involved are Australia, Ireland, Israel, New Zealand, Switzerland, United Kingdom and United States. In addition, five countries made use of ISO 9002 interpretations, but had not generated guidelines.[6] These do not include the myriads of documents generated by consultants or certification bodies for use by their health care clients. Further compounding the problem is that these documents provide conflicting information. Some would have only minor impact on the overall quality management system, but others "would completely alter the perception of the system."[7] The study cited points to several examples of significant discrepancies, e.g., design control, servicing and the definitions of "supplier" and "product" between the various existing documents.

The Problem with the Existing ISO 9000 Documents

In a review of several of the health care guidance documents under development or currently released, e.g., CENITC 251 Health Informatics, NCCLS GP-26A *A Quality System Model for Health Care: Approved Guideline* (10/99), ANSI/AAMI EQ56, none define the term "product."

The organization's product is integral to ISO 9000. ISO 9001:2000 specifies quality system requirements where an organization needs to demonstrate its ability to consistently provide product that meets customer and applicable regulatory requirements as well as enhance customer satisfaction.[8] The use of this term has been a stumbling block for most service sectors who believe that they do not provide "product." ISO 9000:2000 defines product as the "result of a process," and identifies four generic product categories in a note: services, software, hardware and processed materials. Thus, it is clear that services are, in fact, addressed in the ISO 9000 family of documents. Further, health care clearly involves processes and relates to the use of the term "process."

Design control is another element of major conflict in the existing manuals. Tor Janson and Roland Jonsson of SWEDAC are quoted in *ISO 9000+14000 News* as saying, "The particular version of the standard that is most applicable to a health or dental clinic is ISO 9002, or ISO 9001 for those that perform research and development."[9] Others also believe that only those organizations that develop health care protocols and the like would use ISO 9001. This reflects the misunderstanding of the term "product."

In the new ASQ/AIAG document, the ISO 9000 definition of "product" has been retained, but for health care it has been further refined as "typically the planning, design and delivery of patient care, service, training or other, e.g., research, radiograph…"[10] If you consider this definition, it is clear that primary product of the health care provider is the care plan.[11] The provider must diagnose the patient's problem, "design" and implement the care plan. Saying they are not design-responsible is analogous to saying that the chef is not design-responsible for meal service because he/she did not design the ingredients in the recipe (e.g., "ketchup") or that the airline company is not design-responsible for the flight service because they did not design the aircraft.

In order to make sense of the ISO 9001 standard, it is critical to identify the organization's product. From this, you can then identify the customer and components of the process, i.e., the inputs and outputs. This is also important when seeking third-party certification of the system, as it will be used to define the scope of registration on the certificate. True, the health care provider does not typically design the protocols used, but they design the "product," i.e., health care, that they deliver and for which they are compensated. A scope of registration should accurately define what specific product/service is provided by the organization.

The issue of design control is often further confused with the issue of subcontracted design services. ISO 9001 has been used for two-party contractual situations, i.e., customer and supplier. In this context, one party has to be ultimately "design-responsible" for the product supplied in the transaction. If the customer is not design-responsible for the product they are procuring from the supplier, then the supplier must be. If the supplier chooses to subcontract the design, they must still be responsible for the design to the customer. If, on the other hand, the customer selects a third-party design provider as a condition of the transaction, they are then design-responsible in the contract. This understanding can be particularly helpful in health care, where physicians are typically not employees of the hospital where they practice and where health care is provided to a given patient across a number of providers. This continuum of care can be understood within the ISO 9001 model when you understand the "product" that each provider offers across the continuum.

For example, a patient goes to the doctor with various complaints. The doctor provides a diagnosis, designs and implements a "care plan" for that patient and is compensated for that service. However, the plan may call for X-rays and referrals to various other specialists, rehabilitation or home care services. Each of these provides a service to the patient and is compensated for that service. Thus, each one provides a unique "product" to the customer, i.e., patient. This is a critical issue which goes well beyond the quality management system — that is, typically, no one practitioner is ultimately responsible for the coordination of the health care services across the continuum of care by a number of providers. With no one ultimately in charge of the "quality" of the total care across providers, there can be problems, e.g., prescriptions issued by different providers that have adverse effects when used in combination for the same patient.

Purchased Product

Practitioners have also identified another common problem in health care. Hospitals often run short of supplies on off shifts, e.g., weekends. The method of obtaining replacement supplies is not well understood in the organizations. Years ago, an effective method of inventory management, the "pull" system, was identified in other industries, e.g., retail, automotive. "Pull" is based upon replenishment of stock based upon consumption. In the manufacturing industries, "pull" is an enabler of lean manufacturing, which has proved to be much more effective and efficient than the traditional "mass" production inventory management method, i.e., "push" or replenishment of stock based upon forecast. "Pull" has been incorporated into the new health care guidance document as a recommendation to address the stock-out situations in health care.

An Opportunity To Harmonize

In the new ASQ/AIAG health care guidance document, additions to ISO 9004:2000 have purposely been kept to a minimum to promote its use. Most of the additions provide information on the International Organization for Standardization, common definitions and health care examples for the ISO 9004:2000 generic text. Examples of additional content to drive improvements are error-proofing, control of measuring and monitoring devices (supplemental to ISO 9004), business planning and managing patient care processes.

The stated intent of the document is to:

- Improve the quality and safety of delivered health care through enhanced overall accreditations and process improvements, increasing the value added to the organizations and provided to their customers

- Improve the image of the organizations, increase customer confidence and have a tool to reward quality

- Maintain consistency in the global approach with QS-9000 and other ISO 9001 sector-specific documents (e.g., AS9100 for aerospace, ISO 13485 for medical devices, TL 9000 for telecommunications and ISO 15189 for medical laboratories)

- Develop/incorporate a process that is actionable

- Include terminology and examples familiar to health care personnel

- Minimize/reduce the burden on providers.

It is clearly stated in the document that it does not constitute a set of criteria for third-party certification purposes. In addition, the document will be applicable to health care service providers, but not to medical device manufacturers, clinical laboratories, or regulated sectors, e.g., FDA, which have their own ISO-9000-based technical standards.

The document has been offered to ISO as a baseline document to encourage the harmonization of the conflicts in the existing health care ISO-based documents, It has been written at the most fundamental level for quality systems in order to complement, rather than replace, existing health care sector documents that "assume" the fundamentals and press on with technical content. Last year the European Accreditation (EA) Cooperative announced they were launching a new group to do the same thing. Discussions are now under way to see if these efforts can be combined.

In September 2000, ISO approved an AIAG/ASQ proposal to develop an ISO Industry Workshop Agreement (IWA) document using their HC1 document as a base. Note that ISO changed the name of this new portfolio of documents from ITA to IWA near the time of the IWA 1 publication. The project was approved and an international workshop was held in January 2001 in Detroit. There were about 130 heath care "experts" from at least 17 countries in attendance. The final document was subsequently approved by 89 percent of the voting participants and IWA 1 was published in September 2001. The IWA 1 content is nearly identical to its AIAG/ASQ predecessor.

In 2001, the Institute of Medicine (IOM) published "Crossing the Quality Chasm: A New Health System for the 21st Century." It follows their 2000 report, "To Err Is Human," which reported that up to 98,000 people die annually in the

United States due to systemic preventable medical errors. The focus of the new IOM report is how the health care delivery system can be redesigned to improve care. The report proposes an "agenda" supported by concrete recommendations.

Some people in health care have said that quality improvement principles widely applied in other industries (with significant success) are not applicable in health care. The Committee on the Quality of Health Care in America formed in 1998 and which authored the IOM reports, rightly states that application of these principles to the health care sector is the critical first step in improving patient safety. They recommend that the Agency for Healthcare Research and Quality with others convene workshops involving representatives from health care and other industries. The objective would be to identify and implement stat-of-the-art approaches to address the challenges of redesigning health care on this scale. The new ISO IWA 1 document is a logical answer to this recommendation.

To date, health care organizations that have implemented an ISO 9000-based management system have reported benefits including improvements in customer satisfaction, standardized operations, throughput, cost, purchased product, documentation control, problem solving, patient communications and control of measuring equipment. The ISO 9000-based system also helps with regulatory compliance, risk management and consideration of new initiatives or innovation. IWA notes that, "ISO 9000 does not specifically define 'what' needs to be done by a health professional. That is to be done by consensus of appropriate professionals. Rather, ISO 9000 can be used to ensure that the right activities are carried out consistently and in a controlled manner."

As in sports, you don't win the game without being sound in the fundamentals. We all have a vested interest in the health care sector getting "good" at the fundamentals of their "game." This subject has already been the topic of a lot of interesting discussion. We value your feedback. If you would like to help, discuss this initiative with your own health care providers, and with your company health care benefits people. Together we can make a difference.

Endnotes

1. 1997-1998 ASQ/AIAG Quality Survey.
2. Institute of Medicine, "To Err Is Human," National Academy Press, copyright 2000.
3. The Quality of Health Care I Hospital Activities, report by The Working Party On Quality Care in Hospitals, HOPE, The Subcommittee of Coordination.

4. *Quality Progress*, June 2000, ASQ.

5. The Quality of Health care I Hospital Activities, report by The Working Party On Quality Care in Hospitals, HOPE, The Subcommittee of Co-ordination.

6. "Interpretations and Variations of ISO 9000 in Acute Health Care", I. Sweeney, Irish Society for Quality in Health Care, C. Heaton, CASPE Research.

7. Sweeney and Heaton, ibid.

8. ISO 9001:2000, Clause 1.1.

9. *ISO 9000+14000 News*, International Organization for Standardization (ISO), Vol. 8, No. 2, Mar./Apr., 1999, page 12.

10. Committee Draft 4 — Quality Management Systems — Guidelines for process improvements in health care organizations, Clause 3.1.13, ASQ Health Care Division and AIAG, May 21, 2000.

11. Committee Draft 4, ibid, Clause 0.2.1.

AS9100 Aerospace Quality Management System Standard

by Dale K. Gordon

This chapter will detail the specifics of the aerospace industries Quality Management System standard AS9100. The references included herein are based on the year 2001 version. A full discussion of the 1999 version of the standard is not required, as there is a direct read across from the 1999 version to the 2001 version as far as the aerospace industry-specific requirements are concerned (a cross-reference is provided later in this chapter). Both versions are ISO 9001-based documents, which correspond to the 1994 and 2000 versions respectively. If the 2001 version is purchased prior to December 2003, then both versions will be made available from the Society of Automotive Engineers (SAE).

The oft-asked question is, Why are the ISO 9000 standards insufficient for the aerospace industry and why the need for a separate standard? The answer can best be summed up in the words: safety, reliability and maintainability. While these areas are not unique to the aerospace industry, they have significant impact on the customers' use of the products and services provided throughout the industry. Also, because of the regulated nature of the commercial segment of the industry it was felt that instead of viewing the regulations as additional requirements they should be imbedded in the quality system from the start.

Origins of AS9100

In 1995 several aerospace prime manufacturers came together again under the umbrella of the American Society for Quality (ASQ) and, recognizing the need for better and uniform requirements for the supplier community, created the American Aerospace Quality Group (AAQG). This group's original "aim" was "to procure higher quality, lower cost materials and services, faster and more reliably from a stable long-term supplier base." The first order of business was the creation of a common set of requirements for the industry. The AAQG first discussed the use of ISO 9001 as a stand-alone document. Discussions with the Automotive Industry Action Group (AIAG) around the creation and use of QS-9000 planted firmly the concept that an ISO 9001-based document tailored for aerospace was a doable undertaking. The first product of this attempt was published by SAE in October 1996 as an Aerospace Requirements Document, ARD 9000.

Subsequent to the interim publication, some changes happened within the AAQG. They left the umbrella of ASQ and became an SAE Aerospace Council subcommittee. The AAQG began to see its mission as creating requirements, providing solutions and bringing homogeneity to the quality side of the industry. Refinement of the ARD 9000 document led to a final release by SAE in May of 1997 as AS9000.

While satisfied with the result of AS9000, the AAQG recognized that all the Original Equipment Manufacturers (OEMs) operated in a global economy and they needed to extend and include the worldwide aerospace supplier community. To this end the ISO TC 176 was approached along with other sectors about sector-specific standards. The proposal was rejected at the time as not in concert with the ISO "spirit" and was tabled for further study. In 1998, ISO TC 20 (Aerospace) agreed to sponsor Working Group 11 (WG 11) to create an ISO technical paper for quality systems requirements using AS9000 as a basis along with a corresponding document called prEN 9000-1. Unknown to the AAQG at the time, the European aerospace group known as AECMA developed a similar document to supplement ISO 9001.

The ISO TC 20 WG 11 included the United States, four European countries (England, Spain, France and Germany) and also Brazil, Mexico, Canada, China, Japan and others. All recognized the need and desire to have a specific industry standard. There was one major problem: if published by ISO TC 20 it would take additional time and would lose its "9000" number, as did the similar effort by the worldwide auto industry with the QS-9000 harmonization. So the decision was made to have the harmonized document, that is still based on ISO 9001:1994(E), published by each individual country's aerospace association or standards body. In the United States the harmonized standard is an SAE document, AS9100. In Europe it is AECMA EN9100. It is also to be published in Japan and China as a 9100-numbered document. The 9100 number was acknowledgement of the ISO 9001 origin. All 91xx documents have come to symbolize all the internationally harmonized documents that have been produced by the aerospace industry.

AS9100: 2001

Quality Management Systems – Aerospace – Requirements (based on ISO 9001:2000)

For sake of clarity it is assumed that the reader has an understanding of the ISO 9001:2000 version and will recognize the words and general requirements of that standard. This discussion will center on the aerospace-unique requirements in the AS9100 document. They will appear in bold in this text and the ISO 9000:2000 text appears in italics. The headings are as per the ISO 9000:2000 document.

Foreword

To assure customer satisfaction, aerospace industry organizations must produce, and continually improve, safe, reliable products that meet or exceed customer and regulatory authority requirements. The globalization of the aerospace industry, and the resulting diversity of regional/national requirements and expectations, has complicated this objective. End-product organizations face the challenge of assuring the quality of, and integrating, product purchased from suppliers throughout the world and at all levels within the supply chain. Aerospace suppliers and processors face the challenge of delivering product to multiple customers having varying quality expectations and requirements.

This document standardizes, to the greatest extent possible, quality management system requirements for the aerospace industry. The establishment of common requirements, for use at all levels of the supply chain, by organizations around the world, should result in improved quality and safety, and decreased costs, due to the elimination or reduction of organization-unique requirements and the resultant variation inherent in these multiple expectations.

Structure

This standard includes aerospace requirements applied to, and integrated with, both the ISO 9001:2000 and the ISO 9001:1994 quality management system models. Organizations should select one model for use based on their

current ISO-based quality management system, intentions concerning transition to the ISO 9001:2000 model, contractual requirements and other considerations. The model chosen shall be documented in the organization's quality manual.

It is important to note that the industry professionals that created the standard are passionate about the responsibilities that they have to the people who use and depend upon the products produced by the industry. They understand very clearly that the decisions about "fitness for use" can have dire consequences if not properly carried out. Also, the technologies involved in the industry products and processes, coupled with the depth and dependence of these products on fully integrated systems, means that the ability to inspect quality in the product is almost impossible.

The thing the writers of the standard recognized is that we could make an immediate difference in the proliferation of Quality Management System (QMS) requirements in the industry and throughout the supply chain. This "customization" of basic requirements for QMS processes has caused an excessive amount of effort in both enforcement and application. As the "good quality professionals" that we are, we convinced ourselves that reduction in the variability of these requirements was not only doable, but also necessary.

Introduction

0.1 General

Nothing was added to this section of ISO 9000:2000.

0.2 Process approach

There was no supplementation to this area as the industry has long held that the process approach is a basic tenet of quality in the aerospace industry. However, that said, the industry was very much built on the foundation (and in fact CAA rules require) that all products must be found, and can be proven, to meet their design intent or conformity prior to delivery or application. This means that inspection is necessary when process capabilities are not known or can not be proven.

1 Scope

1.1 General

This standard includes quotations from BSR/ ISO/ASQ 9001:2000, the technical equivalent of ISO 9001:2000 quality management system requirements, and specifies additional requirements for a quality management system for the aerospace industry.

It is emphasized that the quality management system requirements specified in this standard are complementary (not alternative) to contractual and applicable law and regulatory requirements.

Very much like the ISO 9001 document, the AS9100 standard is seen as both an internal requirement and a flow-down requirement from customers to suppliers. Likewise it is recognized that there is a "pecking order" to requirements. Since many aerospace companies fall under the purview of the Federal Aviation Administration (FAA) or other Civil Aviation Authorities (CAA), work for the Department of Defense or other national defense organizations, or the National Aeronautics and Space Agency (NASA) or other space agencies. They are subject to the regulatory, criminal and civil laws that apply to doing business for the flying public and these agencies. AS9100 does not contravene these laws and regulations and is seen to emphasize that they exist and need to be taken into consideration when creating a QMS.

The AS9100 document is rooted in the need to make sure that all suppliers within the aerospace industry supply chain understand that it is a regulated industry and by supplying product or services to this industry they are subject to these same laws and regulations as the OEMs. This is true regardless of whether or not these requirements appear on their purchase order/contract requirements or not. This theme is recurrent throughout the standard and is purposely redundant to emphasize the point.

1.2 Application

Nothing added to this section.

2 Normative reference

Members of ISO (International Organization for Standardization) and IEC (International Electrotechnical Commission) maintain registers of currently valid international standards.

The industry, owing to its military origins, is replete with acronyms, so it was decided to educate the uninformed as much as possible, ISO not excluded.

3 Terms and definitions

Key characteristics: The features of a material, process or part whose variation has a significant influence on product fit, performance, service life or manufacturability.

Here is the first hint of things to come. The aerospace industry took back what it had originally developed. The industry is generally credited with the widespread requirement of performing failure modes effects analysis (FEMAs) to determine the possible failure modes of components and systems during the design process. As the FEMAs were performed, critical features were identified that require special attention and assurance that are correct during the manufacturing and maintenance activities. Also, they provide for risk mitigation plans and the creation of redundant features or systems.

The automotive industry picked up on the need to flow these characteristics through the supply chain when the QS-9000 supplements were created. The aerospace industry recognized the value in the automotive approach and has reapplied it.

4 Quality management system

4.1 General requirements

While in fact there are over 80 additions to the basic ISO 9001 standard in the original AS9100 (1999), the basic premise of the need for a QMS is not argued or debated in the industry. The aerospace industry is one that has coined "system integration" and is a strong believer that system performance is critical to mission success. The ISO 9001:2000 revision has actually reduced the number of aerospace-specific requirements that were originally developed, as the standard is now process focused (which as we all know is the basis of quality).

4.2 Documentation requirements

4.2.1 General

The quality management system documentation shall include:

f) quality system requirements imposed by the applicable regulatory authorities.

Here again, we introduce the aspect of the CAA requirements that the commercial aviation part of the industry must adhere to. In the US Code of Federal Regulations (CFR) 14 part 21, the FAA requires all holders of production certificates to comply with subpart G. Since most of the larger aerospace companies now are operating to one basic quality system for all products — civil, industrial, military and space — the QMS must document all requirements.

The organization shall ensure that personnel have access to quality management system documentation and are aware of relevant procedures. Customer and/or regulatory authorities representatives shall have access to quality management system documentation.

Here the industry felt that it was not enough to just have documented procedures, but that they must be readily available to the personnel performing the work. Time and again audits have revealed that procedures are written and then locked away in the manager's office for fear that the floor personnel will not keep them up to date and create an audit nonconformance.

It is a statement of the obvious perhaps, but not all employees need to know about all of the QMS documentation or all procedures. This is nearly impossible in very large organizations and not always practical in any organization. If we truly believe that people in organizations are supposed to follow a documented and proven process, then a concerted effort must be taken to identify those QMS procedures that are applicable to each individual's job and that they are properly trained on them. Again, this may seem redundant, but this is how problems occur in delivered product, and in aerospace, problems can not be tolerated 30,000 feet in the air (or in "orbit" for that matter).

4.2.2 Quality manual

The organization shall establish and maintain a quality manual that includes

b) the documented procedures established for the quality management system, or reference to them, and

—when referencing the documented procedures, the relationship between the requirements of this international standard and the documented procedures shall be clearly shown.

This may be a bit of overkill perhaps, but the industry felt that it is not our job to decipher the documentation of an organization's QMS. As many of the ISO 9000 pundits will say, the documented system does not have to match the requirements of the standard in format and numbering. Well, we agree with that, but we are not going to waste precious time of the internal and external auditors trying to figure out if a company has all the necessary items documented. So here we are not only asking, but requiring, a roadmap for an organization's procedures. When we are investigating a failure, time is of the essence and we don't wish to waste it reading documents that are not relevant to the process in question.

4.2.3 Control of documents

The organization shall coordinate document changes with customers and/or regulatory authorities in accordance with contract or regulatory requirements.

As said earlier, the CAA may require the organization to submit its documentation of its procedures for assurance of product conformity to the authorities prior to implementation. This statement is to make sure that any changes are also routed through that same approval process. The FAA states in CFR 14 part 21 paragraph 21.147, that the holder of a production certificate shall immediately notify the administrator (FAA) of any change that may affect the inspection, conformity or airworthiness of the product. In some cases the holder of a CAA production approval may also require its suppliers to submit quality manuals or other documents for approval, so it can so comply with CAA requirements throughout the supply chain. Also, some organizations have approval rights over certain types of processes and therefore require any changes to the documentation of these processes to also be approved.

4.2.4 Control of records

The documented procedure shall define the method for controlling records that are created by and/or retained by suppliers.

The ISO 9001:2000 paragraph preceeding this sentence required the creation of documented procedure(s) describing the control of records. The aerospace industry wanted to make it clear that each link in the "chain of evidence," as it were, is solid. We require that an organization not only be responsible for the records it creates, but also control the records created by suppliers that show conformance with requirements, and each subtier supplier in turn be responsible for its suppliers. In some cases this goes right down to the raw materials used and the ore from which it was created. We already know that a defect in a raw material forging can bring down an airplane (see record of investigation of the Sioux City, Iowa, crash of a DC-10 in 1989).

Records shall be available for review by customers and regulatory authorities in accordance with contract or regulatory requirements.

This may be obvious from 4.2.3 above, but since that dealt primarily with changes to documentation and approval of the changes, it was felt that it was not harmful to restate the requirement again in no uncertain terms. Records are sacred to the industry and, when so stated by law or contract, shall be made available to anyone with the authority to ask.

4.3 Configuration management

The organization shall establish, document and maintain a configuration management process appropriate to the product.
NOTE: Guidance on configuration management is given in ISO 10007.

This is a very important requirement within the industry. Since it is not always known what effect changes may have on the product it is important to know and have the level of change and design standard that each part, process and product was created from. Aerospace products can last over 50 years and we have yet to know the limits of some of the products that have been put into service in outer space. With the ability to maintain, repair and overhaul products, the need to maintain configuration management is paramount to keeping the products in service.

5 Management responsibility

ISO 9001:2000 paragraphs 5.1 to 5.4 got away unscathed as it's hard to argue with "motherhood and apple pie." The industry wholly endorsed the concepts and requirements presented.

5.5 Responsibility, authority and communication

5.5.2 Management representative

Top management shall appoint a member of management who, irrespective of other responsibilities, shall have responsibility and authority that includes

d) the organizational freedom to resolve matters pertaining to quality.

Say what you will, but quality personnel from the major aerospace companies wrote the standard and they know from experience that the responsibility they carry is not for the faint of heart. Also, when it comes down to the decision to "fly or not to fly" we don't want schedules or profit to taint someone's judgment (just ask the people at NASA about the space shuttle Challenger disaster). The people responsible for quality must have the organizational freedom to make the hard choices and implement corrections necessary for the protection and safety of the products. This is not a part-time responsibility. Quality managers have gone to jail and been heavily penalized for failure to act in cases where people's lives could have been at stake.

6 Resource management

6.4 Work environment

The organization shall determine and manage the work environment needed to achieve conformity to product requirements.

NOTE: Factors that may affect the conformity of the product include temperature, humidity, lighting, cleanliness, protection from electrostatic discharge, etc.

The NOTE that is added to 6.4 was originally part of a separate aerospace requirement that is now reduced to a note since the year 2000 version covered our concern in general. The note now emphasizes the fact that the work environment can have as much of an effect on product quality as materials and process. Stray static electricity has been known to render complete systems inoperable. Oil from compressed air has been known to corrode some of the exotic alloys used in aircraft. Temperature changes have been known to affect measurements, especially when the tolerances used are in microns and millionths of an inch or centimeter. The industry expects the process designers to have knowledge of the environment as it relates to the product and take every precaution necessary to protect the products and components from unintentional damage.

7 Product realization

7.1 Planning of product realization

In planning product realization, the organization shall determine the following, as appropriate:

> **e) the identification of resources to support operation and maintenance of the product.**

The concept of aftermarket support is very important in the aerospace industry. Even in the space program (with the advent of the space shuttle) aerospace vehicles are not "disposable assets" (except missiles). The cost of engines, airframes and launch vehicles is so great that they must remain in service for long periods and be able to be maintained for a useful life to justify the expense. Even something as complex as the Hubble telescope must be conceived with the notion that it can be repairable and/or upgraded (which in fact it was). So this requirement clearly states that the organization must consider what resources will be required to operate and maintain the product after delivery even if that is not the organization's function. This is especially true of subsystem components that are typically not designed by the end user or vehicle manufacturer.

7.2 Customer-related processes

7.2.2 Review of requirements related to the product

The organization shall review the requirements related to the product. This review shall be conducted prior to the organization's commitment to supply a product to the customer (e.g., submission of tenders, acceptance of contracts or orders, acceptance of changes to contracts or orders) and shall ensure that

> **d) risks (e.g., new technology, short delivery time scale) have been evaluated.**

The premise is straightforward and very important to all types of activities, but especially critical to the tight schedules and the program management principles being employed throughout the aerospace industry. When reviewing contracts and/or requirements for delivery of a product or service one of the things that must be considered is the risks involved with being able to deliver; not the least of which is, Does the organization have enough time to do all the necessary steps of design, manufacture, testing and delivery? Does the time allotted take into account state-of-the-art technologies that may not yet be proven on a production scale? Many an aerospace program has suffered from huge cost overruns or delayed deliveries (years) from trying to "push the envelope" in the design of the product or the manufacturing capabilities. These things must be considered before companies sign on the dotted line. Typically, failure to deliver is considered a "quality" problem even though the product meets all the design requirements.

7.3 Design and development

7.3.1 Design and development planning

The organization shall plan and control the design and development of product.

During the design and development planning, the organization shall determine

a) the design and development stages,

- in respect of organization, task sequence, mandatory steps, significant stages and method of configuration control

Where appropriate, due to complexity, the organization shall give consideration to the following activities:

- structuring the design effort into significant elements;

- for each element, analyzing the tasks and the necessary resources for its design and development. This analysis shall consider an identified responsible person, design content, input data, planning constraints and performance conditions. The input data specific to each element shall be reviewed to ensure consistency with requirements.

Now we get into the really "fun" parts of the standard. Most quality experts will tell you that quality starts with design. Even the late Dr. Deming started the "PDCA cycle" with the plan or design element. In aerospace we feel the importance in design is no different. Here is where the aerospace industry has put a lot of thought and where many of the additional requirements have been placed. This addition to the design and development planning is really a reminder that during product planning these stages need to include the organizational aspects, task sequence and configuration control — in essence, program management of the design process, the critical path and the resources required. The program plan should align with the product performance, customer and regulatory requirements. Some may read these as mandatory requirements, but they are not necessarily so. It depends on the complexity of the design effort and the product involved. Where there are multiple teams designing different aspects of the product, this becomes a necessity and a requirement.

The different design and development tasks to be carried out shall be defined according to specified safety or functional objectives of the product in accordance with customer and/or regulatory authority requirements.

Certainly, it may seem a bit of overkill or being lazy, but the industry does not want to play a guessing game about how the design parameters and tasks satisfy the customer's requirements for product performance and safety. In CAA-certificated products there are specific functional and safety parameters that must be met. This includes such things as fire prevention/containment, the ability to handle lighting strikes and corrosion prevention. Even noncertificated products now have to include such design considerations as the use of environmentally friendly materials and processes in manufacturing.

7.3.3 Design and development outputs

Design and development outputs shall

> **e) identify key characteristics, when applicable, in accordance with design or contract requirements.**

Here is the first use of the key characteristic requirement. Key characteristics can be any characteristic of the part or product. The determination that it is "key" must be made during the design phase and it is an output of the design process. The method of identification can be by any means the company desires when not specified by the customer or contract. In many cases the customer may specify a higher level characteristic of the product that must be met, and the next level design authority must incorporate that characteristic through the design to the lowest level component that will affect that higher level characteristic. In some cases these characteristics may not be measurable at the component level, so they may lead to process characteristics that may be controlled. We are looking to the designers to make sure that the people that have to make or produce the products understand what the important features are. The FEMA process, safety or other similar considerations typically determine these characteristics. It is not acceptable to say "because it is a critical part" all features of the part are key characteristics. If this were true we could never afford to manufacture the items economically enough to stay in business.

All pertinent data required to allow the product to be identified, manufactured, inspected, used and maintained shall be defined by the organization; for example:

> **- drawings, part lists, specifications;**
>
> **- a listing of those drawings, part lists and specifications necessary to define the configuration and the design features of the product;**
>
> **- information on material, processes, type of manufacturing and assembly of the product necessary to ensure the conformity of the product.**

A lot of discussion was held around the word "pertinent." We could not come up with a better word so we left it to the users of the standard to define it. Certainly we expect the design source to define and create the data that identifies the product, such as specifications or product descriptions. Create any necessary process specifications or process control requirements and inspection methods to assure that the design parameters are maintained. If the product is serviceable or needs some maintenance action to maintain its life and performance characteristics in all defined operating conditions, the necessary documentation to do this must also be created.

7.3.4 Design and development review

At suitable stages, systematic reviews of design and development shall be performed in accordance with planned arrangements (see 7.3.1)

c) to authorize progression to the next stage.

The design review process must be an orderly and thorough activity. In the best methods of program management it is necessary to have the outcomes of these reviews discussed at the necessary levels in the program. This will allow acknowledgement of the success of the design effort and the suitability of the design work to be continued or suspended until all design issues or corrective actions required are addressed.

7.3.5 Design and development verification

NOTE: Design and/or development verification may include activities such as:

- performing alternative calculations,
- comparing the new design with a similar proven design, if available,
- undertaking tests and demonstrations, and
- reviewing the design stage documents before release.

This NOTE was added for emphasis on what the aerospace industry believes and knows to be natural outcomes of the design and development processes. It is not a requirement, but it is expected that this is the objective evidence that would be available when reviewing the outcomes of this process. All of these items may not be available, but they would or should exist in some combinations. Design and development verification needs to be appropriate to the product. As the complexity increases, then we expect the outcomes to be more than just having a check of design documents for errors.

7.3.6 Design and development validation

NOTES

- Design and/or development validation follows successful design and/or development verification.
- Validation is normally performed under defined operating conditions.
- Validation is normally performed on the final product, but may be necessary in earlier stages prior to product completion.
- Multiple validations may be performed if there are different intended uses.

This is the same rationale as the verification process. Validation can be defined in terms of the concept of designing a house. The design verification process is the process by which the review is made to see if it is structurally sound, will support the necessary loads and meets all the codes and regulations. Validation is the process by which you make sure the house is what the customer wanted. Is it the right size? Are the rooms properly located? Is there enough pantry space? Are the materials used in accordance with customer needs and wants? This is the "validation" phase of the process.

7.3.6.1 Documentation of design and/or development verification and validation

At the completion of design and/or development, the organization shall ensure that reports, calculations, test results, etc., demonstrate that the product definition meets the specification requirements for all identified operational conditions.

This is a culmination of the above paragraphs. It is well proven that this is a critical task in the design process. It may restate the items presented above, but in these instances we have simply expressed the industry's view of the requirements. Here we are stating that it must be clearly demonstrated that the design verification and validation process was performed and not just by writing reports. The reports must prove that what's in the report really matches the product and that the product will meet the requirements in all conditions (usually this means environmental and operating envelope characteristics). Just as automotive products have to work as well in Alaska as they do in Nevada, the same is true for aerospace products, but even more extreme — from weightless environments to high gravity forces, from desert heat to outer space cold, from airport taxiways to Mach 2 or better flight conditions. Many of these cannot be tested as a completed system in a test cell so the calculations or subsystem tests must support the reality.

7.3.6.2 Design and/or development verification and validation testing

Where tests are necessary for verification and validation, these tests shall be planned, controlled, reviewed and documented to ensure and prove the following:

   a) test plans or specifications identify the product being tested and the resources being used, define test objectives and conditions, parameters to be recorded and relevant acceptance criteria;

   b) test procedures describe the method of operation, the performance of the test and the recording of the results;

   c) the correct configuration standard of the product is submitted for the test;

d) the requirements of the test plan and the test procedures are observed;

e) the acceptance criteria are met.

This requirement is only applicable where design verification and validation is accomplished through testing of components, products and deliverables. This requires rigor in the testing process. Crucial is item "c," which requires that the correct configuration be tested. Many times the design or prototype article is not the same as the production or final design configuration. It needs to be established that the item being tested is fully representative for the purposes of the test.

7.3.7 Control of design and development changes

The organization's change control process shall provide for customer and/or regulatory authority approval of changes, when required by contract or regulatory requirement.

In many cases the customer is involved in the design activity or the approval of the design outputs. This requirement reinforces the need to pass all design changes by the customer as well. What may seem a minor change to the designers from a product standpoint may be a major issue to the customer, based on operating conditions that the designer may not be aware of. For civil aviation products the CAA is the issuer of a type certificate that states that the regulatory authority has reviewed and approved the design. Major changes to these designs must be resubmitted and approved by that same authority.

7.4 Purchasing

7.4.1 Purchasing process

The organization shall be responsible for the quality of all products purchased from suppliers, including customer-designated sources.

In many cases the customer may designate that special process sources or other providers of material or services meet the customer's system requirements or process specification requirements. In many cases the customer has made this determination and designated the use of a particular supplier. However, this determination and designation does not alleviate the responsibility of the receiver of the actual product to determine its fitness for use upon receipt. Also this requirement re-emphasizes that every organization is responsible for subtier suppliers as far down the supply chain as they can go.

Supplier control is an area that has reached the notice of CAA's defense and space customers. They recognize the level of partnering and supplier networks that are involved in delivering aerospace products. As such the industry has maintained or added additional requirements from the original ISO 9001 standard.

The organization shall:

a) **maintain a register of approved suppliers that includes the scope of the approval;**

This requires that there is a list of approved suppliers available and that the list includes what the supplier is approved for (based on demonstrated capability) in terms of work or products.

b) **periodically review supplier performance; records of these reviews shall be used as a basis for establishing the level of controls to be implemented;**

Call it supplier ratings or incoming product quality metrics or whatever, but data must be collected on the performance of the supply chain and how it is performing relative to requirements. The results of these reviews/measures shall be used to determine the level of inspection and oversight necessary for each individual supplier. It is not necessary to do supplier surveillance just for the sake of doing surveillance. Data shall determine the amount and types of oversight that should be invoked as well as the risk involved with the product. Risk is always implicit but also stated elsewhere in the standard.

c) **define the necessary actions to take when dealing with suppliers that do not meet requirements;**

It should be clear in the organization's procedures what actions will be taken when supplier performance falls below specified levels or does not meet the performance level deemed acceptable. Evidence of these actions should also be part of the records that are maintained.

d) **ensure where required that both the organization and all suppliers use customer-approved special process sources;**

This restates what was said in 7.4.1 when customers identify sources to be used, that deviations are not allowed unless customer consent is obtained. In some cases organizations may have to ask if there are special process sources that must be used or obtain the latest approved list from the customer. In some cases this will appear as a contract requirement, but often gets overlooked in application.

e) **ensure that the function having responsibility for approving supplier quality systems has the authority to disapprove the use of sources.**

This is also fairly straightforward. In many cases the quality organization is asked to "approve" suppliers and add them to the register for the organization. Many times the procurement organization may insist on continued use of the supplier for delivery or cost reasons even when the product quality is below standard or there is a significant problem with the supplier's QMS. However, the organization that is assigned to determine "fitness for use" of a supplier shall not be overruled by another.

7.4.2 Purchasing information

Purchasing information shall describe the product to be purchased, including where appropriate.

While the industry does not necessarily like to use "where appropriate," we are trying to cover a lot of ground and need to allow for applications based on the product. When is it appropriate and who determines? Either the customer or the supplier may determine when it is appropriate. Does the customer have to specifically require these items? The answer should be "no." It is appropriate to expect any or all of these if the product or process or service requires this level of control.

d) the name or other positive identification, and applicable issues of specifications, drawings, process requirements, inspection instructions and other relevant technical data;

This is just assuring that all the technical information is communicated to the supplier. Even relevant specifications that are buried inside specifications are important and should be identified. It has been shown time and again that one of the most common causes of product nonconformance is the omission of the total package of requirements through the supply chain.

e) requirements for design, test, examination, inspection and related instructions for acceptance by the organization;

If there are specific requirements that must be met before or upon delivery for design, testing or inspections, this needs to be made clear in the contract requirements. This is especially true if there are specific processes or requirements that must be met rather than leaving it to the supplier's decision.

f) requirements for test specimens (e.g., production method, number, storage conditions) for design approval, inspection, investigation or auditing;

If test articles or verification specimens are required or necessary to determine compliance/approval, then any special marking or handling should be identified in the contract. In some cases this may be a flow-down requirement from the customer.

g) requirements relative to

- supplier notification to organization of nonconforming product and

- arrangements for organization approval of supplier nonconforming material;

There is some work being done by the industry in this area. Some customers have unique reporting requirements and there is required information to be reported. AS9131 is a harmonized process for nonconformance reporting. It defines the requirements for the data, not necessarily the format or media for submittal. Some customers will require electronic submittal. There also need to be clear procedures and documentation on how the organization approves non-conformances from suppliers. Where the approval is delegated based on design ownership, this must to be clear in the flow-down requirements.

> **h) requirements for the supplier to notify the organization of changes in product and/or process definition and, where required, obtain organization approval;**

Aerospace companies have what is referred to as fixed or "frozen" processes. These are typically manufacturing processes that produce flight or reliability critical parts. The reason they are fixed is that the processing itself may induce some characteristic that could affect part performance or life. Once the process is established and proven to have no detrimental affects on the item, it may be frozen so no intentional or unintentional changes can be made without an analysis of the change by the design authority to determine the change effects. This requirement must be sent all the way through the supply chain whenever it is present or invoked.

> **i) right of access by the organization, their customer and regulatory authorities to all facilities involved in the order and to all applicable records; and**

This has been a standard requirement of all defense and civil aviation product contracts for some time. This just keeps the industry from having to restate it. It also applies all the way down through the supply chain.

> **j) requirements for the supplier to flow down to subtier suppliers the applicable requirements in the purchasing documents, including key characteristics where required.**

This again is a restatement of the items mentioned above, but the recurring theme here is that no supplier in the supply chain is immune from these requirements if they are applicable based on the product or service provided. Key characteristics are especially important for the same reasons that we use frozen processes and other methods of controlling critical features (see AS9103 for guidance).

7.4.3 Verification of purchased product

Verification activities may include

> a) obtaining objective evidence of the quality of the product from suppli-

ers (e.g., accompanying documentation, certificate of conformity, test reports, statistical records, process control);

b) inspection and audit at supplier's premises;

c) review of the required documentation;

d) inspection of products upon receipt; and

e) delegation of verification to the supplier, or supplier certification.

The list above is partially guidance and partially requirement. The word "may" means that there are several methods that can be used (either alone or in combination) to satisfy the industry needs for verification of purchased product. However, some method or combination of methods must be chosen and shown to be a robust, supported and effective process. The industry is not interested in a lot of non-value-added inspections. They are often costly and not always effective. However, if the inspection function is delegated, there must be proof that the process is effective at the delegated source. Where documentation is the sole means for acceptance, there must be knowledge that the data creation process for the documentation has integrity.

Purchased product shall not be used or processed until it has been verified as conforming to specified requirements unless it is released under positive recall procedure.

This requirement actually dates back to the military requirement in Mil-Q-9858. This allows companies to accept material or product into their facility and use it under certain conditions while awaiting a verification test or other acceptance test to be performed on a sample or specimen. It can only be used if there is a way to assure that all the material or product can be reclaimed or captured should the test or acceptance data show the product/material to be noncompliant. The organization must guard against even the remote possibility that unapproved material or product gets shipped to a customer.

Where the organization utilizes test reports to verify purchased product, the data in those reports shall be acceptable per applicable specifications. The organization shall periodically validate test reports for raw material.

In the list of verification activities it was shown that data might be used as a means of acceptance for product and material. In the case of raw materials, suppliers typically rely on the test reports from the supplier or broker that is supplying the sheet, bar, tube, billet, shot or other raw product. Testing this material can be time consuming and expensive; however, these materials are literally the building blocks upon which success or failure of aerospace products depend. If it is not right to begin with, there is very little margin left to maintain the product integrity and there is every chance that nonconforming material will make its way into the customer's hands. The industry is requiring that some verification testing of the data be performed on a periodic basis. How often? That probably depends on the volume of purchases, types of materials and knowledge about the data source. One method of compliance that has been effective is to run an SPC chart on the incoming data points and take corrective action when drift is observed. Or if the data is "flat lined" then you know that it is not real data because there has to be some variability between different lots of material. The use of a laboratory that is independent of the data source or one that is approved by a customer is required for validation.

Where the organization delegates verification activities to the supplier, the requirements for delegation shall be defined and a register of delegations maintained.

This supports the list of verification options. When delegation is used as the means of verification, such as certified supplier programs, or "dock to stock" plans or hidden feature approval is given to suppliers, there must be a procedure defining how this delegation is controlled. It is also a direct FAA requirement to maintain a list of these delegations as stated in FAR Part 21.143(b). The list needs to be specific by supplier and part number or other identification of product and the delegation.

Where specified in the contract, the customer or the customer's representative shall be afforded the right to verify at the supplier's premises and the organization's premises that subcontracted product conforms to specified requirements.

This reiterates the requirement that has existed since Mil-Q-9858, that reserves the right of the customer at the highest level to go down into the supply chain as deep as necessary to determine conformance of requirements. This is typically noted or invoked in the terms and conditions of a contract.

Verification by the customer shall not be used by the organization as evidence of effective control of quality by the supplier and shall not absolve the organization of the responsibility to provide acceptable product, nor shall it preclude subsequent rejection by the customer.

Just because an inspector from the customer inspects product in the organization's facility or internally, that is not a final assurance that product meets its requirements. Certainly latent defects and performance issues are hard to address during inspections and the organization cannot use the customer's inspection as their own verification of conformance or substitute it as the inspection process. The customer reserves the right to reject the product upon receipt or use if it is proven not to meet specified requirements, regardless of prior inspections.

7.5 Production and service provision

7.5.1 Control of production and service provision

Planning shall consider, as applicable,

- **the establishment of process controls and development of control plans where key characteristics have been identified;**

When the customer requires the control of key characteristics, it is expected the method of creating control plans and the processes to support process and variation management are developed prior to production and are included in the planning activity.

- **the identification of in-process verification points when adequate verification of conformance cannot be performed at a later stage of realization;**

This requires that some forethought be put into the product planning process when there are hidden features or product characteristics that can not be determined to be conforming at the final stage of completion. The organization should have the necessary inspection or testing points and/or process control methods established to create objective evidence that these types of features are verified in process, as necessary.

- **the design, manufacture and use of tooling so that variable measurements can be taken, particularly for key characteristics; and**

This acknowledges that the tooling decisions (including gauging) are part of the product realization process. This applies not only to key characteristics but to all features, as appropriate. Continuous improvement is greatly facilitated when actual measurements can be taken, rather than "go-nogo" measurements. This says that during planning, the tooling to be used and the corresponding measurement process should allow for the capture of the actual measure to the necessary degree of accuracy to determine the process capability. This is required for key characteristics.

- **special processes (see 7.5.2).**

Planning for special processes is especially important and this probably underemphasizes the point. The sequence of the process to be used and the special process itself can be critical to determining product conformity. In some instances the special processes can be detrimental to the product if not properly controlled or implemented. This requires careful planning and error proofing of the special processes that will be used.

The organization shall plan and carry out production and service provision under controlled conditions. Controlled conditions shall include, as applicable

g) accountability for all product during manufacture (e.g., parts quantities, split orders, nonconforming product);

These are not optional requirements. When are they "applicable"? When the product or process is such that these controls can and should be evident. This requirement is the "positive identification" requirement during all phases of product realization. At no time can the industry stand the possibility of an incomplete product, nonconforming part or unknown quality product being shipped and installed in an aerospace product. The organization needs to maintain positive control over all products during manufacture to assure their identification and status.

h) evidence that all manufacturing and inspection operations have been completed as planned, or as otherwise documented and authorized;

This is related to the item "g" above as well. It conveys the same message and meaning. Not only does the organization have to track the product, but it must maintain the necessary control in documented form to assure that all operations are complete and the product conforms to agreed requirements.

i) provision for the prevention, detection and removal of foreign objects;

This is an area that is essential to aerospace products. Some argue that foreign object prevention should be limited to assemblies or gas paths of engines. This is not correct. Foreign objects can create havoc in any system or component on an aerospace vehicle. Machining chips left in a machined housing can block an oil passage and starve a bearing to failure. Loose objects in a digital control box can short out a circuit board. Dirt and debris can block an air passage that would create false commands to the control mechanisms. A minute piece of dirt in a fan disk forging can bring down an aircraft. At all stages of manufacture, assembly, test and maintenance the prevention and detection of foreign objects is critical.

j) monitoring and control of utilities and supplies such as water, compressed air, electricity and chemical products to the extent they affect product quality; and

This is similar to the NOTE in 6.4, but is worth restating here as well. In this age of digitally controlled manufacturing, what effect will an electrical surge have on product conformity? Does the compressed air used to dry or blow off parts have traces of oil or water that may be corrosive and cause a part failure later? Could chemicals used to process items, if not properly stored or neutralized, attack the materials they are in contact with? Any environmental factor that could create a risk to the product integrity and life must be controlled.

k) criteria for workmanship, which shall be stipulated in the clearest practical manner (e.g., written standards, representative samples or illustrations).

What's the old saying: A picture is worth a thousand words? When trying to explain acceptance criteria, it is best to do so in the simplest of terms with illustrations and pictures wherever possible to show the difference between a conforming product and a nonconforming product so there can be no mistake. Trying to determine the correct wiring or routing of hoses using a schematic is very difficult. Translating two dimensions into three is always difficult. A picture can always do better.

7.5.1.1 Production documentation

Production operations shall be carried out in accordance with approved data. This data shall contain as necessary

a) drawings, parts lists, process flow charts including inspection operations, production documents (e.g., manufacturing plans, traveler, router, work order, process cards); and inspection documents (see 8.2.4.1); and

b) a list of specific or nonspecific tools and numerical control (NC) machine programs required and any specific instructions associated with their use.

This requirement is something that most companies already do. It must be clear what process and tooling methods are used to make the product. This is an important baseline that must be maintained in order to determine that processes are repeatable and what the impact of a change might be. Additionally, it should be very clear to any operator or manufacturing person what the process and tooling are and the special instructions that are needed to use the tooling (gauging) or to operate the equipment.

7.5.1.2 Control of production process changes

Persons authorized to approve changes to production processes shall be identified.

Who is authorized to make changes in the documentation listed in 7.5.1.1? Can the operator make decisions on how to manufacture the product? Is a manufacturing engineer responsible? What is the authority and how is it recorded that the changes are made properly and approved?

The organization shall identify and obtain acceptance of changes that require customer and/or regulatory authority approval in accordance with contract or regulatory requirements.

In those cases where there are fixed or "frozen" processes or process procedures, changes to these may require approval of the customer in accordance with customer requirements. In some cases, the process or procedure is so critical to flight safety that a regulatory requirement may control it and require change approval.

Changes affecting processes, production equipment, tools and programs shall be documented. Procedures shall be available to control their implementation.

Even "seemingly" minor changes in an N.C. program have been known to have disastrous results on product conformity or have other unintentional effects. Even if the process is not customer controlled, all changes must be documented. This extends to the tools and the programs that control them.

The results of changes to production processes shall be assessed to confirm that the desired effect has been achieved without adverse effects to product quality.

Once it is decided to make a change in the processing or tooling, the effects of those changes have to be evaluated. It was shown that even a minor change in the sequencing of operations was the source of latent defects on space vehicles and alike. A change in a plating operation sequence caused cracking on welds on parts of the main engines of the space shuttles, causing costly delays and scrap expense.

7.5.1.3 Control of production equipment, tools and numerical control (N.C.) machine programs

Production equipment, tools and programs shall be validated prior to use and maintained and inspected periodically according to documented procedures. Validation prior to production use shall include verification of the first article produced to the design data/specification.

The process must be proven to be acceptable and consistently produce conforming product. This shall be demonstrated via a first article inspection (FAI). Requirements for FAI and the industry-approved method can be found in SAE standard AS9102. Maintenance processes, scheduled down-time for maintenance and proper methods of maintaining production equipment must be documented and followed.

Storage requirements, including periodic preservation/condition checks, shall be established for production equipment or tooling in storage.

Since many aerospace products are "low volume" production, it is not expected that lines will run continuously or that tooling will be always in service. Tools are put in storage, machines sit idle and gauges are set aside. These must be maintained so that when placed back in service they will function as they did originally. If too much time has passed a FAI may have to be repeated.

7.5.1.4 Control of work transferred, on a temporary basis, outside the organization's facilities

When planning to temporarily transfer work to a location outside the organization's facilities, the organization shall define the process to control and validate the quality of the work.

Every once in a while something unexpected may happen and alternate plans must be made. For example, when a machine breaks down and it's the only one of its kind in the company, it is allowable (indeed prudent for meeting schedules) to find an external source with an identical machine or process. It is still the responsibility of the organization to control the work and oversee the activity and assure the production environment, just like it was being manufactured at the organization's facilities. This includes acceptance of the conformity of the operations or process results.

7.5.1.5 Control of service operations

Where servicing is a specified requirement, service operation processes shall provide for

a) a method of collecting and analyzing in-service data;

Servicing, maintenance or repair activities of a product must be controlled and supported. Aerospace products (except for missiles) are not disposable and typically require a high level of maintenance to remain airworthy. It is just as important to perform these operations correctly as it is to make the original product. It is important to collect service data on the product in service to spot trends and anomalies that may show evidence of a latent defect or process problem (e.g., the celebrated Firestone tire problem on Ford Explorers).

b) actions to be taken where problems are identified after delivery, including investigation, reporting activities and actions on service information consistent with contractual and/or regulatory requirements;

Now that the data has been collected and analyzed, the industry requests and the CAA's require that problems be reported and made known regardless of the implications.

c) the control and updating of technical documentation;

As the product gains time in service, there are improvements, design changes or enhancements to operational requirements that could affect maintenance manuals or overhaul instructions or repair processes. The technical information on the product must be kept current and configurable to all the products in service.

d) the approval, control and use of repair schemes; and

Repair processes must be reviewed, approved and controlled, since only the original design information will be able to determine if the repair can work in specified products and applications. It is expected that repair plans will indicate that they are approved and the authority that approved the repair plan has the knowledge, expertise (and rights) to do so.

e) the controls required for off-site work (e.g., organization's work undertaken at the customer's facilities).

Occasionally, it may be necessary to perform work on the finished product outside of the organization's normal facilities. This may include a repair or retrofit of a product already delivered. The customer expects and the industry requires that all work be done under controlled conditions. If the organization is responsible for the work, then methods of controlling the work, the environment and the acceptance process must be established and documented to the extent necessary. This includes the authority to make changes to the process or methods being used.

7.5.2 Validation of processes for production and service provision

The organization shall validate any processes for production and service provision where the resulting output cannot be verified by subsequent monitoring or measurement. This includes any processes where deficiencies become apparent only after the product is in use or the service has been delivered.

NOTE: These processes are frequently referred to as special processes.

Validation shall demonstrate the ability of these processes to achieve planned results.

The organization shall establish arrangements for these processes including, as applicable

a) defined criteria for review and approval of the processes,

- qualification and approval of special processes prior to use;

This may restate the obvious, but the aerospace industry is so dependent on these highly critical processes for the performance of aerospace products, there should be no doubt about the critical nature of special processes and the need to validate that they are functioning correctly and produce the desired results each and every time.

c) use of specific methods and procedures,

- control of the significant operations and parameters of special processes in accordance with documented process specifications and changes thereto;

Some special processes are so sensitive that the slightest changes in environmental conditions or operating technique can be the cause of significant scrap and product failure. Process parameters such as time, temperature, electricity and cleanliness may have such an effect that they need to be measured and controlled at all times.

7.5.3 Identification and traceability

The organization shall maintain the identification of the configuration of the product in order to identify any differences between the actual configuration and the agreed configuration.

This again brings out the importance of configuration management throughout the life cycle of the product. It is also an admission that, in an aircraft comprised of over 6 million individual parts (on average), from the time of release of the bill of material to assemble the airplane to the time it actually gets built there may be substitutions or changes to the installed material. Some changes may be minor or some may be customer ordered improvements or changes that are transparent to the function and performance of the product. In many cases the actual effects of the change may not be known. In all cases the records shall reflect the actual configuration manufactured/built and it shall be comparable to the required configuration definition.

When acceptance authority media are used (e.g., stamps, electronic signatures, passwords), the organization shall establish and document controls for the media.

Simply put, when stamps, numbers, electronic passwords and the like are used to identify the status of a product as determined by an individual (i.e., inspected, approved, rejected, passed, completed, tested, hold or any other such designation), the organization shall document in a procedure how these methods of identification are controlled. This extends to such items as signatures on certificates and official forms (such as FAA 8130-3 forms).

According to the level of traceability required by contract, regulatory or other established requirement, the organization's system shall provide for:

This is the critical part. First, the requirements for traceability must be determined. These requirements can come in many forms. FAA part 45 has some requirements. The purchase order for individual items may have a requirement. There may be a specification/industry standard that is invoked or there may be a note or specification on a drawing. In almost all cases, the level of traceability of a part is exponential to the criticality of the item in its application. The user must be aware that identical items may have different levels of traceability requirements based on their application.

a) identification to be maintained throughout the product life;

This typically means permanent marking in some fashion. It could also be an attached data plate or other means of identification that will remain with the product at all times. In some cases it will be dictated by specification.

> **b) all the products manufactured from the same batch of raw material or from the same manufacturing batch to be traced, as well as the destination (delivery, scrap) of all products of the same batch;**

The common method is serialization of each individual item with a method for assuring the serial numbers are unique. For some manufacturers the serial numbers may be issued/obtained from the customer. In all cases each serial number issued (at whatever point in the process) must be accounted for and documented regardless of whether it was used, consumed, scrapped, changed or delivered.

> **c) for an assembly, the identity of its components and those of the next higher assembly to be traced;**

When an assembly has a collection of serial numbers, the assembly may be issued a unique serial number of its own that collects the identity of the assembled items it contains. Or, the assembly itself may have a unique identification to record the processes/factors in the assembly process. This identification must be carried through to at least the next higher assembly level.

> **d) for a given product, a sequential record of its production (manufacture, assembly, inspection) to be retrieved.**

Finally, for the completed assembled or manufactured item, there must be records of the operations performed, the sequence in which they were performed and the acknowledgement that they were all completed satisfactorily.

> *NOTE: In some industry sectors, configuration management is a means by which identification and traceability are maintained* **(see 4.3).**

This just points back to the industry-added requirement for a configuration management system. The ISO writers almost described the requirement, but did not go far enough. This shows another reason this standard was created.

7.5.4 Customer property

> *The organization shall exercise care with customer property while it is under the organization's control or being used by the organization. The organization shall identify, verify, protect and safeguard customer property provided for use or incorporation into the product. If any customer property is lost, damaged or otherwise found to be unsuitable for use, this shall be reported to the customer and records maintained (see 4.2.4).*

> *NOTE: Customer property can include intellectual property,* **including customer furnished data used for design, production and/or inspection.**

This was an interesting change. The industry liked the revised wording provided by the TC 176 writers. However, they wanted to make sure that the scope of customer material was clear and that it extended beyond hardware and firmware (paper, models and other tangibles) to software and digital data that may be provided by the customer.

7.5.5 Preservation of product

Preservation of product shall also include, where applicable in accordance with product specifications and/or applicable regulations, provisions for:

a) cleaning;

b) prevention, detection and removal of foreign objects;

c) special handling for sensitive products;

d) marking and labeling including safety warnings;

e) shelf life control and stock rotation;

f) special handling for hazardous materials.

This is another "laundry or punch list" that requires the organization to consider these items if they are affected by something in the list. These are commonly referred to as "stealth" requirements, because they may exist without being very clear as to where they came from. There are a myriad of regulations regarding solvents, fluids, packing materials, electrostatic discharge (ESD), liability markings, etc. that must be known and considered at all times when preserving the items at all stages of production through testing and delivery. Special consideration must be given to cleaning to remove foreign objects (as a result of manufacture) and prevention of packaging/preservation methods from introducing foreign objects. The industry is replete with stories of engine or system failures from tubes that were assembled with the end cap (or dust caps) still installed.

The organization shall ensure that documents required by the contract/order to accompany the product are present at delivery and are protected against loss and deterioration.

The number one cause for delays in product acceptance (by customers) has historically been lost or missing paperwork. The required documents shall be shipped in such a manner as to arrive with the material in a condition to preclude its destruction or loss. The industry hope is that this goes away in the future as the data can be electronically transmitted when the material is received. We are not there yet.

7.6 Control of monitoring and measuring devices

The organization shall maintain a register of these monitoring and measuring devices, and define the process employed for their calibration including details of equipment type, unique identification, location, frequency of checks, check method and acceptance criteria.

Pretty simple really. This is an amplification of an ISO 10012 requirement. Since ISO 10012 is a reference directly in ISO 9001:2000 the aerospace companies wanted to re-enforce the requirement to maintain the integrity of the measuring equipment and the process for maintaining calibration and traceability of the calibration record. It states system requirements that have been around since the enactment of Mil-C-45662.

NOTE: Monitoring and measuring devices include, but are not limited to: test hardware, test software, automated test equipment (ATE) and plotters used to produce inspection data. It also includes personally owned and customer-supplied equipment used to provide evidence of product conformity.

This note was added to re-enforce the fact that measuring equipment is not limited to hard gauging and tooling or test equipment. More importantly it does include the requirement to assure, control and monitor the software and software tools used in testing and product measurement. It also means that *any* gauging used, whether owned by the supplier or not, must be controlled within the supplier's system.

The organization shall ensure that environmental conditions are suitable for the calibrations, inspections, measurements and tests being carried out.

This is a basic calibration requirement that for whatever reason was lost in the year 2000 revision of ISO 9001. It is covered elsewhere in the standard that applies to many aspects of the system (6.4), but it was felt that it was worth re-stating it directly in this area to assure that the requirement to have temperature, humidity and cleanliness control in calibration and use of measuring equipment is not lost.

Where necessary to ensure valid results, measuring equipment shall

f) be recalled to a defined method when requiring calibration.

There is a list of requirements in ISO 9001:2000 that precedes this requirement. But for some reason the need to assure a positive recall system for equipment that requires calibration is not evident. Aerospace cannot even afford the perception that aerospace products were accepted/tested on equipment that was past its point or time limit of assuring conformity. There must be a positive system used to assure the compliance of the equipment at all times. This does not mean that the times and calibration cycles have to be fixed or cannot be changed.

8 Measurement, analysis and improvement

8.1 General

The organization shall plan and implement the monitoring, measurement, analysis and improvement processes needed

> *a) to demonstrate conformity of the product,*

> *b) to ensure conformity of the quality management system, and*

> *c) to continually improve the effectiveness of the quality management system.*

This shall include determination of applicable methods, including statistical techniques, and the extent of their use.

NOTE: According to the nature of the product and depending on the specified requirements, statistical techniques may be used to support:

- design verification (e.g., reliability, maintainability, safety);

- process control;

- selection and inspection of key characteristics;

- process capability measurements;

- statistical process control;

- design of experiment;

- inspection - matching sampling rate to the criticality of the product and to the process capability;

- failure mode and effect analysis.

This note is inserted to support a very general and wide-open statement in ISO 9001:2000 about the use of sampling plans and statistical techniques. Aerospace supports the use of sampling inspection and use of statistical methods in design, process control and product acceptance. They have shown themselves to be more effective than 100 percent inspection or testing. This is additional amplification of aerospace expectations of sampling plans in the document under 8.2.3.

8.2 Monitoring and measurement

8.2.2 Internal audit

The organization shall conduct internal audits at planned intervals to determine whether the quality management system

Detailed tools and techniques shall be developed such as checksheets, process flowcharts or any similar method to support audit of the quality management system requirements. The acceptability of the selected tools will be measured against the effectiveness of the internal audit process and overall organization performance.

The aerospace companies involved with the creation of the aerospace 9100 standard were unanimous in their fervent belief that internal auditing, if properly applied, was a very effective management tool. Some past sins of this requirement in the previous version of ISO 9001 have been improved in this version to keep the requirement from just being a paper excercise within companies. However, aerospace has gone even further to require companies to prove that their internal audit process is robust and effective. The auditing tools used and the results of the audits must be shown to be effective and cause real improvement to the product and or quality system.

Internal audits shall also meet contract and/or regulatory requirements.

This was added as a placeholder in case regulators or customers impose future definitions or requirements for internal auditing. ISO is working on ISO 19011 (to replace ISO 10011) that would apply to all auditing and would be more comprehensive than these current words. (See Chapter 6, The Audit Process.)

8.2.3 Monitoring and measurement of processes

In the event of process nonconformity, the organization shall

a) take appropriate action to correct the nonconforming process;

b) evaluate whether the process nonconformity has resulted in product nonconformity; and

c) identify and control the nonconforming product in accordance with Clause 8.3.

When dealing with process control, we need to understand that most companies are operating integrated systems and processes. When these processes are noncompliant in terms of performance or output then actions need to be taken. It was felt that the standard did not cover process nonconformity, which has a big impact on customer satisfaction. The other issue is the requirement to disposition products that have been through a process that is later found to be nonconforming. The system/procedures must identify how to control this situation and the result.

8.2.4 Monitoring and measurement of product

When key characteristics have been identified, they shall be monitored and controlled.

This supports the concept of key characteristics that was introduced earlier. Key characteristics will show up as symbols on drawings, identified characteristics in performance specifications and/or a flow-down specification such as AS9103, *Management of Key Characteristics,* that details how key characteristics must be managed, controlled and documented.

When the organization uses sampling inspection as a means of product acceptance, the plan shall be statistically valid and appropriate for use. The plan shall preclude the acceptance of lots whose samples have known non-conformities. When required, the plan shall be submitted for customer approval.

This requirement was a difficult trade-off for the industry. The basic premise was that the old Mil-Std-105E sampling plans could not be used in the aerospace industry. We could not accept any plans that did not have an OC curve based on c=0. There are many plans that would be perfectly acceptable based on the type and criticality of the characteristic involved; however, it would not be acceptable from a perception standpoint to say that the industry allows lots of materials with known nonconformities (based on the sample) to be accepted. We did make allowances for suppliers to petition their customers for any special plans or process control techniques to be used in lieu of traditional "accept on zero ... reject on 1" lot sampling plans.

Product shall not be used until it has been inspected or otherwise verified as conforming to specified requirements, except when product is released under positive-recall procedures pending completion of all required measurement and monitoring activities.

Most CAAs, and customers for that matter, want assurance that products meet design requirements before point of use. In some respects it is important that products not even be entered into further production (where traceability can be lost) without verification of acceptability prior to release. In this case the industry recognizes that some testing of samples may take considerable time and product can be released as long as it can be recalled. A classic example is one where a sheet of material must pass a corrosion test (salt spray for example) that can take up to a week to perform. The material can be released to manufacture parts as long as all the items made from the sheet can be found and recalled if necessary if the sample from the material fails the testing. It is the producer's risk to do so and in most cases it is an acceptable risk. But the producer's system must also assure that no items that are released will leave the producer's system without assurance that they conform to design intent.

8.2.4.1 Inspection documentation

Measurement requirements for product or service acceptance shall be documented. This documentation may be part of the production documentation, but shall include

a) criteria for acceptance and/or rejection;

b) where in the sequence measurement and testing operations are performed;

c) a record of the measurement results; and

d) type of measurement instruments required and any specific instructions associated with their use.

When all is said and done and the product has flown away, the only proof left that the product was conforming to its design requirements is the inspection documentation. Those given the responsibility to perform inspections and give assurance are still trusted to be honest and provide accurate accounting of their activities. The industry must have a good accounting of the inspection activity to show and understand the methods used and results of the inspections performed.

Test records shall show actual test results data when required by specification or acceptance test plan.

In most cases where product acceptance is based on testing (physical, mechanical or functional) data can be or is created as a result of the testing. Most testing is performed in accordance with a pre-approved test plan. The data from the testing is to be recorded and retained, not just "pass-fail." It is important to know if the product was marginally accepted and, if there is a subsequent problem with the test equipment, it may be able to determine what product is acceptable and which product is not.

Where required to demonstrate product qualification the organization shall ensure that records provide evidence that the product meets the defined requirements.

In aerospace (and many other products) there are product "qualification" tests and "acceptance" tests. Qualification tests may be performed just once or periodically or after process changes, but in all cases these tests are meant to prove that the product will meet its performance requirements in the total range of the intended application. Many times these are special tests that are performed in the laboratory or in special tests facilities. Sometimes these tests are performed at the component level and in assemblies. In all cases the records of these tests must be kept and they need to show the same information as other inspections and testing would show.

8.2.4.2 First article inspection

The organization's system shall provide a process for the inspection, verification and documentation of a representative item from the first production run of a new part, or following any subsequent change that invalidates the previous first article inspection result.

There must be a process and objective evidence that a first article (not necessarily *the* first article) was inspected for conformance to all of the design characteristics when production is initiated or changes are made. That means each part, component and assembly must have a first article inspection performed. This does not have to be performed on a completed end product per se, but may be performed progressively throughout the production process. First article inspections can satisfy the requirement for "conformity inspections" required by CAAs and for Physical Configuration Audits (PCAs) required on some military contracts. In all cases it is an aerospace requirement.

NOTE: See (AS) (EN) (SJAC) 9102 for guidance.

AS9102 is an industry standard detailing how first articles are to be performed what data is to be collected and how it is to be retained and/or submitted. When invoked on a contract by a customer, AS9102 will indicate how the data is to be recorded and transmitted to the customer when a first article package is completed.

8.3 Control of nonconforming product

NOTE: The term "nonconforming product" includes nonconforming product returned from a customer.

When product is returned from the customer as "noncompliant" or unknown quality it shall be segregated and subject to the same or similar requirements as internally discovered nonconforming products and prevented from inadvertent use until it is properly dispositioned. This is especially true for product that may have been put into service and stressed in an unknown fashion but otherwise appears visually and dimensionally acceptable.

The organization's documented procedure shall define the responsibility for review and authority for the disposition of nonconforming product and the process for approving personnel making these decisions.

This requirement is fairly straightforward. The industry and its customers have always required knowledge of the capabilities and knowledge of the people that are charged with the ability to extend the tolerances or design criteria and pass judgment on material that has not been shown to meet the inspection criteria during manufacture. There must be knowledge of products and process involved and the consequences to the users and programs for extending limits and/or scrapping or reworking and repairing material. The personnel allowed to make these decisions (when it is delegated to a manufacturer) must be limited and controlled.

The organization shall not use dispositions of use-as-is or repair, unless specifically authorized by the customer, if

- the product is produced to customer design, or

- the nonconformity results in a departure from the contract requirements.

Unless otherwise restricted in the contract, organization-designed product which is controlled via a customer specification may be dispositioned by the organization as use-as-is or repair, provided the nonconformity does not result in a departure from customer-specified requirements.

The ability to do material review is still a matter of who holds the design data and can make a proper determination of fitness for use. The requirements of the old Mil-Std-1520B are still evident in aerospace handling of nonconformances. In most cases the design owner or ultimate product owner has the right to disposition nonconformities. Nonconformances detected by suppliers must typically be submitted to the customer. Many of the organizations that are the final vehicle or system integrators do not have all the design data for each component. This document gives by implication ("unless otherwise restricted") the ability to perform nonconformance disposition to the organization that has the design data as long as the resultant decision for rework, repair or use does not affect any customer-stated requirements. The only dispositions a nondesign holder can make of a nonconformance are rework or scrap. Rework is narrowly defined as reprocessing, using the current process without any changes. Repair is processing of the part by approved methods that are outside of the approved manufacturing process to bring it back to design limits and tolerances.

Product dispositioned for scrap shall be conspicuously and permanently marked, or positively controlled, until physically rendered unusable.

The aerospace industry uses very expensive and complex materials. Scrapping out a single item can result in a large loss in terms of cost to an organization. Many of the items that may make an item unusable may not be visible to the naked eye and therefore there is an opportunity for mistakes or abuse in allowing material or product that should be scrap being reintroduced into the end products. This requirement is such that for all scrap material it must be obvious to all concerned that it is scrap and is altered in a fashion that makes it unusable. Product that is incomplete and is scrapped may not have to be mutilated, since it would not be usable in its scrapped condition. On the other hand, completed product must be destroyed to the extent that it cannot be cleaned or have cosmetic work performed to make it look like new before it leaves an organization's facility.

In addition to any contract or regulatory authority reporting requirements, the organization's system shall provide for timely reporting of delivered nonconforming product that may affect reliability or safety. Notification shall include a clear description of the nonconformity, which includes as necessary parts affected, customer and/or organization part numbers, quantity, and date(s) delivered.

NOTE: Parties requiring notification of nonconforming product may include

suppliers, internal organizations, customers, distributors and regulatory authorities.

There must be a defined process for the timely notification of all stakeholders that may be affected by a known nonconformance that was (or may have been) delivered to a customer that affects or could affect reliability or safety of an aerospace product. The reporting is required when safety/reliability effects are unknown so that the holder of the design data can make a determination as to the effect of the nonconformance. The notification needs to be complete enough to assure all parties are cognizant of the situation and actions being taken.

8.4 Analysis of data

The organization shall determine, collect and analyse appropriate data to demonstrate the suitability and effectiveness of the quality management system and to evaluate where continual improvement of the effectiveness of the quality management system can be made. This shall include data generated as a result of monitoring and measurement and from other relevant sources.

The analysis of data shall provide information relating to

   a) customer satisfaction (see 8.2.1),

   b) conformity to product requirements (see 7.2.1),

   c) characteristics and trends of processes and products including opportunities for preventive action, and

   d) suppliers.

8.5 Improvement

8.5.2 Corrective action

A documented procedure shall be established to define requirements for

   g) flow down of the corrective action requirement to a supplier, when it is determined that the supplier is responsible for the root cause; and

   h) specific actions where timely and/or effective corrective actions are not achieved.

In addition to the ISO 9001 requirements for corrective action, the aerospace industry requires that any corrective action process extend from the point of origin or discovery down through the supply chain to the root cause(s) that can be positively identified. When the corrective action response is reported (at any level), it must include the specific actions that will be done, in the interim between discovery of the nonconformance until corrective actions are in place, to assure process or product compliance. This could mean the institution of extra inspections, audits or alternate processes until the root causes are eliminated.

8.5.3 Preventive action

There was no supplementation here. The industry expects that "preventive action" is an integral part of the quality system and the corrective action process.

Many will read this document with the aerospace supplementation to the ISO 9001 document and remark, "why this is just common sense" or " you could read that into the standard if you wanted to." That may be the case, but we, the aerospace industry, don't want to leave the safety and well-being of the men, women and children that use our products every day and whose lives they entrust to us and our products to chance. As the reliability of products get better and better, we begin to take many things for granted. Aerospace travel should not be something we ever take lightly or for granted.

Bibliography

AS/EN/JISQ 9102 Aerospace First Article Inspection Requirement

ISO 9000:2000 Quality management systems – Fundamentals and vocabulary

ISO 9001:2000 Quality management systems – Requirements

ISO 9004:2000 Quality management systems – Guidelines for performance improvements

ISO 10007:1995 Quality management — Guidelines for configuration management

ISO 10011-1:1990 Guidelines for auditing quality systems — Part 1: Auditing

ISO 10011-2:1991 Guidelines for auditing quality systems — Part 2: Qualification criteria for quality systems auditors

ISO 10011-3:1991 Guidelines for auditing quality systems — Part 3: Management of audit programmes

ISO 10012-1:1992 Quality assurance requirements for measuring equipment — Part 1: Metrological confirmation system for measuring equipment

ISO 10012-2:1997 Quality assurance for measuring equipment — Part 2: Guidelines for control of measurement processes

CFR Part 21 Code of Federal Regulations 14 Part 21. US Government Printing Office, Washington, DC (latest version)

TL 9000 Quality Management Standard for Telecommunications

16

*by John W. Walz**

Telecommunications Industry and TL 9000

Developed by the Quality Excellence for Suppliers of Telecommunications (QuEST) Forum, the TL 9000 quality management system (QMS) requirements and measurements represents the adaptation of ISO 9001:2000 for the telecommunications industry.

TL 9000 can support the strategies of quality, supplier management and purchasing managers to reduce product failures. It can be used to meet customer quality and reliability requirements while advanced QMS drives goal setting, planning, phased life cycle, vendor management, functional business alignment, feedback and quality improvements leading to customer satisfaction. It is worth pointing out that earlier releases of TL 9000 used the term "metrics," while the latest release uses the term "measurements" to be more easily understood around the world.

Quality requirements for the rapidly changing telecommunications industry had to be designed around a number of fundamental realities:

- Emphasis on reliability, universal service, system level products
- New technology (transition to add data to voice and the convergence of computers and telecom)
- Globalization

* Also contributing to this chapter is James J. Gerard, see page 635.

- Huge investments
- Reduced regulation
- New business arrangements and partnerships
- New suppliers and customers.

TL 9000 registration requires implementation and compliance to two handbooks: *Requirements* and *Measurements*. TL 9000 embeds 81 additional requirements, commonly referred to as "adders," into ISO 9001:2000, covering all product realization phases.

These added requirements provide direction for suppliers, while intended to make good business sense. The *Measurements Handbook* describes 10 measurements, each having several reportable submeasurements. New requirements for specific quality measurements are to:

- Establish processes to capture and validate individual measurements
- Submit data elements to the measurements administrator
- Address nonconformance in the measurement process
- Provide measurement data for new products and services
- Use data to improve products, services and practices
- Use data on joint customer/supplier improvement teams.

QuEST Forum

Historically, the major telecom service providers (TSPs) have written additional requirements beyond ISO 9000 into their contracts. While most telecom suppliers held third-party registration, few organizations were using their systems to generate effective business improvement. There were a number of reasons why ISO 9001:1994 was insufficient for supplier management in telecom:

- Weak on quality improvement/costs
- Weak on customer-supplier relationships
- Allows minimal application without business improvement for immediate customer sale
- Provides certificate with no level of excellence
- Too much supplier discretion
- No cost-based comparable measurements / benchmarking
- Fails to encourage whole-business registrations

- Too generic (excludes telecom best practices for providing high quality and reliable product and services).

While an improvement, ISO 9001:2000 still failed to address many of the specific needs of TSPs.

The cost of poor quality for software and hardware were high for both suppliers and TSPs. Suppliers were subject to multiple and overlapping standards resulting in increased costs, and joint customer/supplier problem solving needed better and common measurements.

Recognizing that the automotive and aerospace industries developed sector-specific requirements based on ISO 9001:1994 largely out of similar concerns, Bell Atlantic, BellSouth, Pacific Bell and SBC adopted a similar approach, resulting in the founding of QuEST Forum in January 1998.

The Forum is a unique partnership of telecommunications suppliers and TSPs created with the following value proposition: Telecommunications industry quality could be improved if an industry association encouraged uniform quality requirements and standard quality performance and cost-based measurements and reporting throughout the telecommunications supply chain.

The purpose of the Forum was to:

- Provide an environment where TSPs and suppliers can work together to foster continuous improvement of service to the consumer
- Decrease time to market
- Improve service provider-supplier relationships
- Enhance the quality of telecommunications products and services and thereby improve total cost of ownership throughout the supply chain.

QuEST Forum Goals

The following goals were established for the Forum:

1. Foster quality systems that effectively and efficiently protect the integrity and use of telecommunication products in the categories of hardware, software or service.

2. Create and maintain a common set of quality system requirements. Suppliers needed a replacement for the overlapping requirements of Telcordia Technologies (formerly Bellcore), ISO 9000:1994 and Software Engineering Institute Capability Maturity Model (SEI-CMM). They also needed to harmonize overlapping service provider requests for different measurements to run the customer report card evaluations.

3. Define effective performance and cost-based measurements to guide progress and evaluate results of quality system implementation and deployment.

4. Drive continuous improvement from the customer's point of view.

5. Enhance customer/supplier relationships. The telecommunications industry experience with joint problem solving is particularly critical with suppliers and providers who are dependent upon each other to quickly resolve problems and cooperate in finding solutions,

6. Leverage industry conformity assessment to use registrars, rather than customer second-party audits, to determine conformance with QMS requirements.

The QuEST Forum learned valuable lessons from the automotive and aerospace industries in developing sector-specific requirements around ISO 9001:1994. The Forum gained speed by using dedicated resources and established publication and distribution. The Forum considered the automotive industry governance approach and selected a "democratic" approach — a more inclusive approach than the US automobile industry where the Big Three simply prescribed the QS-9000 industry standards to the supplier base. From the beginning, QuEST Forum included suppliers in the handbook development in a similar method as ISO standards development: every company had an equal voice and vote. The QuEST Forum then took QS-9000 a step further and embraced the concept of comparable and auditable measurements.

The Forum adopted an ambitious publication schedule. Key dates for deliverables were:

DATE	DELIVERABLE
May 1999	QSR Handbook 1 published
June 1999	Auditing and Implementation training offered for Requirements and Measurements
November 1999	Measurements Handbook (handbook two) published
January 2000	Measurements system online
January 2000	First registrars approved
January 2000	First suppliers registered
April 2000	Telecommunications Industry Measurements Trend Reports (TIMTR) published
December 2000	ISO 9001:2000 and TL 9000:2000 available
March 2001	TL 9000:2000 Measurements revised

What Is TL 9000?

TL 9000 is a common set of quality system requirements and comparable, reportable measurements designed specifically for the telecom industry, encompassing ISO 9001, Customer/Supplier Quality Plan (CSQP) and other telecom best practices. The *TL 9000 Quality System Requirements Handbook* adds 81 hardware, software and service best practices adders and 19 notes/recommendations. The *TL 9000 Measurements Handbook* has 10 well-defined comparable measurements for hardware, software and service QMSs. The following illustration depicts the TL 9000 model.

Figure 16-1

The TL 9000 Model

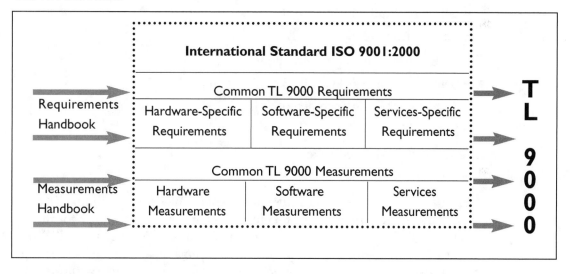

Requirements

This section will cover the first handbook: *TL 9000 Quality System Requirements.* The TL 9000 QMS philosophy is to "raise the bar" over ISO 9001:2000 by increasing the emphasis on industry best practices. Thus TL 9000 requirements are more detailed and descriptive, while ISO 9001 requirements allow for broad supplier discretion. TL 9000 incorporates the following concepts:

• Quality planning as planning (short/tactical, long/strategic) is the key to minimizing variation and customer surprises. Planning requirements have been added to design, customer service and delivery.

• Executive involvement takes place through active participation in setting goals and communicating with customers.

- Reliability is assured through the many requirements added to design control and using a life cycle model as verified by third-party audits of effectiveness.

- Customer satisfaction/continuous improvement adders throughout provide direction.

The TL 9000 sources were debated, modified and voted as the best industry practices and comparable measurements for incorporation into the TL 9000 handbooks. QuEST Forum established a liaison with the TC 176 to ensure that TL 9000 will always be in sync with ISO 9001 updates. Best practices were found in the following Telcordia Technologies (formerly Bellcore) CSQP Generic Requirements (GR):

- Hardware quality management GR179

- Software quality management GR1252

- CSQP GR1202.

The software best practices were found in:

- Software guidance ISO 9000-3

- Software life cycle document ISO 12207

- SEI-CMM.

The services best practices were found in:

- Services guidance ISO 9004-2.

QuEST Forum reviewed over 500 requirements in developing the first TL 9000 release and agreed upon the best 83 requirements and best 26 notes for the TL 9000:1999 QMS Handbook. The 1999 version was again reviewed when ISO was updated, giving us the current 81 added requirements and 19 notes. The purpose of the selection criteria was to add value while not being redundant or unreasonable to implement. Additionally, it could not be proprietary and had to be auditable. More than half of the selection criteria were taken from existing CSQP documents.

There are seven TL 9000 registration options:

1. TL 9000 – HW (hardware QSR and hardware measurements)

2. TL 9000 – SW (software QSR and software measurements)

3. TL 9000 – SC (services QSR and services measurements)

4. TL 9000 – HW/SW

5. TL 9000 – HW/SC

6. TL 9000 – SW/SC

7. TL 9000 – HW/SW/SC.

Each TL 9000 requirement includes:

- ISO clause number (e.g. 4.2.3)
- A letter added that represents "C" for common, "H" for hardware, "S" for software and "V" for services, all linked to the registration options (HW, SW, SC)
- Ordered number starting at one (e.g., 4.2.3.C.1 is the first adder).

The above-referenced TL 9000 categories are defined as follows:

- Common – Applicable to hardware, software and service suppliers
- Hardware – Applicable to hardware suppliers only
- Software – Applicable to software suppliers only
- Services – Applicable to service suppliers only.

The frequency of requirement adders (C, H, S, V) by type and associated registration options are shown below. A review of this table will help you determine how many of the adders are applicable to each type of registration option.

Table 16-1

Adders vs. Registration Options

Requirement Adder type	Registration Options						
	HW	SW	SC	HW/SW	HW/SC	SW/SC	HW/SW/SC
12 HW Only	12			12	12		12
15 SW Only		15		15		15	15
5 SC Only			5		5	5	5
6 HW and SW	6	6		6	6	6	6
4 HW and SC	4		4		4	4	4
39 Common (HW and SW and SC)	39	39	39	39	39	39	39
83 Total	61	60	48	72	66	69	81

Shalls, Shoulds and Notes

The word "shall" indicates mandatory requirements, as in ISO 9001:2000. However, the word "should" indicates a preferred approach, which differs from the ISO 9001 approach. Suppliers choosing other approaches must be able to show that their approach meets the intent of TL 9000. About 20 best practices only use the word "should" and not "shall." These are labeled as "NOTES" to be used as TL 9000 implementation guidance and not intended to be auditable.

The 81 TL 9000 requirements and 19 notes added to ISO 9001:2000 clauses are described below with the clause, number of requirements (Req.) and number of notes. ISO 9000 clauses not listed do not have any additional requirements or notes.

It is important to note that 52 of the additional requirements and 12 of the notes are found in the product realization clause (Clause 7) of ISO 9001:2000.

The TL 9000 adders address:

- Customer orientation
- Continual quality improvement
- Planning for quality
- Life cycle management
- Customer/supplier communication

Table 16-2

ISO 9001:2000 Clause-By-Clause Relationship to TL 9000

ISO 9001:2000 Clause	#Reqs	# Notes
4.2 Control of documents	1	0
5.1 Management commitment	1	1
5.2 Customer focus	2	1
5.4 Planning	3	0
5.5 Administration	1	0
5.6 Management review	1	0
6.2 Human resources	8	0
7.1 Planning of realization processes	9	4
7.2 Customer-related processes	6	2
7.3 Design and/or development	19	5
7.4 Purchasing	1	1
7.5 Production and service operations	16	0
7.6 Control of measuring and monitoring devices	1	0
8.2 Measurement and monitoring	9	1
8.4 Analysis of data	1	0
8.5 Improvement	2	4
Total	**81**	**19**

- Reliability and associated costs
- Software development and life cycle management
- Specialized service functions such as installation and engineering
- Measurement requirements.

These measurement requirements establish processes to capture and validate individual measurements, to submit the data elements to the measurements administrator, address nonconformance in measurements process, provide measurements data for new products and services, use data to improve products, services and practices and establish joint customer/supplier improvement teams.

The quality principles of ISO 9001:2000 are supported by TL 9000 adders in the followings areas:

- Customer-focused organization
- Customer involvement 5.4.2.C.2
- Customer support quality program 7.5.1.C.1
- Customer satisfaction 5.2
- Leadership
- Quality objectives 5.1.C.1
- Involvement of people
- Employee participation 8.5.1.C.2
- Process approach
- Life cycle model 7.1.C.1
- Advanced quality training 6.2.2.C.5
- Process measurement 8.2.2.C.1
- System approach to management
- Long and short-term planning 5.5.2.C.1
- Project plan 7.1.C.3
- Life cycle model 7.1.C.1
- Configuration management plan 7.1.HS.1
- Disaster recovery 7.1.C.5
- Continual improvement
- Quality improvement concepts 6.2.2.C.2
- Quality improvement 5.5, 7.1, 8.5

- Factual approach to decision making
- Process measurement 8.2.2.C.1 (4.20.1.C.1)
- Trend analysis 8.4.C.1 (4.13.2.C.1)
- Mutually beneficial supplier relationship
- Purchasing procedure(s) 7.4.1.C.1 (4.6.1.C.1).

For example, with respect to leadership, Clause 5.1, Management commitment, of ISO 9001:2000 states: "Top management shall establish … the quality policy and quality objectives."

TL 9000 supplements this by adding 5.1.C.1 (4.1.1.C.1), Quality objectives, which states: "Objectives for quality shall include targets for the TL 9000 measurements defined in the TL 9000 Quality System Measurements handbook." Thus top management must now expand the auditable review cycle to address business performance, improvement and benchmarking.

Where ISO 9001:1994 had internal quality records (e.g., employee training), TL 9000:2000 measurement usage is threaded throughout the entire QMS, specifically:

- Management commitment to setting TL 9000 measurements targets (5.1)
- Quality planning for policy deployment and measurements target setting (5.4.2)
- Planning and implementing the measurement and monitoring activities (8.1)
- Provision of resources to achieve measurement targets (6.1)
- Measurement and monitoring of processes necessary to meet customer measurement requirements (8.2.3)
- Measurement and monitoring of product necessary to meet customer measurement requirements (8.2.4)
- Purchasing control to evaluate and select suppliers based on their ability to supply product in accordance with the organization's measurement requirements (7.4.1)
- Analysis of measurements data for gap analysis to measurement targets (8.4)
- Planning for continual measurement improvement of the QMS (8.5.1)
- Corrective action to eliminate the causes of negative deviations from measurement target plans (8.5.2)
- Preventive action to eliminate the potential causes of negative deviations from measurement target plans (8.5.3)

- Internal audit to determine whether the QMS has been effectively implemented and maintained based on measurement performance (8.2.2)

- Management representative reporting to top management on the measurement performance of the QMS (5.5.3)

- Management review of measurement results and findings to ensure the continuing suitability, adequacy and effectiveness of the QMS (5.6)

- Customer focus for top management meetings with key customers on measurement performance as well as customer needs and expectations (5.2)

- Customer satisfaction measurements correlated to measurement performance (8.2.1)

- Planning for continual improvement using industry measurement comparisons (8.5.1)

- General requirements (4.1) to measure, monitor and analyze these processes, and implement action necessary to achieve planned measurement results.

Differences with ISO 9001

TL 9000 has qualitative differences from ISO 9001:2000. As mentioned earlier, ISO 9001:2000 allows for broad supplier discretion. While ISO 9001 requires procedures and records to be in place, it doesn't always specify what subjects the procedures and records should address. TL 9000 is more descriptive (e.g., reliability emphasis). Examples of this include:

- Reliability, not just a broad term like "quality" (e.g., 5.4.2.C.1, Long- and short-term planning, includes product reliability)

- What should be in a quality record (e.g., 8.2.4.HV.2, Inspection and test records, having items a through f)

- What should be in a procedure (e.g., 7.4.1.C.1, Purchasing procedure(s), has subjects a through j).

TL 9000 benefits industry by providing:

- Clearer, less costly QMS implementation due to common industry requirements

- Value-added best practices chosen from the best of the existing major industry requirements

- Easier, less costly audits

- Fewer customer audits
- Robust life cycle management laced through the QMS elements
- Improved "designed in" product reliability
- Assurances to customers that best practices are deployed
- More emphasis on meeting customer contractual requirements.

Reliability is designed in into the product. Quality is planned, not just tested, into the product. Product life cycle management through planning, and customer/supplier communications are also enhanced.

In summary, TL 9000 defines a very comprehensive quality management system for achieving visible customer objectives and provides customers with confidence of a reliable supplier. It is embraced by the supplier to achieve a competitive edge and may be accepted by customers, either in the form of third-party certification or proof of conformance along with the use of measurements.

The following are the added requirements in TL 9000, release 3.0.

TL 9000 Release 3.0

4.2.3.C.1   Control of customer-supplied documents and data

5.2.C.1   Customer relationship development

5.2.C.2   Customer communication procedures

5.4.1.C.1   Quality objectives

5.4.2.C.1   Long- and short-term quality planning

5.4.2.C.2   Customer input

5.4.2.C.3   Supplier input

5.5.3.C.1   Organization performance feedback

6.2.2.C.1   Internal course development

6.2.2.C.1   Quality improvement concepts

6.2.2.C.3   Training requirements and awareness

6.2.2.C.4   ESD training

6.2.2.C.5   Advanced quality training

6.2.2.C.6   Training content

6.2.2.HV.1 Operator qualification

6.4.C.1   Work areas

7.1.C.1	Life cycle model
7.1.C.2	New product introduction
7.1.C.3	Disaster recovery
7.1.C.4	End of life planning
7.1.HS.1	Configuration management plan
7.1.S.1	Estimation
7.1.S.2	Computer resources
7.1.S.3	Support software and tools management
7.1.V.1	Service delivery plan
7.2.3.C.1	Notification about problems
7.2.3.C.2	Problem severity
7.2.3.C.3	Problem escalation
7.2.3.C.4	Customer feedback
7.2.3.H.1	Organization's recall process
7.3.1.C.1	Project plan
7.3.1.C.2	Requirements traceability
7.3.1.C.3	Test planning
7.3.1.S.1	Integration planning
7.3.1.S.2	Migration planning
7.3.2.C.1	Customer and supplier input
7.3.2.C.2	Design and development requirements
7.3.2.H.1	Content of requirements
7.3.2.S.1	Identification of software requirements
7.3.2.S.2	Requirements allocation
7.3.3.S.1	Software design and development output
7.3.3.V.1	Services design and development output
7.3.6.S.1	Release management
7.3.7.C.1	Change management process
7.3.7.C.2	Informing customers

7.3.7.H.1   Component changes

7.3.7.HS.1 Problem resolution configuration management

7.4.1.C.1   Purchasing procedure(s)

7.5.1.V.2   Tool changes

7.5.1.S.3   Replication

7.5.1.V.1   Software used in service delivery

7.5.1.S.2   Patch documentation

7.5.1.C.1   Organization's support program

7.5.1.C.1   Service resources

7.5.1.HS.1 Emergency service

7.5.1.HS.2 Installation plan

7.5.1.S.1   Patch procedure(s)

7.5.2.HV.1 Operational changes

7.5.3.H.1   Traceability for recall

7.5.3.H.2   Traceability of design changes

7.5.3.HS.1 Product identification

7.5.5.HS.1 Packaging and labeling audit

7.5.5.C.1   Antistatic protection

7.5.5.S.1   Software virus protection

7.5.5.H.1   Deterioration

7.6.H.1   Identified equipment

8.2.1.C.1   Customer satisfaction data

8.2.3.C.1   Process measurement

8.2.4.H.1   Periodic retesting

8.2.4.H.2   Content of testing

8.2.4.H.3   Frequency of testing

8.2.4.HV.1 Inspection and test documentation

8.2.4.H.4   Testing of repair and return products

8.2.4.HV.2 Inspection and test records

8.2.4.S.1   Test documentation

8.4.C.1   Trend analysis of nonconforming product

8.4.H.1   Field performance data

8.4.V.1   Service performance data

8.5.1.C.1   Quality improvement program

8.5.1.C.2   Employee participation

8.5.2.S.1   Problem resolution

Measurements

The second handbook, *TL 9000 Quality System Measurements*, requires companies to use measurements that impact on their customer's costs, are visible and reportable to their customers.

In many respects, this has been a missing element of ISO 9001. In the case of the telecom industry, almost all of the companies are public and investors carefully monitor their profits and market position. Telecom companies generally manage by monitoring internal and external business measures focused on costs, sales and market position. The common implementation of formal ISO 9001:1994 management systems did not link any of the quantitative (if any) quality measures to these business measures or their predictors.

TL 9000, on the other hand, requires such mechanisms as necessary to calculate and report a defined set of measurements and measure customer satisfaction. These measurements form the basis for a quality planning and goal-setting process conducted with customers. The goal is a closed loop process, with executive reviews being essential and mandatory to achieve continuous improvement. These external TL 9000 measurements and predictive internal measurements can result in an improvement in the synergy of related information provided to executive management to run the business.

Many customers will use these measures to reduce the cost of ownership throughout the supply chain, potentially impacting supplier profit margins and eventually market share.

The QuEST Forum philosophy was to use TL 9000 to raise the bar on quality management, with increased emphasis on performance measurements as verified by third-party registration. Measurement categories include customer satisfaction and problems, fix response time, delivery, system outages, software aborts and hardware returns.

Suppliers can use these measures to improve their business and customer relations. They will report comparable measurements into a secure industry database repository for benchmarking purposes. By establishing and requiring a consistent set of comparable measurements, the QuEST Forum has achieved an industry first, with the goal of improving the overall telecom industry.

The *Measurements Handbook* is intended to define effective, reportable performance and cost-based measurements to guide progress and evaluate results of quality system implementation and deployment. This evaluation reflects the viewpoints of the supplier, registrar, customers of the supplier and the market.

Why require measurements in a quality management system? TL 9000 measurements provide information for management to gather and use objective evidence, identify improvement opportunities and allocate effective use of resources. The measurement process provides the internal accountability for performance. The use of a common language allows comparisons within the supplier's operations and improves communications with customers. It allows customer feedback to suppliers on relative performance. The database repository provides a means for suppliers to conduct industry benchmarking.

The QuEST Forum attempted only to develop the "vital few" measurements that were relevant and useful to customers and their suppliers.

The sources for TL 9000 measurements were:

- Numerous Regional Bell Operating Company (RBOC) Report Cards
- Telcordia Technologies (formerly Bellcore) Generic Requirements (GR) on GR-929-CORE Reliability and Quality Measurements for Telecommunications Systems (RQMS) [1]
- GR-1315-CORE In-Process Quality Measurements (IPQM) [2].

RQMS data was gathered by each of the CSQP certified suppliers in the switching and transport product families. The QuEST Forum started with more than 200 candidate measurements from existing customer report cards and roughly 60 RQMS measurements used in CSQP and the 15 IPQM measurements.

Renowned quality expert Dr. Joseph Juran pioneered the concept of the "vital few" for the management of quality. Several competing interests had to be addressed by the measurements. Service provider engineers wanted many of the overlapping and subtending RQMS measurements, while customer purchasing managers wanted the "vital few" measurements for business impact and improvement to balance the supplier's price for Requests for Quotes or Information (RFQ / RFI).

Too many quality measurements could weaken or confuse an argument for decisions on life cycle cost comparison rather than first-costs. Suppliers were incurring a business cost in reporting similar but different measurements to different customers for their customer report cards on supplier performance. Those suppliers using the many RQMS for CSQP were not getting business value. Many of the proposed measurements were originally defined to focus on a historical problem root cause. These lower level measurements were discarded as redundant with higher level measurements directly impacting customer costs.

The most important selection criteria was impact on the TSPs and use by customers and suppliers. The impact criteria mainly focused on costs associated with suppliers. The usage criteria were mainly supplier management and comparison. Personnel involved in TSP supplier management wanted a few key measurements, but not many. The TSP's need for measurement comparison and concerns for measurement validity led to the exclusion of the IPQM measurements and the acceptance of "customer-facing" measurements having normalization factors.

Suppliers will be influenced by customers to measure predictive/root cause measurements for current problem areas in the TL 9000 measurements. For example, manufacturing cycle time/interval is predictive of meeting customer requested dates in the light of industry delivery/completion norms.

TL 9000 measurements had to be relevant to customers and suppliers. The measurements are customer/telecom service provider-facing rather than in-process measurements.

They can:

1. Calibrate to TSP end-customer satisfaction

2. Facilitate estimation of customers' cost or pain for poor supplier performance

3. Enhance communications within customer organizations interfacing with the supplier. These attributes allow rich customer/supplier communications on the supplier's impact to end-customers, customer's costs and joint customer/supplier improvement projects.

As mentioned earlier, TL 9000 measurements had to be useful to customers. The measurements were carefully defined to be measurable and comparable, which allows customers to compute their Cost of Poor Quality (COPQ) from supplier performance measurements.

The customers could determine the supplier impact for each defect/incident/delay and then use the supplier measurements to quantify the COPQ for that supplier for a particular time frame. They could then project the COPQ over a product life and add initial cost to arrive at a rough life cycle cost. This may be useful in comparing multiple supplier bids, especially where life cycle costs are greater than first cost differences.

TL 9000 measurements also had to be useful to suppliers if they were to be used in decision making and serve as a focal point for continuous improvement. These measurements complement and correlate to the supplier's internal measurements. Several of the internal measurements should be able to predict TL 9000 measurements. The closed loop use of TL 9000 measurements will help supplier management guide progress to improve processes, products and services and determine whether progress is meeting customer and the industry expectations.

QuEST Forum motivation for establishing common industry measurements was based on favorable experiences in working with individual suppliers on performance trends in critical areas. This experience included some common measurements supporting the world's most reliable national networks.

Thus, for a formal management system, the required addition of reportable measurements was an important QuEST Forum goal. Just as the Malcolm Baldrige National Quality Award structure includes "results," TL 9000 adds the same "results" and improves upon Baldrige with common and normalized measurement definitions for industry comparison. Consequently, the *Measurements Handbook* is expected to have a greater impact than the *Quality System Requirements Handbook*. Customers will move beyond simply requiring third-party certification to working with suppliers in setting measurement targets through a TL 9000 closed loop system.

While other industries also may have some common measures, these typically relate to customer satisfaction as determined by independent agencies such as the American Society for Quality (ASQ), J. D. Powers or Consumer Reports. The oil and gas industry goes further asking companies to contribute purchasing practices performance data to the Juran Institute for benchmarking purposes. TL 9000 takes this further by binding measurement usage to formal management system registration, with registrar oversight through audits. Thus, auditable quality measurements are a unique feature of TL 9000 registration.

Registrars must verify that supplier processes are in place to ensure data validity and integrity in accordance with the TL 9000 quality system measurements definitions and requirements. Registrars also must verify that all supplier measurement responsibilities are met and that all measurement process nonconformances are corrected within the registrar-specified time frame. Registrars must be satisfied that the measurement processes are effective and that the results have been submitted successfully to the QuEST Forum measurements administrator — the University of Texas at Dallas (UTD) — before granting TL 9000 registration.

The Baldrige criteria introduced the important concept of quality system "deployment," which registrars consider in their sampling of quality records and employee interviews. TL 9000 measurements, as reported by specific product categories, are designed to help both the registrar and customers evaluate supplier quality system implementation and results. The TL 9000 measurements provide stakeholders with good ideas as to how evenly continuous improvement has been realized across product categories.

Telecom companies have evolved from essentially a monopoly situation to an atmosphere where robust customer/supplier partnerships are needed to provide enhanced, reliable services to consumers on demand. TL 9000 measurements enhance these customer/supplier relationships through goal setting and joint improvement projects. Customers may ask key suppliers for customer-specific performance trends plotted by "industry mean" for every product category in their contract or registration scope using the QuEST Forum Telecom Industry Measurements Trend Reports (TIMTR).

TIMTR show the comparative benchmarks: industry mean, median, range, best in industry, number of data points and standard deviation. The TL 9000 measurements will allow the TSP to harmonize their supplier assessment processes, commonly called "report cards." Face-to-face meetings can be called to identify joint customer/supplier improvement initiatives.

QuEST Forum defined the selected measurements to be meaningful, comparable and value-added. The definition includes normalization tables, product categories, counting rules and definitions (terminology). Thus, registrar and internal audits can support industrywide definitions in measurement and data collection.

The *Quality Systems Requirements Handbook* links to the *Measurements Handbook* through several requirements:

- Quality Objectives 5.1.1.C.1
- Long- and Short-Term Planning 5.4.2.C.1
- Quality Improvement Program 8.5.1.C.1
- Organization Performance Feedback 5.5.4.C.1
- Field Performance Data 8.4.H.1.

Applicable TL 9000 measurements are determined by the registration option chosen. For example, a hardware supplier that selects registration option HW will collect and use the five common measurements and the single hardware measurement. Here is a summary of the applicable measurements for lother registration options.

Common (HW, SW and / or SC)

- Problem reports (NPR) for critical, major and minor problem reports
- Problem report fix response time (FRT) and overdue fix responsiveness (OFR) for major and minor problem reports
- On-time delivery (OTD) for systems, items and service
- System outage (SO) for HW and SW downtime and outage frequency for both supplier attributable and total.

Hardware (HW)

- Return rates (RR) for field returnable units (normally circuit packs) shipped in their first year and after.

Software (SW)

- Release application aborts (RAA) for three releases, where releases can have one or more software updates
- Software defective updates (SWU) for three releases which could contain both corrections and features, where updates can have one or more patches
- Corrective (CPQ) and feature (FPQ) defective patch quality for three releases.

Services (SC)

- Services quality (SQ) on the rate of successful transactions.

TL 9000 Measurements

TL 9000 product categories define the registration scope, applicable reportable measurements and the individual measurement normalization factors allowing industry comparisons.

1. Problem reports — The NPR measurement is the number of customer problem reports or complaints per normalized unit (e.g., installed system) per month. Problem reports are defined as customer-originated reports that are indicative of the quality of the product delivered. NPR is reported by each product category for HW/SW products by severity level (critical, major and minor) and for all service problems.

2. Problem report fix response time — The FRT measurement represents the percentage of problems resolved on time by month. FRT is reported by each product category for HW/SW products and for service problems fixed on time (major problems are to be fixed within 30 days and minor problems are to be

fixed within 180 days). Note that critical problems are not included as they are worked on a highest priority basis. Overdue problem report fix responsiveness (OFR) is the rate of closure of overdue major and minor H/S problem reports and all service problem reports.

3. On-time delivery — The OTD measurement is the percentage of supplier orders or items completed to the customer's requested date by month. Depending on order type, OTD is reported by each product category at either the order level for systems or services or at the order item level for material only products.

4. System outage — The SO measurement is the number and duration of customer systems outages per normalized unit (e.g., customer capacity) per month. Outages are especially severe problem reports where the customer suffers a complete loss of functionality of all or part of a HW/SW system. The cause of each outage is determined as both supplier-caused and total outages. SO is reported by each product category for annualized outage frequency, annualized downtime, portion attributable to the supplier and overall totals.

5. Return rates — The RR measurement is the number of customer returns per normalized unit (e.g., customer capacity) per month. RR is reported by each HW product category for field returnable units (normally circuit packs) returned. Four measurements are maintained: initial (first six months IRR), first year of service (YRR) of shipment, those after one year of service (LRR) and the normalized first year return (NYR).

6. Release application aborts — The RAA measurement is the cumulative percent of release applications that cannot be installed or are withdrawn. RAA is reported by each SW product category for the three most dominant releases.

7. Software update quality — The SWU measurement is the cumulative percentage of software updates that cannot be installed or are withdrawn. Software updates correct or add to a releases application. SWU is reported by each SW product category for the three most dominant releases.

8. Corrective and feature patch quality — The CPQ and FPQ measurements are the percentage of official corrective and feature patches that are determined to be defective. Patches correct or add to a releases application. CPQ and FPQ are reported by each SW product category for the three most dominant releases.

9. Service quality — The SQ measurement is the rate of successful transactions for installations, maintenance visits, repairs, call center calls and service transactions using specified criteria. SQ is reported by each SC product category.

Eight General Product Families

In order to have industry-comparable measurements, all telecom products were grouped into eight families. Each group is further subdivided into 79 product categories. Those families (and the number of product categories within each family) are:

1. Switching (5)
2. Signaling (3)
3. Transmission (27)
4. Operations and maintenance (7)
5. Common systems (3)
6. Customer premise (11)
7. Services (10)
8. Components and assemblies (13)

For each product category, the applicable measurements and normalization factors or resource unit (such as bandwidth, e.g., OC-1), and other necessary information for compiling measurement reports are listed in the measurements applicability table that can also be found on the Forum web site (www.questforum.org).

Most ISO 9001 registration scope statements are very broad (e.g., "all telecom products"), which has caused confusion among customers trying to understand whether the products they buy actually come from a formal registered quality management system. TL 9000 registration actually requires that the supplier identify the product category and applicable measurements for each of product. This detailed scope information is maintained on the QuEST Forum web site subject to approval by a registrar. It is expected that future customer RFQ / RFI could specify applicable product categories. Some TSPs also plan to provide supplier feedback on the product category level rather than the traditional product family level.

TL 9000 registration scope by registration option, product categories and applicable measurements scheme evaluates results of the quality system implementation and deployment similar to the method used in the Malcolm Baldrige National Quality Award program.

TL 9000 measurements are used by several parties: the supplier itself, registrar, customers and market.

Suppliers using the traditional Plan-Do-Check-Act (PDCA) cycle can now accelerate their improvement with TL 9000 requirements and measurements, as the measurements tie together the most critical processes.

The measurements provide evidence as to how well the quality system is operating. With it the supplier can:

- Evaluate business performance as seen by the customer
- Initiate action in areas that will give the biggest payback
- Diminish performance roadblocks
- Deploy resources to areas that need attention.

Just as the TL 9000 measurements are balanced, suppliers can create the right business balance between product delivery, out of the box quality and product short- /long-term reliability.

The first step in PDCA is long- and short-term planning (5.4.2.C.1). Top management should use both key customer feedback and position on the TIMTR from UTD in setting new quantifiable quality objectives (5.4.1.C.1).

Various organizations within the company can employ their own PDCA cycle with a focus on those applicable TL 9000 measurements for which they have accountability or can exercise control. In some cases, in-process measures may be a predictor for the TL 9000 measurement. Large suppliers, where various portions of the business design and manufacture either the same or different product categories, can now compare results for further insights on new best practices that contribute to improved performance.

Registrars use the supplier measurement results to focus on the critical management system strengths and weaknesses. Registrars can "follow" the measurements throughout the company's various departments instead of relying on a random audit/sampling plan. On occasion, the registrar can follow the management system deployment to new additional product categories. Registrar audit findings can be supported by associated measurement trend fall-downs. Of course, registrars should consider putting unhealthy companies on probation until performance improves, or they may wish to withdraw those registrations entirely.

Customers use supplier measurement results to drive supplier changes. Traditionally major industry suppliers have provided summary data to customers for their report card assessment under existing contracts. Major TSPs have sophisticated supplier management operations. In fact, the major RBOC rank among the highest organizations on some surveys of best-managed TSPs. Their vision is to drive out unnecessary costs in the supply chain. TL 9000 measurements will provide some leverage for this goal. Customer steps in this process include:

1. Provide raw data for supplier aggregation.

2. Collect supplier performance on the customer according to contract.

3. Assign weight and score "grade" for each product category and measurement.

4. Aggregate all scores using the weights for cumulative supplier score.

5. Provide actionable feedback to the supplier and relative rankings to competitors by product category.

6. Communicate quantitatively or qualitatively those areas causing the largest pain/cost to you.

7. Gain supplier commitment to new measurement targets and action plans to close the performance gap.

8. Jointly determine with supplier where joint company improvement teamwork is necessary.

9. Track supplier progress on plans and effectiveness through subsequent measurements.

10. Revise life cycle cost model if necessary.

11. Decide whether continued business is profitable.

The market will use the TIMTR results to reward the best in industry, punish the worst and narrow the range from worst to best. The ASQ Registration Repository System (RRS) provides access to authenticated parties to TIMTR by product categories. The QuEST Forum will track and motivate improved industry performance. QuEST Forum plans to hold annual best practice conferences to reward practices resulting in measurement improvements. Some of these best practices could become future requirement adders.

It is unclear whether companies will cheerlead their own quarterly "best in industry" achievements as only registrars really know the exact data submission. The UTD Measurements Repository System (MRS) is confidential and highly protected and thus is unable to confirm any supplier claims. Also, this quarter's best could find itself being second best during the following quarter.

Some consulting companies have experience in helping telecom suppliers understand their product's market position. TIMTR information could enhance these services.

Responsibilities for TL 9000 measurements have been assigned to make the system work. QuEST Forum has service contracts with UTD and ASQ and agreements with US and Canadian accreditation bodies, as well as contracts with two training providers: STAT-A-MATRIX and Excel Partnership. The QuEST Forum

TSPs have recorded their responsibilities in the *Measurements Handbook* development. The significant roles are discussed.

It is up to the customer to communicate with its suppliers as to when and where TL 9000 compliance or registration is preferred, useful or required. This can be accomplished via letters, public policy, RFI, RFQ and/or contracts. Next, the customer should provide complete raw data to all suppliers on all product categories, otherwise the supplier is not obligated to work with fragmentary records for that customer.

This should include:

- All problems and complaints to proper supplier channels
- Downtime/aborts
- Population data
- Replacement data.

Periodically, the customer should also meet with key suppliers to review measurement performance impacting their organization. The performance trend reviews should include statistics from the TIMTR. If the aggregate does not match expectations, then the customer should challenge or spot-check the supplier's raw data. As a possible meeting outcome, consideration should be given to establishing joint customer/supplier improvement teams. Next, the customer should harmonize supplier performance assessments (report cards) to use TL 9000 measurement definitions. Lastly, the customer should use their supplier assessment findings to award business.

Supplier measurement responsibilities are to:

- Integrate the TL 9000 measurements into the management system.
- Act on evidence with respect to how well the quality system is operating.
- Establish processes to capture and validate measurements through the extension of internal quality audits or internal financial audits.
- Demonstrate measurement process validity to third-party auditors.
- Aggregate customer data by product categories and customer segments.
- Define the registration scope with the Forum administrator (ASQ).
- Receive the confidential product category reporting identifiers for data submission to UTD.
- Present measurements data by product category to management (for internal use).
- Submit monthly data, aggregated by product category to measurements

administrator (UTD) within eight weeks following every quarter. Follow rules in order to maintain confidentiality and security.

- Provide data submission evidence from ASQ to the registrar as required for TL 9000 registration.

- Address nonconformance in measurements process and correct prior submissions.

- Provide measurements data for new products and services within six months of product introduction and first commercial shipment of product.

- Submit data by product category to "key" customers (based on contractual agreements). Every major customer meeting will need specific measurement reports.

- Establish joint customer/supplier improvement teams based on TL 9000 measurements critical to the customer.

ASQ, in its role as Forum administrator, develops and maintains the TL 9000 registration process, tools and techniques called Registration Repository System (RRS) and maintains BS7799 certification for secure systems. ASQ administers TL 9000 registrations and QuEST Forum membership in the RRS. ASQ also updates the supplier's planned TL 9000 registration scope based on final registrar findings. ASQ maintains a double-blind system with UTD to safeguard company specific results. Finally ASQ provides TIMTR access to authenticated parties.

UTD, in its role as measurements administrator, develops and maintains the TL 9000 measurement process, tools and techniques called Measurements Repository System (MRS) and maintains BS7799 certification for secure systems. The MRS processes supplier data in a double-blind system with ASQ to safeguard supplier identities and company-specific results. The MRS checks for missing or out-of-range data and every quarter computes the TIMTR. Finally, UTD manages telecom research using MRS data.

Registrars are certified by US and Canadian accreditation bodies (AB) when their auditors pass the accredited TL 9000 auditor course and when these auditors are witnessed in the field by the AB. Registrars are responsible to ensure supplier compliance to TL 9000 as well as for ensuring that data validity and integrity processes are in place in accordance with the TL 9000 measurements, definitions and requirements.

Registrars also verify that TL 9000 measurements data has been successfully reported to the measurements administrator. Finally, when registration is offered, the registrar confirms the proper scope is on record with the RRS.

The measurements process should be viewed as a short-term investment for a more agile infrastructure to foster business improvements. Whereas most requirement adders require only behavioral changes, measurements may lead to information technology (IT) development with a surprising price tag. Customers already have high expectations that suppliers have the database technology to "slice and dice" trends into root components.

As many industries move to e-commerce, suppliers planning for TL 9000 registration should consider an IT infrastructure that collects every defect, problem or assessment with the specific customer transaction. Besides data collection, the resulting databases should be analyzed and any actionable information reported to the lowest responsible unit for action, with summary information provided for management oversight of the resulting measurements improvement.

In the case of mature quality management systems, in-process data will be able to predict TL 9000 measurements trends. With the proper IT, top management will have information that it can use to make decisions to avoid customer dissatisfaction.

Suppliers benefit considerably from measurements. The key benefit is an enhanced customer/supplier relationship that includes:

- Responding to specific customer issues with objective measures instead of subjective concerns
- Establishment of improvement programs based on well-defined measurements and targets
- Winning customer bids based more on performance than image or past history
- Reduced costs for customer report cards process
- Fewer second-party audits from customers.

Other supplier benefits include a sharper focus on improving products and services based on common industry measures and the ability to understand industry placement with competition.

Future enhancements are planned for the measurements. By expanding QuEST Forum globally with other network service providers or operators, such as British Telecom, worldwide suppliers can expect savings on using these common measurements with other service providers.

The TL 9000 handbooks are considered useful for supplier management of second-tier suppliers (e.g., boards and assemblies). The product category table will be expanded to include a new product family for second-tier suppliers with individual product categories based on hardware complexity and the appropriate normalization factors.

The QuEST Forum has started the next revision of the *Measurements Handbook* based on several pressures: early supplier experience, European inputs, unfinished business for the first version and predelivery measurements.

Fine-tuning from early participants resulted in the normalization factor calculation from the customer view and not the supplier's view. Thus, customer capacity, not supplier architecture, will be the driver for normalization.

European network service providers have long experimented with GR 1315 IPQM & GR 979 RQMS measurements on a voluntary basis, with no plans for supplier comparisons. Their organizations, European IPQM and RQMS Users Group (EIRUS), have agreed to work with QuEST Forum on these overlapping measurements. One possible outcome is the revision of TL 9000 measurements so both North American and European Network service providers will require common measurements.

QuEST Forum is also looking beyond third-party registration to various award criteria. Work is in progress to complete the Business Excellence Acceleration Model (BEAM). The objective is to motivate mature suppliers to strive for world-class performance.

The unfinished business from the *Measurements Handbook* was two noncomparable indicators: outgoing quality and customer costs. The outgoing quality indicator would have suppliers understand the many causes of RR and NPR poor performance. Suppliers could use a variety of in-process measures that correlate to actual RR and NPR rates. These computations could then predict future TL 9000 RR and NPR measurements for the customer to compare against actual. The assumption is that better and more mature quality systems should have better predictions than less mature ones. Supplier predictions would provide the customers more options on deployment.

The second incomplete noncomparable indicator is the cost indicator. This definition would formalize the technique where TSPs analyze the cost of poor quality to compute an estimated cost in dollars per normalized unit (cost factor) for less than perfect product or service performance or imperfection. The customer provides the cost factors for each measurement in each product category to suppliers. The suppliers multiply the cost factor times the number of occurrences to derive the cost indicator. This dollar amount could be added to each customer-specific report by product category and TL 9000 measurement. A roll-up of all cost indicators for the current quarter and possibly a future projection could be computed. This would facilitate customer/supplier discussions on targets for improvement.

Several telecom service providers have accepted large risks with new suppliers for the provisioning of new technology or features. It is believed that a new predelivery measurement for new features could alert each TSP when the risk increases with respect to ability to deliver functionality on time.

Finally, work has started on a telecommunications quality index, which should show industry improvement gain from TL 9000 registration.

Business Excellence Acceleration Model (BEAM)

by James J. Gerard

As noted earlier in this chapter, the QuEST Forum was founded to foster improvements in the quality and reliability of the products and services provided to the telecommunications industry. The TL 9000 Requirements and Measurements Handbooks provide a common basis for a solid quality management system that is designed to meet the basic needs of telecommunications suppliers, customers and ultimately end users; that is, to provide products and services that respond to consumers of the worldwide telecommunications market in the 21st century.

The Forum quickly realized that just meeting customer requirements, through conformity with the TL 9000 requirements and measurements, would not be enough for sustained improvement and overall business success. Focusing on the Forum's strong commitment to customers, through the control and improvement of all business processes, it began work on methodologies that would provide support and guidance to the industry's continual improvement efforts. The goal: overall business excellence throughout the telecommunications industry.

A key road to business excellence is through the use of national recognition programs such as the Malcolm Baldrige National Quality Program, the European Foundation for Quality Management and the many state and local recognition programs. To support these improvement methodologies, the QuEST Forum has developed the Business Excellence Acceleration Model (BEAM) Strategic Planning and Business Improvement Guidance Handbook to assist telecommunication companies in self-assessment and translating the results of these assessments into business improvements. The table of contents includes:

- Introduction
- Managing Continual Business Improvement
- Managing Organizational and Cultural Change
- Encouraging and Managing Innovation
- Technology and Knowledge Management
- Strategic Partnering

- Strategic Supply Chain Management
- Life Cycle Planning and Management
- Optimizing Time-to-Market
- Efficient Product Support and Delivery
- Network Reliability and Availability
- Glossary and Acronyms
- Bibliography.

As noted in Figure 16-2, industry is seeking to move from compliance to ISO 9001:2000 and the added requirements of TL 9000 to a philosophy of benchmarking performance against a common set of performance measures of TL 9000 and ultimately to overall performance excellence.

Figure 16-2

Compliance — Benchmarking — Performance Excellence

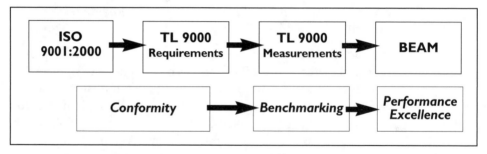

BEAM's intent is: "To identify methods of encouraging and driving business improvement within the global telecommunication market." This does not imply that ISO 9001:2000 and TL 9000 are not valuable quality management systems. On the contrary, they are an essential base that provides a mind-set of consistency and commitment.

Organizations that strive for continued improvement in all facets of their business will, in the long term, outperform those that do not. The BEAM model provides guidelines to assist organizations in moving from a philosophy of conformity to standardized requirements to one of analyzing and improving performance. This is accomplished through suggested methodologies for improving every facet of the business.

There are many very good practices both within and outside of the telecommunications industry. It is not the intent of BEAM to provide the user with lists of these practices, but to provide tools to assist them in planning how they will identify and implement practices. The handbook provides guidance on:

- Key industry issues
- How others have approached key issues
- Suggested references for further information.

While BEAM was initially focused on the telecommunications industry, the philosophies are beneficial to all industries. This is clear when you look at some of the telecommunications industry drivers. They are applicable to all industries.

- Global competition in all facets of the industry
- Global-based economy
- Mergers and acquisitions
- Customer demands for quality in products and services
- Concerns of shareholders and stakeholders
- Technology
- Regulations
- Mobile work force
- Recognition of social accountability issues, including environmental concerns
- Internet growth
- Competitive pressures from parallel industries
- Demands for improved performance at lower prices.

Further information about BEAM is available on the QuEST Forum web site (www.questforum.org).

Conclusion

TL 9000 and the associated third-party registration scheme represents:

- Customer/supplier jointly working to improve telecom quality
- Quality standards consolidation
- An industry adaptation of ISO 9001
- Standardized approach to quality management
- Standardized/visible measurements.

The QuEST Forum membership, consisting of both suppliers and customers, believe this foundation will result in improved supplier performance as measured by customer satisfaction and problems, fix response time, delivery, system outages, software aborts and hardware returns. This in turn will lead to increased market share for both supplier and customer.

TL 9000 defines a very comprehensive quality management system for achieving business objectives. It also provides confidence of supplier reiability. It is likely that many companies will embrace TL 9000 to achieve a competitive edge. More sophisticated customers expect certification and compliance to the measurements.

References

TL 9000 Quality System Requirements (Book One, Release 2.5) ISBN 0-87389-463-4 QuEST Forum and ASQ Press, May 1999

TL 9000 Quality System Requirements (Book Two, Release 2.5) ISBN 0-87389-463-4 QuEST Forum and ASQ Press, November 1999

ISO/IEC 12207, *Information Technology Software Life Cycle Processes*, Geneva, Switzerland, International Organization for Standardization, February 1995.

GR-1202-Core Generic Requirements for a Customer Sensitive Quality Infrastructure, *Telcordia Technologies*, Issue 1, October 1995

GR-1252, Quality System Generic Requirements for Hardware, *Telcordia Technologies*, Issue 1, May 1995.

TR-NWT-000179, Quality System Generic Requirements for Software, *Telcordia Technologies*, Issue 2, June 1993

Application of ISO 9001:2000 to the Construction Industry

by Paul A. Nee

The application of ISO 9000 to the construction industry makes both competitive and business sense in a global marketplace that increasingly rewards efficiency and superior customer service.

Interest in applying ISO 9000 to the construction industry has grown at a steady pace among North American-based companies. Some of that interest has been driven by countries that require ISO 9000 registration to bid on certain types of government and private sector projects. However, the adoption of ISO 9000 by an increasingly diverse stakeholder group from the chemical industry to the health care industry will continue to encourage the use of internationally accepted quality management practices.

The Dorma Experience

Dorma Door Controls, Inc. of Reamstown, Pennsylvania, is a manufacturer of builders hardware products for the construction industry. In January 1991, Dorma decided to pursue certification to ISO 9001:1994 as a "stepping-stone" to a Total Quality Management (TQM) philosophy. In April 1992, Dorma was registered. At the time around 300 registration certificates had been awarded in the United States.

The significance of Dorma's accomplishment was not fully appreciated by the marketplace and there was little customer impact despite the fact that the effort strengthened Dorma's position as the quality leader in the builders hardware industry.

However, Dorma's early success with registration put it in the unique position to become the industry ISO 9000 resource for training customers, competitors and other related companies.

Dorma's market-leading experience has paid off. Many international and domestic customers are now requesting evidence of ISO 9000 registration as a requirement for doing business, a request that promises to be more common than not in the future.

Industry Changes

The application of the ISO 9000 standard to the construction industry requires some interpretation, but the most difficult part of the process for most in this industry will be changing long established ways of doing business.

For example, many companies in the construction industry have poor instructions and inadequate process control. This results in lengthy "punch lists" that must be resolved before the project is complete. Excessive losses are experienced by the contractors due to unsatisfactory work performance. ISO 9000 procedures will help avoid many of these costly and time-consuming problems.

How the Standard Relates to Construction

The following is an explanation of how the ISO 9001:2000 standard can be applied to the construction industry. This is not a comprehensive implementation guide, but should be used as an overview of how a construction-related business approaches registration.

4 Quality Management System

Quality management systems and supporting procedures are documented and followed in most material and hardware manufacturers. On the other hand, some architectural and engineering firms may not have a defined quality system in place. Most construction contractors do not even consider quality systems part of normal construction activities. This clause requires such a system, including developing a quality manual. Documents and records are to be reviewed during construction and at final acceptance.

5 Management Responsibility

5.1 Management Commitment

The majority of construction-related companies do not usually involve executive management in setting and managing the company's quality system. This clause requires management to be committed to improving the quality system.

5.2 Customer Focus

This is a new clause, ensuring that customer needs and expectations are determined and met.

5.3 Quality Policy

Construction management is to make sure the policy includes continual improvement and is understood by those affected.

5.4 Planning

Construction planning is to include measurable objectives that are consistent with the policy.

5.5 Responsibility, Authority and Communication

This describes how to administer the quality management system. Construction-related businesses may be lacking in this area.

Implementing this clause would mean:

- Identifying responsibility, authority, and interrelationships
- A functioning management representative
- Improving communication throughout the organization.

5.6 Management Review

Construction management is to periodically review the quality management system.

6 Resource Management

Construction industry assignments and training are largely based on an apprentice system, with few formal requirements for many jobs. ISO 9000 requires an organization to identify needs, provide training, confirm its effectiveness and maintain appropriate records.

Also, other resources are to be provided as needed.

7 Product Realization

7.1 Planning of Product Realization

Any construction project, no matter the size, must have its processes under control. For example, deciding what equipment to use, making sure that the project meets all applicable building codes and setting criteria for workmanship should be standard procedure. ISO 9000 provides a framework for defining and ensuring that detailed planning is accomplished.

7.2 Customer-Related Processes

Before a contract is signed, ISO 9000 requires that all differences are resolved during a documented contract review session. This clause is critical for engineering and architectural firms and should be an essential part of procedures adopted by all construction-related companies. Implementing ISO 9000 will assure careful review and confirmation of customer requirements, protect other organizations involved in the project and reduce incidents of rework and replacement of product and/or service.

7.3 Design and Development

This clause is primarily the focus of engineering and architectural organizations. ISO 9000 requires that companies have design verification and validation procedures and adequate controls to assure an acceptable design.

7.4 Purchasing

Most construction-related businesses use suppliers they trust, but ISO 9000 offers a more formal system for choosing suppliers. This clause has several advantages for the construction industry. It assures that an approved subcontractor's materials and services are incorporated into a construction project, and it draws project management into the process.

7.5 Production and Service Provision

Current industry practices use an informal system to identify, track and control material entering a construction site. ISO 9000 assures that construction project materials are properly received and identified prior to utilization.

Often construction projects involve customer-supplied materials. ISO 9000 registration formalizes this process.

7.6 Control of Monitoring and Measuring Devices

Building any structure requires the use of numerous measuring devices, from a simple ruler to complex laser surveying equipment. However, ISO 9000 registration does not require that every device be calibrated unless used for verification of quality or acceptance to specification.

8 Measurement, Analysis and Improvement

8.1 General

This clause requires that monitoring and measurement activities needed for conformity are defined, planned and put into use.

8.2 Monitoring and Measurement

A construction foreman is often the principal auditor for a construction project. For many companies, a documented procedure for quality system auditing is a new experience. However, these audits are a valuable quality tool for executive management.

8.3 Control of Nonconforming Product

This is a critical need in construction environments — to avoid unintended use of nonconforming product.

8.4 Analysis of Data

This clause requires analysis of data to determine where quality management system improvements can be made.

8.5 Improvement

A common and recurring problem in the construction industry is failing to address symptomatic or recurring problems during construction. The same "minor detail" problems occur on every job, such as caulking, painting and clean-up. Corrective and preventive action procedures would focus on the root cause of these problems. ISO 9000 helps ensure that past mistakes and inefficient practices are eliminated and continuous improvement is part of the quality system.

The construction industry could benefit from the wide acceptance of ISO 9000. Registered companies working toward the same goals often operate with a higher level of cooperation and customer satisfaction. Construction-related companies will experience improved performance and find fewer mistakes, delays, late penalties and a shorter punch list for rework after the job is complete. For most companies, these efficiencies are payback enough for seeking registration.

ISO 9000 and QS-9000 for the Chemical Industry

18

by James S. Bigelow* and Stephen A. Munden

Introduction

The chemical and process industry (CPI), due to its nature, has some specific considerations when implementing the ISO 9000 series standards. In particular, the CPI is often working with natural raw materials, automated process control is highly developed and many of the processes occur at the molecular level. The latest revisions use more generic language and make the application to our industry easier. The ISO 9000 quality model is highly applicable to the CPI, but some translation is still necessary.

This article will help workers, managers and registrars/certifiers understand the CPI issues that must be addressed. It will:

- Share our combined experience with ISO 9000 in the CPI
- Describe some of the changes necessary to convert from a parts-orientation to a process model
- Help companies with existing registrations in their adoption of the revised standards.

Several years ago, the American Chemistry Council (ACC), formerly the Chemical Manufacturers Association (CMA), suggested that the ISO 9000 model would be appropriate as a uniform model for use between suppliers and cus-

*James S. Bigelow passed away in November 2001.

tomers within the chemical industry. The ACC reasoned that once suppliers built confidence with their customers by using the model, less expense would be associated with auditing each other within the industry.

ISO 9001 and the CPI

Introduction

Differences between ISO 9000:1994 standards and ISO 9001:2000 worthy of note for the CPI include:

- Improved compatibility with the ISO 14000 series standards on environmental management systems
- An emphasis on the involvement of "top management" in the quality management process
- Additional emphasis on meeting regulatory requirements.

0.2 Process Approach

In the revised standard the process approach encompasses all organizational and operational activities. ISO 9001:2000 promotes the adoption of a process approach to quality management in this subclause. In fact, Clause 4.1 actually requires that all the processes needed for the quality management system and their application throughout the organization be identified and described .

The CPI is familiar with manufacturing processes that are often interlinked. The extension of the process approach to business and management activities should, therefore, not cause undue difficulties and should improve the efficiency of the whole organization. It may help to bring down functional hurdles, flatten the structure, further improve and facilitate the integration of the different management systems.

1.2 Application

There is no longer a separate standard, ISO 9002, covering only manufacturing activities. This clause discusses which requirements may be excluded. Only elements of Clause 7 may be excluded, and then only if they do not affect the ability to provide the right products. Much of the CPI has followed ISO 9002 in the past. Applying the revised standard to their systems will require consideration of how to handle "design control." The following table offers several scenarios and possible solutions.

Table 18-1

Design Control — Possible Solutions and Scenarios

Possible Scenario	Comments	Possible Resolution
Customer does not contract with us to do product design. We sell "off-the-shelf" products that we designed at our own risk. That is why we registered to ISO 9002:1994.	The paradigm many companies have followed since 1998 was that if the customer paid for design, follow 9001 (e.g., design a rocket, build it, launch it). Otherwise follow 9002.	The new ISO 9001 QMS does not follow this paradigm. Either include design control in your QMS or see if one of the other scenarios fits your situation.
We did not design the ethylene, ammonia or methanol molecules.	May be superficially true, but we usually write the product design specs that specify acceptable as manufactured purity level, contamination levels, color, etc. Also there are molecules that were designed by man, such as neodo-decanoic acid, which do not exist in nature.	Include design control in your QMS or see if one of the other scenarios fits.
Design is done at another location. We only manufacture the product at this site.	Probably valid. But you may have to explain how you are handling relations with such an "outside supplier" (how you are controlling this "outsourced function").	Exclude design control from your scope. Consider treating this as an "outsourced" process.
Design is not part of the organization we have written into the scope.	Possibly valid. ISO 9001 does not clearly require the organization to include the design function within the scope (unlike QS-9000).	Exclude design control from your scope but treat this as an "outsourced" process.
We manufacture to an industry-standard specification (e.g., 1010 carbon steel, gasoline, SBR rubber, brake fluid).	Probably valid.	Exclude design control from your scope and treat the specifications as documents of external origin.
The customer gives us complete product specifications and we either manufacture to them or select from inventory meeting those specs.	Probably valid.	Exclude design control from your scope and handle this issue as part of "review of requirements related to the product."
We design the process, not the product. The product is just an outcome of setting the process operating conditions. ISO doesn't say anything about controlling process design.	Probably will not be accepted if the auditor understands the process industry. Also, ISO 9004 includes process in the scope of 7.3. It is likely that process design would need to be controlled IF indeed there were no product design function meeting the definition above.	Either include design control in your QMS or see if one of the other scenarios fits your situation.

4 Quality Management System (QMS)

4.1 General Requirements

This section sets out the general requirements for a quality management system. There is a clause here requiring that "outsourced processes" still need to be controlled. The concept of treating outsourced processes is not new in the CPI's use of the ISO 9000 model. Some processes that are commonly outsourced, from the viewpoint of the implementing organization's scope, include human resources, training, purchasing and order review and entry.

4.2.1 General Documentation Requirements

The documentation requirements are less prescriptive than in the 1994 edition. Organizations have more latitude in deciding how formal and extensive their system documentation needs to be. Since most chemical processes are highly complex and technical, it is expected that fairly formal levels of system documentation will be desirable.

4.2.2 Quality Manual

A quality manual is a requirement and the structure of the quality system must be included. In practice, those seeking registration have always been required by their registrars/certifiers to develop a quality manual. In the chemical industry, organizations often refer to overriding standards in their quality manuals. These may include FDA Good Manufacturing Practices, the API Q1 specification or other standard industry practices.

It should be noted that the new standard does not require that the quality manual be a stand-alone document. It is acceptable for it to be combined with other management system documentation. Since regulatory and environmental issues are significant to the CPI, it may well suit companies to have these matters combined in one document.

4.2.3 Control of Documents

Procedures for document control must be documented. Some of the CPI specific documents that should be controlled are specifications, formulas, recipes, standard and emergency operating procedures, laboratory and online test methods, sampling plans, calibration and measurement controls and visual standards. Certain "documents of external origin," such as ASTM test methods, should be included if these documents are spelled out in specifications or contracts. Purchase orders and other information from customers may be treated as external documents, but are more often considered to be quality records.

An issue in the CPI is how to have the current work instruction or procedure available at the point of use. This is often out in the unit, and sometimes in areas that are exposed to the elements. Checklists and "cheat sheets" are sometimes used.

4.2.4 Control of Quality Records

Several clauses of ISO 9001 specifically refer to this section indicating specific records that must be kept. Other clauses may encourage an organization to keep additional quality records, even though they are not specifically identified in the standard. Any type of storage medium is suitable to keep these records, as long as the medium is retrievable and readable for the stated retention period.

5 Management Responsibility

5.1 Management Commitment

This section clarifies management's responsibilities and indicates that management must provide the resources necessary to implement and operate the quality system. This can be applied directly to CPI situations without interpretation.

Top management must demonstrably communicate the importance of meeting customer requirements. In addition, and of particular relevance to the CPI, is the reference in the standard to meeting regulatory and legal requirements. The latter includes environmental, health and safety aspects, including appropriate risk management.

5.2 Customer Focus

This is a new requirement. It may cause difficulties for chemical plants that are remote from their headquarters and sales operations. However, most organizations have already in place some means of including the "voice of the customer" at the plant level. This may include giving customers the ability to access the plant's customer service section directly, joint customer visits with the sales force and having the management representative take on the role of voice of the customer.

5.3 Quality Policy

In large diverse chemical companies, it may be useful to have and use one corporate level quality policy rather than allowing each business unit and site to develop their own. It is acceptable to have stated policies that contain "aspirant" values, that is, those that are not being fulfilled at all times. Unfulfilled policy statements should become automatic change drivers at management review meetings.

5.4 Planning

5.4.1 Quality Objectives

Quality objectives should be documented in some form, perhaps in the quality manual, but more often in supporting documentation such as the company's annual business plan objectives. Measurement of performance against these objectives should be reviewed as part of a continual improvement process.

5.4.2 Quality Management System Planning

Initial planning may include developing the quality policy and the objectives (activities) needed to meet the policy. This may also include determining what processes are needed for the quality management system and how they are to be deployed. Ongoing QMS planning may include action plans to measure the progress and performance of the system.

This is intended to be "high level" planning. The detailed planning that may be needed to meet a customer's contract is covered in Clause 7.1.

5.5 Responsibility, Authority and Communication

5.5.1 Responsibility and Authority

Organization charts, flowcharts and job descriptions may all be useful tools to describe and communicate roles and responsibilities for quality critical functions.

5.5.2 Management Representative

This person(s) should have enough direct or indirect contact with senior management to fulfil the required responsibilities. In the CPI, this person often represents the organization in relationships with customers and suppliers. The management representative often coordinates the preparation of performance information for management reviews and communicates the outcomes of these reviews.

5.5.3 Internal Communication

It is important to communicate to the organization how effectively the QMS is performing. One way to do this is to make sure that the activities of the management reviews are widely circulated.

5.6 Management Review

While it may seem somewhat prescriptive, we believe that the management review frequency should be at least annually, and preferably more often, if a genuine desire exists for continuous improvement. Management reviews should not necessarily be "special events" for review of the quality management system, but rather as part of the continuing monitoring of performance of the business.

Customer complaints and internal statistical measures also ought to be part of these reviews, as well as supplier performance, results from internal and external audits and corrective and preventive actions.

The underlying emphasis of the review should be on the overall effectiveness of the QMS.

6 Resource Management

6.1 Provision of Resources

Management must provide the resources necessary to implement and operate the QMS. In this context resources include people, time and monetary considerations.

6.2 Human Resources

The skills required to perform quality critical jobs should be inventoried and compared to the skills existing in the work force. Training and education are provided to close any gaps. Training plans require a documented procedure and records of training are required.

New to this revision is the requirement that effectiveness of efforts taken to close the identified gaps must be evaluated.

6.3 Infrastructure

Physical resources to assure conformity of product (and ability to meet agreed requirements) must be defined and provided. This may include the equipment, facilities, laboratory testing, utilities, services and other infrastructure typical to the CPI.

6.4 Work Environment

Use suitable production, installation and service equipment. Provide a suitable working environment. (See 4.9.b in the 1994 version.) Typical preventive maintenance plans already used in the CPI should easily satisfy the need for maintenance.

7 Product Realization

7.1 Planning of Realization Processes

Quality planning activities are clearly required. A quality plan in the chemical industry may differ from one in a hard goods industry. This may occur when the same processing equipment (our "hardware") is operated at different conditions (time, temperature, pressure, catalyst, etc.) or with different feedstocks (type and quantity) to produce different products. In some cases multiple grades are offered within a given product family.

Many chemical companies have published product slates and customers order from the product sales specifications. Chemical products vary from near-commodity to high-specialty.

7.2 Customer-Related Processes

The critical issue is for suppliers to evaluate their ability to fulfill orders however they may be received. This includes tenders, contracts and verbal orders. A focal issue for some chemical companies revolves around accepting blanket contracts for more than they can produce, much as the airlines overbook seats on an airplane. When "capability" is used in this section it is not necessarily a statistical process capability, but refers more to the overall ability of the supplier to fulfill the expectations of the customer.

Safety and other considerations require the chemical industry to define the point at which custody transfer takes place. Is the supplier or the customer responsible for the integrity of the product while it is on the way to the customer? Status, Subclause 7.5.3, defines conditions under which product may be "dispatched," and this is addressed further in 7.5.5, Preservation.

7.2.3 Customer Communication

The organization should have established lines of communication and interface with the customer. This may be important in the CPI where "shipment" may involve lining up pipeline connections directly to the customer's tankage.

7.3 Design and/or Development

In the CPI at least three kinds of "design" are common. Most CPI companies maintain fairly major distinctions between process, product and plant engineering or design. All three types could come under an organization's scope of a quality system based on ISO 9001. However, at a minimum, design of the product must be addressed.

In many cases, CPI organizations invent new products from their own initiatives, while seeking new ways to use a molecule. The customer's dollars are not at risk if the product finds no commercial success. These organizations may not wish to impose formal design controls as part of their quality management system, although typically such controls do exist in the organization. See the table in the earlier application discussion in this regard.

It is often difficult to replicate results from lab-scale glassware in pilot plants and commercial plants. If the rules of similitude are not well developed in a given field, then the company may have no choice but to make full-scale trials in their commercial plants. If the design objectives have not been well defined in advance, this can be quite an expensive option.

7.4 Purchasing

No CPI specific issues exist in following the ISO 9000 model for the purchase of conventional raw materials, catalysts and chemicals. Special quality assurance plans should be considered in situations involving bulk shipments, contract terminals and laboratories, exchange agreements, toll processing, the operation of pipeline grids and certain utilities such as process water. Careful consideration should be given to assure that all requirements of the customer are met. CPI organizations are often supplied by upstream units in the same company that are not included in the scope of the quality system. Such sources of supply should be addressed with respect to this element as if they were outside companies.

Although ISO 9000 allows for the customer to include in the contract the right to inspect a subcontractor's operations, customers in the CPI seldom invoke this right.

Changes to a supplier's products or processes that could impact the organization's final product quality may also need to be monitored and controlled.

7.5 Production and Service Operations

Control of Production and Service Provision

Process control in the CPI often carries a different connotation than was intended by the authors of ISO 9000. The term is most often used to describe the systems of sensors, analyzers and control loops employed in our processes. The term has broader meaning in ISO 9000 and is used to describe all the activities to control production, installation and servicing.

Process control is typically an area of strength in the CPI. Automatic control strategies for normal and abnormal operations are usually well defined and documented. Training is often very thorough. The requirement for "suitable maintenance" is sufficiently vague as to explicitly require neither preventive maintenance nor written maintenance procedures.

In the CPI, servicing may occur in such areas as performance specifications, provision for technical service, emergency contacts and other similar functions. It is not intended to include the typical goodwill or customer technical service work that is not billed separately and is considered to be part of the normal conduct of business. Therefore, this clause often does not apply to CPI firms.

7.5.2 Validation of Processes

This is the same as the "special processes" that were covered in 4.9 in the 1994 edition. Oddly, one could argue that all chemical processes are "special" or that none of them are. The requirements are somewhat easier to apply if all or most chemical processes are considered to be "regular processes."

7.5.3 Identification and Traceability

The principle requirement is that you have procedures to identify all raw material, intermediates and finished product throughout your processes. This provides flexibility in the means of identification that is needed in the CPI.

While traceability is only a requirement if specifically stated in a customer's contract, the concept of providing full traceability is a good quality practice to assist in troubleshooting efforts. In addition, if an industry norm calls for traceability, such as FDA-GMP, this should alert the supplier to consider traceability a requirement even if not specifically referenced by the customer. Any blending or comingling of product should be carefully addressed.

Since the status of product from raw materials receipt through to the release of finished product must be known, this is often related to identification and traceability. Direct labeling of products in the CPI is often impossible (until we learn how to bar code every molecule). Therefore the quality plans must identify other procedures to accomplish the same end. Special storage areas for solid products or hold tanks for liquids may be employed. A special case that requires definition is the case in which there is no ability to hold product. Examples are pipeline-linked units, or direct shipments from the supplier's process unit to the customer's process.

7.5.4 Customer Property

This section applies most directly to toll converters or in those cases where the customer provides the raw materials, packaging (including tote bins, rail cars, tank trucks, etc.) or other similar items that are used in your process. The supplier has the obligation to account for and preserve the condition of all that is provided by the customer. In the CPI, these obligations are often spelled out in the contract in terms of loss factors.

7.5.5 Preservation of Product

From a pragmatic viewpoint, packaging, preservation and delivery apply mostly to finished product. However, this clause also applies to internal distribution of raw materials as well as intermediate products. In the CPI, these situations are often addressed as part of process control. In any case, all of the points raised must be covered in one place or the other.

Issues for the CPI include avoiding cross-grade contamination and protecting products from deterioration other than normal aging. As many chemical products are unstable, shelf life and isolation of the products (such as nitrogen blanketing or inhibitor addition) must often be addressed. An issue that is sometimes missed in packaged chemicals is the useful life of the package itself.

Types of storage containers in the CPI are particularly varied and may include caverns, pipelines, ships, rail cars, piles, silos, bags, boxes and crates. Issues that must be addressed include storage pressure and temperature, corrosion allowances, previous contents and the characteristics of the product. Many of these same factors must also be considered for distribution and shipping.

7.6 Control of Measuring and Monitoring Devices

For the CPI, the scope of this section includes lab equipment, on-line analyzers, and equipment in the R&D lab that is used to verify product quality. In-process instrumentation is often used for process control and optimization purposes, rather than verification that product conforms to specified requirements. Many flow, temperature, pressure and level instruments may not need to be included in this requirement.

While the focus is on calibration at prescribed intervals, it is generally accepted that statistical process control (SPC) may be used in the measurement processes. With this system, the equipment need only be taken out of service when SPC indicates the system is out of statistical control. Before the equipment may be put back into service, the cause of the failure must be determined and eliminated. This process will likely include calibration as one of the final steps. It is important for the supplier to document the actual processes used.

National and international reference standards do not exist for many of the tests performed in the CPI. Industry standards are sometimes developed by sections of the industry (for example, ASTM ethylene standards for use with ASTM D3900). However, the supplier often must be responsible for developing, qualifying and maintaining internal standards and reference materials.

Sampling and measurement system variation itself is often a large component of the total process variation experienced in the CPI. It is important, though not a requirement, for suppliers to do statistical studies of measurement capability.

8 Measurement, Analysis and Improvement

8.1 Planning

The proper use of statistical techniques is a requirement, not an option. The supplier is required to identify where statistical tools should be used, and then to provide procedures for their use.

Statistical techniques are widely used in the CPI to determine process and measurement capability, to set specification limits, design sampling plans, make conformance decisions, monitor processes, analyze causes of nonconformance, identify areas for improvement, analyze customer trends and for many other applications.

8.2 Monitoring and Measurement

8.2.1 Customer Satisfaction

Some methods of measuring perceived customer satisfaction must be used. The standard is not prescriptive on what techniques or measures must be used.

A common situation in the CPI is that the corporate offices manage customer surveys and the like, while the ISO registrations occur at the plant level. It is likely that the corporate-level work suffices as long as it is formally considered during management review.

8.2.2 Internal Audit

Many companies in the CPI have practiced internal safety audits for a long time. Internal quality audits are a logical extension of this practice. Internal audits are powerful in driving quality improvement. One is working with the people in the process who are the most knowledgeable of actual or potential problems.

8.2.3 Measurement and Monitoring of Processes

Process performance measurement in manufacturing is a historical strength in the CPI. The key requirement is to use this information to drive improvement. This clause also covers measurement of the performance of the QMS, which in a way is redundant with the internal audit requirements.

High levels of in-process testing are a way of life in the CPI. All testing needed to meet the requirements of the quality plan should be covered either in this section or in the process control section. Close coupling of process units may prevent holding intermediates until testing is complete. In these cases, control plans should provide for the ability to contain the correct downstream inventory if adverse results are later reported. This is often accomplished with process computer data and time lag regression models.

8.2.4 Measurement and Monitoring of Product

Receiving inspection and testing covers both raw materials and customer-supplied materials. Storing bulk materials raises the potential for cross-contamination and this should be addressed in the procedures. Some chemical raw materials, e.g., pipeline shipments, go directly into the process without ever going into inventory and this requires a high level of confidence in your suppliers. Inspection plans for raw materials should be appropriate to their criticality to the process.

Final testing of the finished product should be complete before the product may be "dispatched." Carefully define these aspects of the transaction in the contract to answer questions of ownership and title transfer. The high cost of delays often allows CPI products to move down the supply chain before all the test results are available. In cases of long delivery time, where the product is in transit and can be recalled, it is often desirable to complete testing while the product is in transit. These situations are acceptable practice provided that the supplier and customer have mutually agreed to the actual conditions.

As process capabilities improve, many in the CPI are correlating in-process test results with results on the finished product, thus eliminating some expensive testing. An example might be predicting a product's molecular weight based on reactor measurements, and correlating this by time lags to the finished product. Careful procedure design becomes even more important as this trend increases. Clear communications with the customers are a must.

8.3 Control of Nonconforming Product

Nonconforming product should be segregated into designated tanks, silos, tank cars, hopper cars, warehouse areas, etc. Log notes and product classification systems become very important in tracking this storage.

When product flows are continuous, the absolute isolation of nonconforming product may not be possible. Supplier and customer should have plans to handle these contingencies. In some cases, the customer has the ability to accept the product, given prior notice that it is on the way, along with a description of what to expect. In contrast to the hard goods industry, where parts either fit or don't fit, CPI customers can often accept some deviation, depending on the following factors:

- Nature of the deviation
- Duration and extent of the deviation
- Ability to modify process conditions given sufficient advance notice
- Expenses associated with shutting down and restarting
- Price concession.

This section provides several methods for disposing of nonconforming product, including reworking, acceptance by concession, regrading and scrapping. To this list, the CPI adds blending and recycling, among others.

8.4 Analysis of Data

In most cases in the CPI, analysis of data is not thought of as a separate function but is integrated into the measurements of process and product discussed above.

8.5 Improvement

8.5.2 Corrective Action

Two types of actions are to be considered:

- Correction — disposition of the problem product, perhaps including recall, rework or blending (per Clause 8.3)
- Corrective action — finding and eliminating a root cause so that the problem does not recur.

The organization itself decides whether to correct a nonconformity (contain the problem) or to treat it as corrective action and work to prevent recurrance. This decision is often based on the severity of the problem, the number of repititions, etc. Too often customers send in "Corrective Action Requests" instead of complaints, indicating a fundamental misunderstanding of the standard.

8.5.3 Preventive Action

- Preventive action — eliminating potential causes before a problem ever occurs.

The concept of contingency planning is well developed in the CPI, given the long history of emphasis on safe operations, and this is analogous to taking preventive action.

Corrections, corrective actions and preventive actions should all be included in the management review, not just preventive action as the standard literally requires.

Selecting a Registrar or Certification Body

Many organizations in the CPI decide to proceed beyond implementing an ISO 9000-based quality system to independent third-party registration. Because of the many special issues we have been discussing, it is important to select a registrar carefully. Your relationship with the registrar will likely last several years. Your registrar needs to be cognizant of, and competent concerning, special CPI issues. When you interview potential registrars you will want to ask for references in the CPI.

QS-9000, ISO/TS16949 and ISO 9001

There has been confusion as to how far up the supply chain QS-9000 was supposed to be imposed or applied in the CPI. Many chemical products are at Tiers 3-6 as defined by the Big Three Auto Companies. The recent revision of Production Parts Approval Process (PPAP) has clarified the situation. "Bulk materials," which include chemicals, do not have to go through the PPAP checklist, unless your customer specifically requires it (the prior edition of PPAP required the checklist unless your customer excluded it). Thus, most chemicals are now relieved of this obligation, except in a true Tier 1 sense (e.g., brake fluid).

A Word About ISO 14000 and the CPI

ISO 9001 and ISO 14001 are designed to be fully compatible. While ISO 9000 focuses on the on-purpose product, ISO 14001 addresses the byproducts. Many of the control systems called out in these standards are similar. An organization employing the ISO 9000 and ISO 14000 models should use as many common processes as possible. Some of the common systems may include:

- Development of policies and procedures
- Planning
- Definition of responsibilities

- Training
- Document controls
- Record keeping
- Maintenance plans
- Instrument controls
- Internal auditing
- Corrective and preventive action
- Management review.

The CPI, and specifically the ACC, already have several environmental initiatives such as Responsible Care®. The industry will have to reconcile these activities against the ISO 14001 standard and assess the relative value of compliance and/or registration to ISO 14001.

Conclusion

The chemical and process industries are different from manufactured goods industries and require an appropriate translation of the ISO 9000 standards. The latest revision of ISO 9001 uses more generic language than the earlier version and will be easier for the CPI to use. There are few really new requirements and many clarifications. Guidance has been given for application of ISO 9001 to the CPI to capture both good practices and continuous improvement. The ISO 9000 model is useful for CPI companies.

The 2000 revision increases focus on the voice of the customer and seeking continual improvement, even when following a generic fundamental quality management system.

The Application of ISO 9001:2000 to Software Development

19

By Robert C. Bamford and William J. Deibler II

Introduction

In this chapter, the authors investigate in detail the implications of ISO 9001:2000 for software development organizations. This chapter presents ISO 9001:2000 for individuals who are new to the standard and for individuals who are familiar with the 1994 requirements and need to address changes introduced by the 2000 version.

A Matter of Timing

This chapter is based on newly released versions of the standards:[1]

- ISO 9000[2]
- ISO 9001[3]
- ISO 9004.[4]

Since this chapter includes references to both the 1994 and 2000 versions of these standards, standards are identified both by number and by year of issue (e.g., ISO 9001:1994 and ISO 9001:2000).

Chapter Outline

This chapter begins with a brief review of how previous versions of the standard are perceived by software development organizations. It then examines the ISO 9000:2000 family of standards as it applies to software development organizations. This examination is conducted from three perspectives:

- The members and structure of the family of standards
- The internal structure of ISO 9001:2000
- The requirements of ISO 9001:2000.

The first two perspectives focus on high-level changes. The third perspective steps through key clauses of ISO 9001:2000 and focuses on specific implications for software development organizations. Relevant background information and precedents derived from the use of ISO 9001:1994 are woven into each perspective.

The chapter concludes with two sets of summary recommendations:

- For software development organizations that are in the process of establishing ISO 9001 as a framework for business practices
- For software development organizations that are maintaining business systems that are already aligned with the requirements of ISO 9001. This second set of recommendations focuses on the changes in ISO 9001 that are most likely to require improvements in an organization's policies, procedures, and practices.

The chapter includes six appendices. The first three contain historical information of use to organizations and individuals transitioning to the 2000 version of ISO 9001.

A Brief Review: Been There, Done That

Since this chapter was published in the Third Edition of the *Handbook* in 1997, anecdotal evidence indicates increasing acceptance of ISO 9001:1994 in software development organizations.[5] Whether inspired by customer requirements, competitive pressure or a desire to improve quality and efficiency, software development organizations are coming to understand the value of ISO 9001:1994 as a vehicle for institutionalizing standard software engineering practices. In addition to gaining market recognition and access, these organizations expect to reduce training and facilitate improvement through the establishment of a common baseline for development practices. These organizations are also increasingly receptive to internal audits, as an extension of peer review and software quality assurance,[6] to identify and propagate best practice throughout the organization.

While there is still little government-imposed regulatory pressure, emerging market requirements, particularly in the biomedical, telecommunications and aerospace sectors, position external assessment and registration as a justifiable business expenditure. Beyond providing market access, the value of external assessment and registration for software providers is in its service as a reminder to management of the organization's public commitment to maintain the policies, procedures and standards on which registration and assurance of consistent quality is based.

A software organization seeking guidance on best practice is not limited to ISO 9001. Software organizations can exploit other ISO standards, like ISO 12207 *Standard for Information Technology – Software Life Cycle Processes*[7] and ISO/TR 15504 *Software Process Improvement and Capability Determination*,[8] and non-ISO standards and models, like those offered by the IEEE[9] and the Carnegie Mellon University (CMU) Software Engineering Institute (SEI) *Capability Maturity Model for Software, Version 1.1* (CMM[SM])[10] and its derivative, the Personal Software Process[SM].[11] Concerns about conflicts among these models,[12] particularly between ISO 9001 and the CMM, are being replaced by an understanding of the complementary nature of the models. This growing understanding is a reflection of the ease with which a number of software organizations have transitioned from advanced CMM-based maturity levels to ISO 9001 registration.[13] ISO has also made a new, fundamental commitment to coordinate and harmonize the work products and schedules of its standards-writing subcommittees. One particular outcome of this new commitment is seen in the transfer of responsibility for ISO 9000-3 from TC 176 (Quality Management and Quality Assurance Standards) to JTC 1 SC 7 (Software Engineering Standards).[14]

The table in Appendix D at the end of this chapter suggests how the clauses of ISO 9001:2000 can be grouped based on the life cycle processes defined in ISO/IEC 12207:1995.

A Brief History of ISO 9000-3 and the Application of ISO 9001 to Software

The first version of ISO 9001 was released in 1987.[15]

In 1991, four years later, the member nations of the International Organization for Standardization (ISO) voted to release ISO 9000-3:1991 *Guidelines for the Application of ISO 9001 to the Development, Supply and Maintenance of Software*.[16] In practice with or without the guidance, ISO 9001 had proven applicable to the development of all types of software, including:

- Commercial, off-the-shelf (COTS) software
- Software developed or customized in a contractual situation
- Stand-alone software products (e.g., operating systems, desktop applications)
- Software delivered by any means as part of a system, including firmware.

The second version of ISO 9001 was released in 1994.

Three years passed before a new version of ISO 9000-3 was released in 1997. In chartering the revision to ISO 9000-3:1991, ISO explicitly held changes to a minimum because the impending release of ISO 9001:2000 would render obsolete or eliminate the need for product-specific, nonbinding guidance documents, like ISO 9000-3. The relatively brief — and rapidly shrinking — life expectancy of the revision to ISO 9000-3 made it necessary to expedite the development cycle by tabling known issues that, for whatever reason, would have required extensive discussion to resolve.

The three-year lag, from 1994 to 1997, in the availability of an updated ISO 9000-3 correctly suggests a lack of market pressure for a revision to ISO 9000-3:1991. While it could be construed that the nature of the 1994 revision to ISO 9001 allowed the continued use of ISO 9000-3:1991, a more likely reason for the apparent lack of priority is identified in a 1996 study by Stelzer, Mellis and Herzwurm. Based on data from 36 European software houses that had achieved ISO 9001 registration, the authors concluded that:

"ISO 9000-3[:1991] is not of great help for software houses. Quality managers only read it when they begin to study the ISO 9000 family. When they realize that ISO 9000-3 is as difficult to read as all other parts of ISO 9000, they ignore it and use ISO 9001 instead."[17]

Although ISO 9001:1987 and ISO 9001:1994 are cited as hard to read, Stelzer, Mellis and Herzwurm also report, with some qualification,[18] that:

"Nearly 100 percent of the company representatives [from companies included in the survey] would decide in favor of implementing an ISO 9000 quality system once again. They are convinced that the benefits of installing a quality system exceed the costs."

Perspective 1: The ISO 9000:2000 Family of Standards

The application of ISO 9001:2000 to software is examined first from the perspective of the new makeup of the ISO 9000 family of standards.

In the 2000 release, the number of standards is reduced — eliminating both cost and confusion for adopters of the standard. There are only four documents in the revised family of ISO 9000 standards:

- ISO 9000:2000 *Quality management systems — Fundamentals and vocabulary,* which is normative (must be followed)

- ISO 9001:2000 *Quality management systems — Requirements,* which is normative (must be followed)

- ISO 9004:2000 *Quality management systems — Guidance for performance improvement,* which provides guidance on process improvement for organizations that wish "to move beyond the requirements of ISO 9001:2000 in pursuit of continual improvement of performance"[19]

- ISO 9000-3, *Quality management and quality assurance standards — Guidelines for the application of ISO 9001 to the development, supply, installation and maintenance of computer software.*[20]

The following figure represents the four documents in the 2000 version of the ISO 9000 family.

Figure 19-1

Members of the 2000 Family of ISO 9000 Standards

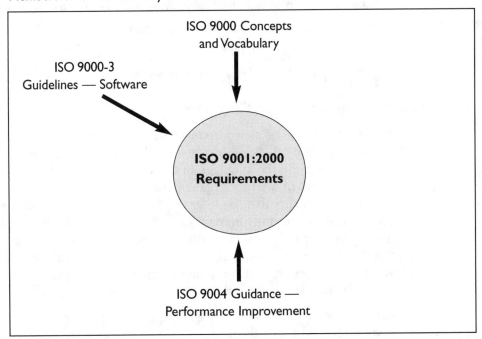

Appendix A in this chapter provides information on the evolution of the ISO 9000 family between 1994 and 2000.

ISO 9001:2000 1.2 Permissible Exclusions

To support the elimination of ISO 9002 and ISO 9003, ISO 9001:2000 Clause 1.2 defines the conditions under which an organization may claim conformity to ISO 9001. The definition of these conditions allows organizations to plan valid exclusions based on information in the standard rather than on anecdotal information garnered from extended negotiation with a registrar. Consistent definitions of conformity and of permissible exclusions are essential if registration and claims of conformity are to be valuable for supplier evaluation and selection.

In Clause 1.2, ISO 9001:2000 institutionalizes the conventions that have evolved since 1987.[21] The rules for excluding requirements are clear and incorporate two criteria:

- The first criterion overrides the second and states that the exclusion can "neither affect the organization's ability, nor absolve it from its responsibility, to provide product that meets customer and applicable regulatory requirements."

- The second criterion is that exclusion applies only to requirements found in ISO 9001:2000 Clause 7, Product realization.

Clause 1.2 goes on to state that exclusions "may be due to the following:

(a) the nature of the organization's product;

(b) customer requirements;

(c) the applicable regulatory requirements."

A Problem: Organization or Company?

In considering ISO's stated requirement that the revision not significantly impact organizations that already comply with the standard[22] (i.e., that are already registered), the language in Clause 1.2 appears to allow an "organization" to be part of a larger organization (e.g., a division in a company). For example, a company that has ISO 9002 registration for manufacturing can continue to claim conformity in manufacturing even if the company also has product engineering and customer service functions. This interpretation is consistent with current usage and it allows many more "organizations" to adopt ISO 9001:2000 conformity (with or without registration) as a public demonstration of commitment to customer satisfaction.

However, at the time this chapter is being written, registrars and accreditation bodies state that under the new rules for exclusion of requirements, if a company includes product engineering and manufacturing functions, they must both be included in the scope of the registration. ISO guidance[23] adds unnecessarily to the confusion by presenting examples of organizations that apply the standard to all of the activities in the organization.

Implications for Software

Since the internal product design and development processes of software engineering organizations are subject to ISO 9001, the determination of permissible exclusions pertains to the relationship between software engineering and the rest of the organization. The key issue associated with exclusion is whether a software engineering organization can claim conformity — with or without seeking registration — unless other organizations in the company, like manufacturing, technical support, hardware engineering, marketing and sales, also achieve conformity.

If exclusion is an issue, the best source of information continues to be the organization's registrar (or candidate registrars) and the guidance provided by ISO.[24]

Perspective 2: The Internal Structure of ISO 9001:2000

The internal structure of ISO 9001:2000 is the basis for the second examination of the application of ISO 9001:2000 to software.

The requirements portion of ISO 9001:2000 is divided into 28 first- and second-level sections and includes 136 instances of the word "shall" — which is the ISO convention for identifying a requirement. By comparison, the requirements in ISO 9001:1994 appear in 66 second- and third-level sections and contain 137 occurrences of "shall." The following table presents the first- and second-level structure of the requirements in ISO 9001:2000.

Table 19-1

First- and Second-Level Structure of ISO 9001:2000 Requirements

4 Quality management systems 4.1 General requirements 4.2 Documentation requirements	7 Product realization 7.1 Planning of product realization 7.2 Customer-related processes 7.3 Design and development 7.4 Purchasing 7.5 Production and service provision 7.6 Control of monitoring and measuring devices
5 Management responsibility 5.1 Management commitment 5.2 Customer focus 5.3 Quality policy 5.4 Planning 5.5 Responsibility, authority and communication 5.6 Management review	
	8 Measurement, analysis and improvement 8.1 General 8.2 Monitoring and measurement 8.3 Control of nonconforming product 8.4 Analysis of data 8.5 Improvement
6 Resource management 6.1 Provision of resources 6.2 Human resources 6.3 Infrastructure 6.4 Work environment	

In ISO 9001:2000, Clause 4, Quality management system, Clause 5, Management responsibility, and Clause 6, Resource management, define requirements for an organizational infrastructure that enables the activities described in Clause 7, Product realization, and Clause 8, Measurement, analysis, and improvement. Clauses 7 and 8 focus on requirements for activities that are directly coupled to the delivery of products and services to customers.

Implications for Software

The revised structure of ISO 9001:2000 provides two opportunities to software development organizations. First, the new structure simplifies the work of assembling the requirements for specific development activities. Second, by defining "production" in a manner that is consistent with both hardware and software processes, the new structure resolves the issues associated with determining the software-related activities to which production applies. Each of these opportunities is discussed in the following paragraphs.

Opportunity 1: Simplification

The revised structure more efficiently segregates requirements associated with activities as they are structured in software organizations. For example, identifying the requirements in ISO 9001:1994 for testing requires consideration of Clauses 4.2.3, Quality planning, (e.g., test planning); 4.4.2, Design and development planning; 4.4.7, Design verification, (e.g., design reviews); 4.4.8, Design validation, (e.g., system test); 4.10.3, In-process inspection and testing; 4.10.4, Final inspection and testing; 4.10.5, Inspection and test records; and 4.11, Control of inspection, measuring and test equipment.

In ISO 9001:2000, comparable requirements are found in Subclauses 7.1, Planning of product realization; 7.3.4, Design and development review; 7.3.5, Design and development verification; 7.3.6, Design and development validation; and 7.6, Control of monitoring and measuring devices.

A second example is in the treatment of requirements related to measurement. ISO 9001:2000 eliminates the overlap and ambiguity associated with ISO 9001:1994 Clause 4.20, Statistical techniques, Clause 4.9 (d)[25] and 4.4.2, Design and development planning.[26]

The new structure of ISO 9001:2000 consolidates requirements for monitoring and measurement in one clause, 8.2. Clause 8.2 and its subclauses are applicable to all processes and call for the "determination of applicable methods," which may include statistical techniques.

Opportunity 2: Resolving the Definition of "Production"

Through careful use of the terms "production," "design and development" and "product realization," the revision resolves one of the most contentious issues associated with the application of ISO 9001:1987 and ISO 9001:1994 to software development: the consistent determination of what activities must satisfy requirements designated by the standard for production. See Appendix C in this chapter for a detailed discussion of the impact, conflicting precedents and convoluted history associated with ISO 9001 and production as applied to software development.

"Production" and ISO 9001:2000

To address the needs of all organizations, technologies, products and markets, ISO 9001:2000 carries forward a structure that distinguishes between "design and development" and "production." Clause 7.3 is titled Design and development. Clause 7.5 is titled Production and service provision.

Table 19-2

Clause 7.5 Production and Service Provision's Subclauses

ISO 9001:2000	Furthers the requirements of ISO 9001:1994
7.5.1 Control of production and service provision	4.9 Process control (the first paragraph and the seven lettered subclauses)
7.5.2 Validation of processes for production and service provision	4.9 Process control (the last four paragraphs)[27]
7.5.3 Identification and traceability	4.8 Product identification and traceability and 4.12 Inspection and test status
7.5.4 Customer property	4.7 Control of customer-supplied product
7.5.5 Preservation of product	4.15 Handling, storage, packaging, preservation and delivery

Note that, of the four clauses that limited themselves to "production" in ISO 9001:1994 (i.e., 4.8, 4.9, 4.11 and 4.12), only 4.11, Control of inspection, measuring and test equipment, is unaccounted for in ISO 9001:2000 Clause 7.5. ISO 9001:2000 Clause 7.6, Control of monitoring and measuring devices, corresponds to ISO 9001:1994 4.11 and defines requirements that apply during all of the realization processes.

The challenge for implementers is to establish how ISO 9001:2000 Clause 7.5, Production and service operations, and its subclauses apply to the software development life cycle.

Get a Life ... Cycle

Clause 7, Product realization, encompasses the elements of an organization's product life cycle, from proposal or requirements gathering to postdelivery support and maintenance. Although activities for product end-of-life are not explicitly referenced in ISO 9001:2000, they are implicitly addressed in Subclause 7.2.2

as part of customer and product requirements review and in Subclause 7.5.1 through "the implementation of defined processes for ... applicable postdelivery activities."

In software engineering, the term "software development life cycle" refers to a subset of the elements of the product life cycle. This subset begins with the receipt of requirements and ends with the delivery of a baseline of the complete product, suitable for replication and distribution to customers. The following figure illustrates how the subclausess of Clause 7.5 apply to a typical product life cycle.

Figure 19-2

Applying the Clauses of ISO 9001:2000 to a Typical Product Life Cycle

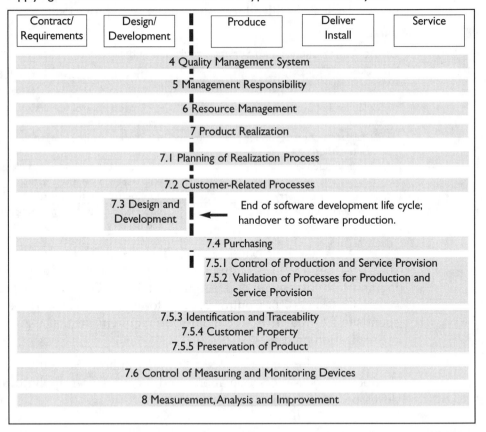

The Application of Clause 7.5 to Software Development Processes

The language in ISO 9001:2000 is sufficient to determine how the subclauses of Clause 7.5 apply to software development. The first two subclauses, 7.5.1 and 7.5.2, do not apply to software development. The remaining three subclauses, 7.5.3, 7.5.4 and 7.5.5, do apply to software development.

ISO 9001:2000 Subclauses 7.5.1 and 7.5.2 refer explicitly to "production and service provision." Both carry forward requirements from ISO 9001:1994 Clause 4.9, Process control, which, based on ISO 9000-3:1997, is not applied to the software development life cycle.

ISO 9001:2000 Subclauses 7.5.3, 7.5.4 and 7.5.5 clearly identify the processes to which their requirements apply.

ISO 9001:2000 Subclause 7.5.3, Identification and traceability, states that "the organization shall identify the product by suitable means throughout product realization."

ISO 9001:2000 Subclause 7.5.4, Customer property, states without qualification that "the organization shall exercise care with customer property while it is under the organization's control or being used by the organization."

The language in ISO 9001:2000 Subclause 7.5.5, Preservation of product, requires that the organization "preserve the conformity of product during internal processing ... Preservation shall also apply to the constituent parts of a product."

Subclauses 7.5.3, 7.5.4 and 7.5.5 contain requirements from clauses of ISO 9001:1994 that are applied to the software development life cycle:

- Subclause 7.5.3 carries forward requirements in ISO 9001:1994 Clause 4.8, Product identification and traceability.

- Subclause 7.5.4 carries forward requirements from ISO 9001:1994 Clause 4.7, Control of customer-supplied product.

- Subclause 7.5.5 carries forward requirements in ISO 9001:1994 Clause 4.15, Handling, storage, packaging, preservation and delivery.

Chapter Outline — Revisited

Referring to the outline presented at the beginning of this chapter, this completes the examination of the ISO 9000:2000 family of standards as they apply to software development organizations from two of three perspectives:

- The members and structure of the family of standards

- The internal structure of ISO 9001:2000.

The remainder of this chapter explores the implications for software development organizations from the third perspective:

- The requirements of ISO 9001:2000.

Perspective 3: The Requirements of ISO 9001:2000 for Software Development

The following paragraphs translate the authors' extensive experience with ISO 9001:1994 into recommendations for maximizing the benefits of ISO 9001:2000 as a benchmark for practical process improvement in software organizations.

The following paragraphs do not address in detail all of the clauses of ISO 9001:2000. They focus on specific requirements, particularly in Clauses 7 and 8, for which additional information directly benefits software development organizations. Whether achieving or maintaining conformity is an organization's goal, all clauses of ISO 9001:2000 are important and require careful consideration.[28]

Defining Quality and Quality Management System

The definitions of "quality" and "quality management system," used throughout ISO 9001, are found in ISO 9000. Quality is "the degree to which a set of inherent characteristics fulfils requirements." A quality management system is defined as "the set of interrelated or interacting elements to direct and control an organization with regard to quality." In practice, a quality management system includes the organizational structure, people, processes, documentation and other resources applied to fulfilling the requirements of customers and any other interested parties (e.g., shareholders, investors, employees and governments).

4 Quality Management System

The requirements in Clause 4.2, Documentation requirements, are of particular relevance to software development organizations, in which the usefulness of processes tends to be perceived as inversely proportional to the amount of procedural documentation.

Too thin. Too rich. Too many procedures?

Subclause 4.2.1, General, points c) and d) define the extent of the procedural documentation required by ISO 9001:2000. Subclause 4.2.1 c) refers to "the documented procedures required by this International Standard." ISO 9001:2000 lists six[29] activities required to be documented in procedures. By comparison, ISO 9001:1994 specifies 19 activities to be documented in procedures. ISO 9001:2000 Subclause 4.2.1 d) requires that the organization's quality management system include "documents needed by the organization to ensure the effective planning, operation and control of its processes." In the context of Subclause 4.2.1 d), "documents" includes all of the work products used in controlling development activities (e.g., plans, schedules, progress review results, meeting minutes, test reports, metrics reports). By reducing explicit requirements for procedures, ISO 9001:2000 focuses software organizations on determining how to achieve results rather than on creating elaborate, overdocumented, unused sets of policies and procedures.

ISO 9001:2000 Subclause 4.2.1 d) generalizes the language of ISO 9001:1994 4.9 a). A documented procedure is necessary if its absence adversely affects quality. For example, missing requirements, disappearing bug fixes and frequent revolving-door releases to SQA of incomplete or bug-ridden versions of software may signal inadequate procedural documentation (or they may be symptoms of inadequate processes, training, resources or management commitment to ensuring that processes are followed). Increasing documentation can exacerbate rather than correct problems.

Streamlining Procedures

Achieving an appropriate level of detail is a critical factor in determining the value of a procedure. Too little information and too much information create similar effects: individuals don't rely on procedures to determine what management wants them to do and procedures are not kept up to date. To address the problems of under and overdocumentation, ISO 9001:2000 Clause 4.2 suggests that the "extent of the quality management system documentation can differ from one organization to another due to … (a) the size of the organization and type of activities … (b) the complexity of processes and their interactions … (c) the competence of personnel." In software development organizations, two of these factors are particularly important in determining an appropriate level of detail.

The first factor is competence of personnel. As the literature suggests, team composition is the most important factor in the success of a software project. Are the software developers application domain experts who have limited software engineering skills or who don't work well together? Competence is also affected by changes in technology, methods and organizational structure, ubiquitous in software development organizations. Is the organization moving from a well-defined structured analysis and design approach to evolving object-oriented methods? Is the organization undergoing rapid change as seen in many Silicon Valley startups and dot-coms? While detailed process documentation may be appropriate for some processes during transitions, once those processes are institutionalized and the work environment stabilizes, reliance on process documentation tends to decrease.

The second factor in determining the appropriate level of documentation is interaction of processes, particularly between software development and other functions of the organization. Processes that cross functional and organizational boundaries need particularly clear and careful definition and documentation. ISO 9001:2000 Clause 5.5.1 reinforces the requirements in Clause 4.2, in stating that, "Top management shall ensure that responsibilities and authorities are defined and communicated within the organization." The importance of cross-functional coordination is further characterized in two subclauses of ISO 9001:2001. Subclause 7.3.1, Design and development planning, requires that the organization "manage the interfaces between groups involved in design and development." Subclause 7.3.3 b) is more specific, stating that "design and development outputs shall ... provide appropriate information for purchasing, production and for service provision."

Cross-functional processes requiring the most attention and potentially the most detailed documentation in conjunction with software development typically include those defining interactions with marketing, systems engineering or customers (for requirements definition, allocation and change management); with system test (for delivery of developer-tested software and receipt of identified problems); with hardware engineering (for coordinating plans and managing dependencies); with manufacturing (for release of completed software product); and with customer support (for providing necessary information and training and for addressing incident reports).[30]

However, if representatives from marketing, development, support and system test meet weekly to manage the development and maintenance of an evolving, off-the-shelf product, the level of documentation related to cross-functional coordination may be minimal.

5 Management Responsibility

Clause 5 contains requirements for "top management," some of which cascade throughout the organization.

While the application of Clause 5 is relatively straightforward, the requirements in Clause 5.2, Customer focus, and 5.4, Planning, can be leveraged to enhance specific software development practices that contribute significantly to the effective and efficient operation of an organization's business practices.

5.2 Customer Focus

In software development, the requirements of Clause 5.2 lead to focus groups, surveys, key customer reviews and systematic methods for requirements gathering and analysis (e.g., joint application development). Clause 5.2 refers to Subclauses 7.2.1, Determination of requirements, related to product and 8.2.1, Customer satisfaction, for specific mechanisms that establish and maintain an organization's customer focus.

Table 19-3

Clause 5

Subclause	Requires that Top Management
5.1, 5.3	Provide evidence of its commitment to ... the quality management system (i.e., establish a quality policy, conduct reviews, ensure resources available).
5.2, 5.4, 5.5.1 and 5.5.3	Ensure that certain activities take place throughout the organizaiton (e.g., customer requirements determined, objectives set, responsibility and authority defined and communicated).
5.5.2	Appoint a management representative.

5.4.1 Quality Objectives

Quality objectives pertain to both product and process. For software, product quality objectives are typically expressed as phase-dependent release criteria (e.g., "For Beta: no severity-A bugs, no more than 3 severity-B bugs," or "All required features are implemented"). Process quality objectives are expressed in relative terms (e.g., rework effort from integration testing as a percent of development effort) and in absolute terms (all code reviews and unit tests completed prior to release to integration test). Product and process quality objectives are established in development policies and procedures as well as in development plans. Subclause 5.4.1 refers to Clause 7.1 Planning of product realization, which requires that the organization determine "quality objectives and requirements for the product."

By acquiring historical data on variability in planning, management in a software organization can establish realistic expectations and objectives for estimating effort and schedules and can institute effective programs to control that variability.

5.4.2 Quality Management System Planning

The requirements of Subclause 5.4.2 of ISO 9001:2000 apply to planning the maintenance and improvement of the whole quality system, which may occur outside the planning associated with a particular product, project or contract. Planning for quality system maintenance and improvement is coordinated with planning for products, described in Clauses 7.1, Planning of product realization, and 7.3.1, Design and development planning.

Subclause 5.4.2 imposes a requirement of particular relevance to organizations with rapidly evolving organizational structures and technologies: "top management shall ensure that the integrity of the quality management system is maintained when changes to the quality management system are planned and implemented." This requirement reinforces the need for management to take appropriate, timely action when change invalidates established policies, procedures, roles, responsibilities and resource availability.

6 Resource Management

Clause 6 provides requirements related to all types of resources: people, infrastructure and the general work environment. ISO 9001:2000 Clause 6.3, Infrastructure, requires that the organization "determine, provide and maintain the infrastructure needed to achieve conformity to product requirements." Examples listed in Clause 6.3 include:

(a) Buildings, workspace and facilities

(b) Process equipment, both hardware and software

(c) Supporting services.

These categories generalize the application of selected elements of ISO 9001:1994 Clause 4.9, Process control.

Process equipment includes all of the software tools associated with product development (e.g., for analysis, modeling, prototyping, planning, reporting, design, coding, configuration management, test and creating documentation and reporting and tracking bugs).

For providers of systems that include hardware and software, process equipment includes prototype and production hardware product for use in software development and testing.

For software development organizations, "supporting services" are varied and may be provided by other parts of the organization (e.g., configuration management, test development and intranet installation and maintenance) or by third parties (e.g., contractors for test or software development, and services for off-site storage or escrow of source code).

For those who have followed the evolution of ISO 9001:2000 through its numerous, public drafts, Clause 6.4 Work environment is a single sentence requiring the organization to "determine and manage the work environment needed to achieve conformity to product requirements."

7 Product Realization

Clause 7, Product realization, is divided into six subclauses. Three of the six define requirements for activities common to all software life cycles:

7.1 Planning of product realization

7.2 Customer-related processes

7.3 Design and development.

Two address specialized activities that support software life cycle activities:

7.4 Purchasing

7.6 Control of monitoring and measuring devices.

Finally, as discussed earlier in this chapter in pages 629-631, parts of Clause 7.5, Production and service provision, apply to software product design and development:

7.5.3 Identification and traceability

7.5.4 Customer property

7.5.5 Preservation of product.

Each of the subclauses of Clause 7 is discussed below.

7.1 Planning of Product Realization

Clause 7.1 includes global requirements for planning all the processes and subprocesses that make up product realization: customer-related processes (Clause 7.2), design and development (Clause 7.3), purchasing (Clause 7.4), production and service provision (Clause 7.5) and control of monitoring and measuring devices (Clause 7.6).

ISO 9001:2000 Clause 7.1 states:

In planning product realization, the organization shall determine the following, as appropriate:

a. Quality objectives and requirements for the product

b. The need to establish processes, documents, and provide resources specific to the product

c. Required verification, validation, monitoring, inspection and test activities specific to the product and the criteria for product acceptance

d. Records needed to provide evidence that the realization processes and resulting product meet requirements.

All of these are appropriate for software development.

By incorporating "specific to the product," Clause 7.1 requires the organization to determine and implement any changes or additions necessary to tailor the organization's standard processes and quality objectives (as documented in the quality management system) for a specific product. Whether any change or amendment is required depends on the nature of the product (e.g., how close it is to a "standard" product) and on the nature of the standard processes (e.g., how flexible and comprehensive they are).[31]

Implications for Software

For software development organizations, the requirements of Clause 7.1 are addressed in combination with the detailed planning requirements found in Clause 7.3.1, Design and development planning. Requirements for the product-specific elements of planning in Clause 7.1 can be addressed in a software development plan by including references or definitions of:

- Applicable "standard" procedures, tools and facilities
- Any new procedures, tools and facilities to be employed in executing the plan.

Change-planning requirements from Clause 5.4.2 b) are also addressed in comprehensive software development plans, which provide for the incorporation of new tools and techniques and any associated skills acquisition (e.g., training, mentoring).

7.2 Customer-Related Processes

Clause 7.2 specifies requirements for the:

- Identification and review of customer requirements
- The management of changes to customer requirements
- Conduct of all customer communication, including the provision of feedback on complaints.

Implications for Software

The language in Subclause 7.2.2 makes ISO 9001:2000 more readily accessible to in-house, commercial and off-the-shelf development organizations. Subclause 7.2.2, paralleling the Requirements Management Key Process Area in the CMM,[32] contains two requirements that support software organizations in dealing with the challenges of product requirements.

The first requirement is in Subclause 7.2.2 c), which requires that the organization ensure it has the ability to meet defined product and process requirements before a commitment is made to the customer (e.g., through a proposal, an accepted order or a product announcement). Typical activities implemented to address this requirement include:

- Engineering participation in the proposal process
- Review and joint authorship (e.g., with marketing) of requirement documents

- Engineering participation in defining product evolution (e.g., product road maps) and in the review and approval of changes to requirements (e.g., through a product management council or a change control committee or board)

- Definitions of the commitments field sales personnel are authorized to make (e.g., for standard products and services), and the conditions under which commitments require review before they are presented to the customer

- Implementation of requirements traceability and any associated tools

- Implementation of a software life cycle such as Joint Application Development (JAD), in which engineering and customer personnel work together to define and develop a product.

The second requirement is in the text above the note:

"Where product requirements are changed, the organization shall ensure that relevant documents are amended and that relevant personnel are made aware of the changed requirements."

The amended documents (in whatever form) are reviewed and approved (as required by Subclause 4.2.3) and serve as triggers for changes to engineering work products (subject to the requirements of Subclause 7.3.7, Control of design and development changes). In the review process, proposed requirements changes are analyzed for impact and feasibility and are translated into revised plans and into changes in priorities and content.

Because of the demonstrated ability of requirement changes to overwhelm development teams, procedures and resources for the systematic analysis and incorporation of requirements, changes are essential to the success of a software project. Providing these resources is particularly challenging when the individuals competent to analyze proposed changes are fully committed to executing the current plan.

7.3 Design and Development

Clause 7.3 contains the requirements for most of the activities carried out by engineering organizations — both hardware and software. ISO 9000:2000 defines "design and development" as the "set of processes that transforms requirements into specified characteristics or into the specification of a product, process or system." This definition can be applied to both traditional hardware life cycle, in which drawings, procedures, bills-of-material, samples, documentation, etc. are the engineering outputs turned over to manufacturing, and software life cycles in which a baseline of the final software product (e.g., source, executables, customer documentation, release notes) is turned over to software production (e.g., manufacturing).

Implications for Software

In software development, "design and development" encompasses the activities from receipt of requirements to the delivery of tested software product to systems integration, to customers or to manufacturing. Software design and development includes the activities associated with the following types of deliverables and activities:

- Planning and life cycle selection and definition
- Functional specification
- High-level design
- Object modeling and associated outputs, such as use cases, class models, sequence diagrams, state charts, and collaboration diagrams
- Detailed/component design
- Unit and integration tests, and associated plans, test cases, test scripts
- Alpha and Beta tests and associated plans and agreements
- User interface model (e.g., for GUI design)
- Prototype for proof of concept
- Design review, inspection and other verification activities
- Source, object and executable code
- Configuration management (as applied to intermediate and final work products).

For software product, "design and development" can also include activities and deliverables provided by other organizations:

- Customer documentation development
- Customer training development
- Product introduction (e.g., for sales channel management, marketing communications, customer support).

Table 19-4 summarizes the subclauses of Clause 7.3 and lists some of the ways in which the requirements specified in these subclauses might be addressed by a software development organization which, like many organizations, derives its software development life cycle from the waterfall model.

7.5 Production and Service Provision

Clause 7.5 contains requirements for product life cycle activities that occur after "design and development." Depending on the nature of the organization and product, these activities include manufacturing, logistics (e.g., warehousing, handling, storage), delivery, (e.g., packing, shipping), installation, and service

Table 19-4

Subclauses 7.3.1 and 7.3.2

Subclause	Summary and Amplification for Software

7.3.1 Design and development planning	***From the Standard***
	Note that Clause 7.1 requires that planning output be provided in a form suitable to the organization's method of operation. Subclause 7.3.1 requires that the output be updated, as appropriate, as the design progresses. Subclause 7.3.1 also lists a minimum set of elements that must be determined during planning:
	    (a) Stages of design and development
	    (b) Appropriate review, verification and validation activities for each stage
	    (c) Responsibilities and authorities for design and development activities.
	
	Scenario for Achieving Compliance
	A software development plan, which identifies goals, requirements, resources, schedules, deliverables, applicable processes, risks, mitigation, dependencies, responsibilities, etc., is created at the beginning of a project. The plan, which is a single document or a collection of documents, divides the work into tasks of a relatively short, manageable size and divides the tasks and activities into stages (e.g., requirements, feasibility, design, test, beta test, release) that allow the organization to assess the project's performance, to determine whether to continue the project and to coordinate the activities of all parts of the organization (e.g., sales, support, hardware).
	
	The schedule is maintained in project management and reporting tools and is updated as frequently as is deemed appropriate (e.g., weekly). Changes to the rest of the plan are documented in meeting minutes (e.g., considered as amendments). The original planning document is updated only when a significant change requires replanning the development effort and obtaining approvals (e.g., from the customer).

7.3.2 Design and development inputs	***From the Standard***
	Subparagraph 7.3.2 requires that inputs relating to product requirements be determined and reviewed to resolve any omissions, ambiguities or inconsistencies. The records of the review are the records referred to in the first sentence of this subparagraph. Generic categories of requirements inputs are listed:
	    (a) Functional and performance requirements
	    (b) Regulatory and legal requirements
	    (c) Applicable information derived from previous designs
	    (d) Any other requirements essential for design and development.
	
	Scenario for Achieving Compliance
	Categories (a) and (b) are supplied by the customer in a statement of work and/or by marketing/engineering in a requirements document. Category (c) includes experience captured as "lessons learned" and work products suitable for reuse or revision. Category (d) includes internally generated requirements for platform and technology, upgradeability and supportability.[34] Applicable standards for documentation or coding are also design and development inputs, used as the basis for verification.
	
	Procedures and plans recognize that, while a complete set of requirements could be available for review at the beginning of a project, requirements can arrive in increments, subject to an ongoing review process.

Table 19-4 (continued)

Subclauses 7.3.3 and 7.3.4

Subclause	Summary and Amplification for Software

7.3.3 Design and development out-puts	***From the Standard***
	Subclause 7.3.3 requires that design and development outputs be:
	    ● Provided in a manner that allows verification against the inputs
	    ● Approved prior to use.
	Subclause 7.3.3 b) requires that the design and development outputs "provide appropriate information for purchasing, production and service provision."
	
	Scenario for Achieving Compliance
	Outputs include use cases, concept of operations documents, prototypes, functional specifications, design specifications, flow charts, block diagrams, test scripts and cases, object interaction diagrams, code, etc. Verification (discussed below with Subclause 7.3.5) includes review, unit testing and intermediate integration and system-level testing. Outputs reference associated input requirements (7.3.3 a) and contain or reference product acceptance criteria (7.3.3 c), which are included in the input requirements.
	
	Use cases, concept or theory of operations documents and specifications for exception handling "specify the characteristics of the product that are essential for its safe and proper use" as required by 7.3.3 d.
	
	Integrated product teams, coordinated planning and mutually agreed-upon document templates ensure that design and development outputs provide downstream organizations — manufacturing, purchasing, customer support and software maintenance — with the information those functions require to perform their roles in product and service provision (subclause 7.3.3 b).

7.3.4 Design and development review	***From the Standard*** Subclause 7.3.4 describes requirements for conducting systematic reviews of "design and development" with the participation of "representatives of functions concerned with the ... stage(s) being reviewed." The purpose of design reviews is two-fold: to "(a) evaluate the ability to meet requirements" and "(b) identify any problems and propose necessary actions." ISO 9000:2000 defines review as "activity undertaken to determine the suitability, adequacy and effectiveness of the subject matter to achieve established objectives." ***Scenario for Achieving Compliance*** In software development, the requirements of Subclause 7.3.4 apply to two types of reviews: project management reviews and technical reviews. Project management reviews include stage, readiness, milestone and periodic reviews of actual progress and completion of activities against the plan. Technical reviews include document review, formal inspection, walkthrough, prototype review, peer review and brainstorming. If any problems are identified in reviews, requirements for exercising corrective action (subparagraph 8.5.2) are applied. Progress reviews are also a mechanism for providing suitable measuring and monitoring of realization processes, as identified in Subclause 8.2.3, Monitoring and measurement of processes. Technical reviews of outputs are also verification activities and are subject to the requirements in subparagraph 7.3.5, Design and development verification.

Table 19-4 (continued)

Subclauses 7.3.5, 7.3.6 and 7.3.7

Subclause	Summary and Amplification for Software
7.3.5 Design and development verification	**From the Standard** ISO 9000:2000 defines "verification" as "confirmation, through the provision of objective evidence, that <u>specified</u> requirements have been fulfilled." This definition is best understood by contrasting it to the definition of "validation," which states that validation is "confirmation, through the provision of objective evidence, that requirements <u>for a specific intended use or application</u> have been fulfilled." "Verification" is conducted stage-to-stage to ensure that design-stage outputs satisfy the requirements of the relevant design-stage inputs. "Validation" is conducted end-to-end to ensure that product satisfies user requirements. **Scenario for Achieving Compliance** The initial design output, a Software Requirements Specification (SRS), is verified against the requirements for intended use. In subsequent stages of design and development, stage outputs are <u>verified</u> against stage inputs. Various methods, including technical reviews, inspections, walkthroughs, unit testing and software integration and integration testing, are identified in the plan for specific work products. Requirements for corrective action (Subclause 8.5.2) are applied to any problems identified in verification.
7.3.6 Design and development validation	**From the Standard** See the "Summary and Amplification for Software" for Subclause 7.3.5, immediately above, for a discussion of the definition of "validation." **Scenario for Achieving Compliance** Validation starts with "SQA" testing and includes alpha test, beta test, and software or system acceptance test. Requirements for corrective action (Subclause 8.5.2) apply to any problems identified in validation. In projects that employ incremental product development, validation occurs as each increment of the product is completed and integrated.
7.3.7 Design and development changes	**From the Standard** Design and development changes includes any changes in design outputs. As an output progresses through the development life cycle, different change mechanisms are typically invoked, but each of the mechanisms is subject to the requirements of Subclause 7.3.7. In software development, the requirements of Subclause 7.3.7 for the control of changes are satisfied through configuration management practices and tools. **Scenario for Achieving Compliance** Proposed changes are submitted through the bug tracking system, which is linked to the configuration management system. Each proposed change is evaluated for impact by representatives of the groups involved in the project (e.g., engineering, test, publications, marketing). Records of the review and approval of change proposals are maintained in the configuration management system as are records of the status of the request (e.g., in review, rejected, accepted, planned, implemented, tested, released). Accepted proposals are planned and implemented by changing affected design outputs (including code and test plans). Design and development changes are handled through the change control process established for managing requirement changes (see Subclause 7.2.2). Software configuration management extends through release to manufacturing or delivery to customers and is also subject to the requirements of Subclause 7.5.3, Identification and traceability.

(e.g., telephone support, maintenance and repair and consulting).

Although the title of this clause contains "production and service provision," several of the subclauses provide requirements that explicitly apply to all aspects of product realization.

Implications for Software

While Subclauses 7.5.1 and 7.5.2 do not apply to software life cycle activities, they do apply to software product-related activities and deliverables typically provided by other organizations.

Table 19-5

Software-Related Activities in Production and Service Provision

Production	Service Provision
• Documentation reproduction	• Distribution of patches and bug fixes
• Software reproduction	• Technical support
• Packaging, warehousing and distribution of physical media and documentation	• Continuation engineering
• Online distribution, including intranet- and extranet-based solutions, of documentation, product, patches, bulletins, etc.	• Field support (e.g., on-site assistance for installation, configuration or troubleshooting)
	• Professional services (e.g., customization, integration with third-party products or existing customer systems, system operation or management)

Service provision can also include postrelease software maintenance activities performed by software engineering:

- Bug fixes
- Patches
- Knowledge transfer (e.g., to support the handover of responsibility to other organizations)
- Initial sales support (e.g., until a field sales support organization is prepared to assume responsibility)
- Initial customer support (e.g., until a technical support organization is prepared to assume responsibility).

Defining and planning the interactions between engineering and technical support represents a significant opportunity to improve customer satisfaction through accurate prioritization and timely resolution of problems, through enhanced communication of status and through the prevention of potential problems.

As described in Table 19-6, Subclauses 7.5.3, 7.5.4 and 7.5.5 provide specific requirements that apply to software life cycle activities.

7.4 Purchasing

Purchasing includes the:

- Evaluation, selection and control of suppliers
- Specification of requirements to suppliers
- Verification of products provided by suppliers.

These suppliers, products and product components may be selected by the organization or specified by the customer.

Implications for Software

For software development and software product, Clause 7.4, Purchasing, applies to the acquisition of:

- Development hardware and software: work stations, integrated development environments, operating systems, configuration management systems, compilers, test tools, debuggers, analytical utilities (e.g., complexity)
- Third-party off-the-shelf software for inclusion in the product (e.g., APIs, operating systems, installation utilities, middleware)
- Third-party development of product or product components
- Third-party testing of product (e.g., certification, verification and validation)
- Third-party services to support product development (e.g., requirements gathering, market surveys, software replication and order fulfillment).

In many cases, software engineering is involved in specifying requirements for purchasing, in identifying candidates, in evaluating the technical capability of candidates, in monitoring and managing supplier performance and in verifying and validating products and services delivered by suppliers.

Purchasing-related activities performed by software engineering are typically coordinated through a purchasing function which is responsible for establishing and administering the overall legal, business relationship with the supplier (e.g., credit and reference checks, terms and conditions, tracking of contractual commitments and the release of funds for payment).

Based on experience with ISO 9001:1994, the requirements of Clause 7.4, Purchasing, apply when there is some form of compensation for the delivery of a product or service. Development partners are not considered suppliers to the organization from a purchasing perspective and are not subject to the requirements for supplier selection, etc.

Table 19-6

Subclauses 7.5.3, 7.5.4 and 7.5.5

Subclause	Summary and Implications for Software

7.5.3 Identification and traceability	**From the Standard**
	Subclause 7.5.3 requires that the organization identify the product and its status. Unique identification of product is related to circumstances in which "traceability is a requirement."
	
	Scenario for Achieving Compliance
	The requirements of Subclause 7.5.3 are addressed primarily through software configuration management practices and tools. These tools and practices ensure that the following are controlled and recorded:
	  - The identification of product components and product-version and source control
	  - Status of identified product and product components with respect to test (e.g., promotion status: ready for integration test, ready for system test).
	
	Traceability refers to the effective control of design and development changes (Subclause 7.3.7). Traceability encompasses tracking:
	  - Change requests (including defect reports) <u>forward</u> from submission to implementation in the product (e.g., Has everything been completed?)
	  - Product changes back to the corresponding approved change request (e.g., Have the right fixes been applied?).

7.5.4 Customer property	**From the Standard** Subclause 7.5.4 contains requirements for the care of customer property – including hardware, software and proprietary information – while it is under the control of or in use by the organization. The customer property may be provided either for incorporation into the product (e.g., shared libraries, APIs, components, data) or for use in the realization of the product (e.g., test data or hardware, documentation and operational data associated with defect reports). **Scenario for Achieving Compliance** Development procedures describe methods for tracking hardware, software and information from receipt and for the use of appropriate, secure repositories. Service procedures address the proper handling of information provided by customers for problem resolution, including information allowing remote access to customer systems and information gathered while accessing those systems.
7.5.5 Preservation of product	**From the Standard** Subclause 7.5.5 contains requirements for preserving the integrity of product and product components during internal processing. **Scenario for Achieving Compliance** For software development, requirements for preserving the integrity of product and product components are addressed through software configuration management, archival practices and tools, and network protection (e.g., virus checking). Preservation of product integrity is closely coupled to control of untested or nonconforming product. Requirements for the control of nonconforming product are defined in Subclause 8.2.4, Monitoring and measurement of product, and Clause 8.3, Control of nonconforming product.

7.6 Control of Monitoring and Measuring Devices

Clause 7.6 contains requirements for the control of test beds, test fixtures, test software and any measuring devices (e.g., oscilloscopes, voltmeters). Devices are to be used in a manner that ensures their capability is consistent with measurement requirements. The clause lists five straightforward requirements, labeled (a) through (e), that apply where necessary.

Clause 7.6 concludes with the explicit requirement that the ability of software used for monitoring and measuring product conformance to specified requirements be confirmed prior to use and reconfirmed as necessary. This clause is intended primarily for software used in production, assembly line and automated test environments.

Implications for Software

In software development, Clause 7.6 applies to test suites, test cases, test scripts, and simulators, as well as the hardware associated with these items.

The requirements to verify the ability of these test tools to detect defects is satisfied by systematic review of test plans, cases and scripts, and by the updating of test suites as new types of defects are reported. For third-party and in-house developed tools, at initial evaluation and as updates are received, the tool is installed in a controlled environment and exercised to ensure that it performs as specified.

Correct test configurations (e.g., hardware, software, parameters) are specified in test plans and procedures. The sequence of tests is specified in a test procedure or plan or in the software development plan. The test hardware and software actually used are identified in the test report. Placing test programs, test data (e.g., input data and expected results), software tools and test results under configuration management control or in a repository maintained in the test tool satisfies the other applicable requirements for protecting the test software from:

- Changes (e.g., adjustments) that would invalidate the test results and the requirements (see 7.6 d)

- Damage or deterioration during handling, maintenance and storage (see 7.6 e).

8 Measurement, Analysis and Improvement

ISO 9001:2000 Clause 8, Measurement, analysis and improvement, contains requirements that pertain to the overall quality system, to processes and to product.

For software organizations, ISO 9001:2000 Clause 8 eliminates the ambiguity of

ISO 9001:1994 Clause 4.20, Statistical techniques, and imposes unequivocal requirements for monitoring and measuring processes and products, and for analyzing the data produced by that monitoring and measuring. The graphs, reports, action items and other results of the monitoring, measuring and analysis are objective evidence that the processes are implemented. Due to the wide range of interpretation of ISO 9001:1994 Clause 4.20, Statistical techniques, ISO 9001:2000 Clause 8 is an area of change that warrants significant attention from organizations seeking to maintain compliance with ISO 9001.

The following table summarizes the stated application of each of the clauses and subclauses in ISO 9001:2000 Clause 8.

Table 19-7

Scope of Application of Requirements of Clause 8

Subclause	Overall Quality System	Processes	Product
8.1 General	•	•	•
8.2 Monitoring and measurement			
8.2.1 Customer satisfaction	•		
8.2.2 Internal audit	•		
8.2.3 Monitoring and measurement of processes		•	
8.2.4 Monitoring and measurement of product			•
8.3 Control of nonconforming product			•
8.4 Analysis of data	•		
8.5 Improvement			
8.5.1 Continual improvement	•		
8.5.2 Corrective action	•	•	•
8.5.3 Preventive action	•	•	•

8.1 General

The requirements for planning monitoring, measurement and analysis are addressed through procedures, development plans and specific test plans (e.g., for "SQA" test, beta test). The development life cycle activities related to measuring and monitoring product and process are discussed above, in conjunction with Subclauses 7.3.4 (progress reviews), 7.3.5 (verification) and 7.3.6 (validation).

8.2 Monitoring and Measurement

Two subclauses of Clause 8.2 describe requirements that apply to the overall quality system: customer satisfaction (8.2.1) and internal audits (8.2.2). While these subclauses affect software development, they describe requirements for activities that are typically independent of the software development life cycle. The remaining two subclauses contain requirements that pertain directly to development life cycle activities.

8.2.3 Monitoring and Measurement of Processes — Implications for Software

In software development, the requirement for monitoring and measuring "to demonstrate the ability of processes to achieve planned results" is addressed at the project or product level through a hierarchy of progress reviews (see Subclause 7.3.4) and reports that allow management to take appropriate corrective (see Subclause 8.5.2) and preventive action (see Subclause 8.5.3).

Project- and product-focused monitoring and measurement are supplemented by the internal audits, management review and preventive action that examine performance across iterations of processes (e.g., across projects or releases) to ensure that the quality system continues to be effective.

In many cases, the project management, requirements management, configuration management, bug tracking and call handling tools automate the collection, synthesis and presentation of data on process performance. Automated reports, which highlight exceptions, are inspected or analyzed by management to determine when action is necessary.

8.2.4 Monitoring and Measurement of Product — Implications for Software

In software development, the requirement for monitoring and measuring "the characteristics of product to verify that product requirements are fulfilled" is addressed through the verification and validation activities discussed above in conjunction with Subclauses 7.3.5 (verification) and 7.3.6 (validation). Typical measurements of product quality include those that quantify characteristics of requirements and functions implemented, work products completed, tests successfully completed and defects found throughout the life cycle and after release.

Project- and product-focused monitoring and measurement of product quality are supplemented by the internal audits (see Subclause 8.2.2), management review (see Clause 5.6) and preventive action (see Subclause 8.5.3), which require an examination of performance across products to ensure that the quality system continues to be effective.

Subclause 8.2.4 contains a critical requirement for software configuration management: "Product release and service delivery shall not proceed until all planned arrangements (see Clause 7.1) have been satisfactorily completed, unless otherwise approved by a relevant authority, and where applicable by the customer." This is addressed in software development through a well-defined release process, which addresses waivers.

The records referenced in 8.2.4 as evidence of product conformity are a by-product of verification, validation and configuration management activities. The records may be in electronic or paper form, and the retention period is determined by the organization's business practices (see Subclause 4.2.4, Control of quality records).

8.3 Control of Nonconforming Product — Implications for Software

For software product, the requirements of Clause 8.3 are addressed through two dependent mechanisms: bug reporting and configuration management.

During development and after release, bug reporting and tracking procedures and tools ensure that specific problems are identified and corrected. Once a work product is made available to individuals other than the author, a mechanism needs to be provided to ensure that identified defects are communicated to the author and that others who have access to the work product are informed of changes, known defects and resolutions. The degree of structure incorporated into the bug-tracking mechanism depends on the frequency of contact between engineers (e.g., within a collocated project team) and on the purpose for which the work product has been made available (e.g., for advance notice, review, integration testing or incorporation into a related work product).

Customer technical support mechanisms typically define how defects in delivered product are reported, evaluated, escalated as appropriate and tracked to closure.

Software configuration management tools and practices ensure that product that does not conform to requirements (e.g., incomplete or untested product) is not *inadvertently* promoted or released.

Requirements for regression testing product after nonconformity has been corrected are defined in Subclause 7.3.7, which states that "changes shall be verified and validated, as appropriate."

8.4 Analysis of Data

The requirements of Clause 8.4 are explicitly defined as applying to activities associated with demonstrating "the suitability and effectiveness of the quality management system and to evaluate where continual improvement of the quality management system can be made." The analysis described in Clause 8.4 considers outputs from monitoring and measurement of processes (see Subclause 8.2.3) and product (see Subclause 8.2.4) along with data related to customer satisfaction and suppliers. As discussed above in conjunction with Subclause 8.2, Monitoring and measurement, systematic analysis of data is an area that warrants attention and which may require significant enhancement by organizations seeking to maintain compliance with ISO 9001. However, as an enabler of improvement, systematic analysis of data also represents a source of significant benefit to organizations.

The results of the analysis are inputs for corrective action (see Subclause 8.5.2), preventive action (see Subclause 8.5.3), management review (see Clause 5.6). The results of the analysis of data are also inputs for planning internal audits (see Subclause 8.2.2) as indicators of current status — and risk.

8.5.1 Continual Improvement

ISO 9000:2000 defines continual improvement as "recurring activity to increase the ability to fulfill requirements." Subclause 8.5.1 finally establishes requirements for this fundamental and potentially intimidating concept. "Continual improvement" is implemented through the "quality policy, quality objectives, audit results, analysis of data, corrective and preventive actions and management review." For software organizations, the analysis of metrics data is a primary driver of preventive action and process improvement.

"Continual improvement" is a concept that has undergone significant change as ISO 9001:2000 has progressed through its various drafts. For those who have followed the evolution of "continual improvement" through the various drafts of the standard, reference to "efficiency" (e.g., improving processes that work) and the incorporation of the Total Quality Management (TQM) concept of "continual improvement" does not appear in ISO 9001:2000.

8.5.2 Corrective Action

Subclause 8.5.2 contains requirements that are invoked whenever a process or product defect or problem is identified. The problem is identified, recorded, communicated and the causes are determined. The organization then evaluates the need for action to ensure that the nonconformity does not reoccur. An appropriate course of action is determined and taken, the results of the action are recorded and the corrective action is reviewed. The criteria for the review of corrective action are those listed in the ISO 9000:2000 definition of "review": suitability, adequacy and effectiveness.

For product problems, the requirements of Subclause 8.5.2 are typically addressed through bug reporting and tracking processes. For third-party-developed product, a supplier corrective action process may also be invoked. Questions about suitability, adequacy and effectiveness are addressed in the planning process. Effectiveness is evaluated in any verification and validation, including regression testing, associated with the corrective action.

Resolution of process problems in a manner that ensures that the nonconformity does not reoccur is frequently handled in real time by a combination of management communication and feedback from verification and validation. For example, progress reviews and test results give appropriate levels of management visibility into an engineer's or manager's need for additional training (e.g., unfamiliarity with writing a design document) and into processes that may be causing the problems (e.g., an engineer cannot check in code in a timely manner because the configuration management tool is not as capable as advertised or because the number of licenses is inadequate).

8.5.3 Preventive Action

The requirements of Subclause 8.5.3 apply to incorporating the results of "lessons learned" into future development activities, projects and products; tools upgrade and implementation; addressing the results of internal audits with respect to opportunities for improvement; and whatever systematic method the organization has in place for capturing, evaluating and implementing improvement ideas (e.g., an engineering council or a software engineering process group). Frequently, the same system used for capturing product bugs and enhancement requests is used to capture process problems and enhancement requests.

Recommendations for Implementers: Establishing ISO 9001 as a Framework

ISO 9001:2000 Clause 3, Fundamentals of quality management systems, presents valuable background information on the principles underlying the adoption of systematic business and software engineering practices. In practice, there are two overriding principles that can guide implementers in software engineering organizations.

Principle 1: ISO 9001:2000 Is a Requirements Specification

The first key principle for implementers to follow is the often-overlooked guidance in ISO 9001:2000 Clause 0.1, General:

"The adoption of a quality management system should be a strategic decision of an organization. The design and implementation of an organization's quality management system is influenced by varying needs, particular objectives, the products provided, the processes employed and the size and structure of the organization.

"It is not the intent of this International Standard to imply uniformity in the structure of quality management systems or uniformity of documentation."

This translates into a recommendation to focus on the definition of software development practices that suit the organization. In the implementation, the standard serves as a checklist for assessing how well the organization's current practices already meet the criteria for compliance.[35] The implementer's assignment is to address any omissions identified in the assessment — in a manner that enhances the ability of the organization to meet its business objectives.

To ensure that the organization achieves full coverage of the requirements in ISO 9001:2000, the implementer studies the standard, digests the results of the assessment and maps the organization's policies, procedures and practices to the requirements of ISO 9001:2000. This mapping may be maintained by the management representative and internal auditors as part of the process for ensuring that compliance with ISO 9001:2000 is achieved and maintained as the quality system and organization evolve. This mapping can also be made available to the registrar's auditor. Based on experience with ISO 9001:1994, this mapping is typically part of the quality manual, as described in ISO 9001:2000 Subclause 4.2.2, Quality manual.

The table in Appendix C in this chapter identifies the relationship between ISO 12207:1997 and ISO 9001:2000 and serves as a starting point for mapping the requirements of ISO 9001:2000 to practices common to software development.

The key processes for implementers to address are the processes that have always challenged software development:

- Requirements management
- Project planning and management — including estimating effort
- Configuration management
- Testing
- Bug reporting and tracking
- Managing third-party development.

About Exclusions

Monitor additional clarification and discussion of the issue of permissible exclusions (see Clause 1.2) to ensure that you include an acceptable portion of the organization in the scope of the implementation.

About Registrars and Their Auditors

The third-party auditor's first responsibility is to examine the quality manual to verify the completeness of the organization's quality system in satisfying the requirements of the standard. The verification of completeness is based solely on the content of ISO 9001:2000 and ISO 9000:2000. Since each organization's quality system is potentially unique, the auditor's job is to recognize compliance based on the information in the quality manual, not to enforce some industry standard practice or conventional wisdom that is established outside the two standards.

If the auditor can't determine how the organization is addressing a particular requirement of ISO 9001:2000, additional information is requested. Internal inconsistencies or omissions may result in an update to the quality manual during this review.

The auditor's second responsibility is to verify through on-site inspection and interviews that:

- The system of policies, procedures and practices defined in the quality manual is implemented throughout the portion of the organization that falls within the scope of the registration

- The evidence provided by the organization demonstrates that these policies, procedures and practices are effective in producing the planned results.

Principle 2: It Is Easier To Achieve Compliance Than To Maintain Compliance

The second key principle for implementers is to ensure that the set of policies, procedures and practices remain current as the organization evolves. During the initial implementation, the implementation team ensures that the set of policies and procedures is sufficiently scaleable and flexible to address all of the software development activities within the organization as they currently occur. For efficiency, the implementation team also ensures that the policies and procedures address software development activities as they will occur in the immediate future. The policies and procedures represent a foundation for sustaining a software organization's culture during periods of high employee turn over and growth.

After the initial implementation has achieved compliance, it is the responsibility of management to ensure that the policies and procedures remain valuable assets and are revised as the organization and its practices evolve (Subclause 5.4.2 b). The systematic evolution of these policies and procedures, with the associated commitment of resources, is a continuing demonstration of management's priority for meeting the needs of customers and employees.

The internal audits (Subclause 8.2.2), management review (Clause 5.6), and corrective (Subclause 8.5.2) and preventive action (Subclause 8.5.3) are the mechanisms built into ISO 9001:2000 to ensure that compliance is maintained. Periodic surveillance audits (typically twice a year) are an additional mechanism for the organization that obtains formal registration as further confirmation of compliance.

Looking beyond ensuring compliance, the system of audits, management review, preventive and corrective action, and employee training (Subclause 6.2.2) can be a significant asset to the organization.

Recommendations for Maintainers in Software Organizations: Addressing the Changes

For anyone who is required to be familiar with the requirements of ISO 9001, the transition from the 1994 version to the 2000 version is significant. These individuals are faced with a completely new structure and approach. Familiar terms like "receiving inspection" and "in-process inspection" are replaced with requirements for measurement and monitoring. In some cases, terms are used with a more narrow definition (e.g., "design and development" and "design review").

The members of ISO, who represent the interests of national industries, imposed requirements that:

"The revision of the ISO 9000 standards will not require the rewriting of an organization's quality management system documentation.

"The 20 elements in the current ISO 9001 will be clearly identifiable in the new process-based structure.

"Organizations that have implemented the current ISO 9000 standards will find it easy to transition to the revised standards."[36]

Based on this stated goal, the mapping of ISO 9001:2000 to ISO 9001:1994 as expressed in ISO 9001:2000, and on more detailed mappings created by studying the text, it is the conclusion of the authors of this chapter that the revision neither adds nor removes requirements.

However, due to past inconsistent interpretation of the standard and variability in the effectiveness of registrar audits, the revision may bring clarification or add emphasis that requires some level of change.[37]

Points to Focus on for Maintainers

The following are some areas that the authors of this chapter identify as likely to require fine-tuning of an organization's quality management system. Appropriate individuals in each organization will have to study and understand the new version of the standard to ensure continuing compliance.

In implementing any changes, consider the same principles listed for implementers of new quality management systems. Implement any changes in a manner that enhances the ability of the organization to meet its business objectives.

The following are presented in no particular order. In the view of the authors of this chapter, points 3, 7, 10 and 15 represent the areas of highest risk and offer the most opportunity for leveraging the revision to improve processes.

Point 1: Provide training and support for all individuals who are required to understand the new standard.

Point 2: Part of the internal audit process (Subclause 8.2.2) is to verify compliance with ISO 9001:2000. If internal auditors have previously been auditing against procedures, the organization needs to determine how this new requirement is to be satisfied (e.g., train some or all internal auditors in the standard, use outside resources).

Point 3: Ensure that mechanisms for measuring customer satisfaction and taking appropriate action are well-defined and consistently understood, implemented and that the data is analyzed. See Subclauses 8.2.1 and 8.4 (a).

Point 4: For corrective action (Subclause 8.5.2), ensure that the organization records the results of the action. In ISO 9001:1994 Clause 4.14.2, the requirement is to record the results of the investigation.

Point 5: Ensure that the organization's policy for quality (however it is expressed) addresses the specific elements in Clause 5.3, particularly as it relates to continual improvement.

Point 6: ISO 9001:2000 Clause 8.5, Continual improvement, is specific in identifying associated practices, many of which should already be in place for ISO 9001:1994: quality policy, quality objectives, audit results, analysis of data, corrective and preventive action and management review. Ensure that they are all in place — particularly preventive action and measurement (see Point 7).

Point 7: Ensure that appropriate monitoring, measurement and data analysis are in place. For organizations seeking to maintain registration, objective evidence of systematic monitoring, measurement and analysis is a potential new focal point for third-party auditors.

Point 8: Ensure that the management review process incorporates the detailed inputs listed in Subclause 5.6.2, Review input, and produces the outputs listed in Subclause 5.6.3, Review output.

Point 9: As part of training (Subclause 6.2.2), ensure that the organization defines mechanisms for evaluating the effectiveness of training (6.2.2 c). This can be as simple as participant evaluations at the completion of a course and periodic solicitation by the training group of management input on training effectiveness. In addition, the organization is required to establish a mechanism for examining this data (Clause 8.4).

Point 10: As required by Subclause 7.3.3 b, ensure that design and development processes provide the information required for downstream processes.

Point 11: Ensure that the management representative carries out the new responsibility to "promote awareness of customer requirements." See Subclause 5.5.2.

Point 12: Ensure that there are processes in place to address handling of confidential information supplied by customers, as specified by Subclause 7.5.4.

Point 13: While there is a new list of quality records (identified by "see 4.2.4"), they correspond to the ISO 9001:1994 quality records except for Subclause 8.5.2, Corrective action, and 8.5.3, Preventive action. Both subclauses require that the organization "record the results of action taken." See also Point 4 above.

Point 14: Ensure that software used for testing is verified before it is put into use — by engineering, manufacturing or support. See Clause 7.6.

Point 15: Monitor additional clarification and discussion of the issue of permissible exclusions (see Clause 1.2).

APPENDIX 19A – Evolution of the ISO 9001 Family of Standards Between 1994 and 2000

ISO 9000:2000 contains the definitions provided in ISO 8402:1994 *Quality management and quality assurance — Vocabulary*[38] as well as the philosophical foundation of ISO 9001:2000, which is described in ISO 9000-1:1994 *Quality management and quality system elements — Guidelines.*[39]

Figure 19-3 summarizes the relationship between the 1994 and the 2000 versions of the ISO 9000 family.[40]

In Figure 19-3, dotted arrows trace the primary evolution of content. With regard to ISO 9000-3, which is connected to both the 1994 and 2000 standards with a solid arrow, a revision is in preparation.

Figure 19-3

The Evolution of the ISO 9000 Family of Standards from 1994 to 2000

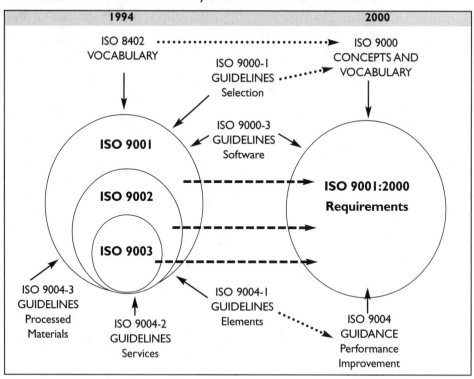

APPENDIX 19B - Background on Claiming Conformity

In the 1987 and 1994 versions of the ISO 9000 family of standards, there are no explicit criteria defining the conditions under which an organization can claim conformity. ISO 9001:1994 states in the introduction that:

"It is intended that these International Standards will be adopted in their present form, but on occasions they may need to be tailored by adding or deleting certain quality-system requirements for specific contractual situations."

ISO 9002:1994 and ISO 9003:1994 provide two mechanisms for identifying to customers when and which requirements are excluded.[41]

Even the three nested standards are, however, inadequate for addressing the variety of ways in which suppliers and customers adopt the standards. In some cases, driven by regulatory requirements, by market requirements or by business needs, only part of an organization seeks to conform to the requirements of the standard (e.g., manufacturing, but not product engineering). In some cases, organizations choose to stage the implementation of compliant processes based on the relative stability of the organization — for example, starting in manufacturing and then, subsequently, extending conformity to engineering and technical support. In other cases, the standards are applied to organizations or parts of organizations offering a specialized service (e.g., contract manufacturing, no product engineering or service; or field service, no manufacturing or product engineering).

Registrars — operating until 1996 without explicit direction from the International Organization for Standardization[42] — apply an effective, common-sense benchmark for determining when activities or functions and the related requirements can be excluded and conformity still claimed. The benchmark is expressed as the ability to write a scope statement that clearly and unambiguously represents to potential customers what activities have been assessed by the registrar and found to meet the requirements of the standard.

Registration-certificate scope statements incorporate one or more of three dimensions: activity, product and location. The registrar audits only those portions of the organization whose activities fall within the defined scope. For example, XYZ Corporation develops client-server and mainframe software in its Sunnyvale CA Software Design Center. Proof of compliance with ISO 9001 is not sought for mainframe software design and development since it is being phased out. In granting registration for the design and development of client-server software, the registrar ignores XYZ's mainframe software design and development processes. The scope statement on the registration certificate states that the certificate is for "The design and development of client-server software at XYZ

Corporation's Sunnyvale CA Software Design Center." The limitation to client-server software development is clearly expressed in the scope statement. The exclusion of mainframe software development is clear from the absence of any reference to it in the scope statement. The ethical dilemma created if XYZ sells products that incorporate both technologies is left to the discretion of the registrar to resolve or to ignore.

In defining permissible exclusions based on organization, geography and product, by convention, registrars do not permit the requirements of common infrastructure clauses of ISO 9001:1994, like 4.1, Management responsibility; 4.5, Document and data control; 4.6, Purchasing; 4.14, Corrective and preventive action; 4.17, Internal quality audits; and 4.18, Training to be excluded. Clauses that address product delivery, like 4.4, Design control, and 4.19, Servicing, can be excluded. Clauses like 4.3, Contract review; 4.10, Inspection and testing; and 4.13, Control of nonconforming product, apply to those product delivery activities (e.g., design and development, manufacturing, servicing) that are not excluded.

Table 19-8

Four Key Clauses on Production in ISO 9001:1994

Clause of ISO 9001:1994	Statement
4.8 Product identification and traceability	… for identifying the product by suitable means from receipt and during all stages of <u>production, delivery and installation</u>.
4.9 Process control	The supplier shall identify and plan the <u>production, installation and servicing</u> processes … and shall ensure that these processes are carried out under controlled conditions.
4.11 Control of inspection, measuring and test equipment	… where test software or comparative references such as test hardware are used as suitable forms of reference, they shall be checked to prove they are capable of verifying the acceptability of product, prior to release for use during <u>production, installation or servicing</u>.
4.12 Inspection and test status	The identification of inspection and test status shall be maintained … throughout <u>production, installation and servicing</u> of the product to ensure that only product that has passed the required inspections and tests … is dispatched, used, or installed.

APPENDIX 19C – Precedents for the Definition of "Production" – Lessons Learned

This appendix provides background information that is intended to give implementers, auditors and standards developers a basis for evaluating conflicting precedents and for proceeding with confidence that their implementations satisfy the requirements of ISO 9001:2000 for clauses related to "production."

In ISO 9001:1994, the term "production" appears in the text of four key clauses.

To lay a complete foundation for understanding the use of production, it is useful to note three other clauses of ISO 9001:1994 that do not limit themselves to any particular product life cycle phases:

- 4.7 Control of customer-supplied product[43]
- 4.10 Inspection and testing[44]
- 4.15 Handling, storage, packaging, preservation and delivery.[45]

In assessing compliance with the requirements of ISO 9001:1994, 4.7 through 4.12 and 4.15 are applied throughout the software development life cycle.

This application of 4.7 through 4.12 and 4.15 is incorporated into the guidance in ISO 9000-3:1991,[46] and ISO 9000-1:1994. ISO 9000-1:1994 Clause 7.4 succinctly characterizes the development of software in the following terms:

"The process of development, supply and maintenance of software is different from that of most other types of industrial products in that there is no distinct manufacturing phase. Software does not "wear out" and, consequently, quality activities during the design phase are of paramount importance to the final quality of the product."

The guidance in ISO 9000-1:1994 recognizes that software product exists in various forms during the phases called "design and development" and, during those phases, requires the same care that hardware product requires in manufacturing.

The software guidance in ISO 9000-3:1997 departs from established conventions and explicitly limits the application of 4.9, Process control, "to the replication, delivery and installation of software items or products." The guidance in ISO 9000-3:1997 for ISO 9001:1994 clause 4.9 adopts the position that production begins when the engineering organization releases product for replication and distribution. This limitation removes unambiguous requirements for designers and developers to follow procedures (ISO 9001:1994 Clause 4.9 c), to manage projects (ISO 9001:1994 Clause 4.9 d), to provide suitable development tools (ISO 9001:1994 Clause 4.9 b) and coding standards (ISO 9001:1994 Clause 4.9 f) and to maintain development tools (ISO 9001:1994 Clause 4.9 g). Implementors in software organizations seeking information on best practice are required to recognize that project management is encapsulated in the statement that "plans shall be updated, as the design evolves,"[47] that coding standards are design inputs[48] or acceptance criteria for design verification activities,[49] and that integrated development environments and work stations are resources.[50] Coupled with the underlying manufacturing orientation of ISO 9001:1994, this change in the application of ISO 9001:1994 Clause 4.9 introduced in ISO 9000-3:1997 has promoted inconsistency, fueled endless debate, sustained those who enjoy raising obstacles, made the standard less accessible and encouraged the role of experts (e.g., consultants and registrars), whose involvement — if not properly constrained — can diminish the organization's feeling of ownership in the quality system.

APPENDIX 19D – Suggested Assignment of ISO 9001:2000 Clauses and Requirements to ISO 12207:1995 Software Life Cycle Processes

The following table suggests the primary relationships between the requirements of ISO 9001:2000 and the life cycle processes of ISO 12207:1995. It should be noted that one of the defined goals of the revision of ISO 12207 is to improve the alignment with ISO 9001.

Table 19-9

Comparison of ISO 12207:1995 and ISO 9001:2000

ISO 12207:1995	ISO 9001:2000
5 Primary life cycle processes	
5.1 Acquisition process	
5.1.1 Initiation	7.4.1
5.1.2 Request-for-proposal [tender] preparation	7.4.2
5.1.3 Contract preparation and update	7.4.2
5.1.4 Supplier monitoring	7.4.1
5.1.5 Acceptance and completion	7.4.3
5.2 Supply process	
5.2.1 Initiation	7.2.1
5.2.2 Preparation of response	7.2.2
5.2.3 Contract	7.2.2
5.2.4 Planning	7.1, 7.3.1, 7.3.2
5.2.5 Execution and control	4.1, 5.5.3, 7.2.3, 7.3.4, 8.2.3, 8.5.2
5.2.6 Review and evaluation	4.2.4, 7.2.2, 7.2.3, 7.3.5, 7.3.6
5.2.7 Delivery and completion	7.5.5
5.3 Development process	
5.3.1 Process implementation	7.3.1, 7.3.2
5.3.2 System requirements analysis	7.3.3, 7.3.5
5.3.3 System architectural design	7.3.3, 7.3.5
5.3.4 Software requirements analysis	7.3.3, 7.3.5
5.3.5 Software architectural design	7.3.3, 7.3.5
5.3.6 Software detailed design	7.3.3, 7.3.5
5.3.7 Software coding and testing	4.2.4, 7.3.3, 7.3.5, 8.2.4
5.3.8 Software integration	4.2.4, 7.1, 7.3.1, 7.3.4, 7.3.5, 8.2.4
5.3.9 Software qualification testing	4.2.4, 7.3.6, 8.2.3, 8.2.4
5.3.10 System integration	4.2.4, 7.3.6, 8.2.3, 8.2.4
5.3.11 System qualification testing	4.2.4, 7.3.6, 7.5.5, 8.2.3, 8.2.4
5.3.12 Software installation	4.2.4, 7.5.1, 7.5.4, 7.5.5
5.3.13 Software acceptance support	4.2.4, 7.3.6, 7.5.1, 8.2.4
5.4 Operation process	
5.4.1 Process implementation	7.1, 7.5.1, 8.5.2
5.4.2 Operational testing	7.5.1, 7.5.4
5.4.3 System operation	7.5.1, 7.5.4

Table 19-9

Comparison of ISO 12207:1995 and ISO 9001:2000 (continued)

ISO 12207:1995	ISO 9001:2000
5.4.4 User support	7.5.1, 8.5.2
5.5 Maintenance process	
5.5.1 Process implementation	7.1, 7.5.1, 8.1, 8.5.2
5.5.2 Problem and modification analysis	7.3.7, 7.5.1, 8.5.2
5.5.3 Modification implementation	4.2.4, 7.3.7, 7.5.1, 8.2.3, 8.2.4
5.5.4 Maintenance review/acceptance	7.2.3, 7.3.7
5.5.5 Migration	7.2.1, 7.2.3
5.5.6 Software retirement	7.2.1, 7.2.3
6 Supporting life cycle processes	
6.1 Documentation process	
6.1.1 Process implementation	4.2.3, 6.3, 7.1, 7.3.1
6.1.2 Design and development	4.2.3, 7.3.2, 7.3.5
6.1.3 Production	4.2.3, 7.5.1
6.1.4 Maintenance	4.2.3, 7.3.7
6.2 Configuration management process	
6.2.1 Process implementation	4.2.3, 5.4.2, 6.3, 7.1, 7.3.1
6.2.2 Configuration identification	4.2.3, 7.3.7, 7.5.3, 8.3
6.2.3 Configuration control	4.2.3, 7.3.7, 8.3
6.2.4 Configuration status accounting	4.2.4, 7.5.3, 8.2.4
6.2.5 Configuration evaluation	8.2.2, 8.2.3, 8.2.4
6.2.6 Release management and delivery	4.2.3, 7.5.5
6.3 Quality assurance process	
6.3.1 Process implementation	5.4.1, 5.4.2, 6, 7.2.2, 8.1, 8.2.2, 8.2.3
6.3.2 Product assurance	7.3.5, 7.3.6, 8.2.4
6.3.3 Process assurance	5.6, 7.3.4, 8.2.2, 8.2.4
6.3.4 Assurance of quality systems	5.6, 8.2.2
6.4 Verification process	
6.4.1 Process implementation	4.2.3, 6, 7.1, 7.2.2, 7.3.1, 7.3.5, 8.1, 8.2.4
6.4.2 Verification	4.2.3, 7.2.2, 7.3.5, 8.2.4
6.5 Validation process	
6.5.1 Process implementation	6, 7.1, 7.3.1, 7.3.6
6.5.2 Validation	4.2.3, 7.3.6
6.6 Joint review process	7.1, 7.3, 8.1, 8.2, 8.5
6.6.1 Process implementation	7.1, 7.3.1, 7.3.4, 8.1, 8.2.3
6.6.2 Project management reviews	7.3.4, 8.2.3, 8.5.2
6.6.3 Technical reviews	7.3.4, 8.2.3, 8.5.2
6.7 Audit process	
6.7.1 Process implementation	5.6.1, 6.1, 7.3.4, 8.1, 8.2.2, 8.2.3, 8.2.4
6.7.2 Audit	5.6.1, 7.3.4. 8.2.2, 8.2.3, 8.2.4
6.8 Problem resolution process	
6.8.1 Process implementation	8.1, 8.4, 8.5.1, 8.5.2
6.8.2 Problem resolution	8.4, 8.5.2

Table 19-9

Comparison of ISO 12207:1995 and ISO 9001:2000 (continued)

ISO 12207:1995	ISO 9001:2000
7 Organizational life cycle processes	
7.1 Management process	
7.1.1 Initiation and scope definition	5.4.2, 6, 7.1, 8.1, 8.5.1
7.1.2 Planning	5.4.2, 6, 7.1, 8.1, 8.5.1
7.1.3 Execution and control	7.1, 8.1, 8.5.1
7.1.4 Review and evaluation	4.2.3, 5.6, 7.3.4, 8.2.2, 8.2.3, 8.2.4
7.1.5 Closure	8.2.4
7.2 Infrastructure process	
7.2.1 Process implementation	4.1, 5.4.2, 6
7.2.2 Establishment of the infrastructure	4.2.2, 5.4.1, 5.4.2
7.2.3 Maintenance of the infrastructure	4.2.2, 5.4.1, 5.4.2
7.3 Improvement process	5.6, 8.2, 8.5
7.3.1 Process establishment	5.6, 8.2.2, 8.5
7.3.2 Process assessment	5.6, 8.2.2
7.3.3 Process improvement	8.5
7.4 Training process	
7.4.1 Process implementation	6.2.2
7.4.2 Training material development	4.2.3
7.4.3 Training plan implementation	6.2.1, 6.2.2

Appendix 19E - Sources of Standards and Information

The following organizations provide information and source documents on the standards and programs described in this chapter.

For the authors of this chapter

Software Systems Quality Consulting

2269 Sunny Vista Drive, San Jose, CA 95128; web: www.ssqc.com; see also www.ssqc.com/ssqcexp.pdf; tel: 1-408-985-4476; fax: 1-408-248-7772.

For the CMM

Software Engineering Institute

Carnegie Mellon University, Pittsburgh, PA 15213-3890; tel: 412-268-7700 or 412 268-6815; fax: 412-268-5758; e-mail: customer-relations@sei.cmu.edu; ftp address: ftp.sei.cmu.edu (for technical reports and documents, including [PAU1] and [PAU2]); web: http://www.sei.cmu.edu/SEI/HomePage.html

For the IEEE standards

IEEE

345 East 47th Street, New York, NY 10017-2394

IEEE Customer Service

445 Hoes Lane, PO Box 1331, Piscataway, NJ 08855-1331; tel: 1-800-678-4333; fax: 1-908-981-9667; web: http://www.computer.org

For TickIT

BSI-DISC TickIT Office

389 Chiswick High Road, London W4 4AL, United Kingdom; tel: 020-8996-9000; fax: 020-8996-7448; e-mail: DISC@BSI.org.uk; web: www.bsi.org.uk/disc/welcome.html

End Notes

[1] International Organization for Standardization, Press Release: Launching of ISO 9000:2000 Series on 15 December, Reference 787, 14 December 2000, www.iso.ch/presse/iso9000_2000.htm

[2] ISO 9000, *Quality management systems – Fundamentals and vocabulary*, International Organization for Standardization, Geneva, Switzerland, December 13, 2000

[3] ISO 9001, *Quality management systems – Requirements*, International Organization for Standardization, Geneva, Switzerland, December 15, 2000

[4] ISO 9004, *Quality management systems – Guidance for performance improvement*, International Organization for Standardization, Geneva, Switzerland, December 15, 2000

[5] For ISO registrations, the annual ISO survey of registrations provides the best source of information. This survey, initiated by Mobil Corporation (see SYM1), was transferred to ISO and evolved into *The ISO Survey of ISO 9000 and ISO 14000 Certificates*. Unfortunately, until ISO began publishing the *The ISO Survey*, the survey focused on geography without providing a breakdown by standard industry classification (SIC).

[6] This reference is to software quality assurance as a management oversight function, not as a test function

[7] ISO/IEC 12207, *Information Technology - Software lifecycle processes*, First edition, ISO/IEC, Geneva, Switzerland, 1995

[8] ISO/TR 15504 *Software Process Assessment*, parts 1 through 9, International Organization for Standardization, Geneva, Switzerland, February 1998

[9] See Appendix E, Sources of Standards and Information for the IEEE

[10] Mark C. Paulk et al., *Capability Maturity Model for Software, Version 1.1*, CMU/SEI-93-TR-24, Software Engineering Institute, Carnegie Mellon University, Pittsburgh PA 15213, February 1993 and Mark C. Paulk et al., *Key Practices of the Capability Maturity Model, Version 1.1*, CMU/SEI-93-TR-25, Software Engineering Institute, Carnegie Mellon University, Pittsburgh PA 15213, March 1993. CMM is registered in the U.S. Patent and Trademark Office. Capability Maturity Model is a registered service mark of Carnegie Mellon University

[11] Personal Software Process is a registered service mark of Carnegie Mellon University

[12] R.C. Bamford and W. J. Deibler, "Comparing, Contrasting ISO 9001 and the SEI Capability Maturity Model," *IEEE Computer*, October 1993, Vol. 26, No. 10, IEEE Computer Society, p. 68 and Mark C. Paulk, *A Detailed Comparison of ISO 9001 and the Capability Maturity Model for Software*, IEEE Software, January, 1995

[13] Mark C. Paulk, Dennis Goldenson, David M. White, *The 1999 Survey of High Maturity Organizations*, CMU/SEI-2000-SR-002, Software Engineering Institute, Carnegie Mellon University, Pittsburgh PA 15213, February 2000, section 2.1 Management Practices

[14] James Moore (chair), Integrated Reporting Spreadsheet, US TAG to ISO/IEC JTC1/SC7, updated: 10 Jan 2001, WG18 Standards and Projects

[15] ANSI/ASQC Q91:1987, *Quality Systems - Model for Quality Assurance in Design/Development, Production, Installation, and Servicing,* American Society for Quality Control, Milwaukee, 1987

[16] ISO 9000-3, *Quality management and quality assurance standards, Part 3: Guidelines for the application of ISO 9001 to the development, supply and maintenance of software, First edition,* International Organization for Standardization, Geneva, Switzerland, 1991

[17] Dirk Stelzer, Werner Mellis, Georg Herzwurm, *Software Process Improvement via ISO 9000?* Results of two surveys among European software houses, Proceedings of the 29th Hawaii International Conference on System Sciences, January 3-6, 1996, Wailea, Hawaii, USA. This document is available on line at:

www.informatik.uni-koeln.de/winfo/prof.mellis/publications/hicscopy.htm

[18] *Software Process Improvement via ISO 9000?* Section 9. While Steltzer et al. report significant process improvement from ISO 9001 for many software houses, they also point out that organizations with well-established processes and management structures documented the status quo and sought registration.

[19] ISO 9001, *Quality management systems – Requirements,* International Organization for Standardization, Geneva, Switzerland, December 15, 2000, Clause 0.3. ISO 9001:2000 Clause 0.3 goes on to define further the relationship between ISO 9001:2000 and ISO 9004:2000:

"ISO 9004:2000 gives guidance on a wider range of management system objectives than does ISO 9001 … [It] is not intended for certification or for contractual purposes."

ISO 9004:2000 Clause 0.3 states that ISO 9004:2000 is "not intended as guidance for compliance with ISO 9001:2000." These statements directly address the frequently expressed misconception that an organization has to provide justification for not implementing guidance found in ISO 9004-1:1994.

[20] James Moore (chair), Integrated Reporting Spreadsheet, US TAG to ISO/IEC JTC1/SC7, updated: 10 Jan 2001, WG18 Standards and Projects

[21] See Appendix B in this chapter for information on the sources and evolution of the conventions for determining permissible exclusions.

[22] See Recommendations for Maintainers in Software Organizations: Addressing the Changes in this chapter for information on ISO's self-imposed restrictions on the impact of changes.

[23] Quality Management and Quality Assurance/Quality Systems, (Draft) Guidance on "Permissible Exclusions" to ISO 9001:2000, ISO/TC 176/SC 2 N485, International Organization for Standardization, Geneva, Switzerland, 26 April 2000

[24] See Appendix E, Sources of Standards and Information for contact information.

[25] Clause 4.9 (d) states that "The supplier should ensure that these processes ... include monitoring and control of suitable process parameters and product characteristics."

[26] Clause 4.4.2 states that "The plans shall be updated as the design evolves" An unstated prerequisite is that processes and progress are monitored.

[27] These clauses relate to "special processes."

[28] See Recommendations for Maintainers: Addressing the Changes in this chapter for ISO's self-imposed requirement that the revision support as seamless a transition as possible from ISO 9001:1994 to ISO 9001:2000.

[29] ISO 9001, *Quality management systems – Requirements* contains six references to "documented procedure": Subclause 4.2.3 (document control), Subclause 4.2.4 (quality records), Subclause 8.2.2 (internal audits), Clause 8.3 (control of nonconforming product), Subclause 8.5.2 (corrective action) and Subclause 8.5.3 (preventive action)

[30] The priority afforded to processes that cross functional boundaries is a consistent theme in each version of the ISO 9000 family, suggested in ISO 9000-1:1994 Clause 4.7 and ISO 9004:1987 Clause 5.2.5.

[31] Similar to the requirements in the Integrated Software Management Key Process Area of the CMM (see *Key Practices of the Capability Maturity Model, Version 1.1* by Mark C. Paulk)

[32] Mark C. Paulk et al., *Key Practices of the Capability Maturity Model, Version 1.1*, CMU/SEI-93-TR-25, Software Engineering Institute, Carnegie Mellon University, Pittsburgh PA 15213, March 1993

[33] The requirements of ISO 9001 apply to all software development life cycles. For information about life cycles, see the following: Waterfall, V Model, Spiral, Object-Oriented Process Life Cycle – OOSP, Prototyping, Unified Process and the Enhanced Unified Process, Incremental (See also: Watts S. Humphrey, *Managing the Software Process*; Roger S. Pressman, *Software Engineering*; Barry Boehm, Wilfred J. Hansen (ed.), CMU/SEI-2000-SR-008 Spiral Development: Experience, Principles, and Refinements; Scott Amblin, "Enhancing the Unified Process," *Software Development*, Vol. 7, No. 10, Oct. 1999, p. 33; UK Department of Trade and Industry, The STARTS Guide)

[34] See ANSI/IEEE Std 830-1984, *IEEE Guide to Software Requirements Specifications*, The Institute of Electrical and Electronics Engineers, Inc., 1984, Subclause 6.3.1.

[35] It is the experience of the authors of this chapter that a well-defined, reasonably efficient, effective set of software development practices satisfies most, if not all, of the requirements of ISO 9001:2000.

[36] ISO/CD1 9001:2000 & ISO/CD1 9004:2000, ISO/TC 176/SC 2/N 415, International Organization for Standardization, Geneva, Switzerland, 30 July 1998, Section 1, "Introduction to the Revision," Clause 1.5, "Structure of the Revised Standards"

[37] See ISO/CD1 9001:2000 & ISO/CD1 9004:2000, ISO/TC 176/SC 2/N 415,

International Organization for Standardization, Geneva, Switzerland, 30 July 1998 Clause 1.3. The issue of variability in the effectiveness of registrar audits has been addressed by ISO in documenting requirements for the operation of accreditation bodies and registrars (see ISO/IEC Guide 61, *General Requirements for Assessment and Accreditation of Certification/Registration Bodies, First edition*, and ISO/IEC Guide 62, *General Requirements for Bodies Operating Assessment and Certification/Registration of Quality Systems, First Edition*) and in facilitating the establishment of the International Accreditation Forum (IAF) as an agency for ensuring that these requirements are adopted and implemented.

[38] ISO 8402:1994, *Quality management and quality assurance - Vocabulary*, International Organization for Standardization, Geneva, Switzerland, 1994

[39] ANSI/ASQC Q9000-1:1994, *Quality Management and Quality System Elements - Guidelines*, American Society for Quality Control, Milwaukee, 1994. Note that the hyphenated number of this document is read as "nine thousand part 1." Unfortunately, renaming ISO 9000-1 as ISO 9000 reintroduces the dual usage of "ISO 9000" as the name of the family and the title of one of the standards in the family.

[40] As of January 10, 2001, a revision of ISO 9000-3:1997 is planned for completion by October 1, 2001. See James Moore (chair), Integrated Reporting Spreadsheet, US TAG to ISO/IEC JTC1/SC7, updated: 10 Jan 2001.

[41] In 1994, incorporating the experience gained in the 1987 versions of the ISO 9000 standards, ISO 9002 and ISO 9003 were rewritten as nearly exact subsets of ISO 9001. The content of clauses selected for exclusion was replaced with a message stating that the clause did not apply. For example, Clause 4.4 Design control is the only clause that does not apply in ISO 9002:1994.

[42] ISO/IEC Guide 61, *General Requirements for Assessment and Accreditation of Certification/Registration Bodies, First edition*, and ISO/IEC Guide 62, *General Requirements for Bodies Operating Assessment and Certification/Registration of Quality Systems, First Edition*, were ISO's first published rules for, respectively, accreditation bodies and registrars. In addition, see contact information for the International Accreditation Forum, IAF, which is the organization of national accreditation bodies that implements these documents.

[43] This clause is applied to any hardware or software provided to development organizations either for inclusion in the product to be returned to the customer or for use in the development of the product.

[44] It is interesting to note that ISO 9001:1994 clause 4.10 contains no explicit limitation, while Clauses 4.11 and 4.12, which support 4.10, each limit themselves to production, installation, and servicing. The clauses of Clause 4.10 are combined with ISO 9001:1994 Clauses 4.4.6, Design review, 4.4.7, Design verification, and 4.4.8, Design validation, to establish the complete requirements for verification and validation in software development.

[45] This clause is applied to all aspects of managing the contents of the configuration management repository during all stages of development and after release.

[46] ISO 9000-3:1991 references elements of ISO 9001:1987 Clause 4.9 in its guidance for design and implementation, configuration management, rules, practices, and conventions, and tools and techniques.

[47] ANSI/ISO/ASQC Q9001:1994, *Quality Systems - Model for Quality Assurance in Design, Development, Production, Installation, and Servicing* Clause 4.4.2

[48] ANSI/ISO/ASQC Q9001:1994, *Quality Systems - Model for Quality Assurance in Design, Development, Production, Installation, and Servicing* Clause 4.4.3

[49] ANSI/ISO/ASQC Q9001:1994, *Quality Systems - Model for Quality Assurance in Design, Development, Production, Installation, and Servicing* Clauses 4.4.5, 4.10.5

[50] ANSI/ISO/ASQC Q9001:1994, *Quality Systems - Model for Quality Assurance in Design, Development, Production, Installation, and Servicing* Clauses 4.1.2.2, 4.4.2

ISO 13485 for the Regulated Medical Device Industry Sector

20

by Edward R. Kimmelman

General

Background

The medical device sector is confronted with a variety of relevant quality system standards that are intended to satisfy organization (manufacturer), customer and regulatory agency objectives. These standards are embodied in:

- Regulations (e.g., the US Quality System Regulation and the Japanese Good Manufacturing Practices Regulation) and
- International standards (e.g., ISO 9001 and ISO 13485) that have been incorporated directly into regulations or that have been voluntarily adopted by medical device manufacturing organizations.

Purpose of This Chapter

This chapter outlines medical device quality system issues created by ISO 9001:2000, the standards community response to this issues and recommended courses of action for individual organizations as they review and, possibly, revise their quality management systems to deal with evolving standards, customer and regulatory requirements.

Key Organizations

Work of ISO TC 210, WG1

ISO Technical Committee (TC) 210, Working Group (WG) 1 is charged with the responsibility to develop international voluntary quality system standards for the medical device sector. It has developed three standards:

- ISO 13485:1996, *Quality systems – Medical devices – Particular requirements for the application of ISO 9001,*

- ISO 13488:1996, *Quality systems – Medical devices – Particular requirements for the application of ISO 9002* and

- ISO 14969:1999, *Quality systems - Medical devices - Guidance on the application of ISO 13485 and ISO 13488.*

The titles of these standards reflect the fact that they are based directly on the 1994 versions of the ISO 9000 series of standards, both in content and format. For example, essentially all of the requirements of ISO 9001:1994 are carried over to ISO 13485:1996, with the addition of particular requirements that are relevant to all medical devices or to some classes of medical devices. Many of these particular requirements come directly from existing regulations.

WG 1 continues to review and update these standards, based on the changing needs of the medical device sector.

Work of GHTF

The Global Harmonization Task Force (GHTF) is an organization comprised of representatives from medical device regulatory agencies in many of the industrialized countries, along with representatives from the medical device industry. The Study Group 3 (SG 3) of the GHTF has succeeded in harmonizing the regulatory quality system requirements in the major markets around the world and is working to promote its work to other countries.

The basis for the GHTF agreement on quality system requirements is ISO 13485:1996. While the quality system regulations in the individual GHTF countries may not follow the format of ISO 13485:1996, the substance of the requirements is consistent with that found in this standard.

Role of TC 176

According to ISO Central Secretariat (ISO/CS) policy, TC 176 has the overall responsibility to manage the development of quality system standards. The ISO/CS, however, has recognized that the medical device sector, due to its heavy regulation worldwide, may require the establishment of standards that are targeted specifically at the sector. As a result, the ISO/CS approved the creation of TC 210 to manage the development of medical device sector-specific documents, with the understanding that TC 176 would still maintain primacy related to quality system standards in general. One of the key overall objectives of TC 176 is to avoid the proliferation of sector-specific quality system standards.

The Interaction Between TC 176 and TC 210, WG1

Over the last six years there has been direct interaction between the two committees as each has developed its own standards. There is now general agreement that the needs of the medical device sector would be best served by a separate quality system standard, based, in great measure, on ISO 9001:2000, with some of the ISO 9001:2000 requirements removed and a number of requirements added. This separate standard would reflect clearly the differences required by the fact that the medical device sector is regulated. As a result the revised ISO 13485 will bear a new title, "Quality management systems – Medical devices – System requirements for regulatory purposes."

Differences Between ISO 9001:2000 and ISO 13485:2003

Divergence of Objectives

The substantive differences between ISO 9001:2000 and the planned ISO 13485:2003 result from the divergence of the objectives of the two standards. TC 210 seeks to maintain ISO 13485 as an easily understood, baseline standard targeted at meeting customer requirements and maximizing the probability that compliant organizations will produce safe and effective products.

While TC 176 professes to share that objective, it is obvious from the requirements that have been added, that TC 176 intends to move the ISO 9000 series of standards closer to the business excellence standards epitomized by quality award systems like the Malcolm Baldrige National Quality Award model. In addition, TC 176 seeks to make compliance to ISO 9001:2000 easier for smaller organizations by reducing the procedural documentation requirements.

Revision of ISO 9000 Series

In 2000, TC 176 published a revised version of the ISO 9000 series of standards. Key elements of this revision included:

- The adoption of the "process approach" to quality management, with the resultant reformatting of ISO 9001:2000 to reflect the key quality system processes (i.e., management, resources, product realization and measurement). Within these major process areas are subprocesses dealing with quality system management planning, management review, human resources, work environment, design and development, purchasing, production, monitoring and measurement, analysis of data, improvement and others.

- The elimination of ISO 9002 and ISO 9003, through the use of an applications approach (ISO 9001:2000, Clause 1.2) that allows the organization to disregard quality system requirements for product realization processes they do not perform (e.g., design and development).

- The refocusing of the objectives of ISO 9001:2000 and ISO 9004:2000, such that ISO 9001:2000 is targeted at a quality management system intended to meet customer requirements, while ISO 9004:2000 is targeted at quality system recommendations for business excellence.

- Within ISO 9001:2000, the strengthening of requirements related to customer satisfaction and continual improvement and the weakening of requirements related to procedural documentation.

- The elimination of ISO 8402 by including relevant quality system definitions in ISO 9000:2000.

Current Dilemma

Representatives of both TC 210, WG 1 and the GHTF, SG 3, after a number of joint working sessions, have concluded that significant requirements contained in ISO 9001:2000 are not appropriate for inclusion in a medical device quality system standard that is intended to be:

- A support for existing international harmonization of quality system regulation and

- A model for countries that are in the process of developing their medical device quality system regulations.

Similarities

Before elaborating on the differences between ISO 9001:2000 and ISO 13485:2003, it is important to point out that there is a great measure of agreement between the two documents. As much as 80 percent of the actual requirements text of ISO 13485:2003 is quoted directly from ISO 9001:2000.

In particular, the format of ISO 13485:2003 is the same, that is, it is based on the "process model." While the actual requirements are not significantly changed by this model, TC 210 found it to be very useful in explaining the relevance of the requirements, since most organizational operations are based on a compilation of processes.

Substantive Differences

The major substantive differences between ISO 9001:2000 and ISO 13485:2003 relate to the following requirement areas:

- Customer satisfaction
- Continual improvement
- Level of procedural documentation.

Continual Improvement

The key issue related to continual improvement is that ISO 9001:2000 requires actual objective evidence of continual improvement of the quality management system, not just objective evidence of the exercise of quality management processes targeted at determining needed continual improvement and the effective actions based on such determinations.

Clause 8.5.1 of ISO 9001: 2000 requires that, "The organization <u>shall continually improve the effectiveness of the quality management system</u> through the use of the quality policy, quality objectives, audit results, analysis of data, corrective and preventive actions and management review" [emphasis added]. Clause 8.5.1 of ISO/CD 13485:2003 is worded as follows, "The organization shall identify and implement any changes necessary to ensure and maintain the continued suitability and effectiveness of the quality management system through the use of the quality policy…"

It is important to note that the processes anticipated by both documents to be used to achieve continual improvement are processes that are familiar to medical device organizations as they are required by most quality system regulations. The inclusion of these examples resulted from comments made by TC 210 during the drafting of ISO 9001:2000.

In early drafts of ISO 9001:2000, Clause 8.5.1 also targeted this requirement at improvement of quality system efficiency, but this was removed at the urging of TC 210, because efficiency is more related to organizational excellence than it is to meeting customer requirements.

Customer Satisfaction

The requirements in ISO 9001:2000 present a number of issues for medical device organizations. One key issue is that ISO 9001:2000 requires objective evidence that there are active processes for determining whether customers are, in fact, satisfied. During the development of ISO 9001:2000, representatives of TC 210 got TC 176 to narrow the definition of customer satisfaction to focus it on whether or not an organization is meeting customer requirements. Unfortunately, even this narrowing of the definition does not overcome the fear that there are widely divergent interpretations among professionals assessing quality management systems as to what "customer satisfaction" really means. In addition, the representatives from TC 210 were not able to get TC 176 to eliminate the use of the term "customer perception" in Clause 8.2.1.

TC 210 feels that the use of the term "customer satisfaction" is not appropriate for ISO 13485:2003, because it is too subjective to use in a standard to be used as the basis for regulation. As a result, ISO 13485:2003 will encourage the use of active processes for gathering customer feedback related to whether or not the organization is meeting customer requirements. It will also require the generation of objective evidence that these systems are being used, with the feedback acted upon. ISO 13485:2003 illustrates such processes as including complaint handling, order handling and contract review.

Level of Procedural Documentation

The key issue here is that ISO 9001:2000 has reduced the number of processes that require documented procedures. It has specifically spelled out a limited number of processes that require documented procedures and it has left it up to the organization to determine whether procedures are needed for all other quality management processes.

In the regulated world of medical devices, documented procedures are used as objective evidence of control of key quality management system processes and it is inappropriate to allow for the flexibility embodied in ISO 9001:2000, especially for processes that could significantly affect the safety and effectiveness of products.

As a result, ISO 13485:2003 will retain the same documented procedure requirements as in the 1996 version of this standard.

What ISO 13485:2003 Will Look Like

ISO 13485:2003 will be a stand-alone standard; it will not make direct references on a section-by-section basis to ISO 9001 as the current version of ISO 13485 does. This approach will go a long way toward disconnecting the two standards and make ISO 13485 less susceptible to future changes in the ISO 9001 standard.

As mentioned earlier in this chapter, ISO 13485:2003 will quote extensively from ISO 9001:2000. As required by ISO policy, these quoted sections will be designated by a distinctive font or font treatment. For particularly important additions or deletions a "NOTE" will be added to the ISO 13485:2003 clause text, pointing out the difference. If the change requires explanation, that information will be provided in an annex to the standard.

ISO 13488 and ISO 14969

What Is ISO 13488?

ISO 13488:1996 is the medical device equivalent of the ISO 9002 standard. ISO 9002 was intended to provide quality management system requirements for organizations that performed all activities, except design and development of products and the processes for providing them. As indicated earlier, TC 176 has decided to eliminate ISO 9002.

Will ISO 13488:2003 Be Published?

Following the lead of TC 176, TC 210 will adopt the applications approach and retire ISO 13488.

The European Union has developed an approach for applying the new version of ISO 9001 to compliance with the conformity assessment requirements of the various new approach directives. They have documented that approach in the Foreword of EN/ISO 9001:2000. It is likely that the European Union will take the same approach with respect to ISO 13485:2003

What Will Happen to ISO 14969?

ISO 14969:1999 is a standard that provides guidance on the application of ISO 13485. It is based on and refers directly to ISO 9000-2, a guidance document published by TC 176. Because TC 176 has decided to eliminate ISO 9000-2, it will republish ISO 14969 as a stand-alone, technical report, following the same organizational structure as ISO 13485:2003.

The technical report is a new kind of ISO document that requires significantly less consensus review and can be published more quickly. ISO/TR 14969:2003 will contain much of the same guidance as in the 1999 version of this document.

Path Forward Recommendations

Key Publication Milestones

ISO 9001:2000 was published in December 2000, with the guidance that the 1994 version of the standard would remain viable until December 2003. Because ISO 13485:1996 refers directly to ISO 9001:1994, WG 1 is under time pressure to publish the approved new version of ISO 13485 by the end of 2002 or the first quarter 2003. WG 1 published the Committee Draft of ISO 13485: 2003 in June 2001 and considered comments on this draft at its meeting in October 2001. The Draft International Standard (DIS) version of ISO 13485:2003 was published in February 2002. WG 1 will consider comments on the DIS during its September

2002 meeting and will publish the final draft international standard for voting by the end of 2002. It is intended that the approved ISO 13485:2003 will be published by the end of the first quarter of 2003.

Such a publication schedule will allow organizations claiming compliance with ISO 13485 to understand the requirements of the new version in time to inform their employees and make any necessary modifications to their quality management systems before the 1994 version of ISO 9001 disappears. This timing will also allow third-party registrars and notified bodies to adjust their assessment procedures and to arrange assessment schedules to ensure no lapses in registrations and an orderly transition.

Determine Standards Strategy

It is important that individual organizations use their management review processes to discuss and determine their quality management system standards compliance objectives. The fundamental question many organizations will be asking is, Should they work for compliance to ISO 9001:2000, ISO 13485:2003, or both?

In the absence of any customer or regulatory requirements to comply with ISO 9001, my recommendation to medical device organizations is to only seek registration to ISO 13485:2003. Such registration will provide objective evidence of compliance with quality management system requirements consistent with meeting customer requirements and those of the major regulatory agencies around the world. The organization may choose to adopt some of the customer satisfaction and continual improvement requirements of ISO 9001 because it feels that it makes good business sense, but if there are no customer or regulatory reasons for registration to this standard, it may be unwise to do so.

Standards Strategy

It is true that some customers and a number of regulatory agencies in smaller countries are not aware of ISO 13485 and may require or request compliance with ISO 9001:2000. The GHTF is doing its best to publicize the value of ISO 13485 to regulatory agencies around the world, but it might be necessary for organizations to educate customers and regulatory agencies. These organizations should avail themselves of materials that are available from the GHTF[1] and the Association for the Advancement of Medical Instrumentation (AAMI)[2], which administers the ISO Secretariat for TC 210.

Negotiations with Registrars and Notified Bodies

It will be important that the organization negotiate with its current registrar or notified body and with others that may offer programs that are more consistent with the organization's objectives. The transition from the 1994 to the 2000 versions of ISO 9001 will likely cause increased demand for quality management system assessments and may lengthen each of these assessments. Getting on the registrar's schedule may be difficult if the organization delays.

If the organization seeks registration to ISO 13485:2003 alone, it will be necessary to determine if the registrar is or plans to be qualified for ISO 13485:2003 for the relevant medical devices. It may be necessary to help the registrar gather information to plan for assessments and, if necessary, educate assessors.

If the organization seeks registration to both ISO 9001:2000 and ISO 13485:2003, it will also be necessary to negotiate with the registrar about the process of assessing for both standards and the costs associated with this process. It will be necessary to determine if dual registration will require more than one assessment, or other significant additional costs.

Internalize Process Approach

One of the things the individual organization can do immediately is to internalize the process approach by reviewing it with top management, developing training programs for affected personnel and beginning to modify high level documentation to reflect this approach. Both ISO 9001:2000 and ISO 13485:2003 have adopted the process approach, so there is little chance that such efforts will be wasted.

Perform "Gap Analysis"

Now that the ISO Central Secretariat has published the DIS version of ISO 13485:2003 it is unlikely that significant substantive changes will be made to this standard as of this writing. The DIS should be satisfactory to use as the basis for an analysis of the organization's current quality management system against revised requirements. Since one of the objectives of ISO 13485:2003 is to maintain the status quo with regard to requirements, it is not likely that an analysis of a compliant quality management system will reveal many "gaps." In any case, starting this process during the third or fourth quarter of 2002, should provide sufficient time for corrective and preventive action before the end of 2003.

If the individual organization seeks compliance with ISO 9001:2000, it should start its gap analysis immediately. Such an analysis may uncover deficiencies related to customer satisfaction and continual improvement processes.

Conclusion

Get Started Right Away

The key for organizations is to begin developing a quality systems strategy right away, keeping in mind the development process for ISO 13485:2003. That should leave enough time to effect an orderly and timely quality management system transition.

End Notes

[1] Global Harmonization Task Force web site: www.GHTF.org.

[2] Association for the Advancement of Medical Instrumentation (AAMI) web site: www.aami.org; contact: Ms. Hillary Woehrle, Secretary TC 210, Hwoehrle@aami.org

CONFORMITY ASSESSMENT AND LABORATORY ACCREDITATION

European Union and Conformity Assessment Requirements

21

by James Kolka

What Is Conformity Assessment?

Conformity assessment includes all activities that are intended to assure the conformity of products to a set of requirements. These activities can include the following:

- Approving product designs
- Testing manufactured products
- Registering a company's quality system
- Accrediting organizations that perform testing and assessment procedures.

In general, conformity assessment includes all market access processes for a product or service that must be followed to bring that product or service to a market.

Governments use conformity assessment procedures to ensure that products sold in their countries meet their laws and regulations and to protect their citizens, public systems and the environment from harm caused by products that enter their country.

Customers benefit from conformity assessment for the same reasons as do governments. Purchasers of products and services can use conformity assessment to identify suppliers whose products can be relied on to comply with critical requirements. Manufacturers, in turn, use conformity assessment procedures to demonstrate to their customers that their products comply with requirements.

The EU's Single Internal Market

The goal of the European Union's single internal market is to promote economic competitiveness and to become a powerful economic trading bloc by removing physical, technical and fiscal barriers to trade. The free internal movement of goods, services, people and capital from one member state to another is essential to economic growth.

Beginning in 1983 and anticipated in the 1985 document, *Completing the Internal Market, White Paper from the European Commission to the Euopean Council*, the European Union has been developing a new approach to regulating products as one way to unify the European market. It has enlisted the aid of key European regional standards organizations to develop EU-wide, "harmonized" standards. The purpose of these standards is to eliminate the jumble of national standards of the individual 15 member states. The European Union identified 300 regulations (later reduced to 286) to implement the single internal market. Among these regulations, were directives dealing with toy safety, machinery, electromagnetic capability, medical devices and others.

> Note: With the addition of Austria, Finland and Sweden, the European Union increased its membership to 15 on January 1, 1995. In 1996 the European Union formalized its assession plans to add 12 new member states in stages. These countries are Poland, Hungary, Czech Republic, Bulgaria, Romania, Slovakia, Estonia, Latvia, Lithuania, Slovenia, Malta and Cyprus. Turkey also is being considered, although further down the road.

These additions would increase the EU's population to over 500 million. US companies already exporting to these nations are finding "CE Marking" stipulated in contracts in anticipation of future EU membership.

Technical Trade Barriers

The trade barriers of most concern to US companies wishing to do business with the European Union are technical barriers. These include different standards for products, duplication of testing and certification procedures for products and differences in the laws of EU member states. These restrict the free movement of products within the European Union.

Goals of the New System

The European Union recognized that, as technical barriers were lowered, a new framework was needed to replace them. The goal of this new framework is to create confidence among the member states in the following:

- Quality and safety of products sold in the European Union
- Overall competence of manufacturers, including their quality procedures
- Competence of the testing laboratories and certification bodies that assess the conformity of products.

The new framework involves EU-wide directives issued by the European Commission that will replace individual member state regulations. It also involves a comprehensive approach to conformity assessment.

This developing system encompasses all aspects of conformity assessment. The European Union refers to it as its Global Approach to Product Certification and Testing. The approach has four major components:

1. EU-wide directives
2. Harmonized standards
3. Consistent conformity assessment procedures
4. Competent certification and testing bodies.

Each component is discussed in detail as follows.

1. EU-wide Directives

As noted in Chapter 2, products in the European Union are classified into two categories: regulated products and nonregulated products.

Nonregulated Products

Most products sold in the European Union are nonregulated products such as paper and furniture. The European Union's strategy for removing technical barriers to nonregulated products is to rely on the principle of mutual recognition of national product standards established in 1979 by the European Court of Justice in the Casis de Dijon decision. According to the principle of mutual recognition, products that meet the requirements of one EU member state can freely circulate in other member states.

An EU purchaser of an nonregulated product (such as paper or manually operated hand tools) can continue to purchase US products specified in terms of US standards. Even if the product remains regulated at the national level and is not subject to harmonized standards, a US product that meets the national requirements of one EU member state may enjoy free circulation throughout the entire European Union through mutual recognition.

Regulated Products

Only a small percentage of the total number of products sold in the European Union are regulated. Regulated products such as medical devices, pressure vessels and personal protective equipment, however, make up approximately 50 percent of US exports to the European Union, according to US Department of Commerce estimates. They include those products that the European Union believes are associated with significant safety, environmental or health concerns.

The EU Council of Ministers is working to remove technical trade barriers for regulated products by issuing EU-level directives. A directive is the official legislation promulgated by the European Commission and approved by the European Parliament and Council. By treaty, it binds all members of the European Union, who are required to convert EU directives into national legislation and regulations. Existing laws and rules that conflict with the directive are invalid and are superseded by EU directives. After a transition period (in most instances), the regulated products must meet the requirements of the new directive.

Old-Approach Directives and New-Approach Directives

Prior to 1989, the European Union issued directives that are now known as old-approach directives. These directives were highly specific, detailing and defining all technical characteristics and requirements of a product. The problem with old-approach directives is that they are complicated, it is expensive to comply with them and they are easily outdated due to technological advances. The term "old approach" also is confusing, because the European Union continues to adopt these types of directives. The 1992 automotive type approval directives, for example, are old-approach directives.

Nevertheless, these directives are binding on all manufacturers. If a company's product falls within the scope of an old-approach directive, it must meet the directive's requirements.

The European Union soon realized that the detailed blueprint it was drafting was slowing its progress in meeting the goals of a single internal market. To expedite the process, the European Union began issuing more "generic-type" directives, known as new-approach directives.

New-approach directives are based on the following four key elements:

- Essential environmental, health and safety requirements
- Presumption of conformity
- Mutual recognition
- Voluntary standards.

Essential Requirements

New-approach directives stipulate the environmental, health and safety requirements a product must meet to be considered safe for the marketplace. These requirements tell a company what must be done to comply with a directive. Technical standards — or the "how-to" specifications — are left to be spelled out by European regional standards organizations and by the member states themselves. The directives do not specifically list technical standards, but they do provide references for all appropriate supporting technical documentation. The number of standards per directive can be considerable. For example, 40 technical committees have drafted 650 technical standards for the machinery directive.

Presumption of Conformity

If a product conforms to European harmonized technical standards that have been adopted into national law, it is assumed that the product conforms to the essential requirements contained in the applicable directive. For example, if a company declares that its product conforms to Committee for European Standardization (CEN) or European Committee for Electrotechnical Standardization (CENELEC) technical standards that apply to the company's product, the product is presumed to conform with the applicable EU directive. (CEN and CENELEC are described in detail later in this chapter.)

Mutual Recognition

Member states must accept products that are lawfully manufactured in any other member state, provided that the product meets EU-wide standards and/or the health, safety and environmental concerns of the receiving state.

The European Union is seeking to apply this principle not only to the acceptance of products, but also to test results and certification activities. Further, it is pushing for Mutual Recognition Agreements (MRAs) with non-EU nations to mutually accept test results and product certifications.

Voluntary Standards

Each new-approach directive provides companies with various options to comply with the essential requirements of the directive. These include a range of conformity assessment procedures. To determine which conformity assessment procedure applies to a product, manufacturers should study the appropriate directive or directives, review the options for conformity assessment and choose the preferred or acceptable option. Depending on the type of product and its potential safety risk, the choices can range from manufacturer's self-certification to the implementation of a full quality assurance system.

Companies also have choices regarding the technical standard(s) to which their product can conform. These include the following:

- They can comply with technical standards appropriate to the directive. Conformance to the technical standard may involve a third-party evaluation; it depends on the specific directive and the procedure chosen for conformity assessment.

- They can conform to a non-European standard or to no standard at all. In this case, the company must demonstrate that its product meets the requirements of the directive, which may involve third-party approval of the demonstration.

In cases where there is a low safety risk, directives may allow a company to self-certify its product. However most conformity assessment options require some third-party involvement in testing and certification.

Some manufacturers abused the self-certification options of the toy safety directive. This resulted in the approval of Council Regulation No. 339/93 on product safety conformity on February 8, 1993. It stipulates that all products must be properly marked and accompanied by documents that indicate product conformity with EU safety requirements. It most cases, this document will be a Declaration of Conformity for an EU new-approach directive.

To be able to assess product compliance with EU legislation, it is important for manufacturers to identify relevant European standards and, where appropriate, third-party testing or certification entities authorized to assess product conformity to the requirements of specific directives. This information should appear on the Declaration of Conformity that accompanies a CE-marked product.

This information is published in the *Official Journal of the European Communities*. For example, the first EU technical harmonization directive to be implemented, covering toy safety, came into effect on January 1, 1990. Reference harmonized standards were formally identified in the *Official Journal* on June 23, 1989. Lists of bodies authorized to carry out EU-type examination as referred to in the toy safety directive were first published over a period of months, beginning June 23, 1990. Currently these directives are republished with periodic updates in the *Official Journal* (http://europa.eu.int/eur-lex/en/oj/ or www.newapproach. org).

Transition Period

In the case of some directives, provisions have been made for a transition period between the implementation of the directive and the date by which companies must comply. The purpose is to allow time for reference standards to be completed and sufficient testing facilities to be qualified and authorized.

For example, under the medical devices directives, transition periods have been established, ranging from two to four years from the date the directive is implemented. This transition period allows manufacturers to continue meeting existing national standards during the transition period. However, they can market only to countries where their product complies with national standards. Under these circumstances, they cannot affix the CE mark and are not guaranteed free circulation for their products among all EU member states.

Manufacturers that meet the new EU-wide directives immediately will be able to sell medical devices throughout the European Union and European Economic Area (EEA). Consequently a number of EU and US medical device manufacturers ignored the transition period and moved to complete certification as soon as possible. This gave them an edge over competitors, allows them to advertise compliance with new EU safety standards, establish an EU-wide marketing presence and increase their market share.

With other directives, such as construction products and telecommunications terminal and satellite earth station equipment, there was no transition period. Since the construction products directive covers a vast range of products and the system for product certification is not fully operational, the lack of a transition period has caused some difficulties in that industry. Interim procedures are now being developed.

Requirements May Include Several Directives

It is possible that a company must conform to more than one directive. For example, a commercial air conditioning manufacturer would have to meet the requirements of five different directives, machinery safety, electromagnetic compatibility, low voltage, pressure vessels and construction products (which covers equipment installed in buildings and building materials).

In another example, compressor-generators are covered by the requirements of the machinery directive. However, the air tank component of this equipment also must meet the requirements of the simple pressure vessels directive. The same is true for suppliers of air brakes that are incorporated into mobile industrial or construction equipment.

Manufacturers who supply components to other producers for incorporation into a machine that is then exported to the European Union may find themselves expected to meet the technical requirements of EU legislation and issue a Declaration of Incorporation to accompany the product in the EU. This type of declaration states that EU safety requirements have been statisfied, but that final CE marking responsibility belongs to the company incorporating the component into its machine.

The European Union also has issued directives that apply to all industry sectors. These include directives on product liability and product safety. Manufacturers will be required to comply with these as well. (See Appendix F for a list of major EU directives.)

Notified Bodies

In addition to requirements, directives also list the appropriate government-appointed organizations, known as notified bodies, that are authorized to certify that a particular product conforms to the requirements of a directive. A notified body might be a testing organization, testing laboratory, the operator of a certification system or even a government agency itself.

A notified body is designated by a competent authority of a member state from among the bodies under its jurisdiction. A competent authority is the national authority in each member country that has overall responsibility for the safety of products.

The name notified body comes from the fact that member states notify the EU Commission as to which bodies in their country are qualified to perform the specific evaluations stipulated in individual directives.

The duties of notified bodies are clearly spelled out in each directive, and lists of notified bodies vary depending on each directive. Every EU country must accept the results of conformity assessments by notified bodies in all other EU countries unless there is cause to believe the product was improperly tested. Notified bodies also are required to carry liability insurance.

The Competence of Notified Bodies

Each member state must have confidence that its notified bodies are competent to declare conformity to a directive. In order to ensure members of the competence of notified bodies, the European Union has developed the Community-wide EN 45000 series standards for certification and testing. The European Union also is developing a Council regulation to guide the creation of notified bodies and their compliance with the EN 45000 series.

Product Certification Versus ISO 9000 Registration

To satisfy the conformity assessment requirements of most EU new-approach directives and to affix the CE mark, a company must receive third-party approval from an EU notified body. Since this product certification approval is not the same as ISO 9000 registration by a registrar, it is critical to ascertain the quality assurance requirements of a directive and establish contact with an EU notified body to make certain that everything is in order. Some US manufacturers have presented ISO 9000 registration to EU authorities and have been denied access to the marketplace because directive requirements and notified body approval have not been met.

It is possible that at least three elements will be necessary. For example, in most cases the EU medical devices directives will require a registered ISO 9000 quality assurance system, augmented by compliance with the EN 46000 requirements (the application of ISO 9000 to medical devices) as guided by an EN medical devices guidance document. In addition, the guidance documents reference key clauses of ISO 9004. Because ISO 9001:2000 is different in structure from the 1994 version, TC 210 (the ISO Technical Committee responsible for health products) is considering replacing the prior structure with a new augmented free-standing ISO 13485, *Quality Systems — Medical Devices — Particular Requirements for the Application of ISO 9001:2000.*

A simple registration to ISO 9001 will not fulfill the requirements of the medical devices directive. A company will require notified body certification of its product and the creation of a medical device vigilance system, in addition to the essential requirements set forth in Annex 1 of the directive. Similar essential requirements are set forth in each EU new-approach directive. In 1995, the European Commission published *The Guide to the Implementation of Community Harmonization Directives Based on the New Approach and the Global Approach.* It contains a chapter outlining the operating procedures and requirements for notified bodies.

The CE Mark

The final result of the product certification process is the CE mark. A notified body is authorized to permit manufacturers to affix the CE mark, which signifies proof that a company has met essential health and safety requirements and the specific conformity assessment requirements to market its product in the European Union. If a directive calls for self-certification (e.g., toy safety, machinery directives, etc.), the manufacturer takes responsibility for affixing the CE mark.

The CE designation, French for "Conformite Europeenne" (European Conformity), is required in order to sell any product manufactured or distributed under the new-approach directives. The CE mark will replace all national marks now used to show compliance with legislated requirements for regulated materials and products.

The requirements for affixing the CE Mark are set forth in each directive. (See Figure 21-1.) Basically, four steps are needed to obtain the mark. They are:

- Conformance with the requirements of the appropriate EU directives

- If quality system registration is required by the directive, official registration with a notified body is required. Until the requirements are integrated with ISO 9001:2000, organizations would register to the appropriate ISO 9000:1994 standard (ISO 9001, ISO 9002 or ISO 9003).

- Documentation of any test data required by the directives
- Necessary certification by the appropriate notified bodies to verify compliance with the directive(s).

Each member state must allow products with the CE mark to be marketed as conforming to the requirements of the directive. The same rules apply — regardless of the product's origin. Products that have been improperly certified will be refused entry or withdrawn from the market.

Figure 21-1

The CE Mark

Information to accompany CE Mark manufacturers in the European Union should be listed in the Declaration of Conformity for certain medical devices. The CE Mark should be accompanied by the identification number of the notified body.

Old-Approach Directives

Old-approach product safety directives, such as those for motor vehicles, tractors and chemicals, contain detailed requirements for standards and test methods, and specify required marks that must be applied to indicate conformance. Products subject to product safety requirements in these areas — as well as to new-approach directives — must bear both the CE mark and other marks required under EU legislation.

Additional Marks

The CE mark alone is sufficient to market a product in the European Union. In some cases, however, customer acceptance of materials and products may hinge on the appearance of one or more additional certification and/or quality marks issued by bodies in that member state.

The CE mark does not preclude the continued existence of national quality or performance marks representing levels of quality, safety or performance higher than those specified in EU legal requirements. Member states cannot require that products bear these marks as a condition of market access, but they can continue to exist on a voluntary basis and can be specified in private commercial contracts.

If a product incorporates a safety element subject to EU legislation requiring the CE mark, but is also subject to national environmental control requirements (recycling, disposal, etc.), manufacturers could be required to obtain additional environmental national marks in order to market the product in a specific EU member state. On June 30, 1999 EU-wide requirements became law for recycling the disposal of packaging waste. It was adopted into national law under the EU Directive on Packaging and Packaging Waste 94/36/EC.

2. Harmonized Standards

The second key component of the European Union's conformity assessment system is harmonized standards. Harmonization refers to the process of creating uniform, EU-wide standards. The European Union believes that harmonized standards are essential to promote trade, not only in Europe but around the world. Standards have been steadily growing in importance and are becoming a strategic issue for business.

Ultimately, the aim of harmonization is a global system, where manufacturers could produce to a single standard, be assessed by a single assessment or testing body and the resulting certificate would be accepted in every market. This is the goal of "make it once, test it once, sell it everywhere."

EU Standards and Regional Standardization Organizations

The essential safety requirements in the EU new-approach directives are broad guidelines only. In addition to issuing directives, the European Union is seeking to harmonize technical requirements by mandating the use of harmonized standards whenever possible. The task of developing specific technical standards to harmonize the many differing national standards of the EU countries into one set of common standards is carried out primarily by three European standard-setting organizations.

These include the European Committee for Standardization (CEN), the European Committee for Electrotechnical Standardization (CENELEC) and the European Telecommunications Standards Institute (ETSI). A fourth organization, the European Organization for Technical Approvals (EOTA), assesses the technical fitness of construction products for their intended use, even when no EU-wide harmonized standard or national standard exists for that product.

These four organizations develop standards according to priorities set by the European Union and its member states. They also consult with existing national and international standardization organizations. CEN and CENELEC have negotiated agreements with the two international standards organizations, the International Organization for Standardization (ISO) and the International Electrotechnical Commission (IEC) to develop new standards.

CEN and CENELEC will develop a new standard when:

- A standard does not already exist under ISO or IEC auspices

- The standard cannot be developed at the international level

- The standard cannot be developed at the international level within a specific time frame.

All member states must conform to each standard once it is formally adopted.

Committee for European Standardization (CEN)

CEN is the Committee for European Standardization (or Normalization, hence the "N"). This nonprofit organization is the world's largest regional standards group. It comprises delegates from 18 Western European countries — the 15 European Union nations plus three member nations of the European Free Trade Association (EFTA). CEN is composed of the national standardization institutes of these 18 countries. (The only nation missing from EFTA is Liechtenstein.)

CEN's main objective is to prepare a single set of European standards in place of numerous national standards. CEN works to remove any standardization differences among its 18 members.

Roles in Testing and Certification

CEN promulgates standards when the European Union passes a directive. It also responds to EU requests to develop a standard when no directive has been issued. When necessary, CEN promulgates new standards that the member countries are obligated to adopt as their own national standards. CEN also creates and implements procedures for the mutual recognition of test results and certification schemes.

CEN and ISO

CEN adopts ISO standards whenever possible and promotes the implementation of ISO and IEC standards. As far as possible, CEN avoids any duplication of work. CEN also works with ISO to draft new standards and has formal agreements with ISO for the exchange of information and for technical cooperation. Following the Vienna Agreement of 1991, CEN and ISO share common planning and have parallel votes during the development of standards and parallel votes for the joint adoption of technical standards.

Types of CEN Standards

CEN publishes its standards in one of the following three ways.

European Standards (or European Norm, hence the EN designation) are totally harmonized, and the 18 member nations of CEN are obligated to adopt these standards as their own national standards. An EN must be implemented at the national level as a national standard and by withdrawing the conflicting national standard.

Manufacturer compliance with European standards is voluntary. But if an EN is met, it is presumed that this also fulfills the requirements of the directive that applies to the manufacturer's product. ENs for a new technology are prepared following specific requests from the European Union and EFTA.

Harmonization Documents (HD) allow for some national deviations in standards. The HD must be implemented at the national level, either by issuing the corresponding national standard or, as a minimum, by publicly announcing the HD number and title. In both cases, no conflicting national standard may continue to exist after a fixed date.

European Pre-standards (prENs) are guidelines for expected ENs or HDs, or guidelines for rapidly developing industries. PrENs may be established as prospective standards in all technical fields where the innovation rate is high or where there is an urgent need for technical advice. CEN members are required to make the prENs available at the national level in an appropriate form and to announce their existence in the same way as for ENs and HDs. However, any conflicting national standards may be kept in force until the prENs is converted into an EN.

European Committee for Electrotechnical Standardization (CEN-LEC)

The European Committee for Electrotechnical Standardization (CENELEC) is CEN's sister organization and is also based in Brussels, Belgium. CENELEC is a nonprofit technical organization working to harmonize standards among its 18 EU and EFTA member countries and is composed of delegates from those countries.

While CEN works closely with ISO to adopt standards on everything but technical issues, CENELEC works with its international counterpart, the International Electrotechnical Commission (IEC). CENELEC maintains an active working agreement with IEC, and 85 percent of the European standards adopted by CENELEC are IEC standards.

The procedures for the development of CENELEC standards are the same as those described for CEN. CENELEC publishes its standards in the same manner as CEN: as European Standards (EN), Harmonization Documents (HD) and European Pre-standards (ENV).

CENELEC Priorities

CENELEC's areas of priorities for developing standards are low-voltage areas, other electric equipment and agreed-upon mandates for standardization from EU and EFTA countries. As mentioned earlier, manufacturers do not have to meet CENELEC standards if their products fulfill the essential requirements of the applicable directive(s). Products that meet CENELEC standards, however, are presumed also to fulfill the requirements of EU directives.

European Telecommunications Standardization Institute (ETSI)

The European Telecommunications Standardization Institute (ETSI) is the third sister organization in the CEN/CENELEC/ETSI regional triumvirate. It promotes European standards for a unified telecommunications system.

ETSI membership is open to all relevant organizations with an interest in telecommunication standardization that belong to a country within the European Confederation of Posts and Telecommunications Administrations. Users, research bodies and others may participate directly in standardization work for Europe.

The process of publishing final ETSI standards is almost identical to the methods used by CEN and CENELEC. The three groups have formed a Joint Presidents' Group to handle common concerns regarding policy and management. The three groups also have signed a cooperation agreement to prevent overlapping assignments and to work together as partners.

Non-European organizations interested in telecommunications are sometimes invited as observers to the technical work of ETSI. In addition, ETSI and the American National Standards Institute (ANSI), the US standardization body, have agreed to an exchange of information concerning their respective work.

3. Consistent Conformity Assessment Procedures

The third component of the EU's overall conformity assessment approach is consistent conformity assessment procedures. The main principle is that, rather than adopting certification procedures on an ad hoc basis, directive-by-directive, as in the past, the European Union in the future will choose from a set of detailed conformity assessment procedures. This plan is called the modular approach.

The Modular Approach

The modular approach to conformity assessment offer several procedures for a manufacturer to demonstrate compliance with directives. These range from a manufacturer's self-declaration of conformity to assessment of a quality system to type-testing of the product by a third party, depending on the health, safety and environmental risks of the product. All future conformity assessment procedures will be based on one or more of these options.

The EU Council outlines the combination of procedures it considers appropriate for each directive and sets the conditions of application. The manufacturers themselves, however, have the final choice as to which of the procedures they will follow. The most recent state of this approach is contained in Council Decision 93/465/EEC of July 22, 1993, entitled *Concerning the Modules for the*

Figure 21-2

Overview — EC 92 Conformity Assessment Procedures — the modules

	MODULES						
	A	**B+C**	**B+D**	**B+E**	**B+F**	**G**	**H**
Product Surveillance: Samples:	○	○			● OR		
Each Product:	○				●	●	
Q.A. Surveillance:			● EN ISO 9002:1994	● EN ISO 9003:1994			● EN ISO 9001:1994
Type Testing:		●	●	●	●		○ Design
Technical Documentation:	①	≠	≠	≠	≠	≠	③
CE Mark Affixed by: Manufacturer:	CE	CE	CE★	CE★	CE★ OR		CE★
Third Party:					CE★	CE★	

○ Supplementary Requirements   ① Required to Be Available   CE CE Mark

● Action by Third Party   ≠ Required by Notified Body

③ Part of Quality System   CE★ CE Mark with the Notified Body Identification Symbol

Figure 21-3

Conformity Assessment Process

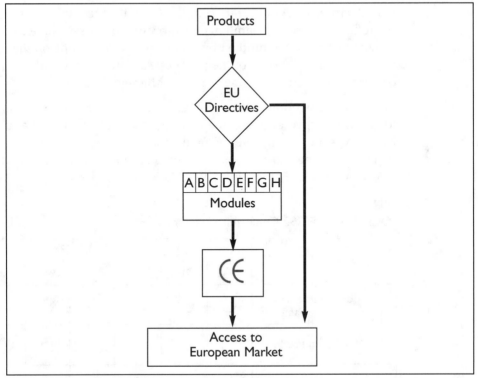

Various Phases of the Conformity Assessment Procedures and the Rules for the Affixing and Use of the CE Conformity Marking Which Are Intended To Be Used in the Technical Harmonization Directives.

Figures 22-2 and 22-3 illustrate the certification options available to comply with the directives. If one or more directives is applicable to a particular product, the directives indicate whether a notified body must be involved, and if so, the extent of that involvement. Apart from module A, the supplier has to involve a notified body for all other modules. The supplier is responsible for maintaining the conformity of its product to all relevant essential requirements.

As stated earlier, ISO 9000 registration alone, without product testing, is not sufficient to meet EU directive requirements. Quality system registration is a component of the conformity assessment requirements for some regulated products. The directives, however, require that products be tested to ensure compliance with the minimum requirements of the directive. In some directives, if a manufacturer has an ISO 9001-registered quality system, it can then self-declare conformity with the technical requirements of the directive, provided that all of the product safety essential requirements have been satisfied.

Description of Modules in Modular Approach

Two main phases in the modular approach exist: the design phase and the production phase. Both phases are covered by modules, which are further broken down into four types of examination:

- Internal control of production
- Type-examination
- Unit verification
- Full quality assurance — EN 29001.

These are examined in more detail below. (See Figure 21-4.)

Internal Control of Production (A)

Internal control of production allows manufacturers to self-declare conformity to the specific standard. Self-declaration is possible for toys, electromagnetic compatibility, some weighing instruments for noncommercial use and most types of machinery, as well as for some types of personal protective equipment, pressure vessels and equipment, recreational craft and low-risk medical devices.

During the design phase, the manufacturer may carry out the procedure for conformity assessment itself. The manufacturer, however, must keep the technical documentation available in a technical construction file for review by the national authorities for at least 10 years after production of the product. This way, assessments and checks can be carried out to determine whether the product complies with the directive.

The producer has to provide insight into the design, the manufacturing process and the performance of the product. The manufacturer must take all the steps necessary to ensure the manufacturing process guarantees that the product constantly complies with the essential requirements.

During the production phase, a notified body carries out testing on specific aspects of the product at random intervals. If allowed by this directive, this module can be used by a manufacturer who chooses to produce, not in accordance with the European standards, but directly in accordance with the essential requirements of the applicable directive and can demonstrate that conformity to those requirements.

Type-Examination (B)

In type-examination, the design phase involves verification by a third party. In this module, the manufacturer has to present the technical documentation and one product type (typical example) to a testing organization of its choice. The testing organization assesses and draws up a type-examination certificate. This module must be supplemented by modules C, D, E or F.

Figure 21-4

Conformity Assessment Procedure Modules

DESIGN	PRODUCTION
A. INTERNAL CONTROL OF PRODUCTION — Manufacturer • Keeps technical documentation at the disposal of national authorities As • Intervention of notified body	Manufacturer • Declares conformity with essential requirements As • Tests on specific aspects of the product • Product checks at random intervals
B. TYPE EXAMINATION — Manufacturer submitts to notified body • Technical documentation • Type Notified body • Ascertains conformity with essential requirements • Carries out tests, if necessary • Issues EU type-examination certificate	**C. CONFORMITY TO TYPE** — Manufacturer • Declares conformity with approved type • Affixes the CE Mark Notified body • Tests on specific aspects of the product • Product checks at random intervals
	D. PRODUCT QUALITY ASSURANCE — EN ISO 9002:1994 - Manufacturer • Operates approved QS-production and testing • Declares conformity with approved type • Affixes the CE Mark EN ISO 9002:1994 - Notified Body • Approves the QS • Carries out surveillance to the QS
	E. PRODUCT QUALITY ASSURANCE — EN ISO 9003:1994 - Manufacturer • Operates approved QS-production and testing • Declares conformity with approved type • Affixes the CE Mark EN ISO 9003:1994 - Notified Body • Approves the QS • Carries out surveillance to the QS
	F. PRODUCT VERIFICATION — Manufacturer • Declares conformity with approved type or essential requirements • Affixes the CE Mark Notified Body • Verifies conformity • Issues certificate of conformity
G. UNIT VERIFICATION — Manufacturer • Submits technical documentation	Manufacturer • Submits product • Declares conformity • Affixes the CE Mark Notified Body • Verifies conformity with essential requirements • Issues certificate of conformity
H. FULL QUALITY ASSURANCE — EN ISO 9001:1994 • Operates approved QS for design EN ISO 9001:1994 • Carries out surveillance to the QS • Validates conformity of the design • Issues EU design examination certificate	Manufacturer • Operates an approved QS for production and testing • Declares conformity • Affixes the CE Mark Notified Body • Carries out surveillance of the QS

Conformity to Type (C)

The manufacturer can self-declare conformity to type with no quality system requirement. The manufacturer draws up a declaration of conformity for the approved type from module B, and keeps this for at least 10 years after manufacture of the last product.

Production Quality Assurance (D)

This module requires third-party certification to ISO 9002, which includes the entire production process except for design. The manufacturer's quality system for production is approved by a testing organization. Then the manufacturer declares that its product matches the approved type.

Product Quality Assurance (E)

This module requires third-party certification to ISO 9003, for inspection and testing. Module E is the same as module D, except that the quality system concerns only the end-production checks.

Product Verification (F)

This module requires testing the product and certifying conformity by a third party. The manufacturer ensures that the production process guarantees the product meets the requirements. Then the manufacturer declares conformity. An approved testing organization checks this conformity. This can take place sometimes by testing each product separately and sometimes by random testing. Finally, the testing organization issues a certificate of conformity.

Unit-Verification (G)

Unit-verification requires the manufacturer to submit technical documents for one-time projects such as the construction of a power plant to regulatory authorities. A notified body must certify the project/product by checking that the production process conforms with essential requirements.

Full Quality Assurance (H)

Full quality assurance requires the manufacturer to operate an approved quality system for design, production and testing, and to be certified to the European quality standard EN ISO 9001/ISO 9001 by a notified body. Manufacturers can avoid expensive, time-consuming product testing by instituting a full quality assurance system according to ISO 9001.

Note: It remains to be seen how the EU will adjust the modular approach with ISO 9000:2000. The modules could remain in their present structure with a small adjustment, e.g., Production Quality Assurance could simply delete the design component of ISO 9001:2000.

Degree of Complexity

As a general rule, the greater the safety risk associated with a product, the more complex the conformity assessment process. For example, in the EU Council *Directive on Personal Protective Equipment*, a manufacturer can probably choose to self-certify a product where the model is simple, the risks are minimal and the user has time to identify those risks safely. Some examples are gardening gloves, gloves for mild detergent solutions, seasonal protective clothing and gloves or aprons for moderate exposure to heat.

Manufacturers, however, must choose either EC type approval ISO 9002:1994, production quality assurance or EC type approval plus EC verification in cases where personal protective equipment is of a complex design, "intended to protect against mortal danger or against dangers that may seriously and irreversibly harm the health..." of individuals, for example, fire protection clothing.

Given a choice between EC type approval plus EC verification or ISO 9001 (minus design), most manufacturers will choose ISO 9001 registration. Under ISO 9001, the manufacturer submits the production quality system for approval, a preferable alternative to the more intrusive EU process of continuously submitting representative samples to a third party for screening.

Additional Requirements

In addition to using the basic framework of the ISO 9000 series, some EU directives have supplemental requirements. For example, to certify under the EU construction products directive, a manufacturer also must comply with the additional requirements of the EN 45000 series of standards. These standards apply to laboratory, testing and certification organizations. Other product sectors for which additional guidelines have been developed are medical devices (EN 46001, *Particular requirements for the application of EN ISO 9001 for medical devices*) and aerospace products (EN 2000, EN 3042). Most likely, similar special requirements will be developed for other directives.

4. Competent Certification and Testing Bodies

The fourth and final component of the EU's comprehensive framework for conformity assessment is the role of certification and testing bodies. The goal of the European Union is to increase confidence of member nations in the work of these organizations so that the results of testing will be accepted throughout the European Union.

In its 1989 presentation, entitled *The Global Approach to Certification and Testing*, the European Union outlined the following major elements of its program for certification and testing bodies:

- The credibility of the manufacturer must be reinforced. This can be achieved by promoting the use of quality assurance techniques.

- The credibility of and confidence in testing laboratories and certification bodies must be enhanced. This can be achieved by developing the EN 45000 series of standards to evaluate the competence of testing laboratories.

- The competence of laboratories and certification bodies is established through an accreditation process based on EN 45000 standards. This accreditation process involves a third-party evaluation and is discussed in more detail in Chapter 22.

According to this system, notified bodies must produce documentation proving they conform to the EN 45000 series. If the notified bodies are not formally accredited, the appropriate national authority in the state member where the notified body is located must produce documentary evidence that the notified body conforms to the relevant standards of the EN 45000 series.

Finally, there is a testing and certification organization at the European level. This organization, called the European Organization for Testing and Certification (EOTC), has the role of promoting mutual recognition agreements in the nonregulated sphere. The EOTC is discussed in detail in Chapter 22.

The European Union and Other Countries

As the European Union moves toward its goal of a unified market and maps out its comprehensive system for product regulation and certification, it also is defining its future relationship with other countries. One of the key components of this relationship is nondiscrimination. This means the same rules apply, regardless of the product's origin. A corollary to this is acceptance of test reports or certificates of conformity from countries outside the European Union. These relationships, however, are still in a developmental phase. The issues discussed in this section include the following:

- Can notified bodies subcontract any of their activities to bodies outside the European Union? How much can be subcontracted?

- Are ISO 9000 registration certificates recognized throughout the European Union?

- Can a notified body be located outside the European Union?

Subcontracting

Can notified bodies subcontract any of their activities to bodies outside the European Union? To some extent the answer is yes. The European Union has proposed new rules for subcontracting and is moving to permit more extensive use of subcontracting. The European Union's general guidelines for subcontracting are stated below:

- EU notified bodies will need to hold subcontractors to the EN 45000 series of standards, including the requirements to maintain records.
- Subcontractors must contract with notified bodies and test to the same standards as the notified body.
- EU notified bodies "cannot subcontract assessment and appraisal activities."
- EU notified bodies remain responsible for any certification activity.
- Notified bodies can subcontract quality assessment audits, provided that they retain responsibility for the audit assessment.

The Guide to the Implementation of Community Harmonization Directives Based on the New Approach and the Global Approach (Brussels, 1995) discusses notified bodies, subcontracting, mutual recognition agreements, etc.

Mutual Recognition

Currently, US companies that achieve ISO 9000 registration obtain whatever recognition their accrediting entity has in the country in which the accreditation entity (i.e., NACCB in the United Kingdom, RAB in the United States) is located. Other countries in the European Union and elsewhere can voluntarily choose to recognize the registration certificate. The registration certificates are not yet governed by EU legislation, and EU-wide recognition is not yet mandatory. Presently, a few national accreditation entities are negotiating mutual recognition agreements to recognize one another's ISO 9000 registrations.

Although the term mutual recognition agreement fairly describes what has been negotiated, it should not be confused with the EU legal term. The EU legal term — Mutual Recognition Agreement — will be governed by an EU legal document and will refer to product-sector Mutual Recognition Agreements negotiated between the European Union and third-party countries (United States, Canada, Japan, etc.). Issues of registrar accreditation and the recognition of registration certificates are discussed in more detail in Chapter 22.

EU/US Mutual Recognition Agreement

On June 21, 1997, the European Union and the United States signed a Mutual Recognition Agreement covering six product sectors: telecommunications equipment, electromagnetic compatibility (EMC), electrical safety, pharmaceutical good manufacturing practice (GMP), medical devices and recreational craft. Under the Framework section of the agreement, each product sector has been developing protocols to implement their sector of the agreement.

For example, after a year the EU and FDA (representing the United States) initiated a three-year transition for the medical devices sector which began on June 1, 1998. One objective of the medical devices sector is to approve Conformity Assessment Bodies (CABs), which will be approved by both FDA and EU Competent Authorities.

In its initial phase, the medical devices eligible for a review under the MRA will be limited to lower risk devices. CABs in the United States and European Union will be authorized to review Class I and many categories of Class II devices. Class II – Tier 3 devices as well as Class III devices will not be subject to the MRA unless they are specifically included by FDA and the European Union.

The MRA also is developing an alert system to share device complaints received by FDA together with complaints received through the European Union's medical devices vigilance system. If a manufacturer experiences a complaint in the European Union or loses the right to CE mark, they should expect a visit from FDA.

The three-year transition period was designed to work out details and build confidence in the EU and US CABs to conduct product reviews and quality system inspections to both parties' satisfaction. It does constitute a significant step forward in sharing regulatory tasks and information.

The European Union also has signed MRAs with Australia and Canada covering medical devices.

Non-EU Notified Bodies

Under the EU system, member states can designate only notified bodies from within the European Union. No subsidiaries or related enterprises located in a third country can perform full third-party product certification and quality system registration except under a legal MRA between the European Union and the government authorities of that country. In addition, their competence must be assessed by third parties, according to the provisions of the EN 45000 series.

MRAs will allow US testing and certification organizations to act as notified bodies in the product areas covered by the MRA. In this way, non-EU notified bodies could award the CE mark for regulated products under the negotiated industry sector.

The European Union and US Conformity Assessment

Increasingly, the global economy is exercising an influence on the standards process. While both the European Union and the United States are major players in international conformity assessment talks, the European Union's influence now takes center stage as it works to harmonize standards and eliminate national barriers to trade. In December 1995, the European Union signed an agreement with MERCOSUR (the common market of Brazil, Argentina, Paraguay and Uruguay) to collaborate on the development of technical standards.

Initially, the European Union directed its energies to critical health and safety issues in the 1985 EU white paper, *Completing the Internal Market, White Paper from the European Commission to the European Council*. More recently, however, EU standards activity is moving beyond the white paper to new areas of concern. In part, this process is being aided by various EU "green papers" that address topics from transportation to telecommunication. It is reasonable to expect this activity to continue and examine most every area of standards activity over the next 20 to 30 years.

The US Response to the European Union

The critical issue for the United States is how to respond to these developments. On the one hand, the European Union and EFTA and their constituent member states have developed a standards structure that uses regional European quasi-legal standards organizations (CEN, CENELEC, ETSI, EOTC) to flesh out product standards. It is a process that fits comfortably into the framework of the EU and European legal code traditions of 17 EU and EFTA member states (only Ireland and the United Kingdom share the English legal system found in the United States). Furthermore, the remaining European nations and most Asian and Latin American nations share those same legal code traditions.

By way of contrast — except for areas of health and safety, where US federal or state agencies have entered the conformity assessment process through regulatory procedures — most American products are manufactured in accordance with industry standards. Industry product sector associations such as API, SAE, ASME, NEMA, etc., have established voluntary quality standards that must be met and approved before a company is entitled to stamp that it has met association standards.

Quite clearly, the two systems do not provide an easy match. The EU system is quasi-legal in structure and a significant part of the US system is private and voluntary. The European Union has made it clear that it wants to interact directly with the US government through a federal agency.

The National Voluntary Conformity Assessment Systems Evaluation (NVCASE) Program is being implemented by the National Institute of Standards and Technology (NIST). NVCASE is designed to serve as the US governmental program that parallels its EU governmental counterparts and officially recognizes US trade associations for product sector standards (see Chapter 22). This mechanism will allow trade associations in turn to recognize US notified body equivalents that can participate in US/EU MRAs.

Whatever the decision, if a conformity assessment procedure is put forth as the US procedure, it will have to be sanctioned by the United States. Likewise, only the European Union can sanction its conformity assessment procedures, government to government.

The Critical Role of Conformity Assessment

The critical role of conformity assessment procedures worldwide is just beginning to emerge. A company's decision to seek ISO 9000 registration should be part of an overall conformity assessment strategy. For example, a company's choice of an ISO 9000 registrar might be limited by an EU directive or US law. Approval of conformity assessment procedures for a specific product might also be required by the European Union.

In the United States, the regulatory process is guided by federal agencies, such as the FDA, the Environmental Protection Agency and the Consumer Product Safety Commission. These agencies drive much conformity assessment activity. Most US products, however, are manufactured to private industry standards such as those adopted by the American Petroleum Institute and the Society of Automotive Engineers.

Despite the complexity of the issues, US business must understand and prepare conformity assessment strategies for the products it sells. While ISO 9000 registration is a significant accomplishment for any company, it may not be sufficient to constitute a comprehensive global market access program.

Conclusion

For those people reading about the European Union and its new structure for the first time, it probably seems like one of Bob Newhart's early comedy routines in which he has Abner Doubleday call a company that sells party games and try to describe his new idea called "baseball."

Naturally, the description of a baseball diamond, outfield, batter, pitcher, home plate, three bases, balls, bats, outs, innings and nine players to a team sounded like total gibberish to the party game company. But what may have been gibberish in 1839 has now become our national pastime.

The European Union's new game may seem confusing and unsettled. From our US perspective, it may not appear to be a level playing field. But it is becoming the playing field. Not understanding its dynamics could mean that a company's team is suited up for football only to discover that the other team is playing baseball.

For example, in 1995 Australia became the first nation to sign a MRA with the European Union, adopting the new approach to medical device regulation. Other nations are expected to follow.

In a similar, but less formal fashion, India, Singapore and Malaysia have adopted several of the European Union's new telecommunication standards. And, as noted earlier in this chapter, MERCOSUR, the common market of southern Latin America, signed a formal agreement to coordinate their technical standards developments.

To understand the EU system, it is necessary to read the directives in depth. Usually more than one directive or set of laws will be involved. Understanding the process will be crucial to becoming an effective competitor in what may become the world's largest market. For those companies that get there early and establish a presence, the monetary rewards could be substantial.

ISO/IEC 17025 and Laboratory Accreditation

22

By Peter S. Unger

Introduction

Internationally, as well as in the United States, considerable debate and confusion exists about the similarities, differences and relationships between laboratory accreditation (usually performed using ISO/IEC 17025, "General requirements for the competence of testing and calibration laboratories") and quality system certification (or registration) to ISO 9001.

Quality system registration certifies that a quality management system meets a defined model (ISO 9001). ISO 9001 certification does not of itself demonstrate the competence of a laboratory to produce technically valid data and results.

Why Is There So Much Confusion?

First, there is a significant problem of semantics. Second, the purposes of each standard are different and thus examination against them gives different levels of assurance. ISO 9001 provides generic requirements for quality management of an organization, irrespective of the product or service it provides.

ISO/IEC 17025 is a standard developed specifically to provide minimum requirements to laboratories on both quality management in a laboratory environment and technical requirements for the proper operation of a laboratory. To the extent that both documents address quality management, ISO/IEC 17025 can be considered as a complementary document to ISO 9001 written in terms most understandable by laboratory managers.

There is, however, a view being expressed that the application of ISO 9001 is sufficient for the effective operation of a laboratory, thus ensuring validity of test data. This opinion has caused some confusion in the laboratory community itself and also, more broadly, among users of laboratory services. The problem is compounded when accreditation of the laboratory by a third party is required.

The Semantics Problem

Terminology used in this area of conformity assessment is in a state of flux, and is confusing or even misleading. The three "tion" words — "accreditation," "certification" and "registration" — are often used interchangeably. The problem is compounded by some very specialized bodies using the words in a different context altogether. The ISO Council Committee on Conformity Assessment (CASCO) is attempting to resolve the semantics problem. The following definitions are still recognized:

- Accreditation — procedure by which an authoritative body gives formal recognition that a body or person is competent to carry out specific tasks

- Certification — procedure by which a third party gives written assurance (certificate of conformity) that a product, process or service conforms to specified requirements

- Registration — procedure by which a body indicates relevant characteristics of a product, process or service, or particulars of a body or person, in an appropriate publicly available list.

Internationally, certification has become the dominant term. However, the common use in the United States is not always in harmony with this international guidance, nor particularly with European practice. The European approach is to label both quality system registrars and product certifiers as certification bodies. There is very little, if any, use of the term registration in Europe, except in the ISO CASCO meaning of the term as a formal listing. So we have certification bodies performing either or both product certification and quality system registration.

There seems to be some agreement in the United States that "accreditation" is a formal recognition that a body is competent to carry out specific tasks, while "certification" is a formal evaluation by a third party that a product conforms to a standard.

"Registration" is the common term in the United States when referring to certification of quality systems. So we have laboratory accreditation defined as a formal recognition that a laboratory is competent to carry out specific tests or specific types of tests, and quality system registration being defined as a formal attestation that a supplier's quality management system is in conformance with ISO 9001. Thus, the American Society for Quality's (ASQ's) Registrar Accreditation Board (RAB) accredits management system certification bodies.

Traditionally, certification in the United States has related to products, processes or services, but because of the European influence we are hearing more references to the certification of quality systems, or the very misleading shorthand, "ISO certified" seen in many advertisements. ISO is vigorously discouraging this type of reference as inappropriate, inaccurate and an infringement on the ISO trademark. Unfortunately, this type of advertising is largely to blame for perpetuating the confusion and perhaps hyping quality system registration beyond that which it can honestly deliver.

ISO/IEC 17025:1999

Unlike the ISO 9000 series, ISO/IEC 17025 was not established primarily as a contractual model for use between suppliers and their customers. Its aims are to:

- Provide a basis for use by accreditation bodies in assessing competence of laboratories
- Establish general requirements for demonstrating laboratory competence to carry out specific tests or calibrations
- Assure correct test and calibration results.

Historically, ISO/IEC 17025 was developed within the framework of third-party laboratory accreditation bodies. Its early drafting was largely the work of participants in the International Laboratory Accreditation Conference (ILAC), and this standard (replacing ISO/IEC Guide 25:1990) was prepared largely as a response to ILAC's need for an International Standard for laboratory accreditation criteria.

To understand the significance and purpose of ISO/IEC 17025 and its relationship to ISO 9001, it is essential that it be viewed in light of its development history — it was initially to assist the harmonization of criteria for laboratory accreditation. ISO/IEC 17025 is now being used by laboratory accreditation bodies throughout the world and is the basis for mutual recognition agreements among accreditation bodies.

Laboratory accreditation is defined as a formal recognition that a testing laboratory is competent to carry out specific tests or specific types of tests. The key words in this definition are "competent" and "specific tests." Each accreditation recognizes a laboratory's technical capability (or competence) defined in terms of specific tests, measurements or calibrations. In that sense, it should be recognized as a stand-alone form of quite specialized technical certification — as distinct from a purely quality management system certification — as provided through ISO 9001.

Laboratory accreditation may also be viewed as a form of technical underpinning for a quality management system in much the same way that product certification could be considered as another form of complementary underpinning for a certified quality management system.

Similarities and Differences

ISO 9001 and ISO/IEC 17025 are used as criteria by third-party bodies, and both contain quality system elements. The elements of ISO 9000 are generic; those of ISO/IEC 17025 are also generic, but more specific to laboratory functions. The textual differences between ISO 9001:1994 and ISO/IEC 17025 are obvious, but when interpreted in a laboratory context, it is generally accepted that the systems elements of the two documents are closely compatible. This is acknowledged in the introduction of ISO/IEC 17025, which states: "Testing and calibration laboratories that comply with this International Standard will therefore also operate in accordance with ISO 9001 or 9002 [the 1994 versions]."

As of this writing it is unclear as to when and if the document will be revised to reflect the changes of ISO 9001:2000. In addition to its system requirements (which are compatible with ISO 9001:1994), ISO/IEC 17025 emphasizes technical competence of personnel for their assigned functions, addresses ethical behavior of laboratory staff, requires use of well-defined test and calibration procedures and participation in relevant proficiency testing programs. ISO/IEC 17025 also provides more relevant equipment management and calibration requirements, including traceability to national and international standards for laboratory functions; identifies the role of reference materials in laboratory work; and provides specific guidance relevant to the output of laboratories — the content of test reports and certificates — together with the records requiring management within the laboratory.

Although ISO/IEC 17025 contains a combination of systems requirements and those related to technical competence, for laboratory accreditation purposes, ISO/IEC 17025 is normally used only as a starting point. ISO/IEC 17025 recognizes in Note 1 of the "Scope" that "It might be necessary to explain or interpret certain requirements in this International Standard to ensure that the requirements are applied in a consistent manner. Guidance for establishing applications for specific fields, especially for accreditation bodies (see ISO/IEC Guide 58:1993, 4.1.3), is given in Annex B."

However, there is another level of technical criteria that must be met for the accreditation of laboratories. That is the technically specific requirements of the individual test methods for which the laboratory's competence is publicly recognized. So the hierarchy of criteria that must be met for laboratory accreditation purposes is:

- ISO/IEC 17025

- Any field-specific criteria

- Technical requirements of specific test methods and procedures.

Apart from comparisons on the similarities and differences between the purposes of ISO 9001 and ISO/IEC 17025 and their use for third-party conformity assessment purposes, it is important to examine the differences in skills and emphasis of auditors involved in quality system certification and assessors for laboratory accreditation assessments.

For quality system certification, emphasis is traditionally placed on the qualifications of the auditor to perform an audit against ISO 9001. A lead auditor is expected to have a thorough knowledge of the requirements of that standard. In current practice internationally, a quality management system audit team should include personnel who have specific technical backgrounds or process familiarity relevant to the organizations being audited, but this is not always possible.

For laboratory accreditation, the assessment team always involves a combination of personnel who have expert technical knowledge of the test or measurement methodology being evaluated for recognition in a specific laboratory, together with personnel who have specific knowledge of the policies and practices of the accreditation body and the general systems applicable to all accredited laboratories. Thus, the laboratory accreditation assessment includes a technical peer-review component plus a systems-compliance component.

There are some other elements of difference in the respective assessment processes. For example, laboratory accreditation involves appraisal of the competence of personnel as well as systems. Part of the evaluation of a laboratory includes evaluation of supervisory personnel, in many cases leading to a recognition of individuals as part of the laboratory accreditation. The technical competence and performance of laboratory technicians may also be witnessed as part of the assessment process. The loss of key personnel may affect the continuing accreditation of the laboratory by the accrediting body. For example, many accreditation bodies recognize key staff whose absence would reduce the laboratory's technical competence and may prompt a reassessment before it would be normally scheduled or result in loss of accreditation.

The final product of a laboratory is test data. In many cases, laboratory accreditation assessments also include some practical testing of the laboratory through various forms of proficiency testing (interlaboratory comparisons or reference materials testing).

Quality system certification is not normally linked to nominated key personnel. The technical competence of managers and process operators is not a defined activity for quality management system audit teams. It is through the documented policies, job descriptions, procedures, work instructions, training requirements of organizations and objective evidence of their implementation that quality system certifiers appraise the people component of a system. Staff turnover is not an issue in maintaining certification.

Fundamental Difference

Quality system registration (ISO 9000) asks:

- Have you defined your procedures?
- Are they documented?
- Are you following them?

Laboratory accreditation asks the same questions but then goes on to ask:

- Are they the most appropriate test procedures to use in the circumstances?
- Will they produce accurate results?
- How have you validated the procedures to ensure their accuracy?
- Do you have effective quality control procedures to ensure ongoing accuracy?
- Do you understand the science behind the test procedures?
- Do you know the limitations of the procedures?
- Can you foresee and cope with any technical problems that may arise while using the procedures?
- Do you have all the correct equipment, consumables and other resources necessary to perform these procedures?

In effect, the registration of a laboratory's quality management system is a component of laboratory accreditation — not a substitute. Quality system registration of a laboratory to ISO 9001 misses a key element — technical validity and competence.

Unfortunately, quality system registration of laboratories is already being seen as an easier route to some form of third-party recognition for a laboratory than full accreditation.

Complementary Functions

Recognizing that there are differences in the purpose, criteria and emphasis of ISO 9001 and ISO/IEC 17025 and their use for conformity assessment purposes, it is worthwhile to consider how the roles of quality system certification and laboratory accreditation can best interact.

Quality system certification for a laboratory should be viewed as a measure of a laboratory's capability to meet the quality expectations of its customers in terms of delivery of laboratory services within a management system model as defined in ISO 9001 — a "quality" job. Secondly, laboratory accreditation should be viewed by customers as an independent reassurance that a laboratory is technically and managerially capable to perform specific tests, measurements or calibrations — a "technically competent" job. If satisfaction is needed on both these characteristics, then a combination of quality system certification and laboratory accreditation may be appropriate.

'In-House' Laboratories

If a laboratory's function is purely for internal quality control purposes within an organization (an "in-house" laboratory) and not requiring any formal output in terms of certificates or reports to external customers (or internal customers within a larger organization requiring formal test reports), it is appropriate for the laboratory to operate within the overall ISO 9001 framework of the parent company. Nevertheless, such laboratories and their senior management may also benefit from the external, independent appraisal provided by the technical assessors used in laboratory accreditation. However, if a laboratory issues certificates or reports certifying that products, materials, environmental conditions or calibrations conform to specific requirements, it may need to demonstrate to its clients or the general community that it is technically competent to conduct such tasks. Laboratory accreditation provides the independent measure of that competence.

Scope of Accreditation/Certification

Organizations may be certified to a quality system standard within very broad industry or product categories. Naturally, organizations with a very narrow product range are certified in these terms.

Laboratories, on the other hand, are accredited for quite specific tests or measurements, usually within specified ranges of measurement with associated information on uncertainty of measurement, and for particular products and test specifications.

Accreditation bodies encourage laboratories to endorse test reports in the name of the accreditation body to make a public statement that the particular test data presented has been produced by a laboratory that has demonstrated to a third party that it is competent to perform such tests.

ISO 9001 is not intended to be used in this way. ISO 9001 addresses the quality management system, not specific technical capability. The use of a quality system certification body's logo should not be used as a certification mark or endorsement as to the conformity of a particular product with its specified requirements. Similarly, it should not be used to endorse the competent performance of tests, calibrations or measurements reported by laboratories. Only a logo or endorsement showing accreditation to ISO/IEC 17025 or equivalent for specific tests or calibrations denotes technical credibility and an expectation of valid results. Laboratories certified to ISO 9001 cannot make the same claim.

The Special Role of Accredited Calibration Laboratories

For more general interaction between certified quality systems and laboratory accreditation, one very significant area is the role that accredited calibration laboratories play in demonstrating traceability to national and international standards of measurement. ISO 9001 requires that "... suppliers shall ... calibrate ... inspection, measuring and test equipment ... against certified equipment having a valid known relationship to nationally recognized standards."

Many calibration certificates presented to quality system auditors contain statements that the measurements or calibrations are "traceable to national standards." Some auditors also insist that suppliers' calibration documents provide cross-reference to the other reference standards used to calibrate their own devices, to provide a documented chain of traceability back to their own national or international standards of measurement. There may be multiple steps, involving various calibration devices, required to demonstrate traceability back to a national standard. This can therefore become a very complex and, in some perceptions, bureaucratic demonstration of traceability by a supplier. The supplier may also have no direct access to information, or influence over, the provider of calibrations for its equipment.

Concentration by auditors on documented statements of traceability of measurement can be viewed as an exercise in "paper traceability, "not "technical traceability" — that is, the calibrations performed on their equipment have been performed by personnel competent to undertake the measurements, under controlled environmental conditions (where appropriate), using other higher accuracy equipment that is maintained and recalibrated within appropriate intervals and backed up by records and other management systems that meet the principles of good laboratory practice embodied in ISO/IEC 17025. Accreditation of the laboratory providing a specialist calibration service provides such reassurance of technical traceability.

As it is a fundamental requirement for accredited calibration laboratories to have their own equipment traceable to national and international standards, both the interest and spirit of the ISO 9001 requirements are thus met when accredited calibration laboratories are used by suppliers. This principle has been recognized in ISO 10012.1, where Clause 4.15 "Traceability" states that "… the supplier may provide the documented evidence of traceability by obtaining his calibrations from a formally accredited source."

European Position

In a statement issued in April 1992, the European Organization for Conformity Assessment (EOTC) declared:

"… the only acceptable stand is to state that QS certification cannot be taken as an alternative to accreditation, when assessing the proficiency of testing laboratories. Not trying to underrate the QS certification procedure, it should nonetheless be underlined that, by being intended as a systematic approach to the assessment of an extremely broad scope of organizations and field of activity, it cannot include technical requirements specific to any given domain."

Conclusion

Before laboratories choose ISO 9001 certification, they should understand whether this type of third-party recognition is really appropriate for the needs of their customers. From the point of view of the user of test data, the quality management systems approach to granting recognition to laboratories is deficient in that it does not provide appropriate assessment of the technical competence of personnel engaged in what can only be described as a very technical activity, nor does it address the specific requirements of particular products or measurements. ISO 9001 states explicitly that they are complementary not alternatives to specified technical requirements.

Users of test data, therefore, should be concerned with both the potential for performing a quality job (quality management system) and technical competence (ability to achieve a technical result). The best available method of achieving these two objectives is through laboratory accreditation bodies, operating themselves to best international practice, requiring laboratories to adopt best practices and by engaging assessors who are expert in the specific tests in which the customer is interested. Acceptance of test data, nationally or internationally, should therefore be based on the application of ISO/IEC 17025 to assure the necessary confidence in the data's validity.

Accreditation according to ISO/IEC 17025 is therefore a more adequate procedure to provide confidence in the professional capabilities of a laboratory than certification of compliance with ISO 9001. Such certification should not be considered to be an alternative to accreditation in the sense that it does not provide a reliable assurance of technical competence. Nevertheless, the confidence associated with certified quality management systems cannot be ignored. Accreditation should thus be operated in such a way that it enables a laboratory, for its scope of accreditation, to demonstrate that its quality management system complies with ISO 9001.

References

Bell, Malcolm. "Laboratory Accreditation," *TELARC Talk*, December 1994.

European Organization for Testing and Certification (EOTC/AdvC/34/92), "Ascertaining the Competence of Test Laboratories, in the Framework of EOTC Agreements Groups," April 15, 1992.

International Laboratory Accreditation Conference Committee 1 on Commercial Applications, "Conformity Assessment: Testing, Quality Assurance, Certification and Accreditation," February 1994.

ISO/IEC Guide 2:1997, "General terms and their definitions concerning standardization and related activities."

ISO/IEC 17025:1999, "General requirements for the competence of testing and calibration laboratories."

Neumann, Lynne. "Validity of Test Data: The Application of ISO ISO/IEC 17025 or ISO 9001," *ILAC Newsletter*, 8, December 1995.

Russell, Anthony J. "Laboratory Accreditation in a World-wide Perspective," Pittcon, March 7, 1994.

ADDITIONAL ISO 9000 APPLICATIONS

Legal Issues with ISO 9000 and the Fastner Quality Act

23

This chapter contains two articles related to legal liability and ISO 9000. The first one, by James W. Kolka, discusses the legal issues arising from ISO 9000's paper trail and customer complaint systems. Kolka describes both the positive potential of an ISO 9000 system in regard to legal issues and potential pitfalls of the system that could prove trying in a legal battle. Kolka also presents a clause-by-clause list of legal liability-related sections of the following ISO 9001:2000 sections:

- 0.1 General
- Section 4
- Section 5
- Section 7

The second article, by Richard B. Stump, discusses the development of the Fastener Quality Act, focusing on the over-10-year journey from the Act's signing through its enactment.

ISO 9000:2000 and Legal Liability

by James W. Kolka

Introduction

Shortly after the ISO 9000 series of standards was published in 1987, several consultants stated that ISO 9001 would provide a great defense in the event of a lawsuit. In addition, prospective US clients were told that insurance companies in the United Kingdom would lower insurance premiums by as much as 20 to 40 percent for companies certified to ISO 9000 by a registered third party. The offer, however, was confined to the United Kingdom and did not extend to companies in the United States.

In addition to the natural benefits of ISO 9000 registration, consultants were looking for another enticement to companies contemplating an ISO 9000 quality management system. Unfortunately, it was a statement without any legal foundation. While it is true that ISO 9000 could provide a defense in the event of a lawsuit, it depends upon the quality of the system and the quality of the paper trail.

The good news about ISO 9000 is that you now have the paper trail in the event of a lawsuit, and the bad news about ISO 9000 is that you now have the paper trail in the event of a lawsuit. Your legal exposure depends upon the quality of the paper trail. If the paper trail contains no evidence that product or services safety was a concern to a company, or that little attention was paid to safety, the paper trail will demonstrate that safety was of little or no concern to the company. Likewise, if the paper trail demonstrates that customer complaints receive little or no attention, this indifference could be harmful in a lawsuit.

In contrast, if the paper trail demonstrates that product safety was a concern and the design control process attended to issues of product safety, this could be extremely helpful in the event of a lawsuit. This is particularly helpful when a lawsuit arises concerning a product that was manufactured several years ago. It then becomes important to demonstrate that product safety was a concern to the company when the product was designed and manufactured. Product design documentation would help to prove that point. It may not eliminate a claim, but it could go a long way toward demonstrating a commitment to safety and limiting damages.

In similar fashion, if a company can demonstrate that it is concerned about customer complaints and has developed a complaint system, this will help to demonstrate that the company pays attention to customer feedback. Just as an ISO 9000 quality management system is only as good as a company makes it, so too is the paper trail. A legally useful paper trail is not the automatic byproduct of an ISO 9000 documented quality management system. It must be created by a preventive law approach.

Areas of Liability Litigation

Long before there was an ISO 9000 quality management system series of standards, there was liability litigation affecting companies. While the areas of litigation can be broken into three areas, they are related to each other. They are set forth below:

- Preproduction — product design, services design, foreseeable use/foreseeable misuse, risk analysis/risk assessment, human factors analysis, instructions and warnings, applicable regulatory requirements and EU directives, applicable industry guidelines and relevant national and international standards

- Production — process controls and process validation, production risk analysis, training, purchasing, supplier management, subcontracting, incoming inspection, materials and component parts, ongoing inspection in testing, nonconforming product or service, corrective and preventive action, internal audits/management review, final inspection and testing, handling, storage

- Postproduction/postsale obligations — delivery, distribution, servicing, proactive postsale surveillance, customer complaints, nonconforming product or service, failure investigation, accident/incident reporting, corrective and preventive action, recalls, regulatory actions.

It quickly becomes apparent that the traditional areas of liability litigation closely parallel elements of the ISO 9001 quality management standard. Consequently, it should not be surprising that ISO 9001 offers information that could be useful in liability litigation. That it took so long is surprising. In one of the first lawsuits involving ISO 9001, Case I H Cotton Picker Fire Products Liability Litigation, plaintiffs' attorneys searched for court cases involving ISO 9000. They found none in 1999 and had to engage an ISO 9000 consultant to learn about the standard to determine if it contained information that was relevant to their lawsuit.

On June 21, 1999, the US District Court for the Eastern District of Arkansas ordered defendant Case Company to turn over ISO manual materials to plaintiffs' attorneys for evaluation. In requesting the ISO manual materials plaintiffs observed that 140 fires occurred between 1994 and 1997 to cotton pickers valued between approximately $90,000 and $200,000. The plaintiffs' brief requesting ISO documentation stated, "The number of fires alone caused alarm and concern. However, the significance of the problem is magnified by the fact that these losses were preventable and that Defendant is doing nothing to correct and prevent the losses as required by its own ISO 9001 program."

The plaintiffs' brief further stated, "...the ISO 9000 standards and its own quality assurance procedures requires that it conduct an analysis of the fires and that it take corrective and preventive action." Consequently, plaintiffs' attorneys requested that the defendant Case Company turn over all other ISO 9000 documents relating to these cotton picker fires. Plaintiffs' legal brief argued that, "Defendant's ISO 9000 quality assurance manual and all other ISO 9000 documents relating to these cotton picker fires are discoverable." They noted, "The manufacturer must have a procedure to process customer complaints to detect, analyze and eliminate potential causes of nonconformance. Lastly, ISO 9000 requires that the documents generated to comply with the certification be submitted to management for review. It is these documents that [plaintiff] seeks to review."

In their legal brief plaintiffs' attorneys stated that they "... seek damages from the defendant for failure to design and manufacture a cotton picker that will perform without catching on fire during normal operations and seek punitive damages for failure to properly investigate the product failures which would have disclosed the product defect and prevented millions of dollars in property losses." Plaintiffs also argued, "If defendant failed to comply with its own ISO 9000 certification, that information is relevant on the issue of negligence and punitive damages. If Defendant complied with its own ISO 9000 procedures, but these procedures are themselves inadequate, [plaintiff] is entitled to discover that information because it also would be relevant on the issue of negligence. Finally, the brief noted that, "[plaintiff] has good cause to believe the Defendant made a conscious decision to deviate from a procedure it established to investigate product failures to cover up the obvious ... It is impossible to determine whether the defendant chose to deviate from its normal course of investigation without a review of the ISO 9000 manual."

The Case I H Cotton Picker Fire Products Liability Litigation illustrates the potential significance of ISO 9000 documentation and procedures to future litigation, and it suggests that organizations should pay close attention to their compliance with their own ISO 9001 quality management system. This litigation also has established significant precedents for future lawsuits.

Plaintiffs' attorneys wanted to examine corrective action review minutes and management review minutes to determine if Case Company had followed its own ISO 9001 corrective action procedures. If not, why not? Since an attorney had been present during the corrective activion review, Case Company argued that the corrective action review minutes fell under attorney client privilege and therefore did not have to be turned over in legal discovery. The US District Court Judge ordered the defendant to turn over the minutes. Defendant Case Company petitioned the US Circuit Court of Appeals for the Eighth Circuit to overturn the judge's order.

On January 24, 2000, the Eighth Circuit Court of Appeals denied the defendant's petition and upheld the district court judge's ruling to turn over the corrective action minutes. In April 2000, the Case Company filed a Writ of Certiorari with the US Supreme Court. On June 5, 2000, the US Supreme Court denied the Writ, thereby upholding the Eighth Circuit Court of Appeals decision that Case had to turn over its minutes of management review and corrective action review to plaintiffs' attorneys. This meant that attorney client privilege did not apply to ISO 9001 records and documentation even though an attorney was present during the corrective action review.

Following a different legal tact, Case submitted a Motion in Limine to US District Court Judge G. Thomas Eisle to prohibit any evidence regarding ISO 9001 from being introduced in the lawsuit. (A Motion in Limine proposes to remove evidence from consideration that is not considered relevant or germane to a lawsuit.) The rationale put forth by Case was that ISO 9001 doesn't contain any specific design specifications for cotton pickers and therefore is irrelevant to the models in question. Case also argued that "its voluntary adherence to ANSI/ISO 9001 as of January 1996 has no relevance to the design of cotton picker models 2055 and 2155, which were no longer in the design phase as of January 1996.

In his ruling Judge Eisle noted, "In contrast, the plaintiffs assert that the ANSI/ISO 9001 ... are relevant to their allegations that Case was negligent in the design and manufacture of models 2055 and 2155 and later in the investigation of the fires that allegedly damaged or destroyed so many of those models. In particular, the plaintiffs claim that Case's failure to use "proper design controls and validation" caused Case to produce "cotton pickers with a transmission and drum drive unit that it knew was generating unacceptably high temperatures ..."

"For example, citing ANSI/ISO standard [subclause] 4.4.4 the plaintiffs contend that Case did not properly document its "duty cycles" or "design envelopes" (which are design parameters for load, speed, and pressure) when choosing the idler bearing that was used in the drum drive for models 2055 and 2155 ..."

"The plaintiffs also allege that Case violated ANSI/ISO standard 4.4.6, 4.4.7 and

4.4.8 when Case: 1) failed to implement design changes after testing of their prototypes revealed unacceptably high temperatures in the drum drive transmission unit, and 2) failed to perform any testing on production models to validate design inputs or customer requirements ..."

"Finally, the plaintiffs claim that if Case had followed ANSI/ISO 9001 standards 4.14.1, 4.14.2 and 4.14.3 during the investigation of the alleged fires, Case would have identified the cause of the cotton picker fires and [taken] corrective and preventive actions which would have prevented a large portion of the fires involved in this litigation ..."

Judge Eisle observed that, pursuant to Federal Rules of Civil Procedure 401 and 402, "all 'relevant' evidence is admissible and evidence is 'relevant' if it has a tendency to make the existence of any fact that is of consequence to the determination of the action more or less probable than it would be without the evidence." He further noted that "the Eighth Circuit has consistently held that compliance or noncompliance with ANSI standards is admissible in strict liability and/or negligence cases to prove a design defect."

Concerning Case Company's argument that the ANSI/ISO 9001 evidence should not be admitted because the plaintiffs have not identified any expert testimony as to this matter, Judge Eisle gave the following response: "In particular, Case asserts that 'whether a given company's policies and procedures are consistent with ISO 9001 and whether the guidelines under that system are being followed is not within the scope of lay knowledge but is a matter of expertise and experience.'"

"The plaintiffs assert that this is a factual issue that they can establish by questioning Case's employees and experts. In particular, the plaintiffs claim that Case's deviation from the ANSI/ISO 9001 standards can be established through the deposition of Case's quality assurance manager. The court finds the plaintiffs' argument to be persuasive. It is therefore ordered that Case's Motion in Limine to prohibit evidence regarding ISO 9001 be, and it is hereby, denied."

Having resolved various procedural issues and points of law, the lawsuits have begun. Farmers in eight states reported 215 fires on two models of Case cotton pickers since 1986. On October 7, 2000, the first lawsuit was won by an Arkansas plaintiff. Individual farmers and their insurance companies are pursuing litigation for the other fires. The case was finally resolved with a class action settlement of plaintiffs with Case Co. on July 19, 1991.

It is useful to review some of the issues raised by the Case cotton picker litigation.

- Product liability litigation exists with or without an ISO 9001 quality management system.

- A company can be held liable if it doesn't follow its own quality management system and that failure to follow its QMS results in property damage or injury to a customer.

- ISO 9001 documentation, records and minutes could provide valuable information in the event of a lawsuit.

- ISO 9000 documentation, records and minutes cannot be shielded from legal discovery by claiming attorney client privilege.

- Information obtained from customer complaints, nonconformities and corrective action generally should result in a design review and possibly a production process review — all relevant elements of an ISO 9001 quality management system should be examined when addressing a customer complaint.

Benefits of an ISO 9001 Quality Management System in the Event of a Lawsuit

Given the difficulty that the Case Company had in the courts with its ISO 9001 quality management system, it raises the question whether an ISO 9001 quality management system is a legal burden. The answer is no. Over the past six years a number of lawsuits have been initiated against companies with no ISO 9001 or ISO 9002 quality management system. Examples of such cases were recorded by John R. Broomfield in his article, "Lawyers Wise up to ISO 9000" in the January - February 1996, *Compliance Engineering*, Vol. 13, No. 1. One of the cases resulted when the collapse of a chaise lounge caused the plaintiff to reinjure a knee that was healing from reconstructive surgery. The retailer attempted to pass blame to the manufacturer, asserting that the assembly instructions were incomplete and confusing. Plaintiff's counsel argued that the manufacturer had ignored The American National Standard for Quality Systems (ANSI/ASQ Q 9001) and that the retailer did not document its training or inspections.

In deposition, the defendants were questioned by plaintiff's attorney using clauses from ISO 9001 that addressed design control, training and inspection and testing. Because the defendants were unable to effectively answer the questions, the case was settled prior to trial with the plaintiff receiving a total of $55,000 from the manufacturer and retailer.

Neither company was registered to one of the three compliance standards available at that time (ISO 9001/2/3) and they were challenged for ignoring those quality standards. Since the case did not go to trial we have no way of knowing whether the judge would have permitted plaintiff's attorney to pursue this line of questioning. The defendants didn't want to risk the possibility that questions might be allowed using clauses from ISO 9001 concerning design control, training and inspection and testing.

Mr. Broomfield's article discussed similar situations where companies not registered to ISO 9001/2/3 were subjected to questions derived from ISO 9001 and ISO 9004. All of these companies chose to settle out of court rather than risk possible embarrassment in a trial where their business processes would be compared to processes derived from an international quality management standard. In a recent conversation with Mr. Broomfield in February 2001, he noted that the forensic engineer and the law firm using ISO 9001 and ISO 9004 to sue nonregistered companies have batted a thousand in litigation over the past six years.

In short, a company or organization could be at greater risk in liability litigation if it has no quality management system. We will return to the subject of the benefits of an ISO 9001 quality management system in the event of a lawsuit at the conclusion of this chapter.

What About Guidance Standards?

In the United States, guidance standards such as ISO 9000 and ISO 9004 are considered components of a series along with ISO 9001. As such, even though these are guidance standards, they can be used to examine issues such as product safety. Further, these guidance standards ask questions that every company should ask itself when establishing a quality management system. In the United States, guidance documents that are part of a series can be used to establish an organization's "due diligence" and "duty of care" and can be used by courts to establish evidence of negligence and/or a design defect. A plaintiff's attorney could argue that the issues raised by ISO 9004 should be considered first by any responsible company before registering to ISO 9001.

This particular issue about the role of guidance standards aggravates a number of consultants who believe that these guidance standards are optional and that the new guidance standard ISO 9004: 2000 was designed solely for performance improvements and was not intended to be used to evaluate an organization's ISO 9001:2000 quality management system. Be that as it may, it is reasonable to expect that plaintiffs' attorneys will argue that ISO 9004: 2000 should be considered before complying with and certifying to ISO 9001: 2000, especially, when there are key issues raised by ISO 9004: 2000 relevant to product or services safety and the day-to-day operations of an organization.

Medical Device

Quality management systems play a different role in a regulated environment. Most notable of these systems is FDA's CGMP Quality System Regulation (QSR), which was published in the October 7, 1996, *Federal Register* and put into effect on June 1, 1997, with design control fully enforced on June 1, 1998. The QSR borrowed heavily from ISO 9001 and ISO 13485 (the application of ISO 9001 to medical devices). It is the QSR that FDA is using to improve quality management systems and the procedures that operate those systems to better safeguard public health in the manufacture of medical devices.

In the regulated sector, the regulatory authority, in this case FDA, inspects medical device manufacturers to determine if they are following the required procedures. Failure to follow procedures could lead to regulatory sanctions ranging all away from a "slap on the wrist" to criminal prosecution of top management accompanied by civil and/or criminal fines.

In between these extremes are other regulatory actions such as shutting down a company's operations through a Permanent Injunction, accompanied by a financial penalty or a notch below that — a Consent Decree of Permanent Injunction. The consent decree allows a company to operate, provided that the company follows the legal path and operational requirements set forth by the FDA and agreed to by a US District Court. FDA oversight can continue from three to five years.

What makes this quality management system oversight different, however, is that FDA's actions are public. FDA's actions and findings are available through the Freedom of Information Act (FOIA) and available on FDA's web site. Consequently, if there are FDA findings that might support a liability lawsuit, the fact that those findings are derived from FDA regulatory sanctions could be very powerful to a jury.

Naturally, the plaintiff must still prove that the medical device affected by FDA regulatory sanctions caused the injury or misdiagnosis alleged to have injured the plaintiff. Nevertheless, these arguments by plaintiff's attorneys would appear to support regulatory findings by the FDA.

An example of an FDA action occurred on November 3, 1999, when Abbott Laboratories received the largest fine in FDA's history — $100 million. To continue manufacturing its in vitro diagnostic medical devices Abbott Laboratories signed a consent decree. The basis of the consent decree was FDA's findings concerning "process validation, corrective and preventive action, and production and process controls." All these findings related to Abbott Laboratories' compliance with FDA's CGMP and its QSR. Clearly, plaintiff's examination of relevant records and documents in Abbott Laboratories' quality management system could provide powerful evidence that could be used for presentation to a jury in a class-action lawsuit.

This underscores the liability exposure that faces companies operating in a regulated environment and underlines the advice often given by medical device insurance companies: "The question is not, If you are sued will you be ready? but, When you are sued will you be ready?"

In another case involving the second largest fine levied by FDA, $60 million, Lifescan, a Johnson & Johnson Co., pleaded guilty to federal criminal charges related to its marketing of a defective diagnostic device for diabetes. The company admitted that it knowingly marketing a blood glucose monitor that could give erroneous blood sugar readings and that it misled patients who reported problems with the monitor. Lifescan admitted that it knew about product defects before it applied to the FDA for marketing approval and a timely recall was not initiated quickly to retrieve the devices.

In both of these instances, with Abbott Laboratories and with Lifescan, class-action lawsuits have been initiated on behalf of plaintiffs who are alleging that they have been injured. In both of these instances, FDA's quality system findings are available to plaintiffs' attorneys. Naturally, plaintiffs will have to establish a causal relationship between the FDA's findings and their injuries, but the quality system data is available to help establish their case.

ISO 9001: 2000 and ISO 9004: 2000

The new version of ISO 9000 establishes new expectations not present in the previous standards. Granted, the various draft versions gradually eliminated the word legal from the text, concentrating on the terms statutory and regulatory. It should be noted, however, that the elimination of legal from the wording does not in any way reduce an organization's legal responsibilities to manufacture safe products, provide safe services, monitor those products and recall those products or services from the marketplace if necessary. The legal requirements for preproduction, production and postproduction/postsale obligations continue.

ISO 9001: 2000 Clauses That Carry Legal Implications

0.1 General

This international standard can be used by internal and external parties including certification bodies to assess the organization's ability to meet customer, regulatory and the organization's own requirements.

5.1 Management Commitment

Top management shall provide evidence of its commitment to the development and implementation of the quality management system and continually improve its effectiveness by

- Communicating to the organization the importance of meeting customer as well as statutory and regulatory requirements.

7.2.1 Determination of Requirements Related to the Product

The organization shall determine

- Statutory and regulatory requirements related to the product.

7.3.2 Design and Development Inputs

Inputs relating to product requirements shall be determined and records maintained (see 4.2.4). The inputs shall include

- Applicable statutory and regulatory requirements.

7.3.3 Design and Development Outputs

The outputs of design and development shall be provided in a form that enables verification against the design and development inputs and shall be approved prior to release.

- Specify the characteristics of the product that are essential for its safe and proper use.

ISO 9004:2000 Clauses That Carry Legal Implications

4.2 Documentation

The nature and extent of the documentation should satisfy the contractual, statutory and regulatory requirements, and the needs and expectations of customers and other interested parties and should be appropriate to the organization. Documentation may be in any form or media suitable for the needs of the organization.

In order to provide the documentation to satisfy the needs and expectations of interested parties management should consider

- Relevant statutory and regulatory requirements.

5.2.2 Needs and Expectations

Examples of customers and end-user needs and expectations, as related to the organization's products, include

- Product safety

- Product liability
- Environmental impact.

In considering its relationship with society, the organization should

- Demonstrate responsibility for health and safety
- Consider environmental impact, including conservation of energy and natural resources
- Identify applicable statutory and regulatory requirements.

5.2.3 Statutory and Regulatory Requirements

Management should ensure that the organization has knowledge of the statutory and regulatory requirements that apply to its products, processes and activities and should include such requirements as part of the quality management system. Consideration should also be given to

- The promotion of ethical, effective and efficient compliance with current and prospective requirements
- The benefits to interested parties from exceeding compliance
- The role of the organization in the protection of community interests.

5.6.2 Review Input

Inputs to evaluate efficiency as well as effectiveness of the quality management system should consider the customer and other interested parties and should include

- Other factors that may impact the organization, such as financial, social or environmental conditions, and relevant statutory and regulatory changes.

7.1.3.3 Product and Process Validation and Changes

Issues to consider should include

- Operating conditions for the product
- Use or application of the product
- Disposal of the product
- Product life cycle
- Environmental impact of the product
- Impact of the use of natural resources including materials and energy.

Process validation should be carried out at appropriate intervals to ensure timely reaction to changes impacting the process. Particular attention should be given to validation of processes

- For high-value and safety critical products
- Where deficiency in product will only be apparent in use
- Which cannot be repeated
- Where verification of product is not possible.

Risk assessment should be undertaken to assess the potential for, and the effect of, possible failures or faults in processes. The results should be used to define and implement preventive action to mitigate identified risks.

Examples of tools for risk assessment should include

- Fault modes and effects analysis
- Fault tree analysis
- Relationship diagrams
- Simulation techniques
- Reliability prediction.

7.3.1 General Guidance

When designing and developing products or processes, management should ensure that the organization is not only capable of considering their basic performance and function, but all factors that contribute to meeting the product and process performance expected by customers and other interested parties. For example, the organization should consider life cycle, safety and health, testability, usability, user-friendliness, dependability, durability, ergonomics, the environment, product disposal and identified risks.

Management also has the responsibility to insure that steps are taken to identify and mitigate potential risk to the users of the products and processes of the organization. Risk assessment should be undertaken to assess the potential for, and the effect of, possible failures or faults in products or processes. The results of the assessment should be used to define and implement preventive actions to mitigate the identified risks. Examples of tools for risk assessment of design and development include

- Design fault modes and effects analysis
- Fault tree analysis
- Reliability prediction
- Relationship diagrams
- Ranking techniques
- Simulation technologies.

7.3.2 Design and Development Input and Output

The organization should identify process inputs that affect the design and development of products and facilitate effective and efficient process performance in order to satisfy the needs and expectations of customers, and those of other interested parties. These external needs and expectations, coupled with those internal to the organization, should be suitable for translation into input requirements for the design and development processes; for example, external inputs such as:

- Changes in relevant statutory and regulatory requirements
- International or national standards
- Industry code of practice.

The preceding examples are not exhaustive, but they do help to illustrate some of the requirements from ISO 9001: 2000 and the breadth and depth of the recommendations contained in ISO 9004: 2000. It is reasonable to expect that an organization would have examined ISO 9004: 2000 prior to contemplating compliance with ISO 9001: 2000. It is what would be expected in the legal system from a responsible company implementing a quality management system.

Conclusion

Clearly, the 2000 version of the ISO 9000 series of standards represents a new set of expectations and requirements. Returning to the question of whether an ISO 9001: 2000 quality management system could provide an excellent defense in the event of a lawsuit, the answer is yes. It will, however, require a proactive preventive law approach by an organization. This could be facilitated by product safety audits, service safety audits, evaluation of safety critical points and safety critical issues, liability exposure audits and a review of documentation, records and minutes.

For example, quite often design engineers create records that could have powerful implications in future lawsuits. In most instances, these engineers in 10 years will not be in their same position, having moved to other positions in the organization, to other companies or retired. Design control records that indicate that product safety was a concern when the product was developed would be extremely helpful to defense attorneys who want to demonstrate that there was a concern for product safety when the product was designed. An absence of records means that defense attorneys will have to reconstruct design history through depositions in an effort to prove the same point. It is an extremely expensive way to defend against a liability claim in a lawsuit. Furthermore, the decision concerning historical facts will rest with a jury. A company with an ISO 9001: 2000 quality management system structured to reduce liability exposure would be in a far more powerful position to defend itself in future litigation.

The Fastener Quality Act

by Richard B. Stump

Introduction

At this point in time, if ever there were a trophy for "The Cure Was Worse Than the Disease Award," the Fastener Quality Act (or The Act) would be one of the strongest candidates. Both the disease and "the cure" are associated with metal fasteners that impact on our well-being every day, as we drive our cars, cross over bridges and fly in airplanes (just to list a few examples of our dependency on proper functioning of products held together by fasteners).

First signed into law in 1990 by President Bush, the original purposes of The Act, were: (1) to protect public safety, (2) to deter introduction of nonconforming fasteners into US commerce and (3) to provide increased assurance to fastener users that products meet stated standards, as a minimum.[1] Upon close examination of the information associated with The Act, a secondary objective emerges to place stricter controls on fasteners produced in foreign countries, some of which were accused of being substandard products "dumped" in the US marketplace. And so began a trek exceeding 10 years from the signing of The Act, perhaps one of the longer waiting periods in US legislative history, for a law to be passed and wait for enactment.

Questions that arise from this episode of the US fastener industry center on these issues:

1. Did the Fastener Quality Act ("the cure"), beginning with its origin in 1990, have substantial impact on fastener manufacturers to cause them to pursue significant product quality and quality system improvements? Or, would quality improvements in the fastener industry have occurred as part of the overall US industry implementation of new (at that time) quality management system standards, such as ISO 9000, AS9000 and QS-9000?

2. Will the high level of quality improvement, so vividly described in the many fastener industry testimonies presented to the US Congress, be maintained or will they erode to a point where history repeats itself?

3. Can the experiences from this fastener industry case study be more widely applied and serve as guidance for other industries as they make decisions for their constituent companies and organizations related to both product quality and quality system requirements?

For many years US industries have searched for the best path to follow to establish quality-system practices for their member companies and suppliers, in order to convince their respective marketplaces that the products and associated services they provide are of the requisite quality. Approaches taken during the last decade include examples such as the US Big Three automotive industry's QS-9000, the aerospace industry's AS9100 and the telecommunications industry's TL 9000. The fastener industry chose to pursue the legislation route to establish quality requirements.

Background

The genesis of the Fastener Quality Act (FQA) began with several tragic product failures occurring during the 1980s. The fastener industry approached the US Congress to take a leadership role in attacking fastener industry malaise, identified as substandard, counterfeit and mismarked fasteners. Congressman John D. Dingell of Michigan, then chairman of the House Subcommittee on Oversight and Investigation, became the champion for the cause.

After two years of studying the extensive list of product failures, the Subcommittee published its seminal report, "The Threat from Substandard Fasteners: Is America Losing Its Grip?" (Committee Print 100-Y). Recognition was given to the Industrial Fasteners Institute (IFI) and the Defense Industrial Supply Center (DISC), among others, for their material assistance in cooperating with the investigation. The Subcommittee's deep concern in its conclusion centered on the imminent probability that a major tragedy would befall US citizens unless vigorous and effective efforts were made to improve fastener quality. [2]

This 1988 Subcommittee Report was later analyzed by the US Department of Commerce (in late 1998 and early 1999) to provide input to the General Counsel in February 1999, titled "The Fastener Quality Act: Assessment and Recommendations," identifying the following salient points:

1. The 1988 report had 29 major findings, 14 of which concerned various parts of the Department of Defense (DoD) related purchases.

2. Of the fastener problems uncovered by the DoD, the major controversy surrounded the issue of substandard grade 8.0 fasteners held out as meeting the Society of Automotive Engineering (SAE) Standard J 429, for grade 8.0 fasteners, but did not.

3. Nearly all of the DoD problems with the grade 8.0 bolts were associated with fasteners imported into the United States. The primary sources of these and other faulty fasteners were identified to originate from manufacturers in Japan, Korea, Poland, Mexico and Spain.

The major problems identified can be grouped as follows:

1. Improper material substitutions

2. Falsification of certificates

3. Inconsistent heat treatments

4. Wrong plating materials

5. Omission of the stress relief processing step

6. Headmarks having no or mismarked performance indicators

7. Dimensional discrepancies (e.g., in 1990 the Defense Industrial Supply Center (DISC) initiated a process to inspect all class 3 threaded fasteners and experienced a 40 percent rejection rate for fasteners made in the late 1980s).

One theory pinpointing a root cause for some of the problems has been posed by an IFI executive as an outgrowth of the OPEC oil embargo during the 1970s, and its impact on the cost of oil in general, and specifically on the cost of quenching oils used in the heat treating process. The oil shortage presented a challenge for fastener manufacturers to make fasteners from substitute low carbon, boron-steels for US commercial grade 8.0 fastener needs. The martensitic, low carbon boron-steels allowed lower heat treating temperatures to be used, conserving the quench oil supply. Lowered temperatures use less heat. Combined, both savings could reduce manufacturing costs and subsequently improve profits. Supplying grade 8.2 bolts for the grade 8.0 version can provide a 30 percent cost advantage in producing the former versus the latter (as provided in the Committee Print 100Y).

Low-carbon, boron-steel fasteners, manufactured using the lower temperature heat-treatment cycles, must be properly identified with grade 8.2 as its numerical marking, as compared to the fasteners previously identified as grade 8.0. By failing to properly make this identification change when producing the low-carbon, boron steel parts, unscrupulous manufacturers and distributors contaminated the US fastener supply base. At this point culling out bogus fasteners was extremely difficult due to the compounding of marking problems, relating to (1) improperly marked, low-carbon boron-steel fasteners, (2) fasteners with no manufacturer's marking and (3) fasteners having manufacturer's markings that were not traceable to any known producer.

The heart of the metallurgical problems centered on an influx of fasteners manufactured to ASTM A 354 "Specification for Quenched and Tempered Alloy Steel Bolts, Studs and Other Externally Threaded Fasteners," and to SAE J 429 "Mechanical and Material Requirements for Externally Threaded Fasteners." The mismarked, low-carbon, boron-steel bolts are characterized as exhibiting a potential for stress relaxation failure. Under certain circumstances, this failure mode can be catastrophic.

At the conclusion of their exhaustive study to provide details regarding the depth and breadth of the fastener quality problems in the United States, the Subcommittee made wide-sweeping recommendations that are too numerous to list here. The following list is a short summary:

1. A fastener held out to meet a consensus standard should indeed meet its requirements as related to fit, form and function.

2. Strength grade, or property class, markings and manufacturer's marks as required by standards shall be present.

3. All manufacturers or private label distributors wishing to introduce fasteners into the stream of commerce of the United States shall register their ID markings with the US Patent and Trade Office; no duplicates allowed.[3]

Round One: The Fastener Quality Act Becomes Law on Friday, November 16, 1990

Then President Bush signed Public Law 101-592, now known as The Fastener Quality Act, a modest 10 pages of legislation! It was heralded as the law to bring under control a situation clearly imperiling every American with the possibility of encountering product failure, injury and even death. The focus on faulty fasteners materialized in a powerful legislative approach to establish and enforce fastener quality.

Government regulation of quality, such as The Act, follows a well-beaten path according to quality guru Joseph Juran.[4] Key ingredients, with the The Act counterparts, are:

1. The Statute: P.L. 101-592 defined the purpose and the subject fasteners to be regulated, established how the regulations ("rules of the game") would unfold and named the Commerce Department as the agency to administer The Act.

2. The Administrator: The Secretary of Commerce was assigned responsibility for compliance to The Act, with the Director of The National Institute of Standards and Technology (NIST) as the administrator to establish the laboratory accreditation program.

3. The Standards: These are the Regulations, required within 180 days of the signing, to implement The Act. They became one of the most contentious parts of The Act, with decisions not reached until over 10 years later.

Another set of standards, controlling fastener test laboratories, was derived from the Regs. NIST Handbook 150, based on ISO Guide 25 and its supplement NIST Handbook 150-18, for fasteners and metals, provided the detailed product support and testing requirements.

4. Test Laboratories: Within 180 days following signing of The Act, a program for laboratory accreditation had to be documented and implementation begun. The sufficient number of accredited fastener testing laboratories to meet FQA needs would not be reached and announced by NIST until 1999. The Accreditation Body Evaluation Program (ABEP) was initiated to allow for private entities (such as A2LA and NADCAP) and foreign government agencies (such as the Japanese Accreditation Board of Conformity Assessment, the United Kingdom Accreditation Service, the Chinese [ROC] National Laboratory Accreditation, et al.) to accredit fastener testing laboratories.

5. Test and Evaluation: At the onset, The Act requirements emphasized final product sampling and test. This was another fastener industry bone of contention, as in-process inspection of fasteners has evolved as the norm for many manufacturers.

6. Regulated Product marks: Fastener head markings are required for fasteners that come under FQA requirements to have these. A registry program is provided for manufacturers wanting unique head markings for their products.

7. Sanctions: The Act remedies and penalties are provided, designating the Office of the Attorney General as the agency to take action on criminal remedies, while the Secretary was assigned to act on civil penalties (up to $25,000 per violation). Criminal penalties of knowingly violating FQA requirements could be a fine and as long as five years imprisonment, or both, for each count. Intentional failure to maintain records results in up to a fine and two years imprisonment, or both, per count.

Controversy surrounding The Act was slow to form. The initial mandate directed the Secretary of Commerce to appoint an advisory committee within 90 days from the signing of The Act, composed of 15 members from a thorough cross-section of fastener industry-related manufacturers, distributors, users and standards organizations, to act as consultants on the regulations and other matters, for both Secretary and Director. The American Society of Mechanical Engineers (ASME) provided the committee chairman. The Fastener Advisory Committee (FAC) was initially chartered for two years beginning in February 1991. Its charter was renewed for two years in 1993 and again in 1995.

The second major task for the initial mandate required FQA regulations (the

Regs) to implement The Act. Agreement on the contents of the Regs became a source of contention for industry representatives versus the NIST group from this point on. At this point, The Act Truly became a government and fastener-industry odyssey.

Round Two: The First FQA Amendment, Public Law 104–113 Appears in March 1996

Part of the Technology Transfer and Advancement Act contained an FQA directive for a final rule (the first of three such notices) to be set with a deadline of November 1996. This time was required for NIST and those fastener industry manufacturers, distributors and user groups to work together to resolve issues with the initial legislation. The initial date for implementation of The Act was set for May 1997. The additional time was needed for NIST to ensure sufficient numbers of accredited fastener-testing laboratories were on board to adequately support proper functioning of The Act.

On April 18, 1997, earlier than the deadline, the implementation date for the FQA Final Rule was moved farther out once more, to July 26, 1998, to allow for the sufficient number of test labs to be accredited by NIST et al. At this point of FQA implementation, NIST's only legally permissible reason for further delay was an insufficient number of laboratory accreditations to support The Act. But, this time was also used by NIST to establish procedures for registering in-process inspection activities of manufacturing facilities that use Quality Assurance Systems (QAS), thus accommodating advances in fastener manufacturing since the 1990 enactment of the The Act.

In addition to the extension, the Federal Notice:[5]

1. Provided provision for fastener manufacturers to use quality assurance systems and Statistical Process Control (SPC)

2. Allowed manufacturers to sell as noncompliant any fastener remaining in their inventories, as all fasteners produced after were to be tested by an accredited laboratory or produced in an approved QAS/SPC manufacturing facility

3. Permitted manufacturers to declare provisional compliance to the FQA if they were certified as operating QAS/SPC fastener production lines. Notice was due no later than May 25, 1999.

April 18, 1997, is also notable for the Industrial Fastener Institute's release of its position statement regarding The Act and regulations.[6] Positions presented were:

1. Repeal the FQA as currently written.

2. If The Act is repealed, a consortium of major fastener purchasers, fastener manufacturers, US DoD, NIST and consensus standard organizations would prepare a biennial report to Congress with evaluations of fastener quality status, safety, standards and need for continuation of this report.

3. Amend the current FQA to simplify or eliminate needless requirements, scope and other provisions that fail to address or obscure the basic issue of substandard and counterfeit fasteners.

So again, on June 30, 1998, NIST further delayed implementation of The Act to October 25, 1998, for the same reason. There were an insufficient number of accredited testing laboratories to adequately support The Act.

Round Three: Public Law 105-234 Creates Exemptions and Allows Further Delay

On August 14, 1998, President Clinton signed into law the "Aircraft Exemption" amendment, allowing fasteners specifically manufactured or altered for use on aircraft to be excluded from The Act, if the quality and suitability of those fasteners had been approved by Federal Aviation Administration programs. And, the law again delayed implementation of the regs until June 1, 1999, or 120 days after the Secretary of Commerce provides a report to Congress that studies:

1. Significant improvements to fastener manufacturing since 1990

2. Comparisons of The Act to other fastener regulatory programs

3. Recommendations for revising The Act that may be warranted because of the changes identified in the first two studies above (1) and (2).

A consequence of this legislation was NIST's sponsorship of a workshop "Changes in Manufacturing Practices for Fasteners," conducted by ASME. The ASME Research Report of the same name concluded:[7]

1. Quality assurance advances, based upon computer control and sensor technology, have allowed fastener manufacturers to produce product with zero defects or Six Sigma precision.

2. Original equipment manufacturers are demanding fastener manufacturers to implement Advanced Quality Systems technology and they are getting a strong, favorable response from the industry.

3. Poor-quality or subpar [fastener] products are not part of current recall and are adequately addressed by today's criminal fraud statutes.

The ASME Workshop Breakout Session to study manufacturing technology concluded that the problems or issues existing with fastener products today were "None," a testimony to ASME's conclusions. A major industry theme came out of this workshop to refocus the FQA initiatives on fraud and severely punish those who engage in intentional fraud in any respect. Public safety would then be protected for today and the future.

Round Four: Public Law 106-34 "FQA Amendments Act of 1999" Signed June 8, 1999

With less than one month to go before US industry was to be required to comply with existing FQA regulations, President Clinton signed Public Law 106-34, the FQA Amendments Act of 1999 on June 8, 1999. The fruits of the labor from countless hours of organized lobbying by fastener industry and associated parties can be seen in the newest versions of the FQA laws and regulations. Significant changes centered on:

1. Elimination of the requirement for NIST to approve organizations that accredit fastener testing laboratories.

2. Fasteners covered under The Act are limited to high-strength parts that are both through hardened and grade marked. Exempt fasteners are further described to provide certainty of which categories are in fact exempt from the FQA regulations.

3. Those manufacturers using quality management systems (QMS) based upon ISO 9000, 9001 or 9002 — such as QS-9000, ISO/TS 16949, AS9100 and TL 9000 — are exempt from the FQA regulations.

4. Accreditation organizations not wanting to follow ISO guidelines for registration and accreditation may submit their own guidance/requirements to NIST to establish how they will accredit bodies to register manufacturing systems as meeting FQA requirements, how they will accredit testing laboratories and how they will approve accreditation bodies to accredit testing laboratories.

5. Reduction of paperwork, record-keeping burdens emerged in allowing companies to transmit and store fastener quality records electronically, and effective control mechanisms are provided to safeguard authentication and prevent against alteration.

6. Fraud issues are heightened through a Department of Commerce "hotline" to be used to report alleged violations of the law. Credible allegations will be forwarded to the Attorney General.

In its July 1999 *Fastener Advisory*, the IFI commented, "This ... has been a 'textbook' example of what a broad coalition of concerned companies, working together, can accomplish in Washington when key Congressional resources are supportive."[8] And later, in the August 1999 issue, the IFI stated, "The new FQA focus is on the prevention of fastener fraud instead of regulating fastener quality through government required inspection, testing and certification. In enacting these changes, Congress expressed its intent that the fastener industry police itself."[9]

Conclusions

What have we learned from this incredible fastener industry trek? First and foremost, the old cliché "Be careful of what you ask for; you might just get it!" had been alive and well within the FQA confines.

But more importantly, as the Secretary of Commerce announced:[10]

1. Congress and the administration recognized the major improvements made by the fastener industry since the FQA was passed in 1990, reducing problems to a fraction of what they were at that time. Even as depositions were made to the Subcommittee on February 25, 1999, for "Unscrewing the Fastener Quality Act" there was an admission from the industry witnesses that they really did not foresee the complexity they would have to deal with as The Act progressed toward implementation.

2. The FQA Amendment reflects many of the recommendations made in the Department of Commerce Report to Congress, headed by Dr. James E. Hill, NIST,[11] which in turn reflected fastener industry input from the ASME-conducted workshop held in Chicago beginning November 9, 1998.

3. Fraud-like criminal offenses are addressed for specific misrepresentations and falsifications. And, the establishment of the new fastener fraud hotline facilitates reporting of alleged fraudulent actions or other violations.

4. NIST will continue to operate a voluntary program to accredit fastener testing laboratories.

5. NIST no longer is responsible for evaluating organizations and subsequently will not maintain the Accredited Laboratory List. Accreditors that operate under international guidelines (ISO/IEC Guide 58 for laboratory accreditors and ISO/IEC Guide 61 for Quality System Registrar Accreditors) may self-declare to NIST, and thereby be eligible to offer accreditation under The Act. Organizations not operating under ISO guidelines may submit their own registrations and accreditation guidelines for review and approval by the Director of NIST.

Ultimately the Fastener Quality Act owes its final status to the well-coordinated lobbying done on the mainstay leaders of Congress to get the major changes to The Act. The critical issues needed to maintain the current, improved methods of functioning within the fastener industry and for their association with major fastener user groups are preserved. Congress was most accommodating to recognize the main requests, to declare victory and go on to other business.

References

[1] From NIST web site http://www.nist.gov/fqa/fqahist.htm.

[2] From the 100th Congress, 2nd Session Committee Print 100-Y, U.S. Government Printing Office Washington, D.C. 1988.

[3] Wilson, C. (1996), "Mechanical Fasteners: Becoming a Regulated Industry," ASTM standardization News, July 1996, pp. 30-33.

[4] Juran, Joseph M. and Godfrey, A., Juran's Quality Handbook, Fifth Edition (New York: McGraw-Hill, 1999) pp. 35.10-35.15.

[5] "NIST Publishes Final Rule for Fastener Quality Act," Quality Digest, June 1998. p. 12.

[6] Industrial Fastener Institute (1997), "IFI Position Statement Regarding The Fastener Quality Act and Its Regulations."

[7] The American Society of Mechanical Engineers, (December 1998), CRTD Vol. 51, "Changes in Manufacturing Practices for Fasteners," November 9-11,1998, Chicago, p.7.

[8] Industrial Fastener Institute, "Fastener Advisory," July 1999, Vol. 8, No. 6, p. 1.

[9] Industrial Fastener Institute, "Fastener Advisory," August 1999, Vol. 8, No.7, p. 1.

[10] Department of Commerce press release #GG 99-79, by Michael E. Newman, "Simpler, More Focused Fastener Quality Act Signed into Law."

[11] Unpublished Department of Commerce Report, "The Fastener Quality Act: Assessment and Recommendations," February 24, 1999.

ISO 9000 in the US Public Sector

by Curtis D. Ricketts

Government involvement with ISO 9000 grew and expanded substantially in the 1990s both at the federal and the local levels. Current activity can be separated into three areas:

- A number of agencies use the standard in their certification/approval activities and in their supplier qualification requirements.

- Other agencies provide assistance to organizations interested in the use of voluntary standards.

- Finally, many agencies have realized the value of implementing ISO 9000-based quality management systems within their own operations.

Examples of each type of activity are presented below.

Approvals and Supplier Qualification

The National Technology Transfer and Advancement Act (NTTAA), P.L.104-113, was signed into law on March 7, 1996. The detailed requirements for federal agencies under the NTTAA are set forth in a circular issued February 19, 1998, by the Office of Management and Budget: OMB Circular A-119 - Federal Register (63 FR 8545).

In summary, the Act directs the National Institute of Standards and Technology (NIST) to:

- Coordinate with other federal agencies as well as with state and local governments to achieve greater reliance on voluntary standards and lessened dependence on in-house standards

- Assist federal agencies in comparing standards used in manufacturing, commerce, industry and educational institutions with the standards developed by the federal government

- Coordinate greater use by federal agencies, states and local governments of private sector standards via the Interagency Committee on Standards Policy (ICSP)

- Emphasize where possible the use of standards developed by private, consensus organizations

- Create guidance on conformity assessment activities.

Many federal agencies have begun to use voluntary standards elements in their supplier requirements. Both the National Aeronautics and Space Administration (NASA) and the Department of Defense (DoD) have dropped government quality system standards in favor of ISO 9000. At the state level, the Arizona Department of Education's procurement agency has required ISO 9000 in a request for proposals (RFP) for a major telecommunications contract.

Department of Defense (DoD)

The DoD provides guidance on the use of the ISO 9000 series standards in contracts. The Defense Standardization Program Office at the Defense Logistics Agency, under the direction of the Under Secretary of Defense (Acquisition, Technology and Logistics), is the proponent for DoD 4120.24-M, "DoD Standardization Program Policies and Procedures." This manual is available on the web at http://www.dsp.dla.mil.

DoD encourages the use of a single quality system in a contractor's facility. The decision gives contractors the option of deciding if they want to use ISO 9000 to satisfy government contractual requirements for quality systems. For new procurements, buying offices may impose commercial standards in contracts. A waiver is required with approval by the Milsetone Decision Authority (MDA) to use military standards in a contract.

Department of Energy (DOE)

The Office of Nuclear and Facility Safety Policy (ONFSP) is responsible for DOE's quality assurance policy and requirements, plus integration with the DOE Safety Management System Policy, P 450.4. DOE's quality assurance requirements are in 10 CFR 830, Subpart A and DOE O 414.1A, Quality Assurance. Guidance directives include: G 414.1-1, G 414.1-2, G 440.1-6 and portions of G 450.4-1.

ONFSP represents DOE's interests on international and national quality standards committees and conformity assessment bodies (third-party quality/environmental management system accreditation) and participates in DOE and contractor QA organizations.

Department of Health and Human Services (HHS)

National Institute for Occupational Safety and Health (NIOSH)

NIOSH is considering ISO 9000 quality standards for implementation in its certification programs by:

- Proposing quality assurance requirements for the respirator approval holder's manufacturing process consistent with international standards, specifically the ISO 9000 guidelines. These international standards would be supplemented by revised respirator specific quality measures, such as quality control plans and product improvement procedures.

- Proposing new quality requirements, such as, mandatory pre-approval audits for new manufacturing sites, more stringent quality sampling plans, critical classification of defects for all type respirators and records retention schedules.

- Proposing to enhance quality monitoring activities by increasing the frequency of both site and product audits, requiring an approval holder to supply free product audit samples for product audits, requiring approval holders to conduct self-audits of their products and present those results to NIOSH, accepting ISO certification in lieu of a NIOSH-performed site audit, employing contract laboratories to do certain tests for the approval program and requiring approval holders to report all customer complaints and noncompliance findings of a serious nature to NIOSH.

Food and Drug Administration (FDA), Center for Devices and Radiological Health (CDRH)

The Food and Drug Administration (FDA) amended its good manufacturing practice regulations pursuant to an international agreement between the United States and the European Community (EC).

The agreement is entitled "Agreement on Mutual Recognition Between the United States of America and the European Community" (MRA). An importing country's authority may normally endorse good manufacturing practice (GMP) inspection reports for pharmaceuticals provided by the exporting authority. The importing authority determines if the exporting country has an equivalent regulatory system. Likewise, an importing country authority may endorse medical device quality system evaluation reports and certain medical device product evaluation reports provided by conformity assessment bodies (CABs) determined to have equivalent assessment procedures.

This regulation became effective on December 7, 1998.

The Global Harmonization Task Force (GHTF)

The Global Harmonization Task Force (GHTF), formed in 1993:

- Encourages convergence in regulatory practices related to ensuring the safety, effectiveness / performance and quality of medical devices
- Promotes technological innovation
- Facilitates international trade.

This is accomplished through the publication and dissemination of harmonized guidance documents on basic regulatory practices. The GHTF also serves as an information exchange forum through which countries with medical device regulatory systems under development can benefit from those with existing systems and/or pattern their practices upon those of GHTF founding members.

National Aeronautics and Space Administration (NASA)

NASA has provided guidance in NASA Procurement Information Circular (PIC) 01-11, May 22, 2001, ISO 9001 Quality Management System Requirements.

NASA's current policy is described in NASA Policy Directive 8730.3. It is NASA policy to contractually require, where appropriate and beneficial to NASA, suppliers comply with the appropriate standard contained in the current version of the ISO 9000 standard series or the American National Standards Institute/American Society for Quality Q9000 series. It is also NASA's policy to contractually require suppliers be third-party certified in those cases where it is determined to be appropriate and beneficial to NASA. For critical space flight hardware and software NASA programs may decide to supplement ISO 9000 with space sector-related quality system requirements depending on the nature of the procurement.

Nuclear Regulatory Commission (NRC)

The NRC is reviewing the ISO 9000 series of standards in connection with its approval responsibilities. The focus of NRC activities in the area of quality assurance is the requirements contained in 10 CFR 50, Appendix B, and the related NRC regulatory guides and industry standards.

Resources

Public sector agencies at all levels are offering assistance to organizations interested in the ISO 9000 standards and their application. The primary federal source for information and assistance is the National Institute of Standards and Technology in the US Department of Commerce.

Many universities and community colleges provide programs ranging from course offerings to consulting. State and local economic development agencies may also offer assistance services.

Department of Commerce

National Institute of Standards and Technology (NIST)

NIST Office of Standards Services

The Office of Standards Services conducts standards-related programs and provides knowledge and services that will strengthen the US economy and improve the quality of life. Its goals are to:

- Ensure recognition and use of US standards domestically and in the global marketplace
- Promote worldwide acceptance of US test and calibration data to facilitate the marketing of US products
- Provide assistance to industry, trade associations and exporters through its operations, training and information programs.

As the focal point for standards and conformity assessment activities in the federal government, the Office of Standards Services (OSS) implements the National Technology Transfer and Advancement Act (NTTAA) by coordinating activities among federal agencies and with the private sector and state and local governments.

NIST Standards Information Center

The Standards Information Center provides research services on standards, technical regulations and conformity assessment procedures for nonagricultural products. The center is a repository for standards-related information in the United States and has access to US, foreign and international documents through its role as the national inquiry point under the World Trade Organization Agreement on Technical Barriers to Trade.

NIST National Voluntary Laboratory Accreditation Program

The National Voluntary Laboratory Accreditation Program (NVLAP) provides third-party accreditation to testing and calibration laboratories. NVLAP is in full conformance with the standards of the International Organization for Standardization (ISO) and the International Electrotechnical Commission (IEC), including ISO/IEC Guides 25 and 58.

NIST Global Standards Program

The Global Standards Program provides technical information and support to federal agencies and industry by:

- Participating in interagency activities to establish US government positions on standards-related aspects of major international agreements

- Participating in the work of international and regional organizations concerned with standardization and conformity assessment

- Recruiting and assigning standards experts to posts at key US embassies and missions to identify and remove technical barriers to trade.

Global Standards also operates the National Voluntary Conformity Assessment Systems Evaluation (NVCASE) program. This program recognizes competent US conformity assessment bodies to provide assurances to foreign governments on the conformity of exported US products.

NIST Interagency Committee on Standards Policy (ICSP)

The ICSP seeks to promote effective and consistent standards policies to foster cooperative participation by the federal government, US industry and other private organizations in standards activities. This includes the related activities of product testing, quality system registration, certification and accreditation.

NIST Manufacturing Extension Partnerships (MEP)

MEP is a nationwide network of not-for-profit centers in over 400 locations nationwide, whose sole purpose is to provide small- and medium-sized manufacturers with the help they need to succeed. Each center has the ability to conduct assessments, provide technical and business solutions, help create successful partnerships and facilitate learning through seminars and training programs.

One example of these centers is the Industrial Extension Service (IES) within North Carolina State University. IES (http://www.ies.ncsu.edu/ieswww/programs/mep) provided over 5000 technical assistance projects in 1999-2000 in management practices, marketing, team building, quality control, information technology, environmental compliance and education.

Department of Agriculture (USDA)

The Livestock and Seed (LS) Program offers audit-based quality management program assistance to the livestock and seed industries based on their experience and expertise with the ISO 9000 series quality management and assurance standards. This program, called the USDA Process Verification Program, focuses on process control instead of end-item examination as a means of ensuring product quality. The service allows producers and processors to market products with USDA-verified quality management systems in each phase of the production cycle. Such third-party-reviewed quality management systems can be used by meat and meat product companies to ensure the quality of their products to international customers.

These programs also allow interested companies a means to verify label claims that pertain to marketing issues, such as breed identification programs, feeding regimes and others.

The LS Program has been appointed to the US TAG to ISO TC 176 to represent the interests of the US agricultural industry in the development of international quality management and assurance standards. The LS Program also is continuing its investment in ISO 9000 training of its employees to ensure its capability to provide technical assistance to US companies that wish to incorporate ISO 9000 quality system management and assurance into their manufacturing processes.

US Department of Transportation

Maritime Administration

National Maritime Resource and Education Center (NMREC)

NMREC will facilitate ISO registration for the maritime industry by identifying registrars, providing preregistration audit assistance as requested by industry through seminars and workshops.

Department of the Treasury

Internal Revenue Service

The Internal Revenue Service issued a ruling on January 6, 2000, allowing businesses a tax deduction for the costs of developing and maintaining quality systems under ISO 9000 registration. A tax advisor should be consulted to determine how this deduction applies. The relevant section of federal income tax regulations is:

Section 162.–Trade or Business Expenses

26 CFR 1.162-1: Business Expenses.

(Also §§ 263, 263A; §§ 1.263(a)-1, 1.263(a)-2, 1.263A-1)

Rev. Rul. 2000-4

Implementation

Federal Agencies

The DoD has led the public sector in the number of registrations to the ISO 9000 standards with approximately two dozen installations registered. NASA is the only federal agency that has registered its entire range of operations and sites to the standards. Several other operations within various federal agencies have also gained registration. Registered installations within federal agencies are:

Installation	Location	
US Army National Guard	Fort Riley	KS
US Army National Guard	Camp Shelby	MS
US Army National Guard	Saginaw	TX
US Army National Guard-CSMS/RSMS-OR	Clackamas	OR
US Army: Anniston Army Depot	Anniston	AL
US Army: Chemical and Biological Defence Command	Aberdeen Proving Ground	MD
US Army: Corps of Engineers	Louisville	KY
US Army: Corps of Engineers (USACE)	McLean	VA
US Army: Corps of Engineers-Portland District	Portland	OR
US Army: Crane Army Ammunition Activity	Crane	IN
US Army: Department of the Army	Watervilet	NY
US Army: ERDEC Surety Office	Aberdeen Proving Ground	MD
US Army: Material Command Treaty Laboratory	Aberdeen Proving Ground	MD
US Army: Medical Research Acquisition Activity	Fort Detrick	MD
US Army: Primary Standards Laboratory	Redstone Arsenal	AL
US Army: Red River Army Depot - Missile Recertification	Texarkana	TX

Installation	Location	
US Marine Corps	Albany	GA
US Marine Corps	Barstow	CA
US Navy	Washington	DC
US Navy	Fort Detrick	MD
US Navy	Jacksonville	FL
US Navy	Washington	DC
US Navy	Cherry Point	NC
NASA Dryden Flight Research Center	Edwards	CA
NASA Ames Research Center	Moffett Field	CA
NASA Jet Propulsion Laboratory	Pasadena	CA
NASA Headquarters	Washington	DC
NASA John F. Kennedy Space Center	Kennedy Space Center	FL
NASA	Greenbelt	MD
NASA	Stennis Space Center	MS
NASA White Sands Test Facility	Las Cruces	NM
NASA	Cleveland	OH
NASA	Hampton	VA
Dyncorp NASA Gsfc/wff	Wallops Island	VA
NASA Ames Research Center	Fairmont	WV
US Department of Commerce Arizona Export Assistance Centers	Phoenix	AZ
US Department of Energy Oak Ridge National Laboratory Isotope Enrichment Facility (managed by Lockheed Martin Energy Research)	Oak Ridge	TN

Installation	Location	
US Coast Guard	Baltimore	MD
US Coast Guard Yard	Baltimore	MD
US Coast Guard, ISC	New Orleans	LA
Federal Reserve Bank of New York	New York	NY
Federal Aviation Administration Logistics Center	Oklahoma City	OK

State and Local

State and local agencies began implementing ISO 9000-based quality systems in the late 1990s. Seven state and local agencies have become registered to the standards. Three more state agencies in California, Louisiana and Nebraska are working toward quality management system implementation and registration. State and local agencies now registered are:

Installation	Location	
Georgia Bureau of Investigation	Decatur	GA
Forensic Services Division, State of North Carolina	Raleigh	NC
Department of Labor, State of Oregon	Salem	OR
Department of Administrative Services		
Information Resources Management Division, City of Crowley		
	Crowley	LA
Lafayette Economic Development Authority	Lafayette	LA
City of Dublin, Ohio	Dublin	OH
Department of Development, New York City	Brooklyn	NY
Metropolitan Transit Authority		

Education

Ten educational institutions have registered all or part of their operations to the ISO 9000 standards. They are:

Installation	Location	
Jefferson County Public Schools	Golden	CO
Sollers Point/Southeastern Technical High School	Baltimore	MD
Liberty Center High School	Liberty Center	OH
School District of Lancaster	Lancaster	PA

York County Area Vocational-Technical School	York	PA
Georgia Institute of Technology, Center for International Standards & Quality	Atlanta	GA
Vincennes University, Northern Indiana Business & Industry	Elkhart	IN
Louisiana State University at Eunice	Eunice	LA
The Metropolitan Community Colleges	Kansas City	MO
University of Dayton Research Institute	Dayton	OH

ENVIRONMENTAL
MANAGEMENT

Chapter 25   The International Environmental Management Standard

The International Environmental Management Standard

25

by James Highlands

An Introduction to ISO 14000

Private industry and regulatory agencies have sought for years to develop voluntary, consensus-based environmental management standards and codes of practice to solve concerns ranging from ozone depletion to deforestation and water pollution.

While some of these programs have been successful at rationalizing burdensome and often redundant country and region-specific environmental compliance requirements, the overall effect of these efforts is still not adequate to allow companies to easily conduct business on a global scale. The ISO 14000 standards provide a rallying point that allows the international business community to get beyond technical, political and geographical barriers to freely participate in the global marketplace.

To be fair, ISO 14000, at least in its early stages, does not produce this "level playing field" by providing companies with internationally accepted targets for effluents release levels and other technical requirements. In their present form, the standards exclude specific effluent and product standards The ultimate promise of ISO 14000 is that wide acceptance will allow companies to prove a high level of environmental stewardship through the establishment of a consistent, documented environmental management system. This environmental management framework drives organizational development that makes environmental considerations part of every employee's job. Market forces are likely to drive the specific standard of excellence in specific industry sectors

Reasons Behind Development

Creating a better internal management system, while a useful and worthy goal, is only part of industry's interest in ISO 14000.

Companies spend an estimated $300 billion globally on environmental protection. In the US market alone, annual environment-related spending is about $150 billion. At this current rate of increase that environmental spending is approximately 3 percent of the US gross domestic product for the year 2000.

This increasing cost of environmental compliance has particularly affected the process and natural resource industries. The Chemical Manufacturers Association (CMA) estimates that environment compliance-related requirements, in addition to remediation spending, now average 15 percent of capital and 5 percent to 10 percent of operating expenses. Environmental compliance costs are similar for petroleum, petrochemicals, paper products, metals, glass and other primary raw material industries.

Business Management Drivers

In addition to bottom-line concerns, companies are changing long-held environmental management axioms. Environmental compliance and remedial site cleanup is no longer viewed as just the cost of doing business. Managing these costs has become an important part of a comprehensive, overall business strategy.

Efforts to minimize waste and to redesign processes, products and packaging to prevent pollution are all part of this new philosophy. Resource productivity — the measure of how efficiently a company uses its capital, labor, energy and raw materials resources — is an important competitive differentiation. Companies whose products and processes make more efficient use of raw materials and energy produced less pollution, consequently resulting in pollution prevention.

Pollution prevention through substitution and process redesign, not end-of-the-pipe waste treatment, is now considered a more acceptable environmental management solution.

Companies that want to compete in the global marketplace must now integrate activities like planning, program implementation and measurement into the same overall process used to manage all business activities. A growing number of companies realize that environmental activities cannot remain a staff responsibility, a lesson only recently learned by quality management professionals. Environmental protection, like quality system management, must be integrated into daily business operations.

Marketplace Advantages

Companies are also discovering that environmentally friendly products have greater marketplace appeal and help customers achieve their own environmental objectives.

For example, more than 90 percent of the total environmental burden associated with the use of cars, refrigerators and washing machines is directly traceable to consumer use. Recyclable product components and other nonpolluting manufacturing systems that address the legitimate environmental concerns expressed by customers will have higher resource productivity and be competitively positioned as tomorrow's market leaders.

Stakeholders, including residents living near manufacturing facilities, customers and the investment community, are also more educated on environmental issues. This group of stakeholders can influence environmental policy to a significant degree. Implementing environmental management systems that protect the environment is an appropriate and ultimately cost-saving response.

Even McDonald's restaurant learned this lesson during the 1980s after it was criticized for the quantities of packaging used in its restaurants. McDonald's agreed to implement aggressive efforts to redesign its packaging as part of a legal settlement with the Environmental Defense Fund. The fast-food giant reduced the annual volume of solid waste it generated by over 10 million pounds per year. The company identified another 35 million to 40 million pounds of additional waste reduction opportunities. Not only did this campaign help create a positive environmental image for McDonalds, the effort reduced the direct business costs.

ISO 14000, Part of an International Trend

Approximately 45 percent of governance requirements used by multinational companies are based on international standards. Europe has taken a leadership position in the development of environmental management standards. The British Standards Institution (BSI) first published a voluntary environmental management standard, designated as BS 7750, in 1991. Other industry groups have also responded to stakeholder pressures to improve environmental performance by developing industry codes of performance.

Even the international business and political community has adopted a code of responsible environmental management principles. In 1991, a United Nations-sponsored sustainable development conference called for internationally recognized environmental practices. The conference published a document known as the International Chamber of Commerce Sustainable Development Charter (ICC Sustainable Development Charter).

The Development of ISO 14000 Standards

In 1990, in response to a request prompted by the United Nations Conference on Environmental Development, the International Organization for Standardization (ISO) formed the Strategic Advisory Group on Environment (SAGE). SAGE's charter was to study the question of whether environmental management was a suitable topic for standardization. By June 1993, ISO had formed Technical Committee (TC) 207 for the development of environmental management standards.

By September 1996, both ISO 14001 *Environmental management systems - Specification with guidance for use* and ISO 14004 *Environmental management systems - General guidelines on principles, systems and supporting techniques* were approved and published. Since that time many of the other standards of the environmental management series have been completed and published. These standards are listed in Figure 25-1. Both ISO 14001 and 14004 are undergoing their first revision at this writing, with final publication expected in 2003 or 2004.

Figure 25-1

ISO 14000 Series Standards

Designation	Title
ISO 14001:1996	*Environmental management systems — Specification with guidance for use*
ISO 14004:1996	*Environmental management systems — General guidelines on principles, systems and supporting techniques*
ISO 14010:1996	*Guidelines for environmental auditing — General principles*
ISO 14011:1996	*Guidelines for environmental auditing — Audit procedures — Auditing environmental management systems*
ISO 14012:1996	*Guidelines for environmental auditing — Qualification criteria for environmental auditors*
ISO 14015:2001	*Environmental assessment of sites and entities*

Figure 25-1

ISO 14000 Series Standards (continued)

Designation	Title
ISO 14020:1998	Environmental labels and declarations — General principles
ISO 14021:1999	Environmental labels and declarations — Self-declared environmental claims
ISO 14024:1999	Environmental labels and declarations — Type I environmental labelling — Principles and procedures
ISO/TR 14025	Environmental labels and declarations — Type III environmental delaractions — Guiding principles and procedures
ISO 14031:1999	Environmental management — Environmental performance evaluation — Guidelines
ISO/TR 14032	Environmental management — Environmental performance evaluation — Case studies illustrating the use of ISO 14031
ISO 14040:1997	Environmental management — Life cycle assessment — Principles and framework
ISO 14041:1998	Environmental management — Life cycle assessment — Goal and scope definition and inventory analysis
ISO 14042:2000	Environmental management — Life cycle assessment — Life cycle impact assessment
ISO 14043:2000	Environmental management — Life cycle assessment — Life cycle interpretation
ISO/TR 14048	Environmental management — Life cycle assessment — Life cycle assessment data documentation format
ISO/TR 14049	Environmental management — Life cycle assessment — Examples for the application of ISO 14041
ISO 14050:1998	Environmental management — Vocabulary
ISO/TR 14061	Information to assist forestry organizations in the use of the environmental management system standards ISO 14001 and ISO 14004
ISO Guide 64	Guide for the inclusion of environmental aspects in products and standards

The ISO 14001 Standard

ISO 14001 is the centerpiece of these standards, providing the requirements that an organization must achieve to have what is internationally agreed to be an Environmental Management System (EMS). The standard is a framework for planning, developing and implementing environmental strategies and related programs in an organization. This framework includes:

- A policy that states a commitment to a specified level of environmental performance
- A planning process to meet this stated performance commitment
- An organizational structure to execute the policy
- Specific objectives and targets
- Specific implementation procedures for meeting these stated objectives
- Communications and training programs to execute the policy commitment
- A measurement and review processes to monitor progress.

ISO 14001 can be used by any organization (regardless of company size or business type) to develop and implement a formalized management process to improve environmental performance. ISO 14001 draws its core elements from proven management systems like the ISO 9000 quality management series. It uses management concepts such as management by objectives, organizational development models and continuous improvement to measure, review, perform root-cause analysis and take corrective action.

Table 25-1

Plan-Do-Check-Act

Plan	Do	Check	Act
Policy	Structure/ responsibility	Monitoring and measurement	Management review
Environmental aspects	Training, competency and awareness	Nonconformance and corrective and preventive action	
Legal and other requirements	Communications	Records	
Objectives and targets	Environmental documentation	Environmental management audit	
Environmental management program	Document control		
	Operational control		
	Emergency preparedness and response		

The standard and its elements or requirements are structured using the Plan-Do-Check-Act, Model (PDCA). Although there was no perfect structure that fit each requirement of the standard, PDCA was quickly recognized as the most widely understood model internationally.

Elements of ISO14001

Management Commitment and Environmental Policy

The most senior level of the organization must:

- Issue a policy statement that includes a commitment to pollution prevention, continuous improvement and environmental legislation and regulations

- Set objectives and targets within its policy statement that commits it to meeting environmental legislative and regulatory requirements.

This policy must be documented, implemented and maintained and communicated to employees and made available to the public.

Planning

The organization must establish and maintain processes to:

- Identify the environmental aspects and impacts of an organization's operations, products and services.

- Identify and have access to the legal and other internally imposed requirements. Organizations may fulfill this requirement when considering environmental aspects and objectives.

- Identify environmental objectives and targets consistent with their stated policy and communicate these to each relevant function within an organization. Planning must also include a commitment to pollution prevention. When establishing environmental objectives, the organization should consider significant environmental aspects, relevant legal requirements, technological and financial aspects, business requirements and stakeholder views.

- Identify environmental management plans and programs to achieve a company's stated objectives and targets.

Implementation Operations:

To effectively implement an environmental management program, an organization must

- Define, document and communicate the organizational structure as well as the roles, responsibilities and authority of all participants. Adequate human resources, technological and financial commitment must also be directed toward implementation. An appointed management representative must be assigned to oversee and review implementation progress.

- Ensure that all employees have the proper training and skills to successfully execute their assigned roles in the implementation process.

- Establish a procedure to communicate internally and externally the environmental aspects of the environmental management system. The system must include a mechanism to receive and act on communications from outside parties.

- Establish operating procedures for those operations related to significant environmental aspects as well as record actual performance data.

- Establish and maintain a document control and archival system that meets both internal and legal requirements.

- Establish operation controls that identify, plan, implement and maintain environmental requirements and procedures. The plan should integrate those activities that are consistent with company environmental policies and objectives.

- Establish an adequate emergency preparedness and response program that is periodically tested for effectiveness.

Checking and Corrective Action

Continuous improvement process requirements in ISO14001 are met by measuring and evaluating implementation performance and effectiveness. The process is key to ensuring that a company is performing in accordance with stated policies and objectives. The key steps in this process are:

- Monitoring and measuring the effectiveness of environmental management activities

- Correcting and preventing areas of nonconformance

- Maintaining training, auditing and review records

- Performing environmental management system audits.

Management Review

Senior management must periodically review the environmental management system to ensure its adequacy and effectiveness. Any nonconformance must be corrected and preventive action taken appropriate to the magnitude of problems

ISO 9001 and ISO 14001

The relationship of ISO 14001 to ISO 14004 differs from that of ISO 9001 to ISO 9004. In the 9000 series, the requirements contained in ISO 9001 represent the basic Quality Management System (QMS), or the minimums for having a QMS, while an optimal or efficient system is contained in the guidance provided in ISO 9004. As such, ISO 9001 can be seen as a subset of ISO 9004. The relationship of ISO 14001 and 14004 differ in that one is not a subset of the other. While the base or fundamental requirements for an EMS are contained in ISO 14001, ISO 14004 does not represent excellence. The role of ISO 14004 is to provide guidance on implementing an EMS (ISO 14001). The tools and/or examples contained in the document (ISO 14004) are not the "how to" for constructing a higher performing system. While the role of ISO 14004 has always been controversial, it provides a useful reference or "how to" for an organization developing an ISO 14001 EMS. Future revisions of ISO 14004 are likely to grow in size as some of the more contentious subjects are discussed and the unique situations for small- and medium-sized enterprises are addressed in the document.

Organizations implementing an ISO 14001 EMS have found their existing ISO 9001 QMS to be extremely helpful in developing their EMS. While EMS systems have taken many different and varying forms from full integration with the existing QMS, many of the existing administrative procedures can be combined or used as a model to develop ISO 14001 procedures. Part of the reason behind this is the fact that both standards, QMS and EMS, use the same approach — process control. Moving away from reliance on final inspection in QMS or tail pipe emissions in EMS to controlling related processes to produce an expected outcome is the underlying goal of both standards.

Customer requirements, needs and expectations drives the ISO 9001 QMS, while significant environmental aspects ("elements of an organization's activities, products or services which can interact with the environment") are used to drive a similar process model in ISO 14001. The primary difference in the 1994 version of ISO 9001 was its use of an activity-based approach (procedures for contract review, design, purchasing etc.), while ISO 14001 requires that you "identify those operations and activities that are associated with the identified significant environmental aspects" and control these processes. This difference has been eliminated with the publication of the 2000 version of ISO 9001, which now embraces a process management model. Beyond this philosophical difference there are many practical similarities between the two systems that make them compatible.

Organizations with an existing ISO 9001 system find that many processes and procedures required by an ISO 14001 EMS have already been addressed in the

QMS. Document control; nonconformance and corrective and preventive actions; monitoring and measurement (calibration); control of records; training, awareness and competence; and parts of process/operational control are shared requirements of both standards. Several of these elements encompass identical controls and could be accommodated through minor changes to existing QMS procedures, while changes to others, such as the qualification of audit personnel, would depend on the nature of the business and the resulting EMS.

Beyond these obvious commonalities are similar elements/requirements in an ISO 9001 QMS and an ISO 14001 EMS. These are elements of the management systems that share similar intent in both standards but may vary in content. While the concept of these elements is often the same in both standards, the differences may cause the use of different procedures, processes, documents or records unique to each system. In some cases an existing ISO 9001 procedure could be used as a model for ISO 14001 when dealing with processes that are similar to those encountered in a quality management system. ISO 9001 users developing an ISO 14001 EMS will find they already have experience with the policy, objectives, structure and responsibility, documentation, operational control, internal audits and management review. The experience organizations gained communicating their QMS policy in their ISO 9001 systems will be useful in communicating their EMS policy.

Of course there are unique elements or requirements in ISO 14001 that are not contained in an ISO 9001 QMS. These requirements reflect the difference in perspective between the two management systems. As previously stated, a QMS is set in motion by customer requirements, while the significant environmental aspects drive an EMS. Consequently, requirements for environmental aspects, legal and other requirements, communications, monitoring and measurement of compliance and emergency preparedness and response tend to be new subjects for the existing ISO 9001 user. However many of these requirements may be addressed in an organization's existing environmental program. Existing laws and regulations have required monitoring and measurement of compliance and emergency preparedness and response for many years as a part of legal compliance. Integrated into a developing EMS they provide an added resource to the existing QMS procedures and experience while maintaining continuity with established practice.

Organizations have also discovered that other existing ISO 9001 QMS procedures or processes can be useful in developing and implementing their ISO 14001 EMS. Processes such as design control are not an explicit requirement of ISO 14001, however it is an ideal process for identifying environmental aspects, both significant and otherwise, of a product and the needed production processes. Work instructions developed to meet ISO 9001 requirements can be modified to control environmental aspects to meet objectives and targets. Handling and storage procedures can also be useful in controlling significant environmental aspects and can integrate legal requirements for some materials. Inspection and test procedures can be modified to accommodate monitoring and measurement requirements for environmental aspects and compliance.

Needless to say organizations with existing ISO 9001 systems have many accessible resources that can be used to develop their ISO 14001 EMS. A little planning, some cooperation between departments and creative thinking can go a long way in both developing, implementing and operating an EMS.

Registration or Certification

Under the RAB/ANSI National Accreditation Program, the registration process for ISO 14001 is similar to that of ISO 9001. It's likely that the organization being audited may not notice the difference. In fact, many registrars offer joint registration. This saves both time and money by allowing an organization to be audited and registered to both ISO 9001 and ISO 14001 simultaneously. Differences between the audit of either system, for the most part, have to do with auditor qualification. EMS auditors need a different set of knowledge than QMS auditors and focus on environmental aspects, laws and regulations. However, many of the administrative elements such as document control and others can be performed by the same auditor evaluating elements of either system in the joint audit process.

The number of organizations registering to ISO 14001 has admittedly been slow in the United States as compared to Europe and Asia, but has begun to accelerate. One reason has been the tendency for many large organizations, such as key automotive manufacturers, to encourage and/or require their suppliers to be compliant to ISO 14001. Consequently, the number of organizations registered to ISO 14001 is beginning to grow swiftly.

Revisions

During the revision of ISO 9001, its compatibility with ISO 14001 was a primary consideration. The two committees responsible for the drafting work now share liaison status and work closely in the development of each other's standards. To some extent this has been driven by ISO's Technical Management Board, which has insisted that the two registration standards, ISO 9001 and ISO 14001, be compatible. Compatibility in this case is defined as undue hardship for an organization with an existing ISO 9001 system to implement an ISO 14001 environmental management system.

Figure 25-2

Growth Comparison: ISO 14001 vs. ISO 9000

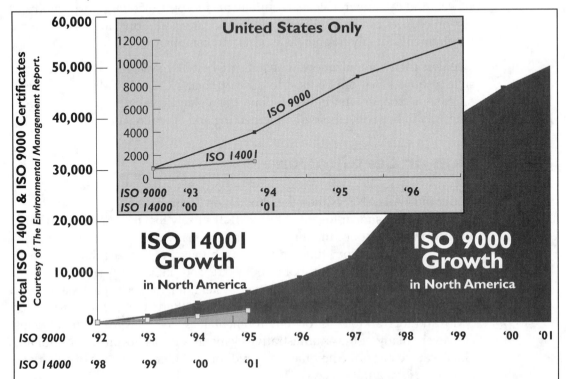

While ISO 14001 shares common management principles with the ISO 9000 standards on quality, it seems to be following its own course with respect to third-party registration trends in the United States and North America as a whole. An Analysis of data by *The Environmental Management Report* shows that ISO 14001 registration gains, though significant since the standard's publication in 1996, do not follow the same explosive growth of the quality standards at comparable certificate milestones.

As a result there is an improved level of compatibility between the recently published ISO 9001:2000 and ISO 14001. ISO 9001:2000 now has a more flexible documentation structure, not necessarily mandating procedures for each process, an area where ISO 14001 has received many compliments. ISO 9001:2000 includes requirements on laws and regulations in policy and design, communications both internal and external, explicit continual improvement requirements and the addition of awareness into the training requirements. The term "organization" as opposed to "supplier" is now used, a recognition that the standards are beginning to transcend the normal customer-supplier relationships as schools and institutions become registered. While ISO 14001 is not the sole driver behind many of these changes, it has been a contributing factor.

Conversely, in 1999 the revision process for ISO 14001 started, as the TC 207 sub-committee began to consider what changes are needed in the recently issued standard. While there has been a resolution that no new requirements will be added during this revision cycle of ISO 14001, the one notable exception is compatibility with the new ISO 9001:2000. During the intervening years a Joint Technical Assistance Group (TAG) between the two committees identified numerous areas where both standards could be revised to improve compatibility for the user. Several of these key areas shared by both standards will need to be considered and possibly changed during the ISO 14001 revision process.

ISO 14001 and Regulation

Representatives of the US Environmental Protection Agency (EPA) have played, and continue to play, a key role in developing and revising ISO 14001.

Over the years the regulatory agencies have mounted a variety of pilot programs aimed at defining the benefits of comprehensive environmental management systems. Several of these initiatives have included attempts to implement facilitywide permitting programs, and several states have formed a Multi State Working Group that participates in the US TAG to TC 207. It remains to be seen whether and/or how the regulatory authorities will weave into current law and regulation (or new legislation) legal mechanisms for industry to evaluate the environmental impacts of their operations and to address those impacts. However, to date, the agency has not formally recognized the standard beyond encouraging its use.

On March 12, 1998, the US EPA issued a position statement for comment in the *Federal Register* regarding environmental management systems, including those based on the ISO 14001 standard.

This EPA document states in part: "Implementation of an EMS has the potential to improve an organization's environmental performance and compliance with regulatory requirements. EPA supports and will help promote the development and use of EMSs, including those based on the ISO 14001 standard, that help an organization achieve its environmental obligations and broader environmental performance goals.

"EPA encourages the use of EMSs that focus on improved environmental performance and compliance as well as source reduction (pollution prevention) and system performance. EPA supports efforts to develop quality data on the performance of any EMS to determine the extent to which the system can help bring about improvements in these areas. EPA also encourages organizations that develop EMSs to do so through an open and inclusive process with relevant stakeholders, and to maintain accountability for the performance of outcomes of their EMSs through measurable objectives and targets. EPA encourages organizations to make information on the actual performance of their environmental management systems available to the public and government agencies. In addition, through initiatives such as Project XL and the Environmental Leadership Program, EPA is encouraging the testing of EMSs to achieve superior environmental performance. At this time, however, EPA is not basing any regulatory incentives solely on the use of EMSs, or certification to ISO 14001."

OPPORTUNITIES AND CHALLENGES

Comparing ISO 9000, Malcolm Baldrige and TQM

26

by Robert G. Grimmett*

Introduction

This chapter compares the ISO 9000:2000 series of standards to the Malcolm Baldrige National Quality Award (MBNQA) guidelines and relates these disciplines to Total Quality Management (TQM). It provides an overview of the two quality initiatives, makes some comparisons and emphasizes the importance of the complementary nature of the two approaches to quality systems and the further pursuit of total quality.

The three core standards of the ISO 9000:2000 series were officially released by the International Organization for Standardization on December 15, 2000. These international standards continue to generate much attention and discussion. This is deserved, but we need to understand what the ISO 9000:2000 series is and what it is not. Such an understanding will contribute significantly to the correct implementation and use of these standards and guidelines on quality systems and management — to meet demands for a process-based quality system applicable to more than traditional manufacturing and to establish a total quality system that has direct and long-term beneficial results for the organization itself. The ISO 9000:2000 series is not intended to be a standard for total quality. It is, however, a uniform, consistent set of system elements and requirements for quality assurance systems and management that can be applied universally

*This chapter was prepared by Dr. Kenneth S. Stephens for the third edition.

within any total quality system. The widespread adoption and implementation of the previous ISO 9000 revisions by companies and nations have brought about harmonization on an international scale. This has fostered the growing impact of quality as a strategic factor in international as well as national and local trade.

As detailed elsewhere in this *Handbook*, the new revisions in the ISO 9000:2000 series consist of standards and a guideline for the performance improvement of quality management systems. The one comprehensive compliance standard is ISO 9001:2000 (see Chapter 4). It specifies the requirements for a quality management system to be used by an organization to achieve customer satisfaction. It is process based and applies to all generic product categories. ISO 9001:2000 is paired with ISO 9004:2000, which provides detailed guidance in not only the establishment of a quality management system but the processes for continual performance improvement.

Additional resources for total quality/management system elements, assessments and criteria for designing, developing and implementing such systems are the various quality awards. Among these are the Deming Prize, the MBNQA, the European Quality Award, other national quality awards, a growing number of institutional and industry sector awards and state quality awards. A major goal of the MBNQA is to increase US competitiveness worldwide. It recognizes US companies for quality and performance excellence. The Award promotes the improvement of organizational performance practices and the sharing of best practices among US organizations. It consists of a set of criteria divided into seven major categories. These categories are further subdivided into 18 examination items, each with one or more areas to address. In assessing the categories and items, a point score scale totaling 1,000 points is established. The criteria for the MBNQA address elements of total quality systems that are not included in the requirements of ISO 9000:2000.

Total quality and its management counterpart, TQM, mean different things to different persons and organizations. These are merely names for discussion, communication, developments and applications. Programs with the TQM label have met with great success. Others with the same label have met with failure. What is significant here is that the nomenclature is not as important as what is being done. It isn't the names that make the programs, but the activities being carried out. It is the philosophies, approaches and attitudes being implemented, and the results being achieved. This is especially true as they pertain to customer and employee satisfaction; continuous improvement and innovation; and quality, productivity, and profitability enhancements.

The ISO 9000 Family and Related Standards

In it broadest aspect, the concept of total quality goes beyond the quality system prescribed by the ISO 9000:2000 series. It also goes beyond the criteria of the MBNQA even though the latter is perhaps more consistent with W. Edwards Deming's concerns about the competitive global marketplace. Deming (1986) warned that the western world needs a "transformation of the American style of management" and not merely a "reconstruction" or "revision." He further pointed out that this new way "requires a whole new structure, from foundation upward." Deming's 14 points for management have significant impact on the management of total quality. We have not yet been successful in incorporating all of these philosophies into systems and programs such as the ISO 9000:2000 series and/or quality awards. Those systems and programs help to point the way and provide partial mechanisms, but there is always the danger that their implementation may represent a "fix" rather than a "transformation."

Comparing the ISO 9000:2000 series requirements and guidelines, the MBNQA criteria and Deming-based TQM philosophies and proposed practices is a difficult task. They have grown closer together in recent years, but emphasis on customer satisfaction and performance improvement in ISO 9000:2000 and performance results in the MBNQA have not yet achieved total convergence with TQM.

Overview of the Two Systems

The ISO 9000 Series — Strengths and Limitations

A detailed technical content overview of the ISO 9000:2000 series is presented in Chapters 3 and 4. The overview presented here will look at the series with a different perspective.

The new ISO 9000:2000 series contains two standards paired with a complementary set of guidelines. The guidelines document could also be seen as a standard in that it is prepared and promulgated by a standards body. All three have the advantages and disadvantages of standards. As a set of standards it is subject to periodic review and revision. The second cycle of that process has been realized recently with the 2000 revisions. We need to understand the standards in order to assure correct and beneficial implementation along with other elements of a total quality system that are not a part of the series. It is extremely important for both organization managers and quality practitioners to understand that the ISO 9000:2000 series is not intended as a standard on total quality. A total quality system must go beyond the ISO 9000:2000 series. This series is one quality system. It may not be the quality system best suited for any given organization. This is discussed subsequently in greater detail.

On the positive side, its strengths lie in its structure. It sets forth a uniform, consistent set of requirements that can be applied universally within limitations of interpretation and individual implementation. It provides a basis for designing, implementing, assessing, improving and registering a Quality Assurance (QA) system. The widespread adoption of the ISO 9000 series provides a common language for international trade with respect to the QA disciplines. It requires a sound, well-documented contractual relationship between the organization and its customers and a well-documented quality system by the organization. ISO 9001:2000 aims to establish a common understanding that a quality management system is in place that will consistently provide product that meets customer and regulatory requirements and further enhance customer satisfaction through continual improvement.

For further understanding, the ISO 9000:2000 series is generic in two significant aspects. It is not product or process specific. It is a set of standards that link the quality system with the basic management process approach common to all organizations. However, the quality system and manual will have to contain specific subsystems related directly to the processes and the generic product categories to which it is being applied. Any quality system is developed and implemented, not in and of itself, but to assist in producing a product. The ISO 9000:2000 series defines four generic product categories: hardware, software, services and processed materials. But in spite of these references to product and process, the ISO 9000:2000 series standards and guidelines do not set standards on product or process. Such standards must be established by the organizations themselves to meet their internal and external customer requirements and made a part of the quality system under ISO 9001:2000 that includes the documentation subsystem.

The ISO 9000:2000 series is not even quality system specific. It does not specify a fixed system beyond the general requirements enumerated for every organization. It provides considerable flexibility to the organization to design and document its own system within the framework of the requirements and then directs attention to evaluating conformance to and improving the performance of that system. This is, perhaps, a good place to dispel the common myth that the ISO 9000:2000 series standards only require that "You say what you do, and do what you say." Yes, you are required to say what you do (i.e., document) and do what you say (i.e., comply), but what you say and do must meet the specific and implied requirements of the standards. You are not at complete liberty to say and do anything you want — if you wish to be found in compliance with ISO 9001:2000.

ISO 9004:2000 Quality Management Systems — Guidelines for Performance Improvement

This standard provides guidance for performance improvement through quality management systems. It is paired with ISO 9001:2000 and is specifically based on the same systems approach. While both standards share a common focus on customer satisfaction, the process approach to quality management, self-development and self-assessment, ISO 9004:2000 is a set of guidelines for organizations that want to move beyond the minimum requirements of customer satisfaction. ISO 9004:2000 incorporates the four basic processes and 23 broad requirements and moves beyond them to detailed requirements for overall performance improvement. It covers guidelines for self-assessment and process methodology for improvement. This standard plays a very special role with respect to the development and assessment of a quality system, especially in comparison with the Malcolm Baldrige National Quality Award. They both have in common an orientation toward self-development and self-assessment. ISO 9004:2000 also approaches the concept of results management as espoused by MBNQA. The standard indicates that the application of quality management principles makes an important contribution to managing costs and risks. They impact revenue, profits and market share along with resource costs. Also ISO 9004:2000, like ISO 9001:2000, is not quality system specific.

This standard is part of the noncontractual or guideline portion of the ISO 9000:2000 series. It contains 27 pages of text, while ISO 9001:2000 has only 14 pages of substantive text.

Some of the criticisms leveled at the old contractual quality assurance models (ISO 9004-1:1994 and ANSI/ASQC Zl.15:1979), primarily in the form of omissions, are included in ISO 9004:2000 as elements of quality systems. These include, among others, more on quality plans, continual performance improvement, quality costs, marketing quality, more on process quality, personnel and motivation and product safety (through references to meet regulatory requirements). It is also interesting to note that in its noncontractual category, two contract-sensitive requirements of ISO 9001 were omitted from ISO 9001-1:1994: contract review and customer-supplied product. They are now included in the 2000 revision.

On the limitation side, as for many standards passing through review, negotiation and consensus, the ISO 9000:2000 series represents a "least common denominator" in its coverage of the quality management disciplines. Everyone should understand this clearly, together with the fact that it is not a standard on total quality. The actual quality system that is optimum for a given organization may go well beyond the requirements of the ISO 9000:2000 series. Indeed, ISO

9004:2000 itself encourages management to go beyond the minimum compliance standards to achieve performance improvement. It is encouraging that many organizations implementing quality systems do, in fact, go beyond the requirements of the standard and incorporate other elements of total quality into their systems.

Some felt that ISO 9004-1:1994 placed too much emphasis on conformance rather than on adequacy and effectiveness. ISO 9004:2000 has added a central focus on top management responsibility to promote policies to increase awareness, motivation and involvement of people. It even has an Appendix A, Guidelines for Self-Assessment. This covers assessment methodologies which approach the MBNQA model with performance maturity levels and a documentation process that will assist in targeting processes for improvements in effectiveness.

As stated earlier, the ISO 9000:2000 series does not represent a total quality system as evidenced by its failure to adequately address the following:

- Quality cost analysis and applications other than as an element in ISO 9004:2000
- Pride in work — and employee participation, involvement and empowerment via project teams and quality circles
- Production/inventory management systems such as JIT and supply train management with TQC
- Innovation of products and processes
- Deming's 14 points for management and the recognition of the necessity for transformation.

Juran (1994) lists the following exclusions from ISO 9000 as essentials to attain world-class quality:

- Training the hierarchy in managing for quality
- A revolutionary rate of quality improvement.

What has been said here must be properly interpreted and understood. It is not so much a criticism of ISO 9000:2000 as a caution not to limit one's quality program to that of ISO 9001:2000 alone.

In fact, other resources for the self-development and self-assessment of total quality/management systems, along with criteria for designing and implementing such systems exist. Among these are the various quality awards such as the Deming Prize, the Malcolm Baldrige National Quality Award and the European Quality Award. The latter, in particular, encourages self-appraisal and assigns 50 percent of the criteria to results in terms of people satisfaction (9 percent), customer satisfaction (20 percent), impact on society (6 percent) and business results (15 percent). See Conti (1991, 1995). See also EFQM (1992a, 1992b).

A further resource for quality system requirements is FDA's current good manufacturing practices (CGMPs). While these apply on a mandatory basis to applicable organizations, they are, nevertheless, available to any organization to study and use. Of significance here is the move toward the ISO 9000 series in recent years. Harmonization of CGMPs with ISO 9001 promotes competitiveness, improves the quality of manufacture and promotes safer and more effective medical devices.

As is now well-known, the Automotive Industry Action Group (AIAG) published a set of requirements entitled *Quality System Requirements, QS-9000* in August 1994, which were revised in later editions. This document is an agreement between the three major American auto manufacturers and five truck manufacturers. QS-9000 contains all of ISO 9001, which is its foundation. An additional section lists some specific requirements of Chrysler, Ford, General Motors and the truck manufacturers. While QS-9000 does not qualify, theoretically, as a "standard" because a consensus process was not used in its development, it does represent an alternate source of information and example for quality system requirements. (See Chapter 13.)

The ISO 9000:2000 series has added or focused more requirements on customer satisfaction, continual performance improvement, top management involvement and leadership, quality cost analysis, long-term cooperative partnerships with suppliers and breakthrough quality improvements. With the addition of additional resources like the MBNQA and incorporation of some missing elements, the resultant system should be better, more dynamic, more comprehensive, more effective and more economical than that of ISO 9001:2000 alone. The present 2000 revision to the ISO 9000 series, within the framework of its intended purpose, addresses many of its previous limitations. For example, the limitation of the "life cycle model" has been replaced with a "process model" and now stands as the basis of the ISO 9000:2000 structure.

The Malcolm Baldrige National Quality Award

The global impact of national and international quality awards is seen in company advertisements, publicity and general literature. The criteria associated with these awards represent an important complement to quality systems as significant alternatives or additional elements of quality systems otherwise promulgated by the ISO 9000 series and its regional and national adoptions — as well as to quality management. Many important quality system elements not covered by the ISO 9000:2000 series are included in the criteria associated with the various quality awards. And while only a select few companies win these awards annually, it is the self-assessment and system development processes, associated with the use of the criteria at the corporation and enterprise levels, that contribute significantly to the spread of quality systems and management.

The three quality awards most sought after are the Deming Application Prize in Japan, the Malcolm Baldrige National Quality Award in the United States and the European Quality Award. In the United States, a growing number of local (institutional, state, city, etc.) quality awards are contributing significantly to the spread of quality concepts. Other developed countries have launched national quality awards, and a growing number of developing countries are also turning to these resources in national quality awards. To illustrate the progress being made in this area of the quality disciplines, following is a discussion of the Malcolm Baldrige National Quality Award and the spread of the MBNQA criteria.

The MBNQA was established in the United States in 1987 by way of the Malcolm Baldrige National Quality Improvement Act of 1987 that was signed by President Reagan on August 20, 1987, becoming Public Law 100-107. The award was named after Malcolm Baldrige, the former Secretary of Commerce, who served from 1981 until his untimely death in 1987. Responsibility for the continuing management of the award is assigned to the National Institute of Standards and Technology (NIST), formerly the US Bureau of Standards), which is an agency of the Department of Commerce. The American Society for Quality (ASQ) assists in administrating the award program under contract to NIST.

The award's role is to help improve organizational performance practices and capabilities and to facilitate communication and sharing of best practices. As a

Figure 26-1

The Baldrige Award Criteria Framework — A System Perspective

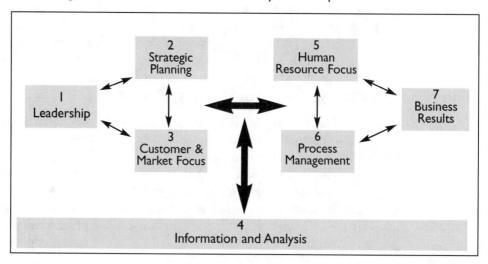

general goal the award promotes awareness of the importance of quality improvement in strengthening US competitiveness. The award's five eligibility categories are manufacturing companies, service companies, small businesses, educational institutions and health care organizations. Up to three winners may be selected per category annually. Recipients may publicize and advertise their awards and are expected to share information about their quality strategies with other US organizations to encourage the spread of quality.

The award is based on a set of criteria for the evaluation of applicants. This set also serves as the basis for self-development and assessment by companies wishing to improve their quality efforts, even when they have no intention of applying for the award. Purposes for the criteria are: (1) to serve as a working tool for planning, training and assessment; (2) to help raise quality performance standards and expectations; and (3) to assist communications and sharing among and within organizations of important quality and operational perform-

Figure 26-2

The Baldrige 2002 Award Criteria — Item Listing

2002 Categories/Items		Point Values
1. Leadership		**120**
1.1 Organizational Leadership	80	
1.2 Public Responsibility and Citizenship	40	
2. Strategic Planning		**85**
2.1 Strategy Development	40	
2.2 Strategy Deployment	45	
3. Customer and Market Focus		**85**
3.1 Customer and Market Knowledge	40	
3.2 Customer Relationships and Satisfaction	45	
4. Information and Analysis		**90**
4.1 Measurement and Analysis of Organizational Performance	50	
4.2 Information Management	40	
5. Human Resource Focus		**85**
5.1 Work Systems	35	
5.2 Employee Education, Training and Development	25	
5.3 Employee Well-Being and Satisfaction	25	
6. Process Management		**85**
6.1 Product and Service Processes	45	
6.2 Business Processes	25	
6.3 Support Processes	15	
7. Business Results		**450**
7.1 Customer-Focused Results	125	
7.2 Financial and Market Results	125	
7.3 Human Resource Results	80	
7.4 Organizational Effectiveness Results	120	
Total Points		**1,000**

Figure 26-3

The Baldrige Award Winners 1988 through 2001

2001
- Clarke American Checks Inc.
- Pal's Sudden Service
- Chugach School District
- Pearl River School District
- University of Wisconsin - Stout

2000
- Dana Corp. - Spicer Driveshaft Division
- KARLEE Company Inc.
- Operations Management International Inc.
- Los Alamos National Bank

1999
- ST Microelectronics Inc.
- Region Americas, BI
- The Ritz-Carlton Hotel Co. LLC
- Sunny Fresh Foods

1998
- Boeing Airlift and Tanker Programs
- Solar Turbines Inc.
- Texas Nameplate Co. Inc.

1997
- 3M Dental Products Division
- Solectron Corp.
- Merrill Lynch Credit Corp.
- Zerox Business Services

1996
- ADAC Laboratories
- Dana Comercial Credit Corp.
- Custom Research Inc.
- Trident Precision Manufacturing Inc.

1995
- Armstrong Building Products Operations
- Corning Telecommunications Products Division

1994
- AT&T Consumer Communication Services
- GTE Directories Corporation
- Wainwright Industries Inc.

1993
- Eastman Chemical Company
- Ames Rubber Corporation

1992
- AT&T Network Systems Group Transmission Systems Business Unit
- Texas Intruments Inc. Defense Systems & Electronics Group
- AT&T Universal Card Services
- The Ritz-Carlton Hotel Company Atlanta, Georgia
- Granite Rock Company

1991
- Solectron Corporation
- Zytec Corporation
- Marlow Industries

1990
- Cadillac Motor Car Division (General Motors)
- IBM Rochester
- Federal Express Corporation
- Wallace Company Inc.

1989
- Miliken & Co.
- Xerox Business Products and Systems

1988
- Motorola
- Commercial Nuclear Fuel Division (Westinghouse)
- Globe Metallurgical

ance requirements. The criteria are built around the following core values: visionary leadership, being customer driven, valuing employees and partners, agility, focus on the future, managing for innovation, management by fact, public responsibility and citizenship, focus on results and creating value, and a systems perspective.

The criteria framework for the award are further categorized into four major dynamic relationships and emphasis categories, as shown in Figure 26-1. The criteria framework is composed of two major triads, Leadership and Results, under the umbrella of Customer and Market Focused Strategy and Action Plans. All actions point to Business Results and the horizontal arrow connects Leadership and Results. At the bottom of Figure 26-1 is the foundation of any performance management system, Information and Analysis. As mentioned in the introduction, these categories are expanded into 18 examination items and 29 areas. The seven major categories are assigned point values to provide a numerical basis for degree of importance and assessment.

The point values assigned to each category are further broken down to point values associated with the 18 examination items, as shown in Figure 26-2. Note that one category alone amounts to 45 percent of the total point values, namely Business Results. This is an area for which ISO 9000 is often criticized for lacking emphasis. ISO 9001:2000 now includes more on results but not to the same degree as MBNQA.

Figure 26-4

The Baldrige Award Application Data

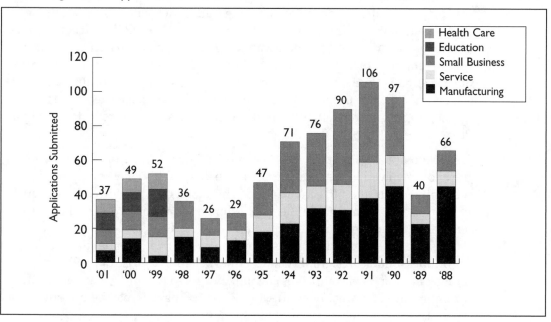

Figure 26-5

The Baldrige Award Site Visit Data, 2001-1988

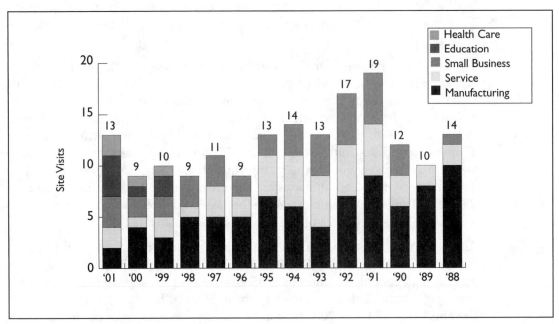

From 1988 through 2000 some 43 companies have received the award. The recipients are shown in Figure 26-3. Since one of the purposes of the award is the sharing of information on quality programs, these companies may be contacted for such information. Application data over this same period is shown in Figure 26-4. The number of applicants reached a peak in 1991 and has declined since. One explanation relates to the awareness of companies, based on their self-assessment, that their programs are not yet ready to meet such high-performance standards. In the assessment of applicants both a paper evaluation (stage 1) and on-site visits (stage 2) are carried out, the latter stage executed for those applicants who score well in the first stage. Site visit data is reflected in Figure 26-5.

Inspection of the data in Figures 26-4 and 26-5 might cause one to ask whether the effort involved in the award process is beneficial if so few companies participate from application to actual award. This alone may be viewed by the quality profession as beneficial in the establishment of a standard for quality excellence. Of further benefit is the recognition of those who have achieved this standard, and the feedback from these companies as encouragement and example for future aspirants. A significant additional benefit is the use of the Baldrige criteria by thousands of companies carrying out self-development and assessment for improving their quality efforts. While the full benefit may be unknown, the number of application guidelines requested has declined. Even with declining applications, the guidelines continue to be in demand at levels well above 100,000 per year. Thus, while the ISO 9000:2000 series stands as a set of requirements for a quality system, the criteria for the MBNQA stands, at least as a de facto standard, for total quality/total quality management. In this respect the self-development and self-assessment of ISO 9004:2000 and MBNQA have a lot in common.

It should be emphasized here that there is no guarantee of financial success in either the use of the ISO 9000:2000 series or the MBNQA. In connection with the MBNQA, sharing success can be overwhelming and self-defeating, if not monitored and controlled carefully. This is true particularly for small companies. The Wallace Company (a 1990 recipient of the award, see Figure 26-3), with some 280 employees, received 60 to 70 requests for information per day after winning the award. Within three months it had 1,000 sign-ups for site visits. See Hart (1993). Shortly after winning the award, the Wallace Company found itself in financial trouble. Some 70 employees were laid off. Company overhead increased by $2 million per year, and customers were unhappy with prices. According to CEO John Wallace, executives were giving speeches all over the United States and not getting sales. The award seemed to distract managers and took their attention away from some crucial parts of running the business. However, on the upside it was seen that employees were able to cope with the cutbacks after the financial problems because of their quality process participation and the openness it fostered. Their attitude of continuous improvement was retained.

ISO 9000 Compared to MBNQA

The ISO 9000:2000 series, as compliance standards, are intended to serve as models for quality assurance systems. The specific guideline, ISO 9004:2000, provides a wider range of objectives of a quality management system for improvement of an organization's overall performance. In this respect it covers more items than the compliance standards, such as cost of quality, marketing, product safety as a regulatory requirement, benchmarking and personnel motivation. The MBNQA is viewed as a higher level standard with respect to principles of total quality and TQM. It gives more specific emphasis on customer management and satisfaction; on results that relate to product and service quality, operations and finances, human resources and suppliers; on employee development and satisfaction; on higher level management involvement and leadership; on competitive benchmarking; and so on. It does not detail certain elements of quality systems as found in the ISO 9000:2000 series compliance standards, such as documentation and document control, inspection, metrology, product traceability, contract review, customer-supplied product, control of nonconforming product, postproduction activities and so on.

In an attempt to compare the two approaches Figure 26-6 identifies the extent to which the requirements of the compliance standards of the ISO 9000:2000 series align with the MBNQA criteria. As seen by this interpretation, 48 percent of the line items in Figure 26-6 for each approach are aligned, indicated by the "very well aligned" symbols. Fifty-two percent are "somewhat aligned," further indicating the multiple alignment of line items in the two approaches.

Comparison of Documentation and Control

The requirements for documentation and control are high for both the ISO 9000:2000 series and MBNQA. However, in ISO 9001:2000, the requirement for documentation is not as pervasive as in the past and limits it to sufficient documentation to ensure effective operation and control of processes. Documentation and control in MBNQA is much more subtle and implied. An organization that demonstrates that MBNQA criteria activities are systematic, well deployed, focused and consistent will require a high level of documentation.

MBNQA has high requirements for results and results measurements. As stated above, 450 out of 1,000 points for the MBNQA are awarded for results. ISO 9000:2000 has initiated focus on results as the proof of organizational performance improvement. The MBNQA requires measured process control; ISO 9000 similarly requires measurement for control of activities needed to assure conformity and achieve improvement.

Comparison of Degree of Prescriptiveness

The degree of prescriptiveness inherent in the two approaches to quality is defined by what and how work is to be done. The MBNQA guidelines spell out what must be done to attain a high score relative to the categories and items defined. It also spells out how each of the "areas to address" should be approached. Otherwise, there is a great deal of latitude within the bounds of the criteria for companies to express their individuality and management style. There is no imposed stereotype. This can be seen by the diversity of the approaches taken by the winners to date.

The ISO 9000:2000 series requirements for the compliance standards are generic, as mentioned earlier. They define specific areas to include in the quality system, essentially the "what" that is considered minimum for compliance. However, the requirements allow much latitude in "how" the system should be set up and how it should operate to accomplish the stated requirements. In this

Figure 26-6

Extent to which ISO 9000:2000 Requirements Align with MBNQA Criteria

Legend: • Very well aligned * Somewhat aligned

ISO 9001:2000	Leadership 1.1	1.2	Strategic Planning 2.1	2.2	Customer, Market 3.1	3.2	Info. Analysis 4.1	4.2	Human Resources 5.1	5.2	5.3	Process Management 6.1	6.2	6.3	Business Results 7.1	7.2	7.3	7.4
4. QMS Requirements	•		*	•	•	*	*	•	•	•		•	•	•	•	*	•	•
5.1 Management Commitment	•		*	*	*		*	*		•		•				*		•
5.2 Customer Focus	*		*	*	•	*	*	*		*		•			•		*	•
5.3 Quality Policy	*		•	*	*		*	*		*		*						*
5.4 Planning			•	*			*					*						
5.5 Responsibility, Authority, Communication	*		•	*	•	*	•	•	•			•	*	*	•		•	•
5.6 Management Review			*		*		*	*	*	*		*				*		*
6.1 Provision of Resources			*				*	*	•			*						*
6.2 Human Resources	•		•	•	*		*	•	•	•	*	•	•		*		•	
6.3 Infrastructure				•			*			*		•	*	•	*		•	
6.4 Work Environment	•		*					*	•	*		*	•	*	•	*	*	
7.1 Planning of Product Realization	•			*			*	*				*				*		*
7.2 Customer-related Processes					•	•	*	*				*	*				•	
7.3 Design and Development					•	*	*	*	*			•	•		*		*	
7.4 Purchasing			*			*	*					•	•	•				
7.5 Production and Service Provision					•		*					*					•	
7.6 Control of Measuring Devices							*					*						
8.1 Measurement, Analysis, Improvement	*		*		•	*	*	*	*	*		*	•	*	•	•	*	•
8.2.1 Customer Satisfaction	•		*		•		•	•		•		•	•	*	•	*	•	•
8.2.2 Internal Audit	•		*	•	*		•	•				•	•	*	•	•	•	*
8.2.3 Monitoring & Measurement Process			*		•	*	*	*	•	*		•	•		•		•	*
8.2.4 Monitoring & Measurement Product			•	*	•	*	•	•	*			•	•		•		•	•
8.3 Control of Nonconforming Product							*	*						*	•		*	•
8.4 Analysis of Data	*		•	*	•	•	•	•		•	*	•	*	•	•	*	*	*
8.5.1 Continual Improvement	•		•	•	•		*	•		•		•	•	•	•		*	*
8.5.2/3 Corrective and Preventive Action	*			•		*	*	•				•	•	•	•		•	•

respect there is also no imposed stereotype. Companies with widely different quality systems have shown compliance and achieved certification. To a certain degree a lot is left to the interpretation of management in setting up the system and the interpretation of the auditors in carrying out the certification process. Where these two interpretations agree sufficiently, registration is achieved. As indicated above, most companies recognize the benefits of exceeding the basic requirements of ISO 9000.

ISO 9000, MBNQA and Total Quality in Summary

As stated in the introduction, there is no standard established for total quality or TQM. One definition of total quality is provided by the study group associated with the 1992 Total Quality Forum and included in Rampey and Roberts (1992) as:

> "Total Quality is ... a people-focused management system that aims at continual increase in customer satisfaction at continually lower real cost. TQ is a total system approach (not a separate area or program), and an integral part of high-level strategy. It works horizontally across functions and departments, involving all employees, top to bottom, and extends backwards and forwards to include the supply chain and the customer chain."

A definition for TQM used by Dr. Kenneth S. Stephens is as follows:

Total Quality Management (TQM) is a process that integrates fundamental management art and techniques with the disciplines, principles, methodologies, activities, approaches and techniques of total (strategic) quality to develop and implement successful business strategies throughout the organization (or any business entity).

Total quality is viewed as:

- A clear focus on customer needs, wants, satisfaction and delight
- Continuous improvement and innovation of all processes, services and products
- Effective utilization, empowerment and recognition of individuals under a team participation approach, including essential programs of education and training, shared values, decisions and benefits
- Sound planning for quality with fact-based decision making, variability reduction, defect prevention and fast response systems that include recognition of the internal customer and the triple role of supplier/processor/customer at all processes
- Integration of and mutual cooperation with suppliers based on longer-term partnership relations

- Sensitivity to competitive comparisons via benchmarking, including "best in class" on noncompetitive but significant processes

- Productivity, cost reduction and profitability enhancements

- Strong leadership by management at all levels with effective creation of policies, vision, mission, values, guiding principles, goals and support communicated and implemented throughout the organization by example, with the establishment of a compatible corporate culture.

The ISO 9000:2000 series standards achieve a great deal by offering a consistent set of requirements that can be applied globally for quality systems. In the same way, the MBNQA criteria prescribe a set of de facto requirements, more closely aligned with the concepts of total quality, and build on the base established by the ISO 9000:2000 series. Therefore, these two approaches are complementary and should be considered jointly in the development of a quality system. However, there are elements of total quality not contained in either of these two approaches. Most of the differences lie in the emphasis, approach and philosophy embodied in Deming's 14 points for management (see Deming, 1986, 1994). The term Deming-based TQM system is used in the following discussion.

Perhaps implied, but never required specifically, is the "transformation" emphasized by Deming. This intangible would be difficult to score or verify. A Deming-based TQM system requires the substantial commitment of personal time and resources of senior managers in "transforming" the organization. Quality cannot be just another aspect of the business; it must become the way business is conducted. While ISO 9000:2000 registration does call for more involved and intensive support by senior management, it is not nearly so demanding as the Deming-based TQM "transformation" initiative. The MBNQA criteria for "Leadership" comes much closer to Deming's expectations.

Deming-based TQM is much more open than MBNQA or ISO 9000. It has no firm requirements other than to improve quality; to decrease costs by less rework, fewer mistakes, fewer delays, better use of machine-time and materials by the use of applied statistics; to improve productivity; to capture the market with better quality and lower price by meeting and/or exceeding customer needs through an understanding of the organization and the effects of current management practices; to remain in business; and to provide jobs and more jobs. It expects the senior managers of an organization to consider management style through a fact-based scientific examination of Deming's 14 points and then prove or disprove the implementation of those points as they apply to the organization. Deming expects senior managers to establish a controlled, customer-focused, continuously improving organization. That kind of organization has requirements, but practical application must define those requirements in a Deming-based TQM system. That is, form should follow function and necessity or potential benefit. Documentation showing how processes are to be accomplished is necessary. But it is up to an organization to document processes to communicate effectively with those who need to know or might benefit from knowing. A Deming-based TQM system leaves the details entirely up to the organization. Deming-based TQM involves the most organizational involvement and organizational change of the three approaches.

Deming urges companies to drive out fear; eliminate slogans, exhortations and management by objective; remove barriers that rob people of pride in workmanship and institute education. These points are not addressed in the ISO 9000:2000 series and are not too explicit in the criteria of MBNQA.

ISO 9000:2000 has several highly specific concerns about inspection and testing that could be at odds with Deming-based TQM. Deming emphasizes that an organization should "cease dependence on inspection to achieve quality." Deming says that companies should "eliminate the need for inspection on a mass basis by building quality into the product in the first place." The ISO 9000:2000 series provides for cases in which in-process control makes later inspection unnecessary, but also emphasizes inspection by requirement. The ISO 9000:2000 series and Deming are in agreement that when inspection and testing are required, those doing the work should be trained and given appropriate equipment.

The ISO 9000:2000 series provides for the use of statistical techniques but does not emphasize them. If statistical process control methods are used, the ISO standard requires that procedures for SPC tools be documented and implemented as documented with appropriate training provided. The basis of Deming-based TQM is statistical understanding.

Deming-based TQM and MBNQA differ greatly in their approaches to benchmarking. Deming recommends that companies spend "time and effort focusing on what customers want and need, not what competitors are doing." Deming says that if you treat your customers right and continuously improve in what you provide to them, your competitors will be watching you, and you will always be ahead of those competitors, because you will be continuously improving while they are trying to catch up to you. Deming favors comparison of quality results and comparison of support-system quality results, but recommends that this comparison be made against the organization's previous record, not as a benchmarking device against competitors' results. Now, both MBNQA and ISO encourage benchmarking to understand the needs and expectations of customers.

Deming is less concerned about measuring customer satisfaction and more concerned about developing a focused, continually improving relationship with customers and suppliers. ISO 9004:2000 is very specific about the achievement of ongoing improvement measured through the satisfaction of customers. While Deming supports organizational leaders helping to improve public quality awareness, it is not a requirement as expressed by MBNQA. On the other hand, MBNQA does require that award recipients share best practices among US organizations of all types.

Deming-based TQM offers little guidance on either the nature of the work or how to set up a system. A Deming-based TQM system creates a learning organization. This learning tenet of TQM makes selecting a Deming-based approach to TQM even more persuasive. Deming provides depth of theory as well as application. Deming points out, "There is no learning without theory." He goes on to say: "All theory is wrong. Some is useful. Of course all theory is wrong! If it were right, it wouldn't be theory, now would it? It would be fact. But without theory, we cannot learn. Experience alone teaches nothing. If we have a theory, then experience can help us to learn."

After an organization has become effective through TQM transformation and has become a learning organization, the use of the MBNQA quality criteria can be an excellent means to improve an already effective organization, even if it doesn't actually apply for the award. However, an organization that applies for the Baldrige Award is likely to put more useful pressure on itself than one using the criteria solely on an internal basis.

It is reasonable for a company to spend some time internally with the MBNQA criteria. The MBNQA criteria are self-descriptive. Even if it is difficult to measure the number of points achieved when self-scoring, the practice is worthwhile. Winning the Baldrige award should not be a company's initial goal. The intent should be to improve. After sufficient improvement has been accomplished, then application should be made for potential recognition.

References

ANSI/ASQC Zl 15 (1979), American National Standard, *Generic Guidelines for Quality Systems*, December 19, 1979, American National Standards Institute, Inc.

Deming, W. E. (1986), *Out of the Crisis*, Cambridge, Massachusetts: Massachusetts Institute of Technology, Center for Advanced Engineering Study.

Deming, W. E. (1994), *The New Economics for Industry, Government, and Education*, 2nd ed., Cambridge, Massachusetts: Massachusetts Institute of Technology, Center for Advanced Engineering Study.

Hart, C. (1993), "What's Wrong and Right With the Baldrige Award," *Chief Executive*, No. 90 (Nov.-Dec. 1993), pp. 36-47.

Peach, R. W. (1994), "Planning the Journey From ISO 9000 to TQM," *ASQC 48th Quality Congress Proceedings*, May 24-26, 1994, Las Vegas, pp. 864-872.

Peach, R. W. (1996), "Putting the ISO 9000 Family of Standards to Use," *ASQC 50th Annual Quality Congress Proceedings*, May 13-15, 1996, Chicago, pp. 351-355.

Rampey, J. and Roberts, H. (1992), "Perspectives on Total Quality," *Proceedings of Total Quality Forum IV November 1992*, Cincinnati, Ohio.

Challenges Facing the ISO 9000 Industry

by Robert W. Peach*

Despite the global impact of ISO 9000, there are a number of challenges that can affect the credibility of the series and its continued acceptance. These challenges include documenting the scope of certification/registration; effectively implementing the requirements for continual improvement, statistical techniques and the system approach to management; maintaining the accuracy of translations and interpretations of the standards; considering alternate routes to registration; dealing with industry-specific adoptions of the ISO standards; applying the ISO 9001 standard to computer software; increasing compatibility with ISO standards for environmental management systems; using the ISO 9000 standards in nonmanufacturing industries; and building on ISO 9001 toward Total Quality Management.

ISO 9000 as an Industry

In a sense, the worldwide activities concerned with implementing the ISO 9000 standards are themselves an "industry." The registrar/certification bodies, accreditation bodies, auditor certification bodies, course provider organizations, consultants, auditors, publishers of trade magazines and books, journalists, university and other academic activities constitute the infrastructure of a full-fledged industry.

Indeed, many organizations that engage in these activities operate internation-

This chapter was originally written by the late Donald W. Marquardt.

ally, with personnel in many countries. ISO 9000 faces the types of challenges typical of a rapidly growing industry. Some of the challenges relate to the integrity and credibility of the industry and its component activities.

The Challenge of Credibility of Registration

Programs for third-party certification/registration of quality systems have grown worldwide and the impact on the global economy has become enormous.

Existing international, regional and national standards and guides for implementation of such third-party programs provide the framework for programs worldwide. This framework includes a requirements standard, core guidance standards and a number of supporting standards. These standards have been prepared by the ISO TC 176 committee. Implementation guides, such as ISO/IEC Guide 62, to be replaced by ISO 17011, have been prepared by the ISO/IEC Committee on Conformity Assessment (CASCO). The elements of these various standards and guides have been adopted by regional bodies such as the European Union and by many nations worldwide.

In addition, many nations have set up implementation programs that reflect the three-tiered concept of certification, accreditation and recognition.

- Quality systems certification/registration bodies (registrars) evaluate quality management systems based on requirement standards.

- Accreditation bodies evaluate the management systems of registrars for conformity to international guides.

- Recognition bodies, usually government affiliated, provide national recognition of the quality systems certification (registration) and accreditation programs, and thus facilitate the establishment of mutual recognition among nations in regulated areas.

The marketplace credibility of this network of international programs rests upon the elements of assurance and ethical principles incorporated in the various standards and guides and their implementation. The high degree of success to date in implementing registration programs around the world indicates that the base of assurance elements and ethical principles is sound, at least in broad outline.

As registration programs become widespread and involve multiple industry/economic sectors and multiple cultures, new complexities are revealed.

The Registrar Accreditation Board (RAB), the US accreditation body, has carefully evaluated the elements of assurance and ethical principles to ensure a credible program, giving due consideration to the complexities of the international system. The three components of these elements are

1. Defining the scope of registration of an organization's quality system (i.e., identifying exclusions, geographic sites, products, portions of the supply chain)

2. Policy, principles and implementation regarding conflict of interest by registrars accredited under the ANSI/RAB program

3. Code of Conduct, confidentiality and ethics, for persons working on behalf of RAB.

All three components are considered essential to achieve the goal of marketplace credibility. The full text of the components is included as a part of Chapter 7.

Some of the key points described in the first component, the scope of registration, are discussed below.

Scope of Registration of an Organization's Quality System

In current practice worldwide there is great variability in the documented definitions of the scopes of quality management system registrations. This variability is observed from organization to organization for a given registrar, from registrar to registrar in a given nation and from one nation to another. The term "registrar" is more commonly used in North America; the term "certification body" is used in Europe and elsewhere.

Greater consistency in defining and documenting the scope of registration is an essential prerequisite to establishing marketplace credibility of quality management system registration, and to negotiating meaningful mutual recognition arrangements among nations.

There are other important benefits beyond the benefits of marketplace credibility, for registrars will benefit if the ground rules for defining scope are consistent for all parties. To adequately describe the scope of registration of an organization's quality system, four basic questions must be answered:

Which Elements of the Standard Are Selected?

The statement of scope should identify the boundaries of the organization's activities that are covered by the registered organization's quality management system. With the discontinuance of the ISO 9002 and ISO 9003 standards in the 2000 publication, all organizations seeking registration/certification are to use ISO 9001. Since not all clauses necessarily apply to all organizations, provision has been made to permit and document appropriate exclusions of specific portions of ISO 9001, but only for Clause 7, Product Realization. Permission for exclusions is contained in Clause 1.2 of ISO 9001. The statement of scope is to identify such exclusions. See Chapter 9 for discussion of the clause exclusion process.

Which Geographic Sites or Operating Units?

The statement of scope should identify the boundaries of the registered organization quality management system, in terms of the geographic location(s) of the facilities and activities, or the operating units involved. An operating unit may be, for example, a regional office or a ship.

Which Products?

The statement of scope should identify the boundaries of the registered quality management system in terms of the commercial product(s) that are processed. The term "products" includes all four generic product categories: hardware, software, processed materials and services.

The customer should be informed whether the product received is processed within the registered system, particularly in situations where the organization may deal with multiple products at the same site or operating unit, and where not all of the products are processed within the registered quality system.

Which Portions of the Supply Chain?

The procedure should inform the customer regarding:

- The starting points of the organization's registered operations (e.g., the raw materials, parts, components, services and intermediate products that are provided by its suppliers)

- The ending points of the organization's registered operations (i.e., the remaining steps on the way to the ultimate consumer that are excluded from the organization's registered operations)

- The nature of the added value that has been provided by the organization's registered operations.

Where the registered quality management system represents only a fraction of the organization's operations, or a fraction of the total added value in the product, this should be stated in registration documentation, and as a consequence, customers are to be made aware of this fact.

Procedures should not allow organizations who wish to be registered, but want to exclude portions of their operations from scrutiny by the registrar, to declare the excluded portions to be operations of their suppliers. It should not matter whether the excluded portions are in another nation, elsewhere in the same nation or simply another part of the same production site.

Procedures for this element of scope would also apply to support functions that are critical to product quality, such as a test laboratory, which may not be included in the organization's registered quality management system.

The Current Status

In practice registration certificates often are deficient because they do not provide definitive answers to the above four questions. Appendix Part 1 of Chapter 7 suggests ways that registrars can implement the above requirements. Four steps in this process are proposed:

1. Each accredited registrar provides information on the face of each registration certificate issued on the four elements discussed above.

2. All publishers of registration lists show the same information.

3. Each registered organization maintains a mechanism to inform customers about the four elements, such as providing copies of registration certifcates when appropriate.

4. Each registrar establishes and maintains procedures and records regarding the above elements.

Policy, principles and implementation regarding conflict of interest by ANSI/RAB-accredited registrars and code of conduct (for persons working on behalf of RAB) appear as Appendix Parts 2 and 3 of Chapter 7.

Responsibilities of the Organizations Involved

ANSI-RAB and the US program do not stand alone. The credibility of registration issues is of international concern.

The implementation of the ethical principles and elements of assurance incorporated in the various standards and guides is clearly important to the credibility of quality management systems registration. Who should take responsibility for these? At a fundamental level, every person involved in any facet of quality management system registration should take personal responsibility.

Specific organizations must have clear responsibilities for implementing the recommended procedures. For example, the code of conduct discussed in Appendix Part 3 of Chapter 7 is to be implemented at the accreditation body level, but corresponding codes of conduct are required of organizations operating at the registration level. The registrar conflict of interest policy and principles discussed in Chapter 7 Appendix Part 2 is to be implemented at the registration level. The scope of registration definition discussed in Chapter 7 Appendix Part 1 is to be implemented jointly by organizations and registrars.

In each instance there are other organizational entities that have defined roles.

For example, registrars audit organizations for conformance; accreditation bodies audit registrars; and recognition bodies have formal processes to establish credibility for recognition.

Those who write international standards (e.g., ISO TC 176) and guides (e.g., ISO CASCO) have their own defined responsibilities. They set the ground rules by means of the standards and guides. Table 22-1 contains a listing of quality management system standards available and projected.

The Challenge of Continual Improvement

The philosophy of quality management and quality assurance has changed over the years. In the 1960s the virtually universal perspective of business managers was, "If it ain't broke, don't fix it."

In that philosophical environment, maintaining the status quo in quality achievement prevailed in most of industry and commerce. Today, the status quo philosophy of the 1960s is giving way to a philosophy of continual improvement. The addition of requirements for continual improvement in ISO 9001:2000 recognizes this change. Continual improvement is increasingly necessary for economic survival in the global economy, and is becoming a widely pursued goal. It is the only reliable route to sustaining marketplace advantage for both customer and supplying organization.

The focus of quality assurance standardization is now on prevention of nonconformities. This requires a "process" focus, which is reflected in the required documentation.

In the first years of use of the ISO 9000 standards an unfortunate status quo mind-set was adopted by many registrars/certifiers and their auditors. Reminiscent of the 1960s, it is characterized by the ditty, "Say what you do, do what you say." This simple advice is correct as far as it goes, but falls far short of the requirements in the ISO 9001 standard, both as originally developed in 1987 and also with the 2000 edition. The status quo mind-set ignores the linked requirements in ISO 9001 to demonstrate continual adequacy of the quality management system for business objectives and customer satisfaction.

While requirements or guidance in accomplishing continual improvement can be found by searching previous ISO 9000 editions, they are much more explicit in ISO 9001:2000. Specific requirements are called out not only in Clause 8.5.1, Continual Improvement, but also in:

0.2 Process approach (such an approach emphasizes the importance of continual improvement of processes ...) Further: The "Act" stage of Plan, Do Check, Act is to take action to continually improve process performance.

5.5.2 The input from the management review is to include information on recommendations for improvement.

5.6.2.3 Review input and output — Management review should include information on recommendations for improvement.

6.1 Provision of resources, and 8.1 Measurement — to continually improve the effectiveness of the QMS.

8.4 Analysis of data — to evaluate where continual improvement of QMS effectiveness can be made.

If the ISO 9000 industry fails to adequately embrace the continual improvement requirements in the ISO 9001 standard, the value of the standards themselves will be seriously compromised in the global marketplace.

The Challenge of Statistical Techniques

From the earliest days of the quality movement, statistical techniques have been recognized as having an important role. In fact, during the 1940s and 1950s, statistical techniques were viewed as the predominant aspect of quality control. During succeeding decades the management system increasingly took center stage. In the 1987 version of ISO 9001, Clause 4.20 on statistical techniques seemed to pay only lip service to its subject. The implementation of quality management standards worldwide has apparently reinforced the deterioration of emphasis on statistical techniques.

It is critical that this situation be remedied, recognizing that statistical techniques and management systems each have their important place in quality. The 1994 version of ISO 9001 contained explicit, meaningful requirements relating to statistical techniques, citing their relation to "process capability" and "product characteristics." These requirements, if conscientiously implemented, would assure that statistical techniques assumed their important place in quality under the ISO 9001 umbrella.

The complete restructuring of ISO 9001 in the 2000 edition provides the opportunity for application of statistical tools during realization stages (design, control of production) and in measurement, analysis and improvement (monitoring and measurement of processes and product). Instead of calling for a single statement of the need for statistical applications, the standard provides ample opportunities to apply statistical techniques to control and measurement. However, in the spirit of allowing organizations the authority to determine the manner in which the requirements of the standard are applied, the present wording of the standard gives the freedom not to make use of statistical methods unless it is clear that the operational situation calls for their use.

Unfortunately, the majority of personnel in the existing infrastructure of auditors, registrars and accreditation bodies, and their supporting consultants, training course providers et. al. have limited knowledge or experience in statistical techniques. Consequently, where many observed that statistical methods received too little emphasis in 1994, that situation is likely to be continued or aggravated. With the resurgence of applications of six-sigma techniques in many organizations, widespread interest in statistical methods may be returning, complementing the requirements of ISO 9001.

The Challenge of Standards Interpretation

In actual application, ISO standards are published by ISO in English and French (and often in Russian), the official ISO languages. ISO requires that "the texts in the different official language versions shall be technically equivalent and structurally identical," (ISO/IEC Directives, Part 1, 1.5, 1989). Sometimes ISO itself publishes standards in languages other than the official languages; then "each is regarded as an original-language version" (ISO/IEC Directives, Part 1, F.3, 1995). "However, only the terms and definitions given in the official languages can be considered as ISO terms and definitions" (ISO/IEC Directives, Part 3, B2.2, 1989).

When a nation "adopts" an ISO standard the standard is first translated by the national body into the national language and processed through the official national procedures for adoption. In the United States the translation issue is minimal, consisting, when deemed necessary, of replacement of British English (the ISO official English) with American English spellings or other stylistic editorial details. In the United States the adoption process follows American National Standards Institute procedures, which ensure the objectivity, fairness, and lack of bias that might favor any constituency; these are requirements for all American national standards.

In situations where the national language is not one of the ISO official languages, ISO has no formal procedure for validating the accuracy of the national body translation. Translating from one language to another always presents challenges when great accuracy of meaning should be preserved. There are many ways in which the meaning may be changed by a translation. Such changes result in different implementations of the standard and are a potential source of nontariff trade barriers in international trade.

The challenge of interpretations of the ISO 9000 standards goes beyond problems of translation into languages other than the official ISO languages. In the global economy many situations of use are encountered; the intended meaning of the standard is not always clear to those applying the standard in some situations of use. For such situations any member body of ISO may choose to set up interpretation procedures. At the time of publication of this *Handbook*, a new international mechanism for developing official ISO interpretations was being tested.

When the situation of use is a two-party contractual situation between the supplier organization and the customer organization, differences of interpretation should normally be revealed and mutually resolved at an early stage (e.g., during contract negotiation and contract review). Official international interpretations become more necessary in third-party certification/registration situations. In that environment, interpretations must be applicable in a wide range of situations, and must not be prejudicial to maintaining a level playing field. Contract negotiations between supplying organization and customer are then free to focus on only those quality management system requirements, if any, that go beyond the scope of the relevant ISO 9000 requirements, plus the technical product specifications.

The Challenge of Alternate Routes to Registration

Organizations differ with regard to the status of their quality management efforts. Some are at an advanced state of implementation and effectiveness. Others have hardly begun. Most are at some intermediate state. The ISO 9001 standard has as a primary purpose the facilitation of international trade. It is, therefore, positioned to ensure a level of effectiveness that is adequate for reducing non-tariff international trade barriers. This required level of effectiveness should increase with time, as improvements in ISO 9001:2000 take effect.

Some organizations have well-established, advanced quality management systems based on an approach that may go well beyond the requirements of ISO 9001. For such organizations, the cost of registration/certification by the usual third-party route may be found to be high compared to the incremental value added to their quality management system.

In the United States, a number of such companies that have major international presence, including but not limited to ones in the electronics and computer industry, have been working to devise an approach that would gain international acceptance. The approach takes full cognizance of existing quality management system status to reduce the cost of certification/registration, while supporting international trade by providing the assurance conferred by accredited certification/registration. The procedures for operation are contained in an annex to IAF Guidance to ISO/IEC Guide 62, requirements for operation of certification/registration systems. These may be incorporated into the text of the guidance document when it is revised as ISO/IEC 17011.

The Challenge of Industry-Specific Adoption and Extension of ISO 9000 Standards

Industry-specific adoption and extensions of the ISO 9000 standards have been made in several sectors of the global economy. Such adoption and extension can be effective in those industries with circumstances where appropriate and consistent ground rules can be developed and implemented consistently industry-wide. While such circumstances have occurred in industries with already well-established, industry-specific or supplier-specific quality management system requirements documents, the opportunity for such extensions may apply to other industries as well.

In the years preceding publication of the 1987 editions of the ISO 9000 standards, various original equipment manufacturers (OEMs) in the automotive industry developed company-specific proprietary quality system requirements. These requirements were part of OEM contract arrangements for purchasing parts, materials and subassemblies from the thousands of suppliers. The OEMs had large staffs of second-party auditors to verify that these OEM-specific requirements were being met.

Upon publication of ISO 9001:1994 the major US OEMs began implementation of QS-9000, which incorporates ISO 9001:1994 verbatim, plus industry-specific supplementary requirements. Some of the supplementary requirements are essentially prescriptive approaches to some of the generic ISO 9001 requirements; others are additional quality system requirements that have been agreed by the major OEMs; a few are OEM-specific. At the time of publication of this *Handbook*, an international supplementary standard for the automotive industry, ISO/TS 16949, was just published. It and QS-9000 are discussed in detail in Chapter 13.

The aerospace industry has followed a similar course, by consolidating and modifying existing industry supplier quality systems requirements around ISO 9001 and adopting Aerospace Quality Management System Standard AS9100. The content and application of AS91000 is described in Chapter 15.

The telecommunications industry established an industry forum (QuEST) and developed TL 9000, a comprehensive supplement to ISO 9001. It is unique in containing industry metrics or measurements that provide a mechanism for uniformly measuring quality throughout the industry. This supplementary document is described in Chapter 16. Even those who are not part of the telecommunications industry should find this industry-specific approach of interest.

The Challenge of Computer Software

The global economy has become permeated with electronic information technology (IT). The IT industry now plays a major role in shaping and driving the global economy. As in past major technological advances, the world seems fundamentally very different, and paradoxically, fundamentally the same. Computer software development occupies a central position in this paradox.

First, it should be noted that computer software development is both an industry and a discipline.

Second, many IT practitioners emphasize that computer software issues are complicated by the multiplicity of ways that computer software quality may be critical in an organization's business. For example:

- The product may be complex software whose functional design requirements are specified by the customer.
- The organization may actually write most of its software product, or may integrate off-the-shelf packaged software from its own suppliers.
- The organization may incorporate computer software/firmware into its product, which may be primarily hardware and/or services.
- The organization may develop and/or purchase from suppliers software that will be used in its own design and/or production processes for its product.

It is important, however, to acknowledge that hardware, processed materials, and services often are involved in an organization's business in these same, multiple ways, too.

There is general consensus worldwide that:

- The generic quality management system activities and associated requirements in ISO 9001 are relevant to computer software, just as they are relevant in other generic product categories (hardware, other forms of software, processed materials and services).
- There are some things that are different in applying ISO 9001 to computer software.
- There is no worldwide consensus as to which things, if any, are different enough to make a difference, and what to do about any things that are different enough to make a difference.

ISO 9000-3 concerning computer software was developed and published as a means to deal with this important, paradoxical issue. This standard provides guidelines for applying ISO 9001 to the development, supply and maintenance of computer software. ISO 9000-3 has been useful and widely used. It offers guidance that enhances understanding of the requirements of ISO 9001. At the time of publication, ISO 9000-3 is undergoing revision to be compatible with ISO 9001:2000. Chapter 19 discusses application of ISO 9001:2000 to software development.

The Challenge of Environmental Management Systems

Environmental management systems and their relation to quality management systems is a classic example of a challenge from the perspective of the ISO 9000 standards. Companies are likely to have to do business under both sets of requirements: the ISO 9000 standards from ISO TC 176 and the ISO 14000 standards from ISO TC 207. The opportunity for mutually beneficial consistency promises important benefits.

These benefits relate to the operational effectiveness of having one consistent management approach in both areas of the business activities, and can translate into cost benefits. The ISO Technical Management Board mandated that TC 176 and TC 207 achieve compatibility of their standards and this objective is being achieved.

In ISO standards development , the compatibility of the ISO 9000 standards and the ISO 14000 standards is one part of the standardization job. The implementation part requires that similar harmonization and compatibility be established in each nation in the infrastructure of accreditation bodies, certification/registration bodies and auditor certification bodies, operating under internationally harmonized guidelines. This topic is discussed in Chapter 25.

The Challenge of Application in Nonmanufacturing Organizations

Since its original publication in 1987, the ISO 9000 series has been manufacturing oriented. This is apparent in the original table of contents of ISO 9001, which follows a manufacturing sequence including design, purchasing, process control, inspection and delivery. In spite of this structure, a considerable number of organizations that do not manufacture a product have applied ISO 9001 to their situations. These included a host of "service industry" organizations with activities supporting manufacturing, such as distribution and office activities, but also other industries such as health care and education. These service applications learned to adapt the ISO 9001 content to their needs.

This situation existed until the publication of ISO 9001:2000, which adopted the "process model" classifying activities into processes such as resources, realization and measurement. This effectively breaks away from a manufacturing sequence, thereby accommodating the needs of all organizations. This opened the way to direct application of ISO 9001 to the host of nonmanufacturing organizations, and already is providing an incentive for even more organizations to use ISO 9001.

The Challenge of Linkage to Total Quality Management

From the earliest days of development of the family of ISO 9000 standards, ISO 9001 was considered to articulate a basic set of quality system requirements that applied to, and were intended to be attainable by, all organizations. ISO 9004 was conceived as a quality management standard (as indicated by its title) containing substantially more elements that were not identified as requirements, but provided a bridge to improved control of all activities in the organization.

The process of starting with ISO 9001 and, having met its requirement, progressing further up the quality systems ladder to ISO 9004, has happened only occasionally. More frequently, organizations looked to the criteria of quality awards (such as the Malcolm Baldrige National Quality Award in the United States) for elements describing a level of quality management capability far exceeding the basic requirements of ISO 9001.

Underlying the difficulty of migrating from ISO 9001 to better things was the lack of compatibility of the clause structures of ISO 9001 and ISO 9004. The instructions received by standards writers for the year 2000 revision was to make ISO 9001 and ISO 9004 a "consistent pair." This not only enables them to be used side by side, but enables the direct and selective application of ISO 9004 content to quality management systems that already meet ISO 9001 requirements. In addition to the new harmony of clause structure, ISO 9004 now has the entire text of ISO 9001 embedded in it, emphasizing the relationship of the two standards. The challenge to the user is to put this structure of the ISO 9000 standards to effective use, resulting in ever-improving quality management capability. A discussion of the content and use of ISO 9004:2000 is contained in Chapter 4.

The ISO quality management standards have never claimed to be the only route to disciplined quality management. A more recent development is Six Sigma methodology, which is gaining momentum throughout business and industry. Impressive cost reduction and quality improvements have been reported by organizations following the Six Sigma methodology, which makes use of customer and financial information for setting targeted objectives, then following carefully planned and methodically executed projects. Cornerstones of the Six Sigma approach include customer focus, disciplined project management and rigorous analysis.

A summary of Six Sigma elements appears in "The Six Sigma Methodology."

ISO 9000 and Six Sigma can and should complement each other. When used in the same organization, they can be most effective if part of a coordinated effort. The technique of following a methodical, structured approach to accomplishing identified goals is common to both Six Sigma and ISO 9000 implementation. This includes top management support and involvement, process control, aiming at full customer satisfaction by meeting all requirements and a structured approach to consistency in conducting all activities.

Operationally, whether solving problems or designing new products or processes, a well-developed and structured quality system will support the efforts of Six Sigma teams. It provides basic process definitions and capabilities, consistent operating procedures and documentation and records that can provide at least initial information for project identification and scoping. The presence of a well-defined quality system in accordance with ISO 9000 provides a mechanism through which the benefits of Six Sigma projects can be institutionalized.

The Six Sigma Methodology

Executing the approach under a directive from top management.

Identifying those quality attributes most important to the customer.

Designing to meet customer requirements, including products, services and the processes that produce them.

Identifying prime opportunities for quality improvement and cost reduction.

Setting very high, but attainable, quality goals — while not perfection, as close to perfection as possible. (Six Sigma, a measure of excellence, expresses substandard quality in parts per million, with goals typically about 3.4 ppm, or less than 1/1000 of 1 percent.)

Providing formal, comprehensive training for those managing and applying the methodology. The highest rank of professional, "Black Belt," attains credentials through training, examination, and a demonstration of competence through effective application of the techniques.

Conducting activities project-by-project, each with defined goals and progress tracking.

Applying the approach to all parts of the organization, not limiting to manufacturing and service activities.

Basing actions on valid data, driving efforts with these data.

Quantifying and reporting the process capability of production, service and administrative operations. Controlling variability (reducing where called for) so that each process is capable of producing product totally within specified requirements.

Removing all internal inefficiencies that may be adversely affecting cost and quality.

Recognizing those whose efforts have contributed to success.

Gearing to maintain progress already made, by formalizing procedures, institutionalizing Six Sigma methodologies and continuing the cycle of improvement.

APPENDICES

Author Biographies

Bamford, Robert

Robert Bamford has an M.A. in mathematics, and has managed training development, technical publications, professional services and third-party software development. His more than 20 years of experience include the implementation of a Crosby-based Total Quality Management System, facilitating quality courses, managing education teams and serving on a corporate quality council.

Bamford is a founding partner of Software Systems Quality Consulting (SSQC). Since 1990, SSQC has specialized in supporting software, hardware, manufacturing and service organizations in the definition and implementation of engineering practices, quality assurance and testing, business process reengineering, ISO 9000 registration and CMM implementation. SSQC offers HM2, a unique, hybrid appraisal method that defines and correlates the position of an organization with respect to both ISO 9001 and CMM. The results of an HM2 assessment are a plan and framework for improving software engineering processes and for implementing the requirements of the two models.

Bamford has developed and published numerous courses, auditing tools, research papers and articles on interpreting and applying the ISO 9000 standards and guidelines and the SEI Capability Maturity Model for Software. His articles have appeared in *Quality Systems Update*, IEEE COMPUTER, *ISO 9000 Handbook*, *CrossTALK* and *Software Marketing Journal*.

He has presented research papers at numerous national and international conferences, including those sponsored by the American Society for Quality (ASQ),

Pacific Northwest Software Quality (PNSQC), the Software Publishers Association (SPA), Software Technology Support Center (STSC), the Software Engineering Institute (SEI) and Software Research Inc.. His courses have been attended by software engineering professionals from many of the country's leading technology companies. His courses have been sponsored for their members by professional associations, including the ASQ, CSU Long Beach's Software Engineering Forum for Training, Semiconductor Equipment and Materials International (SEMI), Software Engineering Institute (SEI), UC Berkeley and UC Santa Cruz. His software development clients have successfully achieved ISO 9000 registration and advanced CMM maturity levels.

Bamford is an active US Technical Advisory Group (TAG) member in the International Organization for Standardization (ISO) Joint Technical Committe (JTC) 1 Subcommittee (SC) 7 - Software Engineering Standards subcommittee, which is responsible for the development and maintenance of ISO 12207, ISO 15504 (SPICE) and ISO 9000-3. He has performed ISO 9000 registration audits as an external resource under contract to BSI.

Bauder, Larry

Larry Bauder has led and assisted two software organizations and a pharmaceutical research group in establishing and maintaining formal quality systems. He has managed the development of training products and written a training development standard for accrediting a technical training organization. He has been a product introduction manager and product launch committee chair for several software products.

Through both success and frustration, as a consultant and as an employee, Bauder has learned from these experiences. He also spent 14 years developing training products and delivering training to manufacturing engineers and product designers on the use of computer-aided design and data management for improvement of products and production.

Bigelow, James S.

The late James S. Bigelow joined TQM Consulting in 1996, after completing 33 years of service with ExxonMobil Chemical Company. During his career with ExxonMobil, he had worldwide assignments in engineering, marketing, product and supply planning and manufacturing before becoming an internal quality consultant in 1982. He was well versed in ISO 9000, QS-9000, the Baldrige Criteria and simple statistical tools, particularly as applied to the chemical and process industries (CPI).

Bigelow co-authored four books as a member of the Chemical and Process Industries Division of the American Society for Quality (ASQ). He was an ASQ Fellow and represented the Chemical and Process Industry Division on ANSI Z-1 Committee on Quality.

Bigelow became a member of the US TAG to ISO Technical Committee (TC) 176 in 1988. He served as chemical industry liaison delegate and was one of the four worldwide team leaders that prepared the revisions to ISO 9001 and 9004 for the year 2000. In 1997, he was awarded the ANSI "Outstanding Professional Achievement Award" for his contributions to the US effort to support ISO 9000.

Bigelow was an examiner for the Malcolm Baldrige National Quality Award and served on the Texas Quality Award Board of Overseers and Panel of Judges. He was ASQ CPID standards chair and served on the Independent Advisory Board of ABS - Quality Evaluations, an ISO 9000 registrar.

Bigelow was educated at Lehigh University and had B.S. degrees in mechanical and electrical engineering. He completed extensive training in quality philosophies, systems and tools, group dynamics, team building, benchmarking and business process reengineering. His hobbies included golf, yacht racing, photography, computers, singing in the church choir and developing his ranch property with his wife Lynne.

Bransky, Joe

Joe Bransky joined General Motors Corporation in 1968 as work standards engineer at Delphi Chassis Operations (formerly New Departure Hyatt Bearings Division) in Sandusky, Ohio. He held various posts in industrial engineering, human resources and manufacturing leading to his appointment as manufacturing manager responsible for production operations at the Sandusky plant. In 1984, he was appointed to the corporate quality staff of General Motors. He worked on various quality improvement initiatives including the development and implementation of the Quality Network, a joint Total Quality partnership of GM management and the UAW. In 1989, he was appointed as director, corporate quality, responsible for corporatewide internal customer satisfaction measurement. In 1991, he was assigned coordination responsibility for the North American Operations Quality Board. In 1995, Bransky was appointed as director, quality systems, which included implementing quality assessment, including ISO and QS-9000, for NAO Manufacturing and Assembly Centers. In 1997, he was also appointed dean of the Quality College for the newly formed General Motors University. Since retiring in January 1999, he has been a quality consultant and was appointed as GM's representative to the QS-9000 Supplier Quality

Requirements Task Force and the ISO/TS 16949 International Automotive Task Force (IATF).

While at GM, Bransky served in various capacities to promote quality initiatives:

- Representative to the Malcolm Baldrige National Quality Award
- Corporate sustaining membership - American Society for Quality
- Conference Board Quality Council III
- Leadership Steering Committee (A partnership of major corporations and universities to promote TQ in higher education)
- Michigan Quality Council Board of Trustees and Executive Board.

Bransky holds a B.S. in education/mathematics from Kent State University in 1965. In 1980, he was appointed as a GM Sloan Fellow at Stanford University, and in 1981 he received a master's degree from the Stanford University Graduate School of Business. In addition he has continued with professional training and certification in quality- and management-related areas including Plexus-ASQ QS-9000 Trainer/Coach Certification.

Bransky is also a member of the Board of Trustees at St. Mary's College, Orchard Lake, Michigan, and resides with his wife Phyllis in Huron, Ohio.

Brumm, Eugenia K.

Eugenia K. Brumm, president of the Quality Records Institute, is an independent consultant and trainer with over 16 years of experience in records management, document control and quality systems. She provides consulting, training seminars and on-site workshops in all areas of records management, specializing in compliance and regulatory records requirements. Through her international seminars and workshops, she has trained over 3,000 people in various aspects of records management techniques and principles, including records inventories, retention schedule development, records protection methods, filing systems, forms management, feasibility analysis, records costing issues, optical disk technology, micrographics and inactive records storage.

Brumm is a former professor from the University of Texas at Austin, where she developed a graduate-level records management program. She has also worked for the nuclear industry, where she developed the records management program, the document control system and the product certification process. She has designed and implemented successful records management programs within quality environments, for private business and industry as well as for local and state government. She is frequently requested as a speaker in ISO 9000 and records management.

Brumm holds a Ph.D. in library and information science from the University of Illinois as well as an M.S. in library science and an M.A. in slavic languages from that same University. She is author of the book *Managing Records for ISO 9000 Compliance*, published by ASQ Quality Press. She has written for *ARMA Records Management Quarterly, Quality Progress, Records and Retrieval Report, Information Management Review, Document Management* and other publications. She is a member of ASQ (American Society for Quality) and ARMA (Association for Record Managers and Administrators) and serves on the ARMA International ISO 9000 Task Force Committee.

Deibler, William J.

William J. Deibler II has an M.S. in computer science and 20-plus years of experience in the computer industry, primarily in the areas of software and systems development, software testing and software quality assurance. Deibler has extensive experience in managing and implementing CMM- and ISO 9001-based process improvement in software engineering environments.

Deibler is a founding partner of Software Systems Quality Consulting (SSQC). Since 1990, SSQC has specialized in supporting software, hardware, manufacturing and service organizations in the definition and implementation of engineering practices, quality assurance and testing, business process reengineering, ISO 9000 registration and CMM implementation. SSQC offers HM2, a unique, hybrid appraisal method that defines and correlates the position of an organization with respect to both ISO 9001 and the CMM. The results of an HM2 assessment are a plan and framework for improving software engineering processes and for implementing the requirements of the two models.

Deibler has developed and published numerous courses, auditing tools, research papers and articles on interpreting and applying the ISO 9000 standards and guidelines and the SEI Capability Maturity Model for Software. His articles have appeared in *Quality Systems Update*, IEEE COMPUTER, *ISO 9000 Handbook, CrossTALK* and *Software Marketing Journal*.

He has presented research papers at numerous national and international conferences, including those sponsored by the American Society for Quality (ASQ), Pacific Northwest Software Quality (PNSQC), the Software Publishers Association (SPA), Software Technology Support Center (STSC), the Software Engineering Institute (SEI) and Software Research Inc.. His courses have been attended by software engineering professionals from many of the country's leading technology companies. His courses have been sponsored for their members by professional associations, including the ASQ, CSU Long Beach's Software Engineering Forum for Training, Semiconductor Equipment and Materials International (SEMI), Software Engineering Institute (SEI), UC Berkeley and UC Santa Cruz. His software development clients have successfully achieved ISO registration and advanced CMM maturity levels.

Deibler is an active US TAG member in the ISO JTC1 SC7 - Software Engineering Standards subcommittee, which is responsible for the development and maintenance of ISO 12207, ISO 15504 (SPICE) and ISO 9000-3. He has performed ISO 9000 registration audits as an external resource under contract to the British Standards Institution (BSI).

Dyczkowsky, Bohdan

Bohdan Dyczkowsky, director of MOYE Company Limited, is a native of Toronto, Ontario. He graduated from the University of Toronto with a B.S. in mechanical engineering. His broad manufacturing experience includes construction, steel fabricating, nuclear and electronics.

Major career accomplishments include serving as the secretary of the Canadian Delegation to the ISO Technical Committee 176 during the development of the first ISO 9000 series. His duties entailed working directly with both the chairman and secretariat of the Technical Committee.

As a trainer, he has developed various RAB accredited lead auditor courses. Additionally he has developed the funding requirements for the Province of Ontario for government funding of ISO 9000 training. As a consultant, he has led numerous companies through to successful ISO 9000 registration on their first audit.

A certified lead auditor with the IRCA in England and the RAB in the United States, he conducts registration audits in over 30 different industry and service sectors. In addition, Dyczkowsky has helped Canadian registrars establish their ISO 9000 registration systems and conducts ISO 9000 audits on behalf of various registrars

Gerard, James J.

James J. Gerard is a management consultant with STAT-A-MATRIX in Cortlandt Manor, New York. His areas of expertise include general methods of project planning/management; quality analysis/problem-solving skills; statistical process control; metrics design; voice of the customer/customer satisfaction; benchmarking; quality function deployment; and operational analysis.

Gerard's experience encompasses 30 years in the telecommunications industry, including positions responsible for quality audits, Total Quality Management (TQM) research and training in Malcolm Baldrige National Quality Award criteria as well as New York State's Excelsior Award. He specializes in the development, maintenance, and training of quality assurance principles, including supplier performance efforts, negotiation, conflict resolution, management of contracts and on-site audits.

Most recently, as executive director, quality assurance (QA) for NYNEX Global Systems–FLAG Project, Gerard's responsibilities included technical and economical analysis of bids from competing consortiums, development and management of the QA organization, negotiation and management of contracts with outside companies for quality inspectors (United States and Japan), on-site audits of contractors and subcontractors (verification of technical ability and ISO 9000 evaluations and follow-up audits) and monitoring of contractor and subcontractor performance. In addition, he was responsible for the negotiation and approval of acceptance procedures for purchased equipment, and management and performance of on-site (United States and Japan) engineering and quality testing of critical equipment to verify compliance.

As staff director in the quality research and support department in the NYNEX Corporate Headquarters, Gerard identified and developed initiatives to improve efficiency and customer focus through the principles of TQM. He was responsible for training on Baldrige Award criteria, as well as Quality Process and QA principles, and for support of NYNEX companies in meeting requirements of the Baldrige and New York State's Excelsior Award. As QA engineering manager for NYNEX Materiel Enterprises, Gerard interviewed, selected, and trained product engineering personnel, developed engineering procedures and procedures for the ethical selection and monitoring of suppliers, managed the QA organization responsible for all New York and New England Telephone products, developed and trained suppliers in QA principles and performed and managed supplier audits.

In addition, Gerard was with New York Telephone for nearly 20 years in engineering and management positions, responsible for customer support, long-range technical and economic planning, and technical, economic and quality evaluation of potential suppliers.

Gerard is a Registrar Accreditation Board (RAB)-certified quality systems lead auditor, licensed professional engineer (NY), former American Society for Quality (ASQ)-certified quality engineer and Excelsior (Quality) Award (NY) past examiner. He holds an M.B.A. from Iona College, B.E.E. from City College of New York and A.A.S. from Bronx Community College.

Gilbert, Ross

Ross Gilbert is the global sourcing and new product introduction leader for the GE Medical Systems Information Technologies, responsible for global supply chain management. Prior to this assignment, he spent 15 years in executive roles within quality management at Kohler Company and General Electric. He has implemented quality improvement and Six-Sigma systems in production, service and administrative operations globally and has been part of all stages of development from initial planning and launch to management of a mature system.

Gilbert is a GE-certified Six-Sigma Master Black Belt. He is also a member of the US Technical Advisory Group (TAG) to ISO TC 176 working on the ISO 9000 standards and was a senior examiner with the Malcolm Baldrige National Quality Award. In addition to sourcing and quality management roles, he has held positions in operations, sales administration and marketing. Gilbert has a B.S. in business from the University of Wisconsin.

Gordon, Dale K.

Dale K. Gordon is director of quality and business improvement for Rolls-Royce PLC's Defense North American Business Unit in Indianapolis. He is chair of the American Aerospace Quality Group and was one of the writers of the AS9100 standard. He earned a bachelor's degree in industrial engineering from General Motors Institute (now Kettering University) in Flint, Michigan, and a master's degree in business administration from Butler University in Indianapolis.

Goult, Rod

Rod Goult, president and CEO of The Victoria Group, has a broad range of experience in both manufacturing and service environments. His specialties are software development and electronics design/manufacture. He is co-author of the internal auditor and ISO 9000-3 course and principal author of the lead auditor program. Goult has worked with companies in the United Kingdom and Sweden on ISO 9001 certification and BABT approvals and has assisted many US companies in achieving ISO 9001 certification as well. Since founding The Victoria Group in 1990, Goult has been a regular contributor to quality-related publications and a frequent speaker at conferences. Goult assisted with the RAB Software Quality Systems Certification Committee and is a member of the international conference on reciprocal auditor certification recognition. A senior member of the American Society for Quality, Goult is both an IRCA-registered lead assessor and an RAB-certified quality systems lead auditor.

Grimmett, Bob

Bob Grimmett is QA manager for the ADE Corporation. He began his standards work in 1977 as a contributor to the manufacturing section of the then ANSI/ASQC Z1.15 (1979) Generic Guidelines for Quality Systems. He subsequently managed large-scale corporate implementation of proprietary and international quality standards in four companies in eight countries and participated in over 500 major systems audits. Grimmett graduated from Rensselaer with bachelor's and master of management engineering degrees and was an MBNQA examiner from 1990 to 1993. Grimmett is an ASQ-certified quality engineer, ASQ-certified quality auditor, an RAB QMS provisional auditor and a reviewer for TC 176. He also served as secretary and treasurer for the Boston Section of the ASQ and is the Region One Councilor for the Quality Audit Division.

Hallenbeck, Lane

Lane Hallenbeck has more than 20 years of technical leadership experience in service and manufacturing organizations. He has worked in the aerospace, semiconductor, defense, automotive, telecommunications, software and construction industries. During his career, he has held such positions as vice president for ABS Quality Evaluations, a management systems registrar, and program manager for TRW Space & Electronics Group.

While with ABS, Hallenbeck was responsible for audit operations and business development. As a founding management team member, he grew the staff from four to more than 100 auditors, serving some 4,000 clients worldwide. His actions helped increase sales 25 percent through the overhaul of business processes, customer service and range of deliverables. His hard work also contributed to the company's annual double-digit growth, including expansion into South American, Asian and European markets. At TRW, he was in charge of the manufacture and assembly of classified DoD and NASA components, meeting tight launch windows and budget parameters.

Having been a principal member of a leading registrar body, Hallenbeck has overseen the implementation of thousands of ISO 9000, QS-9000 and ISO 14000 management systems. This experience, coupled with his proven ability to increase company competitiveness, gives him a special approach when solving customers' unique challenges. He is able to make management systems work from both business and compliance viewpoints. Related areas of expertise include process mapping, supplier management, design-to-manufacturing cycle time reduction and TQM strategies.

Hallenbeck has delivered management system services to some of industry's best-known companies, including General Electric, Sony, IBM, General Dynamics, Delphi Automotive, Quantum, Varian, ABB and Philips.

Hallenbeck holds an M.S. in technology management from Pepperdine University and a B.A. in biology from the University of Colorado at Boulder.

As a founding member of the Independent Association of Accredited Registrars (IAAR), he held the position of president from 1997 to 1999. He is an RAB board member, a member of the Independent International Organization for Certification (IIOC) and was a past program chairman for the ASQ Greater Houston Section. He is also a frequent presenter and subject matter expert at international conformity assessment venues.

Hallenbeck holds quality systems lead auditor certifications through the ASQ and IRCA and is an MAO Supplier Taskforce qualified QS-9000 auditor.

Highlands, James

James Highlands has worked in management systems since 1971 and has experience with a variety of standards including ISO 9000 quality management standards; QS-9000 for the automotive industry; ISO 14000 environmental management standards; the American Society for Mechanical Engineering's (ASME) Division 1 Section III Boiler and Pressure Vessel Code for Nuclear Power Generation; the American National Standards Institute (ANSI) N45.2 Quality Assurance for Nuclear Power Plants, Title 10 Part 50 Appendix "B" of the Code of Federal Regulations; Mil-Q-9858A; and Mil-I-45208A.

Originally qualified as an audit team leader in 1981 to ANSI N45.2.23 and ASME NQA-1 for Bechtel Power Corporation, he has audited hundreds of companies. He is also certified by the RAB and the IRCA as a lead auditor and ASQ as a certified quality auditor.

In 1987 he joined the US Technical Advisory Group (TAG) to ISO's Technical Committee 176 on Quality Management (ISO 9000). For the past three years, he has served as a lead delegate to TC 176 SC 2 on quality management developing the ISO 9001: 2000 standard.

Originally designated the US expert to ISO's Strategic Advisory Group on Environment in 1990, he has served as the vice chairman of the US TAG to ISO TC 207 SC 1 since 1993 and as a lead delegate in the development of ISO 14001 environmental management systems. He is also the chairman of the ANSI Z-1 Committee on EMS and a past member of the ANSI/RAB EMS Accreditation Council developing criteria for accrediting EMS registrars (certifying bodies).

Over the past ten years he has taught (as an instructor for ASQ and other organizations) both public and in-house training courses on: ISO 9001 Implementation; the ISO 9001:2000 Revisions; Internal Auditing; Developing an ISO 14000 Environmental Management System; Integrating ISO 9001 and ISO 14001; ISO 9000 Advance Quality Management; and Making ISO 9000 Profitable. He also worked as a member of ASQ Course Development Team for the Certified Quality Manager Training Program.

He has authored two books on the subject of quality standards and management, *ISO 9000:2000 Revision* and *How to Make Money with ISO 9000*. McGraw-Hill published the books in 1998 and 1999, respectively.

Highlands is a member of the American Society of Mechanical Engineers, American Society of Quality, American National Standards Institute and American Management Society.

He studied metallurgy at Pennsylvania State University and received an M.B.A. in finance and accounting from Southwest University.

Kimmelman, Edward R.

Edward R. Kimmelman provides consultant services in the areas of regulatory submissions, regulatory compliance and quality management systems. During a 35-year career in industry he has served in engineering, product management and senior management positions for the DuPont Co. and the Roche Diagnostics Corp. Kimmelman is a past president of the NCCLS and has served as chairman or the HIMA Standards Section and Science & Technology Section. He is the convener of the ISO TC 210, Working Group 1 on quality systems.

Kimmelman received a B.S. degree in mechanical engineering from Cornell University and a J.D. degree from the Seton Hall University School of Law. He can be reached at 109 Glennside Ave, Wilmington, DE 19803; tel: 302-762-0947; fax: 302-765-3947; e-mail: GPA_ED@msn.com.

Kolka, James W.

James W. Kolka's professional experience spans more than 30 years. During this time he served as a full professor and senior administrator at several public and private universities where his responsibilities ranged from developing interdisciplinary research/teaching programs, serving as vice president for academic affairs, directing strategic planning and managing multimillion dollar state university system budgets. For the past 10 years, he has been working in the quality and environmental fields. He has developed a comprehensive preventive law program that utilizes both the ISO 9001 Quality Management System and the ISO 14001 Environmental Management System to reduce product, services and environmental liability for the US and EU markets.

Kolka specializes in business process improvement and strategic planning in several areas. He has developed integrated regulatory compliance programs for medical devices and medical device packaging for both Europe (CE marking) and the United States (FDA's Quality System Regulation). He also has developed programs for applying ISO 9001 to the health care industry for the United States. For Europe he has developed programs for CE marking for machinery and alternative strategies for dealing with the European Union's Packaging and Packaging Waste Directive. For both the United States and European Union he has developed programs utilizing ISO 9001 and ISO 14001 to reduce liability exposure in the manufacturing and services sectors in both regulated and non-regulated industries. He has conducted more than 300 seminars and workshops for North American, European, Asian and Latin American companies and has written more than 200 articles and five books on the topics of liability, EU Directives and technical standards, ISO 9000, ISO 14000, liability and competitiveness.

Kolka received his B.S. in political science (economics/chemistry) from the University of Wisconsin-Eau Claire. He received his J.D. from the University of Wisconsin-Madison Law School with a background in product liability and environmental law and was admitted to the Wisconsin Bar. He received his Ph.D. in political science and international affairs from the University of Kansas. As a senior administrator, he developed the University of Wisconsin System's statewide Adult Extended Degree Program, served on the American Council on Education's National Commission on Educational Credit and Credentials and was instrumental in creating the Center for International Standards and Quality (CISQ) at Georgia Tech. He was a Ford Foundation Research Fellow in Costa Rica and a Fellow with the American Council on Education in Washington, D.C. Presently, he serves on several advisory committees at Georgia Tech and acts as a standards expert for the European/American Chamber of Commerce. His most recent book, *ISO 9000... A Legal Perspective,* was published in 1998 by ASQ Quality Press and another organization.

Marquardt, Donald W.

Donald W. Marquardt was the leader of the US delegation to TC 176 and chairman of the US Technical Advisory Group (TAG) to TC 176. He was active in TC 176 since its initial meeting in 1980. He served in a variety of international leadership roles in TC 176. He was convener of several working groups, including those that prepared ISO 9000:1987, ISO 9000-1:1994 and ISO 9000-2:1993. Marqardt was chair of the international task force that prepared the Vision 2000 report establishing the strategic intent for implementation and revision of the ISO 9000 standards in the global marketplace of the 1990s. He also chaired the TC 176 Strategic Planning Advisory Group subsequent to the Vision 2000 Task Force.

Marquardt served on the Registrar Accreditation Board (RAB) Board of Advisors, starting in 1990. He was president of Donald W. Marquardt and Associates, established in 1991, which provided consulting and training in the fields of quality management, quality assurance, ISO 9000 standards, strategic planning, applied statistics and organizaitonal change. Marquardt also worked for DuPont Company for 39 years on assignments such as research, management of engineering services and leadership of the DuPont Quality Management and Technology Center, which he organized.

Marquardt was president of the American Statistical Association (ASA) and a former senior examiner for the Malcolm Baldrige National Quality Award. He was a fellow of the American Association of Science, the ASA and ASQ and was an elected member of the International Statistical Institute. His awards include the ANSI Meritorious Service Award, the ASA Founders Award and the ASQ Shewhart Medal. Marquardt passed away in July 1997.

Munden, Steve A.

Steve Munden is manager of technical affairs for Eastman Kodak Company's European, African and Middle Eastern Region, a role which involves having a broad awareness and comprehension of evolving public policies, legislation, standards and conformity assessment regimes. He is also responsible for leading implementation projects within the company to ensure that Kodak continues to meet the highest international standards. Prior to this role, he was instrumental in forming a Company Quality Assurance department within Kodak's

UK subsidiary. This led to Kodak Limited being one of the first organizations to receive companywide registration to ISO 9001. Munden has worked with many international teams implementing management systems concerned with design, product safety and process improvement.

Munden acts as liaison representative to the ISO Technical Committee on Quality Management and Quality Assurance, on behalf of the European Chemical Industry Council (CEFIC). He also represents the Confederation of British Industry on British Standards Institution's (BSI) policy and strategy committee and chairs BSI's management systems sector committee. The latter committee is responsible for overseeing all management systems standards development work within BSI, including design, quality, environment and health and safety management systems.

Munden is an advocate of continuous personal development and is just completing an M.B.A. focusing on technology management. He balances this mechanistic approach to life with a keen interest in philosophy.

Nee, Paul A.

Paul A. Nee is the manager of quality at DORMA Door Controls Inc. of Reamstown, Pennsylvania. He is a graduate of Williamsport Technical Institute in tool design technology and Elizabethtown College in business management. His work experience includes 35 years in inspection, quality control, quality assurance and quality management. Twenty-two years of this experience has been at DORMA Door Controls Inc. For the past five years he has been responsible for the development, implementation and maintenance of the ISO 9001 quality assurance system. In addition, he is the facilitator for total quality management at DORMA. During the past two years, he has presented 35 ISO seminars to construction-related industries and other professional groups.

Nee is author of *ISO 9000 In Construction*, John Wiley and Sons, April 1996, and several articles in *Doors and Hardware* and other periodicals for the construction industry.

Peach, Bill

Bill Peach is a quality consultant with QA International, a provider of quality and technical services in 25 countries. He has served as a research analyst for Robert Peach and Associates, with clients including Allen Bradley, NASA, National Computer Systems, Kodak and Xerox. Prior to that he managed product quality for Florist's Transworld Delivery (FTD), where he managed quality for 23,000 member florists and developed a prevention-oriented quality system, reducing returns and credits by over 50 percent. At Spiegel Inc., as a quality assurance engineer, he coordinated corporate quality assurance efforts in product lines including furniture, jewelry and toys. He is co-author of *Memory Jogger 9000:2000*, published by GOAL/QPC. Peach has a degree in engineering physics from Lehigh University and an M.B.A. with a concentration in operations management and applied statistics from the University of Illinois in Chicago.

Peach, Robert W.

Robert W. Peach is principal of Robert Peach and Associates Inc., Quality Management Consultants, Cary, North Carolina. He was a member of the US delegation to the ISO TC 176 Committee on Quality Assurance at its formation in 1980, and continued serving as convenor of the working group that developed ISO Quality System Standard 9004, *Quality Management and Quality System Elements - Guidelines*. He was the first chairman of the Registrar Accreditation Board, which he helped form and where he served for 10 years..

Peach established the quality assurance activity at Sears Roebuck and Company and managed it for over 25 years. In this capacity, he and his staff worked with quality systems in the plants of hundreds of Sears suppliers. Peach is co-author of *Memory Jogger 9000:2000* and *ISO 9001:2000 - Paraphrased*, published by GOAL/QPC, as well as editor of *The ISO 9000 Handbook*.

For its initial three years, Peach served as project manager of the Malcolm Baldrige National Quality Award Consortium, which administered the awards program managed by the National Institute of Standards and Technology. He chaired the writing of the ANSI/ASQC Z1.15 Standard "Generic Guidelines for Quality Systems," one of the standards upon which ISO 9004 is based.

Peach received degrees from Massachusetts Institute of Technology and the University of Chicago. He is a Fellow of the ASQ, a certified quality engineer and registered professional engineer in quality engineering.

Peterson, Alan J.

Alan J. Peterson is director of product research and development at Plexus Corporation. He has led the product research and development efforts at Plexus since the company's inception. In that role, he has designed training programs for the automotive, aerospace and health care industries in addition to supervising the creation of customized programs for Plexus' clients. He developed training, training materials and selected computer applications for QS-9000,

ISO/TS 16949, TE Supplement, ISO 14000, ISO 9000 and AS9100. He has worked closely with the QS-9000 Supplier Requirements Task Force and the International Automotive Quality Task Force (IATF) and has been manager for the QS-9000 and ISO/TS 16949 Registrar Auditor Certification Programs. He was appointed to the IATF's Training and Exam Commissions and continues to serve on those commissions. Prior to joining Plexus, Peterson served as a department chair at North Dakota State College of Science and was a quality system consultant for North Dakota's university system and department of economic development. In addition, he has served as North Dakota state legislator. Peterson holds a master's degree in English and is currently a doctoral candidate for a Ph.D. in administration and organization development.

Potts, Elizabeth A.

Elizabeth A. Potts is a chemical engineering graduate from the University of Illinois and holds an M.B.A. from Ashland University. She is currently director of manufacturing for Ashland Specialty Chemical Company, Electronic Chemicals Division. Previously, she was director of quality for Ashland Chemical Company. She is the former president of ABS Quality Evaluations, an accredited third-party certifier of management systems to ISO 9000, QS-9000 and ISO 14000. Previously, she was employed as the quality manager for the American Gas Association Laboratories, where she was responsible for product certification inspections, ISO 9000 registration and internal quality program development and implementation. She has also been employed by Babcock & Wilcox as a quality control manager responsible for development and implementation of quality programs for nuclear reactor components and other defense-related components.

Potts is a member of the US Technical Advisory Group to ISO Technical Committee 176 on quality assurance and quality management.

Pratt, Roger C.

Roger C. Pratt held a variety of positions at the Pacific Northwest National Laboratory in Richland, Washington. These included quality training office manager, quality verification department manager, quality assurance systems and audits section manager and quality engineering technical group leader. While serving as department manager he was responsible for developing and implementing an internal QA audit program. As support to the Department of Energy, Pratt provided auditor training not only in Richland but nationwide at DoE sites.

Reid, R. Dan

R. Dan Reid is manager of advanced technology purchasing at GM Powertrain. He was the delegation leader of the International Automotive Task Force (IATF) and a member of the DaimlerChrysler, Ford and GM Supplier Quality Requirements Task Force. He is best known as an author of the three editions of QS-9000, the Quality System Assessment (QSA), ISO Technical Specification 16949, which harmonizes QS-9000 with the equivalent European automotive manuals, and the ISO 9001:2000 revision. In March, he received an "Outstanding Professional Achievement Award" from the US Technical Advisory Group to ISO TC 176 for his work on the ISO 9001:2000 revision. He also worked on the Chrysler, Ford and GM Potential Failure Mode and Effects Analysis, Production Part Approval Process and Advanced Product Quality Planning manuals. He has been a featured speaker at numerous quality conferences in North America, South America, Europe, Asia and Australia and has consulted with other industry sectors including aerospace, telecommunications and health care. Currently he is a contributor to the ASQ Quality Progress Standards column and is a member of the ASQ Editorial Review Board. Most recently, he was a principal author of an AIAG/ASQ ISO 9004-based document for health care, which was approved by ISO as their first Industry Technical Agreement (ITA) project.

Reid was also on the AIAG "Y2K" supplier readiness project team and the General Motors Global "Y2K" core team working on a supplier audit/remediation process. This team won the 2000 GM Chairman's Honors Award. Reid guided the development of sanctioned supplier and third-party auditor training for both QS-9000 and this Y2K program.

He also led or supervised some 40 supplier workshops focused on implementation of "lean" manufacturing concepts, which resulted in immediate productivity improvements and reductions in lead-time, floor space and inventory.

Reid holds master's degrees from Central Michigan University and Christian International and a bachelor's degree from Western Kentucky University. He is listed in the International "Who's Who of Professionals" and is an ASQ-certified quality engineer (CQE), an AIAG-registered QS-9000 internal auditor and a senior member of the ASQ Automotive Division. He is a certified Crosby Quality Education System (QES) instructor, has successfully passed a BSI-sponsored ISO 9000 lead auditor course and Malcolm Baldrige self-assessor training.

Reid is married with four children.

Ricketts, Curtis

Curtis Ricketts has over 19 years of experience in organizational performance and risk assessment including eight years in change management and development of management systems. He has extensive experience in commercial property-casualty insurance and public sector operations.

As quality director and assistant commissioner of administration, Ricketts led the North Carolina Department of Labor to become the first state government agency in the United States to achieve ISO 9001 certification. Additional responsibilities included serving as the agency's planning officer, environmental sustainability officer and as senior executive over the apprenticeship division.

He is a member of the American National Standards Institute ASC Z1 Committee and the US Technical Advisory Group to ISO TC 176 and has played an active role in the ISO 9000 international standards series development. Ricketts is also a former chair of the North Carolina Quality Awards Council (governing body for the state's Baldrige-based quality award).

Curtis holds certifications from the American Society for Quality (ASQ) as a quality manager and as a quality auditor. He is a member of the quality management, service and public sector divisions of ASQ.

Other professional contributions include membership on the State Employee Incentive System review committee, the Quality Resource Advisors and the North Carolina Quality Conference program committee. He is a former member of the Governor's Management Improvement Council, the Performance Management Taskforce on Workforce Development and the Governor's Taskforce on Total Quality Management in State Government. Governor Jim Hunt awarded him The Order of the Long Leaf Pine, the state's highest civilian award, for his work on the TQM taskforce.

Prior to joining the labor department, Ricketts was associated with the North Carolina Department of Insurance, where he managed performance assessments on insurance companies and was the architect of a regulatory audit program that became a national model. He has also worked in the commercial property-casualty insurance industry.

Stump, Richard B.

Richard B. Stump is principal of Consultants in Quality Inc., an ASQ-certified Six Sigma Black Belt, a certified quality engineer and certified quality auditor. Stump has an M.B.A. from Northern Illinois University and a bachelor's degree from Lafayette College. His consulting focuses on implementing quality management systems for clients and eliminating product defects through application of variation analysis, a statistical engineering discipline using the Shainm Techniques. He can be contacted at StumpRB@aol.com.

Tiratto, Joseph

Joseph Tiratto (P.E.) is an international consultant on quality systems, a registered lead auditor with IRCA and RAB and an approved lead auditor instructor. He has bachelor's degrees in naval architecture and marine engineering and mechanical engineering, and has a master's degree in quality management. He is a registered professional engineer, a licensed marine engineer, a chartered engineer (CENG) (United Kingdom) and a registered European engineer (EUR.ING)(EC & EFTA countries). He is a member of the American Society for Quality, the American Society of Mechanical Engineers, the Society of Naval Architects & Marine Engineers and the Institute of Marine Engineers (UK). He is a member of the US TAGs to ISO TC 176, ISO TC 69, IEC/TC 56 and ASQ/ASC Z-1 committee on Quality Assurance. He is a past member and secretary of the board of directors of the RAB.

Tiratto has over 35 years of management experience in engineering, production, operation, quality control, quality assurance and auditing. He has developed and implemented quality systems and has conducted audits to ISO 9000 quality assurance standards in 17 countries worldwide. He directed the development of quality systems for a registrar which met the requirements of the RAB in the United States and the RvA in the Netherlands. He has published papers, authored chapters in handbooks, lectured on ISO 9000 standards and quality system registration and teaches ISO 9000 lead auditor courses.

Unger, Peter S.

Peter S. Unger is president of the American Association for Laboratory Accreditation (A2LA). Previously, he served as vice-president of the Association for 10 years. A2LA is a nonprofit, membership society administering a broad spectrum, nationwide laboratory accreditation system.

Unger served as associate manager of laboratory accreditation at the National Bureau of Standards (now the National Institute of Standards and Technology). He has been involved with laboratory accreditation on the national level since 1978. He began his career with the US General Services Administration on various assignments involving standards writing, testing, quality control and procurement research.

He is chairman of ASTM E-36 on Conformity Assessment and the convener of the working group of the International Laboratory Accreditation Conference (ILAC) on Assessor Qualifications & Competencies.

Unger has a B.S. degree in systems engineering from Princeton University and a master's in environmental management from George Washington University. He is an RAB-certified lead auditor (QO2335) and IRCA-certificated lead assessor (A005890).

Walz, John W.

John W. Walz is the quality and reliability standards senior manager in the supply chain network of Lucent Technologies and is responsible for quality and reliability strategic planning, coordination and implementation within the Lucent supply chain. He also supports the chief quality officer as TL 9000 lead team manager, Lucent delegation manager to the QuEST Forum, Quality Strategy Forum member and quality management systems standards manager.

Walz was formerly technical manager involved in 4ESS and 1A ESS hardware and software development. His career began with Western Electric at Indian Hill, Naperville, Illinios.

He has participated in the introduction of many key processes into AT&T and Lucent: formal quality management systems; product realization gates; policy deployment; quality manuals; process and quality management improvement; quality improvement story; customers' quality requirements; software metrics; customer, internal and supplier quality auditing; Baldrige Award applications and examinations; restructuring to the customer and operating business units; reengineering order management; and currently TL 9000 requirements and metrics development and implementation.

For the QuEST Forum, Walz is the metrics work group secretary and before that the metrics implementation co-chair, helping to deploy the new TL 9000 worldwide telecommunications quality system requirements and metrics.

For the IEEE, he is the secretary of the Computer Standards Activity Board.

Walz earned B.S. and M.S. degrees in electrical engineering from Ohio State University.

He is married to Ann Walz and has two grown children, Sarah Walz and Marion Jaeger, and one grandson, Caleb Jaeger.

His interests are downhill and cross-country skiing, scuba diving, sailing, canoeing and wind surfing.

Whitson, Jerry L.

Jerry L. Whitson's professional experience spans 43 years. This experience includes a variety of quality control positions and consulting assignments, which include such fields as coal liquefaction; manufacturing of computer products, luggage, and toys; compression and injection molding of plastic and rubber; footwear manufacturing; die casting of zinc and magnesium; steel stamping; metal extruding; iron and steel casting; ceramic and brick manufacturing; and missile component manufacturing. Responsibilities included receiving audits; performing process audits of manufactured goods; performing audits of distribution centers; manufacturing operations and final audits of import/export products; performing plant-site audits of both foreign and domestic vendors and defining and implementing consumer service policies. Customer service responsibilities have included frequent visits to points of sale to assist in affirming customer requirements and translating customer feedback into future product. In addition to mechanical inspection and process auditing, Whitson has also been responsible for establishing and/or monitoring both destructive and nondestructive testing procedures and calibration and control of measurement equipment. As a Shainin licensee he solved difficult manufacturing problems and practiced utilization of Shainin statistical problem-solving techniques.

Whitson has been an active member of the American Society for Quality (ASQ) since 1965. He is past chair of the Denver and Middle Tennessee sections and served at the division level as the quality management division vice chair of administration. He has served the national organization as regional director; deputy regional director; national technical program chair for the Annual Quality Congress and Host Committee Chair for the Annual Quality Congress; and served three terms on the National Executive Committee as vice president of conferences and exhibits. He is currently active in establishing local, regional, national and international conferences. Whitson is a frequent speaker for professional society meetings and has presented technical papers for local, regional, national and international conferences. He regularly teaches ASQ certification refresher courses and has taught college courses in quality assurance, engineering management and manufacturing technology.

Whitson holds a B.S. from East Texas Baptist University, is a Fellow of the ASQ, an ASQ-certified reliability engineer (CRE00374), a registered professional quality engineer (QU1604), an ISO 9000 certified assessor (Q94088) and a RAB quality management systems auditor (Q06171).

Wilson, Lawrence A.

Lawrence A. "Larry" Wilson has been a nationally recognized leader and author in the field of quality management/systems for over 45 years. As director of product assurance and safety at the Lockheed Aeronautical Systems Company — Georgia Division, he was responsible for the creation and implementation of one of the first successful Total Quality Management programs in the nation (1985). As directive head of the company's total quality and safety program at this 20,000-plus employee facility, over 2,000 recognized high-quality, heavy-lift, new and modified aircraft (C130, C141 and C5) were delivered to military and commercial customers in the United States and 60-plus countries worldwide.

While on the president's staff at Lockheed, he introduced numerous advanced technical and managerial quality system tools, including the placement of the quality, environmental and safety functions in one control function. He chaired the Lockheed corporate quality committee, established the Lockheed quality technology committee and held the chair and/or office in the Aerospace Industry Association's quality assurance committee and the National Security Industrial Association's quality and reliability assurance committee. He has served on the American National Standards Institute's Z-1 Committee on Quality Assurance, the US Technical Advisory Group (TAG) on ISO 9000 and as a US delegate to the International Standards Organization Committee on Quality Management and Quality Assurance (ISO 9000). He has been a long-standing member of the American Society of Nondestructive Testing and the American Society for Quality. He has also had international leadership responsibility for developing two ISO 9000 quality management system standards, and has authored several books and a software package on ISO 9000 implementation.

He is president of Lawrence A. Wilson & Associates, a successful Atlanta-based consulting and auditing firm that specializes in managing for quality. In this capacity, Dr. Wilson has consulted, lectured, written and instructed nationally and internationally on the latest state of the art in the field of quality management, including TQM, CPI, ISO 9000, MBNQA and quality auditing. He has litigation experience as an expert witness. He is an honorary lifetime member of the National Security Industrial Association and, as leader of the US delegation to ISO TC 176 SC 2, served as international writing group chairman with the ISO TC 176 revision process for ISO 9001 and ISO 9004. He has had specific leadership responsibility for ISO 9004, *Quality management systems — Guidelines for performance improvements*, published in December 2000.

Wilson holds a Ph.D. in statistical/radiation applications in biophysics from Emory University in Atlanta and B.S. and M.S. degrees in the sciences from Kent

State University. He is also a licensed registered professional engineer in quality engineering.

Quality Award Programs

B

Following is a listing of various quality awards presented by different organizations. The Malcom Baldrige National Quality Award is also discussed in Chapter 26.

National Awards

Malcolm Baldrige National Quality Award

National Institute of Standards and Technology
National Quality Program
Route 270 and Quince Orchard Road
Administration Building
Room A635
Gaithersburg, MD 20899
Phone: 301-975-2036
Fax: 301-948-3716
Web: www.quality.nist.gov/

Under the auspices of the Department of Commerce and NIST, up to two awards are given each year to organizations in three major categories: US-based businesses, education organizations serving US citizens and health care organizations serving US citizens. Seven areas of focus are examined: leadership, strategic planning, customer and market focus, information and analysis, human resource focus, process management and business results.

Association for Quality and Participation

Executive Building #200
2368 Victory Pkwy.
Cincinnati, Ohio 45206
Phone: 800-733-3310
Fax: 513-381-0070
Web: www.aqp.org/

The AQP is an international not-for-profit membership association dedicated to improving workplaces through quality and participation practices. The National Team Excellence Awards are presented to the workplace teams that most clearly and effectively demonstrate the principles and techniques of improving quality through participation. Unlike other applications this one requires a video presentation by the team. The presentation covers one completed team project from the current calendar year and tracking it from its origins to implementation, including measurable results. The presentation is judged on the team's ability to explain the process used, and how it reached its conclusions.

The President's Quality Award Program

Office of Executive and Management Development
1900 E St., Room 6468
Washington, DC 20415
Phone: 202-606-5053
Web: www.opm.gov/quality/

The Performance Excellence criteria are similar to the Malcolm Baldrige National Quality Award criteria modified for the government environment. Any part of the executive branch of the federal government with more than 100 full-time federal employees is eligible.

Canada Awards for Excellence

John Perry or Cheryl McAnerin
National Quality Institute
2275 Lakeshore Blvd. W., Suite 307
Toronto, ON M8V 3Y3 Canada
Phone: 416-251-7600
Fax: 416-251-9131
Web: www.nqi.ca/english/awards.htm

The Canada Awards for Excellence is applied to both private and public organizations. There are different awards for different categories of organization. The program uses the Canadian Quality criteria or Healthy Workplace criteria. Organizations are evaluated on their use of quality principles and practices during the previous three years.

European Quality Awards

Applications and criteria for European Quality Awards can be found at www.efqm.org/award.htm. The European Quality Award is given to organizations that show the highest level of commitment to improving business performance and increasing competitiveness. Selection of European Quality Award finalists is based on the highest standards and practice of Total Quality Management and business excellence.

European Quality Prizes are presented to organizations that demonstrate excellence in the management of quality as their fundamental process for continuous improvement. Several prizes are presented for each of the following categories: companies, operational units of companies, public sector organizations, small and medium enterprises. There is additional information for the latter category of applicants at www.eoq.org/SMEAwards.html

State Quality Awards (US)

A number of states have quality awards. Most are available only to organizations based in that particular state. There are usually several awards given for different size companies at different stages in their implementation of quality systems.

Multiple awards are often given in each category. Some awards are based on self-reporting of applicants while others require visits or reviews by evaluators. Many use Malcom Baldrige National Quality Award criteria.

The US Senate Productivity Award is available in several states. In most states, the award is based on the Baldrige criteria. Inquiries should be directed to the relevant US senator's office if the contact information is not listed for a particular state below.

Alabama

Alabama Quality Award
Linda Vincent
Alabama Productivity Center
PO Box 870318
Tuscaloosa, AL 35487
Phone: 205-348-8994
Fax: 205-348-9391
E-mail: Linda@proctr.cba.ua.edu
Web: www.proctr.cba.ua.edu

Arizona

Arizona State Quality Awards
Tim Jones
Arizona Quality Alliance
3737 N. Seventh St., Suite 157
Phoenix, AZ 85014-5079
Phone: 602-636-1383
Fax: 602-636-1377
E-mail: aqa@arizona-excellence.com
Web: www.arizona-excellence.com

Arkansas

Arkansas Quality Awards

Barbara Harvel
1111 W. Capital, Room 1013
Little Rock, AR 72201
Phone: 501-373-1300
Fax: 501-373-1976
Web: www.arkansas-quality.org

California

California Governor's Quality Awards
Stephen V. Brooks
California Center for Quality, Education and Development
1600 Main St., Suite 235
Walnut Creek, CA 94596
Phone: 925-210-9766
Fax: 925-944-3455
Web: www.calepa.ca.gov/Awards/GEELA /default.htm

Eureka Award for Performance Excellence
U.S. Senate Productivity Award (CA only)
The California Prospector Award
The California Challenge
Thomas Hinton
California Council for Quality & Service
PO Box 1235
Poway, CA 92074
Phone: 858-486-0400
Fax: 858-486-8595
E-mail: ccqs@ccqs.org
Web: www.ccqs.org/ccqs/index.htm

Colorado

Better Business Bureau Excellence in Customer Service Award
Carol Odell
Better Business Bureau
25 N. Wahsatch
Colorado Springs, CO 80903
Phone: 719-636-5076, ext. 111

Fax: 719-636-5078
Web: www.coloradosprings.bbb.org

Colorado Performance Excellence Award
Barbara Davis
Colorado Performance Excellence
700 N. Colorado Blvd., #354
Denver, CO 80206
Phone: 303-893-2739
Fax: 303-331-6851
E-mail: bdavis@coloradoexcellence.org
Web: www.coloradoexcellence.org/

Connecticut

Connecticut Award for Excellence
Walter T. Cederholm
PO Box 67
Rocky Hill, CT 06067
Phone: 800-392-2122
Fax: 860-721-8511
E-mail: walter.t.cederholm@us.westing-house.com

Connecticut Quality Breakthrough Award
Connecticut Innovation Prize
Connecticut Quality Improvement Award
Connecticut Quality Leadership Award
Sheila Carmine
Connecticut Quality Improvement Award
Partnership
PO Box 1396
Stamford, CT 06904
Phone: 203-322-9534
Fax: 203-329-2465
E-mail: scarmine@ctqualityaward.com
Web: www.ctqualityaward.org

Delaware

Delaware Quality Award
Zena Tucker
Delaware Quality Consortium

99 Kings Hwy.
Dover, DE 19901
Phone: 302-739-4271
Fax: 302-739-2028
E-mail: ztucker@state.de.us

Florida

Governor's Sterling Award
John A. Pieno Jr.
The Florida Sterling Council
PO Box 13907
Tallahassee, FL 32317
Phone: 850-922-5316
Fax: 850-488-7579
E-mail: pienoj@eog.state.fl.us
Web: www.floridasterling.com

Georgia

Georgia Oglethorpe Award Process
Victoria Currie Taylor
148 International Blvd. N.E.
Suite 650
Atlanta, GA 30303
Phone: 404-651-8405
Fax: 404-651-9377
E-mail: goap@mindspring.com

Hawaii

Hawaii State Award of Excellence
Norm Baker
Chamber of Commerce of Hawaii
1132 Bishop St., Suite 402
Honolulu, HI 96813
Phone: 808-545-4394
Fax: 808-545-4369
E-mail: rona@cochawaii.org

Idaho

Idaho Quality Award
Cliff Long
Idaho Quality Award
Idaho Department of Commerce
700 W. State
Boise, ID 83720
Phone: 208-334-2470
E-mail: clong@idoc.state.id.us
Web: www.idahoworks.com/iqa.html
Web: www.idoc.state.id.us/iqa/iqa.html

Illinois

The Lincoln Awards for Excellence
The Lincoln Foundation for Business
Excellence
820 W. Jackson Blvd., Suite 775
Chicago, IL 60607
Phone: 312-258-5301; 312-258-5252
Fax: 312-258-4066
E-mail: mwrobel@lincolnaward.org
Web: www.lincolnaward.org/

Indiana

State of Indiana Quality Improvement
Award
Task Force Chairperson
BMT
One N. Capitol Ave., Suite 925
Indianapolis, IN 46204
Phone: 800-877-5182; 317-635-3058
Fax: 317-231-7095
E-mail: quality@bmtadvantage.org
Web: www.bmtadvantage.org

Iowa

Iowa Recognition for Performance
Excellence
Gary Nesteby

Director
Woods Quality Center
4401 6th St. SW
Cedar Rapids, IA 52404
Phone: 319-399-6465
Fax: 319-399-6457
E-mail: info@wqc.org
Web: www.wqc.org/

Kansas

Kansas Award of Excellence
John Shoemaker
PO Box 55
Tecumseh, KS 66542
Phone: 800-743-6767; 785-379-5590
Fax: 785-379-5047
E-mail: jshoemaker@qof.com
Web: http://kae.myassociation.com

Kentucky

Commonwealth of Kentucky Quality
Award
Kentucky Quality Council
PO Box 1342
Frankfurt, KY 40602
Phone: 502-695-0066
Fax: 502-695-6824
E-mail: nharnice@kychamber.com
Web: www.kqc.org

Louisiana

Louisiana Quality Award
Corinne Dupui
Louisiana Quality Foundation
Louisiana Productivity Center
PO Box 44172
Lafayette, LA 70504
Phone: 318-482-6767; 337-482-6714
Fax: 318-262-5472

Maine

Margaret Chase Smith Maine State Quality
Award
Andrea Jandebeur
Margaret Chase Smith Quality Association
7 University Dr.
Augusta, ME 04330
Phone: 207-621-1988
Fax: 207-282-6081
E-mail: mqc@maine-quality.org
Web: www.maine-quality.org

Maryland

Maryland Quality Awards
US Senate Productivity Awards (Maryland
only)
Joanne Davis
University of Maryland Center for Quality
and Productivity
4511 Knox Rd., Suite 102
College Park, MD 20740
Phone: 301-403-4413
Fax: 301-403-4478
Web: www.umcqp.umd.edu/

Governor's Quality Awards
Andrea Sutton
Center for Continuous Quality
Improvement
Department of Budget and Management
301 W. Preston St., Room 508
Baltimore, MD 21201
Phone: 410-767-4751
Fax: 410-333-7456

Massachusetts

Massachusetts Performance Excellence
Award
Tyler Fairbank

MassExcellence
Center for Industrial Competitiveness
600 Suffolk St., Fifth Floor
Lowell, MA 01854
Phone: 978-934-2733
Fax: 978-934-4035
E-mail: info@massexcellence.com
Web: www.massexcellence.com

Michigan

Michigan Quality Leadership Award
Bill Kalmar
Oakland University
523 O'Dowd Hall
Rochester, MI 48309
Phone: 248-370-4552
Fax: 248-370-4628
E-mail: kalmar@oakland.edu
Web: www.michiganquality.org

Minnesota

Minnesota Quality Award
Kathryn Mackin
Minnesota Council for Quality
2850 Metro Dr., Suite 519
Bloomington, MN 55425
Phone: 612-851-3181
Fax: 612-851-3183
E-mail: mc4quality@aol.com

Mississippi

Mississippi Quality Award
Duane Hamill
State Board for Community and Junior
Colleges
3825 Ridgewood Rd.
Jackson, MS 39211
Phone: 601-982-6349
Fax: 601-982-6363

E-mail: dhamill@sbcjc.cc.ms.us
Web: www.sbcjc.cc.ms.us/programs.html

Missouri

Missouri Quality Award
Jennifer Kuester
Excellence in Missouri Foundation
PO Box 1085
Jefferson City, MO 65102
Phone: 573-526-1727
Fax: 573-526-1729
E-mail: jkuester@mail.state.mo.us
Web: www.mqa.org

Nebraska

The Edgerton Quality Awards
Nebraska Department of Economic
Development
PO Box 94666
301 Centennial Mall South
Lincoln, NE 68509
Phone: 402-471-3777; 402-471-4167
Fax: 402-471-3365
E-mail: jruff@ded1.ded.state.ne.us
Web: http://assist.neded.org/edgerton/

New Hampshire

Granite State Quality Award
Tom Raffio
Granite State Quality Council
PO Box 29
Manchester, NH 03105
Phone: 603-223-1312
Fax: 603-223-1299
E-mail: quality@gsqc.com
Web: www.gsqc.com

New Jersey

Governor's Award for Performance

Excellence
Quality New Jersey
20 W. State St.
PO Box 827
Trenton, NJ 08625
Phone: 609-777-0940
Fax: 609-777-2798
E-mail: kbiddle@qnj.org
Web: www.qnj.org

New Mexico

New Mexico Quality Awards
Julia Gabaldon
PO Box 25005
Albuquerque, NM 87125
Phone: 505-944-2001
Fax: 505-944-2002
E-mail: qnm@quality-newmexico.org
Web: www.quality-newmexico.org

New York

The Governor's Award for Excellence
The Empire State Advantage
Barbara Ann Harms
Excellence at Work
11 Computer Drive W., Suite 212
Albany, NY 12205
Phone: 518-482-1747
Fax: 518-482-2231
E-mail: ESANewYork@aol.com
Web: http://esaprograms.org/

North Carolina

North Carolina Awards for Excellence
Industrial Extension Service
Margaret O'Brien
North Carolina State University
Campus Box 7902
Raleigh, NC 7902

Phone: 919-515-3940
E-mail: margaret_obrien@ncsu.edu
Web: www.ies.ncsu.edu/qualityaward/
index.cfm

Ohio

Dayton Area Quality Excellence Award
Charlene Marbury
VA Medical Center
4100 W. Third St.
Dayton, OH 45428
Phone: 937-267-3925
Fax: 937-267-5386

Governor's Award for Team Excellence in
Manufacturing
Christine H. Merritt
Ohio Manufacturers' Association
33 N. High St.
Columbus, OH 43215
Phone: 614-224-5111
Fax: 614-224-1012

Ohio Award for Excellence
Thomas Casperson
Ohio Award for Excellence
c/o NCR Corporation
1700 South Patterson Blvd.
Dayton, OH 45479
Phone: 937-445-6556
Fax: 937-445-7336
E-mail: oe200001@ncr.com
Web: www.oae.org

Team Excellence in the Public Sector
John Yesso
Ohio Office of Quality Services
77 S. High St., Seventh Floor
Columbus, OH 43215
Phone: 614-728-2584
Fax: 614-644-6763

Oklahoma

Oklahoma Quality Award
Mike Strong
PO Box 26980
Oklahoma City, OK 73126
Phone: 405-815-5295
Fax: 405-815-5205
E-mail: mike_strong@oklahomaquality.com
Web: www.oklahomaquality.com/

Oregon

Oregon Quality Award
Tricia Hornback
The Performance Center
18640 N.W. Walker Rd.
Suite 1066
Beaverton, OR 97006
Phone: 503-725-2806
Fax: 503-725-2801

Oregon Excellence Awards
Larry Sears
Oregon Partnership for Excellence
c/o Portland General Electric
121 SW Salmon Street, 1WTC-9
Portland, OR 97204
Phone: 503-464-8547
Fax: 503-464-2223
Web: www.oregonexcellence.org/

Pennsylvania

Greater Pittsburgh Total Quality Award
Hank Sobah
Q-NET
Greater Pittsburgh Chamber of Commerce
425 Sixth Ave.
Pittsburgh, PA 15219
Phone: 412-392-4500
Fax: 412-392-4520

Lancaster Chamber Performance Excellence
Award
Betty Rose
The Lancaster Chamber of Commerce and
Industry
PO Box 1558
Lancaster, PA 17608
Phone: 717-397-3531
Fax: 717-293-3159
Web: www.lcci.com

Quality Valley USA Organization
Excellence Award
Ellen Sutjak
Lehigh Carbon Community College
4525 Education Park Dr.
Schnecksville, PA 18078
Phone: 610-799-1537
Fax: 610-799-1762

Keystone Performance Excellence Award
Betty Rose
Keystone Performance Excellence Award
2504 Raleigh Dr.
Lancaster, PA 17601
Phone: 717-560-2910
Fax: 717-581-5261
E-mail: jhrose@ptd.net

Rhode Island

Rhode Island Quality Awards
Brian M. Knight
RACE for Performance Excellence
PO Box 6766
Providence, RI 02940
Phone: 401-454-3030
Fax: 401-454-0056
E-mail: labmk@ids.net

South Carolina

South Carolina Governor's Quality Award
Judy Divita
South Carolina Quality Forum
University of South Carolina, Spartanburg
800 University Way
Spartanburg, SC 29303
Phone: 888-231-0578
Fax: 864-503-5995
E-mail: jdivita@gw.uscs.edu
Web: www.scquality.com

Trident Area Quality Awards
Gloria Palmer-Long
CareAlliance Health Services
125 Doughty St.
Charleston, SC 29403
Phone: 843-724-2251
Fax: 843-973-3058
Web: www.trident.tec.sc.us/tace.html

South Dakota

South Dakota Business Excellence Awards
Mary Anne Hoxeng
South Dakota Chamber of Commerce and
Industry
PO Box 190
Pierre, SD 57501
Phone: 605-224-6161
Fax: 605-224-7198

Tennessee

Greater Memphis Award for Quality
James C. Lippy
The Greater Memphis Association for
Quality
The University of Memphis
213 Alumni Center

Memphis, TN 38152
Phone: 901-678-4268
Fax: 901-678-4301

Tennessee Quality Award
Marie Williams
Tennessee Quality Award
Tennessee Economic Development Center
333 Commerce St.
Nashville, TN 37201
Phone: 800-453-6474
Fax: 615-214-8933
E-mail: tqa@bellsouth.net
Web: www.tqa.org/

Texas

Greater Austin Quality Award
Jim Nelson
Greater Austin Quality Council
PO Box 1967
Austin, TX 78767
Phone: 512-322-5603
Fax: 512-478-2324
Web: www.utexas.edu/courses/kincaid/
gaqc/QCA.html

Houston Awards for Excellence
Tallie Tootle
Houston Awards for Excellence
5225 Katy Freeway, Suite 500
Houston, TX 77007
Phone: 713-341-6114
Fax: 713-867-4922

Northwest Texas Quality Award
Susan Kitchens
PO Box 3070
Amarillo, TX 79116
Phone: 806-351-3206
Fax: 806-351-3327

Texas Award for Performance Excellence
Texas Quality Award
Quality Texas Foundation
PO Box 684157
Austin, TX 78768
Phone: 512-477-8137
Fax: 512-477-8168
E-mail: qualtex@swbell.net
Web: www.texas-quality.org

Utah

Utah Quality Awards
Don Hall
Utah Quality Council
PO Box 271367
Salt Lake City, UT 84127
Phone: 801-825-3336
Fax: 801-825-3337
Web: www.utahqualityaward.org/

Vermont

Vermont Program for Performance
Excellence
Champlain Mill
One Main St.
Winooski, VT 05404
Phone: 802-655-1910
Fax: 802-655-1932
Web: www.vermontquality.org/award.html

Virginia

US Senate Productivity and Quality Award
Bob Bowles
SPQA Board Chair
PO Box 6099
Suffolk, VA 23433
Phone: 757-523-6762

Fax: 757-523-6030
E-mail: rbowles_spqa@yahoo.com
Web: www.paragoncom.com/quality/

Washington

Governor's Award for Quality
Improvement
PO Box 11669
Olympia, WA 98508
Phone: 800-517-8264; 360-445-1357
Fax: 360-664-4250
Web: www.governor.wa.gov/quality/
award/award.htm

Wisconsin

Wisconsin Forward Award
Andrea Weiss
Executive Director
Wisconsin Forward Award, Inc.
14 W. Mifflin St., Suite. 205
Madison, WI 53703
Phone: 608-663-5300
Fax: 608-663-5302
E-mail: weiss@forwardaward.org
Web: www.forwardaward.org

Webliography

The following is a listing of selected ISO 9000 and quality web sites. While this is not a complete list of all resources, it includes many of the most frequently updated sources for information ranging from specific ISO 9000 information to general system or product standard information. These web addresses were accessible at the time of publication, but changes may have occurred since.

American National Standards Institute

http://www.ansi.org/

ANSI Online provides information on a broad spectrum of the latest national and international standards-related activities. There is information on ANSI membership, organizational charts, upcoming ANSI events and the latest standards information. There are a large number of public information materials on the site. Access to the biweekly publication of ANSI can be found at http://web.ansi.org/rooms/ROOM_14/. There are a large number of technical documents on the site; however, many of them are restricted, accessible only by ANSI members or ANSI technical committee members.

American Productivity & Quality Center

http://www.apqc.org/free/

APQC offers white papers, executive summaries, case studies, links, presentations and articles on quality management. While the site is not necessarily focused specifically on ISO 9000, it is a great resource for general quality management information and work practices.

ANSI Public Documents Search

http://www.ansi.org/public/search.asp

ANSI maintains an extensive library of papers, presentations and articles pertaining to the array of supported standards. The search engine allows for targeted research into specific subjects. The reference library (http://www.ansi.org/public/ref_lib.html) provides more general information on the institute and the setting of international standards.

ANSI Conformity Assessment

http://www.ansi.org/public/ca_act.html

This section of the ANSI site provides general guidelines and procedures for assessing conformity to standards. There are sections for various standards, including quality management systems (http://www.ansi.org/public/ca/ca_2.html), and links to sources for the latest information on the current standards and standards in progress.

American Society for Quality

http://www.asq.org

ASQ provides a source of information on ISO 9000 and ISO 14000 standards, QS-9000 requirements and ASQ certification programs. Nonmembers are able to use their on-line resources that share everything from the basics, under "About Quality," to more specific ISO 9000 standards information found under "Standards" and "Certification." Numerous standards, ISO-based books and other sources of standards information can be purchased online from ASQ's "Quality Press."

American Society for Testing and Materials

http://www.astm.org

ASTM prides itself on providing the optimum environment and support for technical committees to develop needed standards and related information. The web site presents a great deal of ISO-related information to aid in this quest. The site carries ASTM news and upcoming events, information for students and educators, training courses, a directory of consultants and a comprehensive standards-based links site.

American Society of Mechanical Engineers

http://www.asme.org

ASME International provides information, courses and numerous membership benefits to those in the mechanical engineering field. There are online journals and press releases coupled with a members only "Student Center" and an "International Center" featuring standards information from around the world.

Association for Quality and Participation

http://www.aqp.org/

AQP is an international not-for-profit membership association dedicated to improving workplaces through quality and participation practices. AQP provides information and training to aid in changing and improving the way businesses operate.

Association of British Certification Bodies (ABCB)

http://www.abcb.demon.co.uk/

The ABCB represent interests of third-party certification bodies according to United Kingdom Accreditation Services, European Co-operation for Accreditation and International Accreditation Forum. ABCB's member-base consists of UKAS accredited third-party certification bodies, or those pursuing UKAS accreditation. The web site contains a directory of members and excellent ISO 9000 implementation guidance for small- and medium-sized businesses.

Automotive Industry Action Group

http://www.aiag.org/quality/index.html

The AIAG is the body responsible for the QS-9000 standards used in the automotive industry. QS-9000 is based on the 1994 edition of ISO 9001 and contains additional requirements that are particular to the automotive industry. The

AIAG site offers access to QS-9000 and related documents as well as many other libraries and services, only some of which are restricted access.

Benchmarking Exchange, The

http://www.benchnet.com

This page is most famous for its informative surveys and polls. At BenchNet users are invited to input their opinions and experiences in numerous surveys on management and quality. Members are able to access BenchNet's Industry Metrics and gain access to help from industry professionals. To go directly to BenchNet's survey and poll results, surfers can steer their browsers to www.industrymetrics.com, which is an easy way to see what has already been collected on business process metrics.

BOOTSTRAP Institute

http://www.iscn.ie/homepages/bootstrap/index.html

Bootstrap's site supports the use of the BOOTSTRAP methodology for the assessment and improvement of the quality of software processes. The site provides an overview of their methodology, taking into account the ISO standard and other initiatives in the quality field.

British Standards Institution

http://www.bsi-global.com/group.xhtml

BSI is the world's oldest national standards body founded in 1901. This profitable corporation is no longer listed as www.bsi.org.uk. BSI provides a broad range of services:

- It is the administrator of the British Standards Society, which participates in the technical committees that write ISO standards.
- It purveys British/European versions of standards.
- It provides a free e-mail update service that will notify subscribers of changes to standards in their areas of interest.
- It provides management consulting, standards implementation consulting and training services worldwide.
- It is one of the largest registration organizations, providing registration and assessment services for small and large companies around the world.

- It provides independent testing, certification and inspection services for products.

Compliance Engineering

http://www.ce-mag.com/

The print magazine covers developments in regulatory compliance for electronics engineers. The online version includes all current and archived articles, an annual reference guide, a calendar and a supplier directory. There are several interactive services and search tools available online that allow users to quickly find and request free information on products and services presented in the magazine.

Department of Defense Single Stock Point for Military Specifications, Standards and Related Publications (DODSSP)

http://www.dodssp.daps.mil/

This is the Department of Defense's (DoD's) Single Stock Point for MilSpecs and Standards. The DoD Single Stock Point was created to centralize the control, distribution, and access to the extensive collection of military specifications, standards, and related standardization documents either prepared by or adopted by the DoD. This site has:

- Military/performance/detail specifications
- Military standards
- DoD-adopted nongovernment/industry specifications and standards
- Federal specifications and standards military handbooks
- Qualified products/manufacturer's lists (QPLs/QMLs)
- USAF/USN aeronautical standards/design standards
- USAF specifications bulletins.

Defense Standardization Program

http://dsp.dla.mil

The DoD Standardization Program uses its web site as a means of distributing information on engineering practices to improve military operational readiness, reduce total ownership costs and reduce acquisition recycle time. The site also lists numerous International Standardization Agreements and the TCP database identifies DoD personnel who participate on technical committees of NGS bodies.

DoE Technical Standards

http://tis.eh.doe.gov/techstds/tspofram.html

This site offers DoE technical standards information including contacts and updates on DoE technical committees, procedures, strategic plans and a complete listing of DoE standards, standards under review, archived standards and ordering information.

European Cooperation for Accreditation

http://www.european-accreditation.org/

The EA site serves as a contact point for the accreditation bodies of the European nations. These bodies are concerned with calibration, measurement and safety as well as with quality management. The database has links to the responsible agencies in each European country.

European Organization for Quality, The

http://www.eoq.org/start.html

The EOQ is the European organization striving for effective improvement of quality management. It is made up of 34 national organizations. This site hosts the journal of the organization as well as other communications and contact information for the national organizations that contribute to global quality standards.

Food and Drug Administration, US Department of Agriculture

http://www.fda.gov/opacom/morechoices/industry/guidedc.htm

Unlike voluntary compliance to standards in many industries, organizations doing business in the food and pharmaceutical industries know that compliance to standards is the law. While structured differently, over 80 percent of the text of the Good Manufacturing Practice (GMP) laws are identical to ISO 9001:1994. GMP laws in force in the United States have parallel regulations in Europe and Asia. FDA departments provide well-written guidelines for the implementation and validation of quality systems in their respective areas.   See http://www.ifpma.org/ich5q.html for a more international perspective.

Global Engineering Documents

http://www.global.ihs.com/

Those in need of engineering standards, military specifications, technical information and regulations, mechanical design specifications, electrical design specifications and news from a wide range of standards — developing organizations — should visit this site. Visitors can sign at the site to receive e-mail newsletters featuring new publications as soon as they become available. Global Engineering Documents is also ANSI's primary distributor for hard copy standards and technical documents and is the parent of www.TechSavvy.com, which provides a searchable database of products, suppliers, specifications and historical data, boasting 87 million parts, records and standards from 460 organizations.

GOAL/QPC

http://www.goalqpc.com/

This nonprofit organization is a management research, publishing and training organization providing products and services enabling people to better manage participative planning, process improvement and innovation. This organization provides several products that aid in implementing quality systems and process improvement. In addition to providing valuable low-cost materials it also has a selection of free materials available for ordering online.

Government-Industry Data Exchange Program

http://www.gidep.org

GIDEP is a cooperative activity between government and industry participants seeking to reduce or eliminate expenditures of resources by making maximum use of information. It is engaged in the exchange of technical information during research, design, development, production and operational phases of the life cycle of systems, facilities and equipment. Any industrial organization that supplies items or services to the US Government or to the Canadian Department of Defence may request participation in GIDEP. An annual utilization report is required in order to maintain participation.

IEEE

http://standards.ieee.org/catalog/olis/subscription.html

The "eye-triple-E" is the world's largest technical professional society and has assumed responsibility for setting standards in electrical engineering, communications and information technology. Most standards can be purchased online.

Independent Association of Accredited Registrars

http://www.iaar.org

IAAR is a nonprofit association of accredited registrars in North America that provides resources for organizations developing their own management assessment based programs. The IAAR works with industry groups, government agencies and other organizations to provide guidance in the appropriate use of international standards, the accreditation process and reliance on accredited registrars. An online listing of its members and contact information for the IAAR can be found at its web site.

Industry Cooperation on Standards and Conformity Assessment

http://www.icsca.org.au

ICSCA is an informally organized group with no charter or dues with members from 44 countries that share the common vision of increased trade and commerce through the appropriate application of industry standards and the belief that such standards should add value to the products affected by them. ICSCA work has been focused upon conformity assessment requirements and agreeing upon ways to improve the global "system" for standards development. ICSCA membership is open to companies and industry associations from all industry sectors. At ICSCA's site visitors will find publicly released documents, news and a "Public Forum" where anyone can participate in electronic debates on ICSCA issues.

Institute of Quality Assurance (IQA)

http://www.iqa.org

IQA provides members with information, training and networking opportunities in the quality arena. Visitors to this site can find numerous sources of ISO 9000 and ISO 14000 information in the "Information Centre," including book reviews, lists of consultants and frequently asked questions. Numerous standards and ISO-based books can also be purchased online at IQA's online bookstore.

International Accreditation Forum

http://www.iaf.nu/

The International Accreditation Forum, Inc. (IAF) is the world association of conformity assessment accreditation bodies and other bodies interested in conformity assessment. Its primary function is to develop a worldwide program of conformity assessment that will promote the elimination of nontariff barriers to trade. IAF promotes the international acceptance of accreditations granted by its MLA signatories, based on the equivalence of accreditation programs. Almost every organization involved in accreditation and registration around the world can be found from this site.

International Automotive Oversight Bureau

http://www.iaob.org

The IAOB is an International Automotive Task Force (IATF) oversight office. IAOB members include DaimlerChrysler Corporation, Ford Motor Company, General Motors and the Automotive Industry Action Group (AIAG). For the latest releases in regard to automotive quality system requirements keep tabs on this site. IAOB online visitors will also find contacts for various IAOB offices, sanctioned interpretations of QS-9000 and communiqués to suppliers from IAOB members.

International Certification Network (IQNet)

http://www.iqnet-certification.com

IQNet is an association of registrars that can administer certificates with the internationally recognized IQNet certificate logo. These organizations work together to provide international certification service to small and large organizations alike. The web site provides a listing of IQNet members, more information on the organization and certification totals for each of its partners.

International Organization for Standardization

http://www.iso.ch

ISO Online is a vehicle for standards creation, distribution and education, which is not surprising coming from the worldwide central office for ISO. This site contains ISO contact information, membership listings, standards and informative Q&As. One of the most helpful features at the site is the "ISO Technical Work" page, which provides lists and links to ISO's numerous technical committees and meeting dates. It is possible to purchase ISO standards "from the source" http://www.iso.ch/iso/en/prods-services/ISOstore/ store.html. However there is no practical difference between those purchased from Switzerland and national versions, except for currency and shipping issues.

International Register of Certificated Auditors (IRCA)

http://www.irca.org

An independent organization within IQA, the IRCA certifies and trains management system auditors. The web site contains information for auditors who are certified or applying for certification and information for training organizations. Downloadable applications for membership and updates on ISO 19011 are also available at the site.

iSixSigma

http://www.isixsigma.com/

This site is loaded with links to free articles, chat and more, covering many areas of quality management. iSixSigma currently provides users with access to a rich collection of online resources, including various communications tools, online forums, timely articles, sample documentation, shopping services, personalized content and branded programming.

ISO 9000 and ISO 14000 from ISO

http://www.iso.ch/iso/en/iso9000-14000/index.html

This is a fairly concise introduction to the standards from the International Organization for Standardization. "The basics" (http://www.iso.ch/iso/en/iso 9000-14000/tour/magical.html) or "The Magical Demystifying Tour of ISO 9000 and ISO 14000" is a particularly informative and entertaining section for the uninitiated.

Home Pages for TC176 and TC207 at ISO Headquarters

http://www.iso.ch/iso/en/stdsdevelopment/tclist/TechnicalCommitteeDeta ilPage.TechnicalCommitteeDetail?TC=176

http://www.iso.ch/iso/en/stdsdevelopment/tclist/TechnicalCommitteeDeta ilPage.TechnicalCommitteeDetail?TC=207

The official home pages of the technical committees are only available to ISO members and standards writers. This site keeps a running tally of activities, including those of subcommittees. These pages are loaded with links to related committees and participants.

TC 176

http://www.tc176.org/

For current ISO 9000 information there is no better place to go than the source. Technical Committee (TC) 176, the committee responsible for developing the ISO 9000 series of standards and guidance documents, offers transition planning guides for ISO 9001:2000, guidance on the documentation requirements of ISO 9001:2000, guidance on terminology and much more to aid in the implementation of the new standard. The site offers general ISO-related news and a detailed listing of each group working under TC 207, its participants and contact information. http://isotc176sc2.elysium-ltd.net/ links to the Quality Systems subcommittee, SC 2.

TC 207

http://www.tc207.org/

This is the home page of TC 207 on Environmental Management — the technical committee responsible for ISO 14000. The site includes a list of current standards for environmental management.

ISO 9000 Translated into Plain English

http://praxiom.com

This site is aimed for those just getting started in the ISO 9000 implementation program and those just considering it. ISO 9000 Translated into Plain English takes visitors through ISO 9000 step-by-step by first explaining the standard, its requirements and its guidelines, and then breaking down the internal audit process and QMS development plans. A perfect "How To" site for QMS coordinators, this site also offers numerous ISO publications and links.

ISO Support Group

http://www.isogroup.simplenet.com/

This site is a resource assisting in the implementation of ISO 9000, QS-9000 or ISO 14000. Visitors can get registration pricing quotes from participating registrars or consulting, auditing and/or training quotes from participating firms. One of the greatest features of the site is the ISO 9000:2000 Auditor's Checklist, which assesses the requirements of the 2000 version of the ISO 9000 standard point-by-point, asking some of the questions necessary for ISO 9000:2000 compliance. Not only is this a great resource for auditors, but it also provides a great preparation tool for those preparing for certification.

ISO Easy

http://www.isoeasy.org

A great source for ISO-related links and basic information, ISO Easy also offers many practical information sources such as a free ISO 9000 mailing list, training resources, consulting services and document preparation services.

ISO 9000 Web Directory

http://www.iso9000directory.com

This site offers a searchable database (for members only) of ISO registered sites, access to technical papers and is home of the International Conference on ISO, along with several other events listed on the site's calendar. The ISO 9000-related links site on this page gives a thorough listing of approximately 150 sites ranging from "General Quality" to "State and Government Quality Awards and Programs."

ISO 14000 Information Center, The

http://www.iso14000.com

One of the best sources for ISO 14000 information on the web, The ISO 14000 Information Center provides a list of ISO 14000 accredited registrars, an overview of the standard, standard purchasing information and numerous resources. Also, the site features a searchable database of companies registered or certified to ISO 14001; however, the database is comprised of site visitors entering their own certification information and thus is an incomplete listing, but constantly growing.

Malcolm Baldrige National Quality Award Program

http://www.quality.nist.gov/

A part of the NIST site, this site provides detailed information on the Malcolm Baldrige National Quality Award Program. Baldrige materials are provided online at no charge.

NSSN: A National Resource for Global Standards

http://www.nssn.org

This site serves as a central point to search for standards and information from many sources and serves as an important gateway connecting those who seek standards to those that supply them. NSSN provides a list of information resources (http://www.nssn.org/information.html), which includes quick links to US government standards and regulatory information sites and listings of all US participation in ISO activities. Also, the site allows users to perform keyword searches or to search by ISO committee or subcommittee for contact information for accredited Technical Advisory Groups. Some of the information is accessible to members only.

National Institute of Standards Technology

http://www.nist.gov/

NIST (formerly known as the National Bureau of Standards) is the government agency responsible for maintaining consistency of measurement throughout the nation. All government standards for calibration and measurement are established by this department. NIST provides training, calibration and measurement services along with standards and calibration materials. The site also offers an extensive selection of publications at no charge for online access. It offers a standards-related news service alongside standards products. An informative historical perspective on the agency can be found at http://museum.nist.gov/.

NIST Office of Calibration Services

http://ts.nist.gov/ts/htdocs/230/233/calibrations

NIST provides, for a fee, the highest order of calibration services available in the United States. It directly links a customer's precision equipment or transfer standards to national and international measurement standards. These services are offered to public and private organizations and individuals alike.

NIST Conformity Assessment

http://ts.nist.gov/ts/htdocs/210/216/assessment.htm

There is a large collection of government guidance documents available on the web through the NIST. A particularly useful selection is on conformity assessment. As part of the Office of Standards Services, the NIST National Voluntary Conformity Assessment Systems Evaluation (NVCASE) Program includes activities related to laboratory testing, product certification and quality system registration. After NVCASE evaluation, NIST provides recognition to qualified US organizations that effectively demonstrate conformance with established criteria. The ultimate goal is to help US manufacturers satisfy applicable product requirements mandated by other countries through conformity assessment procedures conducted in this country prior to export.

NIST Office of Standards Services

http://ts.nist.gov/ts/htdocs/210/210.htm

The Office of Standards Services conducts standards-related programs and knowledge of services that will strengthen the US economy and improve the quality of life. Its goal is to ensure the use and recognition of US standards, test and calibration data domestically and in the global marketplace. Its web site provides information to industry, trade associations and exporters by providing lists of OSS's activities, the Global Standards Program, the Technical Standards Activities Program and the Standards Information Program.

Standard Reference Materials Program

http://ts.nist.gov/ts/htdocs/230/232/232.htm

The SRM program's web site attempts to spread accurate and compatible measurements through the development, certification and distribution of Standard Reference Materials. This program serves as the main contact point for all NIST reference materials activities interfacing with similar efforts in the private sector, other federal agencies and other nations. Thus, the site provides extensive measurement and standards laboratories information, including a list of largely chemical industry-related sties, special publications and catalogs from which to purchase measurement standards and related reference materials.

NIST Manufacturing Engineering Laboratory

http://www.mel.nist.gov/

In addition to being actively involved in several research areas the MEL provides a wide range of guidance and services in manufacturing methods, metrology, calibration and standards.

Quality America Inc.

http://qualityamerica.com

Quality America is the place to get information on statistical process control, document control, American Society for Quality certification materials, SPC training and Six Sigma software, training, consulting and more. The site offers demos of many software products, which are for sale (along with all merchandise) in an online store.

Quality Digest

http://www.qualitydigest.com/

Quality Digest posts articles, features and columns on this site. It is a great place to peruse ISO book and software reviews before making purchases. Quality Digest includes a link to QualNet, an online resource for quality products and services from more than 1,500 quality suppliers.

Quality Network

http://www.quality.co.uk/hometext.htm

For those interested in both ISO 9000 and ISO 14000, this site offers valuable information and advice including sample quality system documentation. Also, for those needing directories of ISO 9000 registrars or auditors, ISO 14000 registrars, EMAS and BS7750 registered companies or accredited EMAS verification organizations, Quality Network has it all along with an extensive list of ISO 9000- and ISO 14000-related links.

Quality Online

http://qualitymag.com/

This is an online version of the monthly business magazine. The magazine covers metrology methods and equipment, software and analytical tools, and quality management. A large number of past articles and news briefs are accessible in the archives. The site also provides downloadable trial versions of some products.

Quality Publishing

http://www.qualitypublishing.com/

Quality America & Quality Publishing provide tools for the quality practitioner. It offers statistical process control and document control software, as well as ASQ certification materials, SPC training, and Six Sigma software, training and consulting.

Quality Resources Online

http://www.quality.org/

Bill Casti, creator of Quality Resources Online, claims his site is "the best quality site around, no bull!" and he just may be right. Whether looking for quality-related employment, information on quality in health care, quality awards, metrology resources or "Insights from Dilbert" this homespun site is one of the most extensive conglomerations of ISO 9000 and quality resources on the web.

QSU Publishing Company

http://www.qsuonline.com/

This is a must to find North American registration totals for ISO 9000 and ISO 14001. Data is available by registrar and top Standard Industrial Codes at www.qsuonline.com. QSU Publishing Company posts the current ISO 9000 Big Ten registrars, a listing of the top firms as determined by total number of active certificates. QSU Publishing Company is the home of *Quality Systems Update*, the 12-year-old premiere industry journal which provides cutting-edge ISO 9000 and QS-9000 content, and *The Environmental Management Report*, a seven-year-old ISO 14001 journal aimed at keeping readers on top of EMS developments. Subscribers can access the contents of current and previous issues of *Quality Systems Update* online as an added bonus of subscription. The site provides information on the *ISO 9000* and *14000 Registered Company Directories North America*, research service and a free registrar contact information page. Co-publisher of this *Handbook*, QSU Publishing Company, formerly a part of The McGraw-Hill Companies, also sells many other quality, environmental and management-related McGraw-Hill books at discounted prices.

QuEST Forum

http://questforum.asq.org

This site supports TL 9000 and is aimed at "Improving Telecommunications Service Worldwide." As you can tell from the URL, the QuEST Forum is administered by ASQ. There is a general public area that provides access to useful information pertinent to the telecommunications industry, including guidelines for registration and proceedings from some of its international meetings. There is also a members area for telecommunication suppliers.

Raad voor Accreditatie (RvA)

http://www.rva.nl

The Dutch accreditation body for certification bodies, inspection bodies, testing bodies, calibration laboratories and proficiency testing, RvA lists all organizations holding RvA accreditation on its web site. Also, visitors at this site can see any suspended, withdrawn or falsely claimed accreditations.

Registrar Accreditation Board

http://www.rabnet.com/index.shtml

All RAB-approved ISO 9000 and ISO 14001 registrars, training course providers and individual auditors can be found here in complete listings or individually through searchable databases. Information on how to become an RAB-approved auditor, registrar or course provider is also available.

RAB Database of Accredited Registrars

http://www.rabnet.com/qr_dir.htm

This is a simple, powerful search engine to access RAB-accredited ISO 9000 registrars. Registrars for ISO 14000 can be found at http://www.rabnet.com/er_dir.htm.

Society of Automotive Engineers

http://www.sae.org

The Society of Automotive Engineers (SAE) is the "Engineering Society for Advancing Mobility in Land, Sea, Air and Space" and is the primary organization providing technical standards for those industries. Measurement and design products and training programs are available for purchase online. The SAE is actively involved in the establishment and harmonization of commercial and military/government standards in the transportation industry. The SAE is the distributor of AS9100: Quality Systems - Aerospace - Model for Quality Assurance in Design, Development, Production, Installation and Servicing

Standards Council of Canada

http://www.scc.ca/

The Standards Council of Canada (SCC) provides numerous ISO resources especially aimed at Canadians implementing the standard. The site includes forums and accreditation information as well as "Infocentre" and "Standards" pages. Users can link from the site to IHS Canada, the exclusive Canadian distributor of ISO and IEC standards.

United Kingdom Accreditation Service

http://www.ukas.com/

UKAS is the sole national body recognized by the British government for the accreditation of testing and calibration laboratories, certification and inspection bodies. A not-for-profit company, limited by guarantee, UKAS operates under a Memorandum of Understanding with the government through the Department of Trade and Industry. UKAS accreditation allows registrars to sell services that are recognized internationally. This service is widely used in North America. UKAS calibration laboratories can be found at http://www.ukas.org.

United States National Committee of IEC

http://web.ansi.org/rooms/room_22

The USNC serves as the US electrotechnical industry interface with the European Committee for Electrotechnical Standardization – CENELEC. The USNC web site provides a calendar of the USNC executive committee, USNC contacts, news, technical information and extensive conglomeration of USNC documents including position papers, presentations, administrative documents and more general organization information. Most of the documents available on this site are for ANSI members only.

W. Edwards Deming Institute

http://caes.mit.edu/deming/resources.html

MIT has links to several free sites that provide resources for quality and process improvement. Deming-related materials are available in several locations from this site.

Training and Consulting Providers

There are a large number of consultants and training organizations that are willing and able to help in the implementation of a quality system. They provide a broad range of services depending on the needs of the organization. The resources below are a starting point for services available around the world. The challenge is finding the services that meet the needs of the organization.

Some companies that provide registration audits also provide consulting or training services. Others do not because they believe it is a conflict of interest. Some registrars recommend consultants or trainers, others do not.

Any trainer or consultant that provides more than "off-the-shelf" training should be willing to discuss specific organizational needs before quoting prices or solutions.

ANSI/RAB keeps a training course provider database that is searchable online at http://www.rabnet.com/qc_dir.htm for Quality Management Systems (QMS) training and

http://www.rabnet.com/ec_dir.htm for Environmental Management Systems (EMS) training course providers.

There are many other capable trainers and consultants that are not registered in the ANSI/RAB database. An overwhelming number can be found on the Internet with a search engine using "ISO train" or "ISO consult" as key words. The following are lists where consultants and trainers have registered. The presence of a provider on a list does not usually constitute an endorsement by the keeper of the list.

http://www.isixsigma.com/co/

http://www.isogroup.simplenet.com/

http://www.isoeasy.org/training.htm

http://www.isoeasy.org/consulti.htm

http://www.quality.org/html/consults.html

There are also a number of resources to find trainers and consultants whose services extend beyond the implementation of ISO 9000.

American Society for Training & Development

www.astd.org

ASTD is a professional organization for trainers and educators. While this is a significant resource for technical training, management and employee development there is little here that is specifically related to ISO 9000 implementation.

Internet Directory of Advisors and Consultants

www.idac.com

This Directory of Advisors and Consultants offers several indexes to help users find US and international consulting groups. The index includes such service areas as industrial engineering, benchmarking, production design and development, product liability and organizational strategy.

International Institute of Consulting and Training

http://consultinginstitute.org

The institute provides contacts and resources in training, consulting and publishing. It focuses on a number of different areas including: metrology, calibration, procedures, gage repair and ISO 17025/Guide 25.

Accredited Registrars

Registrars	ISO 9000	ISO/TS 16949	ISO 14001	Accreditation			
				RvA	RAB	UKAS	SCC
Aboma+Keboma Certificering B.V.	🏳			🏳			
ABS Quality Evaluations, Inc.	🏳	🏳	🏳	🏳	🏳		
ACC-USA, American Certification Corp.	🏳			🏳			
Advanced Waste Management Systems			🏳	🏳	🏳		
Advantica Technologies Ltd.	🏳					🏳	
AEA Quality Advantage Corporation	🏳			🏳			
AFAQ-ASCERT International, Inc.	🏳	🏳	🏳		🏳		
AGS American Global Standards	🏳		🏳		🏳		
Ai Associates			🏳			🏳	
AJA Registrars Ltd.	🏳		🏳			🏳	
American Institute of Quality Registrars	🏳				🏳		
AMTAC Certification Services Ltd.	🏳		🏳			🏳	
Amtri Veritas	🏳		🏳			🏳	
A-Pex International Co. Ltd.	🏳		🏳	🏳			
AOQC Moody International, Inc.	🏳		🏳		🏳		
AOQC Moody International (Canada)	🏳		🏳				
APIQR American Petroleum Inst. Quality Reg.	🏳				🏳		🏳
AQA American Quality Assessors	🏳	🏳	🏳	🏳	🏳		
AQSR International, Inc.	🏳		🏳		🏳		
ASME Am. Soc. of Mech. Engineers	🏳			🏳	🏳		
Aspects Moody Certification Ltd.			🏳			🏳	
ASQR International	🏳	🏳			🏳		
ASR American Systems Registrar	🏳		🏳		🏳		
ASTA Certification Svcs.	🏳		🏳			🏳	

Registrars	ISO 9000	ISO/TS 16949	ISO 14001	Accreditation			
				RvA	RAB	UKAS	SCC
BABT Product Services Ltd.	✓			✓		✓	
Beijing 9000 Certification Ctr for Quality Sys.	✓		✓			✓	
Birmingham Assay Office	✓					✓	
BM TRADA Certification Ltd.	✓		✓				✓
BNQ Bureau de Norm. du Quebec	✓					✓	
BQR Best CERT Quality Regs, Ltd.	✓		✓		✓		
BRE Certification Ltd.	✓					✓	
British Approvals Service for Cables	✓					✓	
British Electrotechnical Approvals Bd.	✓					✓	
British Inspecting Engineers Ltd.	✓					✓	
British Institute of NDT	✓					✓	
BSI	✓	✓	✓			✓	
BSI Inc.	✓		✓	✓	✓		✓
BSI Management Systems Canada Inc.	✓		✓				✓
Bureau of Indian Standards Manak Bhavan	✓			✓			
BVQI Bureau Veritas Quality Intl.	✓	✓	✓	✓	✓	✓	✓
Calidad Mexicana Certificada, A.C.	✓		✓		✓		
Central Certification Service Ltd.	✓		✓			✓	
Centre for Assessment Ltd.	✓					✓	
CEPREI Certification Body	✓		✓		✓		
CERTECH Registration Inc.	✓				✓		
Certificatiebureau Nederland B.V.	✓			✓			
Certification International (UK) Ltd.	✓		✓			✓	
CGSB Canadian General Standards Board	✓						✓
Chamber Certification Assessment Svc. Ltd.	✓					✓	
China Automotive Quality Cert. Ctr.	✓				✓		
CICS Ceramic Industry Cert. Scheme	✓		✓			✓	
Consortium for Auto Reg. Svcs. Ltd.	✓					✓	
CRS Registrars, Inc.	✓		✓		✓		
D.A.S. Certification Ltd.	✓					✓	
DLS Quality Tech. Assoc. Inc.	✓				✓		
DNV Det Norske Veritas Certification, Inc.	✓	✓	✓	✓	✓		
DNV Certification Ltd.	✓		✓		✓	✓	
DQS German Am. Reg. for Mgt. Sys.	✓	✓	✓		✓		
D&T Deloitte & Touche Quality Reg.	✓		✓		✓		
Eagle Registrations, Inc.	✓	✓	✓	✓	✓		
EAQA Ltd.	✓				✓		
EAQA USA Registrars, Inc.	✓				✓		
ECAS B.V.	✓						
Electrical Equipment Certification Svc.	✓					✓	
Electricity Assn. Qual. Assurance Ltd.	✓		✓			✓	
ENTELA, Inc., Quality System Reg. Division	✓	✓	✓		✓		

Registrars	ISO 9000	ISO/TS 16949	ISO 14001	RvA	RAB	UKAS	SCC
Environment & Quality Assur. Intl. Cert. Ctr.	✓				✓		
Environment & Development Foundation			✓	✓		✓	
EQA European Quality Assurance Ltd.	✓		✓			✓	
ERM Cert. & Verification Services Ltd.			✓			✓	
EQR, Quality Registry Inc.	✓			✓			
Ever Win Quality Certification Center	✓		✓		✓		
Excalibur Registrations Inc.	✓	✓			✓		
Fluke Nederland B.V. Standaard Laboratorium	✓		✓				
FM Global	✓						
GASTEC Certification B.V.	✓		✓				
GBJD Registrars Ltd.	✓						
Germanischer Lloyd Certification GmbH	✓						
Global Certification Ltd.	✓		✓	✓		✓	
Government of India ST&QC Directorate	✓			✓			
GRI Global Registrars, Inc.	✓			✓	✓		
Hallmark Quality Assurance Ltd.	✓					✓	
Hangzhow WIT Management Sys. Assessment	✓			✓	✓		
Hong Kong Quality Assurance Agency	✓		✓	✓		✓	
HSB Registration Services	✓			✓	✓		
IMS International Ltd.	✓					✓	
IMS International Mgt. Systems	✓				✓		
Independent European Certification Ltd.	✓					✓	
Indian Register of Shipping	✓			✓			
Industry Sector Certification Ltd.	✓					✓	
INSPEC International Ltd.	✓					✓	
International Certification Services Ltd.	✓					✓	
International Quality Certs. SA de CV	✓				✓		
International Standards Authority	✓				✓		
INTERTEK Testing Servics NA, Inc.	✓	✓		✓	✓	✓	✓
IQSR International Quality System Registrars	✓				✓		✓
ISOQAR	✓		✓		✓	✓	
Japan Audit & Certification Organization	✓		✓			✓	
Japan Automobile Research Institute	✓			✓			
Japan Electrical Safety & Env. Tech. Labs	✓			✓			
Japan Gas Appliances Inspection Association	✓			✓			
Japan Quality Assurance Organization	✓	✓	✓	✓	✓	✓	
Japanese Standards Association			✓			✓	
JIC Quality Assurance Ltd.	✓			✓			
KEMA Quality B.V.	✓			✓			
KEMA Registered Quality, Inc.	✓		✓	✓	✓		
KIWA NV Certificatie en Keuringen	✓			✓			
Koenders Services B.V. Kalibratie Laboratrium	✓		✓	✓			

Registrars	ISO 9000	ISO/TS 16949	ISO 14001	Accreditation			
				RvA	RAB	UKAS	SCC
Korean Foundation for Quality	✓	✓			✓		
Letrina S.A.	✓			✓			
Legal Services Commission	✓					✓	
LLD Inc.			✓		✓		
LRQA Lloyd's Register Q.A. Ltd. UK	✓	✓	✓	✓		✓	
LRQA Lloyd's Register Q.A. Ltd. USA	✓		✓		✓		✓
MALQA Mutuagung Lestari Q.A.	✓					✓	
Marketing Quality Assurance Ltd.	✓					✓	
Meehanite Certification Ltd.	✓					✓	
MKB-Certificatie	✓			✓			
Moody International Certification Ltd.	✓			✓		✓	
MSB Mauritius Standards Bureau	✓			✓			
National Security Inspectorate	✓					✓	
National Weights & Measures Lab.	✓					✓	
Nippon Kaiji Kentei Quality Assurance Ltd.	✓			✓			
Nippon Kaji Kyokai Quality & Envir. Systems	✓			✓			
NQA National Quality Assurance Ltd. UK	✓	✓	✓	✓	✓	✓	
NQA National Quality Assurance Ltd. USA	✓		✓		✓		
NSAI National Standards Authority of Ireland	✓	✓	✓		✓		
NSF International Strategic Registrations Ltd.	✓	✓	✓			✓	
OFGEM (EMES)	✓				✓		
Orion Registrar, Inc.	✓		✓	✓	✓		✓
PJR Perry Johnson Registrars, Inc.	✓		✓	✓	✓	✓	
Premier Assessments Ltd.	✓					✓	
PRI Performance Review Institute Registrar	✓		✓		✓		
Product Authentication Inspectorate Ltd.	✓					✓	
PRO Professional Registrar Org., Inc.	✓		✓		✓		
PSB Certification Pte Ltd.	✓	✓		✓	✓		
QA International Certification Ltd.	✓					✓	
QCB Quality Certification Bureau, Inc.	✓	✓	✓	✓			✓
QMI Quality Management Institute	✓	✓	✓	✓	✓		✓
QSR Quality Systems Registrars, Inc.	✓		✓	✓	✓		
Quality Cert (India) Private Limited	✓			✓			
Quality Certification Ltd.	✓					✓	
Quality & Environmental Cert. Ltd.	✓					✓	
Quality Services International	✓				✓		
QUASAR Quality Systems Assessment Reg.	✓						✓
Quenviro Systems International	✓						✓
Rail Industry Quality Certification Ltd.	✓					✓	
Ronet International Certification Servics Ltd.	✓					✓	
Royal & Sun Alliance Certification Service	✓					✓	

Registrars	ISO 9000	ISO/TS 16949	ISO 14001	Accreditation			
				RvA	RAB	UKAS	SCC
SATRA Quality Assurance Ltd.	✓		✓			✓	
Security Systems & Alarms Inspection Board	✓					✓	
SGS International Certification Services, Inc.	✓	✓	✓	✓	✓		
SGS ICS Canada	✓		✓				✓
SGS United Kingdom ICS Ltd.	✓		✓			✓	
Shanghai Audit Center of Quality Systems	✓			✓	✓		
Signature Management Cert. Services LLC	✓			✓			
SIRA Certification Service	✓		✓			✓	
SIRIM QAS Sdn. Bhd.	✓		✓			✓	
SLSI Sri Lanka Standards Institution	✓			✓			
SABS South African Bureau of Standards	✓	✓	✓	✓			
SQA Smithers Quality Assessments, Inc.	✓		✓	✓	✓		
SRI Steel Related Ind. Quality Syst. Reg.	✓	✓	✓	✓	✓		
Standards Institution of Israel	✓		✓				
Steel Construction Certification Scheme Ltd.	✓					✓	
STR-Registrar LLC	✓				✓		
Sucfinodo	✓			✓			
Telefication B.V.	✓			✓			
Telcordia Quality Registration	✓				✓		
Testing and Certification Specialists Ltd.	✓			✓			
The Health Quality Service	✓					✓	
The Qual. Scheme for Ready Mixed Concrete	✓					✓	
TRA Certification	✓			✓	✓		
TRC The Registrar Company, Inc.	✓				✓		
TUV Essen	✓	✓			✓		
TUV Management Service	✓	✓	✓		✓		✓
TUV Nederland QA B.V.	✓			✓			
TUV Rheinland of North America Ltd.	✓	✓	✓	✓	✓		
TUV UK Quality Assurance Ltd.	✓					✓	
UK Cert. Authority for Reinforcing Steels	✓					✓	
UL Underwriters Laboratories, Inc.	✓		✓	✓	✓	✓	✓
UL Canada	✓		✓				✓
Universal Certification Services Co. Ltd.	✓			✓			
Univ. of Huddersfield Training & Quality Srvs.	✓					✓	
University of Ljubljana	✓		✓	✓			
URS United Registrar of Systems Ltd.	✓		✓			✓	
URS Verification Ltd.			✓			✓	
ViaNoRM B.V.	✓			✓			
Vilnius Metrology Center Calibration Lab.	✓		✓	✓			
VCA Vehicle Certification Agency NA	✓	✓	✓		✓	✓	
VTI Vouching Technical Inspection Ltd.	✓			✓	✓		

Registrars	ISO 9000	ISO/TS 16949	ISO 14001	Accreditation			
				RvA	RAB	UKAS	SCC
World Certification Services Ltd.	☛					☛	
Worldwide Quality Assurance	☛					☛	
Zurich Certification Ltd.	☛		☛			☛	

Registrar Contact Information

Aboma+Keboma Certificering B.V.

Postbus 141
EDE, Netherlands 6710 BC
Phone: +0318-633300; Fax: +0318-632013
E-mail: certificering@aboma.nl
Web: www.aboma.nl

ABS QE

ABS Quality Evaluations, Inc.
16855 Northchase Dr.
Houston, TX 77060 USA
Phone: 281-877-6800; Fax: 281-877-6801
E-mail: qe_cust_serv@eagle.org
Web: www.abs-qe.com

ACC-USA, American Certification Corp.

69 Winn Street
Burlington, MA 01803 USA
Phone: 781-273-4472; Fax: 877-592-5444
E-mail: amcertcorp@aol.com

Advantica Technologies Limited

Ashby Rd.
Loughborough
Leicestershire LE11 3GR United Kingdom
Contact: D Ricketts
Phone: +44-1509-282-000; Fax: +44-1509-283-113

AEA

AEA Quality Advantage Corporation
15 Myers Corner Rd., Suite 1-S
Wappingers Falls, NY 12590-4117 USA
Phone: 845-298-0032; Fax: 845-298-1253
E-mail: sales@aeaquality.com
E-mail: aea@aeaquality.com
Web: www.aeaquality.com

AFAQ-ASCERT

AFAQ-ASCERT International, Inc.
1054 31st St., NW, Suite 320
Washington, DC 20007
Contact: Frederic Sevin
Phone: 202-338-4365 or 800-241-3412; Fax: 202-337-3709
E-mail: frederic.sevin@afaq.org
Web: www.afaq.org

AGS

AGS American Global Standards
300 Esplanade Dr., Suite 1120
Oxnard, CA 93030 USA
Contact: Gary Martel
Phone: 805-983-8200; Fax: 805-983-1227
E-mail: admin@americanglobalstandards.com
Web: www.americanglobalstandards.com

Ai Associates

10 Mill Meadow Way
Etwall
Derbyshire DE65 6NL United Kingdom
Contact: Ian Roberts
Phone: +44-1283-733-190; Fax: +44-1283-733-462

AJA

AJA Registrars Limited
Court Lodge
105 High St.
Portishead
Bristol BS20 9PT United Kingdom
Contact: R Kirton
Phone: +44-1275-849-188; Fax: +44-1275-849-198

American Institute of Quality Registrars

15604 Farmington Rd.
Livonia, MI 48154 USA
Contact: Michael Morse
Phone: 734-422-9789; Fax: 734-421-0353
E-mail: dyaquinto@aiqusa.com

AMTAC

AMTAC Certification Services Limited
Norman Rd.
Broadheath
Altrincham
Cheshire WA14 4EP United Kingdom
Contact: D. Gale
Phone: +44-161-928-8924; Fax: +44-161-927-7359

Amtri Veritas

Hulley Rd.
Macclesfield
Cheshire SK10 2NE United Kingdom
Contact: R. A. Smallwood
Phone: +44-1625-425-421; Fax: +44-1625-434-964

AOQC (Canada)

AOQC Moody International, Ltd. (Canada)
57 Simcoe St., Suite 2H
Oshawa, Ontario L1H 4G4 Canada
Phone: 905-433-2955; Fax: 905-432-9308
E-mail: mti@moodycanada.com
Web: www.moodyint.com

AOQC (USA)

AOQC Moody International, Inc.
24900 Pitkin Road, Suite 200
The Woodlands, TX 77386 USA
Contact: Tom Harris
Phone: 281-367-8764; Fax: 281-367-3496
E-mail: tomh@moodyint.com
Web: www.aoqcmoody.com

A-Pex International Company Ltd.

Quality Assurance Department
4383-326, Asama-cho
Ise-Shi Mie-Ken, Japan 516-0021
Phone: +81-596-248008; Fax: +81-596-248002

APIQR

American Petroleum Institute Quality Registrar
1220 L St., NW
Washington, DC 20005 USA
Contact: Gerardo Uria
Phone: 202-682-8129; Fax: 202-682-8070
E-mail: hans@api.org
E-mail: evanst@api.org
Web: www.api.org

AQA

American Quality Assessors
1107 Belleview Ave.
Columbia, SC 29201 USA
Contact: Patricia Pardue
Phone: 803-779-8150; Fax: 803-779-8109
E-mail: patricia@aqausa.com
E-mail: kelly@aqausa.com
Web: www.aqausa.com

AQSR

AQSR International, Inc.
Automotive Quality Systems Registrar
3025 Boardwalk Dr.
Suite 120
Ann Arbor, MI 48108 USA
Contact: Brad Kitchen
Phone: 888-866-5666 or 734-913-8055; Fax: 734-913-8152
E-mail: bkitchen@aqsr.com
Web: www.aqsr.com

ASME

American Society of Mechanical Engineers
Three Park Ave.
New York, NY 10016-5990 USA
Phone: 212-591-8590 or 212-591-8033; Fax: 212-591-8599 or 212-591-7674
Contact: David Wizda
E-mail: accreditation@asme.org
E-mail: wizdad@asme.org
Web: www.asme.org

AMC

Aspects Moody Certification Ltd.
Suite 6
The Derwent Business Centre
Clarke St.
Derby
DE1 2BU United Kingdom
Contact: J Chalinor
Phone: +44-133-220-2556; Fax: +44-133-220-5067

ASQR

ASQR International Canada
2560 Matheson Blvd. Suite 226
Mississauga, Ontario L4W 4Y9 Canada
Phone: 888-866-5666; Fax: 905-624-7213
E-mail: aqsrca@aqsr.com
Web: www.aqsr.com

ASR

American Systems Registrar
4550 Cascade Rd., SE
Suite 202
Grand Rapids, MI 49546 USA
Contact: Richelle Kinzie
Phone: 888-891-9002; Fax: 616-942-6409
E-mail: staff@asr.9000.net
Web: www.asr.9000.net

ASTA

ASTA Certification Services
ASTA House
Chestnut Field
Rugby
Warwickshire CV21 2TL United Kingdom
Contact: M Swan
Phone: +44-1788-578-435; Fax: +44-1788-573-605

AWM

Advanced Waste Management Systems
6430 Hixson Pike
PO Box 100

Hixson, TN 37343 USA
Phone: 423-843-2206; Fax: 423-843-2310
Contact: Jim Mullican
E-mail: mullican@awm.net
Web: www.awm.net

BABT

BABT Product Services Ltd.
Claremont House
34 Molesey Rd.
Walton-on-Thames
Surrey KT12 4RQ United Kingdom
Contact: A. Binks
Phone: +44-193-225-1244; Fax: +44-193-225-1252

Beijing 9000 Certification Centre

Beijing 9000 Certification Centre for Quality System
PO Box No. 1
Zonghe Building
No. 211, Ban Si Huan Zhong Lu
Haidian District, 100083
Beijing
PR China
Contact: Wang Mei
Phone: +86-10-6233-5123; Fax: +86-10-6233-5213

UK Office
18 Creffield Rd.
Ealing
London W5 3RP United Kingdom
Phone: +44-208-993-7803; Fax: +44-208-932-7471

Birmingham Assay Office

PO Box 151
Newhall St.
Birmingham B3 1SB United Kingdom
Phone: +44-121-262-1043; Fax: +44-121-236-3228
Contact: I. Bayley

BM TRADA

BM TRADA Certification Ltd.
Incorporating CQA

Head Office
Stocking Lane
Hughenden Valley
High Wycombe
Bucks HP14 4NR United Kingdom
Contact: H Taylor
Phone: +44-149-456-5484; Fax: +44-149-456-5487

Office 30
Stirling Business Centre
Wellgreen Place
Stirling FK8 2DZ United Kingdom
Phone: +44-178-645-0891; Fax: +44-178-645-1087

BNQ

Bureau de Normalisation du Quebec
Quality System Registration
333 rue Franquet
Sainte-Foy, Quebec G1P 4C7 Canada
Phone: 418-652-2238; Fax: 418-652-2292
E-mail: bnq@criq.qc.ca
Web: www.criq.qc.ca/bnq

BQR

BestCERT Quality Registrars, Ltd.
55 Lake Street, Suite 240
Gardner, MA 01440
Contact: Sandy Tokola
Phone: 978-630-3993; Fax: 978-630-3909
E-mail: bqriso@aol.com
Web: www.bestcert.org

BRE

BRE Certification Ltd.
Incorporating BRE Certification, LPCB & WIMLAS
Garston
Watford
Herts WD25 9XX United Kingdom
Contact: C Beedel
Phone: +44-192-366-4100; Fax: +44-192-366-4335

British Approvals Service for Cables

23 Presley Way
Crownhill
Milton Keynes MK8 0ES United Kingdom
Contact: J. Senders
Phone: +44-190-826-7300; Fax: +44-190-826-7255

British Electrotechnical Approvals Board

1 Station View
Guildford
Surrey GU1 4JY United Kingdom
Contact: P. D. Stokes
Phone: +44-148-344-5466; Fax: +44-148-344-5477

British Inspecting Engineers Ltd.

Chatsworth Technology Park
Dunston Rd.
Chesterfield
Derbyshire S41 8XA United Kingdom
Contact: P. Smith
Phone: +44-124-626-0260; Fax: +44-124-626-0919

British Institute of NDT

1 Spencer Parade
Northampton NN1 5AA United Kingdom
Contact: J. Thompson
Phone: +44-160-425-9056; Fax: +44-160-423-1489

BSI, Inc.

12110 Sunset Hills Rd., Suite 140
Reston, VA 20190-3231 USA
Contact: Tom Shelley
Phone: 800-862-4977 or 703-464-1931; Fax: 703-437-9001
E-mail: inquiry@bsiamericas.com
E-mail: tom.shelley@bsiamericas.com
Web: www.bsiamericas.com

BSI Management Systems

Head Office
389 Chiswick High Rd.
London W4 4AL United Kingdom

Contact: L. Button
Phone: +44-208-996-9000; Fax: +44-208-996-7400

BSI Management Systems Canada Inc.

17 Four Seasons Place, Suite 102
Toronto, Ontario M9B 6E6 Canada
Contact: Andy Hofmann
Phone: 416-620-9991; Fax: 416-620-9911
E-mail: andy.hofmann@bsiamericas.com
Web: www.bsiamericas.com

Bureau of Indian Standards Manak Bhavan

9 Bahadur Shah Zafar Marg
New Delhi, India 110002
Phone: +91-11-3230131; Fax: +91-11-3239399
E-mail: bis@vsnl.com

BVQI (USA)

Bureau Veritas Quality International (NA) Inc.
515 W. Fifth St.
Jamestown, NY 14701 USA
Contact: Don Burdick
Phone: 800-937-9311 or 716-484-9002; Fax: 716-484-9003
E-mail: info@bvqi.com
E-mail: GSwan@bvqina.com
Web: www.bvqina.com

BVQI (UK)

224 – 226 Tower Bridge Court
Tower Bridge Rd.
London SE1 2TX United Kingdom
Contact: M Littlefair
Phone: +44-207-661-0700; Fax: +44-207-661-0790

Calidad Mexicana Certificada, A.C.

Jose Vasconcelos 83
Col. San Miguel Chapultepec
Mexico D.F. C.P. 11850 Mexico
Contact: Jaime Acosta
Phone: 525-211-8052; Fax: 525-211-6702
E-mail: info@calmecac.com.mx
Web: www.calmecac.com.mx (limited access)

Central Certification Service Ltd.

Tower Court
Irchester Rd.
Wollaston
Northants NN29 7PJ United Kingdom
Contact: S. Luck
Phone: +44-193-366-4000; Fax: +44-193-366-4252

Centre for Assessment Ltd.

CAR (NW) Ltd.
The Wigan Investment Centre
Waterside Dr.
Wigan
Lancs WN3 5BA United Kingdom
Contact: J. McCabe
Phone: +44-194-270-5413; Fax: +44-194-224-4052

CEPREI Certification Body

Wan Juyong
No. 110, Dongguanzhuang Rd.
PO Box 1501-33
Guangzhou GD 510610 China
Phone: 86 20 87236606; Fax: 86 20 87236230
E-mail: info@ceprei.org

CERTECH Registration Inc.

4623 Sherwoodtowne Blvd., Suite 300
Mississauga, Ontario L4Z 1Y5 Canada
Contact: Frank Strohmeier
Phone: 905-273-6338; Fax: 905-273-3378
E-mail: frank@certech.org

Certificatiebureau Nederland B.V.

Postbus 5094
Delft, The Netherlands 2600 GB
Phone: +015-7501630; Fax: +015-7501640
E-mail: contact@certificatiebureau.nl
Web: http://www.certificatiebureau.nl

Certification International (UK) Ltd.

Stratton Park House
Wanborough Rd.
Stratton St.Margaret
Swindon
Wiltshire SN3 4JE United Kingdom
Contact: B. Gill
Phone: +44-179-382-9001; Fax: +44-179-382-9002

CGSB

Canadian General Standards Board
Place du Portage, Phase III, 6B1,
11 Laurier St.
Hull,Quebec K1A 1G6
Phone: 819-956-0398; Fax: 819-956-5740
E-mail: ncr.cgsb-ongc@pwgsc.gc.ca
Web: www.pwgsc.gc.ca/cgsb

Chamber Certification Assessment Services Ltd.

Stowe House
Netherstowe
Lichfield
Staffordshire WS13 6TJ United Kingdom
Contact: A. Brachmanski
Phone: +44-154-325-5144; Fax: +44-154-325-5690

China Automotive Quality Certification Center

PO Box 59
Tianshanlukou, Chenglinzhuang Rd.
Tianjin 300162 China
Contact: Xin Su
Phone: +86-22-8477-1319; Fax: +86-22-2437-0843
E-mail: jwzhang6@sina.com

CICS

Ceramic Industry Certification Scheme Ltd.
Queens Rd.
Penkhull
Stoke-on-Trent ST4 7LQ United Kingdom
Contact: G. Cargill
Phone: +44-178-241-1008; Fax: +44-178-276-4363

Web: www.cicsltd.com
E-mail: info@cicsltd.com

CARS

Consortium for Automotive Registration Services (Quality Assurance) Ltd.
Building 1, St Cross Chambers
Upper Marsh Lane
Hoddesdon
Hertfordshire EN11 8LQ United Kingdom
Contact: A. Jones
Phone: +44-199-244-9002; Fax: +44-199-244-9001

CRS

CRS Registrars, Inc.
135 Chesterfield Lane, Suite 201
Maumee, OH 43537 USA
Contact: Carl Blazik
Phone: 800-891-7333 Ext. 26 or 419-861-1689; Fax: 419-861-1696
E-mail: cfblazik@crsregistrars.com
Web: www.crsregistrars.com

D&T

Deloitte & Touche Quality Registrar Inc.
150 Ouellette Place, Suite 200
Windsor, Ontario N8X 1L9 Canada
Contact: Dan DeMartin
Phone: 888-258-2240 Ext. 714 or 519-967-0388; Fax: 519-967-0324
E-mail: dademartin@deloitte.ca
Web: www.deloitte.ca

D.A.S.

D.A.S Certification Ltd.
6 Amber Court
Belper
Derbyshire DE51 1HG United Kingdom
Contact: D. Smiles
Phone: +44-177-382-8586; Fax: +44-177-382-8586

DLS

DLS Quality Technology Associates, Inc.
100 Main St.
Camillus, NY 13031 USA

Contact: Duane Dodge
Phone: 315-672-3598; Fax: 315-672-3596
E-mail: dlsqual@aol.com
Web: http://hometown.aol.com/dlsqual

DNV Ltd.

DNV Certification Ltd.
Palace House
3 Cathedral St.
London SE1 9DE United Kingdom
Contact: D. Milne
Phone: +44-207-357-6080; Fax: +44-207-357-6048

DNV Inc.

Det Norske Veritas Certification, Inc.
16340 Park Ten Place, Suite 100
Houston, TX 77084 USA
Contact: Yehuda Dror
Phone: 281-721-6818; Fax: 281-721-6903
E-mail: yehuda.dror@dnv.com
Web: www.dnvcert.com

DQS

DQS German American Registrar for Management Systems
3601 Algonquin Rd., Suite 305
Rolling Meadows, IL 60008 USA
Contact: Roger Davis
Phone: 847-797-1860; Fax: 847-797-1876
E-mail: rdavis@dqsusa.com
Web: www.dqscert.com

EAGLE

EAGLE Registrations Inc.
2242 West Schantz Ave.
Dayton, OH 45409 USA
Contact: Chris Shillito
Phone: 937-293-2000; Fax: 937-293-0220
E-mail: eagleiso@aol.com
Web: www.eagleregistrations.com

EAQA Ltd.

Europoint Centre
5-11 Lavington St.
London SE1 0NZ United Kingdom
Contact: Natasha Richards
Phone: +44-207-922-1628; Fax: +44-207-922-1627
E-mail: enquiries@eaqa.demon.co.uk

EAQA

EAQA USA Registrars, Inc.
15475 Chemical Lane
Huntington Beach, CA 92649 USA
Phone: 714-373-3773; Fax: 714-373-3775
E-mail: info@eaqausa.com
Web: www.eaqausa.com

ECAS B.V.

Postbus 17
Roelofarendsveen, Netherlands 2370 AA
Phone: +071-3315781; Fax: +071-3315513
E-mail: info@ecas.nl
Web: www.ecas.nl

Electrical Equipment Certification Service

Health and Safety Executive
Harpur Hill
Buxton
Derbyshire SK17 9JN United Kingdom
Contact: I. Cleare
Phone: +44-12-982-8000; Fax: +44-12-98-28244

Electricity Association Quality Assurance Ltd.

30 Millbank
London SW1P 4RD United Kingdom
Contact: M. Lodge
Phone: +44-207-963-5947; Fax: +44-207-828-9237

ENTELA

Entela, Inc., Quality System Registration Division
2625 Buchanan S.W.
Grand Rapids, MI 49548 USA

Contact: Lisa Hemmer
Phone: 616-222-7979; Fax: 616-222-7999
E-mail: lhemmer@entela.com
Web: www.entela.com

Environment and Development Foundation

Room 212
Building 53
#195 Chung Hsin Rd., Section 4
Chutung, Hsinchu
Taiwan, Republic of China
Contact: N. Yu
Phone: +886-359-16221; Fax: +886-358-20231

Environment & Quality Assurance International

Environment & Quality Assurance International Certification Center
Jae Seung Moon
Grand Bldg. 6F, #229-13
Youngdap-dong Seongdong-ku
Seoul 133-850 South Korea
Phone: +82-2-532-9002; Fax: +82-2-532-9003
E-mail: eqa@chollian.net
Web: www.eqaicc.com

EQA

EQA European Quality Assurance Ltd.
Navigation House
48 Millgate
Newark
Nottinghamshire NG24 4TY United Kingdom
Contact: D. Stack
Phone: +44-16-36-611-226; Fax: +44-1636-611-704
E-mail: eqa@eqa.co.uk
Web: www.eqa.co.uk

EQR

EQR, Quality Registry Inc.
2500 Wilson Blvd.
Arlington, VA 22201-3834 USA
Contact: Miguel Gaitan
Phone: 800-222-9001 or 703-907-7563; Fax 703-907-7966
Web: www.eia.org

ERM

ERM Certification & Verification Services Ltd.
8 Cavendish Square
London W1M 0ER United Kingdom
Contact: B. Kraus
Phone: +44-20-7465-7369; Fax: +44-20-7465-7381

Ever Win Quality Certification Center

216#, Long Bo Office Building A
No. 3 South Lishi Road, Xicheng District
Beijing 100037 P.R. China
Contact: Xu Qing
Phone: +86-106-603-9380; Fax: +86-106-603-9379
E-mail: ewc@public3.bta.net.cn
Web: www.ewqcc.org

EXCALIBUR

Excalibur Registrations, Inc.
20740 Ryan Rd., Suite 100
Warren, MI 48091-2738 USA
Phone: 810-755-9100; Fax: 810-755-9110
Contact: Robert Zanni
E-mail: excalibur9000@ameritech.net
E-mail: wamplerj@earthlink.net
Web: www.excaliburregistrations.com

Fluke Nederland B.V. Standaard Laboratorium

Postbus 1337
Eindhoven, Netherlands 5602 BH
Phone: 040-2675300; Fax: 040-2675300
E-mail: kalibratiedesk@fluke.nl
Web: www.fluke.nl

FM Global

ISO 9000 Registration Department
Factory Mutual Research
PO Box 9102
1151 Boston-Providence Turnpike
Norwood, MA 02062, USA
Phone: 781-255-4972; Fax: 781-762-9375
E-mail: john.hill@fmglobal.com

E-mail: information@fmglobal.com
Web: www.fmglobal.com/approvals

GASTEC Certification B.V.

Postbus 137
Apeldoorn, Netherlands 7300 AC
Phone: +055-5393393; Fax: +055-5393494
E-mail: post@gastec.nl
Web: www.gastec.nl

GBJD

GBJD Registrars Ltd.
9251-8 Yonge St., Suite 310
Richmond Hill, Ontario L4C 9T3 Canada
Phone: 877-256-1967; Fax: 905-727-1730

Germanischer Lloyd Certification GmbH

Postfach 11 16 06
Hamburg, Germany D-20416
Phone: +49-403-61490; Fax: +49-403-6149200
E-mail: bb@germanlloyd.org
Web: http://www.lrqa.com

Global Certification Ltd.

1 Dovecote Close
Westminster Dr.
Kettering
Northamptonshire NN15 6GT United Kingdom
Contact: P. Gibb
Phone: +44-1536-513009; Fax: +44-1536-513024

Government of India, Standardization, Testing & Quality Certification Directorate

Electronics Niketan 6, CGO Complex
Lodi Road
New Delhi, India 110 003
Phone: +91-11-4364757; Fax: +91-11-4363083
E-mail: arveend@hotmail.com

GRI

GRI Global Registrars, Inc.
4700 Clairton Blvd.

Pittsburgh, PA 15236 USA
Contact: Elmer Bennett
Phone: 412-884-2290; Fax: 412-884-2268
E-mail: bennette@globalregistrars.com
E-mail: info@globalregistrars.com
Web: www.globalregistrars.com

Hallmark Quality Assurance Ltd.

Locksley House
Unit 4, Locksley Business Park
39 Montgomery Rd.
Belfast BT6 9JD United Kingdom
Contact: L. Adams
Phone: +44-2890-706766; Fax: +44-2890-706767

Hangzhou WIT Management System Assessment Company

8 Baoshi Rd. (2)
Hangzhou 310007 China
Contact: Rongrong Liu
Phone: +86-571-85211351; Fax: +86-571-85112934
E-mail: lrr@WIT-int.com

Hong Kong Quality Assurance Agency

19/F, K. Wah Centre
191 Java Rd.
North Point, Hong Kong
Contact: H. Ng
Phone: +00-852-2202-9111; Fax: +00-852-2202-9222

HSB

HSB Registration Services
595 East Swedesford Rd.
Wayne, PA 19086 USA
Contact: Janet Kowalski
Phone: 484-582-1419; Fax: 484-582-1802
E-mail: iso_9000@hsb.com
E-mail: janet_kowalski@hsb.com
Web: www.hsbiso.com

IMS Ltd.

IMS International Ltd.
1 TES House

Motherwell Way
West Thurrock
Essex RM20 3XD United Kingdom
Contact: G. Kirk
Phone: +44-153-189-0235; Fax: +44-153-189-0236

IMS Inc.

IMS International Management Systems, Inc.
5420 Bay Center Dr. Suite 200
Tampa, FL 33609 USA
Contact: Steve Pearson
Phone: 813-639-9876; Fax: 813-639-9875
E-mail: mriso9000@ims4iso.com
Web: www.ims4iso.com

Independent European Certification Ltd.

Europa House
65 High St.
Worthing
West Sussex BN11 1DD United Kingdom
Contact: F. Gabbutt
Phone: +44-177-572-2728; Fax: +44-177-571-2227

Indian Register of Shipping Indian Register Quality Systems

52a, Adi Shankaracharya Marg.
Opp. Powai
Lake, Mumbai, India 400 072
Phone: +91-22-570-3627; Fax: +91-22-570-3611
E-mail: irsho@bom3.vsnl.net.in

Industry Sector Certification Ltd.

PO Box 1708
24/50 South Parade
Yate
Bristol BS17 4BB United Kingdom
Contact: C. Doughty
Phone: +44-1454-316-131; Fax: +44-1454-313-163

International Standards Authority

1305 West Arrow Hwy.
San Dimas, CA 91773 USA
Contact: Jamie Topete

Phone: 909-305-4900
E-mail: jamiet@isaregistrar.com
Web: www.isaregistrar.com

INSPEC

INSPEC International Ltd.
Upper Wingbury Courtyard
Wingrave
Aylesbury
Bucks HP22 4LW United Kingdom
Contact: K. Warren
Phone: +44-1296-682-966; Fax: +44-1296-682-909

ICS

International Certification Services Ltd.
Hillcrest House
16 Hillside Close
Paulton
Bristol BS39 7PN United Kingdom
Contact: J. Clift
Phone: +44-1761-411-109; Fax: +44-1761-411-945

IQC

International Quality Certifications, SA de CV
Fernando Adams Gallegos
Joselillo No. 6-A Despacho 908,
Col. El Parque Naucalpan, Edo. de Mexico
C.P. 53390 Mexico
Phone: 525-557-5023; Fax: 525-557-9629

International Standards Accreditation Authority

1305 West Arrow Hwy. #207
San Dimas, CA 91773 USA
Contact: Jim Grace
Phone: 909-305-4900
E-mail: jrgllg@msn.com

INTERTEK (USA)

Intertek Services Corporation
70 Codman Hill Rd.
Boxborough, MA 01719 USA
Contact: Daniel Desilets

Phone: 978-929-2100 x115 or 800-810-1195; Fax: 978-635-8595
E-mail: ddesilet@itsqs.com
Web: www.itsintertek.com

INTERTEK (UK)

Intertek Testing Services Ltd.
25 Savile Row
London W1S 2ES
Tel: +44-20-7396-3400; Fax: +44-20-7396-3480
E-mail: info@itsglobal.com
Web: www.itsglobal.com

IQSR

International Quality Systems Registrars
7025 Tomken Rd., Suite 271
Mississauga, Ontario L5S 1R6 Canada
Contact: Nick Budd
Phone: 905-565-0116 or 800-267-0861; Fax: 905-565-0117
E-mail: nickb@iqsr.com
E-mail: feedback@iqsr.com
Web: www.iqsr.com

ISOQAR (UK)

West Point
501 Chester Rd.
Old Trafford
Manchester M16 9HU United Kingdom
Contact: David Crompton
Phone: +44-161-877-6914; Fax: +44-161-877-6915
Web: www.isoqar.com

ISOQAR (USA)

PO Box 850370
Braintree, MA 02185 USA
Phone: 781-356-6572; Fax: 781-356-0444
E-mail: isoqarusa@isoqar.com
Web: www.isoqar.com

Japan Audit & Certification Organization

Japan Audit & Certification Organization for Environment & Quality
2-17-12 Akasaka
Minato-Ku

Tokyo 107-0052 Japan
Contact: C. Morita
Phone: +81-3-3584-9123; Fax: +81-3-3224-9002

Japan Automobile Research Institute Registration Body (JARI-RB)

Kanda Union Bldg, 3-20 Kandanishiki-cho
Chiyoda-ku, Tokyo 101 Japan
Phone: +81-3-3259-7282; Fax: +81-3-3293-9708

Japan Electrical Safety & Environment Technology Labs

Environment Certification Division
Motoyoyogi Sansan Bld, 33-8 Motoyoyogi
Shibuya-ku, Tokyo 151 Japan
Phone: +81-3-3466-9741; Fax: +81-3-3466-8388
E-mail: shimura@intacc.ne.jp

Japan Gas Appliances Inspection Association QA Center

JIA Building 2nd fl., 4-10
Akasaka
1-CHOME, MINATO-KU
Tokyo 107-0052 Japan
Phone: +81-3-55609561; Fax: +81-3-55609566
E-mail: t.terabe@jia-page.or.jp
Web: www.jia-page.or.jp

Japan Quality Assurance Organization

Akasaka
Minato-Ku
Tokyo 107-0052 Japan
Contact: C. Morita
Phone: +81-3-3584-9123; Fax: +81-3-3224-9002

Japanese Standards Association

Management Systems Enhancement Department
Akasaka Eight One Building
13-5 Nagatacho 2chome
Chiyoda-ku
Tokyo 100 0014 Japan
Contact: Jun Ota
Phone: +81-3-3592-1495; Fax: +81-3-5532-1250

JICQA

JIC Quality Assurance Ltd.
10-4 Haccho-bori 4-chome, Chuo-ku
Tokyo 104-0032 Japan
Phone: +81-35541-2751; Fax: +81-35541-2955
E-mail: matsumura@jicqa.co.jp
Web: www.jicqa.co.jp

KEMA

KEMA Registered Quality, Inc.
4377 County Line Rd., Suite 202
Chalfont, PA 18914 USA
Phone: 215-997-4519, ext. 310; Fax: 215-997-3810
E-mail: cpellegrino@krqusa.com
E-mail: ipeters@krqusa.com
Web: www.kemaregisteredquality.com

KEMA Quality B.V.

Postbus 5185
Arnhem, Netherlands
Phone: +026-3562000; Fax: +026-3525800
E-mail: customer@kema.com
Web: www.kema.com

KIWA NV Certificatie en Keuringen

Postbus 70
2280 AB
Rijswijk, Netherlands
Phone: +070-4144400; Fax: +070-4144420
E-mail: certif@kiwa.nl
Web: www.kiwa.nl

Koenders Services B.V. Kalibratie Laboratorium

Postbus 1189
Almere, Netherlands 1300 BD
Phone: 036-5480101; Fax: 036-5480102
E-mail: olav@koendersgroup.com
Web: www.koendersgroup.com

Korean Foundation for Quality

Byung Yong Lee
FKI Building, 28-1, Yoido-Dong, Youngdungpo-Gu,
Seoul 150-756 Korea
Phone: +82-2-767-9060; Fax: +82-2-767-9090
E-mail: bylee@kfq.or.kr

Legal Services Commission

Supplier Development Group
85 Gray's Inn Rd.
London WC1X 8TX United Kingdom
Contact: R. Willis
Phone: +44-20-7759-0389; Fax: +44-20-7759-0534

Letrina S.A.

21 Egialias & 1, Halepa Street
Paradisos Amarousiou
Attiki GR 151 25 Greece
Phone: +30-1-6848190; Fax: +30-1-6845626
E-mail: letrina@acci.gr

LLD Inc.

500 Grove St.
Third Floor
Herndon, VA 20170 USA
Contact: Mark Birch
Phone: 703-925-0660; Fax: 703-925-9441
E-mail: ems@corp.LLD.com
Web: www.LLD.com

LRQA (UK)

Lloyd's Register Quality Assurance Ltd.
The LRQA Centre
Hiramford
Middlemarch Office Village
Siskin Dr.
Coventry CV3 4FJ United Kingdom
Contact: J. Butler
Phone: +44-24-7688-2399; Fax: +44-24-7630-6055

LRQA (USA)

Lloyd's Register Quality Assurance, Inc.
1401 Enclave Pkwy., Suite 200
Houston, TX 77077 USA
Contact: Jay Freeman
Phone: 281-398-7370; Fax: 281-398-7337
E-mail: sales-usa@lrqa.com
Web: www.lrqausa.com

MALQA

Mutuagung Lestari Quality Assurance
Wijaya Graha Puri
Blok E No. 18 – 19
Jl. Wijaya II
Jakarta 12160 Indonesia
Contact: T. Arifiarachman
Phone: +21-721-0280; Fax: +21-720-2994

Marketing Quality Assurance Ltd.

Operations Directorate
Midsummer House
435 Midsummer Blvd.
Milton Keynes MK9 3BN United Kingdom
Contact: A. James
Phone: +44-1908-231565; Fax: +44-1908-231546

Meehanite Certification (Worldwide) Ltd.

IMMCO House
38 Albert Rd. North
Reigate
Surrey RH2 9EH United Kingdom
Contact: S. Severn
Phone: +44-1737-222-786; Fax: +44-1737-226-644

Moody International Certification Ltd.

Cuckfield House
High St.
Cuckfield
West Sussex RH17 5EL United Kingdom
Contact: B. Dixon
Phone: +44-144-447-2903; Fax: +44-144-445-7324

MKB-Certificatie

Barbarastraat 26
Geleen 6164 HK The Netherlands
Phone: +046-4759931; Fax: +046-4759932
E-mail: mkb.certificatie@worldonline.nl

NQA Ltd. (UK)

National Quality Assurance Ltd.
Trevor Nash
Head Office, Warwick House
Houghton Hall Park, Houghton Regis
Dunstable LU5 5 ZX United Kingdom
Phone: +44-1582-844125; Fax: +44-1582-844103
E-mail: trevor.nash@nqa.com
Web: www.nqa.com

MSB Mauritius Standards Bureau

Old Moka Road
Moka, Mauritius
Phone: +230-433-3648; Fax: +230-433-5051

National Security Inspectorate

Head Office
Queensgate House
14 Cookham Rd.
Maidenhead
Berks SL6 8AJ United Kingdom
Contact: R. Norburn
Phone: +44-870-20-50-000; Fax: +44-1628-773367

Orchard House
Victoria Square
Droitwich
Worcestershire WR9 8DS United Kingdom
Phone: +44-190-577-3131; Fax: +44-190-577-3102

National Weights and Measures Laboratory

Stanton Ave.
Teddington
Middlesex TW11 0JZ United Kingdom
Contact: C. Smith
Phone: +44-208-943-7245; Fax: +44-208-943-7270

Nippon Kaiji Kentei Quality Assurance Ltd. (NKKKQA)

Kaiji Bldg., 2-14-9, Shibaura, Minato-ku
Tokyo 108-0023 Japan
Phone: +81-3-5427-2505; Fax: +81-3-5427-6307
E-mail: nkqa@nkkkqa.co.jp
Web: www.nkkkqa.co.jp

Nippon Kaiji Kyokai (ClassNK) Quality & Environment System Dept.

4-7, Kioi-Cho, Chiyoda-Ku
Tokyo 102 8567 Japan
Phone: +81-3-3230-1201; Fax: +81-3-5226-2012
E-mail: qad@classnk.or.jp
Web: www.classnk.or.jp

NQA

National Quality Assurance, USA
Derek Coppinger
4 PO Square Rd.
Acton, MA 01720 USA
Phone: 800-649-5289 or 978-635-9256; Fax: 978-263-0785
E-mail: edupont@nqa-usa.com
E-mail: dcoppinger@nqa-usa.com
Web: www.nqa-usa.com

NSAI (Ireland)

National Standards Authority of Ireland
Glasnevin
Dublin 9 Ireland
Contact: Brian Lynch
Phone: +44-353-1807-3883; Fax: +44-353-1807-3844
E-mail: lynchb@nsai.ie
Web: www.nsaicert.com

NSAI (USA)

National Standards Authority of Ireland
402 Amherst St.
Nashua, NH 03063 USA
Phone: 603-882-4412; Fax: 603-882-1985
E-mail: richb@nsaieast.com
Web: www.nsaicert.com

NSF ISR

NSF International Strategic Registrations, Ltd.
789 N Dixboro Rd.
Ann Arbor, MI 48105 USA
Contact: Suzie Fourne
Phone: 734-827-6876 or 888-NSF-9000; Fax: 734-827-6801
E-mail: fourne@nsf-isr.org
E-mail: information@nsf-isr.org
Web: www.nsf-isr.org

OFGEM (EMES)

Electricity Meter Examining Service
Ofgem Technical Directorate
3 Tigers Rd.
Wigston
Leicestershire LE18 4UX United Kingdom
Contact: D. Rice
Phone: +44-116-258-1401; Fax: +44-116-258-1403

Orion

Orion Registrar, Inc.
PO Box 5070
7850 Vance Dr., Suite 210
Arvada, CO 80003 USA
Contact: Kaci Fults
Phone: 303-456-6010; Fax: 303-456-6681
E-mail: info@orion-iso.com
E-mail: pburck@orion-iso.com
Web: www.orion-iso.com/index.htm

PJR

Perry Johnson Registrars, Inc.
26555 Evergreen Rd., Suite 1340
Southfield, MI 48076 USA
Contact: Terry Boboige
Phone: 800-800-7910; Fax: 248-358-0882
E-mail: pjr@pjr.com
Web: www.pjr.com

Premier Assessments Ltd.

Suite 6
The Derwent Business Centre
Clarke St.
Derby DE1 2BU United Kingdom
Contact: J. Canning
Phone: +44-1332-202556; Fax: +44-1332-205067

PRI

Performance Review Institute Registrar
161 Thornhill Rd.
Warrendale, PA 15086-7527 USA
Contact: Jim Borczyk
Phone: 724-772-7170; Fax: 724-772-1699
E-mail: jborczyk@sae.org
E-mail: pri@sae.org
Web: www.pri.sae.org

PRO

Professional Registrar Organization, Inc.
3150 Livernois, Suite 270
Troy, MI 48083 USA
Phone: 248-743-6900 or 800-793-4408; Fax: 248-743-0661
E-mail: proregistrar@aol.com
E-mail: Charles_Schleyer@earthtech.com
Web: www.proregistrar.com

Product Authentication Inspectorate Ltd.

Conyngham Hall
Knaresborough
North Yorkshire HG5 9AY United Kingdom
Contact: S. Roberts
Phone: +44-1423-799-128; Fax: +44-1423-799-121

PSB Certification Pte. Ltd.

3 Science Park Drive #03-12 PSB Annex
Singapore 118223 Singapore
Phone: +65-8701280; Fax: +65-8720531
E-mail: enquiries@psbcert.com
Web: www.psbcert.comenquiries@psbcert.com

QA International Certification Ltd.

Cleveland Hall
Cleveland St.
Darlington
County Durham DL1 2PE United Kingdom
Contact: A. Duffield
Phone: +44-1325-384-272; Fax: +44-1325-480-980

QCB

Quality Certification Bureau, Inc.
9650 - 20 Ave.
Suite 103, Advanced Technology Centre
Edmonton, Alberta T6N 1G1 Canada
Phone: 800-268-7321; Fax: 780-496-2464
E-mail: qcbinc@qcbinc.com
Web: www.qcbinc.com/

QMI

Quality Management Institute
90 Burnhamthorpe Rd. W, Suite 300
Mississauga, Ontario L5B 3C3 Canada
Phone: 905-272-3920; Fax: 905-272-3942
E-mail: clientservices@qmi.com
Web: www.qmi.com

Quality & Environmental Certification Ltd.

10 Thyme Court
Farnborough
Hampshire GU14 9XT United Kingdom
Contact: A.M. Pryce
Phone: +44-125-254-5336; Fax: +44-125-254-5702

Quality Cert (India) Private Limited

12, Gandhi Road Gill Nagar, Choolaimedu
Chennai, India 600 094
Phone: +91-44-4839574 ; Fax: +91-44-3723600
E-mail: qcert@vsnl.com

Quality Certification Ltd.

Conyngham Hall
Knaresborough

North Yorkshire HG5 9AY United Kingdom
Contact: S. Roberts
Phone: +44-1423-799-128; Fax: +44-1423-799-121

Quality Services International

12350 Southwest 132nd Court, Suite 206
Miami, FL 33186 USA
Contact: Celso Alvarado
Phone: 786-293-2053; Fax: 786-293-9137
E-mail: qsicelso@aol.com
Web: www.qsiamerica.com

Quenviro Systems International

5-44th Avenue
Edmunston, New Brunswick E3V 2Z8 Canada
Contact: Martin Richer
Phone: 506-736-6918; Fax: 506-736-6908

QSR

Quality Systems Registrars, Inc.
13873 Park Center Rd., Suite 217
Herndon, VA 20171 USA
Contact: Scott Kleckner
Phone: 703-478-0241; Fax: 703-478-0645
E-mail: qsrdr@msn.com
E-mail: timl@qsr.com
Web: www.qsr.com

QUASAR

Quality Systems Assessment Registrar
Head Office, 7250 W Credit Ave.
Mississauga, Ontario L5N 5N1 Canada
Phone: 905-542-0547; Fax: 905-542-1318
E-mail: info@cwbgroup.com
Web: www.cwbgroup.com/english/quasar.htm

Rail Industry Quality Certification Ltd.

PO Box 464
London Rd.
Derby DE24 8ZL United Kingdom
Contact: L. Fitch
Phone: +44-1332-262737; Fax: +44-1332-263692

Ronet International Certification Services Ltd.

Maor 27
Emek Hefer 38830 Israel
Contact: R. Tuchfeld
Phone: +00972-(0)4-637-1466; Fax: +00972-(0)4-637-1463

Royal & Sun Alliance Certification Services

17 York St.
Manchester M2 3RS United Kingdom
Contact: E. Haynes
Phone: +44-161-235-3000; Fax: +44-161-235-3001

SATRA

SATRA Quality Assurance Ltd.
SATRA House
Rockingham Rd.
Kettering
Northants NN16 9JH United Kingdom
Contact: A. Cromwell
Phone: +44-1536-410-000; Fax: +44-1536-410-626

Security Systems and Alarms Inspection Board

Suite 3
131 Bedford St.
Norty Shields
Tyn nad Wear NE29 6LA United Kingdom
Contact: G. Tate
Phone: +44-191-296-3242; Fax: +44-191-296-2667

SGS ICS Canada

SGS International Certification Services Canada, Inc.
6275 Northam Dr., Unit 2
Mississauga, Ontario L4V 1Y8 Canada
Contact: Robert Morris
Phone: 800-636-0847 or 905-676-9595; Fax: 905-676-9519
E-mail: robert_morris@sgs.com
Web: www.sgs.ca

SGS ICS

SGS International Certification Services, Inc.
Meadows Office Complex,

201 Route 17 N
Rutherford, NJ 07070 USA
Phone: 800-747-9047; Fax: 201-935-4555
E-mail: sgsics@attglobal.net
Web: www.sgsicsus.com

SGS United Kingdom Ltd.

SGS Yarsley International Certification Services Ltd.
2 Hutton Close Business Park
South Church Enterprise Park
Bishop Auckland
Co Durham DL14 6XG United Kingdom
Contact: W. Clough
Phone: +44-138-877-6677; Fax: +44-138-877-6691

Shanghai Audit Center of Quality Systems

Zhang Ji Nong
L.T. Square, 35F
North Cheng Du Rd.
Shanghai 200003 China
Phone: 86-21-6360-8125; Fax: 86-21-6360-3395
E-mail: sqcasac@online.sh.cn

Signature Management Cert. Services, LLC

211 Donelson Pike, Suite 6
Nashville, TN 37214-0287
Phone: 615-232-8300; Fax: 615-232-8302
E-mail: ric-signature@worldnett.att.net
Web: http://www.signature9000.com

SIRA Certification Systems

South Hill
Chislehurst
Kent BR7 5EH United Kingdom
Contact: I. Knott
Phone: +44-208-467-2636; Fax: +44-208-295-1990

SIRIM

SIRIM QAS Sdn. Bhd.
Bangunan 4, Kompleks SIRIM
1, Persiaran Dato Menteri
Peti Surat 7035

40911 Shah Alam
Selangor Darul Ehsan
Malaysia
Contact: Parma Iswara Subramaniam
Phone: +60-3-556 7400; Fax: +60-3-550 9439

SLSI

Sri Lanka Standards Institution
P.O. Box 17
No. 17, Victoria Place
(Off Elvitigala Mawatha)
Colombo, Sri Lanka 08
Phone: +94-1-671567-72; Fax: +94-1-671579
E-mail: slsidg@mail.ac.lk
Web: http://www.naresa.ac.lk/slsi/profile.htm

SABS-NETFA

South African Bureau of Standards
PO Box 144
Olifantsfontein, South Africa 1665
Phone: +27-11-3162005; Fax: +27-11-3164979

SQA

Smithers Quality Assessments, Inc.
425 W Market St.
Akron, OH 44303-2099 USA
Phone: 330-762-4231; Fax: 330-762-7447
E-mail: sqa@smithersmail.com
Web: www.smithersregistrar.com

SRI

Steel Related Industries Quality System Registrars
2000 Corporate Dr., Suite 580
Wexford, PA 15090-7605 USA
Phone: 724-934-9000; Fax: 724-934-6825
E-mail: mail@sriregistrar.com
Web: www.sriregistrar.com

Standards Institution of Israel

The Quality and Certification Division
42 Chaim Levanon Street
Tel Aviv, Israel 69977

Phone: +972-3-6465114 ; Fax: +972-3-6465114
E-mail: dafna@sii.org.il
Web: http://www.sii.org.il

Steel Construction Certification Scheme Ltd.

4 Whitehall Court
London SW1A 2ES United Kingdom
Contact: P. Mould
Phone: +44-20-7839-8566; Fax: +44-20-7976-1634

STR

STR-Registrar LLC
Jim Galica
PO Box A
24 Scitico Rd.
Somersville, CT 06072 USA
Phone: 860-763-7013; Fax: 860-763-7017
E-mail: james.galica@str-r.com
Web: www.str-r.com

Sucfinodo (P.T. Superintending Company Indonesia)

JL Raya Pasar Minggu Kav 34
Jakarta, Indonesia 12780
Phone: +62-21-7983666 ; Fax: +62-21-7987015
E-mail: scisics@indosat.net.id

Telcordia

Telcordia Quality Registration
Peter Ortolani
3 Corporate Place
Piscataway, NJ 08854 USA
Phone: 732-699-3739; Fax: 732-336-2244
E-mail: portolan@telcordia.com
E-mail: mfaccone@telcordia.com
Web: www.telcordia.com

Telefication B.V.

Edisonstraat 12a
Zevenaar, Netherlands 6902 PK
Phone: 0316-582780; Fax: 0316-582789

Testing and Certification Specialists (Pty) Ltd

Private Bag X191
Pretoria, South Africa 0001
Phone: +27-12-4287911; Fax: +27-12-3441568

The Health Quality Service

15 Whitehall
London SW1A 2DD United Kingdom
Contact: A. Payne
Phone: +44-20-7389-1000; Fax: +44-20-7389-1001

The Quality Scheme for Ready Mixed Concrete

3 High St.
Hampton
Middlesex TW12 2SQ United Kingdom
Contact: C. Head
Phone: +44-20-8941-0273; Fax: +44-20-8979-4558

TRA-CD

TRA Certification
PO Box 1081
700 East Beardsley Ave.
Elkhart, IN 46514 USA
Contact: Rob Podawiltz
Phone: 219-264-0745; Fax: 219-264-0740
E-mail:info@trarnold.com
E-mail: rpodawiltz@trarnold.com
Web: www.tra-cd.com

TRC

The Registrar Company, Inc.
PO Box 516186
8111 LBJ Freeway, Suite 675
Dallas, TX 75251-6186 USA
Phone: 972-783-7194 or 800-966-3291; Fax: 972-783-8953
E-mail: trcquality@aol.com
E-mail: jenni@theregistrarco.com
Web: www.theregistrarco.com

TÜV Essen

11 Brighton Rd., Second Floor
Clifton, NJ 07012 USA
Contact: John Wilson
Phone: 800-888-4630; Fax: 408-441-7111
E-mail: info@tuvessen.com
Web: www.tuvessen.com

TÜV

TÜV Management Service, A Division of TÜV America
5 Cherry Hill Dr.
Danvers, MA 01923 USA
Contact: David Dougherty
Phone: 978-739-7000; Fax: 978-762-8414
E-mail: ddougherty@tuvam.com
Web: www.tuvglobal.com

TÜV Nederland QA B.V.

Postbus 120
Best, The Netherlands 5680 AC
Phone: +0499-339500; Fax: +0499-339509
E-mail: info@tuv.nl
Web: www.tuv.com

TÜV Rheinland

TÜV Rheinland of North America, Inc.
12 Commerce Rd.
Newtown, CT 06470 USA
Contact: Jodi Espinal
Phone: 203-426-0888; Fax: 203-426-4009
E-mail: jespinal@us.tuv.com
Web: www.tuv.com

TÜV UK

TÜV UK Quality Assurance Ltd.
Surrey House
Surrey St.
Croydon CR9 1XZ United Kingdom
Contact: B. Anderson
Phone: +44-20-8686-3400; Fax: +44-20-8686-3045

UK Certificating Authority for Reinforcing Steels

Pembroke House
21 Pembroke Rd.
Sevenoaks
Kent TN13 1XR United Kingdom
Contact: B. Bowsher
Phone: +44-1732-450000; Fax: +44-1732-455917

UL Canada

Underwriters Laboratories of Canada
7 Crouse Rd.
Scarborough, Ontario M1R 3A9 Canada
Phone: 416-757-3611; Fax: 416-757-8915
E-mail: customerservice@ulc.ca
Web: www.ulc.ca

UL (USA)

Underwriters Laboratories, Inc.
1285 Walt Whitman Rd.
Melville, NY 11747-3081 USA
Phone: 847-272-8800; Fax: 847-272-8129
E-mail: registrar@ul.com
Web: www.ul.com

Universal Certification Services Co., Ltd.

13th floor, Radio Administration Building
Huanqiang Road, South, Shenzhen
Shenzhen, P.R. China 518033
Phone: +86-755-3202710; Fax: +86-755-3202712
E-mail: sqcc@sqcc.com
Web: http://www.sqcc.com

University of Huddersfield Training and Quality Services

Holly Bank Campus
Holly Bank Rd.
Lindley
Huddersfield HD3 3BP United Kingdom
Contact: J. Mothersdale
Phone: +44-1484-478-234; Fax: +44-1484-478-289

University of Ljubljana

Faculty of Electric Engineering Laboratory of Metrology and Quality
Trzaska 25
Ljubljana, Slovenia 1000
Phone: +386 (0)1 4768 223; Fax: +386 (0)1 4264 633
E-mail: janko.drnovsek@fe.uni-lj.si
Web: www.fe.uni-lj.si

URS (USA)

United Registrar of Systems Ltd.
Unit 4
7 Lyndale Ave.
Webster, MA 01570 USA
Phone: 508-943-1642 Fax: 508-943-1642
E-mail: bqa@os.com
Web: www.urs.co.uk

URS (UK)

URS, United Registrar of Systems Ltd.
United House
Station Rd.
Cheddar
Somerset BS27 3AH United Kingdom
Contact: D. Riggs
Phone: +44-193-473-3388; Fax: +44-193-473-3399
Web: www.urs.co.uk

URS Verification Ltd.

Alpha Tower
7th Floor
Suffolk St.
Queensway
Birmingham B1 1YQ United Kingdom
Contact: D. C. Tuberfield
Phone: +44-121-693-3785; Fax: +44-121-693-3791

VCA (UK)

Vehicle Certification Agency
1 The Eastgate Office Centre
Eastgate Rd.
Bristol BS5 6XX United Kingdom

Contact: Alastair Farwell
Phone: +44-117-952-4106; Fax: +44-117-952-4104
E-mail: alastair_farwell@vca.gov.uk

VCA (USA)

Vehicle Certification Agency North America
17250 Newburgh Rd., Suite 140
Livona, MI 48152 USA
Phone: 734-591-1605; Fax: 734-591-1705
Web: www.vca.gov.uk
E-mail: vca@wwnet.com

ViaNoRM B.V.

Postbus 1476
Nieuwegein, The Netherlands 3430 BL
Phone: +030-6087980; Fax: +030-6087982
E-mail: info@norm.nl
Web: http://www.norm.nl

Vilnius Metrology Center Calibration Laboratory

S. Dariaus ir S. Giréno. st. 23
Vilnius, Lithuania 2038
Phone: +370-2-306276; Fax: +370-2-233727
E-mail: vmc@taide.lt

VTI, Vouching Technical Inspection Ltd

Building 2, Floor 2
No.48 North Sanhuan West Road
Beijing, P.R. China 100086
Phone: +86-10-6216-1559; Fax: +86-10-6216-1371

World Certification Services Ltd.

1 Bridge Rd.
Blundellsands
Liverpool L23 6SB United Kingdom
Contact: B. Slocombe
Phone: +44-151-924-7474; Fax: +44-151-924-7477

Worldwide Quality Assurance

3 Sunningdale
Woodham Village
Newton Aycliffe

County Durham DL5 5TS United Kingdom
Contact: P. Raymond
Phone: +44-1325-13233; Fax: +44-1325-307089

Zurich Certification Ltd.

54 Hagley Rd.
Edgbaston
Birmingham B16 8QP United Kingdom
Contact: R. Payne
Phone: +44-121-456-1311; Fax: +44-121-456-1754

Note: It is the customer's responsibility to verify that the registrar has the capability to assess the customer's business. A registrar may evaluate only a portion of the full range of possible activities in a particular category.

Acronyms and Glossary

Acronyms

AACB	Australian Association of Certification Bodies
AAB	Argentine Accreditation Body
AAMI	Association for the Advancement of Medical Instrumentation
ABCB	Association of British Certification Bodies
ABS QE	ABS Quality Evaluations, Inc.
ACIL	American Council of Independent Laboratories
AENOR	Asociación Española de Normalización y Certificación (Spanish Association for Normalization and Certification)
AES	American European Services, Incorporated
AFAQ	Association Française pour l'Assurance de la Qualité (French Accreditation Body and Quality System Registrar)
AFNOR	Association Française de normalisation (French Standards Association)
A.G.A	A.G.A. Quality, a service of International Approval Services (American Gas Association)
AIAG	Automotive Industry Action Group

AIB	Association des Industriels de Belgique (Belgian Organization for Quality System Assessment)
AICQ	Italian Association for Quality
ANSI	American National Standards Institute. Adopts but does not write American standards. Assures that member organizations that do write standards follow rules of consensus and broad participation by interested parties. ANSI is the US member of ISO.
APEC	Asia Pacific Economic Cooperation
API	American Petroleum Institute
APLAC	Asia Pacific Laboratory Accreditation Cooperation
AQAP	Allied Quality Assurance Publication
ASC	Accredited Standards Committee
ASME	American Society of Mechanical Engineers
ASQ	American Society for Quality. A technical society of over 130,000 individual and 1,000 corporate members in the United States and 63 countries. Publishes quality-related American national standards.
ASTD	American Society for Training and Development
ASTM	American Society for Testing and Materials
A2LA	American Association for Laboratory Accreditation
BEC	British Electrotechnical Committee
BQR	Bellcore Quality Registration
BSA	Bulgarian System for Accreditation
BSI	British Standards Institution. The United Kingdom's standards development body and member body to ISO.
BSI Management Systems	BSI Management Systems. The world's largest accredited registration body, headquartered in the United Kingdom. Organizationally separate from the standards development function.
BSR	Board of Standards Review
BVQI	Bureau Veritas Quality International North America, Inc.

CAG	Chairman's Advisory Group
CAI	Cesky Institute pro Akreditaci (Czech Accreditation Institute)
CASCO	Committee on Conformity Assessment
CASE	Conformity Assessment Systems Evaluation, now NVCASE (See separate listing)
CD	Committee Draft
CDRH	Center for Devices and Radiological Health, US Food and Drug Administration
CEAA	Canadian Environmental Auditing Association
CE Mark	Conformité Européene (official French name for the European Community mark)
CEB/BEC	Comité Électrotechnique Belge/Belgisch Elektrotechnisch Comité (Belgian Electrotechnical Committee)
CEI	Comitato Electrotecnico Italiano (Italian Electrotechnical Committee)
CEN	Comité Européen de Normalisation (European Committee for Standardization). Publishes regional standards (for EU and EFTA) covering nonelectrical and nonelectronic subject fields.
CENELEC	Comité Européen de Normalisation Électrotechnique (European Central Secretariat, Committee for Electrotechnical Standardization) Publishes regional standards (for EU and EFTA) covering electrical/ electronic subject fields.
CGA	Canadian Gas Association
cGMP	Good Manufacturing Practice (US Food and Drug Administration 21CFR820)
CGSB	Canadian General Standards Board
CICS	Ceramic Industry Certification Scheme, Ltd.
CMA	Chemical Manufacturers Association, formerly the American Chemistry Council
CNACR	China National Accreditation Committee for Quality System Registration Bodies

CQA	Certified Quality Auditor
CSA International	Canadian Standards Association
CVMA	Canadian Vehicle Manufacturers' Association
DAR	Deutscher Akkreditierungs Rat (German Accreditation Council)
DEK	Dansk Elektroteknisk Komité (Danish Electrotechnical Committee)
DESC	Defense Electronics Supply Center, Department of Defense (US)
DFARS	Department of Defense Federal Acquisition Regulation Supplement (US)
DFQ	Danish Society for Quality
DGO	Deutsche Gesellschaft fur Qualitat (German Society for Quality)
DHHS	Department of Health and Human Services (US)
DIN	Deutsches Institut für Normung (German Standards Institute)
DIS	Draft International Standard
DTI	Department of Trade and Industry (UK)
DKE	Deutsche Elektrotechnische Kommission im DIN und VDE (German Electrotechnical Commission)
DNV	Det Norske Veritas
DOC	Department of Commerce (US)
DoD	Department of Defense (US)
DOE	Department of Energy (US)
DOT	Department of Transportation (US)
DQS	Deutsche Gesellschaft Zur Zertifizierung Qualitatssiche – Rungssystemen MBH (German Association for Certification of Quality Assurance Systems)
DS	Dansk Standardiseringsrad (Danish Standards Association)
DSM	Department of Standards (Malaysia)

EAC	European Accreditation of Certification
EARA	Environmental Auditors Registration Association
EEC	European Economic Community (comprises EU and EFTA countries)
EFQM	European Federation for Quality Management. An organization of upper-level managers concerned with quality.
EFTA	European Free Trade Association. A group of nations whose goal is to remove import duties, quotas and other obstacles to trade and to uphold nondiscriminatory practices in world trade. Current members are Austria, Finland, Iceland, Norway, Sweden and Switzerland.
ELOT	Hellenic (Greek) Organization for Standardization
EMS	Environmental Management System
EN	European Norm
ENAC	Entidad National de Acreditacion, (Spain)
ENTELA	Entela, Inc., Quality System Registration Division
EOQ	European Organization for Quality, formerly EOQC (European Organization for Quality Control). An independent organization whose mission is to improve quality and reliability of goods and services primarily through publications, conferences and seminars. Members are quality-related organizations from countries throughout Europe, including Eastern-bloc countries. ASQ is an affiliate society member.
EOTA	European Organization for Technical Approvals
EOTC	European Organization for Testing and Certification. Set up by the EU and EFTA to focus on conformity assessment issues in the nonregulated spheres.
EPA	Environmental Protection Agency (US)
EQS	European Committee for Quality Assurance Assessment and Certification. The function of EQS is to harmonize rules for quality system assessment and certification (registration), facilitate mutual recognition of registrations and provide advice and counsel to other committees in the EOTC framework on matters related to quality system assessment and certification.

ETCI	Electro-Technical Council of Ireland
ETSI	European Telecommunications Standards Institute
EU	European Union. The EU is a framework within which member states have agreed to integrate their economies and eventually form a political union. Current members are Belgium, Denmark, France, Germany, Greece, Ireland, Italy, Luxembourg, Netherlands, Portugal, Spain and the United Kingdom.
FAA	Federal Aviation Administration, US Department of Transportation
FAR	Federal Acquisition Regulation
FDA	Food and Drug Administration, US Department of Health and Human Services
FDIS	Final Draft International Standard
GATT	General Agreements on Tariffs and Trade
GMP	Good Manufacturing Practices (US Food and Drug Administration)
GQCQ	Quebec Quality Certification Group
GSA	General Services Administration
HAACP	Hazard Analysis and Critical Control Point Procedures followed by US Food and Drug Administration
HIMA	Health Industry Manufacturers Association
HOKLAS	Hong Kong Laboratory Accreditation Scheme
IAAC	Interamerican Accreditation Cooperation
IAAR	Independent Association of Accredited Registrars
IAF	International Accreditation Forum
IAR	International Accreditation Registry
IATCA	International Auditor and Training Certification Association
IATF	International Automotive Task Force
IANZ	International Accreditation, New Zealand
IBN/BIN	Institut Belge de Normalisation/Belgisch Instituut voor Normalisatie (Belgian Institute for Standardization)

ICSP	Interagency Council on Standards Policy (US)
IEAA	International Environmental Auditing Association
IEC	International Electrotechnical Commission. A worldwide organization that produces standards in the electrical and electronic fields. Members are the national committees, composed of representatives of the various organizations which deal with electrical/electronic standardization in each country. Formed in 1906.
IEEE	Institute of Electrical and Electronic Engineers
IIOC	Independent International Organization of Certification
ILAC	International Laboratory Accreditation Cooperation
INMETRO	Instituto Nacional de Metrologia, Normalizatcao e Qualidade Industrial (National Institute for Metrology, Standardization and Industrial Quality, Brazil)
IPQ	Instituto Português da Qualidade (Portuguese Quality Institute)
IQA	Institute for Quality Assurance. A British organization of quality professionals; operates a widely-recognized system of certification for auditors of quality systems.
IQNET	International Certification Network of Quality System Assessment and Certification bodies
IRCA	International Register of Certified Auditors
ISO	International Organization for Standardization (Organisation Internationale de Normalisation). A worldwide federation of 140 national standards bodies. ISO produces standards in all fields, except electrical and electronic (which are covered by IEC). Formed in 1947.
IT	Information Technology
ITA	International Trade Administration (US)
ITM	Inspection du Travail et des Mines (Luxembourg inspecting body)
ITQS	Recognition Arrangement for Assessment and Certification of quality systems in the information technology sector
JAB	Japan Accreditation Board for Conformity Assessment

JAS-ANZ	Australia/New Zealand accreditation service for quality system registrars
KEMA	Keuring Van Electrotechnische; KEMA Registered Quality, Inc., Netherlands
LPCB	The Loss Prevention Certification Board Limited
LRQA	Lloyd's Register Quality Assurance
MBNQA	Malcolm Baldrige National Quality Award
MET	MET Laboratories, Inc.
MLA	Multilateral Recognition Agreement
MoU	Memorandum of understanding; a written agreement among a number of organizations covering specific activities of common interest. There are a number of MOUs covering mutual recognition of quality system registrations in which one of the signatories is a non-European registrar.
MRA	Mutual Recognition Agreement. A company holds the title of a certificate issued by a signer of an MRA. The other signer recognizes the certification performed, and an attestation of equivalence signed by both certification bodies will be delivered to the company upon request.
MTC	Manufacturing Technology Center
NACCB	National Accreditation Council for Certification Bodies. This is the British authority for recognizing the competence and reliability of organizations that perform third-party certification of products and registration of quality systems. Formed in 1984, it is the world's second such organization.
NAC-QS	Comité National pour L'Accreditation des Organismes de Certification (Belgian organization responsible for the accreditation of quality system registrars)
NACE	Nomenclature Générale des Activités Économique dans les Communautés Européennes
NAP	National Accreditation Program operated jointly by ANSI and RAB to accredit ISO 9000 registrars and course providers. Does not provide product certification.
NATA	National Association of Testing Authorities (Australia)
NATO	North Atlantic Treaty Organization

NCCLS	National Committee for Clinical Laboratory Standards
NCSCI	National Center for Standards and Certification Information, National Institute of Standards and Technology (US)
NEC	Nederlands Elektrotechnisch Comité (Dutch Electrotechnical Committee)
NEMA	National Electrical Manufacturers Association
NEN	Netherlands Standardization Institute
NIST	National Institute of Standards and Technology, US Department of Commerce
NNI	Nederlands Normalisatie Instituut (Dutch Normalization Institute)
NQA	National Quality Assurance, Ltd.
NQI	National Quality Institute, Canada
NRC	Nuclear Regulatory Commission (US)
NSAI	National Standards Authority of Ireland
NSF	NSF International
NTIS	National Technical Information Service (US)
NVCASE	National Voluntary Conformity Assessment System Evaluation, formerly the CASE Program (US)
NVLAP	National Voluntary Laboratory Accreditation Program, NIST, US Department of Commerce
NWIP	New Work Item Proposal
OEM	Original Equipment Manufacturer
OSHA	Occupational Safety and Health Administration, US Department of Labor
OTSQR	OTS Quality Registrars, Inc.
PAC	Pacific Accreditation Cooperation
PASC	Pacific Area Standards Cooperation
prEN	Proposed European Norm
PRI	Performance Review Institute Mobility industry registration affiliate of SAE

QA	Quality Assurance
QM	Quality Management
QMS	Quality Management System
QS	Quality System
QSR	Quality Systems Registrars, Inc.
QuEST	Quality Excellence for Suppliers of Telecommunications
RAB	Registrar Accreditation Board. A US organization whose mission is to recognize the competence and reliability of registrars of quality systems, and the operation of the NAP.
RvA	Raad voor Accreditatie (Dutch Council for Accreditation). The Dutch authority for recognizing the competence and reliability of organizations that perform third-party certification of products, accreditation of laboratories and registration of quality systems. The first such organization, formed in 1980.
SABS	South African Bureau of Standards
SAC	Singapore Accreditation Council
SADCA	South African Development Cooperation in Accreditation
SAE	Society of Automotive Engineers
SANAS	South African National Accreditation System
SC	Subcommittee
SCC	Standards Council of Canada
SCS	Sira Certification Service/Sira Test & Certification Ltd. (UK)
SDO	Standards Development Organization
SGLC	Standards Group Leadership Council
SIC	Standard Industrial Classification code
SINCERT	Accreditamento Organismi Certificazione (Italy)
SME	Small- or Medium-sized Enterprise
SPC	Statistical Process Control
Sub-TAG	Subgroup of a Technical Advisory Group
TAAC	Trade Adjustment Assistance Centers

TAG	Technical Advisory Group. A term used specifically in the United States for groups that are responsible for input on international standards within their respective scopes; other countries may use other terms.
TC	Technical Committee
TELARC	Testing Laboratory Registration Council (New Zealand)
TickIT	Refers to British "tick" or check mark and Information Technology, the UK quality system registration scheme for software companies
TG	Task Group
TQM	Total Quality Management
TR	Technical Report (ISO document designation)
UKAS	United Kingdom Accreditation Service
UL	Underwriters Laboratories
UNI	Ente Nazionale Italiano di Unificazione (Italian national association for standardization)
USNC	US National Committee
UTE	Union Technique de l'Électricité (French electrotechnical union)
WD	Working Draft
WG	Working Group (International committee usage); Writing Group (national usage)
WTO	World Trade Organization

Glossary

Also see ASQ web page: http://www.asq.org/info/glossary/definition.html

Accreditation: Procedure by which an authoritative body formally recognizes that a body or person is competent to carry out specific tasks. (ISO/IEC Guide 62)

Accreditation Mark: An insignia that indicates accreditation. Only accredited certification bodies and the companies they certify are allowed to use an accreditation mark. Nonaccredited certification bodies and the companies they certify may not.

Assessment: An estimate or determination of the significance, importance or value of something.

Assessment Body: Third party that assesses products and registers the quality systems of suppliers.

Assessment System: Procedural and managerial rules for conducting an assessment leading to issue of a registration document and its maintenance.

Audit: Systematic, independent and documented process for obtaining audit evidence and evaluating it objectively to determine the extent to which audit criteria are fulfilled. (ANSI/ISO/ASQ Q9000:2000)

Audit Program: Set of one or more audits planned for a specific time frame and directed toward a specific purpose. (ANSI/ISO/ASQ Q9000:2000)

Auditee: Organization being audited. (ANSI/ISO/ASQ Q9000:2000)

Auditor: Person with the competence to conduct an audit. (ANSI/ISO/ASQ Q9000:2000)

CE Mark: (Conformité Européenne) The mark of approval used by the European Union. This mark signifies that the equipment complies with all applicable directives and product standards.

Certification: Procedure by which a third party gives written assurance that a product, process or service conforms to specified requirements. (ISO/IEC Guide 2)

Certified: The quality system of a company, location or plant is certified for compliance to ISO 9000 after it has demonstrated such compliance through the audit process. When used to indicate quality system certification, it is interchangeable with registration.

Compliance: An affirmative indication or judgment that the supplier of a product or service has met the requirements of the relevant specifications, contract or regulation; also the state of meeting the requirements. (ANSI/ASQC A3)

Conformity: Fulfillment of a requirement (ANSI/ISO/ASQ Q9000:2000)

Conformity Assessment: Conformity assessment includes all activities that are intended to assure the conformity of products to a set of standards. This can include testing, inspection, certification, quality system assessment and other activities.

Continual Improvement: The ongoing improvement of products, service or processes through incremental and breakthrough improvements.

Contractor: The organization that provides a product to the customer in a contractual situation.

Convention: A customary practice, rule or method. (ASQ Quality Auditing Technical Committee)

Corrective Action: Action to eliminate the causes of a detected nonconformity or other undesirable situation. (ANSI/ISO/ASQ Q9000:2000)

Customer: Organization or person that receives a product. (ANSI/ISO/ASQ Q9000:2000)

Design Review: A formal, documented, comprehensive and systematic examination of a design to evaluate the design requirements and the capability of the design to meet these requirements and to identify problems and propose solutions.

EN 45000: A series of standards set up by the European Union to regulate and harmonize certification, accreditation and testing activities. National accreditation structures and inspection body standards are still being developed.

Finding: A conclusion of importance based on observation(s).

Follow-up Audit: An audit whose purpose and scope are limited to verifying that corrective action has been accomplished as scheduled and to determining that the action effectively prevented recurrence.

Grade: Category or rank given to different quality requirements for products, processes or systems having the same functional use. (ANSI/ISO/ASQ Q9000:2000)

Inspection: Conformity evaluation by observation and judgment accompanied as appropriate by measurement, testing or gauging. (ANSI/ISO/ASQ Q9000:2000)

Modules: The European Union has devised a conformity assessment system, consisting of modules, to handle the diversity of testing, inspection and certification activities. Modules in the "modular approach" range from manufacturer declaration—through a variety of routes involving design and type approval—to full third-party certification.

Nonconformity: The nonfulfillment of a specified requirement.

Notified Body: A testing organization that has been selected to perform assessment activities for (a) European Union directive(s). It is approved by the competent authority of its member state and notified to the European Commission and all other member states.

Organization: A company, corporation, firm, enterprise or association, or part thereof, whether incorporated or not, public or private, that has its own functions and administration

Organizational Structure: The responsibilities, authorities and relationships, arranged in a pattern, through which an organization performs its functions.

Procedure: A specified way to perform an activity

Process: A set of interrelated resources and activities which transform inputs into outputs.

Process Quality Audit: An analysis of elements of a process and appraisal of completeness, correctness of conditions and probable effectiveness.

Product: The result of activities or processes. (ISO 8402:1994)

Product Quality Audit: A quantitative assessment of conformance to required product characteristics. (ANSI/ASQC A3)

Protocol Agreement: An agreement signed between two organizations that operate in different but complementary fields of activity and that commit themselves to take into account their respective assessment results according to conditions specified in advance.

Purchaser: The customer in a contractual situation

Qualification Process: Process to demonstrate the ability to fulfill specified requirements. (ANSI/ISO/ASQ Q9000:2000)

Quality: Degree to which a set of inherent characteristics fulfills requirements. (ANSI/ISO/ASQ Q9000:2000)

Quality Assurance: Part of quality management focused on providing confidence that quality requirements will be fulfilled. (ANSI/ISO/ASQ Q9000:2000)

Quality Audit: A systematic and independent examination to determine whether quality activities and related results comply with planned arrangements and whether these arrangements are implemented effectively and are suitable to achieve objectives.

Quality Control: Part of quality management focused on fulfilling quality requirements. (ANSI/ISO/ASQ Q9000:2000)

Quality Management: Coordinated activities to direct and control an organization with regard to quality. (ANSI/ISO/ASQ Q9000:2000)

Quality Manual: Document specifying the quality management system of an organization. (ANSI/ISO/ASQ Q9000:2000)

Quality Plan: Document specifying which procedures and associated resources shall be applied by whom and when to a specific project, product, process or contract. (ANSI/ISO/ASQ Q9000:2000)

Quality Planning: Part of quality management focused on setting quality objectives and specifying necessary operational processes and related resources to fulfill the quality objectives. (ANSI/ISO/ASQ Q9000:2000)

Quality Policy: Overall intentions and direction of an organization related to quality, as formally expressed by top management. (ANSI/ISO/ASQ Q9000:2000)

Quality Surveillance: The continuing monitoring and verification of the status of procedures, methods, conditions, products, processes and services and the analysis of records in relation to stated references to ensure that requirements for quality are being met. (ANSI/ASQC A3)

Quality System: The organizational structure, procedures, processes and resources needed to implement quality management.

Quality System Audit: A documented activity to verify, by examination and evaluation of objective evidence, that applicable elements of the quality system are suitable and have been developed, documented and effectively implemented in accordance with specified requirements. (ANSI/ASQC A3)

Quality System Review: A formal evaluation by management of the status and adequacy of the quality system in relation to quality policy and/or new objectives resulting from changing circumstances. (ANSI/ASQC A3)

Registered: A procedure by which a body indicates the relevant characteristics of a product, process or service, or the particulars of a body or person, in a published list. ISO 9000 registration is the evaluation of a company's quality system against the requirements of a standard in the ISO 9000 family.

Registration: Procedure by which a body indicates relevant characteristics of a product, process or service, or particulars of a body or person, and then includes or registers the product, process or service in an appropriate publicly available list. (ISO/IEC Guide 2) In the United States, the term used in the context of management systems to avoid confusion with product certification.

Registration Document: Documentation that a supplier's quality system conforms to specified standards. Issued by an assessment body.

Requirement: Need or expectation that is stated, generally implied or obligatory. (ANSI/ISO/ASQ Q9000:2000)

Root Cause: A fundamental deficiency that results in a nonconformance and must be corrected to prevent recurrence of the same or similar nonconformance.

Service: The result generated by activities at the interface between the supplier and the customer and by supplier internal activities to meet the customer needs.

Service Delivery: Those supplier activities necessary to provide the service.

Software: An intellectual creation consisting of information, instructions, concepts, transactions or procedures.

Software Product: Complete set of computer programs, procedures and associated documentation and data designated for delivery to a user. (ISO 9000-3, Clause 3.2)

Specification: Document stating requirements. (ANSI/ISO/ASQ Q9000:2000)

Subcontractor: An organization that provides a product to the supplier.

Supplier: Organization or person that provides a product. (ANSI/ISO/ASQ Q9000:2000)

Survey: An examination for some specific purpose; to inspect or consider carefully; to review in detail

Testing: A means of determining an item's capability to meet specified requirements by subjecting them to a set of physical, chemical, environmental or operating actions and conditions. (ANSI/ASQC A3)

Top Management: Person or group of people who directs and controls an organization (ANSI/ISO/ASQ Q9000:2000)

Traceability: Ability to trace the history, application or location of that which is under consideration. (ANSI/ISO/ASQ Q9000:2000)

Validation: Confirmation, through the provision of objective evidence, that the requirements for a specific intended use or application have been fulfilled. (ANSI/ISO/ASQ Q9000:2000)

Verification: Conformation, through the provision of objective evidence, that specified requirements have been fulfilled. (ANSI/ISO/ASQ Q9000:2000)

ISO 9001:2000

Introduction

0.1 General

The adoption of a quality management system should be a strategic decision of an organization. The design and implementation of an organization's quality management system is influenced by varying needs, particular objectives, the products provided, the processes employed and the size and structure of the organization. It is not the intent of this International Standard to imply uniformity in the structure of quality management systems or uniformity of documentation.

The quality management system requirements specified in this International Standard are complementary to requirements for products. Information marked "NOTE" is for guidance in understanding or clarifying the associated requirement.

This International Standard can be used by internal and external parties, including certification bodies, to assess the organization's ability to meet customer, regulatory and the organization's own requirements.

The quality management principles stated in ISO 9000 and ISO 9004 have been taken into consideration during the development of this International Standard.

0.2 Process approach

This International Standard promotes the adoption of a process approach when developing, implementing and approving the effectiveness of a quality management system, to enhance customer satisfaction by meeting customer requirements.

For an organization to function effectively, it has to identify and manage numerous linked activities. An activity using resources, and managed in order to enable the transformation of inputs into outputs, can be considered as a process. Often the output from one process directly forms the input to the next.

The application of a system of processes within an organization, together with the identification and interactions of these processes, and their management, can be referred to as the "process approach".

An advantage of the process approach is the ongoing control that it provides over the linkage between the individual processes within the system of processes, as well as over their combination and interaction.

When used within a quality management system, such an approach emphasizes the importance of

a) understanding and meeting requirements,

b) the need to consider processes in terms of added value,

c) obtaining results of process performance and effectiveness, and

d) continual improvement of processes based on objective measurement.

The model of a process-based quality management system shown in Figure 1 illustrates the process linkages presented in clauses 4 to 8. This illustration shows that customers play a significant role in defining requirements as inputs. Monitoring of customer satisfaction requires the evaluation of information relating to customer perception as to whether the organization has met the customer requirements. The model shown in Figure 1 covers all the requirements of this International Standard, but does not show processes at a detailed level.

NOTE   In addition, the methodology known as "Plan-Do-Check-Act" (PDCA) can be applied to all processes. PDCA can be briefly described as follow.

Plan: establish the objectives and processes necessary to deliver results in accordance with customer requirements and the organization's policies.

Do: implement the processes.

Check: monitor and measure processes and product against policies, objectives and requirements for the product and report the results.

Act: take actions to continually improve process performance.

0.3 Relationship with ISO 9004

The present editions of ISO 9001 and ISO 9004 have been developed as a consistent pair of quality management system standards which have been designed to complement each other, but can also be used independently. Although the two International Standards have different scopes, they have similar structures in order to assist the application as a consistent pair.

ISO 9001 specifies requirements for a quality management system that can be used for internal application by organizations, or for certification, or for contractual purposes. It focuses on the effectiveness of the quality management system in meeting customer requirements.

ISO 9004 gives guidance on a wider range of objectives of a quality management system than does ISO 9001, particularly for the continual improvement of an organization's overall performance and efficiency, as well as its effectiveness. ISO 9004 is recommended as a guide for organizations whose top management

Figure 1

Model of a process-based quality management system

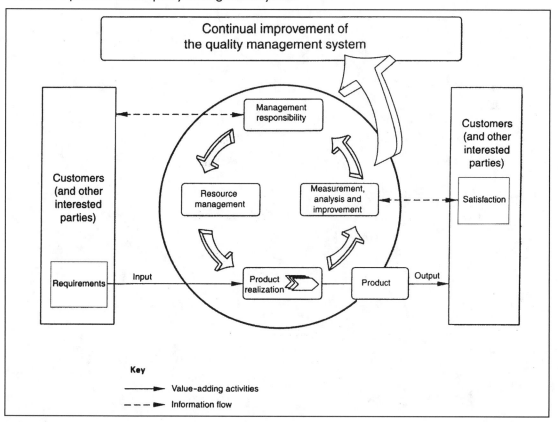

wishes to move beyond the requirements of ISO 9001, in pursuit of continual improvement of performance. However, it is not intended for certification or for contractual purposes.

0.4 Compatibility with other management systems

This International Standard has been aligned with ISO 14001:1996 in order to enhance the compatibility of the two standards for the benefit of the user community.

This International Standard does not include requirements specific to other management systems, such as those particular to environmental management, occupational health and safety management, financial management or risk management. However, this International Standard enables an organization to align or integrate its own quality management system with related management system requirements. It is possible for an organization to adapt its existing management system(s) in order to establish a quality management system that complies with the requirements of this International Standard.

International Standard ISO 9001:2000(E)

Quality management systems – Requirements

1 Scope

1.1 General

This International Standard specifies requirements for a quality management system where an organization

a) needs to demonstrate its ability to consistently provide product that meets customer and applicable regulatory requirements, and

b) aims to enhance customer satisfaction through the effective application of the system, including processes for continual improvement of the system and the assurance of conformity to customer and applicable regulatory requirements.

NOTE   In this International Standard, the term "product" applies only to the product intended for, or required by, a customer.

1.2 Application

All requirements of this International Standard are generic and are intended to be applicable to all organizations, regardless of type, size and product provided.

Where any requirement(s) of this International Standard cannot be applied due to the nature of an organization and its product, this can be considered for exclusion.

Where exclusions are made, claims of conformity to this International Standard are not acceptable unless these exclusions are limited to requirements within clause 7, and such exclusions do not affect the organization's ability, or responsibility, to provide product that meets customer and applicable regulatory requirements.

2 Normative reference

The following normative document contains provisions which, through references in this text, constitute provisions of this International Standard. For dated references, subsequent amendments to, or revisions of, any of these publications do not apply. However, parties to agreements based on this International Standard are encouraged to investigate the possibility of applying the most recent edition of the normative document indicated below. For undated references, the latest edition of the normative document referred to applies. Members of ISO and IEC maintain registers of currently valid International Standards.

ISO 9000:2000, Quality management systems – Fundamentals and vocabulary.

3 Terms and definitions

For the purposes of this International Standard, the terms and definitions given in ISO 9000 apply.

The following terms, used in this edition of ISO 9001 to describe the supply chain, have been changed to reflect the vocabulary currently used:

supplier ⟶ organization ⟶ customer

The term "organization" replaces the term "supplier" used in ISO 9001:1994, and refers to the unit to which this International Standard applies. Also, the term "supplier" now replaces the term "subcontractor".

Throughout the text of this International Standard, wherever the term "product" occurs, it can also mean "service".

4 Quality management system

4.1 General requirements

The organization shall establish, document, implement and maintain a quality management system and continually improve its effectiveness in accordance with the requirements of this International Standard.

The organization shall

a) identify the processes needed for quality management system and their application throughout the organization (see 1.2),

b) determine the sequence and interaction of these processes,

c) determine criteria and methods needed to ensure that both the operation and control of these processes are effective,

d) ensure the availability of resources and information necessary to support the operation and monitoring of these processes,

e) monitor, measure and analyse these processes, and

f) implement actions necessary to achieve planned results and continual improvement of these processes.

These processes shall be managed by the organization in accordance with the requirements of this International Standard.

Where an organization chooses to outsource any process that affects product conformity with requirements, the organization shall ensure control over such processes. Control of such outsourced processes shall be identified within the quality management system.

NOTE   Processes needed for the quality management system referred to above should include processes for management activities, provision of resources, product realization and measurement.

4.2   Documentation requirements

4.2.1 General

The quality management system documentation shall include

a) documented statements of a quality policy and quality objectives,

b) a quality manual,

c) documented procedures required by this International Standard,

d) documents needed by the organization to ensure the effective planning, operation and control of its processes and

e) records required by this International Standard (see 4.2.4).

NOTE 1   Where the term "documented procedures" appears within this International Standard, this means that the procedure is established, documented, implemented and maintained.

NOTE 2   The extent of the quality management system documentation can differ from one organization to another due to

a) the size of organization and type of activities,

b) the complexity of processes and their interactions, and

c) the competence of personnel.

NOTE 3   The documentation can be in any form or type of medium.

4.2.2 Quality manual

The organization shall establish and maintain a quality manual that includes

a) the scope of the quality management system, including details of and justification for any exclusions (see 1.2),

b) the documented procedures established for the quality management system, or reference to them, and

c) a description of the interaction between the processes of the quality management system.

4.2.3 Control of documents

Documents required by the quality management system shall be controlled. Records are a special type of document and shall be controlled according to the requirements given in 4.2.4.

A documented procedure shall be established to define the controls needed

a) to approve documents for adequacy prior to issue,

b) to review and update as necessary and re-approve documents,

c) to ensure that changes and the current revision status of documents are identified,

d) to ensure that relevant versions of applicable documents are available at points of use,

e) to ensure that documents remain legible and readily identifiable,

f) to ensure that documents of external origin are identified and their distribution controlled, and

g) to prevent the unintended use of obsolete documents, and to apply suitable identification to them if they are retained for any purpose.

4.2.4 Control of records

Records shall be established and maintained to provide evidence of conformity to requirements and of the effective operation of the quality management system. Records shall remain legible, readily identifiable and retrievable. A documented procedure shall be established to define the controls needed for the identification, storage, protection, retrieval, retention time and disposition of records.

5 Management responsibility

5.1 Management commitment

Top management shall provide evidence of its commitment to the development and implementation of the quality management system and continually improving its effectiveness by

a) communicating to the organization the importance of meeting customer as well as statutory and regulatory requirements,

b) establishing the quality policy,

c) ensuring that quality objectives are established,

d) conducting management reviews, and

e) ensuring the availability of resources.

5.2 Customer focus

Top management shall ensure that customer requirements are determined and are met with the aim of enhancing customer satisfaction (see 7.2.1 and 8.2.1).

5.3 Quality policy

Top management shall ensure that the quality policy

a) is appropriate to the purpose of the organization,

b) includes a commitment to comply with requirements and continually improve the effectiveness of the quality management system,

c) provides a framework for establishing and reviewing quality objectives,

d) is communicated and understood within the organization, and

e) is reviewed for continuing suitability.

5.4   Planning

5.4.1 Quality objectives

Top management shall ensure that quality objectives, including those needed to meet requirements for product [see 7.1 a)], are established at relevant functions and levels within the organization. The quality objectives shall be measurable and consistent with the quality policy.

5.4.2 Quality management system planning

Top management shall ensure that

a) the planning of the quality management system is carried out in order to meet the requirements given in 4.1, as well as the quality objectives, and

b) the integrity of the quality management system is maintained when changes to the quality management system are planned and implemented.

5.5   Responsibility, authority and communication

5.5.1 Responsibility and authority

Top management shall ensure that responsibilities and authorities are defined and communicated within the organization.

5.5.2 Management representative

Top management shall appoint a member of management who, irrespective of other responsibilities, shall have responsibility and authority that includes

a) ensuring that processes needed for the quality management system are established, implemented and maintained,

b) reporting to top management on the performance of the quality management system and any need for improvement, and

c) ensuring the promotion of awareness of customer requirements throughout the organization.

NOTE   The responsibility of a management representative can include liaison with external parties on matters relating to the quality management system.

5.5.3 Internal communication

Top management shall ensure that appropriate communication processes are established within the organization and that communication takes place regarding the effectiveness of the quality management system.

5.6   Management review

5.6.1 General

Top management shall review the organization's quality management system, at planned intervals, to ensure its continuing suitability, adequacy and effectiveness. This review shall include assessing opportunities for improvement and the need for changes to the quality management system, including the quality policy and quality objectives.

Records from management reviews shall be maintained (see 4.2.4).

5.6.2 Review input

The input to management review shall include information on

a) results of audits,

b) customer feedback,

c) process performance and product conformity,

d) status of preventive and corrective actions,

e) follow-up actions from previous management system, and

f) recommendations for improvement.

5.6.3 Review output

The output from the management review shall include any decisions and actions related to

a) improvement of the effectiveness of the quality management system and its processes,

b) improvement of product related to customer requirements, and

c) resource needs.

6 Resource management

6.1 Provision of resources

The organization shall determine and provide the resources needed

a) to implement and maintain the quality management system and continually improve its effectiveness, and

b) to enhance customer satisfaction by meeting customer requirements.

6.2 Human resources

6.2.1 General

Personnel performing work affecting product quality shall be competent on the basis of appropriate education, training, skills and experience.

6.2.2 Competence, awareness and training

The organization shall

a) determine the necessary competence for personnel performing work affecting product quality,

b) provide training or take other actions to satisfy these needs,

c) evaluate the effectiveness of the actions taken,

d) ensure that its personnel are aware of the relevance and importance of their activities and how they contribute to the achievement of the quality objectives, and

e) maintain appropriate records of education, training, skills and experience (see 4.2.4).

6.3 Infrastructure

The organization shall determine, provide and maintain the infrastructure needed to achieve conformity to product requirements. Infrastructure includes, as applicable

a) buildings, workspace and associated utilities,

b) process equipment (both hardware and software), and

c) supporting services (such as transport or communication).

6.4 Work environment

The organization shall determine and manage the work environment needed to achieve conformity to product requirements.

7 Product realization

7.1 Planning of product realization

The organization shall plan and develop the processes needed for product realization. Planning of product realization shall be consistent with the requirements of the other processes of the quality management system (see 4.1).

In planning product realization, the organization shall determine the following, as appropriate:

a) quality objectives and requirements for the product;

b) the need to establish processes, documents, and provide resources specific to the product;

c) required verification, validation, monitoring, inspection and test activities specific to the product and the criteria for product acceptance;

d) records needed to provide evidence that the realization processes and resulting product meet requirements (see 4.2.4).

The output of this planning shall be in a form suitable for the organization's method of operations.

NOTE 1   A document specifying the processes of the quality management system (including the product realization processes) and the resources to be applied to a specific product, project or contract, can be referred to as a quality plan.

NOTE 2   The organization may also apply the requirements given in 7.3 to the development of product realization processes.

7.2   Customer-related processes

7.2.1 Determination of requirements related to the product

The organization shall determine

a) requirements specified by the customer, including the requirements for delivery and post-delivery activities,

b) requirements not stated by the customer but necessary for specified or intended use, where known,

c) statutory and regulatory requirements related to the product, and

d) any additional requirements determined by the organization.

7.2.2 Review of requirements related to the product

The organization shall review the requirements related to the product. This review shall be conducted prior to the organization's commitment to supply a product to the customer (e.g. submission of tenders, acceptance of contracts or orders, acceptance of changes to contracts or orders) and shall ensure that

a) product requirements are defined,

b) contract or order requirements differing from those previously expressed are resolved, and

c) the organization has the ability to meet the defined requirements.

Records of the results of the review and actions arising from the review shall be maintained (see 4.2.4).

Where the customer provides no documented statement of requirement, the customer requirements shall be confirmed by the organization before acceptance.

Where product requirements are changed, the organization shall ensure that relevant documents are amended and that relevant personnel are made aware of the changed requirements.

NOTE In some situations, such as internet sales, a formal review is impractical for each order, instead the review can cover relevant product information such as catalogues or advertising material.

7.2.3 Customer communication

The organization shall determine and implement effective arrangements for communicating with customers in relation to

a) product information,

b) enquiries, contracts or order handling, including amendments, and

c) customer feedback, including customer complaints.

7.3   Design and development

7.3.1 Design and development planning

The organization shall plan and control the design and development of product.

During the design and development planning, the organization shall determine

a) the design and development stages,

b) the review, verification and validation that are appropriate to each design and development stage, and

c) the responsibilities and authorities for design and development.

The organization shall manage the interfaces between different groups involved in design and development to ensure effective communication and clear assignment of responsibility.

Planning output shall be updated, as appropriate, as the design and development progresses.

7.3.2 Design and development inputs

Inputs relating to product requirements shall be determined and records maintained (see 4.2.4). These inputs shall include

a) functional and performance requirements,

b) applicable statutory and regulatory requirements,

c) where applicable, information derived from previous similar designs, and

d) other requirements essential for design and development.

These inputs shall be reviewed for adequacy. Requirements shall be complete, unambiguous and not in conflict with each other.

7.3.3 Design and development outputs

The outputs of design and development shall be provided in a form that enables verification against the design and development input and shall be approved prior to release.

Design and development outputs shall

   a) meet the input requirements for design and development,

   b) provide appropriate information for purchasing, production and for service provision,

   c) contain or reference product acceptance criteria, and

   d) specify the characteristics of the product that are essential for its safe and proper use.

7.3.4 Design and development review

At suitable stages, systematic reviews of design and development shall be performed in accordance with planned arrangements (see 7.3.1)

   a) to evaluate the ability of the results of design and development to meet requirements, and

   b) to identify any problems and propose necessary actions.

Participants in such reviews shall include representatives of functions concerned with the design and development stages(s) being reviewed. Records of the results of the reviews and any necessary actions shall be maintained (see 4.2.4).

7.3.5 Design and development verification

Verification shall be performed in accordance with planned arrangements (see 7.3.1) to ensure that the design and development outputs have met the design and development input requirements. Records of the results of the verification and any necessary actions shall be maintained (see 4.2.4).

7.3.6 Design and development validation

Design and development validation shall be performed in accordance with planned arrangements (see 7.3.1) to ensure that the resulting product is capable of meeting the requirements for the specified application or intended use, where known. Wherever practicable, validation shall be completed prior to the delivery or implementation of the product. Records of the results of validation and any necessary actions shall be maintained (see 4.2.4).

7.3.7 Control of design and development changes

Design and development changes shall be identified and records maintained. The changes shall be reviewed, verified and validated, as appropriate, and approved before implementation. The review of design and development changes shall include evaluation of the effect of the changes on constituent parts and product already delivered.

Records of the results of the review of changes and any necessary actions shall be maintained (see 4.2.4).

7.4 Purchasing

7.4.1 Purchasing process

The organization shall ensure that purchased product conforms to specified purchase requirements. The type and extent of control applied to the supplier and the purchased product shall be dependent upon the effect of the purchased product on subsequent realization or the final product.

The organization shall evaluate and select suppliers based on their ability to supply product in accordance with the organization's requirements. Criteria for selection, evaluation and re-evaluation shall be established. Records of the results of evaluations and any necessary actions arising from the evaluation shall be maintained (see 4.2.4).

7.4.2 Purchasing information

Purchasing information shall describe the product to be purchased, including where appropriate

  a) requirements for approval of product, procedures, processes and equipment,

  b) requirements for qualification of personnel, and

  c) quality management system requirements.

The organization shall ensure the adequacy of specified purchase requirements prior to their communication to the supplier.

7.4.3 Verification of purchased product

The organization shall establish and implement the inspection or other activities necessary for ensuring that purchased product meets specified purchase requirements.

Where the organization or its customer intends to perform verification at the supplier's premises, the organization shall state the intended verification arrangements and method of product release in the purchasing information.

7.5 Production and service provision

7.5.1 Control of production and service provision

The organization shall plan and carry out production and service provision under controlled conditions. Controlled conditions shall include, as applicable

  a) the availability of information that describes the characteristics of the product,

  b) the availability of work instructions, as necessary,

  c) the use of suitable equipment,

  d) the availability and use of monitoring and measuring devices,

  e) the implementation of monitoring and measuring devices, and

  f) the implementation of release, delivery and post-delivery activities.

7.5.2 Validation of processes for production and service provision

The organization shall validate any processes for production and service provision where the resulting output cannot be verified by subsequent monitoring or measurement. This includes any processes where deficiencies become apparent only after the product is in use or the service has been delivered.

Validation shall demonstrate the ability of these processes including, as applicable

  a) defined criteria for review and approval of the processes,

  b) approval of equipment and qualifications of personnel,

  c) use of specific methods and procedures,

  d) requirements for records (see 4.2.4), and

  e) revalidation.

7.5.3 Identification and traceability

Where appropriate, the organization shall identify the product by suitable means throughout product realization.

The organization shall identify the product status with respect to monitoring and measurement requirements.

Where traceability is a requirement, the organization shall control and record the unique identification of the product (see 4.2.4).

NOTE In some industry sectors, configuration management is a means by which identification and traceability are maintained.

7.5.4 Customer property

The organization shall exercise care with customer property while it is under the organization's control or being used by the organization. The organization shall identify, verify, protect and safeguard customer property provided for use or incorporation into a product. If any customer property is lost, damaged or otherwise found to be unsuitable for use, this shall be reported to the customer and records maintained (see 4.2.4).

NOTE   Customer property can include intellectual property.

7.5.5 Preservation of product

The organization shall preserve the conformity of product during internal processing and delivery to the intended destination. This preservation shall include identification, handling, packaging, storage and protection. Preservation shall also apply to the constituent parts of a product.

7.6   Control of monitoring and measuring devices

The organization shall determine the monitoring and measurement to be undertaken and the monitoring and measuring devices needed to provide evidence of conformity of product to determined requirements (see 7.2.1).

The organization shall establish processes to ensure that monitoring and measurement can be carried out and are carried out in a manner that is consistent with the monitoring and measurement requirements.

Where necessary to ensure valid results, measuring equipment shall

a) be calibrated or verified at specified intervals, or prior to use, against measurement standards traceable to international or national measurement standards; where no such standards exist, the basis used for calibration or verification shall be recorded;

b) be adjusted or re-adjusted as necessary;

c) be identified to enable the calibration status to be determined;

d) be safeguarded from adjustments that would invalidate the measurement result;

e) be protected from damage and deterioration during handling, maintenance and storage.

In addition, the organization shall assess and record the validity of the previous measuring results when the equipment is found not to conform to requirements. The organization shall take appropriate action on the equipment and any product affected. Records of the results of calibration and verification shall be maintained (see 4.2.4).

When used in the monitoring and measurement of specified requirements, the ability of computer software to satisfy the intended application shall be confirmed. This shall be undertaken prior to initial use and reconfirmed as necessary.

NOTE   See ISO 10012-1 and ISO 10012-2 for guidance.

8 Measurement, analysis and improvement

8.1 General

The organization shall plan and implement the monitoring, measurement, analysis and improvement processes needed

a) to demonstrate conformity of the product,

b) to ensure conformity of the quality management system, and

c) to continually improve the effectiveness of the quality management system.

This shall include determination of applicable methods, including statistical techniques, and the extent of their use.

8.2 Monitoring and measurement

8.2.1 Customer satisfaction

As one of the measurements of the performance of the quality management system, the organization shall monitor information relating to customer perception as to whether the organization has met customer requirements. The methods for obtaining and using this information shall be determined.

8.2.2 Internal audit

The organization shall conduct internal audits at planned intervals to determine whether the quality management system

a) conforms to the planned arrangements (see 7.1), to the requirements of this International Standard and to the quality management system requirements established by the organization, and

b) is effectively implemented and maintained.

An audit programme shall be planned, taking into consideration the status and importance of the processes and areas to be audited, as well as the results of previous audits. The audit criteria, scope, frequency and methods shall be defined. Selection of auditors and conduct of audits shall ensure objectivity and impartiality of the audit process. Auditors shall not audit their own work.

The responsibilities and requirements for planning and conducting audits, and for reporting results and maintaining records (see 4.2.4) shall be defined in a documented procedure.

The management responsible for the area being audited shall ensure that actions are taken without undue delay to eliminate detected nonconformities and their causes. Follow-up activities shall include the verification of the actions taken and the reporting of verification results (see 8.5.2).

NOTE   See ISO 10011-1, ISO 10011-2 and ISO 10011-3 for guidance.

8.2.3 *Monitoring and measurement of processes*

The organization shall apply suitable methods for monitoring and, where applicable, measurement of the quality management system processes. These methods shall demonstrate the ability of the processes to achieve planned results. When planned results are not achieved, correction and corrective action shall be taken, as appropriate, to ensure conformity of the product.

8.2.4 *Monitoring and measurement of product*

The organization shall monitor and measure the characteristics of the product to verify that product requirements have been met. This shall be carried out at appropriate stages of the product realization process in accordance with the planned arrangements (see 7.1).

Evidence of conformity with the acceptance criteria shall be maintained. Records shall indicate the person(s) authorizing release of product (see 4.2.4).

Product release and service delivery shall not proceed until the planned arrangements (see 7.1) have been satisfactorily completed, unless otherwise approved by a relevant authority and, where applicable, by the customer.

8.3 Control of nonconforming product

The organization shall ensure that product which does not conform to product requirements is identified and controlled to prevent its unintended use or delivery. The controls and related responsibilities and authorities for dealing with nonconforming product shall be defined in a documented procedure.

The organization shall deal with nonconforming product by one or more of the following ways;

  a) by taking action to eliminate the detected nonconformity;

  b) by authorizing its use, release or acceptance under concession by a relevant authority and, where applicable, by the customer;

  c) by taking action to preclude its original intended use or application.

Records of the nature of nonconformities and any subsequent actions taken, including concessions obtained, shall be maintained (see 4.2.4).

When nonconforming product is corrected it shall be subject to re-verification to demonstrate conformity to the requirements.

When nonconforming product is detected after delivery or use has started, the organization shall take action appropriate to the effects, or potential effects, of the nonconformity.

8.4 Analysis of data

The organization shall determine, collect and analyse appropriate data to demonstrate the suitability and effectiveness of the quality management system and to evaluate where continual improvement of the effectiveness of the quality management system can be made. This shall include data generated as a result of monitoring and measurement and from other relevant sources.

The analysis of data shall provide information relating to

a) customer satisfaction (see 8.2.1),

b) conformity to product requirements (see 7.2.1),

c) characteristics and trends of processes and products including opportunities for preventive action, and

d) suppliers.

8.5 Improvement

8.5.1 Continual improvement

The organization shall continually improve the effectiveness of the quality management system through the use of the quality policy, quality objectives, audit results, analysis of data, corrective and preventive actions and management review.

8.5.2 Corrective action

The organization shall take action to eliminate the cause of nonconformities in order to prevent recurrence. Corrective actions shall be appropriate to the effects of the nonconformities encountered.

A documented procedure shall be established to define requirements for

a) reviewing nonconformities (including customer complaints),

b) determining the causes of nonconformities,

c) evaluating the need for action to ensure that nonconformities do not recur,

d) determining and implementing action needed,

e) records of the results of action taken (see 4.2.4), and

f) reviewing corrective action taken.

8.5.3 Preventive action

The organization shall determine action to eliminate the causes of potential non-conformities in order to prevent their occurrence. Preventive actions shall be appropriate to the effects of the potential problems.

A documented procedure shall be established to define requirements for

a) determining potential nonconformities and their causes,

b) evaluating the need for action to prevent occurrence of nonconformities,

c) determining and implementing action needed,

d) records of results of action taken (see 4.2.4), and

e) reviewing preventive action taken.

Annex A

(informative)

Correspondence between ISO 9001:2000 and ISO 14001:1996
Table A.1 – Correspondence between ISO 9001:2000 and ISO 14001:1996

ISO 9001:2000			ISO 14001:1996
Introduction			Introduction
General	0.1		
Process approach	0.2		
Relationship with ISO 9004	0.3		
Compatibility with other management systems	0.4		
Scope	1	1	**Scope**
General	1.1		
Application	1.2		
Normative reference	2	2	**Normative references**
Terms and definitions	3	3	**Definitions**
Quality management system	4	4	**Environmental management systems requirements**
General requirements	4.1	4.1	General requirements
Documentation requirements	4.2		
General	4.2.1	4.4.4	Environmental management system documentation
Quality manual	4.2.2	4.4.4	Environmental management system documentation
Control of documents	4.2.3	4.4.5	Document control
Control of records	4.2.4	4.5.3	Records
Management responsibility	5	4.4.1	Structure and responsibility
Management commitment	5.1	4.2	Environmental policy
		4.4.1	Structure and responsibility
Customer focus	5.2	4.3.1	Environmental aspects
		4.3.2	Legal and other requirements
Quality policy	5.3	4.2	Environmental policy
Planning	5.4	4.3	Planning
Quality objectives	5.4.1	4.3.3	Objectives and targets
Quality management system planning	5.4.2	4.3.4	Environmental management programme(s)
Responsibility, authority and communication	5.5	4.1	General requirements
Responsibility and authority	5.5.1		
Management representative	5.5.2	4.4.1	Structure and responsibility
Internal communication	5.5.3	4.4.3	Communication

Table A.1 – Correspondence between ISO 9001:2000 and ISO 14001:1996

ISO 9001:2000			ISO 14001:1996
Management review	5.6	4.6	Management review
General	5.6.1		
Review input	5.6.2		
Review output	5.6.3		
Resource management	6	4.4.1	Structure and responsibility
Provision of resources	6.1		
Human resources	6.2		
General	6.2.1		
Competence, awareness and training	6.2.2	4.4.2	Training, awareness and competence
Infrastructure	6.3	4.4.1	Structure and responsibility
Work environment	6.4		
Product realization	7	4.4	Implementation and operation
		4.4.6	Operational control
Planning of product realization	7.1	4.4.6	Operational control
Customer-related processes	7.2		
Determination of requirements related to the product	7.2.1	4.3.1	Environmental aspects
		4.3.2	Legal and other requirements
		4.4.6	Operational control
Review of requirements related to the product	7.2.2	4.4.6	Operational control
		4.3.1	Environmental aspects
Customer communication	7.2.3	4.4.3	Communications
Design and development	7.3		
Design and development planning	7.3.1	4.4.6	Operational control
Design and developments inputs	7.3.2		
Design and development outputs	7.3.3		
Design and development review	7.3.4		
Design and development verification	7.3.5		
Design and development validation	7.3.6		
Control of design and development changes	7.3.7		
Purchasing	7.4	4.4.6	Operational control
Purchasing process	7.4.1		
Purchasing information	7.4.2		
Verification of purchased product	7.4.3		
Production and service provision	7.5	4.4.6	Operational control
Control of production and service provision	7.5.1		
Validation of processes for production and service provision	7.5.2		
Identification and traceability	7.5.3		

Table A.1 – Correspondence between ISO 9001:2000 and ISO 14001:1996

ISO 9001:2000			ISO 14001:1996
Customer property	7.5.4		
Preservation of product	7.5.5		
Control of monitoring and measuring devices	7.6	4.5.1	Monitoring and measurement
Measurement, analysis and improvement	8	4.5	Checking and corrective action
General	8.1	4.5.1	Monitoring and measurement
Monitoring and measurement	8.2		
Customer satisfaction	8.2.1		
Internal audit	8.2.2	4.5.4	Environmental management system audit
Monitoring and measurement of processes	8.2.3	4.5.1	Monitoring and measurement
Monitoring and measurement of product	8.2.4		
Control of nonconforming product	8.3	4.5.2	Nonconformance and corrective and preventive action
		4.4.7	Emergency preparedness and response
Analysis of data	8.4	4.5.1	Monitoring and measurement
Improvement	8.5	4.2	Environmental policy
Continual improvement	8.5.1	4.3.4	Environmental management programme(s)
Corrective action	8.5.2	4.5.2	Nonconformance and corrective and preventive action
Preventive action	8.5.3		

Table A.2 – Correspondence between ISO 14001:1996 and ISO 9001:2000

ISO 14001:1996			ISO 9001:2000
Introduction	—	0	Introduction
		0.1	General
		0.2	Process approach
		0.3	Relationship with ISO 9004
		0.4	Compatibility with other management systems
Scope	1	1	Scope
		1.1	General
		1.2	Application
Normative references	2	2	Normative references
Definitions	3	3	Terms and definitions
Environmental management system requirements	4	4	Quality management system
General requirements	4.1	4.1	General requirements
		5.5	Responsibility, authority and communication
		5.5.1	Responsibility and authority
Environmental policy	4.2	5.1	Management commitment
		5.3	Quality policy
		8.5	Improvement
Planning	4.3	5.4	Planning
Environmental aspects	4.3.1	5.2	Customer focus
		7.2.1	Determination of requirements related to the product
		7.2.2	Review of requirements related to the product
Legal and other requirements	4.3.2	5.2	Customer focus
		7.2.1	Determination of requirements related to the product
Objectives and targets	4.3.3	5.4.1	Quality objectives
Environmental management programme(s)	4.3.4	5.4.2	Quality management system planning
		8.5.1	Continual improvement
Implementation and operation	4.4	7	Product realization
		7.1	Planning of product realization
Structure and responsibility	4.4.1	5	Management responsibility
		5.1	Management commitment
		5.5.1	Responsibility and authority
		5.5.2	Management representative
		6	Resource management
		6.1	Provision of resources

Table A.2 – Correspondence between ISO 14001:1996 and ISO 9001:2000

ISO 14001:1996			ISO 9001:2000	
		6.2	Human resources
		6.2.1	General
		6.3	Infrastructure
		6.4	Work environment
Training, awareness and competence	4.4.2	6.2.2	Competence, awareness and training
Communication	4.4.3	5.5.3	Internal communication
		7.2.3	Customer communication
Environmental management system documentation	4.4.4	4.2	Documentation requirements
		4.2.1	General
		4.2.2	Quality manual
Document control	4.4.5	4.2.3	Control of documents
Operational control	4.4.6	7	Product realization
		7.1	Planning of product realization
		7.2	Customer-related processes
		7.2.1	Determination of requirements related to the product
		7.2.2	Review of requirements related to the product
		7.3	Design and development
		7.3.1	Design and development planning
		7.3.2	Design and development inputs
		7.3.3	Design and development outputs
		7.3.4	Design and development review
		7.3.5	Design and development verification
		7.3.6	Design and development validation
		7.3.7	Control of design and development changes
		7.4	Purchasing
		7.4.1	Purchasing process
		7.4.2	Purchasing information
		7.4.3	Verification of purchased product
		7.5	Production and service provision
		7.5.1	Control of production and service provision
		7.5.3	Identification and traceability
		7.5.4	Customer property
		7.5.5	Preservation of product
		7.5.2	Validation of processes for production and service provision
Emergency preparedness and response	4.4.7	8.3	Control of nonconforming product

Table A.2 – Correspondence between ISO 14001:1996 and ISO 9001:2000

ISO 14001:1996			ISO 9001:2000
Checking and corrective action	4.5	8	Measurement, analysis and improvement
Monitoring and measurement	4.5.1	7.6	Control of monitoring and measuring devices
		8.1	General
		8.2	Monitoring and measurement
		8.2.1	Customer satisfaction
		8.2.3	Monitoring and measurement of processes
		8.2.4	Monitoring and measurement of product
		8.4	Analysis of data
Nonconformance and corrective and preventive action	4.5.2	8.3	Control of nonconforming product
		8.5.2	Corrective action
		8.5.3	Preventive action
Records	4.5.3	4.2.4	Control of records
Environmental management system audit	4.5.4	8.2.2	Internal audit
Management review	4.6	5.6	Management review
		5.6.1	General
		5.6.2	Review input
		5.6.3	Review output

Annex B

(informative)

Correspondence between ISO 9001:2000 and ISO 9001:1994

Table B.1 – Correspondence between ISO 9001:1994 and ISO 9001:2000

ISO 9001:1994	ISO 9001:2000
1 Scope	1
2 Normative reference	2
3 Definitions	3
4 Quality system requirements [title only]	
4.1 Management responsibility [title only]	
4.1.1 Quality policy	5.1 + 5.3 + 5.4.1
4.1.2 Organization [title only]	
4.1.2.1 Responsibility and authority	5.5.1
4.1.2.2 Resources	6.1 + 6.2.1
4.1.2.3 Management representative	5.5.2
4.1.3 Management review	5.6.1 + 8.5.1
4.2 Quality system [title only]	
4.2.1 General	4.1 + 4.2.2
4.2.2 Quality system procedure	4.2.1
4.2.3 Quality planning	5.4.2 + 7.1
4.3 Contract review [title only]	
4.3.1 General	
4.3.2 Review	5.2 + 7.2.1 + 7.2.2 + 7.2.3
4.3.3 Amendment to a contract	7.2.2
4.3.4 Records	7.2.2
4.4 Design control [title only]	
4.4.1 General	
4.4.2 Design and development planning	7.3.1
4.4.3 Organizational and technical interfaces	7.3.1
4.4.4 Design input	7.2.1 + 7.3.2
4.4.5 Design output	7.3.3
4.4.6 Design review	7.3.4
4.4.7 Design verification	7.3.5
4.4.8 Design validation	7.3.6
4.4.9 Design changes	7.3.7
4.5 Document and data control [title only]	
4.5.1 General	4.2.3
4.5.2 General document and data approval and issue	4.2.3
4.5.3 Document and data changes	4.2.3
4.6 Purchasing [title only]	

Table B.1 – Correspondence between ISO 9001:1994 and ISO 9001:2000

ISO 9001:1994	ISO 9001:2000
4.6.1 General	
4.6.2 Evaluation of subcontractors	7.4.1
4.6.3 Purchasing data	7.4.2
4.6.4 Verification of purchased product	7.4.3
4.7 Control of customer-supplied product	7.5.4
4.8 Product identification and traceability	7.5.3
4.9 Process control	6.3 + 6.4 + 7.5.1 + 7.5.2
4.10 Inspection and testing [title only]	
4.10.1 General	7.1 + 8.1
4.10.2 Receiving inspection and testing	7.4.3 + 8.2.4
4.10.3 In-process inspection and testing	8.2.4
4.10.4 Final inspection and testing	8.2.4
4.10.5 Inspection and test records	7.5.3 + 8.2.4
4.11 Control of inspection, measuring and test equipment [title only]	
4.11.1 General	7.6
4.11.2 Control procedure	7.6
4.12 Inspection and test status	7.5.3
4.13 Control of nonconforming product [title only]	
4.13.1 General	8.3
4.13.2 Review and disposition of nonconforming product	8.3
4.14 Corrective and preventive action [title only]	
4.14.1 General	8.5.2 + 8.5.3
4.14.2 Corrective action	8.5.2
4.14.3 Preventive action	8.5.3
4.15 Handling, storage, packaging, preservation & delivery [title only]	
4.15.1 General	
4.15.2 Handling	7.5.5
4.15.3 Storage	7.5.5
4.15.4 Packaging	7.5.5
4.15.5 Preservation	7.5.5
4.15.6 Delivery	7.5.1
4.16 Control of quality records	4.2.4
4.17 Internal quality audits	8.2.2 + 8.2.3
4.18 Training	6.2.2
4.19 Servicing	7.5.1
4.20 Statistical techniques [title only]	
4.20.1 Identification of need	8.1 + 8.2.3 + 8.2.4 + 8.4
4.20.2 Procedures	8.1 + 8.2.3 + 8.2.4 + 8.4

Table B.2 – Correspondence between ISO 9001:2000 and ISO 9001:1994

ISO 9001:2000	ISO 9001:1994
1 Scope	1
1.1 General	
1.2 Application	
2 Normative reference	2
3 Terms and definitions	3
4 Quality management system [title only]	
4.1 General requirements	4.2.1
4.2 Documentation requirements [title only]	
4.2.1 General	4.2.2
4.2.2 Quality manual	4.2.1
4.2.3 Control of documents	4.5.1 + 4.5.2 + 4.5.3
4.2.4 Control of records	4.16
5 Management responsibility [title only]	
5.1 Management commitment	4.1.1
5.2 Customer focus	4.3.2
5.3 Quality policy	4.1.1
5.4 Planning [title only]	
5.4.1 Quality objectives	4.1.1
5.4.2 Quality management system planning	4.2.3
5.5 Responsibility, authority and communication [title only]	
5.5.1 Responsibility and authority	4.1.2.1
5.5.2 Management representative	4.1.2.3
5.5.3 Internal communication	
5.6 Management review [title only]	
5.6.1 General	4.1.3
5.6.2 Review input	
5.6.3 Review output	
6 Resource management [title only]	
6.1 Provision of resources	4.1.2.2
6.2 Human resources [title only]	
6.2.1 General	4.1.2.2
6.2.2 Competence, awareness and training	4.18
6.3 Infrastructure	4.9
6.4 Work environment	4.9
7 Product realization [title only]	
7.1 Planning of product realization	4.2.3 + 4.10.1
7.2 Customer-related processes [title only]	
7.2.1 Determination of requirements related to the product	4.3.2 + 4.4.4
7.2.2 Review of requirements related to the product	4.3.2 + 4.3.3 + 4.3.4
7.2.3 Customer communication	4.3.2
7.3 Design and development [title only]	

Table B.2 – Correspondence between ISO 9001:2000 and ISO 9001:1994

ISO 9001:2000	ISO 9001:1994
7.3.1 Design and development planning	4.4.2 + 4.4.3
7.3.2 Design and development inputs	4.4.4
7.3.3 Design and development output	4.4.5
7.3.4 Design and development review	4.4.6
7.3.5 Design and development verification	4.4.7
7.3.6 Design and development validation	4.4.8
7.3.7 Control of design and development changes	4.4.9
7.4 Purchasing [title only]	
7.4.1 Purchasing process	4.6.2
7.4.2 Purchasing information	4.6.3
7.4.3 Verification of purchased product	4.6.4 + 4.10.2
7.5 Production and service provision [title only]	
7.5.1 Control of production and service provision	4.9 + 4.15.6 + 4.19
7.5.2 Validation of processes for production and service provision	4.9
7.5.3 Identification and traceability	4.8 + 4.10.5 + 4.12
7.5.4 Customer property	4.7
7.5.5 Preservation of product	4.15.2 + 4.15.3 + 4.15.4 + 4.15.5
7.6 Control of monitoring and measuring devices	4.11.1 + 4.11.2
8 Measurement, analysis and improvement [title only]	
8.1 General	4.10.1 + 4.20.1 + 4.20.2
8.2 Monitoring and measurement [title only]	
8.2.1 Customer satisfaction	
8.2.2 Internal audit	4.17 + 4.20.1 + 4.20.2
8.2.3 Monitoring and measurement of processes	4.17 + 4.20.1 + 4.20.2
8.2.4 Monitoring and measurement of product	4.10.2 + 4.10.3 + 4.10.4 + 4.10.5 + 4.20.1 + 4.20.2
8.3 Control of nonconforming product	4.13.1 + 4.13.2
8.4 Analysis of data	4.20.1 + 4.20.2
8.5 Improvement [title only]	
8.5.1 Continual improvement	4.1.3
8.5.2 Corrective action	4.14.1 + 4.14.2
8.5.3 Preventive action	4.14.1 + 4.14.3

Bibliography

[1] ISO 9000-3:1997, *Quality management and quality assurance standards – Part 3: Guidelines for the application of ISO 9001:1994 to the development, supply, installation and maintenance of computer software.*

[2] ISO 9004:2000, *Quality management systems – Guidelines for performance improvements.*

[3] ISO 10005:1995, *Quality management – Guidelines for quality plans.*

[4] ISO 1006:1997, *Quality management – Guidelines to quality in project management.*

[5] ISO 1007:1995, *Quality management – Guidelines for configuration management.*

[6] ISO 10011-1:1990, *Guidelines for auditing quality systems – Part 1: Auditing.*

[7] ISO 10011-2:1991, *Guidelines for auditing quality systems – Part 2: Qualification criteria for quality systems auditors.*

[8] ISO 10011-3:1991, *Guidelines for auditing quality systems – Part 3: Management of audit programmes.*

[9] ISO 10012-1:1992, *Quality assurance requirements for measuring equipment – Part 1: Metrological confirmation system for measuring equipment.*

[10] ISO 10012-2:1997, *Quality assurance for measuring equipment – Part 2: Guidelines for control of measurement processes.*

[11] ISO 10013:1995, *Guidelines for developing quality manuals.*

[12] ISO/TR 10014:1998, *Guidelines for managing the economics of quality.*

[13] ISO 10015:1999, *Quality management – Guidelines for training.*

[14] ISO/TR 10017:1999, *Guidance on statistical techniques for ISO 9001:1994.*

[15] ISO 14001:1996, *Environmental management systems – Specification with guidance for use.*

[16] IEC 60300-1: — *Dependability management — Part 1: Dependability programme management.*

[17] *Quality Management Principles Brochure.*

[18] *ISO 9000 + ISO 14000 News* (a bimonthly publication which provides comprehensive coverage of international developments relating to ISO's management system standards, including news of their implementation by diverse organizations around the world).

[19] Reference websites:

http://www.iso.ch
http://www.bsi.org.uk/iso-tc176-sc2

Index

A

D

H

I

K

L

N

Q

R

S

U